Environmental Regulation

Editorial Advisory Board
Little, Brown and Company
Law Book Division

Richard A. Epstein
James Parker Hall Distinguished Service Professor of Law
University of Chicago

E. Allan Farnsworth
Alfred McCormack Professor of Law
Columbia University

Ronald J. Gilson
Professor of Law
Stanford University

Geoffrey C. Hazard, Jr.
Sterling Professor of Law
Yale University

James E. Krier
Earl Warren DeLano Professor of Law
University of Michigan

Elizabeth Warren
William A. Schnader Professor of Commercial Law
University of Pennsylvania

Bernard Wolfman
Fessenden Professor of Law
Harvard University

Environmental Regulation

Law, Science, and Policy

1995 Supplement

Robert V. Percival
*Professor of Law
Robert Stanton Scholar and
Director, Environmental Law Program
University of Maryland School of Law*

Alan S. Miller
*Executive Director, Center for Global Change
University of Maryland*

Christopher H. Schroeder
*Professor of Law
Duke University School of Law*

James P. Leape
*Senior Vice President
World Wildlife Fund*

Little, Brown and Company
Boston   New York   Toronto   London

Copyright © 1995 by Robert V. Percival,
Alan S. Miller, Christopher H. Schroeder,
and James P. Leape

All rights reserved. No part of this book may be reproduced in any form or by any electronic or mechanical means including information storage and retrieval systems without permission in writing from the publisher, except by a reviewer who may quote brief passages in a review.

Library of Congress Catalog Card No. 92-70815

ISBN 0-316-69915-2

ICP

Published simultaneously in Canada
by Little, Brown & Company (Canada) Limited

Printed in the United States of America

Contents

Acknowledgments	xix
Authors' Note	xxi
Table of Cases	xxiii

— 1 —
Environmental Values and Policies: An Introduction 1

A.	ENVIRONMENTAL PROBLEMS AND PROGRESS	1
	Public Opinion and Political Support for Environmental Protection	1
	What Should Be Considered an "Environmental Problem"?	2
B.	AMERICAN ENVIRONMENTALISM: SOURCES AND VALUES	3
	Religious Organizations and Environmental Concerns	3
	Human Rights and Environmental Protection	3
	The Environmental Justice Movement	4
	Environmental Philosophy: A Pathfinder	10
	Executive Order 12898	12
	Notes and Questions	18
	Tensions Between Biocentric and Homocentric Philosophies	19

v

Contents

	Oil Drilling and ANWR	19
C.	ECONOMICS AND THE ENVIRONMENT	21
	The Tragedy of the Commons and Free Market Environmentalism	21
	Tragedy of the Commons and Fisheries Management	22
D.	ECOLOGICAL PERSPECTIVES	24
	Ecosystems, Complexity, and Uncertainty	24
	Loy, Dredging for Lessons from the Tragedy in Prince William Sound	24
	Notes and Questions	27

— 2 —
Environmental Law: A Structural Overview — 31

A.	SOURCES OF ENVIRONMENTAL LAW	32
	Common Law Roots	32
	Private Nuisance	33
	Foreseeability, Strict Liability, and Groundwater Pollution: The *Cambridge Water Co.* Case	33
	The Chicago River and the *Missouri v. Illinois* Decision	34
	The Environmental Effects of Ocean Dumping	35
	Environmental Statutes	35
	Responsibilities versus Resources: The Case of EPA	37
	State Administration of Federal Programs	37
	Constitutional Limits on Federal Control of State Regulation	38
	Unfunded Mandates Legislation	41
	Federal Preemption of State Common Law	42
	Intergovernmental Relations in Environmental Decision-making	43
B.	APPROACHES TO REGULATION: ASSESSING THE OPTIONS	44
	Regulation and Its Alternatives	44
	Insurance as a Mechanism for Controlling Environmental Risk	45
	Market Forces, Informed Consumers, and Green Marketing	45
	Provisions of the Oil Pollution Act of 1990	46
	Impact of OPA 90	46

		Solomon, U.S. Oil Spills Have Declined Sharply, Study Says: Stiffer Federal Law Is Cited	47
		Notes and Questions	48
		Uncertainty, Flexibility, and Complexity	50
		Oil Spill Liability and Section 311 of the Clean Water Act	51
		Uniformity versus Flexibility: Technology-Based Regulation	51
		Regulation, Innovation, and Technology Forcing	52
		Economic Incentive Approaches to Regulation	54
		Fragmented Regulatory Authorities	55
		Public Law and Control of Lead Poisoning	55
C.	THE REGULATORY PROCESS: A PREVIEW		57
		Theories of Agency Decision-making	57
D.	ENVIRONMENTAL REGULATION: SOME ADDITIONAL THEMES		58
		Winners and Losers	58
		Regulatory Strategies Reflect Different Assessments of Goals and Means	58

— 3 —
‖ *Waste Management and Pollution Prevention* ‖   61

A.	WASTE MANAGEMENT AND THE POLLUTION PROBLEM		62
		Waste Management and the Pollution Problem	62
B.	STATUTORY AUTHORITIES AFFECTING WASTE MANAGEMENT		63
		EPA's Pollution Prevention Strategy	63
C.	THE RCRA REGULATORY PROGRAM		63
	1.	RCRA: An Introduction	63
		RCRA Reauthorization	63
	2.	What Substances are "Solid Wastes"?	63
		Definition of "Solid Wastes"	63
	3.	Identifying "Hazardous Waste"	65
		The Mixture and Derived-from Rules After *Shell Oil*	65
		Used Oil Listing	67
		Incinerator Ash: A Postscript	67
		City of Chicago v. Environmental Defense Fund	68
		Notes and Questions	77
	4.	Avoiding TSD Status	78

Contents

		The Importance of EPA Guidance	78
	5.	The RCRA Land Disposal Ban	79
		Further Implementation of the RCRA Land Ban	79
	6.	Subtitle D and the Regulation of Municipal Waste Disposal	80
		Subtitle D	80
		EPA's Municipal Landfill Standards	81
D.	CERCLA LIABILITY		81
	3.	"Release of Hazardous Substance"	81
		Eagle-Picher Industries v. EPA	81
		No Quantitative Threshold for Hazardous Constituents	82
		CERCLA Petroleum Exclusion	82
		Can a Sale of a "Product" Also Be the Disposal of a Hazardous Substance?	82
	4.	Strict, Joint, and Several Liability	82
		The *Alcan* Decision	82
		United States v. Alcan Aluminum Corp.	*83*
		Notes and Questions	91
		In re Bell Petroleum Services, Inc.	*93*
		Notes and Questions	104
	5.	Responsible Parties	105
		A. Owners and Operators	105
		Operator Liability	105
		Owners and Operators "At the Time of Disposal"	106
		Nurad, Inc. v. William E. Hooper & Sons Co.	*106*
		Notes and Questions	112
		Liability of Contractors as Operators	113
		"Innocent Sellers" and the Third Party Defense	114
		"All Appropriate Inquiry" and the Innocent Purchaser Defense	114
		Property Transfer Statutes	116
		New Jersey's Environmental Cleanup Responsibility Act	116
		B. Generators	117
		Liability of Generators	117
		CERCLA's Anti-Indemnification Provision: Section 107(e)(1)	119
		Asbestos Abatement and CERCLA Section 104(a)(3)(B)	119
		Problem Exercise: CERCLA Liability	119
		C. How Expansively Should CERCLA's Liability Net Be Cast?	121

		Liability of Transporters	121
		Lender Liability After *Fleet Factors*	121
		Lender Liability Under CERCLA	*122*
		Notes and Questions	124
		Liability of Successor Corporations	125
		Liability of State and Local Governments	126
		Settlements and Contribution	126
	6.	Response Cost and Damages to Natural Resources	127
		Recovery of Response Costs	127
		Calculating Natural Resource Damages	128
		Settlements of Natural Resource Damages Claims	128
E.	REMEDIATION OF ENVIRONMENTAL CONTAMINATION UNDER CERCLA AND RCRA		128
	1.	The CERCLA Cleanup Process	128
		NPL Listing Decisions	128
		Progress of Superfund Cleanups	129
		Superfund Reauthorization	129
	2.	RCRA Corrective Action Requirements	132
		RCRA Corrective Action	132
F.	FUTURE OF WASTE MANAGEMENT		133
	1.	The Search for Disposal Alternatives	133
		Commerce Clause Limitations	133
		Chemical Waste Management, Inc. v. Hunt	*134*
		Notes and Questions	140
		Oregon Waste Systems, Inc. v. Department of Environmental Quality	*140*
		Notes and Questions	149
		Fort Gratiot Sanitary Landfill, Inc. v. Michigan Department of Natural Resources	*152*
		Notes and Questions	160
		C & A Carbone, Inc. v. Town of Clarkstown	*161*
		Notes and Questions	169
		Limits on Local Opposition to Siting	170
		The Search for a High-Level Repository	170
		Constitutional Limits on Federal Coercion of State Siting	171
		New York v. United States	*171*
		Notes and Questions	182
	2.	Waste Reduction: Federal and State Initiatives	183
		Encouraging Source Reduction	183
		State and Local Waste Reduction Activities	184

Contents

— 4 —
Regulation of Toxic Substances   185

A.	THE TOXIC SUBSTANCE PROBLEM	186
	Environmental Releases of Toxic Substances	186
	Significance of Toxic Releases	186
B.	STATUTORY AUTHORITIES FOR REGULATING TOXICS	188
	New Legislation	188
C.	UNCERTAINTY AND THE DILEMMA OF PREVENTATIVE REGULATION	189
	2. Coping with Uncertainty: The Road to Risk Assessment	189
	OSHA Regulation after the *Benzene* Decision	189
	AFL-CIO v. OSHA	*189*
	Notes and Questions	202
	Introduction to Risk Assessment Techniques	203
	3. Hazard Identification and Toxicity Testing	204
	The Controversy over Procedures for Identifying Carcinogens	204
	TSCA's Premanufacture Review Process	209
	Advances in Toxicology	209
	Regulation of Toxic Substances: A Pathfinder	209
D.	HOW SAFE IS "SAFE"?	210
	1. Risk-Benefit Balancing	210
	Risk-Benefit Balancing	210
	EPA's Lead Phasedown Decision	211
	The *Lockout/Tagout* Decision	211
	Lockout/Tagout and "Risk/Risk" Tradeoffs	212
	How Much Is It Worth to Prevent a Death?	214
	Risk Disaggregation	214
	2. Feasibility-Limited Regulation	215
	OSHA's Lead Standard	215
	Feasibility Under the OSH Act	215
	AFL-CIO v. OSHA	*215*
	Notes and Questions	221
	Feasibility Under the Safe Drinking Water Act	222
	American Water Works Association v. EPA	*223*
	Notes and Questions	229
	3. Health-Based (Zero, Significant, or De Minimis) Risk	230
	The Delaney Clause and De Minimis Risk	230
	Naturally Occurring Carcinogens	231
	Section 112 of the Clean Air Act	231
	Risk Assessment Legislation, the Contract With	

		America, and Objections to Quantitative Risk Assessment	232
		The Risk-Benefit Trade-offs Enabled by QRA are Unjustified	233
		QRA Ignores Differences Among Risks	234
		Is Risk Assessment Too Conservative?: The Dioxin Reassessment	234
		Reassessments of Radiation Risks	237
		The Relationship Between Risk Assessment and Risk Management	237
		The Risk Assessment and Management Commission	237
E.	ALTERNATIVES TO CONVENTIONAL REGULATORY APPROACHES		238
	1.	Informational and Burden-Shifting Approaches	238
		Informational Strategies and Agency Research Needs	238
		The Nutrition Labeling and Education Act	238
		California's Proposition 65	239
		Emergency Planning and Community Right-to-Know Act	240
	2.	Common Law Liability	241
		Asbestos Litigation	241
		Santiago v. Sherwin-Williams Co.	241
		Agent Orange	242
		Radiation Exposure Compensation Act	242
		Admission of Expert Testimony	242
		Daubert v. Merrell Dow Pharmaceuticals, Inc.	*243*
		Notes and Questions	253
		Impact of the Jury System	254

— 5 —
The Regulatory Process 255

A.	ESTABLISHING REGULATORY PRIORITIES		256
	1.	Reducing Risk as a Method for Setting Priorities	256
		Reducing Risk	256
		Regulatory Priorities and Hazardous Waste Dumpsites	257
	2.	Agency-Forcing Mechanisms	257
		Citizen Suits and Statutory Deadlines	257
		Petitions to Initiate Rulemaking	258

Contents

B. THE RULEMAKING PROCESS AND REGULATORY OVERSIGHT ... 259
   1. The Rulemaking Process ... 259
        Rulemaking Proceedings: Ossification and the Contract With America ... 259
        Negotiated Rulemaking ... 259
        Generic Approaches to Rulemaking ... 260
   2. Presidential Oversight of Rulemaking ... 260
        Regulatory Review in the Clinton Administration ... 260
        Executive Order 12866 ... *261*
        Notes and Questions ... 271
        Regulatory Review and the Clean Air Permit Regulations ... 272
        Legal Bounds on Executive Oversight ... 272
        The Bush Administration's Regulatory Freeze ... 273
C. JUDICIAL REVIEW AND THE REGULATORY PROCESS ... 274
        Associational Standing ... 274
        Lujan v. Defenders of Wildlife and the Future of Environmental Standing ... 275
        Lujan v. Defenders of Wildlife ... *275*
        Notes and Questions ... 295
        Chevron Deference and the Scope of Judicial Review ... 298
        Judicial Hostility to Environmental Concerns ... 298

— 6 —
Air Pollution Control ... *299*

A. THE AIR POLLUTION PROBLEM ... 300
        Air Pollution Trends ... 300
B. THE CLEAN AIR ACT: ORIGIN AND PRINCIPLES ... 300
        Air Pollution Control: A Pathfinder ... 300
        The Clean Air Act and the 104th Congress ... 301
C. NATIONAL AMBIENT AIR QUALITY STANDARDS ... 301
        Efforts to Force Revision of the Ozone Standard ... 301
        The SO_2 Standard ... 301
        Revisions of Other NAAQSs ... 302
D. STATE IMPLEMENTATION PLANS ... 302
        The Clean Air Act's New National Permit System ... 303
E. THE NONATTAINMENT PROBLEM ... 304
        Air Quality Trends: A Clean Air Report Card ... 304
        A FIP for the South Coast Basin ... 304

Contents

	The SCAQMD's RECLAIM Program	306
	Nonattainment, SIP Revisions, and the 1990 Amendments	307
	Natural Resources Defense Council, Inc. v. EPA	*308*
	Notes and Questions	313
F.	INTERSTATE AIR POLLUTION	315
	The Acid Deposition Problem	315
	The Acid Rain Control Program	315
	The Emissions Trading Program: An Update	316
G.	MOBILE SOURCE CONTROLS: A TECHNOLOGY-FORCING VENTURE	321
	Clean Fuels Program	321
	Onboard Vapor Recovery Controls	322
	Update on the California Standards Option	323
	Motor Vehicle Manufacturers Association v. New York State Department of Environmental Conservation	*324*
	Notes and Questions	340
H.	PREVENTION OF SIGNIFICANT DETERIORATION	342
	The "Top-Down" Approach to BACT	342
	The "WEPCO Fix"	343
	Visibility Protection in National Parks	343
I.	AIR TOXICS	343
	Revisions to NESHAPs	343
	EPA's Source Category List and Schedule for Issuance of Standards	344
	The Proposed HON Rule: MACT Regulations for SOCMI	344
	Incentives for Early Reduction	346

— 7 —
‖ Water Pollution Control ‖   347

A.	THE WATER POLLUTION PROBLEM	348
	Water Quality Trends	348
B.	STATUTORY AUTHORITIES FOR CONTROLLING WATER POLLUTION	349
	Clean Water Act Reauthorization	349
C.	EFFLUENT LIMITATIONS ON POINT SOURCE DISCHARGES	349
	Defining Point Sources Subject to Permit Requirements	349

xiii

Contents

	United States v. Plaza Health Laboratories, Inc.	*350*
	Notes and Questions	365
	Storm Water Discharges	366
	Effluent Limitations: The State of the Art	367
	Sewage Sludge Standards	368
	Sewage Treatment	368
D.	WATER QUALITY-BASED CONTROLS	369
	Water Quality Standards	369
	Sediment Quality Criteria	370
	Impact of Water Quality Standards on Permit Limits	370
	Total Maximum Daily Loadings (TMDLs)	370
	Water Quality Certification Under Section 401	371
	PUD No. 1 of Jefferson County v. Washington Department of Ecology	*371*
	Notes and Questions	386
	Water Quality Criteria for Toxics	387
	Judicial Review of Approval of State ICSs	387
	Lead Contamination from Gun Clubs	388
E.	CONTROL OF POLLUTION FROM NONPOINT SOURCES	388
	Nonpoint Pollution Problems	388
	The Food Security Act of 1985	388
	Section 1455b of the CZMA	389
	State Land Use Controls and Water Quality	389
	Lucas v. South Carolina Coastal Council	389
	Lucas v. South Carolina Coastal Council	*390*
	Notes and Questions	408
	A Note on Post-*Lucas* Decisions by the Federal Circuit	414
	Regulatory Exactions and Takings Claims	417
	Dolan v. City of Tigard	*417*
	Notes and Questions	434
F.	WETLANDS PROTECTION AND THE SECTION 404 PERMIT PROGRAM	435
	Letting the Sea Back In	435
	Scope of the Section 404 Program	436
	Wetland Identification and Delineation	437
	The Section 404 Permit Process	438
	"No Net Loss" and New Approaches to Wetlands Protection	439
G.	ENVIRONMENTAL ENFORCEMENT: THE CASE OF THE CLEAN WATER ACT	439
	Environmental Enforcement	439
	Monitoring and Detecting Violations	439
	Self-Monitoring and Environmental Audits	440

Clean Air Act Bounty Provisions	441
Missing Data from Continuous Emissions Monitoring	441
Enforcement Authorities and Policies	441
Criminal Enforcement	442
Citizen Suits in the Aftermath of *Gwaltney*	443
"Permit Shields" and the Clean Water Act	443
Atlantic States Legal Foundation, Inc. v. Eastman Kodak Co.	*444*
Notes and Questions	448
Federal Facilities Compliance Docket	449
The Federal Facility Compliance Act of 1992	449

— 8 —
Protection of Public Resources — 453

A.	THE NATIONAL ENVIRONMENTAL POLICY ACT	454
	Proposed Abolition of the CEQ	454
	Under What Circumstances Must an EIS Be Prepared?: Trade Agreements	454
	Public Citizen v. U.S. Trade Representative	*455*
	Notes and Questions	461
	Major Federal Action	462
	Significantly Affecting the Quality of the Environment	463
	Emergencies and the EIS Requirement	463
	Is the EIS Adequate?: Consideration of Alternatives	464
	Quality of Analysis: Conservation Biology and the Ecosystems Approach	464
	Adequacy of the Analysis in an EIS: Environmental Justice Concerns	465
	"Tiering"	466
	NEPA Statistics: An Update	466
B.	CONSERVATION OF ENDANGERED SPECIES	466
	Why Should We Conserve Endangered Species?	466
	Taxol	466
	The "God Squad" and the Spotted Owl	467
	Species Listings	467
	What's Happened to Listed Species?	468
	Review of Federal Actions: Section 7 and Endangered Salmon	469
	An Ecosystem Approach to Species Management	469

Contents

	Extraterritorial Application of the ESA	470
	Protection Against Private Action: Section 9	471
	Babbitt v. Sweet Home Chapter of Communities for a Great Oregon	*472*
	Notes and Questions	489
C.	PUBLIC RESOURCE MANAGEMENT AND THE ENVIRONMENT	491
	Private Development of Public Resources	491
	The Spotted Owl Controversy, the God Squad, and the Pacific Forest Plan	492
	Assessment of the Endangered Species Act	495
	Approaches to Protection of Biodiversity, the Earth Summit, and the Biodiversity Convention	495

— 9 —
‖ *International Environmental Law* ‖   *499*

A.	INTRODUCTION TO INTERNATIONAL ENVIRONMENTAL LAW	500
	The Rio "Earth Summit"	500
	International Environmental Law: A Pathfinder	503
	UNCED, Draft Declaration of Principles	503
	The International Whaling Commission	503
B.	PROTECTION OF THE GLOBAL ATMOSPHERE	505
	1. Ozone Depletion	505
	Accelerating the Phaseout	505
	CFC Tax and Freon Smuggling	507
	The Ozone Backlash	507
	An Alternative Explanation for Ozone Depletion	508
	2. Global Climate Change	508
	Intergovernmental Panel on Climate Change, Scientific Assessment	508
	The Long-term Impact of Climate Change	509
	Legal and Policy Responses to Global Warming	510
	The Rio Climate Convention	510
	Framework Convention on Climate Change	*511*
	Notes and Questions	516
C.	INTERNATIONAL TRADE AND THE ENVIRONMENT	520
	The Environmental Impact of Trade Liberalization	520
	The Tuna-Dolphin Controversy and the GATT	521
	GATT: Dispute Settlement Panel Report on U.S. Restrictions on Imports of Tuna	*522*

		Notes and Questions	532
		NAFTA and the Environment	535
	2.	International Trade in Hazardous Substances	536
		Policy Issues	536
		The Basel Convention	537
		Multinational Corporate Policies	537
		Dow Chemical Co. v. Alfaro	537
D.	INTERNATIONAL DEVELOPMENT POLICY AND THE ENVIRONMENT		538
		Effect of Development on Environmental Quality	538
	1.	Federal Agencies and the Extraterritorial Application of Environmental Law	538
		Extraterritorial Application of NEPA	538
		Environmental Defense Fund, Inc. v. Massey	*538*
		Notes and Questions	546
		Extraterritorial Application of the Endangered Species Act	547
	2.	International Financial Institutions and the Environment	547
		A. Debt-for-Nature Swaps and the Preservation of Tropical Forests	547
		The Rio Earth Summit	547
		Debt-for-Nature Swaps	549
		Preservation of Tropical Forests	549
		B. Multilateral Development Banks	549
		Brazil's Polonoroeste Project	549
		The Global Environmental Facility	549
		The Evolution of World Bank Environmental Policy	551
E.	FUTURE DIRECTIONS FOR INTERNATIONAL ENVIRONMENTAL LAW		551
		Linking the International Environmental Agenda with Human Rights	551
		Population, the Environment, and the Cairo Conference	552

— 10 —
‖ Conclusion ‖ 555

		Earth Day 1995: The 25th Anniversary	555
A.	ENVIRONMENTAL PROGRESS		556
		A Moment on the Earth and "Ecorealism"	556
B.	ENVIRONMENTAL PROSPECTS		557

Contents

The Valdez Principles Become the CERES Principles	557
Consensus-Building Partnerships and EPA's "Common Sense" Initiative	558
Securities Law and the Environment	558
United Paperworkers International Union v. International Paper Co.	559
Notes and Questions	568
The Greening of American Business?	569

Acknowledgments

The authors gratefully acknowledge the permissions granted to reproduce the following materials.

Loy, Dredging for Lessons from the Tragedy in Prince William Sound, Washington Post, February 15, 1993, p. A3. Wesley Loy is an Anchorage Daily News business reporter who wrote this story for the Washington Post.

Rose, Chart on Strategy Comparison. Vol. 1991:1 Duke L.J., page 24, Copyright © 1991, Duke University School of Law. Reprinted with permission.

Solomon, U.S. Oil Spills Have Declined Sharply, Study Says; Stiffer Federal Law Is Cited, The Wall Street Journal, August 24, 1992, p. A5A. Reprinted by permission of the Wall Street Journal, Copyright © 1992 Dow Jones & Company, Inc. All rights reserved worldwide.

Toles, copyright © 1995 The Buffalo News. Reprinted with permission of Universal Press Syndicate. All rights reserved.

Authors' Note

This supplement provides a comprehensive updating of the material contained in *Environmental Regulation: Law, Science and Policy.* It incorporates significant developments in environmental law that have occurred since publication of the parent text. During this period the courts have continued to play an active role in interpreting the environmental statutes and in fleshing out constitutional limits on environmental regulation. The Supreme Court decided six environmental cases during its 1993-94 Term: cases interpreting RCRA, CERCLA, the Clean Water Act, and the takings clause of the Fifth Amendment, and two cases involving commerce clause limits on state regulation of interstate waste disposal. While the Court decided only one major environmental case (involving the Endangered Species Act) during its 1994-95 Term, the lower courts continue to handle an active environmental docket. Excerpts from several new cases are included in this supplement.

Few significant changes have been made in the federal environmental statutes, despite considerable congressional attention. Efforts to reauthorize some of the major federal environmental statutes failed in both the 102d and 103d Congresses. The only pieces of environmental legislation enacted by the 103d Congress were the California Desert Protection Act and the reauthorization of the Marine Mammal Protection Act. However, the Republican sweep of the 1994 congressional elections may usher in broad changes in the environmental laws. The Republicans' "Contract With America" includes measures that could radically alter environmental law and policy: a regulatory moratorium, risk assessment and cost-benefit analysis requirements, restrictions on unfunded mandates, and requirements that the government compensate landowners when regulation adversely affects property values. These proposals are described in this supplement.

Authors' Note

To forestall radical change in the environmental laws, the Clinton administration is seeking to reduce regulatory burdens through administrative changes, while threatening vetoes of unacceptable legislation. The President has also issued executive orders creating a new regulatory review process and directing agencies to be more responsive to environmental justice concerns. Excerpts from these executive orders are included in the supplement.

Also included are a description of the new World Trade Organization, which was established as a result of the successfully concluded Uruguay Round of the General Agreement on Tariffs and Trade, and its potential impact on environmental regulations. A decision by a GATT panel that may presage how the new organization will respond to environmental concerns also is incorporated in the supplement.

Using This Supplement

This supplement has been written so that each section of material in it can be read after the reader has read the portion of the parent text that covers the same subject matter. For that purpose, each section of material in the supplement is preceded by a heading that identifies the page range of the parent text that covers the corresponding material, together with a description of the subject matter being covered. Our aim has been to minimize the amount of scanning back and forth from book to supplement that is necessary in order to incorporate the new material, as well as to compose text in the supplement that can be read by itself with comprehension. The one exception to this practice is material in Chapter 3F, which is written to replace the corresponding book text (pp. 384-406).

We would like to express our deep appreciation to Jeanne Grasso, Lauren McKeen, Maureen O'Doherty, Brian Kelly, John Shipley, Dorothy C. Alevizatos and Michael K. Levy, who provided us with research assistance, and to Laura Mrozek for her outstanding administrative and secretarial help. We also would like to express our abiding gratitude to the remarkable people at Little, Brown and Company, who allowed us to incorporate late-breaking developments to ensure the timeliness of this supplement, and particularly to Bob Caceres, our manuscript editor. As always, we welcome any comments, criticisms, or suggestions.

Robert V. Percival
Alan S. Miller
Christopher H. Schroeder
James P. Leape

July 1995

Table of Cases

Principal Cases are in italics.

Abate v. AC & S Inc., 241
Adams v. EPA, 387
Adkins v. Thomas Solvent Co., 33
Adoption of N.J.A.C. 7:26B, In re, 116
AFL-CIO v. OSHA, 185, *189*, 213, *215*, 260
Alabama Power Co. v. EPA, 316
Alaska Center for the Envt. v. Browner, 371
Alaska Center for the Envt. v. Reilly, 370, 371
Alaska Sport Fishing Assn. v. Exxon Corp, 128
Alcan Aluminum Corp., United States v. (990 F.2d 711 (2d Cir. 1993)), 92
Alcan Aluminum Corp., United States v. (964 F.2d 252 (3d Cir. 1992)), 61, 82, *83*, 91-93, 104
AM Intl., Inc. v. International Forging Equip. Corp., 119
American Auto. Mfrs. Assn. v. Comm, Mass. Dept. of Envtl. Prot., 342
American Dental Assn. v. Martin, 213, 214
American Lung Assn. v. EPA (No. 92-5316), 302
American Lung Assn. v. EPA (No. 91-4114), 301
American Paper Inst. v. EPA, 369
American Waterworks Assn. v. EPA, 186, *223*
A & N Cleaners & Launderers, Inc., United States v., 114
Anne Arundel Co., Maryland v. EPA, 128
Apache Powder Co. v. United States, 128
Arkansas-Platte & Gulf Parnership v. Dow Chem. Co., 42-43
Arrowhead Refining Co., United States v., 118
Ashland Oil v. Sonford Prods. Corp., 124
Association of Natl. Advertisers v. Lungren, 46
Atlantic States Legal Found. v. Eastman Kodak Co., 443, *444*
AVX Corp., United States v., 274

Babbitt v. Sweet Home Chapter of Communities for a Great Oregon, 454, *472*
Baldwin v. Fish and Game Commn. of Mont., 150
Ballard v. Tomlinson, 33
Bean v. Southwestern Waste Mgmt. Corp., 9, 10

xxiii

Table of Cases

Beazer East, Inc. v. EPA, Region III, 78, 79
Beazer East, Inc. v. Mead Corp., 119
Beck v. United States Dept. of Comm., 297
Bell Petroleum Servs., In re 61, *93*, 104
B.F. Goodrich v. Murtha, 126
BFI Medical Waste Systems v. Whatcom County, 159
Bice v. Leslie's Poolmart, Inc., 42
Blue Circle Cement, Inc. v. Board of County Commrs., 170
Borowski, United States v., 442
Boyd v. Browner, 19
Brace, United States v., 436
Bradley Mining Co. v. EPA, 128
Broderick Inv. Co., United States v., 104, 114

C & A Carbone, Inc. v. Town of Clarkstown, 160
Cadillac of Fairview, Cal., Inc. v. United States, 118
California v. American Standard, 240
Calvert Cliffs Coordinating Comm. v. United States Atomic Energy Commn., 463
Cambridge Water Co. v. Eastern Counties Leather, 33
Carolina Transformer Co., United States v., 125
Catellus Dev. Corp. v. United States, 118
Central Arizona Water Conservation Dist. v. EPA, 343
Chemical Specialties Mfg. Assn. v. Allenby, 239
Chemical Waste Mgmt. v. EPA, 79-80
Chemical Waste Mgmt. v. Hunt, 132, *133,* 159, 169
Chemical Waste Mgmt. v. Templet, 160
Cipollone v. Liggett Group, Inc., 42
City of Chicago v. Environmental Defense Fund, 68
Clean Air Implementation Project v. United States EPA, 272, 303
Coalition Against Columbus Center v. City of New York, 305
Coalition for Clean Air v. Southern Cal. Edison Co., 304
Colorado Envtl. Coalition v. Lujan, 297
Committee of Dental Amalgam Alloy Mfrs. v. Henry, 240
Committee to Save Mokelumne River v. East Bay Util. Dist., 350
Concerned Area Residents for the Env. v. Southview Farm, 366
Connecticut Coastal Fisherman's Assn. v. Remington Arms Co., 388, 443
Cose v. Getty Oil Co., 82
Creppel v. United States, 417

Daigle v. Shell Oil Co., 127
Daubert v. Merrell Dow Pharms., Inc. (113 S. Ct. 2786), 186, 242, *243,* 253-54, 465
Daubert v. Merrell Dow Pharms., Inc. (43 F.3d 1311), 254
Daubert v. Merrell Dow Pharms., Inc. (951 F.2d 1128), 242
Dolan v. City of Tigard, 347, *417*
Dow Chemical Co. v. Alfaro, 537

Eagle-Picher Indus. v. EPA, 81
East Bibb Twigs Neighborhood Assn. v. Macon-Bibb County Planning and Zoning Commn., 9
El Pueblo Para el Aire y Agua Limpio v. County of Kings, 10
Endangered Species Comm. v. Babbitt, 470
Environmental Council of Sacramento, Inc. v. EPA, 305
Environmental Defense Fund v. City of Chicago, 67
Environmental Defense Fund v. Massey, 499, 500

Table of Cases

Environmental Defense Fund v. Thomas, 302
Environmental Transp. Sys., Inc. v. ENSCO, 127

Feikema v. Texas, Inc., 43
Fleet Factors Corp., United States v., 121, 124
Florida Rock Indus., Inc. v. United States (21 Cl. Ct. 161), 415
Florida Rock Indus., Inc. v. United States (18 F.3d 1560), 415
FMC Corp. v. United States Dept. of Commerce, 105
Fort Gratiot Sanitary Landfill, Inc. v. Michigan Dept. of Natural Resources, 151, 159, 160
Frye v. United States, 253

Gade v. National Solid Wastes Mgmt. Assn., 43
General Elec. Co. v. AAMCO Transmissions, Inc., 117
Georgine v. American Chem. Prods. Inc., 241
Goodner Bros. Aircraft, Inc., United States v., 67
Government Suppliers Consolidating Servs. v. Bayh, 159
Gurley, United States v., 106
Gwaltney of Smithfield, Ltd. v. Chesapeake Bay Found., Inc., 443, 452

Hardage, United States v., 127
Harley-Davidson, Inc. v. Ministar, Inc., 119
Hayashi, United States v., 490
Hazardous Waste Treatment Council v. EPA, 67
Hecla Mining Co. v. EPA, 388
Hemingway Transport, Inc., In re, 115
Hines Lumber Co. v. Vulcan Materials Co., 114
Hodel v. Virginia Surface Mining & Reclamation Assn., Inc., 39
Hoffman Homes, Inc. v. Administrator, U.S. EPA, 436
Hughes v. Oklahoma, 150
Hunt v. Chemical Waste Mgmt., 133

Idaho v. I.C.C., 463
Ilco, Inc., United States v., 64
Industrial Union Dept., AFL-CIO v. American Petroleum Inst., 203, 214
Ingredient Communication Council, Inc. v. Lungren, 239
International Fabricare Institute v. EPA, 204-206, 208, 222
International Union, UAW v. OSHA (976 F.2d 749), 211
Inernational Union, UAW v. OSHA (37 F.3d 665), 212

Jones-Hamilton Co. v. Beazer Materials & Serv., 118
Joslyn Mfg. Co. v. Koppers Co., Inc., 113, 119
Juniper Dev. Group v. Kahn, 115
Just v. Marinette, 414

Kaiser Aluminum & Chem. Corp. v. Catellus Dev. Corp., 113, 121
Kane v. United States, 119
Kelley v. EPA, 61, 124-125
Kelley v. Selin, 170, 466
Kelley v. Tiscornia, 124
Kent Co., Delaware Levy Court v. EPA, 128
Kerr-McGee Chem. Corp. v. Lefton Iron & Metal Co., 114, 126
Ketchikan Pulp Co., United States v., 449

Table of Cases

Keystone Bituminous Coal Assn. v. DeBenedictis, 410
Key Tronic Corp. v. United States, 127

Lake Cumberland Trust, Inc., v. EPA, 387
Lansford-Coaldale Joint Water Auth. v. Tonolli Corp., 105
Leather Indus. of Am. v. EPA, 368
Les v. Reilly, 186, 230
Lincoln Properties, Ltd. v. Higgins, 126
Long Beach Unified Sch. Dist. v. Godwin Cal. Living Trust, 106
Lopez, United States v., 39-41
Louisiana-Pacific Corp v. Asarco, Inc., 81, 82
Loveladies Harbor, Inc. v. United States (21 Cl. Ct. 153), 412, 415
Loveladies Harbor, Inc. v. United States (27 F.3d 1545), 414
Loveladies Harbor, Inc. v. United States (28 F.3d 1171), 416
Lowe v. Sporicidin, Intl., 43
Lucas v. South Carolina Coastal Council, 347, 389, *390,* 408, 411, 412, 414, 415, 416
Lujan v. Defenders of Wildlife (Lujan II), 255, *275,* 297, 470, 547
Lujan v. National Wildlife Fed., 275, 295

Madison Gas & Elec. Co. v. EPA, 316
McLamb, United States v., 124
Medical Waste Assocs., Inc. v. Maryland Waste Coalition, Inc., 303
Medical Waste Assocs. Ltd. Partnership
  v. Mayor and City Council of Baltimore, 160
Mexico Feed and Seed Co., United States v., 125
Minnesota Pesticide Info. & Educ., Inc. v. Espy, 462
Missouri v. Illinois, 34
Mobil Oil Corp. v. EPA, 66
Monongahela Power Co. v. Reilly, 316
Morrison v. Olson, 451
Motor Vehicle Mfrs. Assn. v. New York State Dept. of Envtl. Conservation (17 F.3d 521), *324*
Motor Vehicle Mfrs. Assn. v. New York State Dept. of Envtl. Conservation (810 F. Supp. 1331), 324
Motor Vehicle Mfrs. Assn. v. New York State Dept. of Envtl. Conservation (No. 92-CV-869), 341-342

National Gypsum Co. v. EPA, 128
National Solid Wastes Mgmt. Assn. v. Alabama Dept. of Envtl. Mgmt., 133
National Wildlife Federation v. Burlington Northern Railroad, 490
National Wildlife Federation v. EPA, 37
Natural Resources Defense Council. *See* NRDC
NEPA Coalition of Japan v. Aspin, 546
New York v. Reilly, 273
New York v. United States, 38, 61, *171*
Niecko v. Emro Marketing Co., 119
Nollan v. California Coastal Commn., 417
Northeast Doran, Inc. v. Key Ban of Maine, 125
Northwest Envtl. Advocates v. City of Portland, 370
Northwest Forest Reserve Council v. Espy, 494
NRDC v. EPA (16 F.3d 1395), 369
NRDC v. EPA (22 F.3d 1125), *308*
NRDC v. EPA (25 F.3d 1063), 67
NRDC v. EPA (966 F.2d 1292), 366
NRDC v. Reilly (781 F. Supp. 806), 367
NRDC v. Reilly (976 F.2d 36), 344

Table of Cases

NRDC v. Reilly (983 F.2d 259), 323
NRDC v. Texaco, 443
Nurad, Inc. v. William E. Hooper & Sons Co., 61, *106*, 112-113

Old Bridge Chem. v. New Jersey Dept. of Envtl. Protection, 65
Oregon Waste Systems, Inc. v. Department of Envtl. Quality, *140*, 159, 169
Owen Elec. Steel Co. v. Browner, 64-65

Pacific Northwest Generating Coop. v. Brown, 469
Pacific Rivers Council v. Thomas, 469
Palila v. Hawaii Dept. of Land & Natural Resources, 471
Papas v. Upjohn Co., 43
Penn Central Transp. Co. v. New York City, 408, 409, 410
Pennsylvania v. West Virginia, 149
Pennsylvania Dept. of Envtl. Resources v. United States Postal Serv., 452
People v. Blech, 119
Philadelphia v. New Jersey, 132
Plaza Health Labs., Inc., United States v., 350
Portland Audubon Socy. v. Oregon Lands Coalition, 272, 296, 493
Pozsgai, United States v., 437
Price v. United States Navy, 127
Public Citizen v. Kantor, 462
Public Citizen v. Office of the U.S. Trade Representative (5 F.3d 549), 453, *455*
Public Citizen v. Office of the U.S. Trade Representative (970 F.2d 916), 454, 521, 546
Public Citizen v. Young, 230
PUD No. 1 of Jefferson County v. Washington Dept. of Ecology, 371, 387
Puerto Rico Sun Oil Co. v. EPA, 387

Reeves v. Stake, 151
Resources Ltd. Inc. v. Robertson, 464
R.I.S.E. v. Kay, 10
Riverside Bayview Homes, Inc., United States v., 40
Roosevelt v. E. I. DuPont de Nemours, Inc., 568
Rylands v. Fletcher, 34

Santiago v. Sherwin-Williams, 241
Save Our Community v. United States EPA, 436
Seattle Audubon Society v. Lyons, 494
Shell Oil Co. v. EPA, 65, 67
Sierra Club v. Costle, 272-273
Sierra Club v. EPA, 81, 368
Sierra Club v. Marita, 465
Smith v. United States, 546
South Carolina v. O'Leary, 464
South Dakota v. Dole, 38
Southeast Ark. Landfill, Inc. v. Arkansas, In re, 159
Southern Florida Water Mgmt. Dist., United States v., 463
Sweet Home Chapter of Communities for a Great Oregon, Babbitt, v., 454, 471
Synthetic Organic Chem. Mfrs. Assn. v. Secretary, Dept. of Health and Human Servs., 206

Tabb Lakes, Ltd. v. United States, 415
Tex Tin Corp. v. EPA, 129
3550 Stevens Creek Assocs. v. Barclays Bank of Cal., 119

xxvii

Table of Cases

Tippins, Inc. v. USX Corp., 119
Trustees for Alaska v. Fink, 315

Union Gas Co. v. Pennsylvania, 125
United Paperworkers Intl. Union v. International Paper Co., 559
United States v. _____. *See* name of defendant.
United States Dept. of Energy v. Ohio, 449, 450, 452

Villegas, United States v., 366

Waste System Corp. v. County of Martin, Minnesota, 160
Weitzenhoff, United States v., 443
Welch v. Board of Supervisors of Rappahanock County, 368
Westwood Pharmaceuticals, Inc. v. National Fuel Gas Distrib. Corp., 114
Weyerhaeuser Co. v. Costle, 412
Whitney Benefits, Inc. v. United States, 412
Wickard V. Filburn, 39-40
William Recht Co., United States v., 443
Wisconsin Elec. Power Co. v. Reilly, 343
Worm v. American Cyanamid Co., 43

Yee v. City of Escondido, 409

Environmental Regulation

=1=
Environmental Values and Policies: An Introduction

> All across this country, there is a deep understanding rooted in our religious heritage and renewed in the spirit of this time that the bounty of nature is not ours to waste. It is a gift from God that we hold in trust for future generations.
>
> —*President Bill Clinton**

> What is ultimately at stake in the environmental justice debate is everyone's quality of life. The goal is equal protection, *not* equal pollution.
>
> —*Deeohn Ferris***

President Clinton's affirmation of the moral dimensions of environmental protection policy in his first Earth Day address is reminiscent of the quotation from his predecessor on page 1 of the parent text. This chapter reviews new developments in environmental policy and philosophy, including the growth of the environmental justice movement and the decline of global fisheries. By focusing attention on the way environmental risks are distributed across society, the environmental justice movement is raising fundamental issues of fairness that have broad implications for environmental policy. The decline of global fisheries illustrates the tragedy of the commons and the difficulty of controlling access to common resources.

A. ENVIRONMENTAL PROBLEMS AND PROGRESS

Public Opinion and Political Support for Environmental Protection (pp. 2-3). The political climate that previously favored strong environ-

---

*Earth Day address, April 21, 1993.
**Program Director, Environmental Justice Project, Lawyer's Committee for Civil Rights Under Law.

mental protection measures has changed dramatically. While there is little indication that public support for the environment has waned, those who argue that regulation has gone too far take comfort from opinion polls reporting unrecedented public hostility toward government. A poll taken in August 1994 found that 91 percent of respondents had little or no faith in the ability of government to deal with the country's problems (18 percent had no confidence and 73 percent responded that they had only a little confidence in government). Government Garners Low Marks in Poll, N.Y. Times, Aug. 21, 1994, at 35.

What does seem to be eroding is the long-standing bipartisan nature of political support for environmental protection. Republicans in Congress are far less likely to support environmental legislation than in past decades. Even before the 1994 congressional elections, the League of Conservation Voters rated the environmental voting records of both Republican senators and congressmen in the 103d Congress as averaging only 19 out of 100, while Senate Democrats averaged 75 and House Democrats 68. Mathews, Scorched Earth: Why the Hill Has Become an Environmental Disaster Area, Wash. Post, Oct. 18, 1994, at A17. The political clout of national environmental organizations also may be on the wane. Environmental groups have experienced a decline in financial support from the public, which they attribute in part to the election of a president who was not threatening to roll back environmental progress. Aeppel, Green Groups Enter a Dry Season as Movement Matures, Wall St. J., Oct. 21, 1994, at B1; Schneider, Big Environment Hits a Recession, N.Y. Times, Jan. 1, 1995, at F4.

Now that the Republicans have taken control of both houses of Congress, the 104th Congress will be decidedly less sympathetic toward environmental interests. The new Speaker of the House, Newt Gingrich, has called the Environmental Protection Agency "the biggest job-killing agency in inner-city America." Lee, Gingrich Lashes Out at EPA; Browner Praises Its Efforts, Wash. Post, Feb. 17, 1995, at A23. Deeming the last two decades of environmental policy "absurdly expensive," the Speaker has called for a "very profound rethinking of what we want to do collectively as a species in order to save the environment." Cushman, Congressional Republicans Take Aim at an Extensive List of Environmental Statutes, N.Y. Times, Feb. 22, 1995, at A14. As discussed below, a variety of legislative proposals that would sharply restrict environmental regulation are moving rapidly through Congress.

What Should Be Considered an "Environmental Problem"? (pp. 12-13). In February 1993 Russian scientists conducted an experiment in which an orbiting mirror was used to reflect sunlight to illuminate an area of the Earth that was then in darkness. Proponents of the experiment argue that this technology could be used to extend growing

1. Environmental Values and Policies   Pages 18-20

seasons at extreme latitudes and to save electricity. Bill McKibben argues that environmentalists should be "screaming about" such proposals, for "what more basic assault can be mounted on our environment than changing its cadence?" McKibben, Light Up the Sky? Are We Crazy?, N.Y. Times, Feb. 20, 1993, at 19. Should such a proposal be viewed as creating an environmental problem? Why or why not? See also Goodnight Moon, N.Y. Times, May 11, 1993, at A20 (editorial decrying a proposal to orbit a mile-wide satellite that would flash advertisements to Earth in the night sky).

B. AMERICAN ENVIRONMENTALISM: SOURCES AND VALUES

Religious Organizations and Environmental Concerns (pp. 17-18). For an argument that the Christian religious tradition embodies respect for the environment founded on praise for the divine creation of nature, see Susan Bratton, The "New" Christian Ecology, in After Earth Day: Continuing the Conservation Effort 204 (M. Oelschlager, ed. 1992). Religious groups increasingly are emphasizing mankind's responsibility for the environment. In late 1992 the Roman Catholic Church adopted a new catechism that for the first time states that abuse of the environment will be considered a sin by the Church. Riding, New Catechism for Catholics Defines Sins of Modern World, N.Y. Times, Nov. 17, 1992, at A1. A coalition called the Religious Partnership for the Environment has been active in urging Catholic, Jewish, and Protestant congregations to incorporate environmental concerns into their worship. D. Gonzalez, Religions Are Putting Faith in Environmentalism, N.Y. Times, Nov. 6, 1994, at 34.

Human Rights and Environmental Protection (pp. 18-20). In April 1992, Yale Law School sponsored a conference entitled "Earth Rights and Responsibility: Human Rights and Environmental Protection." The conference, which attracted nearly 300 environmentalists, human rights advocates, theologians, scientists, and philosophers, focused on the question of what, if any, environmental rights should be recognized. Participants considered whether humans should have a right to a healthy environment, environmental rights of future generations, and the rights of ecosystems. Conference proceedings were published in Earth Rights and Responsibilities: Human Rights and Environmental Protection, Conference Report (April 1992).

Pages 22-24　　　　　　　　1. Environmental Values and Policies

The Environmental Justice Movement (pp. 22-24). One of the most significant developments in the environmental field in recent years has been the growth of the environmental justice movement. The following Note describes the history of this movement and why it is having a growing influence on environmental policy decisions.

The Environmental Justice Movement

Environmental hazards are not evenly distributed across society. Poor communities and communities of color are exposed to disproportionate levels of environmental risk. Whether due to racism or other factors, the uneven distribution of environmental risks is rapidly becoming one of the most important issues in the environmental field. Questions concerning fairness in the distribution of environmental hazards pose a fundamental challenge to public policy makers. In many disputes, the manner in which risks are distributed may be even more important than the aggregate level of risk.

A Brief History. The environmental justice movement began in 1982 in Warren County, one of the poorest counties in North Carolina, when local officials decided to locate a PCB landfill in a predominately African-American neighborhood. Residents protested vehemently as trucks delivered PCB-contaminated soil to the landfill. In the nonviolent civil disobedience campaign that ensued, over 500 were arrested, including Walter E. Fauntroy, who was then the Delegate to Congress from Washington, D.C., and the Reverend Dr. Benjamin F. Chavis, Jr., executive director of the United Church of Christ Commission for Racial Justice (CRJ), who later became the executive director of the NAACP. The activists were unsuccessful, but their actions promoted a merging of interests between civil rights advocates and environmentalists.

As a result of the Warren County protests, Delegate Fauntroy asked the General Accounting Office (GAO) to investigate the racial and socioeconomic composition of communities surrounding the four major hazardous waste landfills in the South. The 1983 GAO study, "Study of Hazardous Waste Landfills and their Correlation with Racial and Economic Status of Surrounding Communities," found that three of the four largest landfills in the South were in predominantly African-American communities.

In 1987 the CRJ, under the leadership of Dr. Chavis, sponsored a nationwide study to look at the location of sites containing hazardous wastes and the racial and socioeconomic characteristics of persons living near those sites. The results of the landmark study, "Toxic Wastes and Race in the United States: A National Report on the Racial and Socio-

1. Environmental Values and Policies — Pages 22-24

Economic Characteristics of Communities with Hazardous Waste Sites," followed the pattern found in the South. Among the major findings:

- Race proved to be the most significant among variables associated with the location of commercial hazardous waste facilities, with household income being second.
- Communities with the greatest number of commercial hazardous waste facilities had the highest composition of minority residents.
- Three out of the five largest commercial hazardous waste landfills in the United States were located in predominantly black or Hispanic communities. These three landfills accounted for 40 percent of the total estimated commercial landfill capacity in the nation.
- Three out of every five black and Hispanic Americans lived in communities with uncontrolled toxic waste sites.
- Uncontrolled toxic waste sites were disproportionately concentrated in black and Hispanic communities.

Numerous other local, regional, and national studies have confirmed this pattern. These studies have served as a rallying point for poor and minority communities. Atgeld Gardens in Chicago provides a good example.

About ten years ago, Hazel Johnson organized a group called People for Community Recovery (PCR) with the aim of cleaning up Atgeld Gardens, a dilapidated housing project with 10,000 people, nearly all African-American. Despite the image its name might evoke, Atgeld Gardens is built atop a former landfill whose odors still rise through the residents' basements decades after the landfill was closed. It is also surrounded on all sides by various sources of pollution: a hazardous waste incinerator, seven landfills, chemical plants, a paint factory, two steel mills, and lagoons filled with contaminants that emit 30,000 tons of poisons into the air each year. Johnson's group has made some headway—PCR successfully warded off yet another landfill and was effective in getting asbestos removed from homes—but progress has been slow. While Atgeld Gardens has one of the highest cancer rates in the nation, it is not unique. Similar problems face residents in Homer and Wallace, Louisiana; Columbia, Mississippi; Williamsburg, New York; Institute, West Virginia; and hundreds of other communities around the country.

In 1990 the University of Michigan's School of Natural Resources convened a conference on Race and the Incidence of Environmental Hazards that brought together scholar-activists and civil rights leaders. In the aftermath of the conference, participants met with various congressional and federal officials and were instrumental in the creation of EPA's Environmental Equity Workgroup. The Workgroup was charged with assessing the evidence that minority and low-income communities bear a disproportionate amount of environmental burdens and with considering what EPA might do about any identified disparities.

In 1991, the CRJ organized the First National People of Color Environmental Leadership Summit, with the goal of developing a comprehensive national action agenda to help reshape and redirect environmental policy-making in the United States to embrace concerns of minority Americans. This Summit helped to galvanize the grassroots movement and to encourage minority groups to wage a national campaign for environmental justice in their communities. "Principles of Environmental Justice" were adopted by the whole conference (see below). A "Call to Action" was also adopted that called for the embodiment of the Principles in grassroots social and political work within minority communities.

Principles of Environmental Justice

Environmental justice . .

1. affirms the sacredness of Mother Earth, ecological unity and the interdependence of all species, and the right to be free from ecological destruction.
2. demands that public policy be based on mutual respect and justice for all peoples, free from any form of discrimination or bias.
3. mandates the right to ethical, balanced and reponsible uses of land and renewable resources in the interest of a sustainable planet for humans and other living things . . .
5. affirms the fundamental right to political, economic, cultural and environmental self-determination of all peoples . . .
7. demands the right to participate as equal partners at every level of decision-making including needs assessment, planning, implementation, enforcement and evaluation.
8. affirms the right of all workers to a safe and healthy work environment, without being forced to choose between an unsafe livelihood and unemployment . . .
12. affirms the need for urban and rural ecological policies to clean up and rebuild our cities and rural areas in balance with nature, honoring the cultural integrity of all our communities, and providing fair access for all to the full range of resources . . .
16. calls for the education of present and future generations which emphasizes social and environmental issues, based on our experience and an appreciation of our diverse cultural perspectives.

1. Environmental Values and Policies   Pages 22-24

17. requires that we, as individuals, make personal and consumer choices to consume as little of Mother Earth's resources and to produce as little waste as possible; and make the conscious decision to challenge and reprioritize our lifestyles to insure the health of the natural world for present and future generations.

In response to the environmental justice movement, EPA established an Office of Environmental Equity. In July 1992, EPA released a report entitled "Environmental Equity: Reducing Risk for all Communities." EPA's report found that levels of exposure to some environmental pollutants vary with socioeconomic status and race and that there are clear differences by race in disease and death rates. EPA concluded, however, that the data were insufficient to determine the relationship between environmental health effects, race, and income. The report recommended that EPA (1) give higher priority to issues of environmental equity; (2) incorporate considerations of environmental equity into the risk assessment process; (3) selectively review and revise permit and grant procedures as well as monitoring and enforcement to address high concentrations of risk in minority and low-income communities; and (4) improve the level of communication with such communities and increase efforts to involve them in policy-making.

Critics charged that EPA's report overstated the lack of data on the concentration of environmental risks in minority and poor communities and failed to suggest actions to promote greater equity. Dr. Benjamin Chavis called the report itself an "inequity."

Shortly after the release of the EPA report, the National Law Journal (NLJ) published the results of its investigation into the relationship between race and the enforcement of environmental laws. The NLJ report generally found that penalties against environmental violators in minority areas were lower than those imposed for violators in largely white areas. The report's major findings include the following:

- Penalties under hazardous waste laws were about 500 percent higher at sites having the greatest white population than penalties at sites with the greatest minority population.
- Penalties under federal environmental laws regulating air and water pollution and waste disposal were 46 percent higher in white communities than in minority communities.
- Abandoned hazardous waste sites in minority areas took 20 percent longer to be placed on the National Priority List for Superfund cleanup than those in white areas.
- In more than half of the ten regions that administer EPA programs around the country, cleanup of Superfund sites began

from 12 to 42 percent later in minority communities than in white communities.
- In minority communities, EPA chose containment (the capping or walling off of a hazardous dumpsite) 7 percent more frequently than permanent treatment (the cleanup method preferred under the law); in white communities, EPA ordered permanent treatment 22 percent more often than containment.

Evidence of the worsening of disparities in facility siting patterns is provided by a study updating data in the landmark 1987 report by the United Church of Christ Commission for Racial Justice (CRJ). The new study, released in August 1994, compared data from the 1980 and the 1990 census with information on the location of 530 off-site hazardous waste treatment, storage, or disposal facilities operating in the early 1990s and found that racial disparities in the location of these facilities had increased since the data considered in the 1987 study. B. Goldman and L. Fitton, Toxic Wastes and Race Revisited (1994). The study found that "people of color were 47 percent more likely than whites to live near a commercial hazardous waste facility." Noting that 115 of these facilities were new since the 1987 report, the study suggests that stricter environmental regulation actually may have contributed to siting disparities by making it more difficult to site disposal facilities in environmentally aware areas where political and economic power are the greatest.

A study released in April 1994 disputes the notion that waste facilities are sited in a racially discriminatory fashion. The study, performed by the University of Massachusetts and funded by WMX Technologies, Inc., the nation's largest waste disposal firm (formerly called Waste Management, Inc.), found that hazardous waste facilities were more likely to be found in white, working-class neighborhoods than in minority communities. This result was largely a product of the study's use of census tracts rather than zip codes to assess the distribution of facilities. Census tracts are much smaller units of analysis (encompassing about 4,000 persons) than the zip codes (which can include as many as 70,000 persons) used in the CRJ's 1987 study. Two Reports Dispute Claims that Siting of Commercial Facilities Discriminatory, 24 Env. Rep. 2100 (1994).

Sources of Environmental Injustice. The causes of the disproportionate distribution of environmental risk are a subject of considerable controversy. In their quest to set acceptable levels of risk, policy-makers have rarely paid attention to the way risks are distributed. Race, poverty, and political disenfranchisement clearly have some influence on the distribution of risk. Poor communities and communities of color generally have fewer resources and less political clout than wealthy white neighborhoods. The mainstream environmental movement, historically white and

1. Environmental Values and Policies — Pages 22-24

middle- or upper-class in its orientation, rarely focused on issues of concern to minorities or the poor during the 1960s, '70s and '80s.

Some argue that the distribution of locally undesirable land uses is the product not of racism but of other factors such as the desire of many poor communities for development and jobs. Residents of such communities, on the other hand, often insist that they were misled by developers. See, e.g., Bean v. Southwestern Waste Management Corp., 482 F. Supp. 673 (S.D. Tex. 1979), affd. without opinion, 782 F.2d 1038 (5th Cir. 1986) (court found statistical evidence insufficient to establish intentional race discrimination in the selection of a solid waste disposal site even though the community was originally told that a shopping mall or steel mill was being constructed).

Dr. Robert Bullard, a professor of sociology at the University of California-Riverside, calls it "environmental blackmail" when a community is encouraged to accept the environmental risks of a new facility because it purportedly will provide jobs. Bullard's book, Dumping in Dixie: Race, Class, and Environmental Quality (Westview Press, 1990) contains case studies of communities in which a majority of residents initially were willing to accept health risks in exchange for jobs. Nevertheless, after facilities had been completed in their communities, two thirds of the residents felt that employment opportunities had not improved and that the burdens caused by the facilities outweighed the benefits.

Developers also argue that siting decisions are more heavily influenced by zoning restrictions and hydrology than the socioeconomic characteristics of residents. The poor and minorities often have inherited hazards by moving into older or industrial sections of cities, where decrepit factories and other facilities were built long before anyone worried about pollution. Professor Vicki Been of NYU Law School has conducted empirical studies of the distribution of locally undesirable land uses over time. Her research suggests that the disproportionate impact of such facilities on minorities and the poor is in large part a product of demographic changes that occur *after* facilities have been sited. Been, Locally Undesirable Land Uses in Minority Neighborhoods: Disproportionate Siting or Market Dynamics?, 103 Yale L.J. 1383 (1994).

Legal Remedies for Environmental Injustice. Efforts to use existing law to combat environmental injustice have met with little success. While constitutional challenges have been brought on four legal theories (denial of equal protection of the law, violations of procedural or substantive due process, and claims of uncompensated takings of private property), the courts have yet to uphold a challenge based on constitutional claims. See, e.g., East Bibb Twiggs Neighborhood Association v. Macon-Bibb County Planning and Zoning Commission, 706 F. Supp. 880 (M.D. Ga. 1989), affd., 896 F.2d 1264 (11th Cir. 1990) (court found no proof of discriminatory intent behind placement of a non-putrescible landfill in a black community); R.I.S.E. v. Kay, 768 F. Supp. 1144 (E.D. Va. 1991) (judge dismissed a discrimination claim even though three prior landfills located in the contested area had been placed where populations within a one mile radius were between 95 percent and 100 percent black; the population within a half-mile of the challenged site was 64 percent black); *Bean*, 482 F. Supp. 673.

In light of the bleak prospects for constitutional claims, plaintiffs have turned to suits under state law or have concentrated instead on political action, community education, and advocacy of legislative remedies. For example, when Waste Management, Inc. attempted to site a hazardous waste incinerator near its hazardous waste landfill in Kettleman City, California, the predominantly Latino community launched a campaign of opposition with the help of the California Rural Legal Assistance Foundation (CRLAF). Community residents wrote 119 letters opposing the facility—in Spanish. After county officials answered the letters—in English—and approved the incinerator, a judge agreed that the community had been left out of the process and required that the environmental impact documents be prepared in Spanish. El Pueblo Para el Aire y Agua Limpio v. County of Kings, No. 366045 (Cal. Sup. Ct., Dec. 30, 1991).

Some states have changed their siting laws to combat disparities in exposure to environmental risks. In 1993 Arkansas enacted an Environmental Equity Act that creates a rebuttable presumption against the siting of any "high impact solid waste management facility" within 12 miles of an existing facility. This presumption can be overcome either by showing that no other geologically suitable site exists in the region or that "incentives have prompted the host community to accept the siting of the facility." Ark. Stat. Ann. §8-6-1504 (1993).

Efforts to seek legal redress for environmental justice concerns also are focusing on Title VI of the Civil Rights Act of 1964, 42 U.S.C. §2000d. Title VI prohibits discrimination on the basis of race, color or national origin in any program or activity receiving federal financial assistance. After reversing a policy that deemed Title VI inapplicable in the context of environmental justice concerns, EPA's Office of Civil Rights has commenced investigations of possible Title VI violations. These include allegations of discrimination in the permitting of waste disposal facilities by Mississippi and Louisiana authorities. Regulations issued by EPA to implement Title VI can be found at 40 C.F.R. §7.35.

ENVIRONMENTAL JUSTICE: A PATHFINDER

Literature on environmental justice is developing at a rapid pace. Among the most important studies documenting that environmental risks are disproportionately concentrated in minority communities are General Accounting Office, Siting of Hazardous Waste Landfills and Their Correlation with Racial and Economic Status of Surrounding Communities (1983); R. Bullard, Dumping in Dixie; Race, Class, and Environmental Quality (Westview Press, 1990); Commission on Racial Justice, United Church of Christ, Toxic Waste and Race in the United States: A National Report on the Racial and Socio-Economic Characteristics of Communities with Hazardous Waste Sites (1987); Environmental Racism: Issues and Dilemmas (B. Bryant and P. Mohai, eds. 1991). EPA's assessment of this data is contained in the EPA report Environmental Equity: Reducing the Risk for All Communities (July 1992). See also B. Goldman and L. Fitton, Toxic Wastes and Race Revisited (1994), and R. Bullard, Unequal Protection: Environmental Justice and Communities of Color (1994).

Several articles have focussed on issues of environmental justice, including Poirier, Environmental Justice/Racism/Equity: Can We Talk?, 96 W. Va. L. Rev. 1083 (1994); Bullard, Race and Environmental Justice in the United States, 18 Yale J. Intl. L. 319 (1993); Foster, Race(ial) Matters: The Quest for Environmental Justice, 20 Ecology L.Q. 721 (1993); O'Reilly, Environmental Racism, Site Cleanup and Inner-City Jobs: Indiana's Urban In-fill Incentives, 11 Yale J. Reg. 43 (1994). Bullard, The Threat of Environmental Racism, 7 Nat. Res. & Envt. 23 (1993); Cole, Empowerment as the Key to Environmental Protection: The Need for Environmental Poverty Law, 19 Ecology L. Q. 619 (1992); Godsil, Remedying Environmental Racism, 90 Mich. L. Rev. 394 (1991); Lazarus, Pursuing "Environmental Justice": The Distributional Effects of Environmental Protection, 87 Nw. U. L. Rev. 101 (1993). See also the numerous articles in three symposia: Environmental Equity: Confronting Racial Injustice in Land Use Patterns, 2 Land Use F. 3 (1993); Urban Environmental Justice, 21 Fordham Urb. L.J. 425 (1994); and Environmental Justice, 5 Md. J. Cont. L. Issues 1 (1993-94); Symposium, Class, Race and Environmental Regulation, 63 U. Colo. L. Rev. 839 (1992); Symposium, Environmental Equity in the 1990s: Pollution, Poverty, and Political Empowerment, 1 Kan. J.L. & Pub. Poly. 1 (1991). See also the treatise Race and the Incidence of Environmental Hazards: A Time for Discourse (B. Bryant and P. Mohai, eds. 1992).

A quarterly newsletter reporting on developments in the environmental justice movement is Race, Poverty & the

Environment, published jointly by the California Rural Legal Assistance Foundation and the Earth Island Institute. Subscriptions are available from Earth Island Institute, 300 Broadway, Suite 28, San Francisco, California 94133, at a cost of $15 for four issues. Extensive materials prepared for the March 1993 Symposium on Civil Rights and the Environment: Bridging the Disciplines, including a Legal Compendium summarizing litigation raising environmental justice issues, is available from the Environmental Justice Project of the Lawyers Committee for Civil Rights Under Law, 1400 I St., N.W., Washington, D.C. 20005. A directory of groups working to promote environmental justice, which contains a useful annotated bibliography, is available from the Charles Stuart Mott Foundation, (810) 766-1766. R. Bullard, People of Color Environmental Groups, 1994-1995 Directory (1994).

Clinton Administration Executive Order. The Clinton administration has sought to require agencies to incorporate environmental justice concerns in their actions by issuance of the following executive order.

> *Executive Order 12898*
> *Federal Actions to Address Environmental Justice in Minority Populations and Low-Income Populations*
> **59 Fed. Reg. 7629 (1994)**

By the authority vested in me as President by the Constitution and the laws of the United States of America, it is hereby ordered as follows:

Section 1-1. Implementation

1-101. *Agency Responsibilities.* To the greatest extent practicable and permitted by law, and consistent with the principles set forth in the report on the National Performance Review, each Federal agency shall make achieving environmental justice part of its mission by identifying and addressing, as appropriate, disproportionately high and adverse human health or environmental effects of its programs, policies, and activities on minority populations and low-income populations in the United States and its territories and possessions, the District of Columbia, the Commonwealth of Puerto Rico, and the Commonwealth of the Mariana Islands.

1-102. *Creation of an Interagency Working Group on Environmental Justice.* (a) Within three months of the date of this order, the Administra-

1. Environmental Values and Policies — Pages 22-24

tor of the Environmental Protection Agency ("Administrator") or the Administrator's designee shall convene an interagency Federal Working Group on Environmental Justice ("Working Group"). The Working Group shall comprise the heads of the following executive agencies and offices, or their designees: (a) Department of Defense; (b) Department of Health and Human Services; (c) Department of Housing and Urban Development; (d) Department of Labor; (e) Department of Agriculture; (f) Department of Transportation; (g) Department of Justice; (h) Department of the Interior; (i) Department of Commerce; (j) Department of Energy; (k) Environmental Protection Agency; (l) Office of Management and Budget; (m) Office of Science and Technology Policy; (n) Office of the Deputy Assistant to the President for Environmental Policy; (o) Office of the Assistant to the President for Domestic Policy; (p) National Economic Council; (q) Council of Economic Advisers; and (r) such other Government officials as the President may designate. The Working Group shall report to the President through the Deputy Assistant to the President for Environmental Policy and the Assistant to the President for Domestic Policy.

(b) The Working Group shall:

(1) provide guidance to Federal agencies on criteria for identifying disproportionately high and adverse human health or environmental effects on minority populations and low-income populations;

(2) coordinate with, provide guidance to, and serve as a clearinghouse for, each Federal agency as it develops an environmental justice strategy as required by section 1-103 of this order, in order to ensure that the administration, interpretation and enforcement of programs, activities and policies are undertaken in a consistent manner;

(3) assist in coordinating research by, and stimulating cooperation among, the Environmental Protection Agency, the Department of Health and Human Services, the Department of Housing and Urban Development, and other agencies conducting research or other activities in accordance with section 3-3 of this order;

(4) assist in coordinating data collection, required by this order;

(5) examine existing data and studies on environmental justice;

(6) hold public meetings as required in section 5-502(d) of this order; and

(7) develop interagency model projects on environmental justice that evidence cooperation among Federal agencies.

1-103. *Development of Agency Strategies.* (a) Except as provided in section 6-605 of this order, each Federal agency shall develop an agency-wide environmental justice strategy, as set forth in subsections (b) - (e) of this section that identifies and addresses disproportionately high and adverse human health or environmental effects of its program, policies, and activities on minority populations and low-income populations. The environmental justice strategy shall list programs, policies, planning and public participation processes, enforcement, and/or rulemakings related to human health or the environment that should be revised to, at a minimum: (1) promote enforcement of all health and environmental statutes in areas with minority populations and low-income populations; (2) ensure greater public participation; (3) improve research and data collection relating to the health of and environment of minority populations and low-income populations; and (4) identify differential patterns of consumption of natural resources among minority populations and low-income populations. In addition, the environmental justice strategy shall include, where appropriate, a timetable for undertaking identified revisions and consideration of economic and social implications of the revisions.

(b) Within four months of the date of this order, each Federal agency shall identify an internal administrative process for developing its environmental justice strategy, and shall inform the Working Group of the process.

(c) Within six months of the date of this order, each Federal agency shall provide the Working Group with an outline of its proposed environmental justice strategy.

(d) Within ten months of the date of this order, each Federal agency shall provide the Working Group with its proposed environmental justice strategy.

(e) Within 12 months of the date of this order, each Federal agency shall finalize its environmental justice strategy and provide a copy and written description of its strategy to the Working Group. During the 12 month period from the date of this order, each Federal agency, as part of its environmental justice strategy, shall identify several specific projects that can be promptly undertaken to address particular concerns identified during the development of the proposed environmental justice strategy, and a schedule for implementing those projects.

(f) Within 24 months of the date of this order, each Federal agency shall report to the Working Group on its progress in implementing its agency-wide environmental justice strategy.

(g) Federal agencies shall provide additional periodic reports to the Working Group as requested by the Working Group.

1-104. *Reports to the President.* Within 14 months of the date of this order, the Working Group shall submit to the President, through the Office of the Deputy Assistant to the President for Environmental Policy and the Office of the Assistant to the President for Domestic Policy, a report that describes the implementation of this order, and includes the final environmental justice strategies described in section 1-103(e) of this order.

1. Environmental Values and Policies   Pages 22-24

Sec. 2-2. Federal Agency Responsibilities for Federal Programs
Each Federal agency shall conduct its programs, policies, and activities that substantially affect human health or the environment, in a manner that ensures that such programs, policies, and activities do not have the effect of excluding persons (including populations) from participation in, denying persons (including populations) the benefits of, or subjecting persons (including populations) to discrimination under, such programs, policies, and activities, because of their race, color, or national origin.

Sec. 3-3. Research, Data Collection, and Analysis
3-301. *Human Health and Environmental Research Analysis.* (a) Environmental human health research, whenever practicable and appropriate, shall include diverse segments of the population in epidemiological and clinical studies, including segments at high risk from environmental hazards, such as minority populations, low-income populations and workers who may be exposed to substantial environmental hazards.

(b) Environmental human health analyses, whenever practicable and appropriate, shall identify multiple and cumulative exposures.

(c) Federal agencies shall provide minority populations and low-income populations the opportunity to comment on the development and design of research strategies undertaken pursuant to this order.

3-302. *Human Health and Environmental Data Collection and Analysis.* To the extent permitted by existing law, including the Privacy Act, as amended (5 USC §552a):

(a) Each Federal agency, whenever practicable and appropriate, shall collect, maintain, and analyze information assessing and comparing environmental and human health risks borne by populations identified by race, national origin, or income. To the extent practical and appropriate, Federal agencies shall use this information to determine whether their programs, policies, and activities have disproportionately high and adverse human health or environmental effects on minority populations and low-income populations;

(b) In connection with the development and implementation of agency strategies in section 1-103 of the order, each Federal agency, whenever practicable and appropriate, shall collect, maintain and analyze information on the race, national origin, income level, and other readily accessible and appropriate information for areas surrounding facilities or sites expected to have a substantial environmental, human health, or economic effect on the surrounding populations, when such facilities or sites become the subject of a substantial Federal environmental administrative or judicial action. Such information shall be made available to the public, unless prohibited by law; and

(c) Each Federal agency, whenever practicable and appropriate, shall collect, maintain, and analyze information on the race, national origin, income level, and other readily accessible and appropriate information for areas surrounding Federal facilities that are: (1) subject to the reporting requirements under the Emergency Planning and Community Right-To-Know Act, 42 U.S.C. §§11001-11050 as mandated in Executive Order No. 12856; and (2) expected to have a substantial environmental, human health, or economic effect on surrounding populations. Such information shall be made available to the public, unless prohibited by law.

Sec. 4-4. Subsistence Consumption of Fish and Wildlife

4-401. *Consumption Patterns.* In order to assist in identifying the need for ensuring protection of populations with differential patterns of subsistence consumption of fish and wildlife, Federal agencies, whenever practicable and appropriate, shall collect, maintain, and analyze information on the consumption patterns of populations who principally rely on fish and/or wildlife for subsistence. Federal agencies shall communicate to the public the risks of those consumption patterns.

4-402. *Guidance.* Federal agencies, whenever practicable and appropriate, shall work in a coordinated manner to publish guidance reflecting the latest scientific information available concerning methods for evaluating the human health risks associated with the consumption of pollutant-bearing fish or wildlife. Agencies shall consider such guidance in developing their policies and rules.

Sec. 5-5. Public Participation and Access to Information

(a) The public may submit recommendations to Federal agencies relating to the incorporation of environmental justice principles into Federal agency programs or policies. Each Federal agency shall convey such recommendations to the Working Group.

(b) Each Federal agency may, whenever practicable and appropriate, translate crucial public documents, notices, and hearing relating to human health or the environment for limited English speaking populations.

(c) Each Federal agency shall work to ensure that public documents, notices, and hearings relating to human health or the environment are concise, understandable, and readily accessible to the public.

(d) The Working Group shall hold public meetings, as appropriate, for the purpose of fact-finding, receiving public comments, and conducting inquiries concerning environmental justice. The Working

1. Environmental Values and Policies   Pages 22-24

Group shall prepare for public review a summary of the comments and recommendations discussed at the public meetings.

Sec. 6-6. *General Provisions*

6-601. *Responsibility for Agency Implementation.* The head of each Federal agency shall be responsible for ensuring compliance with this order. Each Federal agency shall conduct internal reviews and take such other steps as may be necessary to monitor compliance with this order.

6-602. *Executive Order 12250.* This Executive order is intended to supplement but not supersede Executive Order 12250, which requires consistent and effective implementation of various federal laws prohibiting discriminatory practices in programs receiving Federal financial assistance. Nothing herein shall limit the effect or mandate of Executive Order No. 12250.

6-603. *Executive Order No. 12875.* This Executive order is not intended to limit the effect or mandate of Executive Order No. 12875 [which is designed to reduce the imposition of unfunded mandates on state, local, and tribal governments and to streamline the waiver application process for them].

6-604. *Scope.* For purposes of this order, Federal agency means any agency on the Working Group, and such other agencies as may be designated by the President, that conducts any Federal program or activity that substantially affects human health or the environment. Independent agencies are requested to comply with the provisions of this order.

6-605. *Petitions for Exemptions.* The head of a Federal agency may petition the President for an exemption from the requirements of this order on the grounds that all or some of the petitioning agency's programs or activities should not be subject to the requirements of this order.

6-606. *Native American Programs.* Each Federal agency responsbility set forth under this order shall apply equally to Native American programs. In addition, the Department of the Interior, in coordination with the Working Group, and, after consultation with tribal leaders, shall coordinate steps to be taken pursuant to this order that address Federally-recognized Indian Tribes.

6-607. *Costs.* Unless otherwise provided by law, Federal agencies shall assume the financial costs of complying with this order.

6-608. *General.* Federal agencies shall implement this order consistent with, and to the extent permitted by, existing law.

6-609. *Judicial Review.* This order is intended only to improve the internal management of the executive branch and is not intended to, nor does it create any right, benefit, or trust responsibility, substantive or procedural, enforceable at law or equity by a party against the United

States, its agencies, its officers, or any person. This order shall not be construed to create any right to judicial review involving the compliance or noncompliance of the United States, its agencies, its officers, or any other person with this order.

NOTES AND QUESTIONS

1. The executive order directs each federal agency to "make achieving environmental justice part of its mission by identifying and addressing, as appropriate, disproportionately high and adverse human health or environmental effects of its programs, policies and activities on minority and low-income populations." How should agencies go about determining what constitutes disproportionately high and adverse health or environmental effects?

2. The executive order directs agencies to collect and consider improved data on the impact of environmental and human health risks on minority and poor communities. What sort of data would be most useful for agencies to gather?

3. Each agency is required by the executive order to develop an environmental justice strategy that outlines plans to revise agency rules or policies to promote environmental justice. What should agencies include in their strategies?

4. Some indication of the types of activities agencies may pursue to promote environmental justice may be provided by a plan announced by EPA Region I in May, 1994. The plan is the product of an environmental justice working group convened in 1991 by Region I, which covers the New England area. It pledges to triple the number of environmental inspections in minority and low-income communities and to funnel at least $1 million in enforcement penalties to environmental projects to benefit such communities. Region I Sets Environmental Justice Plan: More Inspections Eyed in Low-Income Areas, 25 Env. Rep. 62 (1994). EPA's three-member Environmental Appeals Board, which hears appeals of permit decisions by the agency's regional offices, also is beginning to hear challenges based on environmental justice concerns. Environmental Justice Becomes Newest Issue Facing Agency's Administrative Appeals Board, 24 Env. Rep. 1970 (1994).

5. What new avenues of redress, if any, does the executive order create for the victims of environmental injustice?

6. How should the following ongoing environmental justice controversies be resolved? EPA is being sued by a group of 87 African-American former residents of a contaminated Texarkana, Texas subdivision demolished as part of a superfund cleanup. The former residents claim that they were coerced by EPA into selling their property to the govern-

1. Environmental Values and Policies   Pages 28-35

ment for below fair market value. Boyd v. Browner, No. 94-0893 (D.D.C. 1994). The plaintiffs cite letters from EPA officials stating that if they forced the government to exercise its power of eminent domain they would receive less money because their property would be appraised based on its location "within an environmentally unsafe area." The plaintiffs maintain that this constitutes discriminatory treatment because EPA made no similar threat when it relocated the residents of the white, dioxin-contaminated community of Times Beach, Missouri. The plaintiffs' lawyer is seeking assistance from EPA's National Environmental Justice Advisory Council, a 25-member advisory panel established in November, 1993. Lavelle, Help Sought from "Green" Justice Panel, Natl. L.J., Oct. 31, 1994, at A16.

In another case, minority residents of a lead-contaminated public housing project in Portsmouth, Virginia are arguing that EPA's failure to relocate them is discriminatory. Located next to a foundry formerly used to recycle lead railroad parts, the Washington Park housing project has been on EPA's National Priorities List for more than a decade because of alarming levels of lead contamination. While EPA plans to buy out the owners of nearby private homes, minority residents of the housing project will have to be content with a soil cleanup around their apartment buildings. The Portsmouth Housing Authority has offered to relocate residents to other public housing projects in the community as units become available, but the other projects are notoriously crime-ridden. Lavelle, Poor Residents Say EPA Hasn't Gotten the Lead Out, Natl. L.J., Oct. 24, 1994, at A1.

Tensions Between Biocentric and Homocentric Philosophies (pp. 24-27). The tensions between biocentric and homocentric philosophies of environmental protection are explored in Bryan Norton, Toward Unity Among Environmentalists (Oxford University Press 1991). Norton, a professor of philosophy at the Georgia Institute of Technology, argues that the sharp differences between these philosophic traditions have generated considerable, and unnecessary, friction among environmentalists. Professor Norton maintains that these differences can be set aside and agreement achieved among environmentalists if they focus on developing pragmatic solutions to environmental problems rather than concentrating on philosophic differences. For a contrasting view, see Martin Lewis, Green Delusions; An Environmentalist Critique of Radical Environmentalism (Duke University Press 1992).

Oil Drilling and ANWR (pp. 28-35). Pressures to open ANWR to drilling will undoubtedly resurface for several reasons. First, the new chairman of the House Natural Resources Committee and the Senate Energy Committee are both Alaskans who strongly favor opening ANWR to drilling. Second, due to declining domestic oil production, U.S. oil imports are now at all-time record levels. In August, 1994 they averaged more than 10 million barrels a day, accounting for a record 58 percent of domestic demand. Peak in Oil Imports, N.Y. Times, Aug. 18, 1994, at D7. Residents of Alaska and the state government have a large financial interest in opening ANWR to drilling. Declining production from the Prudhoe Bay oil field is substantially reducing the amount of royalties the state of Alaska receives, which have funded 85 percent of the state government budget since 1977. The state, which has no income tax, uses this oil money to provide residents with generous annual checks, which averaged $950 per resident in 1993. Dellios, Falling Oil Royalties End Royal Lifestyles, Denver Post, Oct. 2, 1994, at 34A.

It also may be argued that making domestic oil production difficult will only ensure that more oil is produced in areas with lax environmental controls to the detriment of the global environment. For example, in October 1994 a massive oil pipeline spill occurred in the Russian arctic, releasing several times more oil than spilled by the Exxon Valdez. Verhovek, Ruptured Pipeline Spreading Hot Oil in Russia's Arctic, N.Y. Times, Oct. 25, 1994, at A1; Rosett, Big Oil-Pipeline Spill in Russia May Be a Sign of Things to Come, Wall St. J., Oct. 27, 1994, at A17. Some of the oil that had been flowing through this dangerously antiquated pipeline came from an arctic field newly opened by a U.S. oil company: Just a month before the spill, Conoco, Inc. commenced production in the remote Timan Pechora oilfields as part of the first joint U.S.-Russian venture north of the Arctic circle. Herbert, Conoco Starts Pumping Deep in Arctic Russia, Sept. 1, 1994, at D4.

Clinton administration officials have been considering ways to place ANWR permanently off-limits to oil drilling. In August 1994, reports surfaced that the administration was considering a plan to manage ANWR in a coordinated partnership with the nearby Vunntut and Ivvavik National Parks in Canada. This ecosystem management approach could provide protection for migrating caribou under international auspices. Reports that these options were being considered generated heated denunciations by Alaskan officials. "It's unthinkable, it's unbelievable," declared Alaska Governor Walter Hickel, because "it would lock up ANWR forever." Noah and McCoy, U.S. Mulls Plan for Alaskan Refuge That Could End Hopes for Oil Drilling, Wall St. J., August 16, 1994, at A2.

In March 1995, the Clinton administration outlined a plan to lift the ban on exports of oil from Alaska's North Slope. Noah, Clinton Outlines Plan to Lift Export Ban on the Oil From Alaska's North Slope, Wall St. J., Mar. 2, 1995, at A4. Environmentalists fear that lifting the export ban actually would increase pressure to open ANWR to drilling. A provision opening a portion of ANWR to drilling is included in budget legislation that was approved by the House in spring 1995 and that is expected to be approved by the Senate. Despite his opposition to opening ANWR to drilling, President Clinton has not announced whether he would veto the budget legislation because of its ANWR provision. Kenworthy, Refuge May Be Approved for Drilling, Wash. Post, May 23, 1995, at A3.

C. ECONOMICS AND THE ENVIRONMENT

The Tragedy of the Commons and Free Market Environmentalism (pp. 42-46). In its Spring 1992 issue, the Harvard Journal of Law & Public Policy published articles prepared for a Federalist Society symposium on free market environmentalism. Reviewing the history of the tragedy of the commons concept in economic literature, Jim Krier noted that economist Harold Demsetz had demonstrated in a 1967 article that the root of the problem is the difficulty of coordinating human behavior. Krier argues that Demsetz, Hardin, and the free market environmentalists have all begged the difficult question posed by this insight by "implicitly arguing that a community plagued by noncooperation can improve its condition by cooperating." Krier, The Tragedy of the Commons, Part Two, 15 Harv. J.L. & Pub. Poly. 325, 338 (1992). Krier notes that because the public must organize in order to get the government to intervene to protect the commons, the problems of free riders and factional influence persist. Because "markets themselves depend on an active governmental role," Krier finds no reason to believe that the same governmental failures that plague regulatory programs will not plague the establishment and oversight of new natural resources markets. Id. at 341-342. In a companion article, Michael Blumm argues that markets are a poor vehicle for making the kind of value choices that are at the root of most environmental controversies because "markets assume the wisdom of current preferences and the fairness of existing wealth distributions." Blumm, The Fallacies of Free Market Environmentalism, 15 Harv. J.L. & Pub. Poly. 371, 388 (1992). Professor Blumm holds out more hope for the use of markets to lower the cost of implementing environmental policy decisions. For further criticism of economists' devotion to the satisfaction of human preferences see McAdams, Relative Preferences, 102 Yale L.J. 1 (1992). McAdams explores the ways in which pervasive human concern for relative status may lead to socially wasteful investments and why some forms of regulation may be justified as efficient means for limiting such wasteful investments.

Tragedy of the Commons and Fisheries Management (pp. 42-46). Fisheries have long been considered to provide a classic illustration of the problems of managing the commons. See Gordon, The Economic Theory of a Common-Property Resource: The Fishery, 62 J. Pol. Econ. 124 (1954). Concern that overfishing is causing sharp declines in global fisheries is prompting some nations to experiment with measures to "privatize" the commons.

In the early 1970s several nations unilaterally expanded their territorial waters to the 200-mile limit in an effort to win greater control over coastal fisheries where 90 percent of fish are caught. This produced enormous turmoil between foreign fishing fleets, but the 200-mile limit eventually was incorporated in the 1982 International Law of the Sea Convention, which entered into force in November 1994. Congress extended U.S. territorial waters to the 200-mile limit in 1976 when it enacted the Magnuson Fishery Conservation and Management Act, 16 U.S.C. §1801 et seq. However, the increased protection from foreign competition in this zone spurred a dramatic expansion of the U.S. fishing industry. Aided by low-interest government loans, the domestic fishing industry added new boats and sophisticated new equipment at a rapid clip. As the U.S. commercial fishing fleet expanded, severe overfishing depleted the stocks of scores of species of fish. In 1994 the National Marine Fisheries Service estimated that 45 percent of fish stocks for which data are available are overfished, and some species are found at less than 10 percent of optimum levels. Holmes, Biologists Sort the Lessons of Fisheries' Collapse, 264 Science 1252 (1994).

Similar problems are occurring throughout much of the world as the global fishing industry doubled in size between 1970 and 1990, causing too many boats to chase fewer and fewer fish. See Emerson, Fished Out, Newsweek, Apr. 25, 1994, at 30. The global catch has been in decline since 1989 when it reached a peak of 82 million tons. It is estimated that worldwide fishing capacity exceeds sustained levels by 100 percent. War at Sea, The Times (London), July 27, 1994, at 15. The Worldwatch Institute estimates that 90 percent of all jobs in the fishing industry will disappear over the next twenty years unless dramatic new conservation measures are imposed. Nuttall, World's Fishing Fleets Face Ruin as Catches Disappear, The Times (London), July 27, 1994, at 7.

The Magnuson Act attempts to prevent overfishing by creating eight regional fishery management councils to develop conservation and management plans for regional fisheries. These plans, which are subject to review and approval by the Secretary of Commerce, are to include measures to "prevent overfishing while achieving, on a continuing basis, the optimum yield from each fishery for the U.S. fishing industry." 16 U.S.C. §1851(a). But fisheries management plans (FMPs)

1. Environmental Values and Policies — Pages 42-46

have not succeeded in stopping overfishing of many species. For example, the New England fishery management council imposed quotas on catches of cod, haddock, and yellowtail flounder in 1977, but dropped them in 1982 just as the fishing fleet was expanding dramatically. As cod catches fell by more than 50 percent during the next four years, scientists urged that new limits be imposed. But these pleas were rejected by a council dominated by industry representatives. Meier, Fight in Congress Looms Over Fishing, N.Y. Times, Sept. 19, 1994, at A1. Only after a lawsuit was brought by an environmental group did the council in 1993 adopt a plan to freeze the number of fishing vessels and to limit their days of fishing. By 1994, with the cod, haddock, and yellowtail flounder fisheries nearing the point of "commercial extinction," the council issued an emergency order virtually closing the formerly rich Georges Bank to fishing. Daly, New England Fishermen Cry Foul, Wash. Post, Dec. 14, 1994, at A3.

Critics charge that the presence of fishing industry representatives on the councils creates obvious conflict of interest problems. However, the Magnuson Act expressly waives conflict-of-interest laws for private individuals serving on the councils, permitting industry representatives to set policies that can directly affect their financial interests. Id. With the expansion of the U.S. fishing fleet, pressures to permit harvesting at unsustainable levels are intense. Carl Sarfina, director of marine conservation at the National Audubon Society maintains that "in fisheries where people have paid attention to the scientific recommendations, there are still fish around. In fisheries where the scientists have routinely been ignored or the most optimistic gloss has been put on the data, we have declines." Holmes, Biologists Sort the Lessons of Fisheries' Collapse, 264 Science 1252 (1994).

Because fish stocks are subject to natural fluctuations and are affected by a variety of factors, such as pollution and habitat destruction, it is not easy to determine precisely what levels of catch are sustainable. The migration of species over vast distances also makes it difficult to gauge precisely the state of fisheries. See Holden, Tuna Stock: East Meets West, 265 Science 1525 (1994) (apparent decline of Atlantic bluefin tuna may be due to migration from eastern to western Atlantic). These uncertainties make conservation more difficult when the burden of proof is placed on advocates of lower harvest levels.

To protect the Alaska halibut fishery, the 1994 season was limited to two 24-hour periods in which thousands of boats engaged in a frenzied competition for fish, despite horrendous weather conditions. Bernton, U.S. to Revamp System for Harvesting Halibut in Alaska, Wash. Post, Sept. 29, 1994, at A3. After several deaths and many lost vessels in the storms that coincided with these brief windows, the fishery management council decided to adopt a radical new approach to preserving the fishery. Beginning in 1995, a limit will be imposed on the total catch and halibut fisherman will receive transferable quotas that they may use or sell to the highest bidder. The quota allocations are to be based in part on the recipients' historic catches. New Zealand, Iceland, Canada, and Australia also are experimenting with transferable quota systems. While some oppose these schemes for fear that they will help large fishing corporations dominate the industry, others believe that they will help promote conservation by effectively privatizing the commons and allocating it to those who value it most. Less efficient firms may sell their quotas to those willing to pay a higher price while pocketing the proceeds as a kind of rough compensation for exiting the fishery.

As a result of the emergency closure of the Georges Bank, those who formerly fished there now are moving elsewhere, increasing competition for fish in other areas, such as off the coast of Rhode Island. To avoid overfishing in areas that remain open, the Commerce Department has proposed a $2 million pilot program to buy back boats from New England fishermen. Fishing Fleets Are Battling Over Territory Along Coast, N.Y. Times, Mar. 5, 1995, at A25.

D. ECOLOGICAL PERSPECTIVES

Ecosystems, Complexity, and Uncertainty (pp. 56-67). The complexity of ecosystems and the difficulty scientists have in predicting environmental effects of human intervention is well illustrated by efforts to assess the impact of the *Exxon Valdez* oil spill. Following the spill, scientists made an unprecedented effort to study its effects, spending more than $100 million and conducting more than 100 studies. While these studies have produced rich results, there is still considerable uncertainty concerning the spill's impact nearly four years after it occurred. The article below summarizes the results of these studies, which provide an excellent contemporary illustration of the difficulty of tracing environmental effects in complex ecosystems.

> *Loy, Dredging for Lessons from the Tragedy in Prince William Sound*
> **Wash. Post, Feb. 15, 1993, at A3**

Nearly four years after the wreck of the *Exxon Valdez*, visitors to Alaska's coastline would be hard-pressed to find much sign of the nearly 11 million gallons of oil that spread over an area about 15 times the

1. Environmental Values and Policies Pages 56-67

size of Rhode Island. But the largest tanker spill in U.S. history has left a legacy that won't fade for years, if not decades, government scientists now say.

In the months following March 24, 1989, when the supertanker ran aground, the catastrophe attracted an army of biologists and sundry specialists who turned Prince William Sound and outlying coastal areas into a gigantic laboratory. At least $100 million was spent on research, making it the most studied oil spill in history. Many of the findings, however, had been cloaked in secrecy, waiting to be used as evidence against Exxon Corp. in the event of a trial. But in late 1991, Exxon settled with the United States and Alaska governments for more than $1 billion.

Two weeks ago, about 500 scientists, lawyers and environmentalists gathered in Anchorage for the first thorough airing of more than 100 studies of the disaster. Many prompted concern, as scientists reported that oil continues to seep from beneath coastal sediments, some birds seem to have forgotten how to breed, some fish stocks are producing mutated offspring and some of the massive cleanup effort may have done more harm than good.

Nonetheless, most of the oil has dissipated. A National Oceanic and Atmospheric Administration (NOAA) analysis estimates that: 50 percent biodegraded on beaches or in the water; 20 percent evaporated; 14 percent was recovered; 12 percent is at the bottom of the sea, mostly in the Gulf of Alaska; 3 percent lies on shorelines; and less than 1 percent still drifts in the water column.

Most beaches in the oil's path look as clean as they did before the tanker hit Bligh Reef. No species are extinct. The commercial fishing industry has not collapsed. And some experts now caution against overestimating the scope of the damage. "There are a lot of people who are too ready to blame everything on the oil spill," said Mark Fraker, a biologist with the Alaska Department of Fish and Game. "There's a lot we just don't know."

That includes precise counts of dead wildlife. Thousands of oiled carcasses were stored in freezers in Anchorage for later analysis. But researchers needed an array of techniques to better estimate the total kill, ranging from computer modeling to a controversial bird study in 1990 in which 219 live specimens were killed, fitted with radio transmitters, dunked in crude oil and then cast adrift to see where they ended up. Federal biologists defended the use of freshly killed birds, saying the frozen birds would not have the same buoyancy characteristics.

Seabirds were the biggest casualties, dying en masse up to 500 miles from the spill site. More than 36,000 bird corpses were collected, but scientists now believe between 375,000 and 435,000 died, the most ever documented in the history of oil pollution at sea. The common murre, a diving shorebird, was hardest hit; an estimated 300,000 of Alaska's 12 million murres were killed. Scientists also estimate that about 900 bald eagles were killed—about 11 percent of those in the spill area.

Sea otters, the cuddly media symbol of the spill, were another major casualty. Between 3,500 and 5,500 of Alaska's estimated 150,000 sea otters died after their fur became fouled with oil.

Commercially important fish species fared comparatively well—including salmon and herring stocks. Yet scientists report dramatic harm to the long-lived, deep-dwelling rockfish. Normally, rockfish carcasses are rarely seen, but boaters throughout oiled waters found and collected them. Necropsy results on a few rockfish confirmed oil had killed the bottom-dwellers.

Other questions may never be answered. What, for example, became of 14 killer whales that once swam in Prince William Sound? About 182 killer whales in nine families used the sound before the spill. Since then, one well-studied family has lost 14 members, including some females that left calves. It is not clear whether the spill killed the whales, which in years past have been spotted with bullet wounds, possibly inflicted as the whales stole fishing lines.

And what of the harlequin duck, which has all but stopped reproducing in oiled areas? Scientists suspect their breeding habits have been hampered by continued eating of oil-contaminated mussels, but that's not a certainty, said Fraker.

Also unresolved is the question of how some cleanup techniques affected the coast. Exxon hired a fleet of local fishing boats and assembled giant, barge-mounted spray guns to scrub miles of contaminated beaches with hot water during the summer of 1989. NOAA researchers now believe the unusual high-pressure, hot-water spraying may have done more harm than good. The water, up to 140 degrees, basically cooked small organisms and greatly slowed the recovery of those areas compared to a few oiled shorelines left unscrubbed at the request of researchers. The idea behind the washing was to push oil into the water, where it could be skimmed. But NOAA researchers believe a considerable amount of oil clinging to sediments just sank to the bottom of biologically rich tidal zones.

For the future, one major concern is what to do about abundant blue mussel beds, spared vigorous cleanup to let tide and waves do the job. Now many mussels beds overlay oil-bearing sediments, and the contaminated but oil resistant mussels are providing a fresh source of oil for the birds and young sea otters that eat them.

Hard-hit murre colonies are likely to struggle for years, as well. Murre colonies normally begin their summer egg-laying almost simultaneously, staying densely packed to ward off gulls and ravens. Biologists

1. Environmental Values and Policies   Pages 56-67

suspect the oil spill killed many experienced adults, throwing off their breeding rhythm and leaving chicks more exposed to predators and stormy seas.

Fish experts also worry that high egg mortality and genetic deformities like curved spines and eye tumors could haunt commercially vital pink salmon and herring stock for generations. Another problem is the heavy toll the spill and cleanup took on *Fucus*, the dominant tidal algae that provides food and cover to many creatures, including young fish.

How much more research should be conducted to study those and other issues is a touchy subject in Alaska. Many environmentalists are urging the federal-state trustee council charged with managing the billion-dollar settlement to buy coastal lands threatened by logging, and not spend the money on further investigations.

Opinions differ widely. Many state and federal government scientists believe oil will haunt Prince William Sound and other coastal areas of Alaska for many years. They bemoan the fact that information on the number and habits of many species was sketchy before the spill, forcing researchers to glean what conclusions they could by comparing creatures living in an oiled area to those in unoiled areas.

But some researchers, such as David Kennedy, an oil spill expert with NOAA, argue that the spill simply wasn't as bad as previously thought. Prince William Sound was so clean and healthy to begin with, said Kennedy, that it was able to recover from the massive spill far more quickly than could a more polluted marine system, such as the Chesapeake Bay. "There is not a total recovery yet," he said. "There are holes. But the potential for recovery is tremendous."

NOTES AND QUESTIONS

1. As the article notes, while the *Exxon Valdez* oil spill has been the most studied oil spill in history, considerable uncertainty remains concerning its environmental effects. What questions are scientists unable to answer with confidence? Why would policymakers want answers to such questions?

2. What factors have contributed to the uncertainties that surround assessment of the spill's impact? To what extent are these uncertainties the product of a lack of data? To what extent are they the result of incomplete scientific understanding of biological processes?

3. How much more study should be conducted to improve understanding of the spill's environmental effects? Do you agree with the environmentalists who argue that it would be more productive for settlement money to be used to buy threatened land than to fund further

expensive studies of the spill's impact? In May 1993, the federal and state trustees administering the spill fund agreed to spend $38.7 million to buy 42,000 acres of Alaskan coastland threatened by logging operations. Oil-Spill Trustees Back a Land Deal, N.Y. Times, May 16, 1993, at A21. In August, 1994, a group of 10,000 commercial fishermen was awarded $286.8 million in compensatory damages from Exxon for economic losses they suffered due to declines in fish catches and the reduced values of fishing permits. The plaintiffs had sought $895 million in damages.

4. Scientists from NOAA and Exxon disagree sharply over the long-term effects of the *Exxon Valdez* oil spill. At a meeting of the American Society for Testing and Materials in April 1993, NOAA scientists maintained that it may take up to 10 years for Prince William Sound to recover, while representatives of Exxon argued that the cleanup already had been successful. Each side accused the other of misinterpreting data, taking data out of context, and ignoring other relevant data. Exxon Calls Recovery of Sound Complete, But NOAA Says Species Still Affected by Oil, 23 Env. Rep. 3235 (1993). For a discussion of the differences between the Exxon and NOAA scientists, see Stone, Dispute Over *Exxon Valdez* Cleanup Data Gets Messy, 260 Science 749 (1993).

5. As technological advances improve our ability to detect and measure environmental conditions, scientists are acquiring a better understanding of the complex processes that regulate ecosystems. For example, data collected by satellites that record atmospheric conditions have enabled scientists to determine that more than 13 million tons of dust is blown across the Atlantic Ocean from Africa each year to the Amazon rain forest, where it serves as an important nutrient supplement. As a result, scientists are less inclined to view the Amazon rain forests as self-sufficient ecosystems, and now emphasize that rain forest protection strategies must also consider the forests' links to drought conditions on a continent thousands of miles away. Simons, Winds Toss Africa's Soil, Feeding Lands Far Away, N.Y. Times, Oct. 29, 1992, at A1.

6. The dynamism of ecosystems, economies, and human societies has inspired some scientists, particularly those associated with the Santa Fe Institute, to pursue cross-disciplinary studies focusing on what some are touting as a new field of science called "complexity." Studies of complexity, which rely heavily on computer experiments with large models, seek to determine whether these systems exhibit self-organizing properties that fall between orderly behavior and deterministic chaos. For a nontechnical introduction to this work see M. Waldrop, Complexity: The Emerging Science at the Edge of Order and Chaos (1992) and R. Lewin, Complexity: Life at the Edge of Chaos (1992).

7. Scientists are warning that the West African lake that killed 1,700 people (in 1986, it released a giant bubble of carbon dioxide—see

1. Environmental Values and Policies   Pages 56-67

note 6, p. 66 of the parent) continues to threaten residents of nearby villages. Lake Nyos in Cameroon is recharging with carbon dioxide faster than had been expected and could again release a killer gas bubble. Scientists are proposing to build a piping system that would continuously pipe gas-laden waters to the surface, where the carbon dioxide could be slowly vented. Funding is being sought for the system, which is estimated to cost about $500,000. Killer Lakes Threaten to Strike Again, 264 Science 26 (1994).

8. Are there any circumstances in which humans would be justified in destroying the last remaining samples of a life form? For the past several years, a controversy has raged over whether scientists should deliberately destroy the last remaining samples of the smallpox virus. For centuries, smallpox caused millions of deaths until the discovery of a vaccine and a concentrated effort to eradicate the disease succeeded in 1977. The only remaining samples of variola, the virus that causes smallpox, are being held in tightly-guarded research laboratories in Atlanta and Moscow. Siebert, Smallpox Is Dead, Long Live Smallpox, N.Y. Times Mag., Aug. 21, 1994, at 31. While the molecular structure of the three strains of the virus has been extracted and recorded, some virologists argue that further study of the virus could provide additional, useful scientific information. In September, 1994, the World Health Organization agreed that the remaining samples of the virus should be destroyed on June 30, 1995. However, in January, 1995, the organization voted to grant the virus an indefinite reprieve. Altman, Lab Samples of Smallpox Win Reprieve, N.Y. Times, Jan. 19, 1995, at A15.

=2=
Environmental Law: A Structural Overview

[Environmental policy has been] absurdly expensive, created far more resistance than was necessary, and misallocated resources on emotional and public relations grounds without regard to either scientific, engineering or economic rationality. [EPA] may well be the biggest job-killing agency in the inner city in America today.

—*Speaker of the House Newt Gingrich**

The 104th Congress is critically reexamining the fundamental premises of the environmental law constructed over the last 25 years. This reexamination will be influenced by the message the voters sent in November 1994, an expression of anger and concern about economic insecurity. . . . Our basic challenge is not from the 104th Congress, but from a rising generation of citizens who demand that regulations produce results and that environmental programs serve society.

—*J. William Futrell, President of the Environmental Law Institute*†

While the basic structure of environmental law has not changed significantly since publication of the parent text, dramatic changes are in the offing as a result of the Republican sweep of the 1994 congressional elections. The Republican Party's campaign manifesto, the "Contract With America," includes measures that would radically alter existing environmental laws and the process by which regulations are issued. Several of these measures are moving rapidly through Congress, including a regulatory moratorium, risk assessment and cost-benefit analysis requirements, restrictions on unfunded mandates, and requirements that the government compensate landowners when regulation adversely affects property values. This chapter describes the dramatic shift in the political climate that previously had favored environmental regulation.

---

* Speech at the National Environmental Policy Institute, Feb. 16, 1995.
† The Winter of Our Discontent, 12 Envtl. Forum 56 (1995).

2. **Environmental Law: A Structural Overview**

FIGURE S-2.1

> THE ENVIRONMENTALISTS ARE ALWAYS COMPLAINING, BUT LET'S LOOK AT THE RECORD.
>
> OUR AIR IS CLEANER, OUR WATER PURER, OUR FOOD SAFER.
>
> THE ENVIRONMENTAL LAWS HAVE BEEN A SUCCESS.
>
> SO NOW WE CAN REPEAL THEM.
>
> THE UNWRITTEN CONTRACT.—
>
> BY TOLES FOR THE BUFFALO NEWS

It reviews the new unfunded mandates legislation, the effect of the Oil Pollution Act of 1990, and efforts to give private industry greater flexibility in complying with environmental regulations.

A. SOURCES OF ENVIRONMENTAL LAW

Common Law Roots (pp. 74-75). Professor William Jones has argued that the Restatement's approach of singling out abnormally dangerous activities for strict liability is flawed on both theoretical and practical grounds. Jones argues that strict liability generally should apply "whenever the owner permits mischief to escape from the bounds of its property," even if the risk of harm is commonplace or small, as long as the victim cannot "avoid the harm by adopting suitable precautions." Jones, Strict Liability for Hazardous Enterprise, 92 Colum. L. Rev. 1705, 1779 (1992).

2. Environmental Law: A Structural Overview — Pages 83-84

Private Nuisance (pp. 74-77). The traditional common law requirement for a private nuisance is a substantial and unreasonable interference with the private use and enjoyment of land. Is a decline in property values caused by proximity to a polluted site actionable at common law even if there is no proof that the pollution has seeped onto plaintiffs' property? In Adkins v. Thomas Solvent Co., 487 N.W.2d 715 (Mich. 1992), the Michigan Supreme Court held that 22 property owners who live near a contaminated site could not recover for the diminution of their property values in the absence of evidence that contaminants had migrated to their property. The court reasoned that

> [i]f any property owner in the vicinity of the numerous hazardous-waste sites that have been identified can advance a claim seeking damages when unfounded public fears of exposure cause property depreciation, the ultimate effect might be a reordering of the polluter's resources for the benefit of persons who have suffered no cognizable harm at the expense of those claimants who have been subjected to a substantial and unreasonable interference in the use and enjoyment of property.

487 N.W.2d at 727. Two dissenting justices argued that depreciation of property values can constitute interference with the use and enjoyment of property when it can be shown to be the normal consequence of a defendant's conduct.

Foreseeability, Strict Liability, and Groundwater Pollution: The **Cambridge Water Co.** *Case (pp. 83-84).* The difficulty of using common law nuisance actions to redress contamination of groundwater is illustrated by Cambridge Water Co. v. Eastern Counties Leather, 1 All E.R. H.L. 53 (1994). A leather company's repeated spillage of perchloroethene (pce) over a period of several decades resulted in contamination of an aquifer used by the Cambridge Water Co. to supply drinking water. As a result of the contamination, the water company had to discontinue use of the aquifer and develop an alternative water supply. The water company sued and was awarded a judgment of approximately £1 million by a British Court of Appeal. The court held the leather company strictly liable for the damage it had caused. Citing Ballard v. Tomlinson, 29 Ch. D. 115 (1885) (see p. 83, note 10 of parent), the court deemed it unimportant whether the leather company could foresee that its accidental spillages would cause groundwater contamination in violation of modern water quality standards.

The House of Lords then allowed an appeal and reversed the Court of Appeal's decision. After noting that *Ballard* did not involve harm that was unforeseeable, Lord Goff concluded that "foreseeability of harm is indeed a prerequisite of the recovery of damages in private

Pages 83-84 **2. Environmental Law: A Structural Overview**

nuisance, as in the case of public nuisance." Id. at 72. He then considered whether the leather company could be held liable under the rule in Rylands v. Fletcher, 3 H.L. 330 (1868), imposing strict liability for harm caused by abnormally dangerous activities. However, he found that "foreseeability of damage of the relevant type should be regarded as a prerequisite of liability in damages under the rule" in Rylands v. Fletcher. 1 All E.R. H.L. 76 (1994). Finding that the leather company could not reasonably have foreseen the damage that it caused the water company, Lord Goff concluded that the leather company could not be held liable.

Although it can be argued that groundwater pollution is now far more readily foreseeable than in the past, this decision will make it difficult to use the common law to recover for groundwater pollution caused by activities that commenced long ago. While Cambridge Water Co. argued that the leather company should at least be held liable for releases of pce that continued after the discovery of the aquifer contamination, Lord Goff rejected this argument, noting that the pce that actually had reached the groundwater probably had been released at a time when the contamination was not foreseeable.

The Chicago River and the Missouri v. Illinois Decision (pp. 90-94). In the last 20 years the condition of the Chicago River has improved considerably, as described in Valente, The Chicago River, Long an Eyesore, Now Draws Tourists, Wall Street J., Nov. 13, 1992, at A1. "Fifty species of fish, including carp, perch and salmon, have returned. But the late Mayor Richard Daley's 1973 prediction that downtown office workers someday would barbecue their catch for lunch remains a bit far off." Id. at A6. Bubbly Creek, an arm of the Chicago River, still bubbles a bit from the waste Chicago slaughterhouses dumped there during the era of the Missouri v. Illinois decision. Some idea of the horrendous condition of the creek in the early 1900s can be garnered from Upton Sinclair's description of it in The Jungle:

> [I]t is really a great open sewer, a hundred or two feet wide. One long arm of it is blind, and the filth stays there forever and a day. The grease and chemicals that are poured into it undergo all sorts of strange transformations, which are the cause of its name; it is constantly in motion, as if huge fish were feeding in it, or great leviathans were disporting themselves in its depths. Bubbles of carbonic acid will rise to the surface and burst, and make rings two or three feet wide. Here and there, the grease and filth have caked solid, and the creek looks like a bed of lava; chickens walk about on it, feeding, and many times an unwary stranger has started to stroll across, and vanished temporarily. The packers used to leave the creek that way, till every now and then the surface would catch fire and

2. Environmental Law: A Structural Overview   Pages 103-112

burn furiously, and the fire department would have to come and put it out.

U. Sinclair, The Jungle 97 (1906).

The Environmental Effects of Ocean Dumping (pp. 94-96). The Missouri v. Illinois decision illustrates the difficulty of tracing environmental effects when pollutants are dispersed over great distances. Proponents of ocean dumping often argued that deep water sewage dumping would have scant environmental impact because the pollutants would be diluted and widely dispersed. However, scientists recently have found evidence that contaminants from ocean dumping have entered the food chain through bottom-dwelling organisms. Studies conducted at an ocean dumpsite 115 miles off the coast of New Jersey in 8,000 feet of water found elevated levels of sewage sludge in worms, sea urchins, and sea cucumbers collected near the dumpsite. Organisms collected at a downstream site 45 miles away also had elevated levels of the contaminants, though the intensity of the contamination was only half that at the dumpsite. Naj, Sewage Dumped Offshore Is Found in Tiny Animals, Wall St. J., Nov. 12, 1992, at B6; Sullivan, Sewage Bacteria in Food Chain, N.Y. Times, Nov. 17, 1992, at C11.

Environmental Statutes (pp. 103-112). While Congress has made few significant changes in the environmental statutes since the publication of the parent text, dramatic change is in the offing during the 104th Congress. The 102d and 103d Congress enacted only a handful of pieces of environmental legislation. In 1992 Congress enacted the Federal Facility Compliance Act, P.L. 102-386, and the Community Environmental Response Facilitation Act, P.L. 102-426, which addressed problems of environmental contamination at federal facilities. The former specifies that states may collect civil penalties from federal agencies who violate hazardous waste regulations, while the latter seek to accelerate federal property transfers by requiring agencies to identify uncontaminated portions of federal property. Congress also adopted the Comprehensive National Energy Policy Act, P.L. 102-486, which will encourage energy conservation by expanding national energy efficiency standards, requiring federal agencies to invest in energy efficiency improvements, and promoting renewable energy alternatives. Another piece of environmental legislation is the Residential Lead-Based Paint Hazard Reduction Act, known as Title X of the Housing and Community Development Act of 1992, P.L. 102-550. This law seeks to promote abatement of lead-paint hazards in federally-assisted housing, while requiring home sellers to disclose lead paint hazards to prospective buyers or renters beginning in October 1995. The Water Resources

Development Act of 1992, P.L. 102-580, reserves greater federal water resources for the protection of fish and wildlife in California.

Despite the election of a president who campaigned on a platform decidedly more sympathetic to environmental regulation, Congress blocked all but one of the many pieces of environmental legislation the administration put forward during the 103d Congress. Clinton administration efforts to elevate EPA to cabinet status and to abolish the Council on Environmental Quality failed to win adoption. The only environmental measures enacted were the reauthorization of the Marine Mammal Protection Act and the California Desert Protection Act, which was passed only after a filibuster was broken by a single vote on the final day of the legislative session. As a result, the 103d Congress has been dubbed "the worst environmental Congress" since the advent of the modern environmental movement. Kenworthy and Lee, Environmental Bills Still Due, Wash. Post, Sept. 16, 1994, at A4.

A variety of factors contributed to the surprising inability of Congress to enact new environmental legislation. First, other legislative priorities of the new administration, including the budget, health care reform, and the crime bill, eclipsed efforts to enact new environmental laws. Cushman, Few Environmental Laws Emerge from 103d Congress, N.Y. Times, Oct. 3, 1994, at B12. Second, opponents of environmental regulation successfully promoted "killer amendments" designed to make it far more difficult for government to implement regulatory programs. These amendments included measures requiring government to compensate landowners when regulations adversely affect property values, mandating risk assessment and cost-benefit analysis before new regulations could be imposed, and barring regulations that require state and local governments to undertake new programs without providing federal funding. Dubbed by environmentalists the "unholy trinity," this combination of groups concerned about property rights, businesses promoting risk assessment, and state and local officials upset about unfunded mandates proved to be a politically potent combination that ultimately may prevail following the Republican sweep of the 1994 congressional elections.

In 1994 extraordinary bipartisan coalitions labored mightily to produce consensus proposals to reform the Superfund program and the Safe Drinking Water Act. These efforts generated surprising agreement on legislation that had broad support from businesses, environmental interests, and state and local officials. Comprehensive Superfund reform bills were approved by five committees in the House and Senate. Legislation to reauthorize the Safe Drinking Water Act passed each house overwhelmingly, as did bills to reform the Mining Law of 1872. But all of these measures died as Congress approached adjournment in October 1994. Ultimately these efforts were defeated

2. Environmental Law: A Structural Overview   Pages 118-119

by the running of the clock and the growing expectation of conservative Republicans that the November 1994 elections would strengthen their hand, making it worthwhile to block all remaining legislation.

Now that the Republicans have taken control of both houses of Congress, the 104th Congress is decidedly less sympathetic toward environmental interests. In March 1995 Congress enacted legislation making it more difficult for federal mandates to be imposed on state and local governments unless Congress provides the funding to comply with them. (This legislation is described below.) In May 1995 the House passed legislation that would substantially weaken the Clean Water Act. Other legislative proposals that would dramatically revise the environmental laws are moving rapidly through Congress: Proposed legislation to impose a regulatory moratorium and to require that future regulations meet risk assessment and cost-benefit criteria (see Chapter 5 of this supplement); proposals to make it more difficult for plaintiffs to prevail in tort litigation (see Chapter 4); the proposed Clean Water Act revisions and the "takings" legislation that would require compensation of landowners whose property values are adversed affected by regulation (see Chapter 7); efforts to restrict endangered species listings and to boost timber harvests on federal lands through appropriations riders (see Chapter 8).

Responsibilities versus Resources: The Case of EPA (p. 112). EPA's responsibilities are defined by 14 separate federal statutes. Nearly 40 congressional committees and subcommittees have jurisdiction over various aspects of EPA's programs or budget. Shortly after assuming office, EPA Administrator Carol M. Browner told a congressional committee that she had found an agency with a "total lack of management, accountability and discipline" that had wasted considerable sums, particularly as a result of poorly managed government contracts. EPA in Sad Shape, New Boss Testifies, Wash. Post, Mar. 11, 1993, at A18. More than one of every six new employees hired by EPA in recent years has been hired for the Agency's Office of the Inspector General.

State Administration of Federal Programs (pp. 118-119). In December 1992, the D.C. Circuit held that EPA is required to initiate proceedings to withdraw state authority to administer the federal Safe Drinking Water Act once EPA determines that a state is not in compliance with the statute. National Wildlife Federation v. EPA, 980 F.2d 765 (D.C. Cir. 1992). The court's decision was a product of a challenge to EPA regulations declaring that the Agency had the discretion to decline to initiate withdrawal proceedings even after making a formal finding that a state's program does not comply with the Act. While this decision may provide additional leverage for those seeking closer federal oversight of state programs, it also may simply encourage EPA to avoid making formal findings concerning a state's compliance with the Act. The court recognized that EPA has wide discretion in making the threshold finding of noncompliance that triggers EPA's duty to commence withdrawal proceedings.

EPA has threatened to withdraw the authority of nine states to administer Safe Drinking Water Act programs because of the states' failure to meet a June 30, 1994 deadline for issuing standards regulating 38 contaminants. Nine States Could Face Loss of Primacy Unless Programs Improved, EPA Official Says, 25 Env. Rep. 858 (1994). Several of the states have responded to EPA by providing new schedules for coming into compliance with the requirements, making it unlikely that EPA actually will assume primacy over the programs. States Considered Unlikely to Lose Primacy Because of Failure of SDWA Reauthorization, 25 Env. Rep. 1217 (1994).

Constitutional Limits on Federal Control of State Regulation (pp. 118-119). While the Tenth Amendment has not been much of an obstacle to efforts to impel states to administer federal environmental programs, the Supreme Court has recognized that Congress can go too far. In New York v. United States, 112 S. Ct. 2408 (1992) (see Chapter 3 of this Supplement), the Supreme Court held that the federal government could not constitutionally require states to "take title" to low-level radioactive waste if they failed to meet a federal deadline to site a waste disposal facility or to arrange to participate in an interstate compact giving them access to such a facility: "Whether one views the take title provision as lying outside Congress' enumerated powers, or as infringing upon the core of state sovereignty reserved by the Tenth Amendment, the provision is inconsistent with the federal structure of our Government established by the Constitution." 112 S. Ct. at 2429. In reaching this decision, the Court reviewed the mechanisms Congress can properly use to persuade states to administer federal programs. Congress can attach conditions on the receipt of federal funds, a device that effectively has produced a national speed limit and uniform minimum drinking age. South Dakota v. Dole, 483 U.S. 203 (1987). When it can regulate private activity under the Commerce Clause, Congress also can offer states the choice of regulating according to federal standards or having state law preempted by federal regulation. New York v. United States, 112 S. Ct. at 2423-2424. But Congress cannot directly require states to regulate on its behalf without violating principles of federalism. In her majority opinion in New York v. United States, Justice O'Connor sought to justify this distinction as necessary to maintain accountability in government.

2. Environmental Law: A Structural Overview   Pages 118-119

> When Congress encourages state regulation rather than compelling it, state governments remain responsive to the local electorate's preferences; state officials remain accountable to the people. But where the Federal Government directs the States to regulate, it may be state officials who will bear the brunt of public disapproval, while the federal officials who devised the regulatory program may remain insulated from the electoral ramifications of their decision.

112 S. Ct. at 2424.

In April 1995 the Supreme Court issued a surprising decision that may presage more significant limits on federal regulatory authority. For the first time in nearly 60 years the Court overturned a federal law for exceeding Congress's authority under the Commerce Clause. In United States v. Lopez, 115 S. Ct. 1624 (1995), the Court held, by a bare 5-to-4 majority, that Congress does not have the authority under the Commerce Clause to prohibit the possession of firearms in the vicinity of schools.

In *Lopez* the Court confirmed that Congress has the authority to regulate three broad classes of activities under the Commerce Clause. These include "the use of the channels of interstate commerce" and intrastate activities that threaten "the instrumentalities of interstate commerce, or persons or things in interstate commerce," 115 S. Ct. 1629. The third class of activities that may be subject to federal regulation is "activities having a substantial relation to interstate commerce," id. at 1629-1630. Noting that it previously had been unclear how substantial this relationship must be, the Court announced that the "proper test" is "whether the regulated activity 'substantially affects' interstate commerce." Id. at 1630.

While it is unclear to what extent *Lopez*'s "substantially affects" test will impose new restrictions on federal regulatory authority, Chief Justice Rehnquist's majority opinion suggests that Congress will have little problem regulating economic or commercial activity. He emphasized that the Gun-Free School Zones School Act had "nothing to do with 'commerce' or any sort of economic enterprise, however broadly one might define those terms." Id. at 1630-1631. Citing with approval Hodel v. Virginia Surface Mining & Reclamation Assn., Inc., 452 U.S. 264 (1981), which upheld federal regulation of intrastate coal mining under the Surface Mining Control and Reclamation Act, the Chief Justice stated that "[w]here economic activity substantially affects interstate commerce, legislation regulating that activity will be sustained." 115 S. Ct. at 1630. Significantly, the Chief Justice did not question the validity of even Wickard v. Filburn, 317 U.S. 111 (1942), which he described as "the most far-reaching example of Commerce Clause authority over intrastate activity," because it "involved economic activity in a way that the possession of a gun in a school zone does not." 115 S. Ct. at 1630. In *Wickard* the Court upheld federal regulation of the production and consumption of home-grown wheat because of its effect on the price and market for wheat sold in interstate commerce. If *Wickard* remains good law, then *Lopez* apparently will not significantly restrict federal authority to regulate virtually any commercial activity.

The more difficult questions include what impact the decision will have on federal authority to regulate noncommercial activity and how courts can distinguish between commercial and noncommercial activity. Can actions that cause environmental harm be subject to federal regulation if they are not the product of commercial activities? Is the impact of environmental harm on interstate commerce a sufficient basis for assertion of federal regulatory authority over noncommercial activities? Can the federal government regulate land use that causes environmental damage if it is not deemed related to commercial activity? Justice Breyer and three other dissenting justices argue that it will be difficult, if not impossible, to find a principled means for distinguishing commercial from noncommercial conduct. Id. at 1653. While the Chief Justice acknowledged the difficulty of determining "whether an intrastate activity is commercial or noncommercial," 115 S. Ct. at 1633, he concluded that such "legal uncertainty" was a necessary price to pay to ensure that Congress's enumerated powers have "judicially enforceable outer limits," id. In a concurring opinion, Justice Kennedy proposes to address such uncertainty by inquiring as to "whether the exercise of national power seeks to intrude upon an area of traditional state concern." However, environmental law is replete with instances where matters traditionally viewed as local concerns eventually have been subjected to national regulation because of the failure of state or local authorities to address burgeoning environmental problems.

The Court also noted that the statute invalidated in *Lopez* contained "no jurisdictional element which would ensure, through case-by-case inquiry, that the firearm possession in question affects interstate commerce." 115 S. Ct. at 1631. This would appear to distinguish *Lopez* from cases arising under the Clean Water Act, whose jurisdiction extends to "waters of the United States," 33 U.S.C. §1362(7), defined as waters whose use or misuse could affect interstate commerce. United States v. Riverside Bayview Homes, Inc., 474 U.S. 121 (1985). However, it is possible that the Court's articulation of a "substantially affects" test in *Lopez* may restrict the jurisdictional breadth of the Act by requiring demonstrations of more substantial effects on commerce before activities can be regulated under the Act.

Because of the uncertainty it creates, *Lopez* undoubtedly will generate new challenges to federal regulation. However, there are early indications that its impact may be largely symbolic. Five days after deciding

2. Environmental Law: A Structural Overview   Page 119

Lopez, the Court unanimously reversed a Ninth Circuit decision that had restricted the reach of federal antiracketeering legislation on Commerce Clause grounds. United States v. Robertson, 115 S. Ct. 1732 (1995). Moreover, Justices Kennedy and O'Connor, two of the five justices in the *Lopez* majority, cautioned that the Court should exercise "great restraint" before determining that Congress has exceeded its authority. 115 S. Ct. at 1634 (Kennedy, J., concurring). Noting the economic transformation that has occurred during the last two centuries, they concluded that "Congress can regulate in the commercial sphere on the assumption that we have a single market and a unified purpose to build a stable national economy." Id. at 1637.

Unfunded Mandates Legislation (p. 119). State and local officials have become increasingly upset about the cost of implementing federal requirements that are not accompanied by federal funding. Efforts to comply with the Safe Drinking Water Act, discussed in Chapter 4 (pp. 575-579), have been particularly costly for municipalities. Arguing that it is unfair for the federal government to impose "unfunded mandates," state and local officials lobbied Congress for legislation restricting this practice. In an effort to defuse these concerns, President Clinton in October 1993 issued Executive Order 12875, 58 Fed. Reg. 58093, which prohibits federal agencies from issuing regulations that impose unfunded mandates not required by statute unless the agency informs the Office of Management and Budget of its efforts to consult with state and local governments and its justification for the mandate. It also directs federal agencies to process applications from state and local governments for regulatory waivers within 120 days to the extent permitted by law.

In March 1995, Congress overwhelmingly approved legislation making it more difficult to impose federal mandates on state and local governments. The legislation, known as the Unfunded Mandate Reform Act of 1995, requires that more detailed cost estimates be provided for federal mandates and makes it easier for opponents of such provisions to defeat them in Congress. The law requires the Congressional Budget Office (CBO) to provide estimates of the future cost of legislative mandates if they exceed $50 million annually for state or local governments or the private sector. Mandates estimated to cost state or local governments more than $50 million annually may be stricken from legislation by any member of Congress, who can raise a point of order demanding such unless federal funding is provided or the mandate is specifically approved by a majority vote. Mandates for which future federal funding is promised are to expire if the funding is not subsequently provided.

The legislation also imposes new requirements on agencies issuing regulations that impose federal mandates. The law requires federal agencies, prior to publishing a notice of proposed rulemaking, to prepare assessments of the anticipated costs and benefits of any mandate that may cost state or local governments or the private sector more than $100 million annually. It also prohibits federal agencies from issuing regulations containing federal mandates that do not employ the least costly method or that do not have the least burdensome effect on governments or the private sector, unless the agency publishes an explanation of why the more costly or burdensome method was adopted. These provisions are subject to judicial review if the underlying agency action already is reviewable in court.

Congress exempted from the unfunded mandates legislation laws protecting civil or constitutional rights and measures necessary for national security or to implement international treaty obligations. Amendments to exempt radioactive waste regulations or to prevent relaxation of rules that would put private business at a disadvantage with competing governmental entities were defeated.

The unfunded mandates legislation does nothing to repeal any existing federal mandates. House Speaker Newt Gingrich has vowed to set aside one day each month, dubbed "Corrections Day," for the House to consider repeal of such provisions on an individual basis. One reporter noted that " 'Corrections Day' could prove to be a lobbyist's dream by opening the door to special interest legislation designed to circumvent federal regulations." Rogers, House Approves Bill Aimed at Curbing State Mandates, Wall St. J., Feb. 2, 1995, at A20.

Federal Preemption of State Common Law (pp. 119-122). In Cipollone v. Liggett Group, Inc., 112 S. Ct. 2608 (1992), a badly divided Supreme Court wrestled with claims of federal preemption of state common law. A plurality of the Court held that the federal law that has required warning labels on cigarettes since 1969 preempts only "claims based on a failure to warn and the neutralization of federally mandated warnings to the extent that those claims rely on omissions or inclusions in [a defendant's] advertising or promotions," but not "claims based on express warranty, intentional fraud and misrepresentation or conspiracy." 112 S. Ct. at 2625. The plurality in *Cipollone* stated that failure-to-warn claims that rely on testing or research practices unrelated to advertising and claims based on false representations of material facts or concealment of material facts are not preempted.

The Eighth, Tenth, and Eleventh Circuits have interpreted *Cipolone* to mean that the Federal Insecticide, Fungicide, and Rodenticide Act (FIFRA) preempts state common law actions for failure to warn about the hazardous properties of pesticides, even if plaintiffs allege noncompliance with FIFRA labeling requirements. Bice v. Leslie's Poolmart, Inc., 39 F.3d 887 (8th Cir. 1994); Arkansas-Platte & Gulf Partnership v.

2. Environmental Law: A Structural Overview Pages 122-123

Van Water & Rogers, Inc., 981 F.2d 1177 (10th Cir. 1993); Papas v. Upjohn Co., 985 F.2d 516 (11th Cir. 1993). The Fourth Circuit has adopted a narrower view that would permit state common law claims based on breaches of FIFRA-created duties, Lowe v. Sporicidin, Intl., 47 F.3d 124 (4th Cir. 1995), while preempting claims that companies should have issued warnings in addition to those contained in federally-approved FIFRA labels. Worm v. American Cyanamid Co., 5 F.3d 744 (4th Cir. 1993).

The difficulties courts have in applying preemption analysis are illustrated by the Supreme Court's sharply divided decision in Gade v National Solid Wastes Management Association, 112 S. Ct. 2374 (1992). The Court split 4-1-4 in finding that the Occupational Safety and Health Act had preempted state regulations governing the training, testing, and licensing of workers at hazardous waste sites. A four-member plurality of the Court found implicit preemption as a result of regulations adopted by OSHA. Reiterating the longstanding presumption against implicit preemption, Justice Kennedy concurred in the judgment on the ground that preemption was mandated by the express terms of the Occupational Safety and Health Act.

Preemption claims have been less successful under statutes that do not contain express preemption provisions. In Feikema v. Texaco, Inc., 16 F.3d 1408 (4th Cir. 1994), the Fourth Circuit rejected arguments that RCRA's scheme of hazardous waste regulation preempts state common law nuisance and trespass actions for damages due to contamination of soil and groundwater from leaks of petroleum products. However, the court did hold that a consent decree between the defendant and EPA that specified cleanup obligations precluded a state common law claim for injunctive relief.

The Unfunded Mandate Reform Act enacted in March 1995 provides that committee reports accompanying any bill or joint resolution should include "an explicit statement on whether the bill or joint resolution, in whole or in part, is intended to preempt any State, local, or tribal law, and if so, an explanation of the reasons for such intention."

Intergovernmental Relations in Environmental Decision-making (pp. 122-123). As the former head of Florida's Department of Environmental Regulation, Carol Browner, the EPA Administrator, has pledged to make a special effort to improve EPA's relations with the states. In November 1992, the U.S. Advisory Commission on Intergovernmental Relations published a report arguing that intergovernmental decision-making in the environmental area "may be approaching gridlock." The report, entitled Intergovernmental Decisionmaking for Environmental Protection and Public Works, reviewed conflicts between federal environmental regulations and state and local projects. It found that federal environmental regulations "often are complex, conflicting, difficult to apply, adversarial, costly, inflexible, and uncertain," causing "delay, wasted effort and money, lost opportunities to accommodate both environmental protection and infrastructure objectives, prolonged litigation, and more process without necessarily providing more environmental protection." U.S. Advisory Comm. on Intergovernmental Relations, Intergovernmental Decisionmaking for Environmental Protection and Public Works iii (1992).

State government officials have been increasingly vociferous in opposing federal regulatory mandates. Legislatures in 14 states have called for a "conference of states" to propose constitutional amendments that will shift greater power from the federal government to the states. One proposal likely to be considered would allow federal laws to be nullified upon a vote of two-thirds of state legislatures. Despite the enactment of unfunded mandates legislation in Congress in March 1995, polling data indicates that most Americans believe the federal government should have more responsibility than the states for protecting the environment. This notion was endorsed by a margin of 50 percent to 38 percent by respondents in a Wall Street Journal/NBC News Poll in January 1995. Hunt, Federalism Debate Is as Much About Power as About Principle, Wall St. J., Jan. 19, 1995, at A19.

B. APPROACHES TO REGULATION: ASSESSING THE OPTIONS

Regulation and Its Alternatives (pp. 128-130). As the text emphasizes, collective action to protect common resources can take many forms, not all of which rely entirely on government intervention. For example, sport fishers have been concerned about the declining numbers of North Atlantic salmon returning to spawn in rivers in Europe and North America. Recognizing that a salmon worth $15 to a commercial fisher can generate $500 to $1,000 in recreational fishing revenue, some sport fishing groups have begun to consider paying commercial fishers not to catch their yearly quotas of salmon. A plan to buy up Greenland's commercial quota and to pay fishers to start other occupations or to tag fish for scientists is currently under consideration in light of the success of a similar program in the Faroe Islands. Rosewicz, Paying Off Fishermen May Restore Salmon, Wall St. J., Aug. 25, 1992, at B1.

2. Environmental Law: A Structural Overview   Pages 130-133

Insurance as a Mechanism for Controlling Environmental Risk (p. 130). Environmental insurance reportedly has been enjoying a resurgence during the past year as new firms have entered a market from which many other firms previously had withdrawn. While many insurance companies that had discontinued environmental coverage remain on the sidelines, the market for environmental insurance has been stimulated by the decision of a major banking company in June 1992 to require all its borrowers to purchase insurance against environmental liabilities. Steinmetz, Insurers Discover Pollution Can Bolster Bottom Line, Wall St. J., Aug. 19, 1992, p. B4.

Market Forces, Informed Consumers, and Green Marketing (pp. 130-133). In response to concerns that companies were engaging in deceptive "green advertising," the Federal Trade Commission (FTC) in July 1992 adopted guidelines governing the use of environmental claims in advertising and marketing. The guidelines, which apply to any claims about the environmental attributes of products or packaging, are designed to offer guidance to companies and are not enforceable regulations. 57 Fed. Reg. 36,363 (1992). The guidelines address the use of terms such as "degradable," "recyclable," or "ozone safe" in advertising and comparative environmental marketing claims. For an argument that the FTC guidelines are inadequate because they lack precision and enforcement muscle and that legislation should be enacted to give EPA the authority to police environmental advertising, see Grodsky, Certified Green: The Law and Future of Environmental Labeling, 10 Yale J. on Reg. 146 (1993). While noting that some private organizations have been formed to provide certification of environmental product claims, Grodsky maintains that current life-cycle analyses of environmental effects are inadequate.

Joined by 32 states, the FTC filed an administrative complaint charging that the General Electric Company had engaged in false advertising by not disclosing that light bulbs the company promoted as energy savers provided less light. General Electric settled the complaint by agreeing to stop the practice and to pay a $165,000 penalty. Stipp, GE Will Change Promotion of Bulb as Energy Saver, Wall St. J., Nov. 10, 1992, at B9.

Eighteen states have laws that regulate "green marketing" claims. California's statute is the most detailed. It prohibits the use of terms such as "recycled," "ozone friendly," and "biodegradable" unless products meet certain specifications. For example, to be identified as "recycled," a product must contain at least ten percent of post-consumer material. Woo, California Recycling Label Law Is Upheld by U.S. Appeals Court, Wall St. J., Nov. 22, 1994, at B10. Advertisers challenged the California law on grounds that it violated their First Amendment rights, but the court upheld the statute, noting that states have the authority to prevent deceptive advertising. Association of National Advertisers v. Lungren, 44 F.3d 726 (9th Cir. 1994).

The European Community (EC) has adopted an ambitious eco-labeling program to identify environmentally friendly products based on analyses of their life cycle effects. Products deemed environmentally superior will be identified with a flower logo containing an "E" in the flower's pistil. It is anticipated that EC governments will be required to purchase products with the E label. The project was inspired in part by Germany's Blue Angel labeling program, which now covers nearly 4,000 products in 75 categories. Simons, 12 Countries, 340 Million Shoppers, One Planet, N.Y. Times, April 11, 1993, at E5.

Provisions of the Oil Pollution Act of 1990 (pp. 138-139). The Oil Pollution Act of 1990 (OPA 90) is now codified at 33 U.S.C. §§2701-2761. West Publishing has included it in its Selected Environmental Law Statutes Educational Edition, which you may wish to consult to see how Congress addressed the questions discussed in the case study. The provisions limiting liability are contained in §1004 of OPA 90, 33 U.S.C. §2704. The Oil Spill Liability Trust Fund is created by 26 U.S.C. §9509. A provision expressly disavowing any intent to preempt state liability requirements with respect to oil spills and removal activities is contained in §1018 of OPA 90, 33 U.S.C. §2718.

Provisions governing what parties are liable under the statute are contained in §1002, 33 U.S.C. §2702. Congress ultimately decided to extend liability only to owners or operators of vessels and *not* to cargo owners. The conference committee dropped the provision contained in the House bill that would have made owners of oil carried in bulk liable. Thus the last sentence on page 138 of the parent text is in error. Ship owners and operators are liable for the costs of removing the oil, for damages to natural resources and real or personal property, and for the increased costs of providing public services during or after removal activities. Provisions phasing in the double hull requirement are codified in the federal shipping code at 46 U.S.C. §3703a.

Impact of OPA 90 (pp. 139-140). While it may still be too early for a definitive assessment of the impact of OPA 90, shipping industry observers have been eager to volunteer their impressions. Most shipping companies, including the owners of foreign-flag tankers, reportedly are responding positively to the new regulatory requirements of OPA 90 by "constructing new double-hulled tankers and developing detailed oil-spill contingency plans and training programs for ship's personnel." Anderson, Oil Pollution Act Fouls the Regulatory Waters, Wall St. J.,

2. Environmental Law: A Structural Overview   Pages 139-140

Feb. 20, 1992, at A14. While the threat of increased liability reportedly has contributed to a 10 percent increase in published freight rates, the decision not to extend liability to cargo owners is proving "counterproductive," according to one observer. "First, it undermines the efforts of responsible ship owners to modernize their vessels to meet or exceed current safety standards; second, it provides no incentive for the cargo owners to do business only with responsible shipping companies. If cargo owners can escape liability in the event of a spill, there is no incentive to charter safer, but perhaps more expensive tankers." Id. Contrast these views with the following report, written six months later.

> ### Solomon, U.S. Oil Spills Have Declined Sharply, Study Says; Stiffer Federal Law Is Cited
> Wall St. J., Aug. 24, 1992, at A5A

HOUSTON—The number of oil tanker spills in U.S. waters has fallen sharply since the beginning of 1991, possibly because of stricter federal and state rules that raise liability levels, a study finds. Last year, tankers spilled 55,000 gallons of oil or petroleum products, the lowest level in 14 years, according to a report from Golob's Oil Pollution Bulletin, a Cambridge, Mass., newsletter. There weren't any major spills in the first half of 1992, the study says.

Richard Golob, publisher, said the findings "may indicate the beginning of a long-term trend of reduced oil spillage." He credits the federal Oil Pollution Act of 1990, enacted in the aftermath of the 10.9-million-gallon *Exxon Valdez* oil spill in Alaska's Prince William Sound in March 1989. In many cases, the law specifies unlimited liability for tanker owners in the event of a spill. The law also requires that any new vessels be equipped with double hulls, and it phases in the rule for existing tankers. The act also requires operating, safety, crew and maintenance changes. Laws in about 19 states also impose unlimited liability.

"Shipowners are running scared to death of liability," said Arthur McKenzie, director of the Tanker Advisory Center in New York. "When you do that, then you try to pick ships that might not get you in trouble so quick."

When the legislation was debated, many tanker operators said the new laws would drive responsible shippers out of U.S. waters for fear of liability and encourage underfinanced "rust buckets" with little to lose in U.S. waters. But just the opposite has happened, Mr. McKenzie said. He recently compiled a report on tanker quality in which he ranks vessels on a scale of one to five, with five as the highest, based on a ship's age, its frequency and types of accidents, and the quality of the owner. In January, 1989, two months before the *Valdez* spill, ships coming into U.S. waters averaged a rating of 3.4. By March 1992, the rating was 3.6.

"The penalties are so heavy that companies are more careful than they were," said John Lichtblau, chairman of the Petroleum Industry Research Foundation Inc. in New York. The industry-supported group completed a study in June for the Department of Energy and found a "sea change" of improved operational procedures, "safety provisions and inspection routines" among tanker operators.

"There are signs of a marked improvement in the quality of tonnage employed in U.S. trades," the report says. Few tanker companies have pulled out of the U.S., and the threat of inferior ships run by "uncaring owners for unscrupulous charterers" hasn't materialized. Mr. McKenzie said that in the U.K. and much of Europe, the quality of vessels is much lower because of looser regulations.

NOTES AND QUESTIONS

1. Can the sharp decline in oil spills in U.S. waters fairly be attributed to the enactment of OPA 90? Some of the key requirements of the Act have yet to take effect. The requirement that tankers operating in U.S. waters have double hulls will be phased in over a 20-year period that began in 1995. Double hull regulations are contained in 57 Fed. Reg. 36,222 (1992). Oil spills from large tankers in U.S. waters remain rare. While there were three incidents that accounted for the 55,000 gallons spilled in 1991, the Coast Guard reports that in each subsequent year there has been only one spill. The 1992 spill released 98,725 gallons, nearly double the amount spilled in 1991, but the 1993 spill released only 33,558 gallons and the 1994 incident spilled only 35,700 gallons. What do you think accounts for the decline in oil spills in U.S. waters?

2. As noted above, it had been argued that because OPA 90 does not extend liability to cargo owners, "there is no incentive to charter safer, but perhaps more expensive tankers." Anderson, Oil Pollution Act Fouls the Regulatory Waters, Wall St. J., Feb. 20, 1992, at A14. Thus, many predicted that the market would not support investments in safer tankers and that OPA 90 could prove counterproductive. Can you give any reasons why this prediction apparently has not been accurate?

3. Note the article's conclusion that due to looser regulations the quality of vessels operating in the United Kingdom and Europe is much less than that of vessels operating in the United States. Between December 1992 and February 1993, major oil spills occurred in Spain, the Shetland Islands, Indonesia, and Estonia. Wells, Machalaba, and Solo-

mon, Unsafe Oil Tankers and Ill-Trained Crews Threaten Further Spills, Wall S. J., Feb. 12, 1993, at A1. On January 5, 1993, the *Braer*, a U.S.-owned supertanker, broke up off the coast of Scotland, spilling twice as much oil as the *Exxon Valdez*. Lag in Carrying Out Oil Pollution Act Leaves U.S. Waters at Risk, Witnesses Say, 23 Env. Rep. 2685 (1993). In response to this spill, the British government is considering the adoption of tougher safety regulations and restrictions on the movement of oil tankers in environmentally sensitive areas. Schmidt, Shetland Critics Urge New Regulation of Tankers, N.Y. Times, Jan. 14, 1993, p. A14.

4. The regulatory provisions of OPA 90 have been influential throughout the world. The International Maritime Organization has adopted regulations that will require all new oil tankers to have double hulls or equivalent safety features beginning in July 1993. The regulations were adopted after the organization released a study showing that double hulls would prevent any oil spillage in 80 percent of cases in which tankers ran aground. Hudson, Tanker Safety Plans Are Mulled as Oil Spill Threatens Shetlands, Wall St. J., Jan. 8, 1993, at A7B. "Spurred by the 1989 *Exxon Valdez* disaster off Alaska and [OPA 90], naval architects from Japan to Denmark are now competing to come up with ways to build a safer supertanker." Id. Construction of the world's first supertanker with a double hull was completed at a Danish shipyard on December 30, 1992.

5. In December 1994 financial responsibility regulations imposed by OPA 90 became effective. These regulations prohibit oil tankers from docking in U.S. ports unless they have certificates of financial responsibility from the Coast Guard demonstrating that they have ten times more liability insurance ($1,500 per gross ton) than previously required. This means that supertankers that carry 200,000 to 350,000 tons of crude oil need more than $300-500 million in liability insurance. Despite fears that this requirement would disrupt the shipment of oil to the United States, Salpukas, Shift in Insurance to Cover Oil Ships May Disrupt Flow, N.Y. Times, Dec. 12, 1994, at A1, no serious problems were reported after the regulations became effective. More than a thousand oil tankers have received certificates of financial responsibility from the Coast Guard. Oil Supplies Unaffected by Tanker Rules, N.Y. Times, Dec. 29, 1994, at D4.

6. In September 1995 a federal jury ordered the Exxon Corporation to pay $5 billion in punitive damages for the Exxon Valdez oil spill. This award was premised on a jury finding that Exxon acted recklessly in employing a captain with a serious drinking problem. Exxon Ordered by Federal Court Jury to Pay $5 Billion in Punitive Damages, 25 Env. Rep. 1029 (1994). The award, which represents an amount slightly less than one year's net profits for the company, comes on top of more than $2.5 billion Exxon has paid in cleanup costs and $1 billion in

settlements with federal and state governments. Exxon is appealing the punitives damages award.

Uncertainty, Flexibility, and Complexity (pp. 159-161). Environmental regulation's complexity has become an important subject in its own right. Representatives of small businesses are particularly upset about the difficulty of determining what complex environmental regulations require of them. Carlson, Small Firms Spend Much Time, Money Complying with Environmental Rules, Wall St. J., June 15, 1992, at B1. Assisting businesses in deciphering environmental regulations has become a growth industry. Tannenbaum, Government Red Tape Puts Entrepreneurs in the Black, Wall St. J., June 12, 1992, at B2.

Peter Schuck has addressed the causes and consequences of the trend toward legal complexity. Schuck, Legal Complexity: Some Causes, Consequences, and Cures, 42 Duke L.J. 1 (1992). Schuck defines "a legal system as complex to the extent that its rules, processes, institutions, and supporting culture possess four features: density, technicality, differentiation, and indeterminacy or uncertainty." 42 Duke L. J. at 3. He argues that in addition to the transaction costs it engenders, complexity increases the costs of governance by making it more difficult to formulate and gain agreement on rules, while contributing to popular alienation from the legal system. Schuck acknowledges that complexity is in part an indirect result of a desire to tailor legal rules to diverse circumstances (what he calls "external rationality"). But he maintains that another powerful force generating complexity is the fact that "the main producers, rationalizers, and administrators of law—legislators and their staff, bureaucrats, litigants, lawyers, judges, and legal scholars—generally benefit from complexity while bearing few of its costs" (what he calls "internal rationality"). 42 Duke L.J. at 26. Schuck recognizes that complexity has its limits. Eventually it generates such high costs that informal simplification strategies are employed to minimize costs. He recommends greater focus on the way the costs and benefits of complexity are distributed and consideration of legal rules that mimic informal simplification strategies or that tax those who specially benefit from complexity. While conceding that few legal simplification efforts have worked precisely as envisioned, Schuck maintains that it is worth trying in light of the importance of the problems he identifies.

Schuck's insights are particularly valuable for understanding why environmental regulation has not lived up to popular expectations. His observations on the ways in which the political economy of complexity can explain the poor implementation of important regulatory statutes, 42 Duke L.J. at 25-31, are consistent with William Rodgers' insights into the regulatory process, discussed on pages 189-190 of the parent text.

Ian Ayres and John Braithwaite have been exploring strategies for

2. Environmental Law: A Structural Overview — Pages 163-165

making regulation more responsive to the diversity of the regulated community. In their book Responsive Regulation: Transcending the Deregulation Debate (Oxford University Press, 1992) they discuss the difficulties of tailoring regulatory strategies to the diverse characteristics of regulatory targets. One strategy that they discuss is enforced self-regulation, which directs individual firms to draft their own rules, subject to some form of certification. These privately written rules can then be publicly enforced; for example, under the Clean Water Act EPA can penalize firms for violating their privately drafted oil spill prevention rules.

In March 1995 President Clinton announced a series of measures to ease the burden of regulation on businesses by increasing regulatory flexibility. The changes are designed to blunt a Republican drive to roll back federal regulation by saving industry billions of dollars in annual compliance costs. The proposals would expand the Clean Air Act's emissions trading program to cover other pollutants and would extend this approach to efforts to control water pollution and smog, while giving small businesses a grace period for complying with regulations. They also would adopt a tiered approach to the listing of hazardous wastes that would base the severity of regulation on the relative severity of the risks posed by the waste. EPA has been directed to select 50 demonstration projects in which companies will be allowed to bypass existing pollution control regulations by designing plans that achieve even greater reductions in pollutants through other methods. Remarks by President Clinton at Custom Print, Mar. 16, 1995.

Oil Spill Liability and Section 311 of the Clean Water Act (pp. 161-163). In April 1994 the Coast Guard announced a pilot program to issue "tickets" to dischargers who spill less than 100 gallons of oil. The tickets can be served on violators immediately by Coast Guard officials. The alleged violators then would have the option of paying the "ticket" within 30 days or seeking an administrative hearing. 59 Fed. Reg. 16,558 (1994).

Uniformity versus Flexibility: Technology-Based Regulation (pp. 163-165). Professor Carol Rose has outlined a hierarchy of management strategies for common resources. She argues that the strategy with the least net costs depends on the level of pressure on the resources. Rose, Rethinking Environmental Controls: Management Strategies for Common Resources, 1991 Duke L.J. 1. When there is little pressure on congestible resources, a DO-NOTHING strategy initially has the least net costs, as illustrated in Figure S-2.2. As resource use increases, a zoning approach that excludes certain uses from certain areas (KEEPOUT) has the least net costs. At still greater levels of pressure on common resources, regulations that prescribe the ways in which the resources can be used

Pages 163-165   2. Environmental Law: A Structural Overview

FIGURE S-2.2
Strategy Comparison

Pressure on Resource
Source: 1991 Duke L.J. 1, 24.

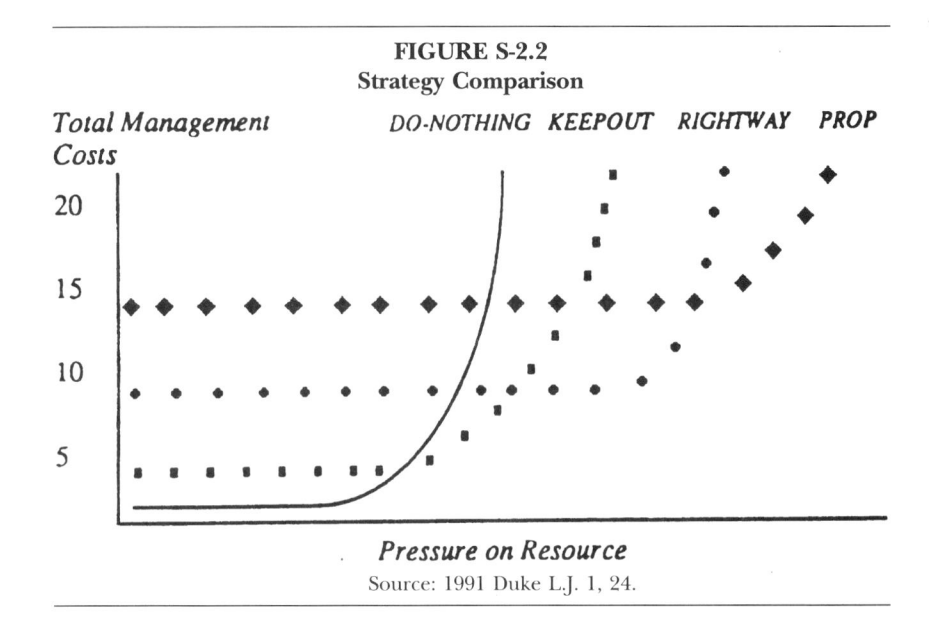

(RIGHTWAY) have the lowest management costs. Finally, at very high levels of pressure on congestible resources, a strategy that creates transferable property rights (PROP) to promote efficient resource use has the least net costs. Professor Rose argues that environmental policy is currently making a partial transition from RIGHTWAY to PROP in the air pollution area. Her model implies that the answers to the questions debated by Ackerman/Stewart and Latin depend on how far to the right we are along the horizontal axis of pressure on resources. If her hypothesis about the relative shape of the cost curves is accurate, then Ackerman/Stewart (as advocates of PROP) have the better of the argument if resource pressures have grown beyond the point at which RIGHTWAY has greater costs than PROP, while Latin is right if we are to the left of this point, where RIGHTWAY has lower costs than PROP. Professor Rose also notes that much of the criticism of PROP is based on concern for its distributional impact and fears that it may sacrifice some of the moral force of RIGHTWAY by promoting the notion of "rights to pollute." Although she suggests some approaches for addressing these problems, Professor Rose emphasizes that more attention must be paid to the norm-formation impact of environmental management strategies.

Regulation, Innovation, and Technology Forcing (pp. 165-173). The 1990 Clean Air Act Amendments appear to have been successful in their efforts to stimulate the development of cleaner fuels. For example,

2. Environmental Law: A Structural Overview   Pages 165-173

in June 1992, the Chevron Corporation announced that it had developed a new formula for manufacturing diesel fuel that would meet California's stringent new emission standards at substantially lower cost than previously anticipated. Rose, Chevron Develops Diesel-Fuel Formula That Meets California's New Standard, Wall St. J., June 3, 1992, at A5. The announcement came only a day after Unocal Corporation had announced that it would withdraw from the California diesel fuel market because of the expense of meeting the new regulations. Rose, Unocal Will End California Sales of Diesel Fuel, Wall St. J., June 2, 1992, at A9.

As noted in the parent text, estimates by regulatory targets of the prospective costs of regulation often prove to be exaggerated. In a pattern similar to that observed in the lead phasedown regulations discussed on page 167, industry estimates of the costs of complying with the acid rain control program in the 1990 Clean Air Act Amendments have quickly proved to be substantially overstated. By 1992 EPA had reduced its cost estimate of the acid rain control program to $3 billion per year from the $4-5 billion estimate it employed when the legislation was adopted. EPA then estimated that emissions allowances would trade for only $275 per ton instead of previous estimates of $500 to $750 per ton. EPA Issues Final Rules for Utilities on Acid Rain, Wall St. J., Oct. 27, 1992, at A18. In fact, allowances cost much less, selling for an average of only $132 at the March 1995 auction.

The question of how regulatory incentives best can be structured to encourage companies to develop more sophisticated environmental protection technologies remains an important one. It can be financially risky for companies to invest in the development of more sophisticated treatment technology in advance of regulation that requires its use. When EPA failed to regulate medical waste disposal as stringently as had been expected, Waste Management, Inc. was forced to write off a $70 million investment in medical waste incineration capacity. Bailey, How Two Garbage Giants Fought Over Medical Waste, Wall St. J., Nov. 17, 1992, at B6.

EPA has successfully promoted a new approach for stimulating the development of energy-efficient technologies. The Agency's Golden Carrot program, funded by a consortium of electric utilities, offered $30 million to the appliance manufacturer who won a contest to develop a refrigerator 25 to 50 percent more efficient than current standards require. Utilities contributed to the program based on calculations of the financial savings the efficiency gains would provide each utility. The Whirlpool Corporation won the competition, which generated 14 firm proposals from manufacturers, by demonstrating that its design can achieve the greatest reduction in energy consumption per dollar invested. Holusha, Whirlpool Takes Top Prize in Redesigning Refrigerator, N.Y.

Pages 165-173　　2. Environmental Law: A Structural Overview

Times, June 30, 1993, at D4. The program is an outgrowth of EPA's Green Lights program, which is designed to reduce pollution by stimulating voluntary commitments to increase the energy efficiency of lighting. EPA is considering extending this program to air conditioners, washers, dryers, and water heaters. Id.

The Clinton Administration has indicated that it will play a more active role in establishing government-industry partnerships to develop new technologies. In February 1993, President Clinton announced the formation of a "clean car" task force that will establish research programs to develop a nonpolluting automobile through cooperation among auto manufacturers, fuel suppliers, and related industries. The Partnership for a New Generation of Vehicles seeks to produce within ten years a commercially viable prototype vehicle that will have a fuel efficiency three times better than today's generation of automobiles. In October 1994 the participants in the project reported that they had made greater progress than expected during the first year of the program. Project to Develop Super-Efficient Auto Makes Progress in First Year, Officials Say, 25 Env. Rep. 1222 (1994).

Economic Incentive Approaches to Regulation (pp. 173-177). Interest in the development of economic incentive approaches to environmental regulation continues to increase, particularly as pressures to reduce the federal budget deficit encourage lawmakers to search for new sources of revenue. A report issued by the World Resources Institute (WRI) in November 1992 estimated that a strategy of shifting the revenue burden of taxation from economic "goods" to environmental "bads" could raise between $100 to $180 billion per year. "Congestion tolls on urban highways could generate $40 to $100 billion, carbon taxes would yield $30 to $50 billion, and solid-waste charges could raise another $5 to $10 billion." R. Repetto, R. Dower, R. Jenkins, and J. Geoghegan, Green Fees: How a Tax Shift Can Work for the Environment and the Economy 11 (World Resources Inst. 1992). These additional revenues could permit the government to reduce marginal tax rates on economically productive activities like labor, producing $45 to $80 billion in net economic benefits annually. Id. The WRI report estimated that effluent charges, charges on environmentally damaging activities or products, and the reduction of tax benefits and subsidies for resource exploitation could generate nearly $40 billion in extra revenue each year. Id. at 83.

Another strong endorsement for greater reliance on economic incentive approaches to regulation is contained in Stavins and Grumbly, "The Greening of the Market: Making the Polluter Pay," in Mandate for Change 197 (W. Marshall and M. Schram, eds. 1993). Stavins and Grumbly recommend consideration of volume-based charges for disposal of household garbage, a carbon tax, increased gasoline taxes,

2. Environmental Law: A Structural Overview   Pages 180-184

and the use of deposit-refund systems to encourage proper disposal of hazardous materials. The Clinton Administration ultimately rejected a carbon tax because its disproportionate impact on certain types of fuels would make it particularly harsh on regions of the country heavily dependent on those fuels, making enactment politically difficult. Instead, the administration proposed an energy tax based on the energy content of all fuels as measured in British thermal units (Btus). The proposal quickly was abandoned in the face of stiff political opposition.

Scientists interested in ecological economics have proposed the use of what they call "flexible environmental assurance bonds" as a means of dealing with uncertainty concerning the environmental effects of human activity. This approach would involve "charging an economic agent directly for known environmental damages and levying an assurance bond equal to the current best estimate of the largest potential future environmental damage." Costanza and Cornwell, The 4P Approach to Dealing with Scientific Uncertainty, 34 Environment 13, 16 (Nov. 1992). "Portions of the bond (plus interest) would be returned if and when the agent could demonstrate that the suspected worst-case damages had not occurred or would be less than was originally assessed." Id. at 17.

Fragmented Regulatory Authorities (pp. 179-180). EPA has responded to concern about the difficulties of pursuing coordinated regulatory responses to cross-media contamination by forming 13 "clusters," teams of staffers from the various program offices who work together on regulation of the same industry, pollutant, or resource. Seven of these clusters are industry- or issue-specific (pulp and paper, petroleum refining, oil and gas production and exploration, printing, transportation, small communities, environmental equity); two are pollutant-based (lead and nitrogen) and four are resource protection clusters (groundwater, habitat, contaminated media, indoor air). By combining staffers from different program offices, the Agency hopes to be able to focus on the greatest sources of risk, to encourage multimedia compliance, to improve communication, and to reduce duplicative data-gathering. Cleland-Hamnett and Retzer, Crossing Agency Boundaries, Envtl. Forum, Mar.-April 1993, at 17.

A treatise published by the Environmental Law Institute contains an industry-by-industry assessment of the ways in which the various pollution control and natural resource laws interact in their application to various industries, Environmental Law Institute, Sustainable Environmental Law (1993).

Public Law and Control of Lead Poisoning (pp. 180-184). The pervasive nature of the lead contamination problem was illustrated in the summer of 1992 when sandblasting of the Williamsburg Bridge in New York City spread a rain of lead paint chips on a Bronx neighborhood. A survey of lead contamination in areas near the Williamsburg, Manhattan, and Brooklyn Bridges subsequently found lead levels in excess of the 1,000 ppm guideline for lead in soil employed by the Centers for Disease Control. Samples taken from Bronx playgrounds ranged from 17,586 ppm to 46,092 ppm lead. Myers, Study Finds Soil Tainted by Lead in a Playground, N.Y. Times, Dec. 27, 1992, at 33. While the mayor of New York City established a task force to investigate the contamination and to recommend remediation, efforts to clean up the lead-contaminated soil had not begun more than six months after the sandblasting.

Evidence that the neurological damage done by lead persists over time continues to mount. Longitudinal studies of children in Boston and Australia demonstrated that the reduced IQ associated with lead poisoning in infants persists into the school years and is independent of a child's socioeconomic status. Baghurst, et al., Environmental Exposure to Lead and Children's Intelligence at the Age of Seven Years, 327 New Eng. J. Med. 1279 (1992). Efforts by lead industry consultants to discredit the pioneering lead poisoning research of Dr. Herbert Needleman proved unsuccessful when an investigatory panel cleared Dr. Needleman of charges of scientific misconduct. Panel Clears Needleman of Misconduct, 256 Science 1389 (1992).

In August 1992, the Health Care Financing Administration announced that it would require state agencies to conduct lead screening of all children assisted by the Medicaid program. Pear, U.S. Orders Testing of Poor Children for Lead Poisoning, N.Y. Times, Sept. 13, 1992, at A1. More than six million children under the age of six are in the Medicaid program. The government directive was criticized because it allows states to continue to use a cheaper, less accurate screening test that is not sensitive to blood lead levels below 25 micrograms per deciliter, even though the level of medical concern for lead recognized by CDC is 10 micrograms per deciliter.

On Oct. 28, 1992, President Bush signed the Residential Lead-Based Paint Hazard Reduction Act, Pub. L. No. 102-550, better known as Title X of the Housing and Community Development Act of 1992. Title X, which adds a new title to the Toxic Substances Control Act, is being heralded by environmentalists as the most comprehensive approach to abatement of lead paint hazards in two decades. The legislation requires sellers or lessors of residential property to disclose the presence of any known lead-based paint hazards to prospective buyers or lessees beginning in October 1995. It requires the establishment of requirements for certification and licensing of lead paint abatement contractors, and it requires OSHA to promulgate worker protection regulations governing lead exposure in the construction industry. Recognizing the enormity of the lead-paint problem, Title X moves away from the approach of requiring abatement of any and all lead-based paint in favor of a more targeted approach designed to focus on the worst hazards first. See Alliance to End Childhood Lead Poisoning, Understanding Title X: A Practical Guide to the Residential Lead-Based Paint Hazard Reduction Act (1993).

In September 1994 EPA announced that it would consider requiring that it be given 90 days' advance notice before lead or lead compounds could be used, imported, or processed for any significant new use. 59 Fed. Reg. 49,484 (1994). Acting pursuant to its authority under section 5(a)(2) of the Toxic Substances Control Act, EPA indicated that the purpose of such a rule would be to give the agency an opportunity to evaluate the intended new use of lead to prevent unreasonable risks to public health or the environment.

As a result of the *Johnson Controls* decision, most corporations that had policies banning women of childbearing age from hazardous jobs have eliminated them, while attempting to educate employees about workplace risks. Labor Letter, Wall St. J., Oct. 27, 1992, at A1.

C. THE REGULATORY PROCESS: A PREVIEW

Theories of Agency Decision-making (pp. 185-190). Mark Seidenfeld has argued that the role of administrative agencies in our system of government can best be understood by applying "civic republican" theory, which views "the Constitution as an attempt to ensure that government decisions are the product of deliberation that respects and reflects the values of all members of society." Seidenfeld, A Civic Republican Justification for the Bureaucratic State, 105 Harv. L. Rev. 1512, 1514 (1992). By falling "between the extremes of the politically over-responsive Congress and the over-insulated courts," agencies are the "prime candidates to institute a civic republican model of policymaking," Seidenfeld argues. Id. at 1542. He maintains that agencies are better equipped than directly elected officials or legislators to engage in "deliberative decisionmaking informed by the values of the entire polity" because of their "greater expertise" and the "fewer immediate political pressures" they face. Id. at 1515.

Seidenfeld emphasizes the important function performed by the president, Congress and the courts in reviewing agency actions. Howard Latin suggests that these reviewing entities need to be more creative in anticipating agency behavior. Focusing on the difficulty of getting agencies to implement regulatory legislation, Latin argues that legislators must pay more careful attention "to the institutional incentives of agencies and to the professional and personal incentives of regulators. . . ." Latin, Regulatory Failure, Administrative Incentives, and the New Clean Air Act, 21 Envtl. L. 1647 (1991). Professor Latin has identified eight "laws" of administrative behavior that he believes explain the limits of legislative control of agencies:

1. In conflicts between political considerations and technocratic requirements, politics usually prevails.
2. Agencies avoid making regulatory decisions that would create severe social or economic dislocation.
3. Agencies avoid resolving disputed issues unless they can render scientifically credible judgments.
4. Agencies will not meet statutory deadlines if budget appropriations, personnel, information, or other resources are inadequate.
5. Regulators are influenced by disciplinary norms that may conflict with statutory mandates.
6. Bureaucrats are conditioned by criticism or other forms of negative feedback.
7. Agency behavior is partly conditioned by manipulative tactics of regulated parties.
8. Administrators of multiple-purpose statutes usually "simplify" the decisional process to emphasize only one or two statutory goals.

Id. at 1651-1652.

D. ENVIRONMENTAL REGULATION: SOME ADDITIONAL THEMES

Winners and Losers (p. 194). The winners and losers theme is particularly timely in light of the growing interest in environmental justice issues, as discussed above, and the debate in the 104th Congress over whether environmental regulation hurts the economy and sacrifices jobs.

Regulatory Strategies Reflect Different Assessments of Goals and Means (p. 195). The moral outrage perspective that has led some to criticize emissions trading schemes is illustrated by reaction to the first sale of emission allowances under the 1990 Clean Air Act Amendments. In May 1992, the Wisconsin Power & Light Company sold emission allowances to the Tennessee Valley Authority and the Duquesne Light Company. A representative of a consumer protection group criticized the sale by arguing: "Clean air should be protected, not traded and sold like a used car. What's next, the L.A. police department trying to buy civil rights credits from Wisconsin?" An economist responded: "I'm not quite sure what people are complaining about. We want to accomplish our environmental goals with the least pain possible to the economy." Pollution Swap, Time, May 25, 1992, at 22.

3
Waste Management and Pollution Prevention

With all of its flaws, Superfund remains at the heart of a bold strategy to deal with one of our most intractable and pervasive environmental problems. By motivating industry to develop and implement effective cleanup technologies while simultaneously regulating toxic waste disposal by risk, Superfund represents an alternative we cannot afford to lose without repercussions that extend far beyond the program's current scope. At the same time, it is clear that the current program not only wastes precious time and scarce resources, but has lost the confidence of virtually all of its key stakeholders. Without effective and timely reform, this confidence—and the program's political viability over the long term—cannot be restored.

—*Rena I. Steinzor**

RCRA and CERCLA are becoming the most frequently litigated areas of federal environmental law. This chapter reviews EPA's continued struggle to define "solid waste" and "hazardous waste" and the denouement of the incinerator ash controversy, which was resolved ultimately by the Supreme Court's decision in City of Chicago v. Environmental Defense Fund. It considers decisions fleshing out the limits of CERCLA liability, including the Third Circuit's *Alcan* decision, the Fourth Circuit's *Nurad* decision, the Fifth Circuit's *Bell Petroleum* decision, and the D.C. Circuit's *Kelley* decision. The chapter concludes by reviewing Supreme Court decisions that address constitutional limits on environmental regulation, including decisions invalidating state efforts to restrict interstate waste disposal, and New York v. United States, which struck down a portion of the federal scheme to require states to take responsibility for disposal of low-level radioactive waste.

---

* The Reauthorization of Superfund: Can the Deal of the Century Be Saved?, 25 Env. L. Rep. 1009 (1995).

3. Waste Management and Pollution Prevention

A. WASTE MANAGEMENT AND THE POLLUTION PROBLEM

Waste Management and the Pollution Problem (pp. 201-206). The amount of waste generated in the United States each year continues to grow. EPA estimates that 206.9 million tons of municipal solid waste was generated in 1993, a four percent increase over the amount generated in 1990. In 1980, approximately 151 million tons of waste was generated in the United States, nearly double the 88 million tons generated in 1960. Thus, Americans now generate waste at a rate of 4.4 pounds per person per day, a substantial increase over the 2.7 pounds per person per day in 1960. These figures do not include waste from industrial processes.

The rate of recycling of municipal solid waste has increased to 22 percent in 1993 from 13 percent in 1988 and 7 percent in 1960. Because of increased recycling, the volume of waste remaining to be disposed decreased to 162 million tons from 163 million tons in 1990. Only 62.4 percent of this waste was sent to landfills in 1993 (a decline from 73 percent in 1988) and 20 percent was incinerated, an increase from 14 percent in 1988.

An anthropologist who directs the University of Arizona's garbage project challenges conventional notions about what types of household waste take up the most landfill space. W. Rathje and C. Murphy, *Rubbish!* (1992). Based on excavations at garbage dumps, the Arizona project found that polysterene foam takes up less than one percent of landfill space, and diapers no more than 1.4%. Paper waste was estimated to occupy more than 40 percent of landfill space, followed by construction debris and yard waste. One of the most surprising findings of the garbage project's excavations is that biodegradation of paper waste and organic materials takes far longer than expected in landfills. The researchers argue that landfills "are not vast composters, rather they are vast mummifiers." Their book provides a useful historical overview of waste management practices in the United States. It reports that until New York City began systematic garbage collection in 1895, waste was simply piled up in the streets, which rose at a rate of almost five feet per century due to the accumulation of garbage. It also describes the wide variations in waste streams in different countries. While the U.S. waste stream contains far more packaging materials, in the aggregate the United States produces one third less waste than Mexico because the Mexican waste stream contains far more food waste.

3. Waste Management and Pollution Prevention — Pages 235-239

B. STATUTORY AUTHORITIES AFFECTING WASTE MANAGEMENT

EPA's Pollution Prevention Strategy (pp. 213-214). As noted in the parent text (p. 213), part of EPA's Pollution Prevention Strategy has been a program encouraging companies to agree to the goal of reducing emissions of 17 highly toxic chemicals by 33 percent by the end of 1992 and by 50 percent by the end of 1995. As of December 1994, EPA reported that more than 1,300 companies had agreed to participate in the program, which EPA believes will succeed in its ultimate goal of reducing aggregate emissions by 50 percent by the end of 1995. June Decision Planned on Voluntary Program to Cut Toxic Chemical Use, EPA Official Says, 25 Env. Rep. 1562 (1994).

C. THE RCRA REGULATORY PROGRAM

1. RCRA: An Introduction

RCRA Reauthorization (pp. 214-220). Reauthorization of RCRA is not high on the current legislative agenda in Congress. The most likely legislative changes in this area are bills authorizing states to impose restrictions on interstate shipments of waste. In 1994 the U.S. House and Senate approved different versions of flow control legislation that would have allowed some state or local restrictions on the movement of waste. However, Congress adjourned before the bills could be reconciled. Satterfield, High Hopes and Failed Expectations: The Environmental Record of the 103d Congress, 25 Env. Rep. 10,089 (1995).

2. What Substances Are "Solid Wastes"?

Definition of "Solid Wastes" (pp. 235-239). EPA continues to wrestle with how to revise its definition of "solid waste" to encourage genuine recycling while regulating activities that threaten harm. In October 1992, EPA announced the formation of a task force to develop a less complex definition of "solid waste" that would eliminate disincentives to recycling. Task Force Planned by EPA to Tackle Redefining Solid Waste to Foster Recycling, 23 Env. Rep. 1541 (1992). In April 1993, EPA convened a roundtable to solicit ideas for improving the definition of "solid waste."

In April 1994, EPA's Definition of Solid Waste Task Force issued a report proposing to exempt certain recycling activities from regulation under Subtitle C of RCRA. Task Force Suggests New Recycling Plan in Definition of Solid Waste Under RCRA, 24 Env. Rep. 2221 (1994). Materials returned to original production processes without reclamation and materials recycled in a manner similar to manufacturing would be exempt if secondary materials were neither burned, placed on land, or used to produce fuel. The report proposed to establish a four-part classification scheme for recycling operations: (1) direct reuse off-site of spent materials and precious metals recovery, (2) on-site recycling, (3) intracompany recycling and product stewardship, and (4) commercial recycling off-site. Notification, biennial reporting, and use of a special manifest would be required for facilities seeking an exemption from Subtitle C. Commercial off-site recycling would be regulated more stringently with prior government approval required before operations could commence. To prohibit what EPA calls "toxics along for the ride," EPA would determine if levels of hazardous constituents in recycled products were greater than levels in virgin material.

Industry representatives have criticized the approach proposed by the task force as too complicated. They argue that all on-site recycling of hazardous waste should be exempted from Subtitle C requirements so long as regulatory authorities are notified of the operations and land storage does not occur prior to recycling. EPA officials are still considering what approach to formulate as a proposed rule. Simplified Approach Adopted by Agency in Attempt to Revise Solid Waste Definition, 24 Env. Rep. 1655 (1994).

Courts also have continued to wrestle with the definition of solid waste. In United States v. Ilco, Inc., 996 F.2d 1126 (11th Cir. 1993), the Eleventh Circuit held that lead parts reclaimed from spent car and truck batteries for recycling purposes are solid wastes subject to regulation under RCRA. While the recycler argued that it had never discarded the lead plates and groups removed from old batteries it had purchased, the court emphasized that the fact that "[s]*omebody* has discarded the battery in which these components are found . . . does not change just because a reclaimer has purchased or finds value in the components." 996 F.2d at 1131 (emphasis in original). In Owen Electric Steel Co. v. Browner, 37 F.3d 146 (4th Cir. 1994), the Fourth Circuit held that slag (produced by a steel mill) that is "cured" on the ground for six months prior to being sold for use as a road base material is, despite its ultimate reuse, "discarded material" subject to regulation under RCRA. The court observed that "the fundamental inquiry in determining whether a byproduct has been 'discarded' is whether the byproduct is *immediately* recycled for use in the same industry; if not, then the byproduct is justifiably seen as 'part of the waste disposal

3. Waste Management and Pollution Prevention   Pages 240-242

problem,' *AMC I,* 824 F.2d at 1186, and therefore as a 'solid waste.' " 37 F.3d at 150 (emphasis in original).

States remain free under RCRA to define more expansively what constitutes solid or hazardous waste. In Old Bridge Chemicals v. New Jersey Department of Environmental Protection, 965 F.2d 1287 (3d Cir. 1992), the Third Circuit rejected an industry challenge to New Jersey regulations that expressly include materials recycled as effective substitutes for commercial products within the state's definition of "solid waste," even though these materials are excluded from EPA's definition. As a result of its more expansive definition of "solid waste," New Jersey subjects a broader class of materials to RCRA's manifest system. Industry petitioners argued that this interfered with interstate commerce. The Third Circuit rejected these arguments and found that Congress had not intended to preempt more stringent state regulations, that the New Jersey standards did not create any direct conflict with regulations of other states, and that they imposed no greater burden on interstate than on intrastate commerce.

3. *Identifying "Hazardous Waste"*

The Mixture and Derived-from Rules After **Shell Oil** *(pp. 240-242).* Following the *Shell Oil* decision, EPA sought to reinstate the mixture and derived-from rules on an emergency basis, as the court indicated would be permissible pending a new round of notice-and-comment rulemaking. However, the vice president's Council on Competitiveness, which is discussed in Chapter 5 (p. 700-701), saw this as an opportunity to force EPA to cut back drastically on the scope of the RCRA program. After a bitter battle, the Council agreed to let EPA temporarily reinstate the mixture and derived-from rules on the condition that the Agency also propose major changes in the RCRA program.

On April 30, 1992, EPA reinstated the mixture and derived-from rules while proposing a new Hazardous Waste Identification Rule (HWIR). The proposed HWIR would employ one of two alternative approaches for moving the RCRA program toward a risk-based approach that would vary the stringency of regulation with the degree of danger posed by certain wastes. 57 Fed. Reg. 21,450.

One proposal, dubbed the concentration-based exemption criteria (CBEC) proposal, would permit listed wastes, mixtures, and derived-from wastes to be exempted from some hazardous waste management requirements once their concentrations of certain hazardous constituents fell below certain levels. This approach essentially would implement EPA's long-standing desire to devise a means for determining when the concentrations of hazardous constituents in wastes have been so greatly reduced as to no longer warrant management as hazardous waste. In order to determine what constitutes a de minimis level of hazardous constituents for the CBEC approach, EPA proposed five options: relying on health-based numbers (e.g., Safe Drinking Water Act MCLs) adjusted by factors of 100, 10, or 1; using levels corresponding to BDAT; or using BDAT capped with health-based numbers. 57 Fed. Reg. 21,457-21,458.

EPA's second approach, called the expanded characteristics option (ECHO), would treat most listed, mixed, and derived-from wastes like characteristic wastes by providing that they would not be deemed hazardous unless they exhibited one of the hazardous characteristics. This approach would radically revise the RCRA program by largely abandoning the listing approach in favor of expanded reliance on the regulated community to determine if their wastes exhibit hazardous characteristics. EPA also proposed to vary the stringency of regulations applicable to certain wastes based on the levels of hazardous constituents in them. This would subject waste to a continuum of management controls, rather than the two-tiered system currently in effect. In an unusual provision inserted at the insistence of the Competitiveness Council, EPA provided that its current mixture and derived-from rules would expire automatically on April 28, 1993 if EPA failed to take final action on proposed revisions to them.

EPA's proposed Hazardous Waste Identification Rule drew more than 600 comments and a lawsuit challenging reinstatement of the mixture and derived-from rules. Environmental groups and waste management officials from 40 states were particularly critical of the proposed HWIR. The Hazardous Waste Treatment Council and the Sierra Club estimated that the proposal could have exempted 90 percent of listed hazardous wastes from RCRA Subtitle C regulation. Proposed HWIR Rule Withdrawn by EPA; Huge Number of Negative Comments Cited, Env. Rep. 1491, 1493 (1992). Congress responded by adopting an amendment that removed the April 28, 1993 sunset provision and directed EPA to take until October 1994 to revise the mixture and derived-from rules. In September 1992, EPA's HWIR proposal was withdrawn suddenly after the Bush Administration learned that several prominent Democrats had scheduled a press conference to denounce the proposal and make it an issue in the 1992 presidential campaign. Schneider, Campaign Concerns Prompt White House to Drop Waste Plan, N.Y. Times, Sept. 30, 1992, at A1.

In Mobil Oil Corp. v. EPA, 35 F.3d 579 (D.C. Cir. 1994), the D.C. Circuit held that Congress's action temporarily reinstating the mixture and derived-from rules rendered moot a lawsuit challenging EPA's reinstatement of them. Congress had directed EPA to revise the mixture and derived-from rules by October 1, 1994, but EPA missed the deadline.

3. Waste Management and Pollution Prevention   Pages 251-252

After several deadline suits were brought, EPA agreed in November 1994 to a consent decree establishing a new schedule for revising the rules. The schedule requires EPA to propose revisions to the mixture and derived-from rules by August 15, 1995 and to adopt final rules by December 15, 1996. Settlement Requires Partial Revision of Mixture, Derived-From Rules by Late 1996, 25 Env. Rep. 1472 (1994).

In an effort to achieve consensus concerning how to revise the mixture and derived-from rules, EPA convened a federal advisory committee that failed to reach consensus after 18 months of negotiations. EPA is attempting to determine through risk assessments if it can determine "bright line" levels of hazardous constituents that should subject industrial process waste or contaminated media to Subtitle C regulation. The agency expects to issue a rule dealing with contaminated media by the fall of 1996. Simplified Approach Adopted by Agency in Attempt to Revise Solid Waste Definition, 25 Env. Rep. 1655 (1994).

Because the D.C. Circuit denied EPA's supplemental motion asking the court to clarify that the *Shell Oil* decision is not retroactive, many persons penalized for RCRA violations have been able to overturn past EPA enforcement actions. In June 1992, the Eighth Circuit reversed criminal convictions obtained under RCRA for illegal waste dumping, finding that *Shell Oil*'s invalidation of the mixture rule applies retroactively. United States v. Goodner Brothers Aircraft, Inc., 966 F.2d 380 (8th Cir. 1992). However, the court refused to overturn a companion conviction for failing to report the release of a hazardous substance under CERCLA.

Used Oil Listing (p. 244). As noted in the parent text, in Hazardous Waste Treatment Council v. EPA, 861 F.2d 270 (D.C. Cir. 1988), the D.C. Circuit vacated EPA's determination not to list used oil as a hazardous waste because the court found that the perceived "stigma" associated with the listing was not relevant under the statute. Following this decision, EPA reconsidered the matter and again determined not to list used oil as a hazardous waste. 57 Fed. Reg. 21,524 (1992). The agency decided that engine oils already are subject to regulation as characteristic wastes and that other oils are not hazardous with sufficient frequency to warrant listing. In Natural Resources Defense Council v. EPA, 25 F.3d 1063 (D.C. Cir. 1994), EPA's decision was upheld by the D.C. Circuit, which noted that the agency retains considerable discretion in determining when to list a particular waste as hazardous.

Incinerator Ash: A Postscript (pp. 251-252). As expected, the City of Chicago sought Supreme Court review of the Seventh Circuit's decision in Environmental Defense Fund v. City of Chicago, 948 F.2d 345 (7th Cir. 1991). In light of the conflicting decisions by the U.S. Courts of Appeals for the Second and Seventh Circuits, the Supreme Court asked for the views of the U.S. Solicitor General. In the course of preparing his amicus brief, the Solicitor General persuaded EPA Administrator William Reilly to issue a new memorandum determining that section 3001(i) of RCRA exempts incinerator ash from regulation under Subtitle C. While EPA previously had taken the position that section 3001(i) was not intended to affect whether ash should be considered a hazardous waste, the memorandum issued on September 18, 1992 stated that section 3001(i) "arguably extended the regulatory exclusion for ash derived from the incineration of household waste to similar residues generated by resource recovery facilities from the incineration of household waste *and* nonhazardous commercial and industrial solid waste." Noting that section 3001(i) specifies that certain resource recovery facilities are not considered to be "treating, storing, disposing of, or otherwise managing" hazardous waste, the memorandum states that "[n]othing ordinarily is 'disposed of' when a resource recovery facility receives or stores a nonhazardous solid waste, and the burning of such waste generally is regarded as a type of treatment under RCRA. As a result, since MWC [municipal waste combustion] ash ordinarily is the only waste 'disposed of' by such a facility, Congress arguably intended that MWC ash not be regarded as a hazardous waste." William K. Reilly, Exemption for Municipal Waste Combustion Ash From Hazardous Waste Regulation Under RCRA Section 3001(i), Sept. 18, 1992.

In line with the Solicitor General's recommendation, the Supreme Court vacated the Seventh Circuit's decision in November 1992 and remanded the case for reconsideration in light of the EPA Administrator's new interpretation of section 3001(i). On remand, the Seventh Circuit reaffirmed its previous decision finding that the ash was not exempt. The Supreme Court then granted review and reached the following decision.

City of Chicago v. Environmental Defense Fund
114 S. Ct. 1588 (1994)

Justice SCALIA delivered the opinion of the Court.

We are called upon to decide whether, pursuant to §3000(i) of the Solid Waste Disposal Act (Resource Conservation and Recovery Act of 1976 (RCRA)), as added, 98 Stat. 3252, 42 U.S.C. §6921(i), the ash generated by a resource recovery facility's incineration of municipal solid waste is exempt from regulation as a hazardous waste under Subtitle C of RCRA.

3. Waste Management and Pollution Prevention Pages 251-252

II

RCRA is a comprehensive environmental statute that empowers EPA to regulate hazardous wastes from cradle to grave, in accordance with the rigorous safeguards and waste management procedures of Subtitle C, 42 U.S.C. §§6921-6934. (Nonhazardous wastes are regulated much more loosely under Subtitle D, 42 U.S.C. §§6941-6949.) Under the relevant provisions of Subtitle C, EPA has promulgated standards governing hazardous waste generators and transporters, see 42 U.S.C. §§6922 and 6923, and owners and operators of hazardous waste treatment, storage, and disposal facilities (TSDF's), see 42 U.S.C. §6924. Pursuant to §6922, EPA has directed hazardous waste generators to comply with handling, record-keeping, storage, and monitoring requirements, see 40 CFR pt. 262 (1993). TSDF's, however, are subject to much more stringent regulation than either generators or transporters, including a 4-to-5 year permitting process, see 42 U.S.C. §6925; 40 CFR pt. 270 (1993); U.S. Environmental Protection Agency Office of Solid Waste and Emergency Response, The Nation's Hazardous Waste Management Program at a Crossroads, The RCRA Implementation Study 49-50 (July 1990), burdensome financial assurance requirements, stringent design and location standards, and, perhaps most onerous of all, responsibility to take corrective action for releases of hazardous substances and to ensure safe closure of each facility, see 42 U.S.C. §6924; 40 CFR pt. 264 (1993). "[The] corrective action requirement is one of the major reasons that generators and transporters work diligently to manage their wastes so as to avoid the need to obtain interim status or a TSD permit." 3 Environmental Law Practice Guide §29.06[3][d] (M. Gerrard ed. 1993) (hereinafter Practice Guide).

RCRA does not identify which wastes are hazardous and therefore subject to Subtitle C regulation; it leaves that designation to EPA. 42 U.S.C. §6921(a). When EPA's hazardous waste designations for solid wastes appeared in 1980, see 45 Fed. Reg. 33084, they contained certain exceptions from normal coverage, including an exclusion for "household waste," defined as "any waste material . . . derived from households (including single and multiple residences, hotels and motels)," id., at 33120, codified as amended at 40 CFR §261.4(b)(1) (1992). Although most household waste is harmless, a small portion—such as cleaning fluids and batteries—would have qualified as hazardous waste. The regulation declared, however, that "[h]ousehold waste, including household waste that has been collected, transported, stored, treated, disposed, recovered (e.g., refuse derived fuel) or reused" is not hazardous waste. Ibid. Moreover, the preamble to the 1980 regulations stated that "residues remaining after treatment (e.g., incineration, thermal treatment) [of household waste] are not subject to regulation as a hazardous waste." 45 Fed. Reg. 33099. By reason of these provisions, an incinerator that burned only household waste would not be considered a Subtitle C TSDF, since it processed only nonhazardous (i.e., household) waste, and it would not be considered a Subtitle C generator of hazardous waste and would be free to dispose of its ash in a Subtitle D landfill.

The 1980 regulations thus provided what is known as a "waste stream" exemption for household waste, ibid., i.e., an exemption covering that category of waste from generation through treatment to final disposal of residues. The regulation did not, however, exempt MWC ash from Subtitle C coverage if the incinerator that produced the ash burned anything *in addition to* household waste, such as what petitioner's facility burns: nonhazardous industrial waste. Thus, a facility like petitioner's would qualify as a Subtitle C hazardous waste generator if the MWC ash it produced was sufficiently toxic, see 40 CFR §§261.3, 261.24 (1993) though it would still not qualify as a Subtitle C TSDF, since all the waste it took in would be characterized as nonhazardous. (An ash can be hazardous, even though the product from which it is generated is not, because in the new medium the contaminants are more concentrated and more readily leachable, see 40 CFR §§261.3, 261.24, and pt. 261, App. II (1993).)

Four years after these regulations were issued, Congress enacted the Hazardous and Solid Waste Amendments of 1984, Pub. L. 98-616, 98 Stat. 3221, which added to RCRA the "Clarification of Household Waste Exclusion" as §3001(i), §223, 98 Stat., at 3252. The essence of our task in this case is to determine whether, under that provision, the MWC ash generated by petitioner's facility—a facility that would have been considered a Subtitle C generator under the 1980 regulations—is subject to regulation as hazardous waste under Subtitle C. We conclude that it is.

Section 3001(i), 42 U.S.C. §6921(i), entitled "Clarification of household waste exclusion," provides:

> A resource recovery facility recovering energy from the mass burning of municipal solid waste shall not be deemed to be treating, storing, disposing of, or otherwise managing hazardous wastes for the purposes of regulation under this subchapter, if—
> (1) such facility—
> (A) receives and burns only—
> (i) household waste (from single and multiple dwellings, hotels, motels, and other residential sources), and
> (ii) solid waste from commercial or industrial sources that does not contain hazardous waste identified or listed under this section, and
> (B) does not accept hazardous wastes identified or listed under this section, and

3. Waste Management and Pollution Prevention   Pages 251-252

(2) the owner or operator of such facility has established contractual requirements or other appropriate notification or inspection procedures to assure that hazardous wastes are not received at or burned in such facility.

The plain meaning of this language is that so long as a facility recovers energy by incineration of the appropriate wastes, *it* (the *facility*) is not subject to Subtitle C regulation as a facility that treats, stores, disposes of, or manages hazardous waste. The provision quite clearly does not contain any exclusion for the *ash itself.* Indeed, the waste the facility produces (as opposed to that which it receives) is not even mentioned. There is thus no express support for petitioners' claim of a waste-stream exemption.[1]

Petitioners contend, however, that the practical effect of the statutory language is to exempt the ash by virtue of exempting the facility. If, they argue, the facility is not deemed to be treating, storing, or disposing of hazardous waste, then the ash that it treats, stores, or disposes of must itself be considered nonhazardous. There are several problems with this argument. First, as we have explained, the only exemption provided by the terms of the statute is for the *facility*. It is the facility, *not the ash*, that "shall not be deemed" to be subject to regulation under Subtitle C. *Unlike* the preamble to the 1980 regulations, which had been in existence for four years by the time §3001(i) was enacted, §3001(i) does not explicitly exempt MWC ash generated by a resource recovery facility from regulation as a hazardous waste. In light of that difference, and given the statute's express declaration of national policy that "[w]aste that is . . . generated should be treated, stored, or disposed of so as to minimize the present and future threat to human health and the environment," 42 U.S.C. §6902(b), we cannot interpret the statute to permit MWC ash sufficiently toxic to qualify as hazardous to be disposed of in ordinary landfills.

Moreover, as the Court of Appeals observed, the statutory language does not even exempt the *facility* in its capacity as a *generator* of hazardous waste. RCRA defines "generation" as "the act or process of producing

---

1. The dissent is able to describe the provision as exempting the ash itself only by resorting to what might be called imaginative use of ellipsis: "even though the material being treated and disposed of contains hazardous components before, during, and after its treatment[,] that material shall not be deemed to be . . . hazardous." In the full text, quoted above, the subject of the phrase "shall not be deemed . . . hazardous" is *not* the material, but the *resource recovery facility,* and the complete phrase, including (italicized) the ellipsis, reads "shall not be deemed to be *treating, storing, disposing of, or otherwise managing* hazardous *wastes.*" Deeming a facility not to be engaged in these activities with respect to hazardous wastes is of course quite different from deeming the output of that facility not to be hazardous.

71

hazardous waste." 42 U.S.C. §6903(6). There can be no question that the creation of ash by incinerating municipal waste constitutes "generation" of hazardous waste (assuming, of course, that the ash qualifies as hazardous under 42 U.S.C. §6921 and its implementing regulations, 40 CFR pt. 261 (1993)). Yet although §3001(i) states that the exempted facility "shall not be deemed to be treating, storing, disposing of, or otherwise managing hazardous wastes," it significantly omits from the catalogue the word "generating." Petitioners say that because the activities listed as exempt encompass the full scope of the facility's operation, the failure to mention the activity of generating is insignificant. But the statute itself refutes this. Each of the three specific terms used in §3000(i)—"treating," "storing," and "disposing of"—is separately defined by RCRA, and none covers the production of hazardous waste. The fourth and less specific term ("otherwise managing") is also defined, to mean "collection, source separation, storage, transportation, processing, treatment, recovery, and disposal," 42 U.S.C. §6903(7)—just about every hazardous waste-related activity *except* generation. We think it follows from the carefully constructed text of §3001(i) that while a resource recovery facility's management activities are excluded from Subtitle C regulation, its generation of toxic ash is not. . . .

Petitioners contend that our interpretation of §3001(i) turns the provision into an "empty gesture," since even under the pre-existing regime an incinerator burning household waste and nonhazardous industrial waste was exempt from the Subtitle C TSDF provisions. If §3001(i) did not extend the waste-stream exemption to the product of such a combined household/nonhazardous industrial treatment facility, petitioners argue, it did nothing at all. But it is not nothing to codify a household waste exemption that had previously been subject to agency revision; nor is it nothing (though petitioners may value it as less than nothing) to *restrict* the exemption that the agency previously provided which is what the provision here achieved, by withholding all waste-stream exemption for waste processed by resource recovery facilities, even for the waste stream passing through an exclusively household-waste facility.

We also do not agree with petitioners' contention that our construction renders §3001(i) ineffective for its intended purpose of promoting household/nonhazardous-industrial resource recovery facilities, see 42 U.S.C. §§6902(a)(1), (10), (11), by subjecting them "to the potentially enormous expense of managing ash residue as a hazardous waste." It is simply not true that a facility which is (as our interpretation says these facilities are) a hazardous waste "generator," is also deemed to be "managing" hazardous waste under RCRA. Section 3001(i) clearly exempts these facilities from Subtitle C TSDF regulations, thus enabling

3. Waste Management and Pollution Prevention   Pages 251-252

them to avoid the "full brunt of EPA's enforcement effort under RCRA." Practice Guide §29.05(1). . . .

RCRA's twin goals of encouraging resource recovery and protecting against contamination sometimes conflict. It is not unusual for legislation to contain diverse purposes that must be reconciled, and the most reliable guide for that task is the enacted text. Here that requires us to reject the Solicitor General's plea for deference to the EPA's interpretation, cf. Chevron U.S.A., Inc. v. Natural Resources Defense Council, Inc., 467 U.S. 837, 843-844 (1984), which goes beyond the scope of whatever ambiguity §3001(i) contains. Section 3000(i) simply cannot be read to contain the cost-saving waste stream exemption petitioners seek.

For the foregoing reasons, the judgment of the Court of Appeals for the Seventh Circuit is *Affirmed.*

Justice STEVENS, with whom Justice O'CONNOR joins, dissenting.

The statutory provision in question is a 1984 amendment entitled "Clarification of Household Waste Exclusion." To understand that clarification, we must first examine the "waste exclusion" that the amendment clarified and, more particularly, the ambiguity that needed clarification. I therefore begin with a discussion of the relevant pre-1984 law. I then examine the text of the statute as amended and explain why the apparent tension between the broad definition of the term "hazardous waste generation" in the 1976 Act and the more specific exclusion for the activity of incinerating household wastes (and mixtures of household and other nonhazardous wastes) in the 1984 amendment should be resolved by giving effect to the later enactment.

I

When Congress enacted the Resource Conservation and Recovery Act of 1976 (RCRA), it delegated to the Environmental Protection Agency (EPA) vast regulatory authority over the mountains of garbage that our society generates. The statute directed the EPA to classify waste as hazardous or nonhazardous and to establish regulatory controls over the disposition of the two categories of waste pursuant to Subtitles C and D of the Act. 42 U.S.C. §6921(a). To that end, the EPA in 1980 promulgated detailed regulations establishing a federal hazardous waste management system pursuant to Subtitle C.

Generally, though not always, the EPA regulations assume that waste is properly characterized as hazardous or nonhazardous when it first becomes waste. Based on that characterization, the waste is regulated under either Subtitle C or D. Household waste is regarded as nonhazardous when it is first discarded and, as long as it is not mixed with hazardous waste, it retains that characterization during and after its treatment and disposal. Even though it contains some materials that would be classified as hazardous in other contexts, and even though its treatment may produce a residue that contains a higher concentration of hazardous matter than when the garbage was originally discarded, such waste is regulated as nonhazardous waste under Subtitle D. Thus, an incinerator that burns nothing but household waste might "generate" tons of hazardous residue, but as a statutory matter it still is deemed to be processing nonhazardous waste and is regulated as a Subtitle D, rather than Subtitle C, facility.

Section 261.4(b)(1) of the EPA's 1980 regulations first established the household waste exclusion. See 45 Fed. Reg. 33120 (1980). The relevant text of that regulation simply provided that solid wastes derived from households (including single and multiple residences, hotels and motels) were "not hazardous wastes." The regulation itself said nothing about the status of the residue that remains after the incineration of such household waste. An accompanying comment, however, unambiguously explained that "residues remaining after treatment (e.g. incineration, thermal treatment) are not subject to regulation as hazardous waste." Id., at 33099. Thus, the administrative history of the 1980 regulation, rather than its text, revealed why a municipal incinerator burning household waste was not treated as a generator of hazardous waste.

The EPA's explanatory comment contained an important warning: if household waste was "mixed with other hazardous wastes," the entire mixture would be deemed hazardous. Yet neither the comment nor the regulation itself identified the consequences of mixing household waste with other wastes that are entirely *nonhazardous*. Presumably such a mixture would contain a lower percentage of hazardous material than pure household waste, and therefore should also be classified as nonhazardous—assumptions that are not inconsistent with the EPA's warning that mixing household waste "with other *hazardous* wastes" would terminate the household waste exemption. The EPA's failure to comment expressly on the significance of adding 100 percent nonhazardous commercial or industrial waste nevertheless warranted further clarification.

Congress enacted that clarification in 1984. Elaborating upon the EPA's warning in 1980, the text of the 1984 amendment—§3001(i) of RCRA, 42 U.S.C. §6921(i)—made clear that a facility treating a mixture of household waste and "solid waste from commercial or industrial sources that does not contain hazardous waste," §6921(i)(1)(A)(ii), shall not be deemed to be treating hazardous waste. In other words,

3. Waste Management and Pollution Prevention   Pages 251-252

the addition of *non*hazardous waste derived from other sources does not extinguish the household waste exclusion.

The parallel between the 1980 regulation and the 1984 statutory amendment is striking. In 1980 the EPA referred to the exclusion of household waste "in all phases of its management." Similarly, the 1984 statute lists *all phases* of the incinerator's management when it states that a facility recovering energy from the mass burning of a mixture of household waste and other solid waste that does not contain hazardous waste "shall not be deemed to be treating, storing, disposing of, or otherwise managing hazardous wastes." See 42 U.S.C. §6921(i). Even though that text only refers to the exemption of the facility that burns the waste, the title of the section significantly characterizes it as a *waste* exclusion. Moreover, the title's description of the amendment as a "clarification" identifies an intent to codify its counterpart in the 1980 regulation. . . .

II

The relevant statutory text is not as unambiguous as the Court asserts. There is substantial tension between the broad definition of the term "hazardous waste generation" in §1004(6) of the Act and the household waste exclusion codified by the 1984 amendment: both provisions can be read to describe the same activity. The former "means the act or process of producing hazardous waste." 90 Stat. 2799; 42 U.S.C. §6903(6). Read literally, that definition is broad enough to encompass the burning of pure household waste that produces some hazardous residue. The only statutory escape from that conclusion is the 1984 amendment that provides an exemption for the activity of burning household waste. Yet that exemption does not distinguish between pure household waste, on the one hand, and a mixture of household and other nonhazardous wastes, on the other. It either exempts both the pure stream and the mixture, or it exempts neither.

Indeed, commercial and industrial waste is by definition nonhazardous: in order for it to fall within the exclusion created by the 1984 amendment, it must not contain hazardous components. As a consequence, the only aspect of this waste stream that would ordinarily be regulated by Subtitle C of RCRA is the ash residue. EPA could reasonably conclude, therefore, that to give any content to the statute with respect to this component of the waste stream, the incinerator ash must be exempted from Subtitle C regulation.

The exemption states that a facility burning solid waste "shall not be deemed to be treating, storing, disposing of, or otherwise managing hazardous wastes for the purposes of regulation under this subchapter" if two conditions are satisfied. As long as the two conditions are met—even though the material being treated and disposed of contains hazardous components before, during, and after its treatment—that material "shall not be deemed to be . . . hazardous." By characterizing both the input and the output as not hazardous, the 1984 amendment excludes the activity from the definition of hazardous waste generation that would otherwise apply. For it is obvious that the same activity cannot both subject a facility to regulation because its residue is hazardous and exempt the facility from regulation because the statute deems the same residue to be nonhazardous.[8]

Thus, if we are to be guided only by the literal meaning of the statutory text, we must either give effect to the broad definition of hazardous waste generation and subject all municipal incinerators that generate hazardous ash to Subtitle C regulation (including those that burn pure household waste) or give effect to the exclusion that applies equally to pure household waste and mixtures that include other nonhazardous wastes. For several reasons the latter is the proper choice. It effectuates the narrower and more recently enacted provision rather than the earlier more general definition. It respects the title of the 1984 amendment by treating what follows as a "clarification" rather than a repeal or a modification. It avoids the Court's rather surprising (and uninvited) decision to invalidate the household waste exclusion that the EPA adopted in 1980,[9] on which municipalities throughout the Nation have reasonably relied for over a decade. It explains why the

---

8. The Court characterizes my reading of the text as "imaginative use of ellipsis," because the subject of the predicate "shall not be deemed to be . . . hazardous" is the recovery facility rather than the residue that is disposed of after the waste is burned. That is true, but the reason the facility is exempted is because it is not "deemed to be . . . disposing of . . . hazardous wastes." Thus it is the statutorily deemed nonhazardous character of the object of the sentence—wastes—that effectively exempts from Subtitle C regulation the activity and the facility engaged in that activity. If, as the statute provides, a facility is not deemed to be disposing of hazardous wastes when it disposes of the output of the facility, it must be true that the output is deemed nonhazardous.

9. Although the first nine pages of the Court's opinion give the reader the impression that the 1980 regulatory exclusion for pure household waste was valid, the Court ultimately acknowledges that its construction of the statute has the effect of "withholding all waste-stream exemption for waste processed by resource recovery facilities, even for the waste stream passing through an exclusively household-waste facility." Of course, it is not the 1984 amendment that casts doubt on the validity of the regulation, but the Court's rigid reading of §1004(6)'s definition of the term "hazardous waste generation" that has achieved that result. Since that definition has been in the Act since 1976, the Court utterly fails to explain how the 1984 amendment made any change in the law.

legislative history fails to mention an intent to impose significant new burdens on the operation of municipal incinerators. Finally, it is the construction that the EPA has adopted and that reasonable jurists have accepted.

The majority's decision today may represent sound policy. Requiring cities to spend the necessary funds to dispose of their incinerator residues in accordance with the strict requirements of Subtitle C will provide additional protections to the environment. It is also true, however, that the conservation of scarce landfill space and the encouragement of the recovery of energy and valuable materials in municipal wastes were major concerns motivating RCRA's enactment. Whether those purposes will be disserved by regulating municipal incinerators under Subtitle C and, if so, whether environmental benefits may nevertheless justify the costs of such additional regulation are questions of policy that we are not competent to resolve. Those questions are precisely the kind that Congress has directed the EPA to answer. The EPA's position, first adopted unambiguously in 1980 and still maintained today, was and remains a correct and permissible interpretation of the Agency's broad congressional mandate.

Accordingly, I respectfully dissent.

NOTES AND QUESTIONS

1. When Administrator Reilly issued his new interpretation of the effect of section 3001(i) on incinerator ash, the president of the Integrated Waste Management Association hailed it as "a major breakthrough for solid waste managers in communities nationwide." Noting that there are 142 municipal incinerators in the United States that manage 16 percent of the municipal waste stream, he declared that the Administrator's decision "confirms what the scientific evidence has revealed for the past decade—namely that MWC ash is not hazardous and can be safely managed in [municipal] landfills." Ash from Combustion of Municipal Waste to Be Considered Non-Hazardous, EPA Says, 23 Env. Rep. 1459, 1460 (1992). Is this an accurate characterization of the Administrator's memorandum?

2. If household waste can contain hazardous constituents, why would EPA have sought to grant it a waste-stream exemption from regulation as hazardous waste under Subtitle C?

3. In light of the Court's decision, would ash produced by an incinerator that burned *only* household waste and *no* other materials be exempt from Subtitle C regulation? Would it have been prior to the 1984 amendment that added §3001(i) to RCRA? What did the addition of §3001(i) accomplish, according to Justice Scalia?

4. Justice Scalia notes that municipal incinerators whose ash becomes a hazardous waste will be subject only to the Subtitle C regulations applicable to generators and not to Subtitle C's more onerous requirements for TSDs. Does this mean that the Court's decision will not impose substantial additional costs on incinerators?

5. In the wake of the Court's decision, EPA has been considering alternative management strategies for incinerator ash. In May 1994 the agency issued guidance stating that incinerator ash be tested for hazardous constituents four times a year beginning in August 1994, using the Toxicity Characteristic Leaching Procedure (TCLP). EPA is developing land disposal treatment standards for ash that is determined to be hazardous. In January 1995, EPA announced that incinerator operators could combine fly ash and bottom ash prior to testing to determine if the waste exhibits a hazardous characteristic. The agency based this decision on the notion that ash does not become a waste until it leaves the combustion facility. Because bottom ash usually is less toxic than fly ash, the decision is expected to mean that most incinerator ash will not exhibit a hazardous characteristic when tested. EPA Says Municipal Incinerator Owners Can Combine Fly, Bottom Ash for Testing, 25 Env. Rep. 1841 (1995). If ash does not become a waste until it leaves the combustion facility, could incinerator operators treat ash that flunks the TCLP to render it nonhazardous prior to shipping it off-site without having to comply with Subtitle C of RCRA?

4. Avoiding TSD Status

The Importance of EPA Guidance (pp. 259-260). As noted in the text, important regulatory interpretations often appear in EPA guidance documents not published in the Federal Register. This practice is criticized in Tabler and Shere, The EPA's Practice of Regulation by Memorandum, in The Environmental Law Manual 32 (T. Garrett, ed. 1992). A contemporary illustration of the practice is provided by Beazer East, Inc. v. EPA, Region III, 963 F.2d 603 (3d Cir. 1992). In *Beazer East* a company argued that its 80-foot wide, concrete-lined aeration basins should be considered to be tanks rather than surface impoundments that are subject to more stringent regulation under RCRA. EPA's regulations define "tank" as "a stationary device, designed to contain an accumulation of hazardous waste, which is constructed primarily of non-earthen materials (e.g., wood, concrete, steel, plastic) which provide structural support." 40 C.F.R. 260.10. As EPA has recognized, this definition "has caused numerous problems for the RCRA enforcement program because it uses subjective terms, such as 'primarily' and 'provide

3. Waste Management and Pollution Prevention — Pages 277-280

structural support.' " EPA, The Nation's Hazardous Waste Management Program at a Crossroads 65 (1990).

In an effort to clarify this definition for EPA enforcement personnel, an acting director of the agency's Office of Solid Waste issued a memorandum, known as the "Weddle memorandum," that interprets the definition of "tank" to require that a device be able to support itself when removed from the ground and filled to capacity with the material it was intended to contain and that non-earthen materials provide the primary structural support. In *Beazer East* the owner of the concrete-lined basin conceded that it could not meet the test outlined in the Weddle memorandum. However, the company argued that it had been deprived of adequate notice of this interpretation because it was contained in a guidance document that had not been published in the Federal Register. Noting that EPA's interpretation was reasonable and consistent with the language of the regulation, the Third Circuit rejected the company's argument and affirmed the penalties that had been imposed on it.

5. *The RCRA Land Disposal Ban*

Further Implementation of the RCRA Land Ban (pp. 277-280). While EPA generally employed the BDAT approach to set treatment standards for listed waste subject to the RCRA land ban, for characteristic waste it adopted a different approach. As noted in the text (p. 279), EPA's "third-third" land ban rule was controversial because the Agency asserted, but generally did not exercise, the authority to require treatment of characteristic waste to reduce hazardous constituents to levels below which a waste no longer would exhibit a hazardous characteristic. Both industry groups and environmentalists challenged the regulations in court. The industry groups argued that EPA did not have the authority to require treatment at levels below which a waste would no longer be considered hazardous. The environmental groups argued that EPA had such authority and was required to exercise it more vigorously to satisfy the requirements of the land disposal ban. In Chemical Waste Management v. EPA, 976 F.2d 2 (D.C. Cir. 1992), the D.C. Circuit rejected the industry arguments, holding that EPA had the authority to require hazardous wastes to be treated even to levels below those at which the wastes would be considered to exhibit a hazardous characteristic.

The court observed that the land ban in section 3004(m)(1) of RCRA directs EPA to specify treatment methods that would "substantially diminish the toxicity of the waste" in order to minimize short-term and long-term hazards. While noting that it previously had expressed the view that it might be unreasonable to require treatment of wastes that pose "no threat to human health or the environment," the court concluded that the land ban gave EPA authority "to reduce risks beyond those presented by the [hazardous] characteristics themselves." 976 F.2d at 14.

The court also rejected NRDC's claim that dilution could not be a form of treatment for ignitable, corrosive, or reactive hazardous wastes. So long as it meets the objectives of section 3004(m)(1), dilution is permissible, the court concluded. 976 F.2d at 15. However, the court found that EPA had failed to demonstrate that dilution met these objectives for ignitable or reactive wastes or for corrosive wastes whose hazardous constituents would present a continuing threat even after dilution. It also overturned EPA's efforts to exempt "decharacterized wastes" managed in wastewater treatment systems or underground injection wells from treatment under the RCRA land ban.

EPA had to modify its land ban regulations in response to the court's decision. The Agency estimated that billions of gallons of decharacterized wastes currently managed in underground injection wells or wastewater treatment systems required additional treatment at a potential cost of hundreds of millions of dollars. The Chemical Manufacturers Association and the American Petroleum Institute sought Supreme Court review of the D.C. Circuit's decision, but the Court declined to hear the case. In May 1993, EPA promulgated an emergency rule establishing interim treatment standards to replace the regulations vacated by the D.C. Circuit. 58 Fed. Reg. 29,860 (1993). In September 1994 EPA adopted its final "Phase II" land disposal restrictions rule. 59 Fed. Reg. 47,982 (1994). For a discussion of the rule, see Van Voorhees, Kastner and Day, Universal Treatment Standards Adopted; Restrictions Imposed for Toxicity Characteristic Organics, Newly Listed Wastes, 25 Env. Rep. 1231 (1994).

EPA is expected to propose its "Phase III" land disposal restrictions in early 1995 to implement the D.C. Circuit's "third/third" decision. Later in 1995 EPA plans to propose its "Phase IV" land disposal restrictions.

6. *Subtitle D and the Regulation of Municipal Waste Disposal*

Subtitle D (p. 283). Only about 4 percent of industrial waste is regulated under RCRA Subtitle C, even after excluding mining wastes and wastes from oil and gas operations that generally have been exempted from Subtitle C regulation. The other 96 percent of industrial waste (subtitle D waste) includes many wastes that can pose significant environmental hazards. Given their enormous volume, Subtitle D wastes may in the aggregate pose an even greater threat to the environment than the small volumes of waste regulated as hazardous under Subtitle C.

Many states have eschewed RCRA's all-or-nothing approach by subjecting broad classes of "nonhazardous" industrial waste to an intermediate level of regulation more stringent than Subtitle D, but less stringent than Subtitle C. For example, after ten years of effort, Pennsylvania has adopted comprehensive regulations governing the management of industrial wastes not considered hazardous under RCRA's federal standards. These regulations require disposal facilities to use liners and to conduct groundwater monitoring, and they direct waste generators to analyze source reduction strategies. Dernbach, The Other Ninety-Six Percent, The Environmental Forum, Jan.-Feb. 1993, at 10.

EPA's Municipal Landfill Standards (pp. 284-286). EPA's Subtitle D standards for municipal landfills were generally upheld by the D.C. Circuit in Sierra Club v. EPA, 992 F.2d 337 (D.C. Cir. 1993). Over Judge Mikva's dissent, the court held that EPA had the discretion not to set numeric limits for toxics in sewage sludge when it is codisposed with municipal waste even though the Clean Water Act imposes such limits when sludge alone is disposed. But the court agreed with environmental groups that RCRA required all municipal landfills, regardless of their size or location, to conduct groundwater monitoring.

D. CERCLA LIABILITY

Because of the broad reach of its liability provisions, it is not surprising that CERCLA appears to be generating more litigation than any other environmental statute. This is reflected in several important decisions discussed below that have continued to flesh out CERCLA's liability provisions.

3. *"Release of Hazardous Substance"*

Eagle-Picher Industries v. EPA (pp. 295-297). The Ninth Circuit has held that slag from copper smelting is not exempt from CERCLA, based on the same reasoning used by the D.C. Circuit in the *Eagle-Picher* case. Louisiana-Pacific Corp. v. Asarco, Inc., 6 F.3d 1332 (9th Cir. 1993).

Pages 297-298   3. Waste Management and Pollution Prevention

No Quantitative Threshold for Hazardous Constituents (pp. 297-298). Courts continue to reject arguments that some threshold level of hazardous constituents should be required before a substance can be considered to fall within the ambit of CERCLA's liability provisions. See, e.g., United States v. Alcan Aluminum Corp., 964 F.2d 252, 259-261 (3d Cir. 1992), discussed below, which outlines what may be a more promising avenue for limiting CERCLA liability.

CERCLA Petroleum Exclusion (p. 298). As noted in the parent text, courts have interpreted CERCLA's petroleum exclusion narrowly. In Cose v. Getty Oil Co., 4 F.3d 700 (9th Cir. 1993), the Ninth Circuit held that crude oil tank bottoms did not fall within CERCLA's petroleum exclusion. The court found a large conceptual difference between releases of petroleum and the delivery of petroleum-related waste material to a disposal facility.

Can the Sale of a "Product" Also Be the Disposal of a Hazardous Substance? (p. 300). In the case discussed in note 5 of the parent text (p. 300), a jury found that smelter slag was a "product" for purposes of Washington's Products Liability Act. The smelter operator contended that this finding precluded the imposition of CERCLA liability because it had simply sold a product rather than disposing of a hazardous substance. On appeal, the Ninth Circuit rejected this argument. The court concluded that the sale of smelter slag could simultaneously be both the sale of a product and the disposal of a hazardous substance because the slag was a "material[] [its] producer[] wanted to get rid of whether [it] could sell them or not." Louisiana-Pacific Corp. v. Asarco, Inc., 6 F.3d 1332, 1341 (9th Cir. 1993).

4. Strict, Joint, and Several Liability

The Alcan *Decision (pp. 301-312).* PRPs have continued to search for ways to avoid what they perceive to be the unfairness of joint and several liability. Having had little success in court, they have sought to appeal to the court of public opinion by publicizing cases in which small firms have been shouldered with heavy liabilities. See, e.g., Hamilton, Shouldering Toxic Waste Cleanup Costs, Wash. Post, Jan. 18, 1993, at D1. Recall that *Picillo* left open the possibility that PRPs could obtain an apportionment of liability if they could make an adequate factual showing. What is the necessary showing? Consider the next case.

3. Waste Management and Pollution Prevention   Pages 301-312

United States v. Alcan Aluminum Corp.
964 F.2d 252 (3d Cir. 1992)

Before: GREENBERG and SCIRICA, Circuit Judges, and DEBEVOISE, District Judge
GREENBERG, Circuit Judge.

[The United States charged Alcan and 20 other defendants for response costs incurred in cleaning up the Susquehanna River. Only Alcan refused to settle, and on May 8, 1991, the district court entered judgment against Alcan in the amount of $473,790.18, which was the difference between the full response costs the government had incurred in cleaning the Susquehanna River and the amount the government had recovered from the settling defendants.]

I. FACTS AND PROCEDURAL HISTORY

. . . The Butler Tunnel Site (the "Site") is on the NPL. . . . [It] includes a network of approximately five square miles of deep underground mines and related tunnels, caverns, pools and waterways bordering the east bank of the Susquehanna River in Pittston, Pennsylvania. The mine workings at the Site are drained by the Butler Tunnel (the "Tunnel"), a 7,500-foot tunnel which feeds directly into the Susquehanna River.

The mines are accessible from the surface by numerous air shafts or boreholes. One borehole (the "Borehole") is located on the premises of Hi-Way Auto Service, an automobile fuel and repair station situated above the Tunnel. The Borehole leads directly into the mine workings at the Site. . . .

Alcan . . . manufactures aluminum sheet and plate products in Oswego, New York. From 1965 through at least 1989, Alcan's manufacturing process involved the hot-rolling of aluminum ingots. To keep the rolls cool and lubricated during the hot-rolling process, Alcan circulated an emulsion through the rolls, consisting of 95% deionized water and 5% mineral oil. At the end of the hot-rolling process, Alcan removed the used emulsion and replaced it with unused emulsion.

During the rolling process, fragments of the aluminum ingots, which also contained copper, chromium, cadmium, lead and zinc, hazardous substances under CERCLA, broke off into the emulsion. In an effort to remove those fragments, Alcan then filtered the used emulsion prior to disposing of it, but the filtering process was imperfect and hence some fragments remained. According to Alcan, however, the level of these compounds in the post-filtered, used emulsion was "far below the EP toxic or TCLP toxic levels and, indeed, orders of magnitude below ambient or naturally occurring background levels. Moreover, the trace quantities of metal compounds in the emulsion [were] immobile. . . ." The Government does not specifically challenge Alcan's assertion that the used emulsion contained only low levels of these metallic compounds, as it contends that this fact is irrelevant to Alcan's liability under CERCLA.

From mid-1978 to late 1979, Alcan contracted with [another company] to dispose of at least 2,300,950 gallons of used emulsion from its Oswego, New York, facility. During that period, [that other company] disposed of approximately 32,500-37,500 gallons (or five 6,500-7,500 gallon loads) of Alcan's liquid waste through the Borehole into the Site. [Alcan contended, and the government did not contest, that it did not know that its emulsions were being disposed of in this manner.]

In September 1985, approximately 100,000 gallons of water contaminated with hazardous substances were released from the Site into the Susquehanna River. It appears that this discharge was composed of the wastes deposited into the Borehole in the late 1970's. Between September 28, 1985, and January 7, 1987, EPA incurred significant response costs due to the release and the threatened release of hazardous substances from the Site. . . .

The Government . . . moved for summary judgment against Alcan, the only non-settling defendant, to collect the balance of its response costs. Alcan cross-moved for summary judgment, arguing that its emulsion did not constitute a "hazardous substance" as defined by CERCLA due to its below-ambient levels of copper, cadmium, chromium, lead and zinc, and further contending that its emulsion could not have caused the release or any response costs incurred by the Government. . . .

II. Discussion

B. *CERCLA Contains No Quantitative Requirement in Its Definition of "Hazardous Substance":*

[Alcan first argued that "it should not be held liable for response costs incurred by the Government in cleaning the Susquehanna River because the level of hazardous substances in its emulsion was below that which naturally occurs and thus could not have contributed to the environmental injury." After examining the statute, the legislative history and other court decisions, the court concluded that CERCLA contains no requirement that some threshold quantity of a covered hazardous substance exist.]

It may be that Congress did not intend such an all-encompassing definition of "hazardous substances," but this argument is best directed at Congress itself. If Congress had intended to impose a threshold requirement, it could easily have so indicated. We should not rewrite the statute simply because the definition of one of its terms is broad in scope. . . .[13]

In Alcan's view, the district court's construction of the statute is at odds with environmental policy because it imposes liability on generators of allegedly "hazardous" substances although the substances pose no real threat to the environment. Alcan's argument, though superficially appealing, is flawed. First, as noted above, the Government responds to "releases" that threaten environmental safety. Thus, it is the *release alone* that must justify the response costs, not the particular waste generated by one given defendant. Here, there is no question but that a release occurred. Second, the fact that a single generator's waste would not in itself justify a response is irrelevant in the multi-generator context, as this would permit a generator to escape liability where the amount of harm it engendered to the environment was minimal, though it was significant when added to other generators' waste. Accordingly, we find that the district court's construction of the statute furthers important environmental goals.

D. *Causation*

Alcan maintains that, if we decline to construe the determination of "hazardous substance" to encompass a concentration threshold, we must at least require the Government to prove that *Alcan's emulsion*

---

13. EPA's statement that it does not consider a waste to be "hazardous" for purposes of the Resource Conservation and Recovery Act ("RCRA") unless that waste exists in a form "capable of causing substantial harm if mismanaged," 57 Fed. Reg. 1, 12 (January 2, 1992), does not alter our conclusion. . . . RCRA's goals differ from CERCLA's, and we do not construe EPA's comments as indicating that the Agency also imputes a threshold concentration requirement into the definition of hazardous substance under section 101(14) of CERCLA, especially in the face of plain statutory language indicating otherwise.

There is some force to Alcan's argument that this definition of "hazardous substances" is so broad that it encompasses virtually everything and thereby eviscerates the meaning of "hazardous." However, our holding with respect to divisibility of harm as discussed below should assuage Alcan's fear that liability under CERCLA will be as far-reaching as the definition of hazardous substances.

caused or contributed to the release or the Government's incurrence of response costs. The Government contends, and the district court . . . agreed, that the statute imposes no such causation requirement, but rather requires that the plaintiff in a CERCLA proceeding establish that the *release* or *threatened release* caused the incurrence of response costs; it underscores the difficulty CERCLA plaintiffs would face in the multi-generator context if required to trace the cause of the response costs to each responsible party.

1. Plain Meaning

The plain meaning of the statute supports the Government's position. . . . [S]ection 107 imposes liability upon a generator of hazardous substances who contracts with another party to dispose of the hazardous substances at a facility "from which there is a *release, or threatened release which causes the incurrence of response costs.*" 42 U.S.C. §9607 (emphasis supplied). The statute does not, on its face, require the plaintiff to prove that the generator's *hazardous substances* themselves caused the release or caused the incurrence of response costs, rather it requires the plaintiff to prove that the *release or threatened release* caused the incurrence of response costs, and that the defendant is a generator of hazardous substances at the facility.

2. Legislative History

[After reviewing CERCLA's legislative history, the court finds that] Congress considered and rejected a requirement that the plaintiff establish that the defendant's waste caused or contributed to the release or the incurrence of response costs.

3. Jurisprudence

Further, virtually every court that has considered this question has held that a CERCLA plaintiff need not establish a direct causal connection between the defendant's hazardous substances and the release or the plaintiff's incurrence of response costs. For example, in New York v. Shore Realty Corp. [parent text, p. 312], the defendant, an owner of a facility, asked the Court of Appeals for the Second Circuit to read this "causation" requirement into section 107(a). The court declined that invitation and held, "section 9607(a)(1) unequivocally imposes strict liability on the current owner of a facility from which there is a release or threat of release without regard to causation." . . .

3. Waste Management and Pollution Prevention   Pages 301-312

The court of appeals in United States v. Monsanto Co., 858 F.2d 160 (4th Cir. 1988), cert. denied, 490 U.S. 1106 (1989), extended *Shore Realty*'s analysis to generators of hazardous waste. The court of appeals there rejected a similar argument that the CERCLA plaintiff was required to establish that the waste the defendant generator sent to the facility caused or contributed to the environmental harm, observing that Congress deleted the causation language from CERCLA precisely because it was aware of the difficulties plaintiffs would confront in the multi-generator context if required to prove such a connection. It held, "in deleting causation language from section 107(a), we assume as have many other courts, that Congress knew of the synergistic and migratory capacities of leaking chemical waste, and the technological infeasibility of tracing improperly disposed waste to its source." Id. at 170 (footnote omitted). . . .

F. Divisibility of Harm

The foregoing conclusions that (1) there is no quantitative threshold in the definition of hazardous substances and (2) the plaintiff need not establish a causal connection between a given defendant's waste and the release or the incurrence of response costs would initially appear to lead to unfair imposition of liability. As Alcan asserts, this definition of "hazardous substances" effectively renders everything in the universe hazardous, including, for example, federally approved drinking water. When this definition is read in conjunction with the rule that specific causation is not required, CERCLA seemingly would impose liability on every generator of hazardous waste, although that generator could not, on its own, have caused any environmental harm.[25]

While Alcan's assertion is of considerable strength, the Government's rebuttal is equally forceful. It notes that individual defendants

---

25. Dean Prosser's hornbook highlights the paradox of liability where acts harmless in themselves together cause damage, observing:

> A very troublesome question arises where the acts of each of two or more parties, standing alone, would not be wrongful, but together they cause harm to the plaintiff. If several defendants independently pollute a stream, the impurities traceable to each may be negligible and harmless, but all together may render the water entirely unfit for use. The difficulty lies in the fact that each defendant alone would have committed no tort. There would have been no negligence, and no nuisance, since the individual use of the stream would have been a reasonable use, and no harm would have resulted.

William L. Prosser, The Law of Torts, §52, at 322 (4th ed. 1971).

must be held responsible for environmental injury brought about by the actions of multiple defendants, even if no single defendant itself could have produced the harm, for otherwise "each defendant in a multi-defendant case could avoid liability by relying on the low concentrations of hazardous substances in its waste, while the plaintiff is left with the substantial clean-up costs associated with the defendants' accumulated wastes." The Government reasons that this strong public interest in forcing polluters in the multi-generator context to pay outweighs a defendant's interest in avoiding liability even if that defendant has not acted in an environmentally unsound fashion when its actions are viewed without regard to the actions of others. . . .

We find some merit in the arguments advanced by both the Government and Alcan. Accordingly, in our view, the common law principles of joint and several liability provide the only means to achieve the proper balance between Alcan's and the Government's conflicting interests and to infuse fairness into the statutory scheme without distorting its plain meaning or disregarding congressional intent. . . .

. . . In determining whether the imposition of joint and several liability upon Alcan is proper, so that it may be held liable for the Government's full response costs less what had been recovered from the settling defendants, we turn to the Restatement (Second) of Torts for guidance.

Section 433A of the Restatement provides that, when two or more joint tortfeasors acting independently cause a distinct or single harm for which there is a reasonable basis for division according to the contribution of each, each is subject to liability only for the portion of the harm that the individual tortfeasor has caused. It states,

> (1) Damages for harm are to be apportioned among two or more causes where
> (a) there are distinct harms, or
> (b) there is a reasonable basis for determining the contribution of each cause to a single harm.
> (2) Damages for any other harm cannot be apportioned among two or more causes.

Similarly, section 881 sets forth the affirmative defense based upon the divisibility of harm rule in section 433A:

> If two or more persons, acting independently, tortiously cause distinct harms or a single harm for which there is a reasonable basis for division according to the contribution of each, each is subject to liability only for the portion of the total harm that he has himself caused.

However, where joint tortfeasors cause a single and indivisible harm for which there is no reasonable basis for division according to the contribution of each, each tortfeasor is subject to liability for the entire harm. Section 875 recites:

> Each of two or more persons whose tortious conduct is a legal cause of a single and indivisible harm to the injured party is subject to liability to the injured party for the entire harm.

Obviously, of critical importance in this analysis is whether a harm is divisible and reasonably capable of apportionment, or indivisible, thereby subjecting the tortfeasor to potentially far-reaching liability.[27]

Under the Restatement, where a joint tortfeasor seeks to apportion the full amount of a plaintiff's damages according to that tortfeasor's own contribution to the harm, it is the tortfeasor's burden to establish that the damages are capable of such apportionment. As the comments concerning this issue explain, the burden of proving that the harm is capable of apportionment is placed on the tortfeasor to avoid:

> the injustice of allowing a proved wrongdoer who has in fact caused harm to the plaintiff to escape liability merely because the harm which he has inflicted has combined with similar harm inflicted by other wrongdoers, and the nature of the harm itself has made it necessary that evidence be produced before it can be apportioned. In such a case the defendant may justly be required to assume the burden of producing that evidence, or if he is not able to do so, of bearing full responsibility. As between the proved tortfeasor who has clearly caused some harm, and the entirely innocent plaintiff, any hardship due to lack of evidence as to the extent of the harm should fall upon the former.

Comment on Section 433 B subsection (2).

These provisions underscore the intensely factual nature of the "divisibility" issue and thus highlight the district court's error in granting summary judgment for the full claim in favor of EPA without con-

---

27. Interestingly, the drafters of the Restatement found that joint pollution of water is typically subject to the divisibility rule. They write:

> There are other kinds of harm which, while not so clearly marked out as severable into distinct parts, are still capable of division upon a reasonable and rational basis, and of fair apportionment among the causes responsible. . . . *Such apportionment is commonly made in cases of private nuisance, where the pollution of a stream . . . has interfered with the plaintiff's use and enjoyment of his land.*

Section 433 A., Comment d (emphasis supplied). See, e.g., Somerset Villa, Inc. v. Lee's Summit, 436 S.W.2d 658 (Mo. 1968).

ducting a hearing. For this reason, we will remand this case for the court to determine whether there is a reasonable basis for limiting Alcan's liability based on its personal contribution to the harm to the Susquehanna River.

Our conclusions on this point are completely consistent with our previous discussion on causation, as there we were concerned with the Government's burden in demonstrating liability in the first instance. Here we are dealing with Alcan's effort to avoid liability otherwise established. We observe in this regard that Alcan's burden in attempting to prove the divisibility of harm to the Susquehanna River is substantial, and the analysis will be factually complex as it will require an assessment of the relative toxicity, migratory potential and synergistic capacity of the hazardous waste at issue. But Alcan should be permitted this opportunity to limit or avoid liability. If Alcan succeeds in this endeavor, it should only be liable for that portion of the harm fairly attributable to it.

Alcan maintains that there is no need for a hearing because, not only is the harm divisible, but its relative contribution to the injury to the Susquehanna River is zero. According to Alcan, "[i]t is technically impossible to have a release or threatened release such that a clean-up would be authorized or justified under the National Contingency Plan as a result of the addition of the metal compounds in the Alcan emulsion to the Butler Site. When one adds two materials that have the same concentrations of an element or compound, the net result is the *same* concentration. It can never result in a higher concentration." Appellant's Br. at 18 (emphasis in original). Alcan's Reply Brief similarly asserts that "below ambient levels of any substance can never cause or contribute to a release or response costs."

The district court did not specifically address this argument. Indeed, in light of their belief that [a previous ruling in this litigation] was dispositive of the arguments advanced by Alcan in this case, neither the magistrate judge nor the district court engaged in any factual investigation concerning the divisibility of the environmental harm caused to the Susquehanna River as a result of the release of hazardous substances from the Borehole. However, we are not the proper forum to consider Alcan's argument as we have no way of determining whether the trace levels of metallic compounds in Alcan's used emulsion became concentrated and thereby posed an environmental threat. Furthermore, there may be other circumstances bearing on this issue of which we are not even aware. Thus, the district court should re-evaluate Alcan's contention in light of the facts developed in the hearing on this issue.[29]

---

29. In this vein, we also reject the Government's argument that a hearing is unnecessary because Alcan has admitted that its emulsion was "commingled"

3. Waste Management and Pollution Prevention   Pages 301-312

In sum, on remand, the district court must permit Alcan to attempt to prove that the harm is divisible and that the damages are capable of some reasonable apportionment. We note that the Government need not prove that Alcan's emulsion caused the release or the response costs. On the other hand, if Alcan proves that the emulsion did not or could not, *when mixed with other hazardous wastes,* contribute to the release and the resultant response costs, then Alcan should not be responsible for *any* response costs. In this sense, our result thus injects causation into the equation but, as we have already pointed out, places the burden of proof on the defendant instead of the plaintiff. We think that this result is consistent with the statutory scheme and yet recognizes that there must be some reason for the imposition of CERCLA liability. Our result seems particularly appropriate in light of the expansive meaning of "hazardous substance." Of course, if Alcan cannot prove that it should not be liable for any response costs or cannot prove that the harm is divisible and that the damages are capable of some reasonable apportionment, it will be liable for the full claim of $473,790.18.

NOTES AND QUESTIONS

1. In a conclusion to its opinion, the *Alcan* court repeated that Alcan can limit its liability if it can establish "that the harm is capable of reasonable apportionment" and that it can avoid liability altogether if it "can establish that the hazardous substances in its emulsion could

---

with the other generators' waste: "commingled" waste is not synonymous with "indivisible" harm. We observe that some courts have held that a generator may present evidence that is has paid more than its "fair share" in a contribution proceeding, expressly permitted under 42 U.S.C. §9613(f)(2). In a sense, the "contribution" inquiry involves an analysis similar to the "divisibility" inquiry, as both focus on what harm the defendant caused. However, we believe that this inquiry . . . is best resolved at the initial liability phase and not at the contribution phase since it involves precisely relative degrees of *liability.* Thus, if the defendant can prove that the harm is divisible and that it only caused some portion of the injury, it should only be held liable for that amount. In our view, the logical consequence of delaying the apportionment determination may well be drastic, for it seems clear that a defendant could easily be strong-armed into settling where other defendants have settled in order to avoid being held liable for the remainder of the response costs. Indeed, in this case the court determined that Alcan, one of 20 defendants, was liable for $473,790.18 in response costs, although the total response costs amounted to $1,302,290.18. Thus, although Alcan comprised only 5% of the defendant pool, it was required by the court to absorb over 36% of the costs. Furthermore, Alcan's share of the liability seems to be disproportionate on a volume basis as well. We also point out that contribution will probably not be available from a settling defendant in an action by the United States. 42 U.S.C. §9613(f)(2).

not, when added to other hazardous substances, have caused or contributed to the release or the resultant response costs," 964 F.2d at 271. Precisely what will Alcan have to show to establish that the harm is capable of apportionment? How difficult will it be to make such a showing? Would proof that its wastes contained no more than "background" levels of hazardous constituents be sufficient to absolve Alcan of all liability? What more, if anything, would Alcan be required to prove to avoid liability?

2. Even if a company cannot prove that its wastes could not have caused or contributed to a release, does *Alcan* hold some promise for certain contributors? Suppose a generator conceded that its waste contained hazardous substances above background levels, but asserts that the volume of its waste was small in comparison with the total volume discharged into the environment. It offers to prove that if its waste had been the only waste released into the environment, response costs would have been no more than 5 percent of the actual total. Should a court entertain such evidence and, if the generator sustains its burden of proof, limit that generator's liability to 5 percent? Can a generator who can show that its wastes were placed in a particular location at a site where little or no migration of wastes has occurred limit its liability? How about a generator who claims that its wastes had unique chemical properties that were unlikely to change or to alter the chemical properties of other wastes when commingled with them?

3. How will *Alcan* affect the government's ability to prevail against PRPs in CERCLA cases? Because it appears to open the door to a new line of attack on joint and several liability, PRP lawyers are greeting *Alcan* with the same enthusiasm that lawyers for RCRA TSDs greeted the *American Mining Congress (AMC)* decision (parent text, p. 229), see text, pp. 237-239. This enthusiasm increased when the Second Circuit reached a similar result in another case involving Alcan in April 1993. United States v. Alcan Aluminum Corp., 990 F.2d 711 (2d Cir. 1993). While the court rejected Alcan's argument that it could escape CERCLA liability entirely if it could show that its releases did not exceed background levels of contaminants, the court agreed that Alcan might be able to escape joint and several liability if it could show that any harm caused by its releases was divisible. Lawyers for PRPs are citing *Alcan* at every turn. Like *AMC*, *Alcan's* ultimate impact probably will be far narrower than PRPs hope. However, if *Alcan* gives PRPs the ability to raise "factually complex" issues at the liability phase, see 964 F.2d at 270 n.29 (divisibility inquiry "is best resolved at the initial liability phase"), *Alcan* may create a procedural obstacle that impedes swift settlement of CERCLA cases.

4. Consider the following prediction:

3. Waste Management and Pollution Prevention — Pages 301-312

If *Alcan*'s holding becomes widely followed, EPA response cost actions will become more like private party contribution actions. Potentially responsible parties will need to retain toxicologists, environmental chemists, and cleanup cost specialists to aid in proving the harm caused by a particular waste. These experts will need to create an allocation of damages model that quantifies the relative toxicity of their clients' wastes, and the effect those wastes had on the site and on cleanup costs.

Harris and Milan, Avoiding Joint and Several Liability Under CERCLA, 23 Env. Rep. 1726, 1728 (1992). Do you agree that this is a likely consequence of *Alcan*?

5. In *Alcan,* approximately two million gallons of oil wastes containing hazardous substances had been dumped into the Borehole, including more than 30,000 gallons of Alcan's waste. The company that dumped Alcan's waste in the Borehole collected liquid waste from numerous industrial facilities and occasionally commingled Alcan's waste with other waste. Why did the court reject the notion that this commingling makes the harm indivisible? Even if the *hazardous substances* in Alcan's wastes were in such low concentrations that they could not have caused environmental damage, if the presence of Alcan's wastes increased the likelihood of a *release* of the other wastes in the Borehole, can Alcan be held jointly and severally liable?

6. In a portion of the opinion not reproduced above, the court argues that requiring some threshold level of hazardous constituents before bringing a hazardous substance within CERCLA's ambit would "permit a polluter to add to the total pollution but avoid liability because the amount of its own pollution was minimal." 964 F.2d at 260. If a hazardous substance released into a heavily polluted river actually contains lower concentrations of hazardous constituents than those already in the river, has the release in any sense added to the pollution problem? Cf. EPA's "net/gross" policy, discussed in the text on page 893.

7. Even if the harm is indivisible, a defendant can still bring an action for contribution against nonsettling defendants under section 113(f) of CERCLA. In contribution actions courts may allocate response costs on the basis of equitable considerations. Was Alcan's real problem in this case the fact that it was the only PRP who refused to settle, thus leaving it "holding the bag" and unable to seek contribution against the other PRPs because of section 113(f)(2)'s bar on contribution actions against settlors?

8. Despite the *Alcan* decisions, there had been no reported multi-generator case in which a PRP had succeeded in convincing a court that the harm caused by a hazardous substance release was divisible, until the Fifth Circuit decided the following case.

| *In re Bell Petroleum Services, Inc.* |
| 3 F.3d 889 (5th Cir. 1993) |

Before JOLLY and DUHE, Circuit Judges, and PARKER, District Judge.
E. GRADY JOLLY, Circuit Judge:

The Environmental Protection Agency (EPA) seeks to recover its response costs under the Comprehensive Environmental Response, Compensation and Liability Act (CERCLA) because of a discharge of chromium waste that contaminated a local water supply. Sequa Corporation appeals from the imposition of joint and several liability, challenges the EPA's decision to provide an alternate water supply system to the area in which the groundwater was contaminated by the chromium discharge, and contests the calculation of prejudgment interest and the application of the proceeds of the EPA's settlement with its co-defendants. . . .

I

In 1978, a citizen in the Odessa, Texas area complained about discolored drinking water. The Texas Water Commission conducted an investigation. It ultimately focused on a chrome-plating shop that was operated successively from 1971 through 1977 by John Leigh, Western Pollution Control Corporation (hereinafter referred to as Bell), and Woolley Tool Division of Chromalloy American Corporation (which later merged with Sequa), at 4318 Brazos Street, just outside the city limits of Odessa. The investigation showed that during the chrome-plating process, finished parts were rinsed, and the rinse water was pumped out of the building onto the ground.

In 1984, the EPA designated a 24-block area north of the Brazos Street facility as a Superfund site—"Odessa Chromium I." It authorized a response action pursuant to its authority under CERCLA §104, 42 U.S.C. §9604, and entered into a cooperative agreement with the State of Texas. The State was to perform a remedial investigation, feasibility study, and remedial design work for the site, with the EPA reimbursing the State for 90 percent of the costs. The remedial investigation revealed that the Trinity Aquifer, the only source of groundwater in the area, contained elevated concentrations of chromium.

A "focused" feasibility study (FFS) was undertaken to evaluate the need to provide an alternative water supply pending completion of the remaining portion of the feasibility study and implementation of final remedial action. The FFS concluded that the City of Odessa's water system should be extended to provide service in the Odessa Chromium

I area. On September 8, 1986, the EPA Regional Administrator issued a Record of Decision (ROD), finding that city water service should be extended to the site. Pursuant to the cooperative agreement, the State, through its contractor, designed and constructed the system, which was completed in 1988.

II

In December 1988, the EPA filed a CERCLA cost-recovery action against Bell, Sequa, and John Leigh, which was consolidated with an adversary proceeding the EPA had filed against Bell in Bell's bankruptcy case. The EPA sought to recover direct and indirect costs it incurred in studying, designing, and constructing the alternate water supply system. . . .

[T]he district court held that Sequa is jointly and severally liable for $1,866,904.19, including the costs of studying, designing, and constructing the alternate water supply system. In addition, Sequa is jointly and severally liable for all future costs incurred by the EPA in studying, designing, and implementing a permanent remedy. . . .

IV. JOINT AND SEVERAL LIABILITY

Since CERCLA's enactment, the federal courts have struggled to resolve the complicated, often confusing, questions posed by the concept of joint and several liability, and its application under a statute whose provisions are silent with respect to the scope of liability, but whose legislative history is clear that common law principles of joint and several liability may affect liability. The issue is one of first impression in this Circuit.

A. *Common Law: The Restatement of Torts*

Although joint and several liability is commonly imposed in CERCLA cases, it is not mandatory in all such cases. United States v. Monsanto Co., 858 F.2d 160, 171 (4th Cir. 1988). Instead, Congress intended that the federal courts determine the scope of liability in CERCLA cases under traditional and evolving common law principles, guided by the Restatement (Second) of Torts. United States v. Alcan Aluminum Corp. (*Alcan-Butler*), 964 F.2d 252, 268 (3d Cir. 1992); O'Neil v. Picillo, 883 F.2d 176, 178 (1st Cir. 1989); Allied Corp. v. Acme Solvents Reclaiming,

Inc., 691 F. Supp. 1100, 1116 (N.D. Ill. 1988); United States v. Chem-Dyne Corp., 572 F. Supp. 802, 810 (S.D. Ohio 1983).

Section 433 of the Restatement provides that:

(1) Damages for harm are to be apportioned among two or more causes where

    (a) there are distinct harms, or
    (b) there is a reasonable basis for determining the contribution of each cause to a single harm.

(2) Damages for any other harm cannot be apportioned among two or more causes.

Restatement (Second) of Torts, §433A.

The nature of the harm is the key factor in determining whether apportionment is appropriate. Distinct harms—e.g., where two defendants independently shoot the plaintiff at the same time, one wounding him in the arm and the other wounding him in the leg—are regarded as separate injuries. Although some of the elements of damages (such as lost wages or pain and suffering) may be difficult to apportion, "it is still possible, as a logical, reasonable, and practical matter, . . . to make a rough estimate which will fairly apportion such subsidiary elements of damages." Id., comment b on subsection (1).

The Restatement also discusses "successive" harms, such as when "two defendants, independently operating the same plant, pollute a stream over successive periods of time." Id., comment c on subsection (1). Apportionment is appropriate, because "it is clear that each has caused a separate amount of harm, limited in time, and that neither has any responsibility for the harm caused by the other." Id.

The final situation discussed by the Restatement in which apportionment is available involves a single harm that is "divisible"—perhaps the most difficult type of harm to conceptualize. Such harm, "while not so clearly marked out as severable into distinct parts, [is] still capable of division upon a reasonable and rational basis, and of fair apportionment among the causes responsible. . . . Where such apportionment can be made without injustice to any of the parties, the court may require it to be made." Id., comment d on subsection (1). . . .

In sum, the nature of the harm is the determining factor with respect to whether apportionment is appropriate. Ultimately, the decision whether to impose joint and several liability turns on whether there is a reasonable and just method for determining the amount of harm that was caused by each defendant (or, in some cases, by an innocent cause or by the fault of the plaintiff). The question whether the harm to the plaintiff is capable of apportionment among two or more causes is a question of law. Restatement (Second) of Torts, §434(1)(b). Once it has been determined that the harm is capable of being apportioned among the various causes of it, the actual apportionment of damages is a question of fact. Id., §434(2)(b) & comment d.

Section 433B of the Restatement sets forth the burdens of proof. As a general rule, the plaintiff must prove that the defendant's tortious conduct caused the harm. Id., §433B(1). As we have already noted, however, this rule does not apply in CERCLA cases. See note 4, supra. Nevertheless, subsection (2) of §433B, which sets forth the burdens of proof with respect to apportionment, does apply and provides as follows:

> Where the tortious conduct of two or more actors has combined to bring about harm to the plaintiff, and one or more of the actors seeks to limit his liability on the ground that the harm is capable of apportionment among them, the burden of proof as to the apportionment is upon each such actor.

As explained in the comment, this rule applies only to "a proved wrongdoer who has in fact caused harm to the plaintiff." Id., comment d on subsection (2). Thus, the rule stated in subsection (2) will not permit a defendant to escape liability altogether, but only to limit its liability, if it can meet its burden of proving the amount of the harm that it caused. If it is unable to do so, it is liable for the full amount of the harm. According to the Restatement, the typical case to which this rule applies "is the pollution of a stream by a number of factories which discharge impurities into it." Id., comment c on subsection (2).

Comment e notes that there is a possibility that the rule stated in subsection (2) may cause disproportionate harm to defendants where each of a large number of them contributes a relatively small and insignificant part to the total harm. For example, "if a hundred factories each contribute a small, but still uncertain, amount of pollution to a stream, to hold each of them liable for the entire damage because he cannot show the amount of his contribution may perhaps be unjust." Id., comment e on subsection (2). The comment, however, expresses no conclusion with respect to the applicability of this illustration, noting that such a case had not arisen. . . .

To summarize, our review of the jurisprudence leads us to conclude that there are three distinct, although closely-related, approaches to the issue of joint and several liability. The first is the "*Chem-Dyne* approach," which relies almost exclusively on the principles of the Restatement (Second) of Torts. Under that approach, a defendant who seeks to avoid the imposition of joint and several liability is required to prove the amount of harm it caused.

The second approach, the "*Alcan* approach," [United States v.

Alcan Aluminum Corp., 990 F.2d 711 (2d Cir. 1993)] is adopted by the Second and Third Circuits. Although that approach also relies on the Restatement, it recognizes that, under the unique statutory liability scheme of CERCLA, the plaintiff's common law burden of proving causation has been eliminated. Under the Restatement, the plaintiff must first prove that the defendant's conduct was a substantial factor in causing the harm; the defendant may limit its liability by proving its contribution to the harm. In contrast, the *Alcan* approach suggests that a defendant may escape liability altogether if it can prove that its waste, even when mixed with other wastes at the site, did not cause the incurrence of response costs.

The third approach is the "moderate" approach taken in United States v. A & F. Materials Co., Inc., 578 F. Supp. 1249 (S.D. Ill. 1984). Under that approach, the court applies the principles of the Restatement in determining whether there is a reasonable basis for apportionment. If there is not, the court may impose joint and several liability; the court, however, retains the discretion to refuse to impose joint and several liability where such a result would be inequitable.

Although these approaches are not entirely uniform, certain basic principles emerge. First, joint and several liability is not mandated under CERCLA; Congress intended that the federal courts impose joint and several liability only in appropriate cases, applying common-law principles. Second, all of the cases rely on the Restatement in resolving the issues of joint and several liability. The major differences among the cases concern the timing of the resolution of the divisibility question, whether equitable factors should be considered, and whether a defendant can avoid liability for all, or only some portion, of the damages. Third, even where commingled wastes of unknown toxicity, migratory potential, and synergistic effect are present, defendants are allowed an opportunity to attempt to prove that there is a reasonable basis for apportionment (although they rarely succeed); where such factors are not present, volume may be a reasonable means of apportioning liability.

With respect to the timing of the "divisibility" inquiry, we believe that an early resolution is preferable. We agree with the Second Circuit, however, that this is a matter best left to the sound discretion of the district court. We also agree with the majority view that equitable factors, such as those listed in the Gore amendment, are more appropriately considered in actions for contribution among jointly and severally liable parties, than in making the initial determination of whether to impose joint and several liability. We therefore conclude that the *Chem-Dyne* approach is an appropriate framework for resolving issues of joint and several liability in CERCLA cases. Although we express no opinion with respect to the *Alcan* approach, because it is not necessary with respect to the issues we are faced with in this case, we nevertheless recognize that the Restatement principles must be adapted, where necessary, to implement congressional intent with respect to liability under the unique statutory scheme of CERCLA.

C. *Application of Joint and Several Liability*

We now turn to consider the application of these traditional and evolving common law principles of joint and several liability to the facts of this case.

First, we conclude that the district court erred in determining that there is no reasonable basis for apportionment. We reject the EPA's assertion that the clearly erroneous standard of review applies to these findings of the district court. According to the Restatement, "the question whether the harm to the plaintiff is capable of apportionment among two or more causes is a question of law." Restatement (Second) of Torts, §434.

In the district court, the EPA contended that there was no reasonable basis for apportionment, because the harm to the Trinity Aquifer was a single harm, and that a single harm is the equivalent of an indivisible harm, thus mandating the imposition of joint and several liability. Apparently now recognizing the lack of support for that position, the EPA on appeal acknowledges that apportionment is available, at least theoretically, when there is a reasonable basis for determining the contribution of each cause to a single harm. It asserts, however, that Sequa failed to meet its burden of proof on that issue. Sequa responds that the district court was misled by the EPA's incorrect view of the law, and erroneously required it to prove a *certain*—as opposed to *reasonable*—basis for apportionment.

Essentially, the question whether there is a reasonable basis for apportionment depends on whether there is sufficient evidence from which the court can determine the amount of harm caused by each defendant. If the expert testimony and other evidence establishes a factual basis for making a reasonable estimate that will fairly apportion liability, joint and several liability should not be imposed in the absence of exceptional circumstances. The fact that apportionment may be difficult, because each defendant's exact contribution to the harm cannot be proved to an absolute certainty, or the fact that it will require weighing the evidence and making credibility determinations, are inadequate grounds upon which to impose joint and several liability.

Our review of the record convinces us that Sequa met its burden of proving that, as a matter of law, there is a reasonable basis for apportionment. This case is closely analogous to the Restatement's illustrations in which apportionment of liability is appropriate. For example, where cattle owned by two or more defendants destroy the plaintiff's crops, the damages are apportioned according to the number of cattle owned by each defendant, based on the reasonable assumption that the respective harm done is proportionate to that number. Thus, the Restatement suggests that apportionment is appropriate even though the evidence does not establish with certainty the specific amount of harm caused by each defendant's cattle, and even though there is a possibility that only one of the defendant's cattle caused all of the harm, while the other defendant's cattle idly stood by. Likewise, pollution of a stream by two or more factories may be treated as divisible in terms of degree, and apportioned among the defendants on the basis of evidence of the respective quantities of pollution discharged by each.

As is evident from our previous discussion of the jurisprudence, most CERCLA cost-recovery actions involve numerous, commingled hazardous substances with synergistic effects and unknown toxicity. In contrast, this case involves only one hazardous substance—chromium—and no synergistic effects. The chromium entered the groundwater as the result of similar operations by three parties who operated at mutually exclusive times. Here, it is reasonable to assume that the respective harm done by each of the defendants is proportionate to the volume of cromium-contaminated water each discharged into the environment.

Even though it is not possible to determine with absolute certainty the exact amount of chromium each defendant introduced into the groundwater, there is sufficient evidence from which a reasonable and rational approximation of each defendant's individual contribution to the contamination can be made. The evidence demonstrates that Leigh owned the real property at the site from 1967 through 1981, and conducted chrome-plating activities there in 1971 and 1972. In 1972, Bell purchased the assets of the shop and leased the property from Leigh. It continued to conduct similar, but more extensive, chrome-plating activities there until mid-1976. In August 1976, Sequa purchased the assets from Bell, leased the property from Leigh, and conducted similar chrome-plating activities at the site until late 1977. In response to the EPA's motion for summary judgment, Sequa introduced evidence regarding chrome flake purchases during each operator's tenure. It also introduced evidence with respect to the value of the chrome-plating done by each, as well as summaries of sales. Given the number of years that had passed since the activities were conducted, the records of these activities were not complete. However, there was testimony from various witnesses regarding the rinsing and wastewater disposal practices of each defendant, and the amount of chrome-plating activity conducted by each.

During the Phase III hearing, Sequa introduced expert testimony regarding a volumetric approach to apportionment. The first expert, Henderson, calculated the total amount of chromium that had been introduced into the environment by Leigh, Bell, and Sequa, collectively and individually. The second expert, Mooney, calculated the amount of chromium that would have been introduced into the environment by each operator on the basis of electrical usage records.

In addition to rejecting apportionment because of competing theories, the district court also rejected volume as a basis for apportionment, because there was no method of dividing the liability among the defendants which would rise to any level of fairness above mere speculation. It stated that each of the proposed apportionment methods involved significant assumption factors, because records had been lost, and because the theories differed significantly.

The existence of competing theories of apportionment is an insufficient reason to reject all of those theories. It is true, as the district court noted, that the records of chrome-plating activity were incomplete. However, under the facts and circumstances of this case, and in the light of the other evidence that is available, that factor may be taken into account in apportioning Sequa's share of the liability. Finally, the fact that Sequa's experts relied on certain assumptions in forming their opinions is not fatal to Sequa's ability to prove that there is a reasonable basis for apportionment. Expert opinions frequently include assumptions. If those assumptions are well-founded and reasonable, and not inconsistent with the facts as established by other competent evidence, they may be sufficiently reliable to support a conclusion that a reasonable basis for apportionment exists.

In sum, we conclude that the district court erred in imposing joint and several liability, because Sequa met its burden of proving that there is a reasonable basis for apportioning liability among the defendants on a volumetric basis. We therefore remand the case to the district court for apportionment. . . .

PARKER, District Judge, concurring in part and dissenting in part:

I. JOINT AND SEVERAL LIABILITY

I cannot agree with the majority's holding on the joint and several liability/quantitative apportionment issue in this case. I do agree that the determination of whether the type harm involved in this case is *capable* of quantitative apportionment is a question of law. And the majority is correct that the single chromium harm suffered by the Trinity Aquifer is the sort theoretically *capable* of apportionment. However, while Sequa met its *legal* burden of establishing that the type harm involved is capable of apportionment, it failed to meet its *factual* burden relative to apportionment. If proof exists by which the fact-finder could determine, on a reasonable basis, the extent of environmental injury attributable to a party, then certainly that party is entitled to escape the heavy hand of joint and several liability and to have its liability restricted to its actual, quantitative contribution to the single harm. The majority correctly places the burden of proof on the party seeking such a finding, to produce credible evidence to meet its burden. But the majority confuses the distinction between the *legal* burden that the single harm at issue caused is of a type capable of apportionment, and the *factual* burden of proving the amount of harm attributable to a particular party. ("Our review of the record convinces us that Sequa met its burden of proving that, as a matter of law, there is a reasonable basis for apportionment." This case is closely analogous to the Restatement's illustrations in which apportionment of liability is appropriate.)

The gist of the majority opinion is this legal fallacy: because the evidence is clear that Sequa did not cause 100 percent of the harm to the aquifer, Sequa *must* be entitled to a finding by the district court apportioning the amount of harm attributable to it under the Restatement (Second) of Torts, §433. We are not to approach our analytical task from that end. The majority's "rule of thumb" miscasts the role of the district court and eviscerates the very concept of joint and several liability.

I agree with the majority that certainty is not required. What is required is proof by a preponderance of the evidence. The majority properly embraces the applicability of the Restatement (Second) of Torts to this case, but then seeks to divorce itself from the applicable preponderance of the evidence standard of proof so as to mandate that the district court "pick a number" apportioning liability.

Civil cases are decided by a preponderance of the evidence because such proof affords a *reasonable basis* for decision. In other words, while *certainty* of proof is not required in civil cases, probability is. Evidence by "51 percent," or to the extent of "more likely than not," is deemed sufficiently reliable for resolution of civil disputes. But proof by *less than this amount* is unacceptably speculative; and amounts to mere *possibility*, not probability. . . . If proof by a preponderance of the evidence is to be abandoned in CERCLA apportionment cases, the district court is at least entitled to guidance regarding the level of possibilities that is acceptable. Will 10 percent do? 20 percent? 30 percent? . . .

The majority remands the case to the district court for a finding apportioning liability on a volumetric basis. Such was, however, precisely the purpose of Phase III of the trial. In Phase III of the trial, the district

3. Waste Management and Pollution Prevention   Pages 301-312

court heard approximately 400 pages of testimony from 19 witnesses, three of whom were experts. The district court reviewed over 150 exhibits: 80 new exhibits were admitted during Phase III of the trial, and the district court allowed for the more than 70 exhibits from Phase I to also be used during Phase III.

A review of the record reveals that Sequa attempted to climb the preponderance hill by focusing on several potential methods of achieving a reasonable basis for quantitative apportionment of liability on a *volumetric* basis.

Under one proffered method of such apportionment by a Sequa expert, the expert assumed that Sequa's *electrical* usage for plating operations was 30 percent of its total electrical usage, while, in contrast, he attributed to both Bell and Leigh a plating percentage of 50 percent of their respective total electrical usages. But the bases for this expert's electrical percentage assumptions were effectively refuted by other evidence in the case.

Sales records served as the springboard for another proffered method of apportionment. The sales record approach suffered fatally from Sequa's ability to produce only scattered invoices.

An attempt was then made to compare the defendants' *expense* records. However, the only expense records for Sequa demonstrated that it purchased 3,500 pounds of chromic acid flake within a three-month period in 1977. Sequa's other records were destroyed. Any attempt to extrapolate from the three-month period in 1977 would have been at best speculative.

A Sequa expert also assumed that Sequa had no waste disposal after the installation of a catch tank. The credibility of this assumption was fatally eroded by contrary evidence—of substantial overflows, spills of plating solution, leaks in the plating tanks, and plating solution dumped by Sequa.

Indeed, the *only* evidence the district court could view with any comfort was evidence of relative *times of facility ownership* and the periods of plating activity by the defendants. Yet, the apportionment import of even this evidence was reduced to mere speculation when attempts were made to prove the *actual level, or quantity,* of plating activity conducted during the known periods of time. In the language of the majority's cited example of cows in the field: the defendants evidenced what periods of time each farmer had cows in the field, but failed to demonstrate to any degree above speculation *how many cows* each farmer had in the field. . . .

In my opinion, the following is the appropriate appellate court approach to this case.

First, we should hold that the district court was not clearly erroneous in its finding that Sequa failed to meet its burden of proof on the factual, quantitative apportionment issue—of Sequa's proportionate responsibility for the single chromium harm suffered by the aquifer. Then, we should reject the district court's conclusion that, in this case, it did not need to consider the fairness of the proposed consent decrees relative to Sequa's SARA-bestowed, equitable cost allocation rights. See 42 U.S.C. §9613(f)(1). I think we must address the impact of the consent decrees on the defendants' statutory equitable cost allocation rights—in light of the alternative, *equitable* "apportionment" finding reasonably rendered by the district court. This approach is consistent with the caselaw on appropriate contribution analyses. And my approach certainly offers a much better prospect for bringing this protracted and expensive litigation to an end than does a remand to the district court for more (essentially redundant) proceedings.

NOTES AND QUESTIONS

1. How does the court's approach to CERCLA's joint and several liability differ from that of the *Alcan* courts? How does it differ from the approach advocated by Judge Parker in dissent?

2. Under which of these approaches—*Alcan*, the *Bell Petroleum* majority, or Judge Parker's approach—would a defendant have a better chance of escaping liability entirely? What sort of evidence would a defendant have to produce in order to escape joint and several liability under each approach?

3. On remand, the district court in *Bell Petroleum* held Sequa liable for only four percent of the total liability in the case. United States v. Bell Petroleum Services, 1994 WL 235536 (W.D. Tex. March 11, 1994). This amounted to only approximately $68,000 of the $1.7 million in response costs and prejudgment interest that had been incurred. While the district judge indicated that he was convinced that Sequa's share of the contamination actually was much greater than four percent, he interpreted the Fifth Circuit's decision as precluding him from taking additional evidence on apportionment.

4. Would the result in *Bell Petroleum* have been any different if the contamination at the site had been caused by more than one hazardous substance, as is far more typical in CERCLA cases? How difficult would it be to satisfy the Fifth Circuit's standard for apportionment if several wastes had been commingled at the site?

5. In United States v. Broderick Investment Co., 862 F. Supp. 272 (D. Colo. 1994), a federal district court found harm to be divisible in a CERCLA case based on geographic considerations. Citing *Alcan* and *Bell Petroleum*, the court held that a railroad that owned a portion of land used by a wood treatment facility was liable only for the cost of

3. Waste Management and Pollution Prevention

cleaning up contamination emanating from an impoundment pond located primarily on the railroad's land. The railroad was held not to be liable for remediating a separate contamination plume emanating from a processing plant east of the railroad's land because that plume had neither merged with the pond plume nor migrated onto the railroad's land. For a discussion of the practical impact of *Bell Petroleum*, see Azarmehr, CERCLA Joint and Several Liability: Alive and Well After *Bell Petroleum*, 25 Env. Rep. 1138 (1994).

6. Even if courts generally accept holdings that generators may in theory be able to show divisibility and apportionment, the joint and several liability routinely imposed in Superfund litigation is nevertheless still a good step beyond the common law.

5. *Responsible Parties*

A. Owners and Operators

Operator Liability (p. 317). Even a party who does not own a facility can be held liable as an "operator" under CERCLA §107. In FMC Corp. v. United States Dept. of Commerce, 29 F.3d 833 (3d Cir. 1994), the U.S. government was held liable for contamination caused by a rayon manufacturing plant that had been operated during World War II at the direction of the government's War Production Board. The Third Circuit, sitting en banc, decided by an 8 to 4 vote that the government was liable as an "operator" of the facility under CERCLA. The court noted that it previously had adopted a "substantial control" test to determine when a corporation should be held liable for the environmental violations of another. In Lansford-Coaldale Joint Water Authority v. Tonolli Corp., 4 F.3d 1209 (3d Cir. 1993), the court rejected an "authority-to-control" test that would have imposed operator liability on a corporation that had the capability to control another, even if it was never utilized. Instead, the court adopted what it termed an "actual control" test that holds one company liable for the violations of another only "when there is evidence of substantial control exercised by one corporation over the activities of the other." 4 F.3d at 1221.

In *FMC*, the en banc court found that the government clearly had exercised substantial control over FMC's rayon plant "as the government determined what product the facility would produce, the level of production, the price of the product, and to whom the product would be sold." 29 F.3d at 843. The court distinguished this situation from cases involving "governmental regulatory activities undertaken solely with the purpose of cleaning up hazardous materials. . . ." 29 F.3d at 841. But it rejected the government's argument that regulatory activities can never constitute the basis for CERCLA liability, finding that "the government can be liable when it engages in regulatory activities extensive enough to make it an operator of a facility or an arranger of the disposal of hazardous wastes even though no private party could engage in the regulatory activities at issue." 29 F.3d at 840. The dissenting judges argued that the company that profited from production of the rayon should bear the costs of cleanup, rather than "society as the ultimate beneficiary of the war effort. . . ." 29 F.3d 854 (Sloviter, C.J., dissenting).

In United States v. Gurley, 43 F.3d 1188 (8th Cir. 1994), the Eighth Circuit also adopted an actual control test for determining when individuals can be held liable as operators under section 107(a)(2) of CERCLA. The court held that two elements were required for such liability: (1) that the individual "had the authority to determine whether hazardous wastes would be disposed of and to determine the method of disposal and (2) actually exercised that authority, either by personally performing the tasks necessary to dispose of the hazardous wastes or by directing others to perform those tasks." 43 F.3d at 1193.

Owners of an easement to operate a pipeline over contaminated land are not owners or operators under CERCLA simply by virtue of the fact that they own an easement, according to the Ninth Circuit in Long Beach Unified School District v. Godwin California Living Trust, 32 F.3d 1364 (9th Cir. 1994). The court noted that if the pipeline released hazardous substances or the easement holder played an active role in operating a facility where substances were released, the easement holder could be held liable. However, simply being in a position to prevent contamination is not enough to generate CERCLA liability.

Owners and Operators "At the Time of Disposal" (p. 317). In addition to naming current owners and operators as PRPs, CERCLA also names those who were owners and operators "at the time of disposal." §9607(a)(2). While this language has a straightforward application to those who owned and operated a hazardous waste facility at the time it was actively receiving hazardous substances, CERCLA's expansive definitions and scope once again can produce some possibly surprising results. Consider the following decision.

Nurad, Inc. v. William E. Hooper & Sons Co.
966 F.2d 837 (4th Cir. 1992)

Before WILKINSON, Circuit Judge, WILLIAMS, District Judge, and MACKENZIE, Senior District Judge.
WILKINSON, Circuit Judge.

3. Waste Management and Pollution Prevention   Page 317

I

Plaintiff Nurad, Inc., brought this lawsuit to recover the costs it incurred in removing several underground storage tanks (USTs) from a piece of property it owns in Baltimore, Maryland. From 1905 to 1963, Wm. E. Hooper & Sons Co. (the Hooper Co. or the Company) owned the site and adjacent properties, collectively known as Hooperwood Mills. At some point before 1935, the Hooper Co. began to install tanks for the storage of mineral spirits which it used to coat fabrics in its textile finishing plant. The Company continued to use the tanks for that purpose until 1962, when it shut down its finishing operations. At that time, the Hooper Co. abandoned the USTs and did not remove the mineral spirits.

In 1963, the Hooper Co. sold Hooperwood Mills to Property Investors, Inc. Frank Nicoll, as president and principal shareholder of Property Investors and its successor, Monumental Enterprises, Inc., leased several of the buildings on Hooperwood Mills to various tenants, none of which ever used the USTs. Then in 1976, Monumental Enterprises sold Hooperwood Mills to Kenneth Mumaw, who subdivided the property and sold a portion of it to Nurad.

In all its years at the site, Nurad apparently never used the USTs. In 1987, however, the Maryland Department of the Environment informed Nurad that the tanks had not been properly abandoned and required that they be removed from the ground or filled with sand or concrete within 180 days. Nurad sought assistance with the cleanup from several of the previous owners and tenants of the site, but they all refused. Nurad then hired an environmental consultant and a tank removal contractor to analyze the contents of the tanks and dispose of several of the tanks and the surrounding soil.

In 1990, Nurad filed this CERCLA suit, seeking reimbursement for approximately $226,000 in cleanup costs from former owners of the site (the Hooper Co., Nicoll, Mumaw, and Monumental Enterprises); from former tenants at the site (Allstates Moving & Storage, Raymond B. McMillan, Universal Laboratory Installations, Inc., and Monumental Millwork); and from James Hooper, Jr., and Lawrence Hooper (the Hooper brothers), who were shareholders and directors of the Hooper Co. The district court decided the issues of liability on summary judgment. In its view, only the Hooper Co. was liable under CERCLA for costs incurred by Nurad in removing the tanks. The court found that the tenant defendants did not qualify as "operators" because they did not possess sufficient authority to control the hazardous waste at the facility. Further, the court ruled that certain of the previous owners were not liable because they were not owners "at the time of disposal." According to the district court, "disposal" necessarily

107

contemplated some element of affirmative participation on the part of the defendant, and only the original owner actively dealt with hazardous substances at the site.

Both Nurad and the Hooper Co. appeal.

II

. . . The issues on appeal concern the scope of the terms defining responsible persons under §9607(a)(2) —specifically, the meaning of the terms "owned," "operated" "facility," and "disposal." We think it best to approach the meaning of those terms by considering Nurad's claims against the various parties who were prior owners or tenants at Hooperwood Mills.

A

We shall first address Nurad's claims against the former tenants at the site. [The circuit court affirmed the district court's determination that the tenants were not operators within the meaning of §9607(a)(2) because they lacked the authority to control the USTs pursuant to their leases.]

C

Finally, we address Nurad's claims against the previous owners of the site, the Hooper Co. and Kenneth Mumaw. Neither the Hooper Co. nor Mumaw appeals from the district court's conclusion that they are prior owners of the facility. At oral argument, Mumaw did direct our attention to the fact that he held legal title to the property for only a short period of time. We do not think, however, that the word "owned" is a word that admits of varying degrees. Such equitable considerations as the duration of ownership may well be relevant at a later stage of the proceedings when the district court allocates response costs among liable parties, see 42 U.S.C. §9613(f)(1), but we reject any suggestion that a short-term owner is somehow not an owner for purposes of §9607(a)(2).

Because both the Hooper Co. and Mumaw are prior owners of the facility, we must ask whether recovery against them is nonetheless barred because no "disposal" of hazardous wastes took place on their watch. The district court took a narrow view of the word "disposal," limiting it to disposal by affirmative human conduct. Thus, the court

3. Waste Management and Pollution Prevention

concluded that the Hooper Co. was liable because it actively disposed of hazardous substances and then abandoned them in the USTs. The court held, however, that Mumaw was not liable—even though passive migration of hazardous substances may have occurred during his ownership—since he did not take an active role in managing the tanks or their contents.

We think the district court's restrictive construction of "disposal" ignores the language of the statute, contradicts clear circuit precedent, and frustrates the fundamental purposes of CERCLA. The statute defines "disposal" in 42 U.S.C. §9601(29) by incorporating by reference the definition found in the Resource Conservation and Recovery Act (RCRA). That definition states:

> The term "disposal" means the discharge, deposit, injection, dumping, spilling, leaking, or placing of any solid waste or hazardous waste into or on any land or water so that such solid waste or hazardous waste or any constituent thereof may enter the environment or be emitted into the air or discharged into any waters, including ground waters.

Some of the words in this definition appear to be primarily of an active voice. See Ecodyne Corp. v. Shah, 718 F. Supp. 1454, 1457 (N.D. Cal. 1989). This is true of "deposit," "injection," "dumping," and "placing." Others of the words, however, readily admit to a passive component: hazardous waste may leak or spill without any active human participation. The district court arbitrarily deprived these words of their passive element by imposing a requirement of active participation as a prerequisite to liability.

Indeed, this circuit has already rejected the "strained reading" of disposal which would limit its meaning to "active human conduct." United States v. Waste Ind., Inc., 734 F.2d 159, 164-65 (4th Cir. 1984). In *Waste Industries*, the court held that Congress intended the 42 U.S.C. §6903(3) definition of disposal "to have a range of meanings," including not only active conduct, but also the reposing of hazardous waste and its subsequent movement through the environment. Id. at 164. Here the district court attempted to distinguish *Waste Industries* on the ground that it involved the authority of the Environmental Protection Agency to demand cleanup by former owners and operators under RCRA. The district court thought that the *Waste Industries* definition was necessary to close a loophole in RCRA's environmental protection scheme, see id. at 165, and believed "that the only way for the *Waste Industries* court to preserve the EPA's ability to demand cleanup by the actual former owners and operators was to define 'disposal' in RCRA to cover completely passive repose or movement through the environment." In this CERCLA action, by contrast, the district court noted that the current owner and all prior owners were already defendants and in some cases were liable for cleanup costs.

We think the district court was bound to follow *Waste Industries* in interpreting the term "disposal." It is true that *Waste Industries* interpreted the definition in the context of RCRA, but Congress expressly provided that under CERCLA the term "shall have the meaning provided in section 1004" of RCRA. Moreover, the aim of both RCRA and CERCLA is to encourage the cleanup of hazardous waste conditions. Whether the context is one of prospective enforcement of hazardous waste removal under RCRA or an action for reimbursement of response costs under CERCLA, a requirement conditioning liability upon affirmative human participation in contamination equally frustrates the statutory purpose.

It is easy to see how the district court's requirement of active participation would frustrate the statutory policy of encouraging "voluntary private action to remedy environmental hazards," In re Dant & Russell, Inc., 951 F.2d 246, 248 (9th Cir. 1991). Under the district court's view, an owner could avoid liability simply by standing idle while an environmental hazard festers on his property. Such an owner could insulate himself from liability by virtue of his passivity, so long as he transfers the property before any response costs are incurred. A more conscientious owner who undertakes the task of cleaning up the environmental hazard would, on the other hand, be liable as the current owner of the facility, since "disposal" is not a part of the current owner liability scheme under 42 U.S.C. §9607(a)(1). See *Shore Realty* [parent text, p. 312]. The district court's view thus introduces the anomalous situation where a current owner, such as Nurad, who never used the storage tanks, could bear a substantial share of the cleanup costs, while a former owner who was similarly situated would face no liability at all. A CERCLA regime which rewards indifference to environmental hazards and discourages voluntary efforts at waste cleanup cannot be what Congress had in mind.

The district court's view of the CERCLA definition of disposal is also at odds with CERCLA's strict liability emphasis. The trigger to liability under §9607(a)(2) is ownership or operation of a facility at the time of disposal, not culpability or responsibility for the contamination. See *Monsanto*, 858 F.2d [160] at 168 [(4th Cir. 1988)] ("The traditional elements of tort culpability on which the site-owners rely simply are absent from the statute"); *Shore Realty* [p. 312] (noting that Congress specifically rejected a causation requirement). We must decline therefore to engraft onto the statute additional prerequisites to the reimbursement of response costs which Congress did not place there.

Thus, we hold that §9607(a)(2) imposes liability not only for active involvement in the "dumping" or "placing" of hazardous waste at the

3. Waste Management and Pollution Prevention   Page 317

facility, but for ownership of the facility at a time that hazardous waste was "spilling" or "leaking." The only remaining question is whether a statutory disposal of hazardous waste occurred during the period of Hooper's and Mumaw's ownership.

We think for the following reasons that it did. Initially, the record supports the conclusion that both the Hooper Co. and Mumaw owned the facility at a time when the mineral spirits were "leaking" from the tanks. Nurad has established that the Hooper Co. began to install the USTs some time before 1935 and that mineral spirits reposed in the tanks until they were removed by Nurad in 1988-89. Nurad has further presented uncontroverted evidence that at the time the tanks were removed the soil around several of the tanks was contaminated with mineral spirits. Indeed, the district court found that the "mineral spirits in the excavated soil show an exact chromatographic match" with those in one tank, and that another of the tanks had "corrosion holes in the bottom and was underlain by discolored soils that emanated solvent odors." Neither the Hooper Co. nor Mumaw has pointed to anything to overcome the presumption that the leaking that has occurred was not a sudden event, but the result of a gradual and progressive course of environmental contamination that included these defendants' period of ownership. We do not think in such circumstances that Congress intended to impose upon a CERCLA plaintiff the onerous burden of pinpointing at what precise point a leakage may have begun. This circuit has been careful not to vitiate what was intended as remedial legislation by erecting barrier upon barrier on the road to reimbursement of response costs. As this court emphasized in rejecting a requirement that a CERCLA plaintiff prove a nexus between waste sent by a particular defendant to a particular site and the resulting environmental harm:

> Congress knew of the synergistic and migratory capacities of leaking chemical waste, and the technological infeasibility of tracing improperly disposed waste to its source. . . . To require a plaintiff under CERCLA to "fingerprint" wastes is to eviscerate the statute.

Monsanto, 858 F.2d at 170.

Finally, we agree with the district court that the Hooper Co.'s claim that there was no statutory disposal is especially insubstantial. The Company disposed of hazardous substances at the site by depositing them in the USTs and abandoning them upon closing its finishing plant in 1962. The statute provides that "disposal" includes the "placing" of any hazardous waste "into or on any land" so that such hazardous waste "may enter the environment," 42 U.S.C. §6903(3), and courts have specifically held that depositing hazardous waste into enclosed containers fits this definition. Even if we accept the Hooper Co.'s argument that the storage of useful mineral spirits for active use as a raw material cannot constitute disposal because it is not "waste," see 3550 Stevens Creek Assoc. v. Barclays Bank [parent text, p. 330], we think there clearly was a disposal in 1962 when the Company closed down the finishing plant and abandoned the tanks. At that point, the mineral spirits clearly became "waste," as they were abandoned and were apparently never again used. See 40 C.F.R. §261.2 (defining waste as any "discarded" material, or material which has been "abandoned"). The Hooper Co. is quick to point out that it later "sold" the USTs and their contents to Property Investors, but we agree with the district court that the sale of the previously abandoned tanks to a real estate investor—who had no use for the mineral spirits or the tanks and apparently never used them—cannot reverse the earlier disposal. A defendant who has abandoned hazardous materials at a site cannot escape CERCLA liability by simply labelling a subsequent transfer of the property as a "sale" of the hazardous waste. See United States v. Aceto Agric. Chems. [parent text, p. 323] ("[C]ourts have imposed CERCLA liability where defendants sought to characterize their arrangement with another party who disposed of their hazardous substances as a 'sale' rather than a 'disposal.' ").

III

In sum, Nurad is entitled to reimbursement from some of the prior occupants of Hooperwood Mills, but not from all. We affirm the district court's dismissal of Nurad's claims against each of the tenant defendants and against the Hooper brothers, and we affirm the entry of summary judgment in Nurad's favor against the Hooper Co. We reverse the district court's denial of Nurad's motion for summary judgment as to Mumaw. We remand the case for further proceedings consistent with this opinion.

Affirmed in part, reversed in part, and remanded.

NOTES AND QUESTIONS

1. Do you agree with the court's interpretation of "disposal"? Is it consistent with CERCLA's purpose of holding "responsible parties" liable? Is it fair?

2. Does *Nurad* have any consequences for parties who might assert the innocent landowner defense? Under its reasoning, could a PRP named under section 107(a)(1) also be named under section 107(a)(2)

3. Waste Management and Pollution Prevention   Pages 317-318

if waste on the property continued to leak after the current owner purchased it? If so, would that vitiate the innocent landowner protections enacted by SARA?

3. In the *Nurad* case, suppose that the Hooper Company, which installed and later abandoned the tanks that stored mineral spirits, instead had sold the property to another textile finishing company, which continued to use the tanks in its business. How, if at all, would this have affected Hooper's liability? Would it depend on whether or not the tanks already were leaking at the time of the sale?

4. Will the *Nurad* decision encourage prospective purchasers of real estate to make greater efforts to determine if underground storage tanks are located on property they wish to buy? If the *Nurad* court had imposed liability only on the current owner of the property, could owners who discover environmental hazards on their property escape CERCLA liability by simply selling their property before any response costs are incurred?

5. In Joslyn Manufacturing Co. v. Koppers Co., Inc., 40 F.3d 750 (5th Cir. 1994), the Fifth Circuit refused to apply the *Nurad* rationale to hold liable a company that had owned land contaminated by wood-treating chemicals for two years before selling it. The Koppers Co. had purchased the parcel of land it order to remove the wood-treatment equipment located there for use at one of its other plants. While removing much equipment from the site, Koppers did not operate the wood-treatment facility before selling the land to another company. The Fifth Circuit refused to find Koppers liable in a contribution action brought by the wood treatment company that sold the land to Koppers. The court found no evidence to indicate that disposal had occurred during Koppers' ownership of the site. There was no evidence that any hazardous substances were discharged, moved or dispersed when the wood treating equipment was removed. Nor was there evidence that any hazardous substance had "leaked" or "spilled" during Koppers' ownership. Thus, the court found it unnecessary to decide whether it would follow the Fourth Circuit's *Nurad* decision.

Citing *Nurad*, the wood treatment company argued that it would be bad policy for the court to allow a sophisticated purchaser who knew about the contamination to escape liability through its passivity. However, the court opined that it would be even worse policy to reward the primary contaminator in a contribution action by allowing it to pass "the contaminated property through a series of innocent landowners and then, when the contamination is discovered, demanding contribution from each." 40 F.3d at 762.

Liability of Contractors as Operators (pp. 317-318). In Kaiser Aluminum & Chemical Corp. v. Catellus Development Corp., 976 F.2d 1338

(9th Cir. 1992), a contractor who had excavated contaminated soil and spread it over uncontaminated portions of a site was held liable under section 107(a)(2) as an operator of a facility at the time of disposal. The Ninth Circuit held that "operator" liability under section 107(a)(2) "only attaches if the defendant had the authority to control the cause of the contamination at the time the hazardous substances were released into the environment." The court rejected arguments that contractors could not be held liable as operators. It distinguished Hines Lumber Co. v. Vulcan Materials Co., 861 F.2d 155 (7th Cir. 1988), which held that a contractor who had designed a wood treatment facility was not liable as an operator or arranger, on the ground that "the activity which produced the contamination . . . —the excavation and grading of the development site—occurred *during*, not after, the construction process." 976 F.2d at 1342.

"Innocent Sellers" and the Third-Party Defense (pp. 318-319). Section 101(35)(A) of CERCLA, which contains the innocent purchaser defense, specifies that neither it nor the third-party defense in section 107(b)(3) "shall diminish the liability of any previous owner or operator . . . who otherwise would be liable." The third-party defense also is not available if the cause of a release "occurs in connection with a contractual relationship," including contracts for the sale of real estate. Nevertheless, the Second Circuit has held that a prior owner who left contained hazardous materials on a property can successfully assert a third-party defense against a subsequent purchaser whose actions caused their release. The court held that if the previous owner would not otherwise be liable it can invoke the third party defense unless the property sales contract "somehow is connected with the handling of hazardous substances." Westwood Pharmaceuticals, Inc. v. National Fuel Gas Distribution Corp., 964 F.2d 85, 89 (2d Cir. 1992). Thus the predecessor in title's claim that soil contamination was entirely the result of construction activities by the subsequent purchaser of a property could constitute a valid third-party defense.

"All Appropriate Inquiry" and the Innocent Purchaser Defense (pp. 318-319). The innocent purchaser defense outlined in section 101(35)(B) of CERCLA has been difficult to satisfy in part because parties that conduct "all appropriate inquiry" generally do not have difficulty discovering potential contamination problems. The defense has been rejected by courts for a variety of reasons, including a landowner's failure to inquire about the disposal practices of a business that previously operated on the property, United States v. A & N Cleaners & Launderers, Inc., 854 F. Supp. 229 (S.D.N.Y. 1994), actual knowledge that a lessor discharged waste on the property, United States v. Broderick Investment

3. Waste Management and Pollution Prevention   Pages 318-319

Co., 862 F. Supp. 272 (D. Colo. 1994), and failure to take precautions to prevent damage from hazardous substances known to be present on the site, Kerr-McGee Chemical Corp. v. Lefton Iron & Metal Co., 14 F.3d 321 (7th Cir. 1994).

No appellate decision to date has directly defined what constitutes "all appropriate inquiry" for purposes of the defense. The First Circuit in In re Hemingway Transport, Inc., 993 F.2d 915 (1993), suggested that a developer that acquired land on which leaking drums were subsequently discovered "would be held to an especially stringent level of preacquisition inquiry—on the theory that an acquiring party's failure to make adequate inquiry may itself contribute to a prolongation of the contamination." 993 F.3d at 933. On remand in the case, a bankruptcy court rejected the developer's assertion that the location of the drums in a wetland and the fact that the acquisition occurred in the early 1980s when there was less awareness of problems of environmental contamination should qualify it for the innocent purchaser defense. Juniper Development Group v. Kahn, 174 B.R. 148 (Bankr. D. Mass. 1994). The court stated that even if what the developer did had constituted customary practice in the industry, it was neither a good nor commercially reasonable practice under CERCLA.

In response to complaints that the "all appropriate inquiry" requirement of section 101(35)(B) of CERCLA is too vague for purchasers to rely on, legislation has been proposed that would specify precisely what inquiry a purchaser must undertake to meet this requirement. One bill would define such inquiry as requiring a visual site inspection by an environmental professional, inspection of chain of title documents for the past 50 years, examination of available aerial photographs of the site, inspection of government records of any activities causing the release of hazardous substances, and a check for any Superfund liens.

The vagueness of current liability standards has discouraged development of previously contaminated industrial sites. In an effort to encourage development of such properties, EPA is formulating guidance to assure purchasers of certain properties that they are not buying into mammoth liability problems. In January 1995 EPA Administrator Carol Browner announced that the agency would encourage greater sue of "comfort letters" assuring owners that their properties would not be targets of Superfund enforcement actions. Noah, EPA Plans Rules to Limit Liability of Superfund Sites, Wall St. J., Jan. 26, 1995, at A5. The agency also will issue new criteria making it easier to obtain a "prospective purchaser agreement" that provides similar assurances to buyers of such properties. EPA will provide grants of up to $200,000 each to fund at least 50 projects where cities will develop previously-contaminated properties and the agency will remove approximately 25,000 sites from its current list of 40,000 potential Superfund sites.

Pages 319-322   3. Waste Management and Pollution Prevention

Property Transfer Statutes (pp. 319-322). In 1992 Congress enacted two laws that expand required environmental disclosures when property is transferred. The Residential Lead-Based Paint Hazard Reduction Act, Pub. L. No. 102-550, enacted as Title X of the Housing and Community Development Act of 1992, will require sellers or lessors of residential property to disclose to purchasers or lessors "the presence of any known lead-based paint" on the property commencing in 1995. Sellers and lessors also will have to provide an informational pamphlet on lead paint hazards and give purchasers up to ten days to conduct a lead paint inspection. The Community Environmental Response Facilitation Act, Pub. L. No. 102-426, amends section 120(h) of CERCLA to require federal agencies to identify uncontaminated portions of federal property that is for sale in order to facilitate transfers to private parties. While retaining the requirement that the federal government remediate environmental contamination on such properties, the Act provides that property transfers may occur before the completion of long-term remedial action once cleanup plans have been approved and initiated.

New Jersey's Environmental Cleanup Responsibility Act (pp. 320-321). By the end of 1991, a total of 1,759 remedial actions costing more than $478 million had been undertaken pursuant to New Jersey's Environmental Cleanup Responsibility Act (ECRA). New Jersey officials attribute ECRA's results to the fact that it avoids expensive disputes over who is at fault for contamination by internalizing the cost of cleanup in the property transfer transaction. As the New Jersey Supreme Court has noted, "the statute focuses on the environmental wrong, not the wrongdoer. Identification of the polluter plays no part in the ECRA process, which imposes a 'self-executing duty to remediate.'" In re Adoption of N.J.A.C. 7:26B, 608 A.2d 288, 291 (N.J. 1992).

The New Jersey Supreme Court upheld ECRA regulations that require the cleanup of off-site contamination emanating from a property being transferred and that include within ECRA's coverage contiguous parcels of vacant land controlled by the same owner or operator. The latter was necessary, the court explained, because otherwise "exemption of vacant land contiguous to a plant would provide owners with an incentive to move hazardous wastes from the plant site to that land. Such an exemption would allow owners to sell off the uncontaminated part of the property and abandon the part that is contaminated." Id. at 297. Two dissenting justices argued that requiring cleanup of off-site contamination "converts ECRA's quick and simple determination of liability into a time-consuming and controversial analysis about the source of off-site contamination." Id. at 303 (Garibaldi, J., concurring in part and dissenting in part). The dissenters maintained that this

3. Waste Management and Pollution Prevention   Pages 323-331

actually will delay cleanup by opening the door to disputes over whether or not the source of contamination is located on the property being sold.

In 1993 New Jersey amended its Environmental Cleanup Responsibility Act (ECRA) to relax cleanup standards and streamline the remediation process required by the Act. The new legislation, called the Industrial Site Recovery Act, allows parties to defer remediation of industrial property if the new owner plans to use it for substantially the same purpose. It permits soil cleanups to proceed without prior state approval in most cases and authorizes transfers of partial interests in property without requiring cleanup of an entire site. The law permits the use of substantially lower exposure estimates in calculating cleanup levels required to reduce residual risk, depending upon the expected future use of the land, and it authorizes the use of institutional controls that restrict access to a site as an alternative to permanent remediation. ECRA Reforms Streamline Cleanup Process, Allow DEPE to Adopt Differential Standards, 24 Env. Rep. 364 (1993). The new legislation responds to concerns that ECRA was so stringent that it made old industrial properties almost impossible to sell. Wald, Trenton Acts to Weaken Industrial Cleanup Law, N.Y. Times, June 7, 1993, at B1.

B. GENERATORS

Liability of Generators (pp. 323-331). In General Electric Co. v. AAMCO Transmissions, Inc., 962 F.2d 281 (2d Cir. 1992), the Second Circuit refused to hold major oil companies liable under section 107(a)(3) as "arrangers" for the disposal of waste oil collected by the lessees of their service stations. The court rejected the argument that "arranger" liability should turn on whether a company has the ability or authority to control the waste disposal practices of another even if this authority has not been exercised. While noting that arranger liability can attach even to parties who do not have active involvement in "the timing, manner or location of disposal," the court stated that "there must be some nexus between the potentially responsible party and the disposal of the hazardous substance" that "is premised upon the potentially liable party's conduct with respect to the disposal or transport of hazardous wastes." Finding that "Congress employed traditional notions of duty and obligation in deciding which entities would be liable under CERCLA as arrangers for the disposal of hazardous substances," the court concluded that "it is the *obligation* to exercise control over hazardous waste disposal, and not the mere ability or opportunity to control the disposal of hazardous substances that makes an entity an arranger under CERCLA's liability provision." 962 F.2d at 286. The Second Circuit distinguished *Aceto* by noting that "the oil companies did not own the hazardous substance, nor did they control the process by which waste motor oil was generated." While noting that the oil companies may have encouraged dealers to buy virgin motor oil from them, the court found it significant that they did not require dealers to perform oil changes. A federal district court has held that even an oil company that did require its dealers to perform oil changes is not liable as an "arranger" under CERCLA so long as it did not attempt to control their disposal practices. United States v. Arrowhead Refining Co., 35 E.R.C. 2065 (D. Minn. 1992).

Efforts to convince the Ninth Circuit that the sale of material containing hazardous substances insulated the seller from generator liability were unsuccessful in two cases. In Catellus Development Corp. v. United States, 34 F.3d 748 (9th Cir. 1994), the court held that the seller of spent automotive batteries to a lead reclamation plant could be held liable for arranging for disposal or treatment. Noting that spent batteries would be considered a solid waste under RCRA, the court noted that "all that is necessary is that the [disposal or] treatment be inherent in the particular arrangement, even though the arranger does not retain control over its details." 34 F.3d at 753. See also Cadillac Fairview/California, Inc. v. United States, 41 F.3d 562 (9th Cir. 1994) (rubber companies who sold contaminated styrene back to chemical company supplier for reprocessing could be held liable as arrangers since the reprocessing required removal and release of hazardous substances).

In a case remarkably similar to *Aceto,* the Ninth Circuit has held that a company that hired a chemical formulator to process its chemicals, while retaining ownership of them, was liable for having "arranged for disposal" of chemicals released at the formulator's plant. Jones-Hamilton Co. v. Beazer Materials & Services, 973 F.2d 688 (9th Cir. 1992). The court noted that the contract between the chemical company and the formulator expressly made allowances for a 2-percent chemical loss due to "spillage or shrinkage" and that the chemical company's consultant had been present to help direct the formulator's operations. Unlike *Aceto,* where the government had brought suit, the plaintiff in *Beazer* was the chemical formulator, who brought a contribution action against the chemical company. Charging that its contract required the formulator to indemnify it for all violations of law, the chemical company countersued for indemnification. After taking notice of CERCLA's "truly murky" anti-indemnification provision in section 107(e)(1), the court upheld the indemnification clause of the contract, while noting that it probably

3. Waste Management and Pollution Prevention   Pages 331-334

only covered liability arising out of illegal acts by the formulator and not liability due to the acts of the chemical company itself.

CERCLA's Anti-Indemnification Provision: Section 107(e)(1) (p. 330). The anti-indemnification provision of CERCLA section 107(e)(1), mentioned above, seeks to prevent PRPs from escaping CERCLA liability by contract, while not discouraging companies from purchasing environmental insurance. It provides that "[n]o indemnification, hold harmless, or other similar agreement or conveyance shall be effective to transfer . . . from any person who may be liable for a release or threat of release under this section, to any other person the liability imposed under this section." But it then also provides that "[n]othing in this subsection shall bar any agreement to insure, hold harmless, or indemnify a party to such agreement for any liability under this section." While some courts have viewed these two sentences as contradictory, others have interpreted them to mean that although liability cannot be transferred away from a party liable under CERCLA, PRPs can insure against liability or indemnify each other for it by agreement among themselves. Beazer East, Inc. v. Mead Corp., 34 F.3d 206 (3d Cir. 1994); Joslyn Manufacturing Co. v. Koppers Co., 40 F.3d 750 (5th Cir. 1994); Harley-Davidson, Inc. v. Ministar, Inc., 41 F.3d 341 (7th Cir. 1994); Niecko v. Emro Marketing Co., 973 F.2d 1296 (6th Cir. 1992); AM International, Inc. v. International Forging Equipment Corp., 982 F.2d 989 (6th Cir. 1993) (CERCLA contribution action based on contract not barred, though plaintiff cannot escape CERCLA liability by contract).

Asbestos Abatement and CERCLA Section 104(a)(3)(B) (p. 330). In People v. Blech, 976 F.2d 525 (9th Cir. 1992), the Ninth Circuit rejected an effort by the State of California to recover the expenses of abating an asbestos hazard in state-leased buildings contaminated with asbestos dust as a result of a fire. Citing 3550 Stevens Creek Associates v. Barclays Bank of California, 915 F.2d 1355 (9th Cir. 1990), the court concluded that section 104(a)(3)(B) of CERCLA bars cost recovery by any party for responses to releases of products that are part of the structure of a building when "the resulting exposure is wholly within the structure." 976 F.2d at 527. The Eighth Circuit reached a similar result in Kane v. United States, 15 F.3d 87 (8th Cir. 1994).

Problem Exercise: CERCLA Liability (pp. 331-334). Figure S-3.1, a diagram of the ownership history of the facility owned initially by Industrial Concern, may help you to understand the Problem Exercise.

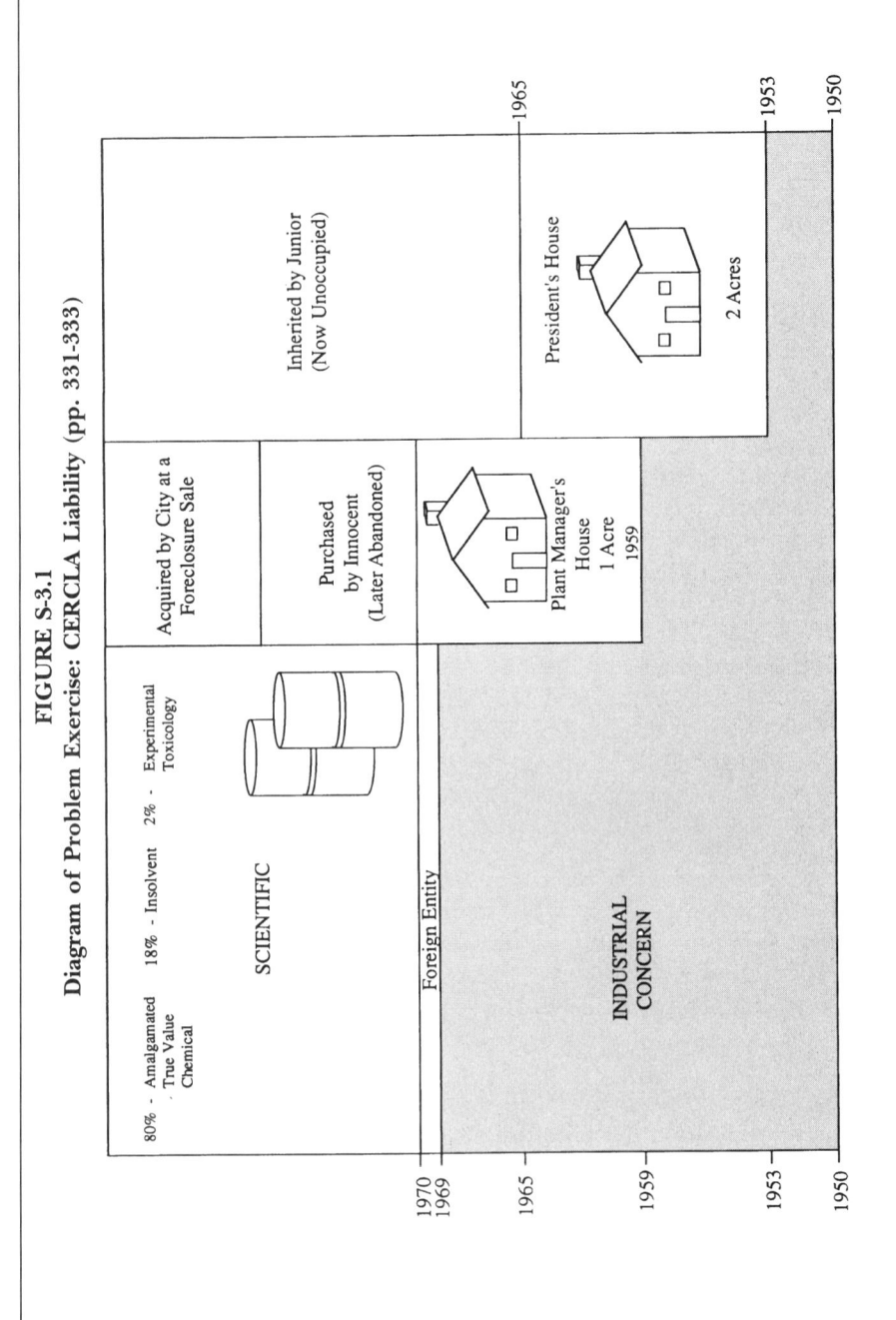

FIGURE S-3.1
Diagram of Problem Exercise: CERCLA Liability (pp. 331-333)

3. Waste Management and Pollution Prevention

C. How Expansively Should CERCLA's Liability Net Be Cast?

Liability of Transporters (p. 334). As noted in the parent text, §107(a)(4) premises transporter liability on the transporter's involvement in the selection of the site where a release occurs. In Tippins, Inc. v. USX Corp., 37 F.3d 87, 90 (3d Cir. 1994), the Third Circuit held that even if a transporter did not make the final decision concerning site selection, section 107(a)(4) "applies if the transporter's advice was a substantial contributing factor in the decision." The court determined that "a transporter selects the disposal facility when it actively and substantially participates in the decision-making process which ultimately identifies a facility for disposal." The transporter held liable in *Tippins* was a company that specialized in the transport and disposal of hazardous substances. The transporter surveyed alternative disposal sites, identified two candidate landfills that would accept the waste, and provided the generator with information concerning disposal costs at each. Although the generator ultimately chose between the two sites, the Third Circuit held the transporter liable because of its substantial participation in the site selection process.

In Kaiser Aluminum & Chemical Corp. v. Catellus Development Corp., 976 F.2d 1338 (9th Cir. 1992), a contractor who excavated contaminated soil and spread it over uncontaminated portions of a site was held liable as a transporter of hazardous substances under section 107(a)(4) of CERCLA. The court rejected arguments that transporter liability could not attach unless the substances were taken to another site. "Whether a transporter moves hazardous material from one parcel of land to another, or whether he simply takes the material from a contaminated area of the same parcel, he has spread the contamination." 976 F.2d at 1343. The court found "no logical basis" for transporter liability "to hinge solely on whether he moves hazardous substances across a recognized property boundary." Id.

Lender Liability After **Fleet Factors** *(pp. 343-345).* EPA published its lender liability interpretive rule in April 1992, a portion of which is reproduced below.

> **Lender Liability Under CERCLA**
> 40 C.F.R. pt. 300, As Amended, 57
> Fed. Reg. 18,344 (April 29, 1992)

§300.1100 Security interest exemption. . . .

(c) *Participation in Management Defined.* The term *participating in the management of a vessel or facility* means that the holder is engaging in acts of facility or vessel management, as defined herein.

(1) *Actions That Are Participation in Management.* Participation in the management of a facility means, for the purpose of section 101(20)(A), actual participation in the management or operational affairs of the vessel or facility by the holder, and does not include the mere capacity to influence, or ability to influence, or the unexercised right to control facility operations. A holder is participating in management, while the borrower is still in possession of the vessel or facility encumbered by the security interest, only if the holder either:

(i) Exercises decisionmaking control over the borrower's environmental compliance, such that the holder has undertaken responsibility for the borrower's hazardous substance handling or disposal practices; or

(ii) Exercises control at a level comparable to that of a manager of the borrower's enterprise, such that the holder has assumed or manifested responsibility for the overall management of the enterprise encompassing the day-to-day decisionmaking of the enterprise with respect to:

(A) Environmental compliance or

(B) All, or substantially all, of the operational (as opposed to financial or administrative) aspects of the enterprise other than environmental compliance. Operational aspects . . . include functions such as that of facility or plant manager, operations manager, chief operating officer, or chief executive officer. Financial or administrative aspects include functions such as that of credit manager, accounts payable/receivable manager, personnel manager, controller, chief financial officer, or similar functions.

(2) *Actions That Are Not Participation in Management—*

(i) *Actions at the Inception of the Loan or Other Transaction.* No act or omission prior to the time that indicia of ownership are held primarily to protect a security interest constitutes evidence of participation in management within the meaning of section 101(20)(A). A prospective holder who undertakes or requires an

3. Waste Management and Pollution Prevention   Pages 343-345

environmental inspection of the vessel or facility in which indicia of ownership are to be held, or requires a prospective borrower to clean up a vessel or facility or to comply or come into compliance (whether prior or subsequent to the time that indicia of ownership are held primarily to protect a security interest) with any applicable law or regulation, is not by such action considered to be participating in the vessel or facility's management. Neither the statute nor this regulation requires a holder to conduct or require an inspection to qualify for the exemption, and the liability of a holder cannot be based on or affected by the holder not conducting or not requiring an inspection.

(ii) *Policing and Workout.* Actions that are consistent with holding ownership indicia primarily to protect a security interest do not constitute participation in management for purposes of section 101(20)(A) of CERCLA. The authority for the holder to take such actions may, but need not, be contained in contractual or other documents specifying requirements for financial, environmental, and other warranties, covenants, conditions, representations or promises from the borrower. Loan policing and workout activities cover and include all activities up to foreclosure and its equivalents, as provided in 40 CFR 300.1100(d)(1).

(A) *Policing the Security Interest or Loan.* A holder who engages in policing activities prior to foreclosure will remain within the exemption provided that the holder does not by such actions participate in the management of the vessel or facility as provided in 40 CFR 300.1100(c)(1). Such actions include, but are not limited to, requiring the borrower to clean up the vessel or facility during the term of the security interest; requiring the borrower to comply or come into compliance with applicable federal, state, and local environmental and other laws, rules and regulations during the term of the security interest; securing or exercising authority to monitor or inspect the vessel or facility (including on-site inspections) in which indicia of ownership are maintained, or the borrower's business or financial condition during the term of the security interest; or taking other actions to adequately police the loan or security interest (such as requiring a borrower to comply with any warranties, covenants, conditions, representations or promises from the borrower).

(B) *Work Out.* A holder who engages in work out activities prior to foreclosure and its equivalents will remain within the exemption provided that the holder does not by such action participate in the management of the vessel or facility as provided in 40 CFR 300.1100(c)(1). For purposes of this rule, "work out" refers to those actions by which a holder, at any time prior to foreclosure and its equivalents, seeks to prevent, cure, or mitigate a default by the borrower or obligor; or to preserve, or prevent the diminution of, the value of the security. Work out activities include, but are not limited to, restructuring or renegotiating the terms of the security interest; requiring payment of additional rent or interest; exercising forbearance; requiring or exercising rights pursuant to an assignment of accounts or other amounts owing to an obligor; requiring or exercising rights pursuant to an escrow agreement pertaining to amounts owing to an obligor; providing specific or general financial or other advice, suggestions, counseling, or guidance; and exercising any right or remedy the holder is entitled to by law or under any warranties, covenants, conditions, representations or promises from the borrower.

(iii) *Actions Taken Under CERCLA section 107(d)(1)*. Notwithstanding 40 CFR 300.1100(c)(1), a holder does not participate in the management of a vessel or facility by taking any response action under section 107(d)(1) of CERCLA or under the direction of an on-scene coordinator.

NOTES AND QUESTIONS

1. What result in *Fleet Factors* itself if the new interpretive rule had been applicable? See United States v. Fleet Factors Corp., 819 F. Supp. 1079 (S.D. Ga. 1993).

2. EPA's lender liability rule initially was treated as authoritative in several cases. Ashland Oil v. Sonford Products Corp., 810 F. Supp. 1057 (D. Minn. 1993) (lender who helped sell a contaminated site on which it had foreclosed is not liable under CERCLA); Kelley v. Tiscornia, 810 F. Supp. 901 (W. D. Mich. 1993) (bank that appointed two members of borrower's board of directors and that required daily financial reports not liable as an "operator" of borrower's facility under CERCLA absent actual participation in management). In other cases courts reached decisions that were consistent with EPA's rule without expressly relying upon it. United States v. McLamb, 3 F.3d 69 (4th Cir. 1993) (security interest exemption in CERCLA exempts foreclosing bank from liability even though the bank owned the property for several months after foreclosure). However, in Kelley v. EPA, 15 F.3d 1100 (D.C. Cir. 1994), a D.C. Circuit panel, by a 2-to-1 vote, struck down the lender liability regulations on the ground that CERCLA did not delegate to EPA the authority to define through regulation the scope of liability under section 107.

3. The court majority in *Kelley* acknowledged that EPA has author-

3. Waste Management and Pollution Prevention

ity to promulgate a national contingency plan under §105 of CERCLA and to reimburse private parties who undertake cleanup pursuant to EPA administrative orders issued under section 106(a). However, the court held that Congress intended only for the judiciary, and not EPA, to determine liability issues under section 107. In dissent, Judge Mikva argued that because CERCLA's secured lender exemption was ambiguous, EPAs interpretation of it should be entitled to judicial deference under *Chevron.*

4. In response to the *Kelley* decision, EPA is treating the lender liability regulations as though they remain in effect as a policy statement while the agency works to incorporate them in a guidance document to govern agency enforcement proceedings. Noah, EPA Plans Rules to Limit Liability of Superfund Sites, Wall St. J., Jan. 26, 1995, at A5. While EPA's interpretation of lender liability can be used to guide the agency's exercise of enforcement discretion, in light of the *Kelley* decision, what deference, if any, should reviewing courts give to it in private cost recovery actions?

5. In Northeast Doran, Inc. v. Key Bank, 15 F.3d 1 (1st Cir. 1994), the First Circuit held that CERCLA's secured lender exception exempts from liability as an "owner" even a foreclosing mortgagee who had been informed of environmental contamination on the property but who chose not to disclose it to prospective purchasers before the property was auctioned.

Liability of Successor Corporations (p. 345). To prevent corporations from evading liabilities by changing their ownership, successor corporations have been held liable under CERCLA. The Fourth and the Eighth Circuits recently have joined the Third, Sixth, and Ninth Circuits in holding that corporate successors are "persons" within the meaning of CERCLA section 107. United States v. Carolina Transformer Co., 978 F.2d 832 (4th Cir. 1992); United States v. Mexico Feed and Seed Co., Inc, 980 F.2d 478 (8th Cir. 1992). Applying the traditional exceptions to the rule that an asset purchaser does not acquire the liabilities of an asset seller, the courts have held that an asset purchaser can be held liable if it (1) "expressly or impliedly agrees to assume the liability," (2) the transaction is a "de facto" consolidation or merger, (3) the purchaser "is merely a continuation of the selling corporation," or (4) the "transaction was fraudulently entered into in order to escape liability." 980 F.2d at 487. Some courts also have applied a "continuity of enterprise" theory or "substantial continuity approach," under which a successor can be held liable based on consideration of factors such as whether it employs the same employees and supervisors, uses the same production facility, and manufactures the same product. 978 F.2d at 839.

Liability of State and Local Governments (pp. 345-348). The potential liability of state and local governments under CERCLA continues to generate great concern and proposals for legislative amendments. A federal district court contributed to that concern when it held that the State of Pennsylvania may be held liable for contamination of a creek under CERCLA because the state holds title to the creek bed. Union Gas Co. v. Pennsylvania, 35 ERC 1750 (E.D. Pa. 1992). Faced with a somewhat similar claim, a federal court in California has held that a county can assert a valid third-party defense under section 107(b)(3) to avoid CERCLA liability as the owner of sewers and wells from which a contaminant was released. Lincoln Properties, Ltd. v. Higgins, 36 E.R.C. 1217 (E.D. Calif. 1992).

Municipalities continue to be concerned about their potential liability as "arrangers for disposal" of garbage. More than 650 counties and municipalities in 12 states have been faced with contribution claims. Steinzor, The Reauthorization of Superfund: Can the Deal of the Century Be Saved? 25 Envtl. L. Rep. 10,009, 10,022 (1995). This has generated several proposals to limit the CERCLA liability of municipalities. While EPA abandoned an effort to adopt regulations limiting municipal liability, bills to restrict the ability of PRPs to bring contribution actions against local governments and to limit municipal liability have been introduced in both houses of Congress. The consensus Superfund reauthorization legislation that nearly was enacted in 1994 would have limited the liability of all public and private parties that sent municipal solid waste to a Superfund site to ten percent of total cleanup costs. Id. at 10023.

On remand from the Second Circuit, the district court hearing the *Murtha* case ultimately rejected the industry PRPs' effort to join more than a thousand homeowners and small businesses as defendants in contribution actions. The court held that the companies could not rely on generic statistical studies to show the likely presence of hazardous substances in the homeowners' waste, but rather had to prove that the waste actually contained such substances. The mere fact that household waste may contain items made with hazardous substances was not a sufficient basis for finding that disposal of such waste constitutes disposal of a hazardous substance. B.F. Goodrich Co. v. Murtha, 840 F. Supp. 180 (D. Conn. 1993); for a list of the 1,151 parties the industrial PRPs sought to join see the appendices to B.F. Goodrich Co. v. Murtha, 815 F. Supp. 539, 547-561 (D. Conn. 1993).

Settlements and Contribution (pp. 348-350). EPA has greatly expanded its use of de minimis settlements under CERCLA. In fiscal year 1994, the agency completed 42 de minimis settlements with more than

3. Waste Management and Pollution Prevention   Pages 350-351

4,000 parties at 38 different NPL sites. During the previous 13 years, the agency had reached de minimis settlements with approximately 6,000 parties. Administrative Improvement Initiative Leads to Settlements with 4,000 De Minimis Parties, 25 Env. Rep. 1221 (1994).

In actions for contribution under section 113(f) of CERCLA, courts may allocate liability for response costs on the basis of equitable considerations. As explained by the Seventh Circuit in Kerr-McGee Chemical Corp. v. Lefton Iron & Metal Co., 14 F.3d 321 (7th Cir. 1994), these include the relative fault of the parties, relevant "Gore factors" (named after an unsuccessful amendment to CERCLA offered by then Congressman Al Gore), and any contracts between that parties that bear on the allocation of cleanup costs. The Gore factors include: (1) the ability of the parties to demonstrate that their contribution can be distinguished, (2) the amount of the hazardous substance involved, (3) the degree of toxicity of the hazardous substance, (4) the degree of involvement by the parties in generation, transportation, treatment, storage, or disposal, (5) the degree of care exercised by the parties taking into account the characteristics of the hazardous substance, and (6) the degree of cooperation by the parties with government officials to prevent harm. These factors are neither an exhaustive nor a complete list of the considerations courts may take into account in allocating liability. Courts are not required to make pro rata assessments of contribution when one party is primarily at fault. Thus, in Environmental Transportation Systems v. Ensco, Inc., 969 F.2d 503, 508-509 (7th Cir. 1992), the Seventh Circuit held that a trucking company that had dumped a shipment of transformers containing PCBs could not recover in a contribution action against the utility that owned the transformers because the accident had been the fault of the trucking company.

6. *Response Costs and Damages to Natural Resources*

Recovery of Response Costs (pp. 350-351). As discussed in the text, when the government is the party seeking to recover response costs, defendants bear the burden of showing that the response actions are not consistent with the NCP. In United States v. Hardage, 982 F.2d 1436, 1442 (10th Cir. 1992), the Tenth Circuit held that even if a defendant can show that particular response costs were excessive or unreasonable, the government is entitled to recover them unless the action that generated the costs is shown to have been inconsistent with the NCP. The court emphasized that the language of section 107(a)(4)(A) permits recovery of "*all* costs of removal or remedial action incurred . . . not inconsistent with the [NCP]." In Daigle v. Shell Oil Co., 972 F.2d 1527 (10th Cir. 1992), the Tenth Circuit held that persons exposed to hazardous substance releases cannot recover medical monitoring expenses as response costs under section 107(a). In Price v. United States Navy, 39 F.3d 1011 (9th Cir. 1994), the Ninth Circuit also held that medical monitoring costs were not recoverable as response costs under CERCLA. In Key Tronic Corp. v. United States, 114 S. Ct. 1960 (1994), the Supreme Court resolved a split in the circuits by holding that attorney's fees incurred in CERCLA cost recovery actions were not recoverable as "necessary costs of response" within the meaning of §107(a)(4)(B). The Court did permit recovery of fees pertaining to attorneys' activities to identify other potentially responsible parties because these actions significantly benefited the cleanup effort and promoted statutory purposes unrelated to reallocation of costs.

Calculating Natural Resource Damages (pp. 359-362). In March 1994 the Department of Interior issued final rules governing assessment of natural resources damages in cases of major oil spills or releases of hazardous substances ("Type B" regulations). 59 Fed. Reg. 14,261 (1994). In December 1994 the Department proposed revisions to its regulations governing assessment of natural resource damages for small releases ("Type A" regulations). 59 Fed. Reg. 63,300 (1994).

Settlements of Natural Resource Damages Claims (pp. 362-363). In Alaska Sport Fishing Association v. Exxon Corp., 34 F.3d 769 (9th Cir. 1994), the Ninth Circuit held that Exxon's settlement of natural resource damages claims with the federal and state governments (see parent text, p. 362) barred private parties from recovering such damages. The court interpreted the Department of Interior's damage assessment regulations as allowing the government to recover for all loss of use and enjoyment of natural resources on behalf of the public from the time of a release until full restoration of the resources. Thus, it rejected the fishers' claims that Exxon's settlement with the government had provided damages only for residual injury to the resources.

E. REMEDIATION OF ENVIRONMENTAL CONTAMINATION UNDER CERCLA AND RCRA

1. The CERCLA Cleanup Process

NPL Listing Decisions (pp. 364-365). Challenges to EPA's listing of sites on Superfund's National Priorities List (NPL) have been success-

3. Waste Management and Pollution Prevention   Pages 368-370

ful in several cases. NPL listing decisions have been overturned by the U.S. Court of Appeals for the D.C. Circuit due to problems with the evidence EPA relied on in listing the sites or because of irregularities in the procedures EPA used. See Tex Tin Corp. v. EPA, 992 F.2d 353 (D.C. Cir. 1993); National Gypsum Co. v. EPA, 968 F.2d 40 (D.C. Cir. 1992); Anne Arundel County, Maryland v. EPA, 963 F.2d 412 (D.C. Cir. 1992); Kent County, Delaware Levy Court v. EPA, 963 F.2d 391 (D.C. Cir. 1992). In other cases, EPA's listing decisions were upheld. Apache Powder Co. v. United States, 968 F.2d 66 (D.C. Cir. 1992); Bradley Mining Co. v. EPA, 972 F.2d 1356 (D.C. Cir. 1992).

Progress of Superfund Cleanups (pp. 366-368). In October 1992, one year after EPA Administrator William Reilly announced plans to revitalize the Superfund cleanup program, EPA claimed that it had made substantial progress. Revitalization Program One Year Later: Mix of Better Management, "Coming of Age," 23 Env. Rep. 1497 (1992). EPA has now developed what it calls "a new Superfund paradigm," the Superfund Accelerated Cleanup Model (SACM), which is designed to speed up the cleanup process. EPA Memorandum to Regions on Superfund Program Priorities for 1993, 23 Env. Rep. 2670 (1993).

As of March 1995 there were 1,238 sites on the NPL. Clean-up construction had been completed at 282 sites.

Superfund Reauthorization (pp. 368-370). Superfund has become the environmental program that everyone loves to hate. President Clinton's statement in his first Address to Congress in February 1993 that he would "like to use that Superfund to clean up pollution for a change and not just pay lawyers" drew loud applause. A study by the Rand Corporation's Institute for Civil Justice provides one perspective on lawyers' costs: It found that only 12 percent of the monies paid by insurance companies on CERCLA claims paid for cleanup costs; the remainder went toward transactions costs, including the costs of litigation and administration. Elsewhere, however, the study's findings were different. For large industrial concerns, for instance, 78 percent of Superfund expenditures paid for cleanup, while only 21 percent was spent on transactions costs, with three-fourths of that amount going to attorneys. Some observers have interpreted these data to suggest that insurance companies' own hardball litigation tactics have generated a major share of their transactions costs.

Reports on virtually all aspects of the program continue to accumulate as study groups under many different auspices pore over every conceivable aspect of Superfund, always with a view toward recommending changes in the program. In addition to the transactions costs studies, major areas of empirical study include the processes for designating NPL sites and for choosing remediation measures; the efficacy of different remediation measures; the correlation between site priorities, remediation measures, human risk exposure, and the desirability of the measures chosen. For a review of the site and remedy selection processes and citations to reports on the efficacy of different remediation measures, see Ferris and Rees, CERCLA Remedy Selection: Abandoning the Quick Fix Mentality, 21 Ecology L.Q. 785 (1994).

While all aspects of the process have drawn criticism, our inability to develop remediation methods that can actually restore contaminated groundwater to a condition suitable to beneficial uses has been particularly frustrating to both those footing the bill for clean up and those wishing that Superfund live up to its remediation ambitions. A major source of the difficulties in cleaning groundwater are attributable to nonaqueous phase liquids that are heavier than water and which can be absorbed into solid layers surrounding underground aquifers, where they remain highly resistant to removal and yet capable of continuing to contaminate those aquifers through molecular absorption back into the aquifers. It now appears that currently known technologies may be incapable of remediating to contaminant levels required by Superfund standards where nonaqueous phase liquids are present, as they are highly likely to be wherever chemical usage in the area was appreciable and disposal practices consistent with industry customs that prevailed until very recently. See Ferris and Rees at 829-835.

EPA has sponsored research underway to evaluate the risks associated with Superfund sites, and some preliminary results from that ongoing effort have been published. See Hamilton and Viscusi, Human Health Risk Assessments for Superfund, 21 Ecology L.Q. 573 (1994). After a comprehensive analysis of the risk assessment information considered in 78 recent RODs, Hamilton and Viscusi conclude that as between existing risks and future risks, future risks account for over 90 percent of the risk-weighted pathways for the sites in their sample. "Chief among these future risks is the projection that future residents will reside on sites that are not currently residential." Id. at 608. Findings such as these will fuel the ongoing debate over whether site usage controls should play a more prominent role than they have in remediation decisions.

The anticipated expiration of the Superfund tax in 1995 put Superfund reauthorization on the agenda for the 103d Congress. In an effort to influence the reauthorization outcome, an unusual consortium of private parties with significant interests in Superfund came together as the National Commission on Superfund. The Commission did in fact produce a consensus reauthorization proposal, which, after some negotiations, was endorsed by the Clinton Administration. The consensus proposal contained major modifications with respect to cleanup

3. Waste Management and Pollution Prevention   Pages 368-370

standards that retained a national health-based focus, but incorporated adjustments in response to site-specific considerations, including future land use, as well as recognizing technological infeasibility in the remediation selection process. With respect to liability, the consensus proposal would have retained strict, joint, and several liability as the standard in an ultimate judicial resolution, but it also would have provided an attractive prelitigation settlement option to PRPs that would authorize individual assigned shares based on equitable standards identified in the legislation—in effect, offering each PRP a way to resolve its own "several" liability at the outset. For a description of the consensus proposal, see Steinzor, The Reauthorization of Superfund: Can the Deal of the Century Be Saved?, 25 Envtl. L. Rep. 10,009 (1995).

Although the package had broad bipartisan support, it also contained plenty of individual pieces that did not completely satisfy specific constituencies. Because the legislative package did not take form until mid-1994, there proved to be too little legislative time to work through all the points of opposition before the Congress adjourned in October, 1994, for the fall elections, and the legislation failed to get through the Congress. In the closing weeks, disagreements arose over wage rates for work at Superfund sites, groundwater cleanup standards, cost-benefit requirements for cleanups, and insurance company liability. Representative Al Swift (D-Wash), chair of the House subcommittee with jurisdiction over the bill, said he thought "the epitaph should read that it died from too many people wanting a little more . . . whether labor protection, risk assessment, or groundwater [and] that elasticity wasn't there." Superfund: Time Restraints, Wrangling Kill Reform Bill; New Effort to Change CERCLA Promised Next Year, 25 Env. Rep. 1172 (1994).

Several studies by Resources for the Future bring some additional perspective to Rep. Swift's epitaph. The first study examined five different options for CERCLA's liability structure, and whether changes in the status quo would speed up cleanup operations. K. Probst and P. Portney, Assigning Liability for Superfund Cleanups: An Analysis of Policy Options (1992). The study analyzed five alternatives: (1) the status quo; (2) expanding mixed funding for the "orphan shares" of response costs caused by insolvent or recalcitrant parties; (3) releasing PRPs from liability for all sites that accepted both municipal and industrial waste and that were closed at the time CERCLA is amended; (4) releasing PRPs from liability for all sites where waste disposal operations had ceased before January 1, 1981; and (5) releasing PRPs from liability for sites currently on the NPL, relying upon tax monies to fund the entire cleanup. The study finds that "while it is unarguable that changing the liability standards would speed cleanup, it is less clear whether that is the most promising way" to do so. Id. at ix. It cautions that "[a]ny alternative that eliminates Superfund liability for a subset of sites could diminish—if not eliminate—the current incentives PRPs face both to clean up sites not on the NPL, and also to carefully handle hazardous substances not regulated under other statutes." Moreover, it concludes that any modifications to the existing liability scheme will create some new inequities, even as they seek to ameliorate old ones. For example,

> Those PRPs who have already stepped forward and begun to pay for cleanups at sites like those to be released from liability under Options 2 through 5 would be unfairly treated if, as we suspect is likely, they are not reimbursed for the costs they have incurred. This potential inequity would carry with it a very important incentive effect: the message that it may not be wise to comply immediately with environmental laws because, if one hangs back and waits, the law may be changed.

Id. at 46.

In 1995, a second study, cosponsored by RFF and Brookings, examined additional issues raised by these different financing options. K. Probst et al., Footing the Bill for Superfund Cleanups: Who Pays and How? (1995). This study finds a difference of less than four percent between total costs of cleanup under the most expensive option as compared to the least expensive option. This small difference in total costs, however, hides dramatic differences in which companies and industries pay, and how much. "This helps explain why responsible parties find it worth spending time and money to influence the congressional debate."

2. *RCRA Corrective Action Requirements*

RCRA Corrective Action (pp. 370-373). In January 1993, EPA issued a final rule that eased requirements for handling wastes involved in RCRA corrective actions by permitting "remediation wastes" to be managed in a manner less stringent than otherwise would be required by RCRA's land disposal ban. 58 Fed. Reg. 31,114 (1993). The rule defines "remediation wastes" as "all solid and hazardous wastes, and all media (including ground water, surface water, soils and sediments) and debris that contain listed hazardous wastes, or which themselves exhibit a hazardous waste characteristic, that are managed at a facility for the purpose of implementing [RCRA] corrective action requirements."

3. **Waste Management and Pollution Prevention   Pages 384-406**

F. FUTURE OF WASTE MANAGEMENT

1. *The Search for Disposal Alternatives*

Commerce Clause Limitations (pp. 384-406). The existing material on these pages can be replaced with the following.

In 1978, the Supreme Court held that household garbage was "commerce" within the meaning of the Commerce Clause and that New Jersey's attempt to preserve landfill capacity in the state for New Jersey garbage was unconstitutional. Philadelphia v. New Jersey [page 384]. In 1992, the Supreme Court reaffirmed and extended the central holding of Philadelphia v. New Jersey in two separate decisions. The first, Chemical Waste Management v. Hunt, 112 S. Ct. 2009 (1992) (overruling Hunt v. Chemical Waste Management, Inc., 584 So. 2d 1367 (Ala. 1991) [p. 403]), addressed the latest effort of Alabama to close its borders to out-of-state *hazardous* waste being shipped into the hazardous waste facility run by ChemWaste at Emelle, Alabama.

After the volume of out-of-state waste shipped to Emelle increased dramatically (as noted in the text, p. 383), Alabama first responded by enacting a ban on the importation of hazardous waste into the state. This statute was declared unconstitutional. National Solid Wastes Management Association v. Alabama, 910 F.2d 713 (11th Cir. 1990) [p. 396]. In April 1990, the Alabama legislature, sullied but unbowed, enacted new legislation that (a) imposed a "base fee" of $25.60 per ton on all hazardous wastes disposed of in the state, regardless of state of origin; (b) imposed an "additional fee" of $72.00 per ton on all out-of-state waste disposed of in the state; and (c) placed a cap on the amount that could be disposed of in any Alabama facility in any one-year period. The cap provision applies to all facilities that dispose of over 100,000 tons per year. Alabama has only one such facility: Emelle.

Accompanying these provisions were a number of detailed legislative findings, including the following:

> (8) Since hazardous wastes and substances generated in the state compose a small proportion of those materials disposed of at commercial disposal sites located in the state, present circumstances result in the state's citizens paying a disproportionate share of the costs of regulation of hazardous waste transportation, spill cleanup and commercial disposal facilities. Persons, firms or corporations which generate and dispose of such waste and substances in Alabama presently are among the taxpaying citizens of this state who must bear the burden of regulation, inspection, control and clean-up of hazardous waste sites; addressing the public health problems created by the presence of such facilities in the state; and, preserving

this state's environment while those generating this waste in other states and shipping it to Alabama for disposal presently are not. This act attempts to resolve that inequity by requiring all generators of waste being disposed of in Alabama to share in that financial burden.

Ala. Act No. 90-326, §S1, Code §S22-30B-1.1 Legislative Findings.

Emelle's owner and operator, Chemical Waste Management, challenged the statute through the state court system, and ultimately to the United States Supreme Court, which issued the following opinion.

Chemical Waste Management, Inc. v. Hunt
112 S. Ct. 2009 (1992)

JUSTICE WHITE delivered the opinion of the Court.

II

No State may attempt to isolate itself from a problem common to the several States by raising barriers to the free flow of interstate trade.[3] Today . . . we adhere[] to our decision in Philadelphia v. New Jersey, 437 U.S. 617 (1978), where we found New Jersey's prohibition of solid waste from outside that State to amount to economic protectionism barred by the Commerce Clause:

> [T]he evil of protectionism can reside in legislative means as well as legislative ends. Thus, it does not matter whether the ultimate aim of ch. 363 is to reduce the waste disposal costs of New Jersey residents or to save remaining open lands from pollution, for we assume New Jersey has every right to protect its residents' pocketbooks as well as their environment. And it may be assumed as well that New Jersey may pursue those ends by slowing the flow of all waste into the State's remaining landfills, even though interstate commerce may incidentally be affected. But whatever New Jersey's ultimate purpose, it may not be accompanied by discriminating against articles of commerce coming from outside the State unless there is some reason, apart from their origin, to treat them differently.

---

3. [W]hether the business arrangements between out-of-state-generators of hazardous waste and the Alabama operator of a hazardous waste landfill are viewed as "sales" of hazardous waste or "purchases" of transportation and disposal services, "the commercial transactions unquestionably have an interstate character. The Commerce Clause thus imposes some constraints on [Alabama's] ability to regulate these transactions." *Fort Gratiot Sanitary Landfill*, 112 S. Ct. at 2023.

3. Waste Management and Pollution Prevention   Pages 384-406

Both on its face and in its plain effect, ch. 363 violates this principle of nondiscrimination.

"The Court has consistently found parochial legislation of this kind to be constitutionally invalid, whether the ultimate aim of the legislation was to assure a steady supply of milk by erecting barriers to allegedly ruinous outside competition, or to create jobs by keeping industry within the State, or to preserve the State's financial resources from depletion by fencing out indigent immigrants." *Fort Gratiot Sanitary Landfill,* 112 S. Ct. at 2024 (quoting Philadelphia v. New Jersey, supra, at 626-627).

To this list may be added cases striking down a tax discriminating against interstate commerce, even where such tax was designed to encourage the use of ethanol and thereby reduce harmful exhaust emissions, New Energy Co. of Ind. v. Limbach, 486 U.S. 269, 279 (1988), or to support inspection of foreign cement to ensure structural integrity, Hale v. Bimco Trading, Inc., 306 U.S. 375, 379-380 (1939). For in all of these cases, "a presumably legitimate goal was sought to be achieved by the illegitimate means of isolating the State from the national economy." Philadelphia v. New Jersey, supra, at 627.

The Act's additional fee facially discriminates against hazardous waste generated in States other than Alabama, and the Act overall has plainly discouraged the full operation of petitioner's Emelle facility.[4] Such burdensome taxes imposed on interstate commerce alone are generally forbidden: "[A] State may not tax a transaction or incident more heavily when it crosses state lines than when it occurs entirely within the State." Once a state tax is found to discriminate against out-of-state commerce, it is typically struck down without further inquiry.

The State, however, argues that the additional fee imposed on out-of-state hazardous waste serves legitimate local purposes related to its citizens' health and safety. Because the additional fee discriminates both on its face and in practical effect, the burden falls on the State "to justify it both in terms of the local benefits flowing from the statute and the unavailability of nondiscriminatory alternatives adequate to preserve the local interests at stake." Hunt v. Washington Apple Advertising Comm'n, 432 U.S. 333, 353 (1977). "At a minimum such facial discrimination invokes the strictest scrutiny of any purported legitimate local purpose and of the absence of nondiscriminatory alternatives." Hughes v. Oklahoma, 441 U.S. 322, 337 (1979).[5]

---

4. The act went into effect July 15, 1990. The volume of hazardous waste buried at the Emelle facility fell dramatically from 791,000 tons in 1989 to 290,000 tons in 1991.

5. To some extent the State attempts to avail itself of the more flexible approach outlined in, e.g., Brown-Forman Distillers Corp v. New York State Liquor Auth., 476 U.S. 573, 579 (1986), and Pike v. Bruce Church, Inc., 397 U.S. 137, 142 (1970), but this lesser scrutiny is only available "where other

135

The State's argument here does not significantly differ from the Alabama Supreme Court's conclusions on the legitimate local purposes of the additional fee imposed, which were:

> The Additional Fee serves these legitimate local purposes that cannot be adequately served by reasonable nondiscriminatory alternatives: (1) protection of the health and safety of the citizens of Alabama from toxic substances; (2) conservation of the environment and the state's natural resources; (3) provision for compensatory revenue for the costs and burdens that out-of-state waste generators impose by dumping their hazardous waste in Alabama; (4) reduction of the overall flow of wastes traveling on the state's highways, which flow creates a great risk to the health and safety of the state's citizens.

584 So. 2d, at 1389.

These may all be legitimate local interests, and petitioner has not attacked them. But only rhetoric, and not explanation, emerges as to why Alabama targets only interstate hazardous waste to meet these goals. As found by the Trial Court, "although the Legislature imposed an additional fee of $72.00 per ton on waste generated outside Alabama, there is absolutely no evidence before this Court that waste generated outside Alabama is more dangerous than waste generated in Alabama. The Court finds under the facts of this case that the only basis for the additional fee is the origin of the waste." In the face of such findings, invalidity under the Commerce Clause necessarily follows, for "whatever [Alabama's] ultimate purpose, it may not be accomplished by discriminating against articles of commerce coming from outside the State unless there is some reason, apart from their origin, to treat them differently." Philadelphia v. New Jersey, 437 U. S., at 626-627. The burden is on the State to show that "the discrimination is demonstrably justified by a valid factor unrelated to economic protectionism,"[6] and it has not carried this burden.

---

legislative objectives are credibly advanced and there is no patent discrimination against interstate trade." We find no room here to say that the Act presents "effects upon interstate commerce that are only incidental," for the Act's additional fee on its face targets only out-of-state hazardous waste. While no "clear line" separates close cases on which scrutiny should apply, "this is not a close case." Wyoming v. Oklahoma, 502 U.S.—, —, n. 12 (1992).

6. The Alabama Supreme Court found no "economic protectionism" here, and thus purported to distinguish Philadelphia v. New Jersey, based on its conclusions that the legislature was motivated by public health and environmental concerns. 584 So. 2d 1367, 1388-1389 (1991). This narrow focus on the intended consequence of the additional fee does not conform to our precedents, for "[a] finding that state legislation constitutes economic protectionism" may be made on the basis of either discriminatory purpose, or discriminatory effect.

3. Waste Management and Pollution Prevention   Pages 384-406

Ultimately, the State's concern focuses on the volume of the waste entering the Emelle facility. Less discriminatory alternatives, however, are available to alleviate this concern, not the least of which are a generally applicable per-ton additional fee on all hazardous waste disposed of within Alabama, or a per-mile tax on all vehicles transporting hazardous waste across Alabama roads, or an evenhanded cap on the total tonnage landfilled at Emelle, which would curtail volume from all sources. To the extent Alabama's concern touches environmental conservation and the health and safety of its citizens, such concern does not vary with the point of origin of the waste, and it remains within the State's power to monitor and regulate more closely the transportation and disposal of all hazardous waste within its borders. Even with the possible future financial and environmental risks to be borne by Alabama, such risks likewise do not vary with the waste's State of origin in a way allowing foreign, but not local, waste to be burdened.[9] In sum, we find the additional fee to be "an obvious effort to saddle those outside the State" with most of the burden of slowing the flow of waste into the Emelle facility. "That legislative effort is clearly impermissible under the Commerce Clause of the Constitution."

Our decisions regarding quarantine laws do not counsel a different conclusion. The Act's additional fee may not legitimately be deemed a quarantine law because Alabama permits both the generation and landfilling of hazardous waste within its borders and the importation of still more hazardous waste subject to payment of the additional fee. In any event, while it is true that certain quarantine laws have not been considered forbidden protectionist measures, even though directed against out-of-state commerce, those laws "did not discriminate against interstate commerce as such, but simply prevented traffic in noxious articles, whatever their origin." Philadelphia v. New Jersey, supra, at 629.[11] As the Court has stated in Guy v. Baltimore, 100 U.S., at 443:

---

9. The State presents no argument here, as it did below, that the additional fee makes out-of-state generators pay their "fair share" of the costs of Alabama waste disposal facilities, or that the additional fee is justified as a "compensatory tax." The Trial Court rejected these arguments.

11. "The hostility is to the thing itself, not to merely interstate shipments of the thing; and an undiscriminating hostility is at least nondiscriminatory. But that is not the case here. The State of Illinois is quite willing to allow the storage and even the shipment for storage of spent nuclear fuel in Illinois, provided only that its origin is intrastate." Illinois v. General Elec. Co., 683 F.2d 206, 214 (CA7 1982), cert. denied, 461 U.S. 913 (1983); cf. Oregon-Washington Co. v. Washington, supra, 270 U.S., at 96, 46 S. Ct., at 282: Inspection followed by quarantine of hay from fields infested with weevils is "a real quarantine law, and not a mere inhibition against importation of alfalfa from a large part of the country without regard to the condition which might make its importation dangerous."

In the exercise of its police powers, a State may exclude from its territory, or prohibit the sale therein, of any articles which, in its judgment, fairly exercised, are prejudicial to the health or which would endanger the lives or property of its people. But if the State, under the guise of exerting its police powers, should make such exclusion or prohibition applicable solely to articles, of that kind, that may be produced or manufactured in other States, the courts would find no difficulty in holding such legislation to be in conflict with the Constitution of the United States. . . .

The law struck down in Philadelphia v. New Jersey left local waste untouched, although no basis existed by which to distinguish interstate waste. But "[i]f one is inherently harmful, so is the other. Yet New Jersey has banned the former while leaving its landfill sites open to the latter." 437 U.S., at 629. Here, the additional fee applies only to interstate hazardous waste, but at all points from its entrance into Alabama until it is landfilled at the Emelle facility, every concern related to quarantine applies perforce to local hazardous waste, which pays no additional fee. For this reason, the additional fee does not survive the appropriate scrutiny applicable to discriminations against interstate commerce.

Maine v. Taylor, 477 U.S. 131 (1986), provides no additional justification. Maine there demonstrated that the out-of-state baitfish were subject to parasites foreign to in-state baitfish. This difference posed a threat to the State's natural resources, and absent a less discriminatory means of protecting the environment—and none was available—the importation of baitfish could properly be banned. To the contrary, the record establishes that the hazardous waste at issue in this case is the same regardless of its point of origin. As noted in *Fort Gratiot Sanitary Landfill,* "our conclusion would be different if the imported waste raised health or other concerns not presented by [Alabama] waste." Because no unique threat is posed, and because adequate means other than overt discrimination meet Alabama's concerns, Maine v. Taylor provides the State no respite.

III

The decision of the Alabama Supreme Court is reversed, and the cause remanded for proceedings not inconsistent with this opinion, including consideration of the appropriate relief to petitioner.

CHIEF JUSTICE REHNQUIST, dissenting.

Taxes are a recognized and effective means for discouraging the consumption of scarce commodities—in this case the safe environment that attends appropriate disposal of hazardous wastes. Cf. 26 U.S.C.A.

3. Waste Management and Pollution Prevention   Pages 384-406

§§4681, 4682 (Supp. 1992) (tax on ozone-depleting chemicals); 26 U.S.C. §4064 (gas guzzler excise tax). I therefore see nothing unconstitutional in Alabama's use of a tax to discourage the export of this commodity to other States, when the commodity is a public good that Alabama has helped to produce. Nor do I see any significance in the fact that Alabama has chosen to adopt a differential tax rather than an outright ban. Nothing in the Commerce Clause requires Alabama to adopt an "all or nothing" regulatory approach to noxious materials coming from without the State.

In short, the Court continues to err by its failure to recognize that waste—in this case admittedly hazardous waste—presents risks to the public health and environment that a State may legitimately wish to avoid, and that the State may pursue such an objective by means less Draconian than an outright ban. Under force of this Court's precedent, though, it increasingly appears that the only avenue by which a State may avoid the importation of hazardous wastes is to ban such waste disposal altogether, regardless of the waste's source of origin. I see little logic in creating, and nothing in the Commerce Clause that requires us to create, such perverse regulatory incentives. The Court errs in substantial measure because it refuses to acknowledge that a safe and attractive environment is the commodity really at issue in cases such as this. The result is that the Court today gets it exactly backward when it suggests that Alabama is attempting to "isolate itself from a problem common to the several States." To the contrary, it is the 34 States that have no hazardous waste facility whatsoever, not to mention the remaining 15 States with facilities all smaller than Emelle, that have isolated themselves.

There is some solace to be taken in the Court's conclusion that Alabama may impose a substantial fee on the disposal of all hazardous waste, or a per-mile fee on all vehicles transporting such waste, or a cap on total disposals at the Emelle facility. None of these approaches provide Alabama the ability to tailor its regulations in a way that the State will be solving only that portion of the problem that it has created. But they do at least give Alabama some mechanisms for requiring waste-generating States to compensate Alabama for the risks the Court declares Alabama must run.

Of course, the costs of any of the proposals that the Court today approves will be less than fairly apportioned. For example, should Alabama adopt a flat transportation or disposal tax, Alabama citizens will be forced to pay a disposal tax equal to that faced by dumpers from outside the State. As the Court acknowledges, such taxes are a permissible effort to recoup compensation for the risks imposed on the State. Yet Alabama's general tax revenues presumably already support the State's various inspection and regulatory efforts designed to ensure the Emelle facility's safe operation. Thus, Alabamans will be made to pay twice, once through general taxation and a second time through a specific disposal fee. Permitting differential taxation would, in part, do no more than recognize that, having been made to bear all the risks from such hazardous waste sites, Alabama should not in addition be made to pay more than others in supporting activities that will help to minimize the risk. . . .

For the foregoing reasons, I respectfully dissent.

NOTES AND QUESTIONS

1. How did Alabama seek to justify the higher fee it imposed on waste originating out of state? Were the ostensible purposes of the fee legitimate? Why does the Court strike down the differential fee?

2. Why don't the quarantine cases help Alabama's case? Are there any measures that the state could undertake that would promote the purposes allegedly served by the differential tax without violating the nondiscrimination principle?

3. As the Court notes in footnote 9, Alabama ultimately abandoned attempts to justify the additional fee on waste originating out of state as reflecting an underlying cost differential for regulating such waste. Is there anything Alabama could have done to try to defend the fee on the basis of a cost differential?

4. Two Terms later, the Supreme Court revisited the question whether a state could justify a higher fee on waste originating out of state when it decided the following case.

Oregon Waste Systems, Inc. v. Department of Environmental Quality
114 S. Ct. 1345 (1994)

Justice THOMAS delivered the opinion of the Court.

Two Terms ago, in Chemical Waste Management, Inc. v. Hunt, 504 U.S.—(1992), we held that the negative Commerce Clause prohibited Alabama from imposing a higher fee on the disposal in Alabama landfills of hazardous waste from other States than on the disposal of identical waste from Alabama. In reaching that conclusion, however, we left open the possibility that such a differential surcharge might be valid if based on the costs of disposing of waste from other States. Id., at —, n. 9. Today, we must decide whether Oregon's purportedly cost-based surcharge on the in-state disposal of solid waste generated in other States violates the Commerce Clause.

disposal of identical in-state waste. 504 U.S. at —. We deem it equally obvious here that Oregon's $2.25 per ton surcharge is discriminatory on its face. The surcharge subjects waste from other States to a fee almost three times greater than the $0.85 per ton charge imposed on solid in-state waste. The statutory determinant for which fee applies to any particular shipment of solid waste to an Oregon landfill is whether or not the waste was "generated out-of-state." Ore. Rev. Stat. §459.297(1) (1991). It is well-established, however, that a law is discriminatory if it " 'tax[es] a transaction or incident more heavily when it crosses state lines than when it occurs entirely within the State.' " *Chemical Waste*, supra, at — (quoting Armco Inc. v Hardesty, 467 U.S. 638, 642 (1984)). . . .

Respondents argue, and the Oregon Supreme Court held, that the statutory nexus between the surcharge and "the [otherwise uncompensated] costs to the State of Oregon and its political subdivisions of disposing of solid waste generated out-of-state," Ore. Rev. Stat. §459.298 (1991), necessarily precludes a finding that the surcharge is discriminatory. We find respondents' narrow focus on Oregon's compensatory aim to be foreclosed by our precedents. As we reiterated in *Chemical Waste*, the purpose of, or justification for, a law has no bearing on whether it is facially discriminatory. See 504 U.S. at —. See also *Philadelphia*, supra, at 626. Consequently, even if the surcharge merely recoups the costs of disposing of out-of-state waste in Oregon, the fact remains that the differential charge favors shippers of Oregon waste over their counterparts handling waste generated in other States. In making that geographic distinction, the surcharge patently discriminates against interstate commerce.

III

Because the Oregon surcharge is discriminatory, the virtually *per se* rule of invalidity provides the proper legal standard here, not the *Pike* balancing test. As a result, the surcharge must be invalidated unless respondents can "show that it advances a legitimate local purpose that cannot be adequately served by reasonable nondiscriminatory alternatives." New Energy Co. of Indiana v. Limbach, 486 U.S. 269, 278 (1988). See also *Chemical Waste*, supra, at —. Our cases require that justifications for discriminatory restrictions on commerce pass the "strictest scrutiny." *Hughes*, supra, at 337. . . .

At the outset, we note two justifications that respondents have *not* presented. No claim has been made that the disposal of waste from other States imposes higher costs on Oregon and its political subdivisions than the disposal of in-state waste. Also, respondent have not offered any safety or health reason unique to nonhazardous waste from other States for discouraging the flow of such waste into Oregon. Cf. Maine v. Taylor, 477 U.S. 131 (1986) (upholding ban on importation of out-of-state baitfish into Maine because such baitfish were subject to parasites completely foreign to Maine baitfish). Consequently, respondents must come forward with other legitimate reasons to subject waste from other States to a higher charge than is levied against waste from Oregon.

Respondents offer two such reasons, each of which we address below.

A

Respondents' principal defense of the higher surcharge on out-of-state waste is that it is a "compensatory tax" necessary to make shippers of such waste pay their "fair share" of the costs imposed on Oregon by the disposal of their waste in the State. In *Chemical Waste* we noted the possibility that such an argument might justify a discriminatory surcharge or tax on out-of-state waste. See 504 U.S., at —, n.9. In making that observation, we implicitly recognized the settled principle that interstate commerce may be made to " 'pay its way.' " Complete Auto Transit, Inc. v. Brady, 430 U.S. 274, 281 (1977). . . .

At least since our decision in Hinson v. Lott, 8 Wall. 148 (1868), these principles have found expression in the "compensatory" or "complementary" tax doctrine. Though our cases sometimes discuss the concept of the compensatory tax as if it were a doctrine unto itself, it is merely a specific way of justifying a facially discriminatory tax as achieving a legitimate local purpose that cannot be achieved through nondiscriminatory means. . . . Under that doctrine, a facially discriminatory tax that imposes on interstate commerce the rough equivalent of an identifiable and "substantially similar" tax on intrastate commerce does not offend the negative Commerce Clause. Maryland v. Louisiana, 451 U.S. 725, 758-59 (1981). . . .

To justify a charge on interstate commerce as a compensatory tax, a State must, as a threshold matter, "identif[y] the [intrastate tax] burden for which the State is attempting to compensate." *Maryland,* supra, at 758. Once that burden has been identified, the tax on interstate commerce must be shown roughly to approximate—but not exceed—the amount of the tax on intrastate commerce. See, e.g., Alaska v. Arctic Maid, 366 U.S. 199, 204-205 (1961). Finally, the events on which the interstate and intrastate taxes are imposed must be "substantially equivalent"; that is, they must be sufficiently similar in substance to serve as mutually exclusive "prox[ies]" for each other. Armco, Inc. v. Hardesty, 467 U.S. 638, 643 (1984). . . .

3. Waste Management and Pollution Prevention   Pages 384-406

Although it is often no mean feat to determine whether a challenged tax is a compensatory tax, we have little difficulty concluding that the Oregon surcharge is not such a tax. Oregon does not impose a specific charge of at least $2.25 per ton on shippers of waste generated in Oregon, for which the out-of-state surcharge might be considered compensatory. In fact, the only analogous charge on the disposal of Oregon waste is $0.85 per ton, approximately one-third of the amount imposed on waste from other States. See Ore. Rev. Stat. §§459A.110(5), 459A.115 (1991). Respondents' failure to identify a specific charge on intrastate commerce equal to or exceeding the surcharge is fatal to their claim. See *Maryland*, 451 U.S., at 758.

Respondents argue that, despite the absence of a specific $2.25 per ton charge on in-state waste, intrastate commerce does pay its share of the costs underlying the surcharge through general taxation. Whether or not that is true is difficult to determine, as "[general] tax payments are received for the general purposes of the [government], and are, upon proper receipt, lost in the general revenues." Flast v. Cohen, 392 U.S. 83, 128 (1968) (Harlan, J., dissenting). Even assuming, however, that various other means of general taxation, such as income taxes, could serve as an identifiable intrastate burden roughly equivalent to the out-of-state surcharge, respondents' compensatory tax argument fails because the in-state and out-of-state levies are not imposed on substantially equivalent events. . . .

B

Respondents' final argument is that Oregon has an interest in spreading the costs of the in-state disposal of Oregon waste to all Oregonians. That is, because all citizens of Oregon benefit from the proper in-state disposal of waste from Oregon, respondents claim it is only proper for Oregon to require them to bear more of the costs of disposing of such waste in the State through a higher general tax burden. At the same time, however, Oregon citizens should not be required to bear the costs of disposing of out-of-state waste, respondents claim. The necessary result of that limited cost-shifting is to require shippers of out-of-state waste to bear the full costs of in-state disposal, but to permit shippers of Oregon waste to bear less than the full cost.

We fail to perceive any distinction between respondents' contention and a claim that the State has an interest in reducing the costs of handling in-state waste. Our cases condemn as illegitimate, however, any governmental interest that is not "unrelated to economic protectionism," Wyoming v. Oklahoma, 502 U.S. — (1992), and regulating interstate commerce in such a way as to give those who handle domestic articles of commerce a cost advantage over their competitors handling similar items produced elsewhere constitutes such protectionism. See *New Energy,* 486 U.S., at 275. To give controlling effect to respondents' characterization of Oregon's tax scheme as seemingly benign cost-spreading would require us to overlook the fact that the scheme necessarily incorporates a protectionist objective as well. . . .

Respondents counter that if Oregon is engaged in any form of protectionism, it is "resource protectionism," not economic protectionism. It is true that by discouraging the flow of out-of-state waste into Oregon landfills, the higher surcharge on waste from other States conserves more space in those landfills for waste generated in Oregon. Recharacterizing the surcharge as resource protectionism hardly advances respondents' cause, however. Even assuming that landfill space is a "natural resource," "a State may not accord its own inhabitants a preferred right of access over consumers in other States to natural resources located within its borders." *Philadelphia,* 437 U.S., at 627. As we held more than a century ago, "if the State, under the guise of exerting its police powers, should [impose a burden] applicable solely to articles [of commerce] produced or manufactured in other States, the courts would find no difficulty in holding such legislation to be in conflict with the Constitution of the United States." Guy v. Baltimore, 100 U.S. 434, 443 (1880). . . .

Chief Justice REHNQUIST, with whom Justice BLACKMUN joins, dissenting.

Landfill space evaporates as solid waste accumulates. State and local governments expend financial and political capital to develop trash control systems that are efficient, lawful, and protective of the environment. The State of Oregon responsibly attempted to address its solid waste disposal problem through enactment of a comprehensive regulatory scheme for the management, disposal, reduction, and recycling of solid waste. For this Oregon should be applauded. The regulatory scheme included a fee charged on out-of-state solid waste. The Oregon Legislature directed the Commission to determine the appropriate surcharge "based on the costs . . . of disposing of solid waste generated out-of-state." Ore. Rev. Stat. §459.298 (1991). The Commission arrived at a surcharge of $2.25 per ton, compared to the $0.85 per ton charged on in-state solid waste. Ore. Admin. Rule 340-97-110(3) (1993). The surcharge works out to an increase of about $0.14 per week for the typical out-of-state solid waste producer. This seems a small price to pay for the right to deposit your "garbage, rubbish, refuse . . . ; sewage sludge, septic tank and cesspool pumpings or other sludge; . . . manure, . . . dead animals, [and] infectious waste" on your neighbors. Ore. Rev. Stat. §459.005(27) (1991).

3. Waste Management and Pollution Prevention — Pages 384-406

Nearly 20 years ago, we held that a State cannot ban all out-of-state waste disposal in protecting themselves from hazardous or noxious materials brought across the State's borders. Philadelphia v. New Jersey, 437 U.S. 617 (1978). Two Terms ago in Chemical Waste Management, Inc. v. Hunt, 504 U.S. — (1992), in striking down the State of Alabama's $72 per ton fee on the disposal of out-of-state hazardous waste, the Court left open the possibility that such a fee could be valid if based on the costs of disposing of waste from other States. Id., at —, n.9. Once again, however, as in *Philadelphia* and *Chemical Waste Management*, the Court further cranks the dormant Commerce Clause ratchet against the States by striking down such cost-based fees, and by so doing ties the hands of the States in addressing the vexing national problem of solid waste disposal. I dissent.

Americans generated nearly 196 million tons of municipal solid waste in 1990, an increase from 128 million tons in 1975. See U.S. Environmental Protection Agency, Characterization of Municipal Solid Waste in the United States: 1992 Update, p. ES-3. Under current projections, Americans will produce 222 million tons of garbage in the year 2000. Ibid. Generating solid waste has never been a problem. Finding environmentally safe disposal sites has. By 1991, it was estimated that 45 percent of all solid waste landfills in the Nation had reached capacity. 56 Fed. Reg. 50980 (1991). Nevertheless, the Court stubbornly refuses to acknowledge that a clean and healthy environment, unthreatened by the improper disposal of solid waste, is the commodity really at issue in cases such as this, see, e.g., *Chemical Waste Management*, supra, at — (REHNQUIST, C. J., dissenting), and Fort Gratiot Sanitary Landfill, Inc. v. Michigan Dept. of Natural Resources, 504 U.S.—(1992) (REHNQUIST, C. J., dissenting).

Notwithstanding the identified shortage of landfill space in the Nation, the Court notes that it has "little difficulty" concluding that the Oregon surcharge does not operate as a compensatory tax, designed to offset the lack of available landfill space in the State caused by the influx of out-of-state waste. The Court reaches this nonchalant conclusion because the State has failed "to identify a specific charge on *intrastate* commerce equal to or exceeding the surcharge." (emphasis added) The Court's myopic focus on "differential fees" ignores the fact that in-state producers of solid waste support the Oregon regulatory program through state income taxes and by paying, indirectly, the numerous fees imposed on landfill operators and the dumping fee on in-state waste. Ore. Rev. Stat. §459.005 et seq. (1991).

We confirmed in Sporhase v. Nebraska ex rel. Douglas, 458 U.S. 941 (1982), that a State may enact a comprehensive regulatory system to address an environmental problem or a threat to natural resources within the confines of the Commerce Clause. In the context of threatened ground water depletion, we stated that "[o]bviously, a State that imposes severe withdrawal and use restrictions on its own citizens is not discriminating against interstate commerce when it seeks to prevent the uncontrolled transfer of water out of the State." Id., at 955-956. The same point could be made about a "clean and safe environment" in these cases: where a State imposes restrictions on the ability of its own citizens to dispose of solid waste in an effort to promote a "clean and safe environment," it is not discriminating against interstate commerce by preventing the uncontrolled transfer of out-of-state solid waste into the State.

The availability of safe landfill disposal sites in Oregon did not occur by chance. Through its regulatory scheme, the State of Oregon inspects landfill sites, monitors waste streams, promotes recycling, and imposes an $0.85 per ton disposal fee on in-state waste, Ore. Rev. Stat. 459.005 et seq. (1991), all in an effort to curb the threat that its residents will harm the environment and create health and safety problems through excessive and unmonitored solid waste disposal. Depletion of a clean and safe environment will follow if Oregon must accept out-of-state waste at its landfills without a sharing of the disposal costs. The Commerce Clause does not require a State to abide this outcome where the "natural resource has some indicia of a good publicly produced and owned in which a State may favor its own citizens in times of shortage." *Sporhase*, supra, at 957. A shortage of available landfill space is upon us, 56 Fed. Reg. 50980 (1991), and with it comes the accompanying health and safety hazards flowing from the improper disposal of solid wastes. We have long acknowledged a distinction between economic protectionism and health and safety regulation promulgated by Oregon. See H. P. Hood & Sons, Inc. v. Du Mond, 336 U.S. 525, 533 (1949).

Far from neutralizing the economic situation for Oregon producers and out-of-state producers, the Court's analysis turns the Commerce Clause on its head. Oregon's neighbors will operate under a competitive advantage against their Oregon counterparts as they can now produce solid waste with reckless abandon and avoid paying concomitant state taxes to develop new landfills and clean up retired landfill sites. While I understand that solid waste is an article of commerce, *Philadelphia*, 437 U.S., at 622-623, it is not a commodity sold in the marketplace; rather it is disposed of at a cost to the State. Petitioners do not buy garbage to put in their landfills; solid waste producers pay petitioners to take their waste. Oregon solid waste producers do not compete with out-of-state businesses in the sale of solid waste. Thus, the fees do not alter the price of a product that is competing with other products for common purchasers. If anything, striking down the fees works to the disadvantage of Oregon businesses. They alone will have to pay the "nondisposal" fees associated with solid waste: landfill siting, landfill

3. Waste Management and Pollution Prevention   Pages 384-406

clean-up, insurance to cover environmental accidents, and transportation improvement costs associated with out-of-state waste being shipped into the State. While we once recognized that " 'the collection and disposal of solid wastes should continue to be primarily the function of State, regional, and local agencies,' " id., at 621, n.4, quoting 42 U.S.C. §6901(a)(4) (1976 ed.), the Court today leaves States with only two options: become a dumper and ship as much waste as possible to a less populated State, or become a dumpee, and stoically accept waste from more densely populated States.

The Court asserts that the State has not offered "any safety or health reasons" for discouraging the flow of solid waste into Oregon. I disagree. The availability of environmentally sound landfill space and the proper disposal of solid waste strike me as justifiable "safety or health" rationales for the fee. . . .

The State of Oregon is not prohibiting the export of solid waste from neighboring States; it is only asking that those neighbors pay their fair share for the use of Oregon landfill sites. I see nothing in the Commerce Clause that compels less densely populated States to serve as the low-cost dumping grounds for their neighbors, suffering the attendant risks that solid waste landfills present. The Court, deciding otherwise, further limits the dwindling options available to States as they contend with the environmental, health, safety, and political challenges posed by the problem of solid waste disposal in modern society.

NOTES AND QUESTIONS

1. Unlike the Alabama statute, the Oregon law did not specify the level of the surcharge on waste generated in other states. Instead it left the fee to be determined by the state Environmental Quality Commission following a rulemaking proceeding. Why was this insufficient to convince the Court that the fee was nondiscriminatory because it was based on a genuine cost differential? In light of the Court's decision is there any way in which Oregon could have imposed a surcharge on waste generated out of state that would not violate the constitution?

2. Because the Court concluded that the Oregon surcharge was discriminatory, it placed a heavy burden on the state to demonstrate that the law advances a legitimate local purpose that cannot adequately be served by nondiscriminatory alternatives. Why was Oregon unable to justify the fee as necessary to conserve scarce landfill space within a state that had imposed stringent regulations on disposal of its own waste?

3. Efforts to preserve local access to natural resources have faced constitutional obstacles in the past. In Pennsylvania v. West Virginia,

262 U.S. 553 (1923), the Supreme Court struck down a West Virginia statute requiring producers of natural gas to give West Virginia residents preference over nonresident consumers in the purchase of natural gas. The West Virginia legislature had wanted to insulate state residents in the case of gas shortages and believed this was permissible because the gas originated in West Virginia. However, the Court stated that "[n]atural gas is a lawful article of commerce, and its transmission from one state to another for sale and consumption in the latter is interstate commerce." Id. at 596. West Virginia's stated interest in conserving natural resources could not justify the measure because "the purpose of its conservation is in a sense commercial—the business welfare of the State, as coal might be, or timber. . . . If the States have such power a singular situation might result. Pennsylvania might keep its coal, the Northwest its timber, the mining states their minerals. . . . [C]ommerce will be halted at state lines." Id. at 599. In *West Virginia* and similar cases, the states' ostensible purpose was the conservation of a scarce resource. Should landfill capacity be viewed as a resource analogous to natural gas reserves?

4. In a case that some have thought hard to square with the recent Commerce Clause decisions, the Supreme Court has held that Montana could charge an out-of-state license fee for hunting Montana elk that was 25 times larger than the fee charged in-staters. Baldwin v. Fish and Game Commission of Montana, 436 U.S. 371 (1978). *Baldwin* was decided under the Privileges and Immunities Clause, not the Commerce Clause. The Court recognized that states are not "obliged to share those things held in trust for their own people." Id. at 384. Moreover, such policies "manifest the State's special interest in regulating and preserving wildlife for the benefit of its citizens." Id. at 392. However, in a concurring opinion, Chief Justice Burger limited the majority holding by stating that if the wildlife became involved in interstate commerce, then access cannot be restricted in a manner that violates the Commerce Clause.

Professor Tribe has the following to say about *Baldwin:*

> There . . . appear to be some goods and services that a state's citizens, having created or preserved for themselves, are entitled to keep for themselves. Thus Montana's carefully-tended elk herds are akin to public libraries, public schools, state universities, state-supported hospitals, and public welfare programs—things that the Court has suggested that a state may reserve for the use or enjoyment of its citizens. The Court implied in *Baldwin* that it would approve even a total exclusion of nonresident hunters upon a showing by the state that any additional hunting opportunities beyond those Montana chose to reserve to its citizens would endanger the elk population to the point of extinction. [L. Tribe, American Constitutional Law 539 (2d ed. 1988).]

3. Waste Management and Pollution Prevention   Pages 384-406

A year after *Baldwin*, the Court decided Hughes v. Oklahoma, 441 U.S. 322 (1979). At issue was an Oklahoma statute banning the export of minnows caught in state waters. The state defended the ban as a conservation measure. The Court struck down the statute in a 7 to 2 decision. Once wild animals or other natural resources became objects in interstate commerce, said the Court, state laws concerning them had to be judged by the same Commerce Clause standards that are applicable to other items of commerce. While recognizing that conservation was a legitimate state interest, the majority held that the state had not shown its ban to be the least discriminatory means of furthering that interest. "Far from choosing the least discriminatory alternative, Oklahoma has chosen to 'conserve' its minnows in the way that most overtly discriminates against interstate commerce." 441 U.S. at 337-338.

5. In another line of decisions, the Supreme Court has taken a more permissive view of efforts by states to ensure that state-created resources be reserved for use by their citizens. For example, in Reeves v. Stake, 447 U.S. 429 (1980), the Supreme Court upheld a South Dakota statute reserving all cement produced by a state-owned cement plant for use by state residents, in the event orders exceeded supply. According to the Court, "[c]ement is not a natural resource, like coal, timber, wild game, or minerals. . . . It is the end product of a complex process whereby a costly physical plant and human labor act on raw materials. South Dakota has not sought to limit access to the State's limestone or other materials used to make cement." Id. at 443-444. The Court acknowledged that South Dakota's policies "reflect the essential and patently unobjectionable purpose of state government—to serve the citizens of the State." Id. at 442. Suppose the Oregon legislature decided to develop a system of state-owned landfills. Relying on *Reeves*, could it limit access to those facilities for the benefit of its own citizens? See Note, Recycling Philadelphia v. New Jersey: The Dormant Commerce Clause, Postindustrial Natural Resources and the Solid Waste Crisis, 137 U. Pa. L. Rev. 1309 (1989).

6. Could a state avoid the problem of facially discriminatory legislation by simply banning all waste disposal within the boundaries of the state regardless of where the waste was generated? Such a law effectively would require that all waste generated in the state be exported. Could it survive constitutional scrutiny under the Commerce Clause?

7. In the case that follows a state authorized, but did not require, its counties to restrict inflows of solid waste as part of comprehensive waste management plans. A constitutional challenge to the law was decided by the Supreme Court in the decision below.

Fort Gratiot Sanitary Landfill, Inc. v. Michigan Department of Natural Resources
112 S. Ct. 2019 (1992)

JUSTICE STEVENS delivered the opinion of the Court.

I

In 1978 Michigan enacted its Solid Waste Management Act (SWMA). That Act required every Michigan county to estimate the amount of solid waste that would be generated in the county in the next 20 years and to adopt a plan providing for its disposal at facilities that comply with state health standards. Mich. Comp. Laws Ann. §299.425 (Supp. 1991). . . .

On December 28, 1988, the Michigan Legislature amended the SWMA by adopting two provisions concerning the "acceptance of waste or ash generated outside the county of disposal area." Those amendments (Waste Import Restrictions), which became effective immediately, provide:

> A person shall not accept for disposal solid waste . . . that is not generated in the county in which the disposal area is located unless the acceptance of solid waste . . . that is not generated in the county is explicitly authorized in the approved county solid waste management plan. §299.413a.
>
> In order for a disposal area to serve the disposal needs of another county, state, or country, the service . . . must be explicitly authorized in the approved solid waste management plan of the receiving county. §299.430(2).

In February, 1989, petitioner submitted an application to the St. Clair County Solid Waste Planning Committee for authority to accept up to 1,750 tons per day of out-of-state waste at its landfill. In that application petitioner promised to reserve sufficient capacity to dispose of all solid waste generated in the county in the next 20 years. The planning committee denied the application. In view of the fact that the county's management plan does not authorize the acceptance of any out-of-county waste, the Waste Import Restrictions in the 1988 statute effectively prevent petitioner from receiving any solid waste that does not originate in St. Clair County. . . .

3. Waste Management and Pollution Prevention   Pages 384-406

II

Philadelphia v. New Jersey provides the framework for our analysis of this case. Solid waste, even if it has no value, is an article of commerce. . . .

As we have long recognized, the "negative" or "dormant" aspect of the Commerce Clause prohibits States from "advancing their own commercial interests by curtailing the movement of articles of commerce, either into or out of the state." H. P. Hood & Sons, Inc. v. Du Mond, 336 U.S. 525, 535 (1949). A state statute that clearly discriminates against interstate commerce is therefore unconstitutional "unless the discrimination is demonstrably justified by a valid factor unrelated to economic protectionism." New Energy Co. of Indiana v. Limbach, 486 U.S. 269, 274 (1988). . . .

The Waste Import Restrictions enacted by Michigan authorize each of its 83 counties to isolate itself from the national economy. . . . In view of the fact that Michigan has not identified any reason, apart from its origin, why solid waste coming from outside the county should be treated differently from solid waste within the county, the foregoing reasoning would appear to control the disposition of this case.

III

Respondents Michigan and St. Clair County argue, however, that the Waste Import Restrictions—unlike the New Jersey prohibition on the importation of solid waste—do not discriminate against interstate commerce on their face or in effect because they treat waste from other Michigan counties no differently than waste from other States. Instead, respondents maintain, the statute regulates evenhandedly to effectuate local interests and should be upheld because the burden on interstate commerce is not clearly excessive in relation to the local benefits. We disagree, for our prior cases teach that a State (or one of its political subdivisions) may not avoid the strictures of the Commerce Clause by curtailing the movement of articles of commerce through subdivisions of the State, rather than through the State itself.

In Brimmer v. Rebman, 138 U.S. 78 (1891), we reviewed the constitutionality of a Virginia statute that imposed special inspection fees on meat from animals that had been slaughtered more than 100 miles from the place of sale. We concluded that the statute violated the Commerce Clause even though it burdened Virginia producers as well as the Illinois litigant before the Court. We explained:

> This statute [cannot] be brought into harmony with the Constitution by the circumstance that it purports to apply alike to the citizens of all the

States, including Virginia; for, a burden imposed by a State upon interstate commerce is not to be sustained simply because the statute imposing it applies alike to the people of all the States, including the people of the State enacting such statute. If the object of Virginia had been to obstruct the bringing into that State, for use as human food, of all beef, veal and mutton, however wholesome, from animals slaughtered in distant States, that object will be accomplished if the statute before us be enforced.

In Dean Milk Co. v. Madison, 340 U.S. 349 (1951), another Illinois litigant challenged a city ordinance that made it unlawful to sell any milk as pasteurized unless it had been processed at a plant "within a radius of five miles from the central square of Madison," id., at 350. We held the ordinance invalid, explaining:

> This regulation, like the provision invalidated in Baldwin v. Seelig, Inc., in practical effect excludes from distribution in Madison wholesome milk produced and pasteurized in Illinois. The importer . . . may keep his milk or drink it, but sell it he may not.' Id., at 521. In thus erecting an economic barrier protecting a major local industry against competition from without the State, Madison plainly discriminates against interstate commerce.

The fact that the ordinance also discriminated against all Wisconsin producers whose facilities were more than five miles from the center of the city did not mitigate its burden on interstate commerce. As we noted, it was "immaterial that Wisconsin milk from outside the Madison area is subjected to the same proscription as that moving in interstate commerce."

Nor does the fact that the Michigan statute allows individual counties to accept solid waste from out of state qualify its discriminatory character. In the New Jersey case the statute authorized a state agency to promulgate regulations permitting certain categories of waste to enter the State. See 437 U.S., at 618-619. The limited exception covered by those regulations—like the fact that several Michigan counties accept out-of-state waste— merely reduced the scope of the discrimination; for all categories of waste not excepted by the regulations, the discriminatory ban remained in place. Similarly, in this case St. Clair County's total ban on out-of-state waste is unaffected by the fact that some other counties have adopted a different policy.

In short, neither the fact that the Michigan statute purports to regulate intercounty commerce in waste nor the fact that some Michigan counties accept out-of-state waste provides an adequate basis for distinguishing this case from Philadelphia v. New Jersey. . . .

3. Waste Management and Pollution Prevention   Pages 384-406

IV

Michigan and St. Clair County also argue that this case is different from Philadelphia v. New Jersey because the SWMA constitutes a comprehensive health and safety regulation rather than "economic protectionism" of the State's limited landfill capacity. Relying on an excerpt from our opinion in Sporhase v. Nebraska, 458 U.S. 941 (1982), they contend that the differential treatment of out-of-state waste is reasonable because they have taken measures to conserve their landfill capacity and the SWMA is necessary to protect the health of their citizens. That reliance is misplaced. In the Sporhase case we considered the constitutionality of a Nebraska statute that prohibited the withdrawal of ground water for use in an adjoining State without a permit that could only issue if four conditions were satisfied. We held that the fourth condition—a requirement that the adjoining State grant reciprocal rights to withdraw its water and allow its use in Nebraska—violated the Commerce Clause.

As a preface to that holding, we identified several reasons that, in combination, justified the conclusion that the other conditions were facially valid. First, we questioned whether the statute actually discriminated against interstate commerce. Although the restrictive conditions in the statute nominally applied only to interstate transfers of ground water, they might have been "no more strict in application than [other state law] limitations upon intrastate transfers." "Obviously, a State that imposes severe withdrawal and use restrictions on its own citizens is not discriminating against interstate commerce when it seeks to prevent the uncontrolled transfer of water out of the State."

We further explained that a confluence of factors could justify a State's efforts to conserve and preserve ground water for its own citizens in times of severe shortage.[6] Only the first of those reasons—our refer-

---

6. "Moreover, in the absence of a contrary view expressed by Congress, we are reluctant to condemn as unreasonable, measures taken by a State to conserve and preserve for its own citizens this vital resource in times of severe shortage. Our reluctance stems from the confluence of [several] realities. First, a State's power to regulate the use of water in times and places of shortage for the purpose of protecting the health of its citizens—and not simply the health of its economy—is at the core of its police power. For Commerce Clause purposes, we have long recognized a difference between economic protectionism, on the one hand, and health and safety regulation, on the other. Second, the legal expectation that under certain circumstances each State may restrict water within its borders has been fostered over the years not only by our equitable apportionment decrees, but also by the negotiation and enforcement of interstate compacts. Our law therefore has recognized the relevance of state boundaries in the allocation of scarce water resources. Third, although

ence to the well-recognized difference between economic protectionism, on the one hand, and health and safety regulation, on the other—is even arguably relevant to this case.[7] We may assume that all of the provisions of Michigan's SWMA prior to the 1988 amendments adding the Waste Import Restrictions could fairly be characterized as health and safety regulations with no protectionist purpose, but we cannot make that same assumption with respect to the Waste Import Restrictions themselves. Because those provisions unambiguously discriminate against interstate commerce, the State bears the burden of proving that they further health and safety concerns that cannot be adequately served by nondiscriminatory alternatives. Michigan and St. Clair County have not met this burden.[8]

Michigan and St. Clair County assert that the Waste Import Restrictions are necessary because they enable individual counties to make adequate plans for the safe disposal of future waste. Although accurate forecasts about the volume and composition of future waste flows may be an indispensable part of a comprehensive waste disposal plan, Michigan could attain that objective without discriminating between in- and out-of-state waste. Michigan could, for example, limit the amount of waste that landfill operators may accept each year. There is, however, no valid health and safety reason for limiting the amount of waste that a landfill operator may accept from outside the State, but not the amount that the operator may accept from inside the State.

---

appellee's claim to public ownership of Nebraska ground water cannot justify a total denial of federal regulatory power, it may support a limited preference for its own citizens in the utilization of the resource. In this regard, it is relevant that appellee's claim is logically more substantial than claims to public ownership of other natural resources. Finally, given appellee's conservation efforts, the continuing availability of ground water in Nebraska is not simply happenstance; the natural resource has some indicia of a good publicly produced and owned in which a State may favor its own citizens in times of shortage."

7. The other reasons were related to the special role that States have traditionally played in the ownership and control of ground water and to the fact that Nebraska's conservation efforts had given the water some indicia of a good that is publicly produced and owned. There are, however, no analogous traditional legal expectations regarding state regulation of private landfills, which are neither publicly produced nor publicly owned.

8. The dissent states that we should remand for further proceedings in which Michigan and St. Clair County might be able to prove that the Waste Import Restrictions constitute legitimate health and safety regulations, rather than economic protectionism of the State's limited landfill capacity. See post, at 1, 4-5. We disagree, for respondents have neither asked for such a remand nor suggested that, if given the opportunity, they could prove that the restrictions further health and safety concerns that cannot adequately be served by nondiscriminatory alternatives.

3. Waste Management and Pollution Prevention   Pages 384-406

For the foregoing reasons, the Waste Import Restrictions unambiguously discriminate against interstate commerce and are appropriately characterized as protectionist measures that cannot withstand scrutiny under the Commerce Clause. The judgment of the Court of Appeals is therefore reversed.

CHIEF JUSTICE REHNQUIST, with whom JUSTICE BLACKMUN joins, dissenting.

When confronted with a dormant Commerce Clause challenge "the crucial inquiry . . . must be directed to determining whether [the challenged statute] is basically a protectionist measure, or whether it can fairly be viewed as a law directed to legitimate local concerns, with effects upon interstate commerce that are only incidental." Philadelphia v. New Jersey, 437 U.S. 617, 624 (1978). Because I think the Michigan statute is at least arguably directed to legitimate local concerns, rather than improper economic protectionism, I would remand this case for further proceedings.

The substantial environmental, aesthetic, health, and safety problems flowing from this country's waste piles were already apparent at the time we decided Philadelphia. Those problems have only risen in the intervening years. 21 Envt. Rep. 369-370 (1990). In part this is due to increased waste volumes, volumes that are expected to continue rising for the foreseeable future. See United States Environmental Protection Agency, Characterization of Municipal Solid Waste in the United States: 1990 Update 10 (municipal solid wastes have increased from 128.1 million tons in 1975 to 179.6 million tons in 1988, expected to rise to 216 million tons by the year 2000); id. at ES-3 (1988 waste was the equivalent of 4.0 pounds per person per day, expected to rise to 4.4 pounds per person by the year 2000). In part it is due to exhaustion of existing capacity. Id., at 55 (landfill disposals increased from 99.7 million tons in 1975 to 130.5 million in 1988); 56 Fed. Reg. 50980 (1991) (45% of solid waste landfills expected to reach capacity by 1991). It is no secret why capacity is not expanding sufficiently to meet demand—the substantial risks attendant to waste sites make them extraordinarily unattractive neighbors. Swin Resource Systems, Inc. v. Lycoming Cty., 883 F. 2d 245, 253 (CA3 1989), cert. denied, 493 U.S. 1077 (1990). The result, of course, is that while many are willing to generate waste—indeed, it is a practical impossibility to solve the waste problem by banning waste production—few are willing to help dispose of it. Those locales that do provide disposal capacity to serve foreign waste effectively are affording reduced environmental and safety risks to the States that will not take charge of their own waste.

The State of Michigan has stepped into this quagmire in order to address waste problems generated by its own populace. It has done so by adopting a comprehensive approach to the disposal of solid wastes generated within its borders. The legislation challenged today is simply one part of a broad package that includes a number of features: a state-mandated state-wide effort to control and plan for waste disposal, requirements that local units of government participate in the planning process, restrictions to assure safe transport, a ban on the operation of a waste disposal facilities unless various design and technical requirements are satisfied and appropriate permits obtained, and commitments to promote source separation, composting, and recycling. The Michigan legislation is thus quite unlike the simple outright ban that we confronted in Philadelphia.

In adopting this legislation, the Michigan Legislature also appears to have concluded that, like the State, counties should reap as they have sown—hardly a novel proposition. It has required counties within the State to be responsible for the waste created within the county. It has accomplished this by prohibiting waste facilities from accepting waste generated from outside the county, unless special permits are obtained. In the process, of course, this facially neutral restriction (i.e., it applies equally to both interstate and intrastate waste) also works to ban disposal from out-of-state sources unless appropriate permits are procured. But I cannot agree that such a requirement, when imposed as one part of a comprehensive approach to regulating in this difficult field, is the stuff of which economic protectionism is made.

If anything, the challenged regulation seems likely to work to Michigan's economic disadvantage. This is because, by limiting potential disposal volumes for any particular site, various fixed costs will have to be recovered across smaller volumes, increasing disposal costs per unit for Michigan consumers. 56 Fed. Reg. 50987 (1991). The regulation also will require some Michigan counties—those that until now have been exporting their waste to other locations in the State—to confront environmental and other risks that they previously have avoided. Commerce Clause concerns are at their nadir when a state act works in this fashion —raising prices for all the State's consumers, and working to the substantial disadvantage of other segments of the State's population—because in these circumstances " 'a State's own political processes will serve as a check against unduly burdensome regulations.' " Kassel v. Consolidated Freightways Corp. of Delaware, 450 U.S. 662, 675 (1981) (quoting Raymond Motor Transportation, Inc. v. Rice, 434 U.S. 429, 444, n.18 (1978)). In sum, the law simply incorporates the commonsense notion that those responsible for a problem should be responsible for its solution to the degree they are responsible for the problem but not further. At a minimum, I think the facts just outlined suggest the State must be allowed to present evidence on the economic, environmental and other effects of its legislation.

3. Waste Management and Pollution Prevention   Pages 384-406

The Court suggests that our decision[] . . . in Dean Milk Co. v. Madison, 340 U.S. 349 (1951), foreclose[s] the possibility that a statute attacked on Commerce Clause grounds may be defended by pointing to the statute's effects on intrastate commerce. But our decisions in those cases did not rest on such a broad proposition. Instead, as the passages quoted by the Court make clear, in . . . *Dean Milk* the Court simply rejected the notion that there could be a noneconomic protectionist reason for the bans at issue, because the objects being banned presented no health or environmental risk. Dean Milk, 340 U.S., at 354 (the statute "excludes from distribution in Madison wholesome milk"). It seems unlikely that the waste here is "wholesome" or "entirely sound and fit." It appears, instead, to be potentially dangerous—at least the State has so concluded. Nor does the legislation appear to protect "a major local industry against competition from without the State." Ibid. *Dean Milk* [does not] prohibit[] a State from adopting health and safety regulations that are directed to legitimate local concerns. See Maine v. Taylor, 477 U.S. 131 (1986). I would remand this case to give the State an opportunity to show that this is such a regulation. . . .

The modern landfill is a technically complex engineering exercise that comes replete with liners, leachate collection systems and highly regulated operating conditions. As a result, siting a modern landfill can now proceed largely independent of the landfill location's particular geological characteristics. See 56 Fed. Reg. 51009 (1991) (EPA-approved "composite liner system is designed to be protective in all locations, including poor locations"); id., at 51004-51005 (outlining additional technical requirements for only those landfill sites (1) near airports, (2) on floodplains, (3) on wetlands, (4) on fault areas, (5) on seismic impact zones, or (6) on unstable areas). Given this, the laws of economics suggest that landfills will sprout in places where land is cheapest and population densities least. See Alm, "Not in My Backyard:" Facing the Siting Question, 10 EPA J. 9 (1984) (noting the need for each county to accept a share of the overall waste stream equivalent to what it generates so that "less populated counties are protected against becoming the dumping ground of the entire region"). I see no reason in the Commerce Clause, however, that requires cheap-land States to become the waste repositories for their brethren, thereby suffering the many risks that such sites present. . . .

The Court today penalizes the State of Michigan for what to all appearances are its good-faith efforts, in turn encouraging each State to ignore the waste problem in the hope that another will pick up the slack. The Court's approach fails to recognize that the latter option is one that is quite real and quite attractive for many States—and becomes even more so when the intermediate option of solving its own problems, but only its own problems, is eliminated.

For the foregoing reasons, I respectfully dissent.

NOTES AND QUESTIONS

1. Together, *Fort Gratiot, Chemical Waste Management* and *Oregon Waste Systems* severely limit the ability of states to discourage importation of out-of-state solid or hazardous wastes. See, e.g., Government Suppliers Consolidating Services v. Bayh, 753 F. Supp. 769 (D. Ind. 1990) (striking down a two-tier fee system, on a rationale similar to *Chemical Waste Management*'s); BFI Medical Waste Systems v. Whatcom County, 983 F.2d 911 (9th Cir. 1993) (citing *Fort Gratiot* in striking down a law authorizing a county option system similar to that at issue in *Fort Gratiot*). See also In re Southeast Arkansas Landfill, Inc. v. Arkansas, 981 F.2d 372 (8th Cir. 1992) (an Arkansas law limiting the amount of solid waste generated outside regional planning district that landfills within the district could accept violates the Commerce Clause); Chemical Waste Management v. Templet, 967 F.2d 1058 (5th Cir. 1992) (prohibition of import or disposal of hazardous waste originating in foreign nations violates dormant commerce power). But see Medical Waste Associates Limited Partnership v. Mayor and City Council of Baltimore, 966 F.2d 148 (4th Cir. 1992) (city ordinance requiring medical waste incinerator to burn only wastes generated within city does not violate commerce clause).

2. The logic of *Fort Gratiot* has been extended to cover cases in which a county has sought to require that all solid waste generated within its borders be sent to a county-owned waste composting facility. In Waste System Corp. v. County of Martin, Minnesota, 985 F.2d 1381 (8th Cir. 1993), the Eighth Circuit held that such an ordinance was unconstitutional because it discriminated against interstate commerce. While the county argued that the ordinance had only an incidental burden on interstate commerce because it applied only to waste generated within the county, the court found that it prevented out-of-state disposal facilities from competing for the business of disposing of waste generated in the county. The court concluded that even if the county's construction of the composting facility had been motivated by environmental concerns, the county could not seek to protect it from competition by out-of-state facilities.

3. "Flow control" guarantees have been considered important for ensuring the financial viability of new waste disposal projects. Such guarantees typically provide that a particular jurisdiction will ship all, or a substantial portion, of its waste to a particular recycling or disposal facility. In the case below the Supreme Court heard a constitutional challenge to a municipality's flow control ordinance.

3. Waste Management and Pollution Prevention   Pages 384-406

> *C & A Carbone, Inc. v. Town of Clarkstown*
> 114 S. Ct. 1677 (1994)

Justice KENNEDY delivered the opinion of the Court.

As solid waste output continues apace and landfill capacity becomes more costly and scarce, state and local governments are expending significant resources to develop trash control systems that are efficient, lawful, and protective of the environment. The difficulty of their task is evident from the number of recent cases that we have heard involving waste transfer and treatment. See Philadelphia v. New Jersey, 437 U.S. 617 (1978); Chemical Waste Management, Inc. v. Hunt, 504 U.S.—(1992); Fort Gratiot Sanitary Landfill, Inc. v. Michigan Dept. of Natural Resources, 504 U.S.—(1992); Oregon Waste Systems, Inc. v. Department of Environmental Quality of Oregon, 511 U.S.—(1994). The case decided today, while perhaps a small new chapter in that course of decisions, rests nevertheless upon well-settled principles of our Commerce Clause jurisprudence.

We consider a so-called flow control ordinance, which requires all solid waste to be processed at a designated transfer station before leaving the municipality. The avowed purpose of the ordinance is to retain the processing fees charged at the transfer station to amortize the cost of the facility. Because it attains this goal by depriving competitors, including out-of-state firms, of access to a local market, we hold that the flow control ordinance violates the Commerce Clause.

The town of Clarkstown, New York, lies in the lower Hudson River valley, just upstream from the Tappan Zee Bridge and by highway minutes from New Jersey. Within the town limits are the village of Nyack and the hamlet of West Nyack. In August 1989, Clarkstown entered into a consent decree with the New York State Department of Environmental Conservation. The town agreed to close its landfill located on Route 303 in West Nyack and build a new solid waste transfer station on the same site. The station would receive bulk solid waste and separate recyclable from nonrecyclable items. Recyclable waste would be baled for shipment to a recycling facility; nonrecyclable waste, to a suitable landfill or incinerator.

The cost of building the transfer station was estimated at $1.4 million. A local private contractor agreed to construct the facility and operate it for five years, after which the town would buy it for one dollar. During those five years, the town guaranteed a minimum waste flow of 120,000 tons per year, for which the contractor could charge the hauler a so-called tipping fee of $81 per ton. If the station received less than 120,000 tons in a year, the town promised to make up the tipping fee deficit. The object of this arrangement was to amortize the cost of the transfer station: The town would finance its new facility with the income generated by the tipping fees.

The problem, of course, was how to meet the yearly guarantee. This difficulty was compounded by the fact that the tipping fee of $81 per ton exceeded the disposal cost of unsorted solid waste on the private market. The solution the town adopted was the flow control ordinance here in question, Local Laws 1990, No. 9 of the Town of Clarkstown. The ordinance requires all nonhazardous solid waste within the town to be deposited at the Route 303 transfer station. Id. §3.C (waste generated within the town), §5.A (waste generated outside and brought in). Noncompliance is punishable by as much as a $1,000 fine and up to 15 days in jail. §7.

The petitioners in this case are C & A Carbone, Inc., a company engaged in the processing of solid waste, and various related companies or persons, all of whom we designate Carbone. Carbone operates a recycling center in Clarkstown, where it receives bulk solid waste, sorts and bales it, and then ships it to other processing facilities—much as occurs at the town's new transfer station. While the flow control ordinance permits recyclers like Carbone to continue receiving solid waste, §3.C, it requires them to bring the nonrecyclable residue from that waste to the Route 303 station. It thus forbids Carbone to ship the nonrecyclable waste itself, and it requires Carbone to pay a tipping fee on trash that Carbone has already sorted. . . .

The town of Clarkstown sued petitioners in New York Supreme Court, Rockland County, seeking an injunction requiring Carbone to ship all nonrecyclable waste to the Route 303 transfer station. Petitioners responded by suing in United States District Court to enjoin the flow control ordinance. On July 11, the federal court granted Carbone's injunction, finding a sufficient likelihood that the ordinance violated the Commerce Clause of the United States Constitution. C. A. Carbone, Inc. v. Clarkstown, 770 F. Supp. 848 (S.D.N.Y. 1991).

Four days later, the New York court granted summary judgment to respondent. The court declared the flow control ordinance constitutional and enjoined petitioners to comply with it. The federal court then dissolved its injunction.

The Appellate Division affirmed, 587 N.Y.S.2d 681 (2d Dept. 1992). The court found that the ordinance did not discriminate against interstate commerce because it "applies evenhandedly to all solid waste processed within the Town, regardless of point of origin." Id., at 686. The New York Court of Appeals denied petitioners' motion for leave to appeal. 605 N. E. 2d 874 (N.Y. 1992). We granted certiorari, 508 U.S.—(1993), and now reverse.

At the outset we confirm that the flow control ordinance does

3. Waste Management and Pollution Prevention   Pages 384-406

regulate interstate commerce, despite the town's position to the contrary. The town says that its ordinance reaches only waste within its jurisdiction and is in practical effect a quarantine: It prevents garbage from entering the stream of interstate commerce until it is made safe. This reasoning is premised, however, on an outdated and mistaken concept of what constitutes interstate commerce.

While the immediate effect of the ordinance is to direct local transport of solid waste to a designated site within the local jurisdiction, its economic effects are interstate in reach. The Carbone facility in Clarkstown receives and processes waste from places other than Clarkstown, including from out of State. By requiring Carbone to send the nonrecyclable portion of this waste to the Route 303 transfer station at an additional cost, the flow control ordinance drives up the cost for out-of-state interests to dispose of their solid waste. Furthermore, even as to waste originant in Clarkstown, the ordinance prevents everyone except the favored local operator from performing the initial processing step. The ordinance thus deprives out-of-state businesses of access to a local market. These economic effects are more than enough to bring the Clarkstown ordinance within the purview of the Commerce Clause. It is well settled that actions are within the domain of the Commerce Clause if they burden interstate commerce or impede its free flow. NLRB v. Jones & Laughlin Steel Corp., 301 U.S. 1, 31 (1937).

The real question is whether the flow control ordinance is valid despite its undoubted effect on interstate commerce. For this inquiry, our case law yields two lines of analysis: first, whether the ordinance discriminates against interstate commerce, *Philadelphia*, 437 U.S. at 624; and second, whether the ordinance imposes a burden on interstate commerce that is "clearly excessive in relation to the putative local benefits," Pike v. Bruce Church, Inc., 397 U.S. 137, 142 (1970). As we find that the ordinance discriminates against interstate commerce, we need not resort to the *Pike* test.

The central rationale for the rule against discrimination is to prohibit state or municipal laws whose object is local economic protectionism, laws that would excite those jealousies and retaliatory measures the Constitution was designed to prevent. See The Federalist No. 22, pp. 143-145 (C. Rossiter ed. 1961) (A. Hamilton); Madison, Vices of the Political System of the United States, in 2 Writings of James Madison 362-363 (G. Hunt ed. 1901). We have interpreted the Commerce Clause to invalidate local laws that impose commercial barriers or discriminate against an article of commerce by reason of its origin or destination out of State. See, e.g., *Philadelphia*, supra (striking down New Jersey statute that prohibited the import of solid waste); Hughes v. Oklahoma, 441 U.S. 322 (1979) (striking down Oklahoma law that prohibited the export of natural minnows).

Clarkstown protests that its ordinance does not discriminate because it does not differentiate solid waste on the basis of its geographic origin. All solid waste, regardless of origin, must be processed at the designated transfer station before it leaves the town. Unlike the statute in Philadelphia, says the town, the ordinance erects no barrier to the import or export of any solid waste but requires only that the waste be channeled through the designated facility.

Our initial discussion of the effects of the ordinance on interstate commerce goes far toward refuting the town's contention that there is no discrimination in its regulatory scheme. The town's own arguments go the rest of the way. As the town itself points out, what makes garbage a profitable business is not its own worth but the fact that its possessor must pay to get rid of it. In other words, the article of commerce is not so much the solid waste itself, but rather the service of processing and disposing of it.

With respect to this stream of commerce, the flow control ordinance discriminates, for it allows only the favored operator to process waste that is within the limits of the town. The ordinance is no less discriminatory because in-state or in-town processors are also covered by the prohibition. In Dean Milk Co. v. Madison, 340 U.S. 349 (1951), we struck down a city ordinance that required all milk sold in the city to be pasteurized within five miles of the city lines. We found it "immaterial that Wisconsin milk from outside the Madison area is subjected to the same proscription as that moving in interstate commerce." Id., at 354, n. 4. . . .

In this light, the flow control ordinance is just one more instance of local processing requirements that we long have held invalid. . . . The essential vice in laws of this sort is that they bar the import of the processing service. Out-of-state meat inspectors, or shrimp hullers, or milk pasteurizers, are deprived of access to local demand for their services. Put another way, the offending local laws hoard a local resource—be it meat, shrimp, or milk—for the benefit of local businesses that treat it.

The flow control ordinance has the same design and effect. It hoards solid waste, and the demand to get rid of it, for the benefit of the preferred processing facility. The only conceivable distinction from the cases cited above is that the flow control ordinance favors a single local proprietor. But this difference just makes the protectionist effect of the ordinance more acute. In *Dean Milk*, the local processing requirement at least permitted pasteurizers within five miles of the city to compete. An out-of-state pasteurizer who wanted access to that market might have built a pasteurizing facility within the radius. The flow control ordinance at issue here squelches competition in the waste-processing service altogether, leaving no room for investment from outside.

3. Waste Management and Pollution Prevention   Pages 384-406

Discrimination against interstate commerce in favor of local business or investment is *per se* invalid, save in a narrow class of cases in which the municipality can demonstrate, under rigorous scrutiny, that it has no other means to advance a legitimate local interest. Maine v. Taylor, 477 U.S. 131 (1986) (upholding Maine's ban on the import of baitfish because Maine had no other way to prevent the spread of parasites and the adulteration of its native fish species). A number of *amici* contend that the flow control ordinance fits into this narrow class. They suggest that as landfill space diminishes and environmental cleanup costs escalate, measures like flow control become necessary to ensure the safe handling and proper treatment of solid waste.

The teaching of our cases is that these arguments must be rejected absent the clearest showing that the unobstructed flow of interstate commerce itself is unable to solve the local problem. The Commerce Clause presumes a national market free from local legislation that discriminates in favor of local interests. Here Clarkstown has any number of nondiscriminatory alternatives for addressing the health and environmental problems alleged to justify the ordinance in question. The most obvious would be uniform safety regulations enacted without the object to discriminate. These regulations would ensure that competitors like Carbone do not underprice the market by cutting corners on environmental safety.

Nor may Clarkstown justify the flow control ordinance as a way to steer solid waste away from out-of-town disposal sites that it might deem harmful to the environment. To do so would extend the town's police power beyond its jurisdictional bounds. States and localities may not attach restrictions to exports or imports in order to control commerce in other states. Baldwin v. G.A.F. Seelig, Inc., 294 U.S. 511 (1935) (striking down New York law that prohibited the sale of milk unless the price paid to the original milk producer equalled the minimum required by New York).

The flow control ordinance does serve a central purpose that a nonprotectionist regulation would not: It ensures that the town-sponsored facility will be profitable, so that the local contractor can build it and Clarkstown can buy it back at nominal cost in five years. In other words, as the most candid of *amici* and even Clarkstown admit, the flow control ordinance is a financing measure. By itself, of course, revenue generation is not a local interest that can justify discrimination against interstate commerce. Otherwise States could impose discriminatory taxes against solid waste originating outside the State. See Chemical Waste Management, Inc. v. Hunt, 504 U.S.—(1992) (striking down Alabama statute that imposed additional fee on all hazardous waste generated outside the State and disposed of within the State); Oregon Waste Systems, Inc. v. Department of Environmental Quality of Oregon,

511 U.S.—(1994) (striking down Oregon statute that imposed additional fee on solid waste generated outside the State and disposed of within the State).

Clarkstown maintains that special financing is necessary to ensure the long-term survival of the designated facility. If so, the town may subsidize the facility through general taxes or municipal bonds. New Energy Co. of Indiana v. Limbach, 486 U.S. 269, 278 (1988). But having elected to use the open market to earn revenues for its project, the town may not employ discriminatory regulation to give that project an advantage over rival businesses from out of State. . . .

State and local governments may not use their regulatory power to favor local enterprise by prohibiting patronage of out-of-state competitors or their facilities. We reverse the judgment and remand the case for proceedings not inconsistent with this decision.

It is so ordered.

Justice O'CONNOR, concurring in the judgment.

The town of Clarkstown's flow control ordinance requires all "acceptable waste" generated or collected in the town to be disposed of only at the town's solid waste facility. Town of Clarkstown, Local Law 9, §§3(C)-(D) (1990) (Local Law 9). The Court holds today that this ordinance violates the Commerce Clause because it discriminates against interstate commerce. I agree with the majority's ultimate conclusion that the ordinance violates the dormant Commerce Clause. In my view, however, the town's ordinance is unconstitutional not because of facial or effective discrimination against interstate commerce, but rather because it imposes an excessive burden on interstate commerce. . . .

I

. . . Local Law 9 prohibits anyone except the town-authorized transfer station operator from processing discarded waste and shipping it out of town. In effect, the town has given a waste processing monopoly to the transfer station. The majority concludes that this processing monopoly facially discriminates against interstate commerce. In support of this conclusion, the majority cites previous decisions of this Court striking down regulatory enactments requiring that a particular economic activity be performed within the jurisdiction. See, e.g., Dean Milk Co. v. Madison, 340 U.S. 349 (1951) (unconstitutional for city to require milk to be pasteurized within five miles of the city). . . .

Local Law 9, however, lacks an important feature common to the regulations at issue in these cases—namely, discrimination on the basis of geographic origin. In each of the cited cases, the challenged enact-

3. Waste Management and Pollution Prevention   Pages 384-406

ment gave a competitive advantage to local business *as a group* vis-á-vis their out-of-state or nonlocal competitors as a group. In effect, the regulating jurisdiction—be it a State (Pike v. Bruce Church, Inc., 397 U.S. 137 (1970)), a county (Fort Gratiot Sanitary Landfill, Inc. v. Michigan Dept. of Natural Resources, 504 U.S.—(1992)), or a city (*Dean Milk*)—drew a line around itself and treated those inside the line more favorably than those outside the line. . . .

In my view, the majority fails to come to terms with a significant distinction between the laws in the local processing cases discussed above and Local Law 9. Unlike the regulations we have previously struck down, Local Law 9 does not give more favorable treatment to local interests as a group as compared to out-of-state or out-of-town economic interests. Rather, the garbage sorting monopoly is achieved at the expense of all competitors, be they local or nonlocal. That the ordinance does not discriminate on the basis of geographic origin is vividly illustrated by the identity of the plaintiff in this very action: petitioner is a *local* recycler, physically located *in Clarkstown*, that desires to process waste itself, and thus bypass the town's designated transfer facility. Because in-town processors—like petitioner—and out-of-town processors are treated equally, I cannot agree that Local Law 9 "discriminates" against interstate commerce. Rather, Local Law 9 "discriminates" evenhandedly against all potential participants in the waste processing business, while benefiting only the chosen operator of the transfer facility.

. . . Thus, while there is no bright line separating those enactments which are virtually per se invalid and those which are not, the fact that in-town competitors of the transfer facility are equally burdened by Local Law 9 leads me to conclude that Local Law 9 does not discriminate against interstate commerce.

II

That the ordinance does not discriminate against interstate commerce does not, however, end the Commerce Clause inquiry. Even a nondiscriminatory regulation may nonetheless impose an excessive burden on interstate trade when considered in relation to the local benefits conferred. See Brown-Forman Distillers Corp. v. New York State Liquor Authority, 476 U.S. 573, 579 (1986). Indeed, we have long recognized that "a burden imposed by a State upon interstate commerce is not to be sustained simply because the statute imposing it applies alike to . . . the people of the State enacting such statute." Brimmer v. Rebman, 138 U.S. 78, 83 (1891) (internal quotation marks and citation omitted). Moreover, "the extent of the burden that will be tolerated will of course depend on the nature of the local interest involved, and on whether it could be promoted as well with a lesser impact on interstate activities." *Pike*, 397 U.S. at 142. Judged against these standards, Local Law 9 fails.

The local interest in proper disposal of waste is obviously significant. But this interest could be achieved by simply requiring that all waste disposed of in the town be properly processed somewhere. For example, the town could ensure proper processing by setting specific standards with which all town processors must comply.

In fact, however, the town's purpose is narrower than merely ensuring proper disposal. Local Law 9 is intended to ensure the financial viability of the transfer facility. I agree with the majority that this purpose can be achieved by other means that would have a less dramatic impact on the flow of goods. For example, the town could finance the project by imposing taxes, by issuing municipal bonds, or even by lowering its price for processing to a level competitive with other waste processing facilities. But by requiring that all waste be processed at the town's facility, the ordinance "squelches competition in the waste-processing service altogether, leaving no room for investment from outside." . . .

Over 20 states have enacted statutes authorizing local governments to adopt flow control laws. If the localities in these States impose the type of restriction on the movement of waste that Clarkstown has adopted, the free movement of solid waste in the stream of commerce will be severely impaired. Indeed, pervasive flow control would result in the type of balkanization the Clause is primarily intended to prevent. See H. P. Hood & Sons., Inc. v. Du Mond, 336 U.S. 525, 537-538 (1949). . . .

The increasing number of flow control regimes virtually ensures some inconsistency between jurisdictions, with the effect of eliminating the movement of waste between jurisdictions. I therefore conclude that the burden Local Law 9 imposes on interstate commerce is excessive in relation to Clarkstown's interest in ensuring a fixed supply of waste to supply its project.

Justice SOUTER, with whom The CHIEF JUSTICE and Justice BLACKMUN join, dissenting.

The majority may invoke "well-settled principles of our Commerce Clause jurisprudence," but it does so to strike down an ordinance unlike anything this Court has ever invalidated. Previous cases have held that the "negative" or "dormant" aspect of the Commerce Clause renders state or local legislation unconstitutional when it discriminates against out-of-state or out-of-town businesses such as those that pasteurize milk, hull shrimp, or mill lumber, and the majority relies on these cases because of what they have in common with this one: out-of-state proces-

3. Waste Management and Pollution Prevention   Pages 384-406

sors are excluded from the local market (here, from the market for trash processing services). What the majority ignores, however, are the differences between our local processing cases and this one: the exclusion worked by Clarkstown's Local Law 9 bestows no benefit on a class of local private actors, but instead directly aids the government in satisfying a traditional governmental responsibility. The law does not differentiate between all local and all out-of-town providers of a service, but instead between the one entity responsible for ensuring that the job gets done and all other enterprises, regardless of their location. The ordinance thus falls outside that class of tariff or protectionist measures that the Commerce Clause has traditionally been thought to bar States from enacting against each other, and when the majority subsumes the ordinance within the class of laws this Court has struck down as facially discriminatory (and so avails itself of our "virtually *per se* rule" against such statutes, see Philadelphia v. New Jersey, 437 U.S. 617, 624 (1978)), the majority is in fact greatly extending the Clause's dormant reach.

There are, however, good and sufficient reasons against expanding the Commerce Clause's inherent capacity to trump exercises of state authority such as the ordinance at issue here. There is no indication in the record that any out-of-state trash processor has been harmed, or that the interstate movement or disposition of trash will be affected one whit. To the degree Local Law 9 affects the market for trash processing services, it does so only by subjecting Clarkstown residents and businesses to burdens far different from the burdens of local favoritism that dormant Commerce Clause jurisprudence seeks to root out. The town has found a way to finance a public improvement, not by transferring its cost to out-of-state economic interests, but by spreading it among the local generators of trash, an equitable result with tendencies that should not disturb the Commerce Clause and should not be disturbed by us.

NOTES AND QUESTIONS

1. Unlike the surcharges in *Chemical Waste Management* and *Oregon Waste Systems*, the Clarkstown ordinance applied to all solid waste brought within the town's jurisdiction without regard to its point of origin. Why did the Court majority find that the Clarkstown ordinance discriminated against interstate commerce?

2. A private contractor had agreed to build Clarkstown's $1.4 million transfer station and to sell it to the town for one dollar after operating it for five years. Would it have made any difference to the outcome of the case if the city had instead built and owned the facility using municipal funds?

3. In her concurring opinion, Justice O'Connor was more sympathetic to Clarkstown's ordinance, finding that it did not discriminate against interstate commerce. Nevertheless, she voted with the majority to strike it down. What was Justice O'Connor's concern and what would Clarkstown have to do to satisfy her that its ordinance was constitutional?

4. On May 16, 1995, the U.S. Senate, by a vote of 94-to-6, approved S. 534, a bill that would give states the authority to limit interestate shipments of municipal waste and to impose fees on waste originating out of state. Under the bill, states can freeze the amount of municipal solid waste that they receive from other states at 1993 levels and they can ban shipments of such waste to in-state facilities that did not receive waste in 1993. In response to the *Carbone* decision, the bill authorizes municipal authorities in nine states to impose flow control restrictions in order to help preserve the financial viability of certain waste disposal facilities. Legislation on Interstate Waste, Flow Control Passes Senate One Year After Carbone Decision, 26 Env. Rep. 212 (1995).

Limits on Local Opposition to Siting (pp. 406-414). The Tenth Circuit has suggested that RCRA could preempt a local hazardous waste zoning ordinance. In Blue Circle Cement, Inc. v. Board of County Commissioners, 27 F.3d 1499 (10th Cir. 1994), the court ruled that a county requirement that a conditional use permit be obtained before a facility could burn hazardous waste as fuel in a cement kiln would be preempted if it were "a sham, with the purpose and effect simply of frustrating the policy of RCRA to encourage the recycling of hazardous waste and the safe use of [hazardous waste fuels]." 27 F.3d at 1510. The owner of the facility argued that the ordinance amounted to a total ban on such activity because no land in the county could have satisfied the ordinance's requirements. While remanding for further consideration of this argument, the court noted in a footnote that if the county "consisted only of densely populated residential areas, and the hazardous waste activity in fact posed a significant threat to health or safety, a total ban could be upheld as a reasonable exercise of §6929 delegation of authority to state and local authorities to adopt more stringent requirements, including regulations relating to site selection." 27 F.3d at 1508 n.7.

The Search for a High-Level Repository (pp. 414-415). Little progress has been made in the search for a repository for high-level radioactive waste. Despite spending nearly $2 billion studying the Yucca Mountain site, the Department of Energy has yet to determine if it is a suitable repository. If the site is selected, it is unlikely to open before the year 2010. As the operators of nuclear power plants run out of on-site storage space, they are being forced to develop alternative storage sites. Under

3. Waste Management and Pollution Prevention   Pages 414-416

a regulation adopted in 1990, utilities can build new storage sites without performing an environmental impact assessment or holding public hearings, so long as the spent fuel is kept in casks approved by the Nuclear Regulatory Commission. This policy was upheld by the Sixth Circuit in Kelley v. Selin, 42 F.3d 1501 (6th Cir. 1995).

Constitutional Limits on Federal Coercion of State Siting (pp. 414-416). On June 19, 1992, the Supreme Court partially reversed the Second Circuit's decision in New York v. United States, 942 F.2d 114 (2d Cir. 1991), which is discussed on pages 415-416 of the parent text. A portion of the Supreme Court's decision is reproduced below.

> ### New York v. United States
> #### 112 S. Ct. 2408 (1992)

JUSTICE O'CONNOR delivered the opinion of the Court.

Faced with the possibility that the Nation would be left with no disposal sites for low level radioactive waste, Congress responded by enacting the Low-Level Radioactive Waste Policy Act, Pub. L. 96-573, 94 Stat. 3347. Relying largely on a report submitted by the National Governors' Association, Congress declared a federal policy of holding each State "responsible for providing for the availability of capacity either within or outside the State for the disposal of low-level radioactive waste generated within its borders," and found that such waste could be disposed of "most safely and efficiently on a regional basis." §4(a)(1), 94 Stat. 3348. The 1980 Act authorized States to enter into regional compacts that, once ratified by Congress, would have the authority beginning in 1986 to restrict the use of their disposal facilities to waste generated within member States. §4(a)(2)(B), 94 Stat. 3348. The 1980 Act included no penalties for States that failed to participate in this plan.

By 1985, only three approved regional compacts had operational disposal facilities; not surprisingly, these were the compacts formed around South Carolina, Nevada, and Washington, the three sited States. The following year, the 1980 Act would have given these three compacts the ability to exclude waste from nonmembers, and the remaining 31 States would have had no assured outlet for their low level radioactive waste. With this prospect looming, Congress once again took up the issue of waste disposal. The result was the legislation challenged here, the Low-Level Radioactive Waste Policy Amendments Act of 1985.

The 1985 Act was again based largely on a proposal submitted by the National Governors' Association. In broad outline, the Act embodies a compromise among the sited and unsited States. The sited States agreed to extend for seven years the period in which they would accept low level radioactive waste from other States. In exchange, the unsited States agreed to end their reliance on the sited States by 1992.

The mechanics of this compromise are intricate. The Act directs: "Each State shall be responsible for providing, either by itself or in cooperation with other States, for the disposal of . . . low-level radioactive waste generated within the State," 42 U.S.C. §2021c(a)(1)(A), with the exception of certain waste generated by the Federal Government, §§2021c(a)(1)(B), 2021c(b). The Act authorizes States to "enter into such [interstate] compacts as may be necessary to provide for the establishment and operation of regional disposal facilities for low-level radioactive waste." §2021d(a)(2). For an additional seven years beyond the period contemplated by the 1980 Act, from the beginning of 1986 through the end of 1992, the three existing disposal sites "shall make disposal capacity available for low-level radioactive waste generated by any source," with certain exceptions not relevant here. §2021e(a)(2). But the three States in which the disposal sites are located are permitted to exact a graduated surcharge for waste arriving from outside the regional compact—in 1986-1987, $10 per cubic foot; in 1988-1989, $20 per cubic foot; and in 1990-1992, $40 per cubic foot. §2021e(d)(1). After the seven-year transition period expires, approved regional compacts may exclude radioactive waste generated outside the region. §2021d(c).

The Act provides three types of incentives to encourage the States to comply with their statutory obligation to provide for the disposal of waste generated within their borders.

1. *Monetary incentives.* One quarter of the surcharges collected by the sited States must be transferred to an escrow account held by the Secretary of Energy. §2021e(d)(2)(A). The Secretary then makes payments from this account to each State that has complied with a series of deadlines. By July 1, 1986, each State was to have ratified legislation either joining a regional compact or indicating an intent to develop a disposal facility within the State. §§2021e(e)(1)(A), 2021e(d)(2)(B)(i). By January 1, 1988, each unsited compact was to have identified the State in which its facility would be located, and each compact or stand-alone State was to have developed a siting plan and taken other identified steps. §§2021e(e)(1)(B), 2021e(d)(2)(B)(ii). By January 1, 1990, each State or compact was to have filed a complete application for a license to operate a disposal facility, or the Governor of any State that had not filed an application was to have certified that the State would be capable of disposing of all waste generated in the State after 1992. §§2021e(e)(1)(C), 2021e(d)(2)(B)(iii). The rest of the account is to be paid out to those States or compacts able to dispose of all low level radioactive waste generated within their borders by January 1, 1993. §2021e(d)(2)(B)(iv). Each State that has not met the

3. Waste Management and Pollution Prevention   Pages 414-416

1993 deadline must either take title to the waste generated within its borders or forfeit to the waste generators the incentive payments it has received. §2021e(d)(2)(C).

2. *Access incentives.* The second type of incentive involves the denial of access to disposal sites. States that fail to meet the July 1986 deadline may be charged twice the ordinary surcharge for the remainder of 1986 and may be denied access to disposal facilities thereafter. §2021e(e)(2)(A). States that fail to meet the 1988 deadline may be charged double surcharges for the first half of 1988 and quadruple surcharges for the second half of 1988, and may be denied access thereafter. §2021e(e)(2)(B). States that fail to meet the 1990 deadline may be denied access. §2021e(e)(2)(C). Finally, States that have not filed complete applications by January 1, 1992, for a license to operate a disposal facility, or States belonging to compacts that have not filed such applications, may be charged triple surcharges. §§2021e(e)(1)(D), 2021e(e)(2)(D).

3. *The take title provision.* The third type of incentive is the most severe. The Act provides:

> If a State (or, where applicable, a compact region) in which low-level radioactive waste is generated is unable to provide for the disposal of all such waste generated within such State or compact region by January 1, 1996, each State in which such waste is generated upon the request of the generator or owner of the waste, shall take title to the waste, be obligated to take possession of the waste, and shall be liable for all damages directly or indirectly incurred by such generator or owner as a consequence of the failure of the State to take possession of the waste as soon after January 1, 1996, as the generator or owner notifies the State that the waste is available for shipment. §2021e(d)(2)(C).

These three incentives are the focus of petitioners' constitutional challenge.

In the seven years since the Act took effect, Congress has approved nine regional compacts, encompassing 42 of the States. All six unsited compacts and four of the unaffiliated States have met the first three statutory milestones. . . .

Petitioners—the State of New York and the two counties—filed this suit against the United States in 1990. They sought a declaratory judgment that the Act is inconsistent with the Tenth and Eleventh Amendments to the Constitution, with the Due Process Clause of the Fifth Amendment, and with the Guarantee Clause of Article IV of the Constitution. . . . Petitioners have abandoned their Due Process and Eleventh Amendment claims on their way up the appellate ladder; as the case stands before us, petitioners claim only that the Act is inconsistent with the Tenth Amendment and the Guarantee Clause. . . .

Petitioners do not contend that Congress lacks the power to regulate the disposal of low level radioactive waste. Space for radioactive waste disposal sites is frequently sold by residents of one State to residents of another. Regulation of the resulting interstate market in waste disposal is therefore well within Congress' authority under the Commerce Clause. Cf. Philadelphia v. New Jersey, 437 U.S. 617, 621-623 (1978); Fort Gratiot Sanitary Landfill, Inc. v. Michigan Dept. of Natural Resources, 112 S. Ct. 2019, 2023, (1992). Petitioners likewise do not dispute that under the Supremacy Clause Congress could, if it wished, preempt state radioactive waste regulation. Petitioners contend only that the Tenth Amendment limits the power of Congress to regulate in the way it has chosen. Rather than addressing the problem of waste disposal by directly regulating the generators and disposers of waste, petitioners argue, Congress has impermissibly directed the States to regulate in this field.

Most of our recent cases interpreting the Tenth Amendment have concerned the authority of Congress to subject state governments to generally applicable laws. The Court's jurisprudence in this area has traveled an unsteady path. See Maryland v. Wirtz, 392 U.S. 183 (1968) (state schools and hospitals are subject to Fair Labor Standards Act); National League of Cities v. Usery, 426 U.S. 833 (1976) (overruling *Wirtz*) (state employers are not subject to Fair Labor Standards Act); Garcia v. San Antonio Metropolitan Transit Authority, 469 U.S. 528 (1985) (overruling *National League of Cities*) (state employers are once again subject to Fair Labor Standards Act). . . .

This case presents no occasion to apply or revisit the holdings of any of these cases, as this is not a case in which Congress has subjected a State to the same legislation applicable to private parties. Cf. FERC v. Mississippi, 456 U.S. 742, 758-759 (1982).

This case instead concerns the circumstances under which Congress may use the States as implements of regulation; that is, whether Congress may direct or otherwise motivate the States to regulate in a particular field or a particular way. Our cases have established a few principles that guide our resolution of the issue.

I

As an initial matter, Congress may not simply "commandee[r] the legislative processes of the States by directly compelling them to enact and enforce a federal regulatory program." Hodel v. Virginia Surface Mining & Reclamation Assn., Inc., 452 U.S. 264, 288 (1981). In *Hodel*, the Court upheld the Surface Mining Control and Reclamation Act of 1977 precisely because it did not "commandeer" the States into regulating mining. The Court found that "the States are not compelled to enforce the steep-slope standards, to expend any state funds, or to participate in the federal regulatory program in any manner whatsoever. If a State does not wish to submit a proposed permanent program that complies with the Act and implementing regulations, the full regulatory burden will be borne by the federal Government." Ibid. . . .

While Congress has substantial powers to govern the Nation directly, including in areas of intimate concern to the States, the Constitution has never been understood to confer upon Congress the ability to require the States to govern according to Congress' instructions. See Coyle v. Oklahoma, 221 U.S. 559, 565 (1911). . . .

In providing for a stronger central government . . . the Framers explicitly chose a Constitution that confers upon Congress the power to regulate individuals, not States. As we have seen, the Court has consistently respected this choice. We have always understood that even where Congress has the authority under the Constitution to pass laws requiring or prohibiting certain acts, it lacks the power directly to compel the States to require or prohibit those acts. E.g., FERC v. Mississippi, 456 U.S., at 762-766; Hodel v. Virginia Surface Mining & Reclamation Assn., Inc. 452 U.S., at 288-289; Lane County v. Oregon, 7 Wall., at 76. The allocation of power contained in the Commerce Clause, for example, authorizes Congress to regulate interstate commerce directly; it does not authorize Congress to regulate state governments' regulation of interstate commerce.

II

This is not to say that Congress lacks the ability to encourage a State to regulate in a particular way, or that Congress may not hold out incentives to the States as a method of influencing a State's policy choices. Our cases have identified a variety of methods, short of outright coercion, by which Congress may urge a State to adopt a legislative program consistent with federal interests. Two of these methods are of particular relevance here.

First, under Congress' spending power, "Congress may attach conditions on the receipt of federal funds." South Dakota v. Dole, 483 U.S., at 206. Such conditions must (among other requirements) bear some relationship to the purpose of the federal spending, id., at 207-208, and n. 3; otherwise, of course, the spending power could render academic the Constitution's other grants and limits of federal authority. Where the recipient of federal funds is a State, as is not unusual today, the conditions attached to the funds by Congress may influence a State's legislative choices. See Kaden, Politics, Money, and State Sovereignty: the Judicial Role, 79 Colum. L. Rev. 847, 874-881 (1979). *Dole* was one such case: The

Court found no constitutional flaw in a federal statute directing the Secretary of Transportation to withhold federal highway funds from States failing to adopt Congress' choice of a minimum drinking age.

Second, where Congress has the authority to regulate private activity under the Commerce Clause, we have recognized Congress' power to offer States the choice of regulating that activity according to federal standards or having state law preempted by federal regulation. Hodel v. Virginia Surface Mining & Reclamation Assn., Inc., supra, 452 U.S., at 288. See also FERC v. Mississippi, supra, 456 U.S., at 764-765. This arrangement, which has been termed "a program of cooperative federalism," *Hodel*, supra, 452 U.S., at 289, is replicated in numerous federal statutory schemes. These include the Clean Water Act, 86 Stat. 816, as amended, 33 U.S.C. §1251 et seq., see Arkansas v. Oklahoma, 112 S. Ct. 1046, 1054 (1992) (Clean Water Act "anticipates a partnership between the States and the Federal Government, animated by a shared objective"); the Occupational Safety and Health Act of 1970, 84 Stat. 1590, 29 U.S.C. §651 et seq., see Gade v. National Solid Wastes Management Assn., —U.S.—, —, 112 S. Ct. 2374, — (1992); the Resource Conservation and Recovery Act of 1976, 90 Stat. 2796, as amended, 42 U.S.C. §6901 et seq., see United States Dept. of Energy v. Ohio, 112 S. Ct. 1627, 1632 (1992); and the Alaska National Interest Lands Conservation Act, 94 Stat. 2374, 16 U.S.C. §3101 et seq., see Kenaitze Indian Tribe v. Alaska, 860 F.2d 312, 314 (CA 9 1988), cert. denied, 491 U.S. 905 (1989).

By either of these two methods, as by any other permissible method of encouraging a State to conform to federal policy choices, the residents of the State retain the ultimate decision as to whether or not the State will comply. If a State's citizens view federal policy as sufficiently contrary to local interests, they may elect to decline a federal grant. If state residents would prefer their government to devote its attention and resources to problems other than those deemed important by Congress, they may choose to have the Federal Government rather than the State bear the expense of a federally mandated regulatory program, and they may continue to supplement that program to the extent state law is not preempted. Where Congress encourages state regulation rather than compelling it, state governments remain responsive to the local electorate's preferences; state officials remain accountable to the people.

By contrast, where the Federal Government compels States to regulate, the accountability of both state and federal officials is diminished. If the citizens of New York, for example, do not consider that making provision for the disposal of radioactive waste is in their best interest, they may elect state officials who share their view. That view can always be preempted under the Supremacy Clause if it is contrary to the national view, but in such a case it is the Federal Government

3. Waste Management and Pollution Prevention Pages 414-416

that makes the decision in full view of the public, and it will be federal officials that suffer the consequences if the decision turns out to be detrimental or unpopular. But where the Federal Government directs the States to regulate, it may be state officials who will bear the brunt of public disapproval, while the federal officials who devised the regulatory program may remain insulated from the electoral ramifications of their decision. Accountability is thus diminished when, due to federal coercion, elected state officials cannot regulate in accordance with the views of the local electorate in matters not preempted by federal regulation. . . .

With these principles in mind, we turn to the three challenged provisions of the Low-Level Radioactive Waste Policy Amendments Act of 1985. . . .

Construed as a whole, the Act comprises three sets of "incentives" for the States to provide for the disposal of low-level radioactive waste generated within their borders. We consider each in turn.

A

The first set of incentives works in three steps. First, Congress has authorized States with disposal sites to impose a surcharge on radioactive waste received from other States. Second, the Secretary of Energy collects a portion of this surcharge and places the money in an escrow account. Third, States achieving a series of milestones receive portions of this fund.

The first of these steps is an unexceptionable exercise of Congress' power to authorize the States to burden interstate commerce. While the Commerce Clause has long been understood to limit the States' ability to discriminate against interstate commerce, see, e.g., Wyoming v. Oklahoma, 502 U.S.—,— (1992); Cooley v. Board of Wardens of Port of Philadelphia, 12 How. 299 (1851), that limit may be lifted, as it has been here, by an expression of the "unambiguous intent" of Congress. *Wyoming*, supra, 502 U.S., at—; Prudential Ins. Co. v. Benjamin, 328 U.S. 408, 427-431 (1946). Whether or not the States would be permitted to burden the interstate transport of low level radioactive waste in the absence of Congress' approval, the States can clearly do so *with* Congress' approval, which is what the Act gives them.

The second step, the Secretary's collection of a percentage of the surcharge, is no more than a federal tax on interstate commerce, which petitioners do not claim to be an invalid exercise of either Congress' commerce or taxing power. Cf. United States v. Sanchez, 340 U.S. 42, 44-45 (1950); Steward Machine Co. v. Davis, 301 U.S. 548, 581-583 (1937).

The third step is a conditional exercise of Congress' authority under the Spending Clause: Congress has placed conditions—the achievement of the milestones—on the receipt of federal funds. Petitioners do not contend that Congress has exceeded its authority in any of the four respects our cases have identified. . . .

The Act's first set of incentives, in which Congress has conditioned grants to the States upon the States' attainment of a series of milestones, is thus well within the authority of Congress under the Commerce and Spending Clauses. Because the first set of incentives is supported by affirmative constitutional grants of power to Congress, it is not inconsistent with the Tenth Amendment.

B

In the second set of incentives, Congress has authorized States and regional compacts with disposal sites gradually to increase the cost of access to the sites and then to deny access altogether, to radioactive waste generated in States that do not meet federal deadlines. As a simple regulation, this provision would be within the power of Congress to authorize the States to discriminate against interstate commerce. See Northeast Bancorp, Inc. v. Board of Governors, Fed. Reserve System, 472 U.S. 159, 174-175 (1985). Where federal regulation of private activity is within the scope of the Commerce Clause, we have recognized the ability of Congress to offer states the choice of regulating that activity according to federal standards or having state law preempted by federal regulation. . . .

The Act's second set of incentives thus represents a conditional exercise of Congress' commerce power, along the lines of those we have held to be within Congress' authority. As a result, the second set of incentives does not intrude on the sovereignty reserved to the States by the Tenth Amendment.

C

The take title provision is of a different character. This third so-called "incentive" offers States, as an alternative to regulating pursuant to Congress' direction, the option of taking title to and possession of the low level radioactive waste generated within their borders and becoming liable for all damages waste generators suffer as a result of the States' failure to do so promptly. In this provision, Congress has crossed the line distinguishing encouragement from coercion. . . .

The take title provision offers state governments a "choice" of either accepting ownership of waste or regulating according to the instructions of Congress. Respondents do not claim that the Constitu-

3. Waste Management and Pollution Prevention   Pages 414-416

tion would authorize Congress to impose either option as a freestanding requirement. On one hand, the Constitution would not permit Congress simply to transfer radioactive waste from generators to state governments. Such a forced transfer, standing alone, would in principle be no different than a congressionally compelled subsidy from state governments to radioactive waste producers. The same is true of the provision requiring the States to become liable for the generators' damages. Standing alone, this provision would be indistinguishable from an Act of Congress directing the States to assume the liabilities of certain state residents. Either type of federal action would "commandeer" state governments into the service of federal regulatory purposes, and would for this reason be inconsistent with the Constitution's division of authority between federal and state governments. On the other hand, the second alternative held out to state governments—regulating pursuant to Congress' direction—would, standing alone, present a simple command to state governments to implement legislation enacted by Congress. As we have seen, the Constitution does not empower Congress to subject state governments to this type of instruction.

Because an instruction to state governments to take title to waste, standing alone, would be beyond the authority of Congress, and because a direct order to regulate, standing alone, would also be beyond the authority of Congress, it follows that Congress lacks the power to offer the States a choice between the two. Unlike the first two sets of incentives, the take title incentive does not represent the conditional exercise of any congressional power enumerated in the Constitution. In this provision, Congress has not held out the threat of exercising its spending power or its commerce power, it has instead held out the threat, should the States not regulate according to one federal instruction, of simply forcing the States to submit to another federal instruction. A choice between two unconstitutionally coercive regulatory techniques is no choice at all. Either way, "the Act commandeers the legislative processes of the States by directly compelling them to enact and enforce a federal regulatory program," Hodel v. Virginia Surface Mining & Reclamation Assn., Inc., supra, 452 U.S., at 288, an outcome that has never been understood to lie within the authority conferred upon Congress by the Constitution.

Respondents emphasize the latitude given to the States to implement Congress' plan. The Act enables the States to regulate pursuant to Congress' instructions in any number of different ways. States may avoid taking title by contracting with sited regional compacts, by building a disposal site alone or as part of a compact, or by permitting private parties to build a disposal site. States that host sites may employ a wide range of designs and disposal methods, subject only to broad federal regulatory limits. This line of reasoning, however, only underscores the critical alternative a State lacks: A State may not decline to administer the federal program. No matter which path the State chooses, it must follow the direction of Congress.

The take title provision appears to be unique. No other federal statute has been cited which offers a state government no option other than that of implementing legislation enacted by Congress. Whether one views the take title provision as lying outside Congress' enumerated powers, or as infringing upon the core of state sovereignty reserved by the Tenth Amendment, the provision is inconsistent with the federal structure of our Government established by the Constitution. . . .

Much of the Constitution is concerned with setting forth the form of our government, and the courts have traditionally invalidated measures deviating from that form. The result may appear "formalistic" in a given case to partisans of the measure at issue, because such measures are typically the product of the era's perceived necessity. But the Constitution protects us from our own best intentions: It divides power among sovereigns and among branches of government precisely so that we may resist the temptation to concentrate power in one location as an expedient solution to the crisis of the day. The shortage of disposal sites for radioactive waste is a pressing national problem, but a judiciary that licensed extra-constitutional government with each issue of comparable gravity would, in the long run, be far worse.

States are not mere political subdivisions of the United States. State governments are neither regional offices nor administrative agencies of the Federal Government. The positions occupied by state officials appear nowhere in the Federal Government's most detailed organizational chart. The Constitution instead "leaves to the several States a residuary and inviolable sovereignty," The Federalist No. 39, p. 245 (C. Rossiter ed. 1961), reserved explicitly to the States by the Tenth Amendment.

Whatever the outer limits of that sovereignty may be, one thing is clear: The Federal Government may not compel the States to enact or administer a federal regulatory program. The Constitution permits both the Federal Government and the States to enact legislation regarding the disposal of low level radioactive waste. The Constitution enables the Federal Government to preempt state regulation contrary to federal interests, and it permits the Federal Government to hold out incentives to the States as a means of encouraging them to adopt suggested regulatory schemes. It does not, however, authorize Congress simply to direct the States to provide for the disposal of the radioactive waste generated within their borders. While there may be many constitutional methods of achieving regional self-sufficiency in radioactive waste disposal, the method Congress has chosen is not one of them.

JUSTICE WHITE, with whom JUSTICE BLACKMUN and JUSTICE STEVENS join, concurring in part and dissenting in part.

3. Waste Management and Pollution Prevention   Pages 414-416

The Court today affirms the constitutionality of two facets of the Low-Level Radioactive Waste Policy Amendments Act of 1985 (1985 Act) Pub. L. 99-240, 99 Stat. 1842, 42 U.S.C. §2021b et seq. These provisions include the monetary incentives from surcharges collected by States with low-level radioactive waste storage sites and rebated by the Secretary of Energy to States in compliance with the Act's deadlines for achieving regional or in-state disposal, see §§2021e(d)(2)(A) and 2021e(d)(2)(B)(iv), and the "access incentives," which deny access to disposal sites for States that fail to meet certain deadlines for low-level radioactive waste disposal management. §2021e(e)(2). The Court strikes down and severs a third component of the 1985 Act, the "take title" provision, which requires a noncomplying State to take title to or to assume liability for its low-level radioactive waste if it fails to provide for the disposal of such waste by January 1, 1996. §2021e(d)(2)(C). The Court deems this last provision unconstitutional under principles of federalism. Because I believe the Court has mischaracterized the essential inquiry, misanalyzed the inquiry it has chosen to undertake, and undervalued the effect the seriousness of this public policy problem should have on the constitutionality of the take title provision, I can only join [in the parts affirming the Court of Appeals] and I respectfully dissent from the rest of its opinion and the judgment reversing in part the judgment of the Court of Appeals. . . .

[S]een as a term of an agreement entered into between the several States, this measure proves to be less constitutionally odious than the Court opines. First, the practical effect of New York's position is that because it is unwilling to honor its obligations to provide in-state storage facilities for its low-level radioactive waste, *other* States with such plants *must accept* New York's waste, whether they wish to or not. Otherwise, the many economically and socially beneficial producers of such waste in the State would have to cease their operations. The Court's refusal to force New York to accept responsibility for its own problem inevitably means that some other State's sovereignty will be impinged by it being forced, for public health reasons, to accept New York's low-level radioactive waste. I do not understand the principle of federalism to impede the National Government from acting as referee among the States to prohibit one from bullying another.

Moreover, it is utterly reasonable that, in crafting a delicate compromise between the three overburdened States that provided low-level radioactive waste disposal facilities and the rest of the States, Congress would have to ratify some punitive measure as the ultimate sanction for noncompliance. The take title provision, though surely onerous, does *not* take effect if the generator of the waste does not request such action, or if the State lives up to its bargain of providing a waste disposal facility either within the State or in another State pursuant to a regional compact arrangement or a separate contract. See 42 U.S. C. §2021e(d)(2)(C)....

The Court's distinction between a federal statute's regulation of States and private parties for general purposes, as opposed to a regulation solely on the activities of States, is unsupported by our recent Tenth Amendment cases. In no case has the Court rested its holding on such a distinction. Moreover, the Court makes no effort to explain why this purported distinction should affect the analysis of Congress' power under general principles of federalism and the Tenth Amendment. The distinction, facilely thrown out, is not based on any defensible theory.... An incursion on state sovereignty hardly seems more constitutionally acceptable if the federal statute that "commands" specific action also applies to private parties. The alleged diminution in state authority over its own affairs is not any less because the federal mandate restricts the activities of private parties....

The ultimate irony of the decision today is that in its rigid obeisance to "federalism," the Court gives Congress fewer incentives to defer to the wishes of state officials in achieving local solutions to local problems. This legislation was a classic example of Congress acting as arbiter among the States in their attempts to accept responsibility for managing a problem of grave import. The States urged the National Legislature not to impose from Washington a solution to the country's low-level radioactive waste management problems. Instead, they sought a reasonable level of local and regional autonomy consistent with Art. I §10, cl. 3, of the Constitution. By invalidating the measure designed to ensure compliance for recalcitrant States, such as New York, the Court upsets the delicate compromise achieved among the States and forces Congress to erect several additional formalistic hurdles to clear before achieving exactly the same objective. Because the Court's justifications for undertaking this step are unpersuasive to me, I respectfully dissent.

NOTES AND QUESTIONS

1. While upholding most aspects of the Low-Level Radioactive Waste Policy Act (LLRWPA), the Court struck down the "take title" provision as inconsistent with constitutional principles of federalism. Justice O'Connor's analysis appears founded on concern about maintaining political accountability. Do you agree with her analysis that while direct federal regulation leaves the federal government politically accountable, "where the Federal Government directs the states to regulate, it may be state officials who will bear the brunt of public disapproval, while the Federal officials who devised the regulatory program may remain insulated from the electoral ramifications of their decision"?

3. Waste Management and Pollution Prevention   Pages 417-420

   2. Justice White's dissent emphasizes the irony of invalidating part of the LLRWPA on grounds of federalism when enactment of the statute was "very much the product of cooperative federalism" because it "reflected hard-fought agreements among states as refereed by Congress." Is he right when he argues that the majority's decision "gives Congress fewer incentives to defer to the wishes of state officials in achieving local solutions to local problems"?
   3. After the Court announced its decision, a New York official was quoted as stating: "If the state does not have to take ownership and liability for the wastes, there may be less inclination to build a facility for those wastes." Schneider, Decision Is Expected to Ease the Pressure on States, N.Y. Times, June 20, 1992, at A10. Is this precisely what has happened? Nevada closed its site and Washington's Hanford site now will accept waste only from Hawaii and six other northwestern states. Under South Carolina law, the Barnwell facility was closed to waste from states outside the Southeast Compact on June 30, 1994. As a result, 37 states then using the facility had to shift to alternative sites. Yet none of these states had commenced constructing a permanent low-level radioactive waste disposal facility at the time. On December 31, 1995, the Barnwell facility will close entirely. Because it is unlikely that a new facility will open in the Southeast Compact states until at least late 1997, if a site selected in North Carolina is built, generators of low-level radioactive waste in the region may be forced to rely on on-site storage for up to two years. Regional Commission Told of Problems for Generators Forced to Store Wastes, 25 Env. Rep. 1183 (1994).

2. *Waste Reduction: Federal and State Initiatives*

   Encouraging Source Reduction (pp. 417-420).   When it reauthorizes RCRA, Congress is likely to confront the question of what regulatory incentives to provide to encourage source reduction. The EPA's Green Lights program is being expanded to encourage more efficient heating, ventilation, and air conditioning systems. EPA also has developed an Energy Star Program to encourage the development of more energy-efficient products by authorizing manufacturers to display an EPA-developed logo. Computer manufacturers will soon begin marketing machines that "sleep" while not in active use in order to save energy. EPA estimates that because personal computers are used only 20 percent of the time, this new generation of "Energy Star Computers" could save $1 billion per year by the year 2000, while preventing 20 million tons of carbon dioxide emissions, 140,000 tons of sulfur dioxide emissions, and 75,000 tons of nitrogen oxide emissions annually. EPA Energy Star Logo Premieres 1992 EPA J 2

Pages 417-420   3. Waste Management and Pollution Prevention

(July-Aug. 1992). For a summary of federal efforts to encourage pollution prevention in the wake of the enactment of the Pollution Prevention Act, see Stephen M. Johnson, From Reaction to Proaction: The 1990 Pollution Prevention Act, 17 Colum. J. Env. L. 153 (1992). Proposals for a more regulatory approach to pollution prevention are discussed in Lieberman, Planning for Pollution Prevention, 1993 Envtl. Forum 22 (Jan.-Feb. 1993).

Perhaps the most significant regulatory action to encourage source reduction is EPA's issuance of guidance for waste minimization programs to comply with RCRA §§3002(b) and 3005(h). These sections require generators to certify that they have programs in place to reduce the volume and toxicity of their waste. While EPA previously had eschewed implementation of these provisions (text, p. 419), the Agency announced in May 1993 that it intends to require generators to establish waste minimization programs. 58 Fed. Reg. 31,114 (1993).

In October 1993, President Clinton issued Executive Order 12873, 58 Fed. Reg. 54,911, to encourage recycling and waste prevention through federal acquisition policies. It directs all federal agencies to "incorporate waste prevention and recycling in the agency's daily operations and to increase and expand markets for recovered materials through greater Federal Government preference and demand for such products." The position of Federal Environmental Executive, located within EPA, is created to develop government-wide implementation plans that will include revisions of federal product specifications and guidance for the purchase of environmentally preferable products. Agencies also are directed to purchase paper containing at least 20 percent postconsumer materials beginning in 1995 and increasing to 30 percent beginning in 1999.

State and Local Waste Reduction Activities (pp. 420-422).   After foundering because of the absence of well-developed markets for recycled materials, recycling programs have become more profitable as prices for recycled materials have increased substantially. Stipp, Cities Couldn't Give Away Their Trash; Now They Get Top Dollar from Recyclers, Wall St. J., Sept. 19, 1994, at B1. Prices for paper, cardboard, and certain plastics soared to record highs in 1994. While more than 6,700 communities have established programs for curbside collection of recyclable materials, collection costs still exceed the value of the materials collected by most programs. Bailey, Curbside Recycling Comforts the Soul, But Benefits Are Scant, Wall St. J., Jan. 19, 1995, at A1. Some localities are adopting an economic incentive approach to encourage source reduction and recycling by charging residents for garbage disposal by volume. Hanley, Towns Adopt Pay-as-You-Throw Garbage, N.Y. Times, July 14, 1992, at B1.

4
Regulation of Toxic Substances

We have no doubt that the agency acted with the best of intentions. It may well be, as OSHA claims, that this was the only practical way of accomplishing a much needed revision of the existing standards and of making major strides toward improving worker safety and health. Given OSHA's history of slow progress in issuing standards, we can easily believe OSHA's claim that going through detailed analysis for each of the 428 different substances regulated was not possible . . . Unfortunately, OSHA's approach to this rulemaking is not consistent with the requirements of the OSH Act.

—*AFL-CIO v. OSHA**

[T]here are important differences between the quest for truth in the courtroom and the quest for truth in the laboratory. Scientific conclusions are subject to perpetual revision. Law, on the other hand, must resolve disputes finally and quickly.

—*Daubert v. Merrell Dow Pharmaceuticals, Inc.*†

In this chapter we review major developments in toxic substance regulation that have occurred since publication of the parent text. Efforts to reduce human exposure to toxics continue to generate controversy both in and out of court. While environmental and public health groups perceive gaping loopholes in the regulatory safety net, chemical manufacturers decry a regulatory system that imposes huge costs to respond to what they believe may be trivial risks. These issues have produced an uncomfortable juxtaposition of law and science as regulators and the adversary process press for answers science cannot confidently provide.

The chapter discusses the Eleventh Circuit's decision in AFL-CIO v. OSHA, 965 F.2d 962 (11th Cir. 1992), the air contaminants decision,

---

*965 F. 2d 962, 987 (11th Cir. 1992).
†113 S. Ct. 2786 (1993).

which struck down an ambitious effort by OSHA to adopt new and revised standards to control occupational exposure to 428 toxic substances. In addition to illustrating the abiding impact of the Supreme Court's *Benzene* decision, this case highlights the enormous obstacles to efforts to supplant chemical-by-chemical regulation with a more comprehensive approach. Another important decision discussed below is American Water Works Assn v. EPA, 40 F.3d 1266 (D.C. Cir. 1994), which upheld EPA's approach to regulating lead in drinking water. In Les v. Reilly, 968 F.2d 985 (9th Cir. 1992), the Ninth Circuit embraced the rationale of Public Citizen v. Young (text, p. 583) and rejected EPA's effort to create a de minimis exception to the Delaney Clause applicable to food additives. The chapter also explores the conflict that has erupted over the use of animal test data to assess risks to human health. This controversy has embroiled the scientific community in an extended debate over the validity of assumptions commonly employed in risk assessment. After updating experience with California's Proposition 65, the chapter concludes by reviewing the Supreme Court's *Daubert* decision, which addresses the admission of expert testimony in toxic tort litigation.

A. THE TOXIC SUBSTANCE PROBLEM

Environmental Releases of Toxic Substances (p. 433). In 1995, EPA released the results of the Toxics Release Inventory (TRI) for 1993, compiled with data reported under the Emergency Planning and Community Right-to-Know Act (EPCRTKA). Discharges of 2.8 billion pounds of toxic substances were reported, including 1.7 billion pounds released into the air, 289 million pounds released on land, and 271 million pounds released into surface waters. The 1993 data report lower levels of releases to every environmental medium. Reporting required by the Pollution Prevention Act revealed that a total of 33.5 billion pounds of toxic wastes are being generated each year, but that increasing quantities are being recycled or reused for energy recovery. Industrial Releases of Toxic Chemicals Continue to Decline, EPA Administrator Says, 24 Env. Rep. 180 (1993); Lee, Industry Cuts Emissions of Toxic Chemical Waste, Wash. Post, Mar. 28, 1995, at A6.

Significance of Toxic Releases (p. 434). Controversy continues over the significance of environmental toxicants as a threat to human health. A large-scale analysis of cancer data, which was published in 1994, found

4. Regulation of Toxic Substances

that, when smoking-related cancers are excluded from consideration, men born during the 1940s are experiencing a cancer rate more than twice that experienced by their grandfathers. Women born during this period have a cancer rate 30 percent higher than their grandmothers. Davis et al., Decreasing Cardiovascular Disease and Increasing Cancer Among Whites in the United States from 1973 Through 1987, 271 JAMA 431 (1994). The authors of the study concluded that because "increases in cancer have occurred that are not solely linked to aging of the population and smoking patterns," environmental sources of carcinogens should be studied more intensively. The study's results are consistent with those found by Swedish researchers. Adami et al., Increasing Cancer Risk in Younger Birth Cohorts in Sweden, 341 Lancet 773 (1993).

Other epidemiological studies are generating results that are raising concerns about the potential effects of environmental toxicants. A study performed by the New York State Health Department found that women who once lived within a kilometer of large chemical plants had a 62 percent higher risk of developing breast cancer than women who lived elsewhere. Schemo, Intl. Herald Trib., Apr. 14, 1994, at 8. A Norwegian study published in the New England Journal of Medicine in July 1994 found that mothers of children with birth defects were nearly eight times more likely to have a second child with the same defect if they stayed in the same urban area, a risk that dropped dramatically if the women moved. Painter, Strong Environmental Link to Birth Defects Seen, USA Today, July 8-10, 1994, at 1A.

Some epidemiological studies have produced more encouraging results. A study by the Kaiser Foundation Research Institute found no evidence of a link between residues of DDT and breast cancer rates. Taubes, Pesticides and Breast Cancer: No Link?, 264 Science 499 (1994). A Canadian study that measured radon levels in the homes of lung cancer victims found no relationship between radon levels and lung cancer. Stone, New Radon Study: No Smoking Gun, 263 Science 465 (1994). However, a Swedish study published earlier in the year found that people exposed to radon at levels permitted under Canada's looser regulations had an 80 percent greater chance of getting lung cancer than those exposed at the much lower levels recommended in the United States and Sweden. Id.

In their search for environmental causes of cancer and other diseases, scientists are focusing increasingly on a wide range of chemicals found in pesticides, plastics, and other pollutants that affect hormone levels in humans. "Environmental estrogens" and other hormone-modulating pollutants may be linked to a global decline in human sperm counts, a disturbing increase in the rate of testicular cancer, and declines in the reproductive success of many species of wildlife. Stone, Environmental Estrogens Stir Debate, 265 Science 308 (1994); Colborn et al., Developmental Effects of Endocrine-Disrupting Chemicals in Wildlife and Humans, 101 Env. Health Persp. 378 (1993). While dozens of chemicals are known to be capable of disturbing the endocrine system by binding to the estrogen receptor, some scientists argue that the risks are low because most of these chemicals have only a very weak effect on estrogen. Given EPA's recognition that more attention needs to be devoted to assessment of reproductive risks, environmental estrogens are likely to receive more scrutiny in the future.

Concerns about the potential health effects of electromagnetic radiation also are commanding increasing attention. Humans are exposed to extremely low frequency electric and magnetic fields from a variety of sources, including powerlines, video display terminals, and household appliances. Some epidemiological studies have found statistically significant associations between the risk of some cancers and presumed measures of EMF exposure; a few studies have found a relationship between such measures and noncancer health effects. Florig, Containing the Costs of the EMF Problem, 257 Science 468 (1992). However, the exposure estimates used by these studies are subject to considerable uncertainty, and there are many potentially confounding factors that may account for these relationships.

Even as studies with more refined measures of exposure are being conducted, inconsistent findings seem to be the only constant. A study of more than 223,000 electric utility workers in Canada and France found an excess of cases of acute nonlymphoid leukemia, but no evidence that the risk of cancer varied with the level of exposure to EMF. 264 Science 205 (1994). A study of 139,000 electrical utility workers in the U.S. found that workers with mid-level exposures to EMF had a 50 percent greater risk of brain cancer than the lowest-exposure group and that workers with the most exposure were 2.3 times more likely to get brain cancer. However, the study found no increased risk of leukemia at higher exposures. Bishop, Link Between EMF, Brain Cancer Is Suggested by Study at Five Utilities, Wall St. J., Jan. 11, 1995, at B6. Thus, the controversy over the relationship between EMFs and cancer remains, as it was described in 1992, as "plagued by a morass of contradictory data." Stone, Polarized Debate: EMFs and Cancer, 258 Science 1724 (1992).

B. STATUTORY AUTHORITIES FOR REGULATING TOXICS

New Legislation (pp. 436-440). The most significant new federal legislation for control of human exposure to toxics is the Residential Lead-

4. Regulation of Toxic Substances   Pages 477-481

Based Paint Hazard Reduction Act, Pub. L. No. 102-550, enacted as Title X of the Housing and Community Development Act. As noted in Chapter 2 of this Supplement, the legislation adds a new title to the Toxic Substances Control Act to govern lead-paint abatement. It requires sellers or lessors of residential property to disclose any known lead-based paint hazards to prospective purchasers or lessees beginning in 1995. The legislation also mandates federal standards for licensing of lead paint abatement contractors, and it requires OSHA to adopt standards to protect construction workers from exposure to lead hazards.

C. UNCERTAINTY AND THE DILEMMA OF PREVENTATIVE REGULATION

2. Coping with Uncertainty: The Road to Risk Assessment

OSHA Regulation after the Benzene Decision (pp. 477-481). In an effort to shake off the regulatory paralysis induced by its chemical-by-chemical approach to regulation, OSHA in 1988 conducted a single generic rulemaking to amend and update permissible exposure limits (PELs) for hundreds of toxic substances. Known as the air contaminants rule, this rulemaking, which is discussed in the treatment of generic rulemaking in Chapter 5 of the text (p. 686), resulted in the adoption of new PELs for 428 toxic substances, including 164 substances that had not previously been regulated by OSHA. Both industry and labor groups challenged the OSHA regulations, resulting in the following decision by the Eleventh Circuit. The decision illustrates how *Benzene*'s requirement that OSHA make a finding of "significant risk" before regulating toxic substances in the workplace has made it difficult for OSHA to regulate in a comprehensive fashion.

AFL-CIO v. OSHA
965 F.2d 962 (11th Cir. 1992)

Before FAY and COX, Circuit Judges, and JOHNSON, Senior Circuit Judge.
FAY, Circuit Judge:

I. BACKGROUND

The Occupational Safety and Health Act of 1970 ("OSH Act" or "the Act"), 29 U.S.C. §§651-71, was adopted "to assure so far as possible every working man and woman in the nation safe and healthful working conditions." Id. §651(b). To this end, the Act authorizes the Secretary to issue occupational health and safety standards, id. §655, with which each employer must comply. Id. §654. Section 6(a) of the Act provided that in its first two years, OSHA should promulgate "start-up" standards, on an expedited basis and without public hearing or comment, based on "national consensus" or "established Federal standard[s]" that improve employee safety or health. Id. §655(a). Pursuant to that authority, OSHA in 1971 promulgated approximately 425 permissible exposure limits ("PELs") for air contaminants, 29 C.F.R. §1910.1000 (1971), derived principally from federal standards applicable to government contractors under the Walsh-Healey Act, 41 U.S.C. §35.[5] Air Contaminants Proposed Rule, 53 Fed. Reg. 20960, 20962 (1988).

The Act then provides two mechanisms to update these standards. Most new standards or revised existing standards must be promulgated under the requirements of section 6(b) of the OSH Act. 29 U.S.C. §655(b). This section sets forth both procedural requirements and substantive criteria which the standards must meet. In promulgating these standards, OSHA must follow a procedure that is even more stringent than that in the federal Administrative Procedure Act, 5 U.S.C. §553. United Steelworkers v. Marshall, 647 F.2d 1189, 1207 (D.C. Cir. 1980), cert. denied, 453 U.S. 913 (1981). OSHA must provide notice of proposed rulemaking, give interested parties an opportunity to comment, and hold a public hearing if requested. 29 U.S.C. §655(b)(2)-(4). As of 1988, OSHA had issued only twenty-four substance-specific and three "generic" health standards under section 6(b)[7]. . .

On June 7, 1988, OSHA published a Notice of Proposed Rulemaking for its Air Contaminants Standard. 53 Fed. Reg. 20960-21393. In this single rulemaking, OSHA proposed to issue new or revised PELs for over 400 substances. OSHA limited the scope of this rulemaking to those substances for which the ACGIH recommended limits that were either new or more protective than the existing PELs. Id. at 20967. There was an initial comment period of forty-seven days, followed by a thirteen-day public hearing. Interested parties then had until October

---

5. The Walsh-Healey standards, in turn, had been adopted from the 1968 recommendations of the American Conference of Governmental Industrial Hygienists ("ACGIH"). The ACGIH is a private organization consisting of professional personnel who work in governmental agencies and educational institutions engaged in occupational safety and health programs. ACGIH updates its recommendations (called "Threshold Limit Values" or "TLVs") annually. Air Contaminants Proposed Rule, 53 Red. Reg. 20960, 10966 (1988).

7. The three "generic" rulemakings were: Cancer Policy, 29 C.F.R. Part 1990; Access to Employee Exposure and Medical Records Regulation, 29 C.F.R. §1910.20; Hazard Communication Standard, 29 C.F.R. §1910.1200.

4. Regulation of Toxic Substances   Pages 477-481

7, 1988 to submit post-hearing evidence and until October 31, 1988 to submit post-hearing briefs.[8]

OSHA then issued its revised Air Contaminants Standard for 428 toxic substances on January 19, 1989. 54 Fed. Reg. 2332-2983. This standard, which differs from the proposal in several respects, lowered the PELs for 212 substances, set new PELs for 164 previously unregulated substances, and left unchanged PELs for 52 substances for which lower limits had originally been proposed. Id. at 2334. The standard established an approximately four-year period for employers to come into compliance with the new standard using engineering and work practice controls. Id. at 2916. Until that time, employers may use respirators or any other reasonable methods to comply with the standards. Id. at 2915-16. . . .

III. Discussion

In challenging the procedure by which OSHA promulgated the Air Contaminants Standard, a group of industry petitioners complain that OSHA's use of generic findings, the lumping together of so many substances in one rulemaking, and the short time provided for comment by interested parties, combine to create a record inadequate to support this massive new set of PELs. The union also challenges the rulemaking procedure utilized by OSHA for the Air Contaminants Standard. Not surprisingly, however, the union claims that this procedure resulted in standards that are systematically underprotective of employee health. The union further challenges OSHA's decision to limit the scope of the rulemaking to substances for which the ACGIH recommendation was more protective than the current PEL, and thereby to ignore both other air contaminant substances in need of regulation and standards for exposure monitoring and medical surveillance. Moreover, the union argues that there is no record support for a four-year compliance period

---

8. Industry petitioners repeatedly complain about the amount of time allowed for comment in this rulemaking. They claim the time period prevented them from adequately addressing all of the 428 PELs about which they had concerns. From the time of the initial Notice of Proposed Rulemaking to the close of the time allowed for submission of post-hearing evidence, four months elapsed. The OSH Act only provides that 30 days must be allowed for comment after publication of a proposed rule. 29 U.S.C. §655(B)(2). As the statute does not expressly address multi-substance rulemakings, it is unclear from the statute whether thirty days must be provided for each substance in such a rulemaking. However, we are unpersuaded that this time period allowed in this rulemaking was so insufficient as to prevent interested parties from commenting on the proposed rule.

for these standards, given that OSHA itself found that the standards can be met by existing technology.

A. "Generic" Rulemaking

Unlike most of the OSHA standards previously reviewed by the courts, the Air Contaminants Standard regulates not a single toxic substance, but 428 different substances. The agency explained its decision to issue such an omnibus standard in its Notice of Proposed Rulemaking:

> OSHA has issued only 24 substance-specific health regulations since its creation. It has not been able to review the many thousands of currently unregulated chemicals in the workplace nor to keep up with reviewing the several thousand new chemicals introduced since its creation. It has not been able to fully review the literature to determine if lower limits are needed for many of the approximately 400 substances it now regulates.
>
> Using past approaches and practices, OSHA could continue to regulate a small number of the high priority substances and those of greatest public interest. However, it would take decades to review currently used chemicals and OSHA would never be able to keep up with the many chemicals which will be newly introduced in the future.

53 Fed. Reg. at 20963. For this reason, "OSHA determined that it was necessary to modify this approach through the use of *generic* rulemaking, which would simultaneously cover many substances." 54 Fed. Reg. at 2333 (emphasis added).

"Generic" means something "common to or characteristic of a whole group or class; typifying or subsuming; not specific or individual." Webster's Third New International Dictionary 945 (1966). Previous "generic" rulemakings by OSHA have all dealt with requirements that, once promulgated, could be applied to numerous different situations. For example, OSHA's Hazard Communication Standard, 29 C.F.R. §1910.1200, mandates that employers inform employees of potentially hazardous materials. The regulation includes a basic list of substances which employers must treat as hazardous, but requires that the employers themselves also evaluate substances produced in their workplaces to determine if they are potentially hazardous based on available scientific evidence. United Steelworkers v. Auchter, 763 F.2d 729, 732 (3d Cir. 1985). Similarly, OSHA has issued standards regulating employee access to medical and toxic substance exposure records, 29 C.F.R. §1910.20, and setting forth uniform criteria for application in future regulation of exposure to carcinogens, 29 C.F.R. Part 1990.

4. Regulation of Toxic Substances   Pages 477-481

By contrast, the new Air Contaminants Standard is an amalgamation of 428 unrelated substance exposure limits. There is little common to this group of diverse substances except the fact that OSHA considers them toxic and in need of regulation. In fact, this rulemaking is the antithesis of a "generic" rulemaking; it is a set of 428 specific and individual substance exposure limits. Therefore, OSHA's characterization of this as a "generic" rulemaking is somewhat misleading.

Nonetheless, we find nothing in the OSH Act that would prevent OSHA from addressing multiple substances in a single rulemaking. Moreover, because the statute leaves this point open and because OSHA's interpretation of the statute is reasonable, it is appropriate for us to defer to OSHA's interpretation. See Chevron U.S.A., Inc. v. Natural Resources Defense Council, Inc., 467 U.S. 837, 843-45, 864-66 (1984); see also Vermont Yankee Nuclear Power Corp. v. Natural Resources Defense Council, Inc., 435 U.S. 519, 524-25, 543-49 (1978) (Courts should not impose procedural requirements on agencies if not statutorily required.). However, we believe the PEL for each substance must be able to stand independently, i.e., that each PEL must be supported by substantial evidence in the record considered as a whole and accompanied by adequate explanation. OSHA may not, by using such multi-substance rulemaking, ignore the requirements of the OSH Act. Both the industry petitioners and the union argue that such disregard was what in essence occurred. Regretfully, we agree.

B. *Significant Risk of Material Health Impairment*

Section 3(8) of the OSH Act defines "occupational health and safety standard" as "a standard which requires conditions, or the adoption or use of one or more practices, means, methods, operations, or processes, *reasonably necessary or appropriate* to provide safe or healthful employment and places of employment." 29 U.S.C. §652(8) (emphasis added). The Supreme Court has interpreted this provision to require that, before the promulgation of any permanent health standard, OSHA make a threshold finding that a significant risk of material health impairment exists at the current levels of exposure to the toxic substance in question, *Benzene*, 448 U.S. at 614-15, 642; *ATMI* [American Textile Manufacturers Institute, Inc. v. Donovan], 452 U.S. [490], 505-06 [(1981)],[13] "and that a new, lower standard is therefore 'reasonably

---

13. In Industrial Union Department, AFL-CIO v. American Petroleum Institute, 448 U.S. 607 (1980), commonly referred to as the *Benzene* case, a plurality of the Supreme Court vacated OSHA's standard for benzene and set forth the appropriate analysis for reviewing a standard promulgated under the OSH Act. Since that time, the courts of appeals have generally considered that

necessary or appropriate to provide safe or healthful employment and places of employment.' " *Benzene,* 448 U.S. at 615. OSHA is not entitled to regulate *any* risk, only those which present a "significant" risk of "material" health impairment. Id. at 641-42. OSHA must therefore determine: (1) what health impairments are "material," Texas Independent Ginners, 630 F.2d at 407, and (2) what constitutes a "significant" risk of such impairment, *Benzene,* 448 U.S. at 641-42, 655. Moreover, OSHA ultimately bears the burden of proving by substantial evidence that such a risk exists and that the proposed standard is necessary. Id. at 653. The agency "has no duty to calculate the exact probability of harm," id. at 655, or "to support its finding that a significant risk exists with anything approaching scientific certainty," id. at 656. However, OSHA must provide at least an estimate of the actual risk associated with a particular toxic substance, see Public Citizen Health Research Group v. Tyson, 796 F.2d 1479, 1502-03 (D.C. Cir. 1986), and explain in an understandable way why that risk is significant. *Benzene,* 448 U.S. at 646. In past rulemakings, OSHA has satisfied this requirement by estimating either the number of workers likely to suffer the effects of exposure or the percentage of risk to any particular worker.[15] See *ATMI,* 462 U.S. at 503, 505 n.25; Building & Constr. Trades Dept., AFL-CIO v. Brock, 838 F.2d 1258, 1263 (D.C. Cir. 1988); Public Citizen, 796 F.2d at 1502; ASARCO, Inc. v. OSHA, 746 F.2d 483, 488 (9th Cir. 1984).

Once OSHA finds that a significant risk of material health impairment exists at current exposure levels for a given toxic substance, any standard promulgated to address that risk must comply with the requirements of section 6(b)(5) of the OSH Act. 29 U.S.C. §655(b)(5). That section provides that the agency

> in promulgating standards dealing with toxic materials or harmful physical agents under this subsection, shall set the standard which *most adequately assures, to the extent feasible, on the basis of the best available evidence, that no employee will suffer material impairment of health or functional capacity* even if such employee has regular exposure to the hazard dealt with by such standard for the period of his working life. . . .

---

the plurality opinion in *Benzene* was implicitly adopted by a majority of the Court in American Textile Mfrs. Inst. v. Donovan, 452 U.S. 490, 505 n. 25 (1981) (hereinafter *"ATMI"*).

15. The Court in *Benzene* gave an example, stating that "if the odds are one in a thousand that regular inhalation of gasoline vapors that are 2% benzene will be fatal, a reasonable person might well consider the risk significant and take appropriate steps to decrease or eliminate it." *Benzene,* 448 U.S. at 655, 100 S. Ct. at 2871. OSHA has apparently incorporated that example "as a policy norm, at least in the sense of believing that it *must* regulate if it finds a risk at the 1/1000 level." International Union v. Pendergrass, 878 F.2nd 389, 392 (D.C. Cir. 1989).

4. Regulation of Toxic Substances

Id. (emphasis added). In other words, section 6(b)(5) mandates that the standard adopted "prevent material impairment of health to the extent feasible." *ATMI*, 452 U.S. at 512 (emphasis omitted).

1. Material Impairment

In this rulemaking, OSHA grouped the 428 substances into eighteen categories by the primary health effects of those substances, for example, neuropathic effects, sensory irritation, and cancer. See 54 Fed. Reg. at 2402-03. Industry petitioners charge that for several categories of substances OSHA failed to adequately justify its determination that the health effects caused by exposure to these substances are "material impairments." We disagree.

Petitioners cite the category of "sensory irritation" as a particularly egregious example . . . We interpret [OSHA's] explanation as indicating that OSHA finds that although minor irritation may not be a material impairment, there is a level at which such irritation becomes so severe that employee health and job performance are seriously threatened, even though those effects may be transitory. We find that explanation adequate. OSHA is not required to state with scientific certainty or precision the exact point at which each type of sensory or physical irritation becomes a material impairment. Moreover, section 6(b)(5) of the Act charges OSHA with addressing all forms of "material impairment of health *or functional capacity*," and not exclusively "death or serious physical harm" or "grave danger" from exposure to toxic substances. See 29 U.S.C. §§654(a)(1), 655(c). Overall, we find that OSHA's determinations of what constitute "material impairments" are adequately explained and supported in the record.

2. Significant Risk

However, the agency's determination of the extent of the risk posed by individual substances is more problematic. "No one could reasonably expect OSHA to adopt some precise estimate of fatalities likely from a given exposure level, and indeed the Supreme Court has said that the agency has 'no duty to calculate the exact probability of harm.' " International Union UAW v. Pendergrass, 878 F.2d 389, 392 (D.C. Cir. 1989) (quoting *Benzene*, 448 U.S. at 655). Nevertheless, OSHA has a responsibility to quantify or explain, at least to some reasonable degree, the risk posed by *each* toxic substance regulated. See id. ("OSHA necessarily seeks to quantify the risk posed by *each toxic threat*." (Emphasis added.)); see also *Benzene*, 448 U.S. at 614-15 ("We agree . . . that §3(8) requires the Secretary to find, as a threshold matter, that *the toxic substance in question* poses a significant health risk . . ." (Emphasis added.)). Otherwise, OSHA has not demonstrated, and this court cannot evaluate, how serious the risk is for any particular substance, or whether *any* workers will in fact benefit from the new standard for any particular substance. If each of these 428 toxic substances had been addressed in separate rulemakings, OSHA would clearly have been required to estimate in some fashion the risk of harm for each substance. OSHA is not entitled to take short-cuts with statutory requirements simply because it chose to combine multiple substances in a single rulemaking.

However, OSHA's discussions of individual substances generally contain no quantification or explanation of the risk from that individual substance.[18] The discussions of individual substances contain summaries of various studies of that substance and the health effects found at various levels of exposure to that substance. However, OSHA made no attempt to estimate the risk of contracting those health effects. Instead, OSHA merely provided a conclusory statement that the new PEL will reduce the "significant" risk of material health effects shown to be caused by that substance, see, e.g., 54 Fed. Reg. at 2508 (bismuth telluride), without any explanation of how the agency determined that the risk was significant. However, OSHA did make a generic finding that the Air Contaminants Standard as a whole would prevent 55,000 occupational illnesses and 683 deaths annually. Id. at 2725.

Moreover, a determination that the new standard is "reasonably necessary or appropriate," 29 U.S.C. §652(8), and that it is the standard that "most adequately assures . . . that no employee will suffer material impairment of health or functional capacity," id. §655(b)(5), necessarily requires some assessment of the level at which significant risk of harm is eliminated or substantially reduced. See *Benzene*, 448 U.S. at 653. Yet, with rare exceptions, the individual substance discussions in the Air Contaminants Standard are virtually devoid of reasons for setting those individual standards. In most cases, OSHA cited a few studies and then established a PEL without explaining why the studies mandated the particular PEL chosen. For example, the PEL for bismuth telluride appears to be based on a single study that showed almost no effects of any kind in animals at several times that concentration. 54 Fed. Reg. at 2508. Similarly, the PEL for ferrovanadium dust was based on pulmonary changes at exposure levels many hundreds of times higher than OSHA's new standard. Id. at 2510. See also, e.g., iron pentacarbonyl, id. at 2412; cesium hydroxide, id. at 2455; iron salts, id. at 2466; ethylene dichloride,

---

18. The exception is the discussion of the substances regulated as carcinogens. For these substances, OSHA used a mathematical model to quantify the risk posed by each substance. See, e.g., 54 Fed. Reg. at 2677-78 (amitrole).

4. Regulation of Toxic Substances   Pages 477-481

id. at 2484; sulfur tetrafluoride, id. at 2526. For some substances, OSHA merely repeated a boilerplate finding that the new limit would protect workers from significant risk of some material health impairment. For example, OSHA did not cite any studies whatsoever for its aluminum welding fume standard, id. at 2554, or its vegetable oil mist standard, id. at 2601. See also, e.g., starch, id. at 2599-2600.

"While our deference to the agency is at a peak for its choices among scientific predictions, we must still look for *some* articulation of reasons for those choices." *Pendergrass*, 878 F2d at 392 (emphasis added). . . . Mere conclusory statements, such as those made throughout the Air Contaminants Standard, are simply inadequate to support a finding of significant risk of material health impairment.

On the other hand, OSHA established PELs for carbon tetrachloride and vinyl bromide, both carcinogens, at levels where OSHA itself acknowledged that the risk of material health impairment remained significant. 54 Fed. Reg. at 2679-80, 2694. For carbon tetrachloride, OSHA stated that at the new level, "residual risk continues to be significant. . . . 3.7 excess deaths per 1,000 workers exposed over their working lifetimes." Id. at 2680. For vinyl bromide, OSHA stated that the new PEL "will not eliminate this significant risk, because . . . residual risk [at the new level] is 40 excess deaths per 1,000 exposed workers . . . [and thus] is clearly significant." Id. at 2694. The only explanation given by OSHA in the final rule for setting its standard where a significant risk of material health impairment remains was that the time and resource constraints of attempting to promulgate an air contaminants standard of this magnitude prevented detailed analysis of these substances. See id. at 2363, 2694. OSHA did not claim in the final rule that the PELs for these two substances were necessary because of feasibility concerns.

The agency's response to this criticism is unpersuasive. OSHA first contends that quantitative risk analysis using mathematical models like the ones developed for carcinogens was impossible for this rulemaking because no such models exist for non-carcinogens.

> Dose-response models have often been used in the quantitative assessment of the risks associated with exposures to carcinogenic substances. However, less scientific effort has been devoted to models to be used with non-carcinogenic substances. Mathematically precise methods to establish the true no-effect level or to define the dose-response curves have not been developed for most of the more than 400 substances involved in this rulemaking.
>
> Most of the scientific work that has been done was designed to identify lowest observed effect or no-effect levels for a variety of acute effects . . . It is possible to use these data, combined with professional judgment and OSHA's expertise and experience, to determine that signifi-

cant risk exists at current levels of exposure and that a reduction in these levels will substantially reduce this risk of material impairment of health.

54 Fed. Reg. at 2399-2400. Yet, in several previous rulemakings, OSHA apparently succeeded in determining how many workers were exposed to a particular substance or how much risk would be alleviated by a new standard, even though those particular substances were *not* carcinogens. See *United Steelworkers*, 647 F.2d at 1245-51 (lead poisoning); AFL-CIO v. Marshall, 617 F.2d at 646 (byssinosis caused by cotton dust); see also *Building & Constr.*, 838 F.2d at 1263 (asbestosis and cancer). It is therefore unclear whether the lack of a method to quantitatively assess the risk for noncarcinogens is a cause or a result of the agency's approach. In this rulemaking, OSHA concluded that current exposure to 428 substances posed a "significant" risk of material health impairment, and that its new standards were required for most of these substances to eliminate or substantially reduce that risk. It is not unreasonable to require that the agency explain how it arrived at that determination, and, indeed, this is precisely what Congress required.

The agency further claims that no quantification was required because OSHA's final standards " 'fall[] within a zone of reasonableness.' " OSHA Brief at 40-41 (quoting *United Steelworkers*, 647 F.2d at 1207). However, without *any* quantification or *any* explanation, this court cannot determine what that "zone of reasonableness" is or if these standards fall within it.

OSHA also responds by noting that it incorporated "uncertainty" or "safety" factors into many PELs. However, OSHA did not use a uniform safety factor, but instead claims to have made a case-by-case assessment of the appropriate safety factor. 54 Fed. Reg. at 2398-99. "Studies are often of small size and since there is a large variation in human susceptibility, a study because of its small size may not demonstrate an effect that actually exists . . . For this reason, it is not uncommon to set a limit below that level which the study may have indicated showed no effect." Id. at 2365. OSHA claims that use of such uncertainty factors "has been the standard approach for recommending exposure limits for non-carcinogens by scientists and health experts in the field for many years." Id. In this rulemaking, the difference between the level shown by the evidence and the final PEL is sometimes substantial. We assume, because it is not expressly stated, that for each of those substances OSHA applied a safety factor to arrive at the final standard. Nevertheless, the method by which the "appropriate" safety factor was determined for each of those substances is not explained in the final rule.

We find OSHA's use of safety factors in this rulemaking problematic. First, OSHA's use of safety factors in this rulemaking is very similar

4. Regulation of Toxic Substances — Pages 477-481

to the approach criticized by the Supreme Court in *Benzene*. Second, even assuming that the use of safety factors is permissible under the Act and *Benzene*, application of such factors without explaining the method by which they were determined, as was done in this case, is clearly not permitted.

From OSHA's description, safety factors are used to lower the standard below levels at which the available evidence shows no significant risk of material health impairment because of the *possibility* that the evidence is incorrect or incomplete; i.e., OSHA essentially makes an assumption that the existing evidence does not adequately show the extent of the risk. That may be a correct assumption, but beyond a general statement that the use of safety factors is common in the scientific community, OSHA did not indicate how the existing evidence for individual substances was inadequate to show the extent of the risk from those substances. Such a rationale is very reminiscent of the "benefits are likely to be appreciable" rationale rejected in *Benzene* as insufficient to satisfy the agency's obligation under the OSH Act. . . . Comparing OSHA's rationale for using safety factors in this rulemaking with the Court's discussion of their use in the *Benzene* case, we find little appreciable difference.

The Supreme Court in *Benzene* did recognize that absolute scientific certainty may be impossible when regulating on the edge of scientific knowledge, and that "so long as they are supported by a body of reputable scientific thought, the Agency is free to use conservative assumptions in interpreting the data . . . , risking error on the side of overprotection rather than underprotection." Id. at 656. However, the Court also discussed the use of monitoring and medical testing as a "backstop," permitting the agency to "keep a constant check on the validity of the assumptions made in developing the permissible exposure limit, giving it a sound evidentiary basis for decreasing the limit if it was initially set too high." Id. at 658.

The lesson of *Benzene* is clearly that OSHA may use assumptions, but only to the extent that those assumptions have some basis in reputable scientific evidence. If the agency is concerned that the standard should be more stringent than even a conservative interpretation of the existing evidence supports, monitoring and medical testing may be done to accumulate the additional evidence needed to support that more protective limit. *Benzene* does not provide support for setting standards below the level substantiated by the evidence. Nor may OSHA base a finding of significant risk at lower levels of exposure on unsupported assumptions using evidence of health impairments at significantly higher levels of exposure. *Benzene*, 448 U.S. at 656-58; *Texas Indep. Ginners*, 630 F.2d at 409. Overall, OSHA's use of safety factors in this rulemaking was not adequately explained by this rulemaking record.

199

More generally, OSHA defends its failure to make more specific findings for each individual substance, as well as its decision to set the standards for several substances at levels where significant risks of material health impairment remain, by citing its authority to set priorities, 29 U.S.C. §655(g), and the discretion permitted the agency in making policy decisions. There were warning signs of this position in the Notice of Proposed Rulemaking, where OSHA expressed its view that "to review and regulate many substances in a reasonable period requires some narrowing of the issues, focus of analysis, and reducing the length of the discussions in the preamble." 53 Fed. Reg. at 20963. Indeed, the agency stated that "[t]he success of a project to regulate a large backlog of chemicals for which there is a generally recognized need for new or improved employee protection requires some recognition of the need for agency flexibility in several areas," for example, "in less detailed discussion for each substance." Id. Moreover, the agency stated that

> [i]n response to both the court challenges and the need to face difficult issues, OSHA has engaged in detailed and extensive analyses. These have resulted in lengthier preamble discussions and in-depth analyses for all issues . . .
>
> Now that OSHA has reviewed these issues in depth several times, has experience "gained under the . . . law" (sec. 6(b)(5)) on these issues, and has had its analysis upheld in the Courts, somewhat less detailed chemical-by-chemical analyses should be appropriate. The accumulated judicial guidance and agency experience reduces the need for as extensive a discussion of some of the issues.

Id. at 20964. This implies that OSHA need no longer perform detailed analysis and explanation when promulgating PELs because the agency's analysis for other substances has been upheld in prior rulemakings. Besides displaying more than a touch of hubris, this passage reveals a fundamental misperception of the OSH Act and the caselaw interpreting that act.

While OSHA has probably established that most or all of the substances involved do pose a significant risk at some level, it has failed to establish that existing exposure levels in the workplace present a significant risk of material health impairment or that the new standards eliminate or substantially lessen the risk. . . .

[The court then discussed OSHA's findings concerning the feasibility of the new and revised PELs. This portion of the opinion is reproduced in Section D2 below, where feasibility-limited regulation is discussed.]

4. Regulation of Toxic Substances   Pages 477-481

E. *Other Union Issues*

Union petitioners raise several other issues that deserve comment.

1. **Use of ACGIH Recommendations**

The union challenges OSHA's use of the ACGIH recommendations on two grounds. First, OSHA only considered for this rulemaking those substances for which the ACGIH has recommended a limit more protective than the existing PEL. 54 Fed. Reg. at 2372; 53 Fed. Reg. at 20967. The union argues that this decision to limit the scope of this rulemaking in such a way was inconsistent with the agency's duty to set the standards "which most adequately assure[] . . . that no employee will suffer material impairment of health or functional capacity" from exposure to toxic substances. See 29 U.S.C. §655(b)(5). We disagree.

As previously noted, we find nothing in the OSH Act that prohibits OSHA from combining multiple substances in one rulemaking, as long as the statutory requirements are met for each substance. Neither do we find a requirement that OSHA include *all* possible substances in one rulemaking. OSHA has never claimed that this Air Contaminants Standard constituted the total universe of substances needing regulation, and it seems reasonable that some limit needed to be set as to what substances could be considered in this rulemaking. The list of ACGIH recommendations is a rational choice as the source for that limitation. The ACGIH recommendations are clearly well known to industry and the safety and health community. Therefore, we find that the agency's choice to so limit this rulemaking is a valid exercise of OSHA's authority to set priorities for rulemaking. See id. §655(g). The Act is sufficiently flexible to allow OSHA "to initially determine whether or not there will be a standard . . . [and] to process higher priority standards more quickly." National Congress of Hispanic Am. Citizens v. Usery, 554 F.2d 1196 (D.C.Cir. 1977).

Petitioners also challenge OSHA's extensive use of the ACGIH recommendations for individual substances. Petitioners claim that OSHA did no more than adopt wholesale the ACGIH recommendations without independently analyzing the evidence supporting those recommendations. It is not clear from the record if OSHA independently reviewed the individual studies cited by the ACGIH, or merely the ACGIH summary of the data. See 53 Fed. Reg. at 20965 ("OSHA has concentrated its efforts on reviewing summaries of the major studies, with emphasis on the literature used to support the exposure limits proposed by NIOSH and ACGIH. . . ."). However, we do not believe that OSHA is required to independently research all aspects of its rules.

The Act authorizes the agency to employ expert consultants, 29 U.S.C. §656(c), and OSHA is entitled to rely on such consultants, as well as studies in the scientific literature, as a basis for its PELs. See *United Steelworkers*, 647 F.2d at 1217. To that extent, OSHA is entitled to rely on the recommendations and documentation of the ACGIH, as it may rely on any other consulting organizations.

Use of such consultants, however, does not relieve OSHA of the responsibility for making detailed findings, with adequate explanations, for all statutory criteria. The recommendations of a consultant are not always based on the criteria required by the statute. As it is ultimately OSHA's responsibility to make those statutory findings, OSHA must determine, based on the "best available evidence," 29 U.S.C. §655(b)(5), if those statutory criteria have been met, and then set forth the analysis behind that determination in an understandable way.

In this rulemaking, petitioners state that the ACGIH recommendations are not based on the statutory criteria and that OSHA did nothing more than adopt those recommendations without any independent analysis of whether the evidence supporting those recommendations satisfied the statutory criteria. We express no opinion on this claim. However, the dearth of explanation in the rulemaking record for these 428 PELs makes it difficult to determine how the agency arrived at its conclusions. We do note that not all final PELs conformed to the ACGIH recommendation, through approximately ninety percent were identical. On remand, OSHA will be required to carefully review the evidence supporting each of the 428 PELs, and this concern should be addressed at that time.

[The court vacated the air contaminants standard in its entirety. The concluding portion of the court's opinion is reproduced in Section D2 below.]

NOTES AND QUESTIONS

1. The Eleventh Circuit appears to endorse the concept of "generic" rulemaking, at least in theory. The court states that it finds "nothing in the OSH Act that would prevent OSHA from addressing multiple substances in a single rulemaking." Yet the court then harshly criticizes OSHA's approach. What would OSHA have had to do differently in this rulemaking in order to accomplish its goal of updating and expanding the coverage of its PELs in a generic manner? Is it realistic to expect that OSHA could accomplish this in a single rulemaking? Note that, when published, the final air contaminants rule encompassed an entire 651-page volume of the Federal Register. 54 Fed. Reg. 2332-2983 (1989).

4. Regulation of Toxic Substances — Pages 481-486

2. As the court notes, OSHA found that "the Air Contaminants Standard as a whole would prevent 55,000 occupational illnesses and 683 deaths annually." Yet the court concludes that this did not satisfy the *Benzene* decision's requirement that OSHA make "significant risk" findings. Why not? Is the court suggesting that OSHA would have to perform individualized risk assessments for each of the 428 substances?

3. Justice Stevens's plurality opinion in the *Benzene* decision stated that OSHA is free to use conservative assumptions, "risking error on the side of overprotection rather than underprotection," as long as those assumptions "are supported by a body of reputable scientific thought," parent text, p. 472. Why, then, did the Eleventh Circuit reject OSHA's attempt to use safety factors to justify its actions? Is the court suggesting that safety factors are not an appropriate response to scientific uncertainty?

4. What relevance should the ACGIH recommendations have? Should the fact that ACGIH had adopted lower recommended exposure limits for many substances give OSHA more leeway to regulate such substances? Should it permit OSHA to make less detailed findings concerning the significance of the risk? According to an OSHA official, under the carbon monoxide standard reinstated by the Eleventh Circuit's decision, "you can die from carbon monoxide poisoning and still be within OSHA's limit." Swoboda, Some Toxic Substance Rules Being Dropped, Wash. Post, Mar. 23, 1993, at D1.

5. The Eleventh Circuit also found fault with OSHA's findings concerning the feasibility of its new and revised PELs. See Section D2 below.

Introduction to Risk Assessment Techniques (pp. 481-486). Joseph Rodricks, a scientist with the Environ Corporation who has helped develop risk assessment models, has written a useful book explaining how risk assessments are conducted. The book employs the National Research Council's four-step model of the risk assessment process. J. Rodricks, Calculated Risks (1992). In it Rodricks identifies eight standard practices that are used in risk assessments performed by regulatory agencies:

1. In general, data from studies in humans are preferred to animal data for purposes of hazard and dose-response evaluation.
2. In the absence of human data, or when the available human data are insufficiently quantitative or are insufficiently sensitive to rule out risks, animal data will be used for hazard and dose-response evaluation.
3. In the absence of information to demonstrate that such a

selection is incorrect, data from the animal species, strain, and sex showing the greatest sensitivity to a chemical's toxic properties will be selected as the basis for human risk assessment.
4. Animal toxicity data collected by the same route of exposure as that experienced by humans are preferred for risk assessment, but if the toxic effect is a systemic one, then data from other routes can be used.
5. For all toxic effects other than carcinogenicity, a threshold in the dose-response curve is assumed. The lowest NOEL [no observed effects level] from all available studies is assumed to be the threshold for the groups of subjects (humans or animals) in which toxicity data were collected.
6. The threshold for the human population is estimated by dividing the NOEL by a safety factor, the size of which depends upon the nature and quality of the toxicity data and the characteristics of the human population.
7. For carcinogens a linear, no-threshold dose-response model is assumed to apply at low doses . . . .
8. Generally, human exposures and resulting doses and risks are estimated for those members of the population experiencing the highest intensity and rate of contact with the chemical, although other, less exposed subgroups and people experiencing average exposures will frequently be included.

J. Rodricks, Calculated Risks 188-189 (1992). As noted in the text, exposure assessments have been one of the most difficult aspects of the risk assessment process. EPA has revised its guidelines for performing exposure assessments. The new EPA guidelines, which appear at 57 Fed. Reg. 22,889 (1992), combine and update previous exposure assessment guidelines issued by EPA in 1986 and 1988.

3. Hazard Identification and Toxicity Testing

The Controversy over Procedures for Identifying Carcinogens (pp. 508-514). The use of animal bioassays to assess risks to human health continues to be criticized, particularly by scientists representing industry. In International Fabricare Institute v. EPA, 972 F.2d 384 (D.C. Cir. 1992), representatives of a group of chemical companies challenged EPA's establishment of a zero maximum contaminant level goal (MCLG) for two chemicals under the Safe Drinking Water Act. They raised what the court called "a general challenge to the EPA policy of rejecting the existence of safe threshold levels for carcinogens in the absence of

4. Regulation of Toxic Substances

contrary evidence." 972 F.2d at 387. The court rejected their claim that it was arbitrary and capricious for EPA not to consider "new scientific evidence" questioning the appropriateness of assuming no safe threshold of exposure to carcinogens. The evidence in question consisted of a letter published in Science magazine from Bruce Ames and Lois Swirsky Gold, who stated that "low doses of carcinogens appear to be . . . less hazardous than is generally thought" and comments from another scientist about "the difficulties inherent in drawing conclusions about humans from studies done on animals." 972 F.2d at 391.

The court noted that this evidence "boils down to the opinions of a few scientists who, however qualified, are in their own words at odds with what is 'generally thought' about the subject." Id. It found that the arguments made by these scientists largely repeated arguments previously heard and rejected by EPA. While the Agency has pledged to continue consideration of the appropriateness of the no-threshold model, the court concluded that it need not "undertake a more detailed re-justification of its prior position" simply because of "the submission of comments consisting of little more than assertions that in the opinion of the commenters the agency got it wrong." Id.

EPA's policy for establishing MCLGs has been to divide chemical substances into three categories based on how the evidence concerning the carcinogenicity of the chemicals has been evaluated by EPA scientists. EPA's Category I consists of substances classified by the Agency as known or probable human carcinogens, including (1) substances considered to be known human carcinogens based on sufficient human epidemiologic data (Group A), (2) substances considered probable human carcinogens based on limited human epidemiologic data (Group B1), and substances considered probable human carcinogens based on a combination of sufficient evidence in animals and inadequate data in humans (Group B2). Category II consists of substances classified as possible human carcinogens based on limited evidence of carcinogenicity in animals and the absence of human data (Group C). Category III consists of chemicals that are either unclassifiable due to lack of data (Group D) or chemicals for which adequate animal tests or animal and human epidemiological studies found no evidence of carcinogenicity (Group E). EPA's policy has been to set MCLGs at zero for Category I chemicals based on the assumption of no safe threshold for exposure to carcinogens.

In *International Fabricare* industry petitioners maintained that EPA had erroneously placed perchloroethylene (perc) into Group B2 rather than Group C because it had not taken into account "other plausible mechanistic explanations" for the tumors found in animals exposed to perc. While EPA's scientists had not reached a consensus concerning whether the animal data justified classifying perc in Group B2, the court upheld EPA's decision to treat perc as a Group B2 probable human carcinogen. The court agreed with EPA's reasoning that "although there may be 'other plausible mechanistic explanations' for the reported occurrences of cancer, 'the experimental animal evidence identifies the potential for a carcinogenic response in humans unless there is evidence to the contrary'; that is, 'lack of key information does not support the use of the uncertainties to discount the sufficient level of animal evidence.' " 972 F.2d at 398. Thus, the court upheld EPA's decision to set the MCLG at zero.

The *International Fabricare* decision is consistent with the result in Synthetic Organic Chemical Manufacturers Association v. Secretary, Department of Health and Human Services, 720 F. Supp. 1244 (W.D. Cal. 1989), discussed on pages 510-511 of the text. The *International Fabricare* decision indicates that courts will not require EPA to reconsider carcinogen classification decisions on the basis of hypotheses about mechanisms of action until the mainstream scientific community has a clearer understanding of how cancer is caused and greater confidence that certain adverse effects on animals are not predictive of.

Criticism of the use of animal data to assess risks to humans has persisted. See Abelson, Exaggerated Carcinogenicity of Chemicals, 256 Science 1609 (1992) (arguing that the risks of butadiene have been greatly exaggerated because epidemiological data do not confirm the results of animal tests); but cf. Carcinogenicity of Butadiene, 257 Science 1330 (three letters from six scientists accusing the author of the former editorial of selective presentation of data and arguing that epidemiological studies actually confirm the carcinogenicity of butadiene); Stipp, How Sand on a Beach Came to Be Defined as Human Carcinogen, Wall St. J., Mar. 22, 1993, at A1 (maintaining that OSHA has erroneously classified crystalline silica, the primary ingredient of sand, as a carcinogen, when there is no evidence for its carcinogenic potential outside of dusty workplaces); Brinkley, Animal Tests as Risk Clues: The Best Data May Fall Short, N.Y. Times, Mar. 23, 1993, at A1. As a result, efforts to force regulatory agencies to reconsider the way carcinogens are identified and the way risk assessments are conducted are likely to continue.

One major effort in this direction was initiated by the director of the National Toxicology Program (NTP), Dr. Kenneth Olden. In 1992 Dr. Olden asked the NTP's Board of Scientific Counselors to conduct a comprehensive review of existing practices for assessing human health risks. This review had three goals: (1) to ensure that chemicals nominated for testing by NTP were those with the greatest public health significance, (2) to emphasize studies of the mechanisms of toxicity and carcinogenicity, and (3) to develop and validate alternative assays that could reduce the need for long-term animal tests. In July 1992,

4. Regulation of Toxic Substances

the NTP Board released a draft of its report. National Toxicology Program, Final Report of the Advisory Review by the NTP Board of Scientific Counselors (1992). The report concluded that the NTP "places too much emphasis on testing per se, and not enough emphasis on providing the mechanistic interpretation of the significance of the testing results with regard to human health." 57 Fed. Reg. 31,722 (1992). To change this, the NTP advisory board recommended that "[s]tudies directed toward discerning the mechanism(s) of action of the chemical of interest need to be incorporated into, and juxtaposed with, the bioassay in order to place its results into proper perspective." The Advisory Review Report advocated that "results of the bioassay be discussed with regard to their biological significance concerning human health coupled with the requirement to facilitate this by incorporating hypothesis-driven mechanistic research into the testing program." In contrast to the traditional approach of "better safe than sorry," members of the advisory board concluded that "tests which place an emphasis on sensitivity over specificity (i.e., the extent to which noncarcinogens yield negative results) are not appropriate. In what was construed as a powerful endorsement of Bruce Ames's criticism of the maximum tolerated dose approach (MTD) to chemical testing, the advisory board expressed the view that "approximately two-thirds of the NTP carcinogens would not be positive, i.e., not be considered as carcinogens, if the MTD was not used." 57 Fed. Reg. 31,723 (1992). This statement led at least one observer to forecast erroneously a revolutionary change in risk assessment practices that would exonerate most chemicals formerly listed as carcinogens. Gori, Overturning the Verdict on Carcinogens, Wall St. J., Aug. 27, 1992, at A10.

After review of the draft report, the National Toxicology Program (NTP) rejected the advisory board's conclusion that two-thirds of NTP carcinogens would not be positive but for the use of MTD. In a response issued in December 1992, the NTP noted that the two-thirds estimate was based on a single paper "that evaluated only 13 rodent carcinogens studies, too few to justify such general conclusions." 57 Fed. Reg. 61,442 (1992). A study that expanded on this analysis found that "only 18 of 52 (35%) multidose chemicals classified as carcinogens would not be statistically positive if the MTD were excluded." Yet "[f]ifteen of the 18 chemicals not showing statistically significant tumor effects at doses below the MTD nevertheless had numerically elevated tumor rates at these dose levels relative to controls." Id. Noting that "[h]ypotheses about mechanisms of cancer and relevancy of animal responses are not widely accepted for any type of tumor," the NTP rejected the notion that carcinogen identification procedures should be changed in any fundamental manner. "We believe, given our current understanding of mechanisms of carcinogenesis, that currently there are no well-founded generic changes that can be incorporated in test protocols that would impact any default criteria for extrapolation from high dose to low dose in animals, or in scaling to human exposure doses." Id. However, the NTP did pledge "to explore modification or alternatives to the MTD concept, such as DNA repair kinetics, to assist in protocol design and in reducing the number of default assumptions incorporated in conducting risk assessments." Id. The program also agreed that the process for nominating chemicals to be tested should be "revised to include more emphasis on endpoints of toxicity other than carcinogenesis and to get input from a broader audience of nomination sources." 57 Fed. Reg. 61,439 (1992).

Another major study of risk assessment practices reached similar conclusions. After three years of study, a committee of the National Academy of Sciences refused to endorse the notion that the MTD approach to animal testing should be abandoned. National Academy of Sciences, Issues in Risk Assessment 61-64 (1993). Dr. Bernard Goldstein, chairman of the committee, noted that although 6 of the 17 committee members had favored such a shift, the "science isn't there yet." Racz, Science Panel Splits Over Chemical Dose Given to Animals, Wall St. J., Jan. 28, 1993, at B7. Moreover, Dr. Goldstein stated that it may take a decade before scientific advances would permit an entirely new approach for toxicity testing. Id.

While animal tests will continue to play an important role in assessment of risks to human health, this does not mean that the data they generate will be accepted uncritically. Regulatory agencies are likely to evaluate the relevance of animal test results more carefully as understanding of biological mechanisms improves. For example, in 1992 EPA was persuaded that kidney tumors in male rats produced by chemicals that bind to a certain protein (alpha 2 micro globulin) should not be considered evidence of carcinogenic risk to humans in light of certain differences in molecular biology between humans and rats. Marshall, Toxicology Goes Molecular, 259 Science 1394, 1398 (1993). This decision indicates that in some circumstances EPA will be willing to reconsider standard assumptions employed in risk assessment. The key challenge for regulatory policy is to define what must be shown when and by whom to warrant deviation from conventional assumptions about the relevance of animal test data. As noted above, a duty to reconsider standard risk assessment practices "cannot be triggered by the submission of comments consisting of little more than assertions that in the opinions of the commenters the agency got it wrong." International Fabricare Institute v. EPA, 972 F.2d 384, 391 (D.C. Cir. 1992).

4. Regulation of Toxic Substances — Pages 519-520

TSCA's Premanufacture Review Process (p. 516). In October 1992, EPA announced that it had imposed premanufacture restrictions on the use of a nickel compound that is marketed as a substitute for lead in paint. EPA Orders Restrictions for Manufacture of Lead Substitute with Cancer Concerns, 23 Env. Rep. 1275 (1992). The name of the substance and its manufacturer were not disclosed because they were claimed to be confidential business information. EPA had received a premanufacture notification concerning the substance in March 1992, but the PMN did not contain any test data. Based on risk assessments of other nickel compounds, EPA expressed concern that the substance may cause cancer and other adverse health effects in humans. While EPA had considered banning the substance entirely, the Agency's desire to encourage the development of substitutes for lead, a potent human neurotoxin, ultimately resulted in the negotiation of a consent agreement restricting use of the substance. EPA staff expressed the view that the Agency is "more concerned about neurotoxic effects based on human data than long-term cancer risks based on animal studies." Id.

In September 1994 EPA announced that it was considering issuing significant new use rules for lead and lead compounds under section 5(a)(2) of TSCA. 59 Fed. Reg. 49,484 (1994). Such regulations would give EPA the opportunity to evaluate the intended new uses of lead for 90 days in order to determine whether regulatory action was necessary to prevent harm to public health or the environment. This proposal is part of the agency's efforts to reduce further human exposure to lead.

Advances in Toxicology (p. 517). As molecular biologists join the ranks of toxicologists in record numbers, optimism is growing that scientists will be able to develop improved tests for assessing chemical risks. This optimism stems in part from the development of molecular probes that greatly facilitate the detection of toxins, making it easier to study sub-clinical responses to toxic chemicals. Some toxicologists are predicting an eventual shift away from high dose animal testing to studies that rely on engineered models derived from human cells and tissue. See Special Report: Toxicology Goes Molecular, 259 Science 1394 (1993).

Regulation of Toxic Substances: A Pathfinder (pp. 519-520). Two excellent, three-part practitioner's guides to the Toxic Substances Control Act and the Federal Insecticde, Fungicide, and Rodenticide Act appear in Hathaway et al., A Practitioner's Guide to the Toxic Substances Control Act, 24 Env. Rep. 10,207 (Part I), 10,285 (Part II), 10,357 (Part III) (1994), and Fisher et al., A Practitioner's Guide to the Federal

Insecticide, Fungicide, and Rodenticide Act, 24 Env. Rep. 10,449 (Part I), 10,507 (Part II), 10,629 (Part III) (1994).

D. HOW SAFE IS "SAFE"?

1. Risk-Benefit Balancing

Risk-Benefit Balancing (pp. 521-525). The 1992 presidential campaign featured a vigorous, though largely superficial, debate over the impact of environmental regulation on the economy. This generated a flurry of articles addressing whether or not there is a tradeoff between environmental protection and economic values. See, e.g., Stevens, Economists Strive to Find Environment's Bottom Line, N.Y. Times, Sept. 8, 1992, at C1; Moore, Bush's Nonsense on Jobs and the Environment, N.Y. Times, Sept. 25, 1992, at A33; Environmentalism Runs Riot, The Economist, Aug. 8, 1992, at 11; Stay Clean, The Economist, Sept. 5, 1992, at 4. A key, but poorly understood, variable in this debate was the impact of environmental regulation on innovation. In some circumstances regulation has stimulated technological advances that lower compliance and production costs and give more efficient firms a competitive advantage. Stevens, Environmental Rules May Spur Innovation, N.Y. Times, Sept. 8, 1992, at C8. A study of state environmental policies released by MIT's Project on Environmental Politics and Policy in December 1992 found a surprising link between strong environmental regulations and healthy state economies. Meyer, Environmentalism and Economic Prosperity: Testing the Enviro-nmental Impact Hypothesis (1992).

The RCRA wood preserving wastes regulation that had become OMB's favorite example of the most costly regulation per life saved (parent text, pp. 524-525) was modified substantially in November 1992. 57 Fed. Reg. 61,492 (1992). These changes reportedly "addressed most of the industry's concerns," according to a spokesperson for the American Wood Preservers Institute. Standards for Wood Preserving Wastes to Become Less Stringent Under Final Rule, 23 Env. Rep. 1867 (1992). Yet a chart containing OMB's former estimate continues to be circulated widely in order to generate opposition to environmental regulation. Schneider, How a Rebellion over Environmental Rules Grew from a Patch of Weeds, N.Y. Times, Mar. 24, 1993, at A16.

In September 1993 President Clinton revoked Executive Order 12,291 (parent text, p. 523), which had directed agencies to base regulatory decisions on principles of cost-benefit analysis and replaced it with

4. Regulation of Toxic Substances   Pages 545-551

EO 12,866, which establishes a more selective regulatory review process, while continuing to require agencies to conduct cost-benefit analyses of regulations expected to cost industry more than $100 million per year. The new executive order can be found in Chapter 5 of this supplement.

The new Republican majority in Congress is considering legislation to require agencies to base regulatory decisions on the results of risk assessments and cost-benefit analysis. In March 1995, the House of Representatives approved legislation that would impose a temporary moratorium on new regulations, require cost-benefit analyses for regulations with an annual cost exceeding $25 million, and displace all existing environmental standard-setting methods by requiring that all regulations satisfy cost-benefit tests. A Senate committee has cleared similar but more moderate legislation that would require cost-benefit analysis for rules costing more than $100 million per year, while not supplanting existing environmental standard-setting methods. The Senate bill would require that all final regulations be submitted to Congress for 45 days in order to permit a congressional veto.

EPA's Lead Phasedown Decision (pp. 526-533). Data from the Third National Health and Nutrition Examination Survey released in 1994 found that, due largely to EPA's phasedown of lead additives in gasoline, average levels of lead in childrens' blood had declined sharply from 12.8 µg/dl during the 1976-1980 survey period to 2.8 µg/dl during the 1988-1991 survey. Brody et al., Blood Lead Levels in the U.S. Population, 272 JAMA 277, 281 (1994). A study by an EPA economist estimates that each 1 µg/dl reduction in average blood lead concentrations yields monetized net benefits of $17.2 billion per year. Schwartz, Societal Benefits of Reducing Lead Exposure, 66 Env. Health 105, 119 (1994).

The Lockout/Tagout *Decision (p. 545-551).* After additional briefing, the D.C. Circuit decided not to stay the lockout/tagout standard, despite its directive that OSHA adopt a new construction of section 3(8). OSHA made slow progress in complying with the court's mandate. In October 1992, the court noted that OSHA's actions "appear not inconsistent with complete recalcitrance," but it denied a motion by the National Association of Manufacturers seeking to compel OSHA to adopt a new interpretation of section 3(8). International Union, UAW v. OSHA, 976 F.2d 749, 751 (D.C. Cir. 1992). OSHA ultimately declined the court's invitation to employ cost-benefit analysis. In March 1993, OSHA reissued the final lockout/tagout rule, accompanied by a "Supplemental Statement of Reasons" that sought to provide further support for the Agency's adoption of the existing standard. 58 Fed. Reg. 16,612 (1993). The Agency stated that it would employ the following criteria in establishing safety standards:

> A safety standard must substantially reduce a significant risk of material harm; the standard must be technologically feasible in the sense that the protective measures being required already exist, can be brought into existence with available technology, or can be created with technology that can reasonably be developed; the standard must be economically feasible in the sense that industry can absorb or pass on the costs without major dislocation or threat of instability; the standard must be at least as protective as existing national consensus standards; and the standard must be supported by the evidence in the rulemaking record and be consistent with prior agency action.

58 Fed. Reg. at 16,613. Given that "the application of the statutory criteria set forth [above] assures that the agency's discretion is confined and that the standard produces substantial safety benefits at a reasonable cost," OSHA concluded that "formal cost-benefit analysis is not needed to meet the court's constitutional concerns." Id. at 16,614. OSHA also determined that further study of the empirical basis for risk-risk analysis was needed before it could be applied in a rulemaking.

The D.C. Circuit upheld OSHA's decision in International Union, United Automobile Workers v. OSHA, 37 F.3d 665 (D.C. Cir. 1994). The court questioned whether the criteria adopted by OSHA sufficiently channeled the agency's exercise of discretion to satify the nondelegation doctrine. However, it concluded that OSHA's statement that the Act requires it, "once it has identified a 'significant' safety risk, to enact a safety standard that provides 'a high degree of worker protection,'" was sufficient because it permits the agency "to deviate only modestly from the stringency required by §6(b)(5) for health standards." 37 F.3d at 669. Judge Williams went on to criticize OSHA for adopting criteria that in other circumstances "could lead to adoption of a regulation costing billions, yet likely to save few if any lives," but he reserved decision on whether OSHA is required to demonstrate a reasonable relationship between the costs and benefits of rules to address safety hazards. 37 F.3d at 670.

Lockout/Tagout *and "Risk/Risk" Tradeoffs (p. 552).* The "richer is safer" argument articulated by Judge Williams in the *Lockout/Tagout* case has spawned what has become known as "risk/risk" analysis. As noted in the text, in 1992 OMB used this argument to insist that OSHA balance health risks from chemical exposures against health risks from reduced income. OMB did so in the context of a rulemaking to extend OSHA's air contaminants standard to farm workers and the construction and maritime industries. In a letter to OSHA officials in March 1992, James B. MacRae Jr., acting administrator of OMB's Office of Information and Regulatory Affairs, argued that "the positive effect of wealth on

4. Regulation of Toxic Substances

health has been established both theoretically and empirically. Richer workers on average buy more leisure time, more nutritious food, more preventive health care and smoke and drink less than poorer workers. . . . Government regulations often have significant impact on the income and wealth of workers. To the extent that firms cannot pass on regulatory compliance cost increases to consumers, firms will absorb these costs by cutting wages and by reducing employment." Therefore, "OSHA should estimate whether the possible effect of compliance costs on workers' health will outweigh the health improvements that may result from decreased exposure to the regulated substances." Swoboda, OMB's Logic: Less Protection Saves Lives, Wash. Post, Mar. 17, 1992, at A15.

Unlike the *Lockout/Tagout* case, in which the court found that section 6(b)(5) did not apply, the air contaminants rulemaking was conducted under section 6(b)(5). In light of the decision in American Textile Manufacturers Institute v. Donovan (p. 541 of the parent text), can OSHA legally consider "risk/risk" tradeoffs when setting standards to control toxic materials in the workplace under section 6(b)(5)?

In June 1992, OSHA issued the proposed regulations (extending the air contaminants standard to additional industries) that had been delayed by OMB's "risk/risk" objection. 57 Fed. Reg. 26,001 (June 12, 1992). In response to OMB's argument, OSHA solicited public comment on the "risk/risk" theory. The Agency identified eight studies that had purported to estimate the amount of income loss that would cause an extra fatality. These studies generated numbers ranging from $1.8 million to $7.25 million. Id. at 26,005-26,009 (June 12, 1992). However, in light of the decision by the Eleventh Circuit (discussed below) striking down OSHA's initial air contaminants standard, AFL-CIO v. OSHA, 965 F.2d 962 (11th Cir. 1992), OSHA has canceled the public hearings and extended "indefinitely" the comment period on its proposal to extend the standard to the construction, maritime, and agricultural sectors. 57 Fed. Reg. 37,126 (1992).

In January 1993, the Seventh Circuit brushed aside efforts to require OSHA to conduct "risk/risk" analysis. In American Dental Association v. Martin, 984 F.2d 823 (7th Cir. 1993), the court upheld OSHA's regulations governing occupational exposure to bloodborne pathogens despite arguments that OSHA should have considered the lives that would be lost because the regulation would increase the cost of medical care. Judge Posner accepted the theoretical basis for the "risk/risk" argument. He noted that OSHA "exaggerated the number of lives likely to be saved by the rule by ignoring lives likely to be sacrificed by it, since the increased cost of medical care, to the extent passed on to consumers, will reduce the demand for medical care, and some people may lose their lives as a result." 984 F.2d at 826. However, he emphasized that the proponents of "risk/risk" analysis had not made any effort to quantify these "indirects costs" and that OSHA also had ignored indirect *benefits* by considering only deaths prevented and ignoring "the benefits to workers who will be spared illness." Id. These indirect benefits could be particularly large in the case of diseases caused by bloodborne pathogens, since "99 times as many people get Hepatitis B as die from it." Id. In another portion of his opinion, Judge Posner noted that OSHA's cost estimates may overstate the actual costs to the regulated industry, because the indirect costs on which the "risk/risk" argument focuses are the result of industries' being able to shift some of their increased costs to consumers or suppliers.

How Much Is It Worth to Prevent a Death? (pp. 566-567). OSHA's bloodborne pathogens standard was projected to prevent between 113 and 197 deaths per year at an annual cost of $813 million in American Dental Association v. Martin, 984 F.2d 823 (7th Cir. 1993). Judge Posner, writing for the court, noted that the "rule's implicit valuation of a life is high—about $4 million—but not so astronomical, certainly by regulatory standards, as to call the rationality of the rule seriously into question," especially since the diseases to be prevented often affect young people. 984 F.2d at 825.

Risk Disaggregation (p. 569). In *Corrosion Proof Fittings*, asbestos manufacturers convinced the Fifth Circuit to overturn EPA's asbestos ban by disaggregating the risks estimated for each type of product that contained asbestos. By contrast, in American Dental Association v. Martin, supra, the Seventh Circuit refused to require OSHA to disaggregate risks on an industry-by-industry basis in making the "significant risk" findings required by the *Benzene* decision. The Seventh Circuit explained that

> OSHA cannot impose onerous requirements on an industry that does not pose substantial hazards to the safety or health of its workers merely because the industry is a part of some larger sector or grouping and the agency has decided to regulate it wholesale. That would be an irrational way to proceed. But neither is the agency required to proceed workplace by workplace, which in the case of bloodborne pathogens would require it to promulgate hundreds of thousands of separate rules. It is not our business to pick the happy medium between these extremes. It is OSHA's business. If it provides a rational explanation for its choice, we are bound.

984 F.2d at 827. The court found that OSHA's explanation that the risks of infection from bloodborne pathogens do not vary in a readily determinable fashion from industry to industry was sufficiently rational

so as not to require an industry-by-industry disaggregation of risk estimates. OSHA had found that infection risks vary with practices, rather than industries, and it had issued regulations designed to control these practices.

2. Feasibility-Limited Regulation

OSHA's Lead Standard (pp. 570-573). When it adopted its PEL for airborne lead in 1978, OSHA pledged that it eventually would extend the standard to the construction industry. After 14 years of inaction, Congress in 1992 enacted legislation requiring OSHA to extend the lead standard to construction. Title X of the Housing and Community Development Act, Pub. L. No. 102-550. In May 1993 OSHA promulgated an interim final rule extending the lead standard to the construction industry. 58 Fed. Reg. 26,590 (1993).

Feasibility Under the OSH Act (pp. 573-575). The Eleventh Circuit's decision striking down OSHA's air contaminants rulemaking, page 132 of this Supplement, also has important implications for the way feasibility is assessed. The portion of the court's decision that addressed the feasibility of the new and revised PELs is presented below.

AFL-CIO v. OSHA
965 F.2d 962 (11th Cir. 1992)

Before FAY and COX, Circuit Judges, and JOHNSON, Senior Circuit Judge.
FAY, Circuit Judge:

C. Feasibility

The Supreme Court has defined "feasible" as " 'capable of being done, executed, or effected,' " *ATMI* [American Textile Manufacturers Institute, Inc. v. Donovan], 452 U.S. at 508-09 (quoting Webster's Third New International Dictionary 831 (1976)), both technologically and economically, *National Cottonseed,* 825 F.2d at 487; *United Steelworkers,* 647 F.2d at 1264; see also *ATMI,* 452 U.S. at 513 n.31 ("[A]ny standard that was not *economically or technologically* feasible would *a fortiori* not be 'reasonably necessary or appropriate' under the Act." (Emphasis added.)). Again, the burden is on OSHA to show by substantial evidence that the standard is feasible, *United Steelworkers,* 647 F.2d at 1264-67, although OSHA need not prove feasibility with scientific certainty, id.

at 1266.[24] Despite OSHA's repeated claims that it made feasibility determinations on an industry-by-industry basis, it is clear that the agency again proceeded "generically."

1. Technological Feasibility

To show that a standard is technologically feasible, OSHA must demonstrate "that modern technology has at least conceived some industrial strategies or devices which are likely to be capable of meeting the PEL and which the industries are generally capable of adopting." *United Steelworkers*, 647 F.2d at 1266. Further, "the undisputed principle that feasibility is to be tested industry-by-industry demands that OSHA examine the technological feasibility of each industry individually." Id. at 1301. Courts have remanded OSHA determinations where the agency has not sufficiently analyzed the abilities of different industries to meet proposed standards. See *Building & Constr.*, 838 F.2d at 1272-73; Industrial Union Dept., AFL-CIO v. Hodgson, 499 F.2d 467, 480-81 (D.C. Cir. 1974).

In this rulemaking, OSHA first identified the primary air contaminant control methods: Engineering controls are methods such as ventilation, isolation and substitution. 54 Fed. Reg. at 2789. Complementing the engineering controls are work practices and administrative reforms (e.g., housekeeping, material handling or transfer procedures, leak detection programs, training, and personal hygiene). Id. at 2790. Finally, personal protective equipment such as respirators and gloves may become necessary when these other controls are not fully effective. Id. at 2790.

OSHA then organized its discussion of technological feasibility by industry sector using the Standard Industrial Classification (SIC) groupings. The SIC codes classify by type of activity for purposes of promoting uniformity and comparability in the presentation of data. As the codes go from two and three digits to four digits, the groupings become progressively more specific. For example, SIC Code 28 represents "Chemicals and Allied Products," SIC Code 281 represents "Industrial Inorganic Chemicals" and SIC Code 2812 includes only "Alkalies and Chlorine." OSHA primarily relied on the more general two-digit codes in its feasibility analysis. For most of the SIC codes discussed, OSHA provided only a general description of how generic

---

24. The industrial petitioners have suggested that on-site visits, surveys, and computer modeling are improper means of determining whether a proposed standard is feasible. However, OSHA is free to use such techniques to establish that a particular proposed standard is feasible. See American Iron & Steel Inst. v. OSHA, 939 F.2d 975, 980-82, 987-89 (D.C. Cir. 1991).

4. Regulation of Toxic Substances   Pages 573-575

engineering controls might be used in a given sector. Then, relying on this generic analysis, OSHA concluded

> that existing engineering controls are available to reduce exposure levels to the new levels.
> In reviewing the comments and hearing testimony on the technological feasibility of achieving the PELs and other limits, OSHA has found that for the overwhelming majority of situations where air contaminants are encountered by workers, compliance can be achieved by applying known engineering control methods and work practice improvements.

54 Fed. Reg. at 2789. However, OSHA made no attempt to show the ability of technology to meet specific exposure standards in specific industries. Except for an occasional specific conclusion as to whether a particular process control could meet a particular PEL, OSHA merely presented general conclusions as to the availability of these controls in a particular industry. See, e.g., id. at 2802-03 (SIC 32—Stone, Clay, and Glass Products).

OSHA correctly notes that all it need demonstrate is "a general *presumption* of feasibility for *an industry*." *United Steelworkers*, 647 F.2d at 1266 (second emphasis added); see also *ASARCO*, 746 F.2d at 496. However, as this quote indicates, "a general presumption of feasibility" refers to a specific industry-by-industry determination that a "typical firm will be able to develop and install engineering and work practice controls that can meet the PEL in most of its operations." *United Steelworkers*, 647 F.2d at 1272. OSHA can prove this "by pointing to technology that is either already in use or has been conceived and is reasonably capable of experimental refinement and distribution within the standard's deadlines." Id. Only when OSHA has provided such proof for a given industry does there arise "a presumption that industry can meet the PEL without relying on respirators, a presumption which firms will have to overcome to obtain relief in any secondary inquiry into feasibility." Id.

For example, in *United Steelworkers*, the court analyzed whether the agency had provided enough information about the relative abilities of different industries to meet the standard. The court upheld OSHA's rationale with regard to lead smelting industries because OSHA made industry-specific findings and identified specific technologies capable of meeting the proposed limit in industry specific process operations. Id. at 1278-89. As to numerous other industries, however, the court remanded because OSHA's findings lacked a detailed industry- or operation-specific analysis. . . . Thus, it is clear that the concept of "a general presumption of feasibility" does not grant OSHA a license to make overbroad generalities as to feasibility or to group large categories of industries together without some explanation of why findings for the group adequately represent the different industries in that group. We find that OSHA has not established the technological feasibility of the 428 PELs in its revised Air Contaminants Standard.

2. Economic Feasibility

Nor has OSHA adequately demonstrated that the standard is economically feasible. OSHA must "provide a reasonable assessment of the likely range of costs of its standard, and the likely effects of those costs on the industry," id. at 1266, so as to "demonstrate a reasonable likelihood that these costs will not threaten the existence or competitive structure of an industry, even if it does portend disaster for some marginal firms," id. at 1272. The determination of economic feasibility is governed by the same principles as technological feasibility. It must be supported by substantial evidence and OSHA must demonstrate its applicability to the affected industries. See id. at 1301 & n.160.

In this rulemaking, although OSHA ostensibly recognized its responsibility "to demonstrate economic feasibility for *an industry*," 54 Fed. Reg. at 2367 (emphasis added), the agency nevertheless determined feasibility for each industry *"sector"* (i.e., two-digit SIC code), without explaining why such a broad grouping was appropriate. Id. OSHA's economic feasibility determinations therefore suffer from the same faults as its technological feasibility findings. Indeed, it would seem particularly important not to aggregate disparate industries when making a showing of economic feasibility. OSHA admits that its economic feasibility conclusions only "have a high degree of validity on a sector basis," id., as opposed to a subsector or more industry-specific basis. See also id. at 2374 ("OSHA concludes that this approach is accurate on an industry sector by industry sector basis for individual processes."). OSHA then stated that "[t]he costs are sufficiently low per sector to demonstrate feasibility not only for each sector but also for each subsector." Id. at 2367.

However, reliance on such tools as average estimates of cost can be extremely misleading in assessing the impact of particular standards on individual industries. Analyzing the economic impact for an entire sector could conceal particular industries laboring under special disabilities and likely to fail as a result of enforcement. Moreover, for some substances, OSHA failed even to analyze all the affected industry sectors. See, e.g., id. at 2686-89 (perchloroethylene).[28] We find that OSHA has

---

28. We are not foreclosing the possibility that OSHA could properly find and explain that certain impacts and standards do apply to entire sectors of an industry. Two-digit SICs could be appropriate, but only if coupled with a

not met its burden of establishing that its 428 new PELs are either economically or technologically feasible. . . .

E. Other Union Issues

Union petitioners raise several other issues that deserve comment. . . .

3. Four-year Compliance Period

The union also challenges OSHA's decision to allow four years, until December 31, 1992, for the implementation of engineering and work practice controls to bring industry into compliance with the new standards, while in the interim permitting compliance through the use of respirators. . . . In adopting this four-year time period, OSHA stated that the agency's "experience is that for substances of normal difficulty, one to two years is sufficient," 54 Fed. Reg. at 2916, but that a four-year period "takes into account that some employers will have to control several substances and also considers those few substances where compliance may take greater efforts for some employers," id. That conclusory analysis falls short of justifying an across-the-board four-year period of delay, but is fully consistent with OSHA's treatment of this standard as a "generic" standard, without adequate consideration of individual substances or the effect of the new standards on individual industries.

This "generic" four-year compliance period is simply not adequately supported in the record. Unlike other standards where OSHA has exercised its "technology-forcing" authority and required that industries develop the technology to achieve the new standards, see *United Steelworkers*, 647 F.2d at 1264-65, in *this* standard, "OSHA's feasibility analysis was based on what industry is already achieving or what could be achieved with standard 'off-the-shelf' technology, [and] there are few if any cases where OSHA is attempting to force technology." 54 Fed. Reg. at 2366. If the technology exists and is in many cases already being used, it is difficult to understand why four years is required for the implementation of this standard for *all* industries. If OSHA's concern was primarily economic feasibility, that too needed to be addressed for each industry or for each appropriate industrial grouping.

To the extent that there may be any unusual situations in which

---

showing that there are no disproportionately affected industries within the group.

a feasibility problem exists, the OSH Act and the standard itself provide appropriate means of dealing with such problems without resorting to the extreme expedient of an across-the-board four-year compliance period. First, section 6(b)(6) allows an employer to obtain a temporary variance if that employer "is unable to comply with a standard by its effective date because of unavailability of professional or technical personnel or of materials and equipment needed to come into compliance with the standard or because necessary construction or alteration of facilities cannot be completed by the effective date." 29 U.S.C. §655(b)(6)(A)(i). Furthermore, if the rulemaking record establishes that specific industries will need an extended period of time to comply with PELs for certain substances, OSHA could so provide, just as it allows respirator use after December 1992 for four substances in specified operations. 54 Fed. Reg. at 2335, 2916 (carbon monoxide, carbon disulfide, styrene, and sulfur dioxide). We find insufficient explanation in the record to support this across-the-board four-year delay in implementation of this rule.

IV. CONCLUSION

It is clear that the analytical approach used by OSHA in promulgating its revised Air Contaminants Standard is so flawed that it cannot stand. OSHA not only mislabeled this a "generic" rulemaking, but it inappropriately treated it as such. The result of this approach is a set of 428 inadequately supported standards. OSHA has lumped together substances and affected industries and provided such inadequate explanation that it is virtually impossible for a reviewing court to determine if sufficient evidence supports the agency's conclusions. . . .

[A]lthough we find that the record adequately explains and supports OSHA's determination that the health effects of exposure to these 428 substances are material impairments, we hold that OSHA has not sufficiently explained or supported its threshold determination that exposure to these substances at previous levels posed a significant risk of these material health impairments or that the new standard eliminates or reduces that risk to the extent feasible. OSHA's overall approach to this rulemaking is so flawed that we must vacate the whole revised Air Contaminants Standard.

We have no doubt that the agency acted with the best of intentions. It may well be, as OSHA claims, that this was the only practical way of accomplishing a much needed revision of the existing standards and of making major strides towards improving worker health and safety. Given OSHA's history of slow progress in issuing standards, we can easily believe OSHA's claim that going through detailed analysis for

4. Regulation of Toxic Substances   Pages 573-575

each of the 428 different substances regulated was not possible given the time constraints set by the agency for this rulemaking. Unfortunately, OSHA's approach to this rulemaking is not consistent with the requirements of the OSH Act. Before OSHA uses such an approach, it must get authorization from Congress by way of amendment to the OSH Act. Legislative decisions on the federal level are to be made in the chambers of Congress. It is not for this court to undertake the substantial rewriting of the Act necessary to uphold OSHA's approach to this rulemaking.

NOTES AND QUESTIONS

1. The court states that "OSHA made no attempt to show the ability of technology to meet specific exposure standards in specific industries. . ." Must OSHA perform separate studies of the feasibility of controlling each of the 428 substances for each of the industries in which they are used? Given the enormous burden that would be entailed in demonstrating feasibility on an industry-by-industry and substance-by-substance basis, why wasn't OSHA's four-year extended compliance deadline a reasonable compromise approach?

2. Note that the court finds plausible OSHA's claim that "this was the only practical way of accomplishing a much needed revision of the existing standards and of making major strides toward improving worker health and safety." Why, then, did the court invalidate OSHA's standards? Would OSHA have been better off if it had selected several dozen substances and given more careful and more individualized consideration to their risks and the feasibility of controlling them?

3. Why was OSHA's approach opposed by both employers and labor unions? In what respects is the decision a victory for workers? Is it likely to give them more comprehensive protection against exposure to toxic substances in the workplace? Could the decision be used to require OSHA to regulate more aggressively to force companies to develop and to employ new technology to control workplace risks?

4. The court struck down OSHA's air contaminants standard in its entirety, even though no party objected to the PELs OSHA set for many substances. By what authority may a court invalidate PELs not challenged by any party?

5. While Labor Secretary Lynn Martin initially vowed to seek Supreme Court review of the Eleventh Circuit's decision, the decision concerning whether or not to appeal ultimately was left to the incoming Clinton Administration. Although Robert Reich, the Clinton Administration's new Secretary of Labor, reportedly recommended that a petition for certiorari be filed, no appeal was filed by the deadline for seeking Supreme Court review. Thus, the Eleventh

Circuit's decision is now final and binding on OSHA. As a result, the PELs for 212 substances will revert to the initial standards adopted in 1971, and 164 new substances that would have been regulated will escape regulation for now. Representatives of labor unions are using the decision to reinforce their arguments that Congress should adopt comprehensive legislation to reform OSHA. One proposal would authorize OSHA to set PELs at the levels recommended by groups like the ACGIH while requiring that they be updated at three-year intervals. Salwen, U.S. Won't Fight Ruling that Scraps Toxics Standards, Wall St. J., Mar. 24, 1993, at B3.

Feasibility Under the Safe Drinking Water Act (pp. 575-579). As noted in the text, feasibility issues also arise in connection with implementation of the Safe Drinking Water Act, which requires EPA to set maximum contaminant levels (MCLs) as close as feasible to the levels of MCLGs. Economic feasibility is becoming a particularly important issue under the Act as state and local governments resist what they project to be enormous compliance costs. For example, while EPA estimated that compliance with a proposed regulation restricting levels of radon in drinking water would cost $1.6 billion nationwide, the Association of California Water Agencies argues that the costs will be $12 to $20 billion. Abelson, Regulatory Costs, 259 Science 159 (1993). New York City's proposed alternative watershed protection program (parent text, p. 579) has been granted conditional approval by EPA. There are questions concerning whether the SDWA gives EPA the authority to grant such conditional approval and whether the Agency can enforce the 65 conditions it sought to impose when approving New York City's request to waive the filtration requirement.

When it incorporated a feasibility limitation into the Safe Drinking Water Act, Congress imposed some limitations on EPA's discretion by specifying in the statute that "granular activated carbon is feasible for the control of synthetic organic chemicals," 42 U.S.C. §300g-1(b)(5). Thus, in International Fabricare Institute v. EPA, 972 F.2d 384 (D.C. Cir. 1992), the D.C. Circuit had no difficulty rejecting an industry petitioner's claim that EPA had not established the feasibility of an MCL for dibromochloropropane. The court noted that EPA had based its cost of treatment estimates on the use of granular activated carbon, which it described as "per se 'feasible' under section 300g-1(b)(5)." 972 F.2d at 394.

New York City continues its efforts to avoid construction of a filtration system for its drinking water. In December 1994 the city submitted "a plan to regulate everything from new development to the disposal of plowed snow in the vast upstate region that supplies the city's water." Perez-Pena, City Submits Watershed Regulations for

4. Regulation of Toxic Substances   Pages 575-579

State Approval, N.Y. Times, Dec. 29, 1994, at B3. If approved by the state, the plan would give New York City tremendous authority over activities that could be conducted in the city's 2,000-square-mile watershed area. Cities within the watershed area are bitterly opposed to the plan.

Concerns about enforcement of the Safe Drinking Water Act were heightened in January 1995 when two chemists who formerly worked for New York City's Division of Drinking Water Quality Control charged that water quality tests had been deliberately manipulated by their supervisors. The chemists charged that workers had been ordered to avoid taking samples from sites that potentially were contaminated. Finder, With Some Qualms, Water Is Called Safe, N.Y. Times, Jan. 15, 1995, at 29.

As noted in the parent text (p. 578), environmental groups sued EPA to challenge the agency's failure to establish an MCL for lead in drinking water. The D.C. Circuit heard the case and rendered the following decision.

> *American Water Works Association v. EPA*
> 40 F.3d 1266 (D.C. Cir. 1994)

Before GINSBURG and RANDOLPH, Circuit Judges, and SHADUR, Senior District Judge. GINSBURG, Circuit Judge:

I. BACKGROUND

The Safe Drinking Water Act requires the EPA to promulgate drinking water regulations designed to prevent contamination of public water systems. 42 U.S.C. §300g-1(b). A national primary drinking water regulation (NPDWR) is one that specifies for a contaminant with an adverse effect upon human health either an MCL or a treatment technique, and establishes the procedures and criteria necessary to ensure a supply of drinking water that complies with that MCL or treatment technique. 42 U.S.C. §300f(1). An NPDWR is an enforceable standard applicable to all public water systems nationwide. In most of the NPDWRs promulgated to date the EPA has set an MCL for the particular contaminant being regulated. The EPA has the authority, however, to specify a treatment technique in lieu of an MCL if the Administrator finds that it is not "economically or technologically feasible" to determine the level of the particular contaminant in a public water system. 42 U.S.C. §300f(1)(C)(ii).

It is particularly difficult to determine the level of lead in a public

223

water system. Less than one percent of all public water systems draw source water containing any lead. Notice of Proposed Rulemaking: Drinking Water Regulations; Maximum Contaminant Level Goals and National Primary Drinking Water Regulations for Lead and Copper, 53 Fed. Reg. 31,516, 31,526-31,527 (1988). Instead, most lead enters a public water system through corrosion of service lines and plumbing materials containing lead, such as brass faucets and lead solder connecting copper pipes, that are privately owned and thus beyond the EPA's regulatory reach under the Act. System-wide measurement is made still more difficult because the degree to which plumbing materials leach lead varies greatly with such factors as the age of the material, the temperature of the water, the presence of other chemicals in the water, and the length of time the water is in contact with the leaded material. Final Rule: Maximum Contaminant Level Goals and National Primary Drinking Water Regulations for Lead and Copper, 56 Fed. Reg. 26,460, 26,463-26,466, 26,473-26,476 (1991). Indeed, lead levels in samples drawn consecutively from a single source can vary significantly. Id. at 26,473-26,476. Measurement difficulties aside, treatment is made problematic because chemicals added to the drinking water supply in order to reduce the corrosion of pipes can increase the levels of other contaminants subject to MCLs. Id. at 26,486-26,487.

Recognizing the peculiar difficulty of establishing an MCL for lead in public water systems, the EPA proposed regulations that distinguish between control of lead in source water and control of lead due to corrosion. First, the EPA proposed an MCL for lead in source water, to be measured at the point where the water enters the distribution system. Second, the EPA proposed to require a treatment technique—an "optimal corrosion control treatment" supplemented with a program of public education—to be tailored specifically by each public water system in such a way as to minimize lead contamination in drinking water without increasing the level of any other contaminant to the point where it violates the NPDWR for that substance. 53 Fed. Reg. at 31,537-31,538.

The EPA solicited comments on this two-part monitoring and treatment proposal and on several alternatives that it was not then proposing. One such alternative was to require each public water system to replace the lead service lines it owns or controls that, after treatment to reduce corrosion, still contribute a significant amount of lead to tap water. Id. at 31,546, 31,547-31,548. Under this approach the EPA would erect a "rebuttable presumption" that the public water system "owns or controls and therefore can replace, the lead components up to the wall of the building served." 53 Fed. Reg. at 31,548.

In the final rule the EPA abandoned its two-part monitoring and treatment proposal in favor of a rule under which all large water systems must institute corrosion control treatment, while smaller systems must do so only if representative sampling indicates that lead in the water exceeds a designated "action level." 56 Fed. Reg. at 26,550 (to be codified at 40 C.F.R. §141.81(d) & (e)). The agency also adopted a schedule that allows a public water system five or more years to comply with the regulation, depending upon the number of persons it serves, see id. at 26,480 (codified at 40 C.F.R. §141.81(a)); see also id. at 26,479-26,480, 26,494-26,497. The EPA required larger systems to come into compliance sooner than smaller systems because they are generally more sophisticated technically and have a greater impact upon the purity of drinking water; also the states, which are responsible for implementing the regulation, would benefit from experience gained with larger systems before reviewing treatment plans for smaller systems. The EPA exempted from the rule all transient noncommunity public water systems, such as those in restaurants, gas stations, and motels. 40 C.F.R. §141.80(a)(1).

Unlike the proposed rule, the final rule requires each public water system to replace each year at least 77 of the lead service lines it controls that when tested exceed a designated action level. 40 C.F.R. §141.84(b) & (d). A public water system is said to "control" a service line if it has "authority to set standards for construction, repair, or maintenance of the line, authority to replace, repair, or maintain the service line, or ownership of the service line." 40 C.F.R. §141.84(e). The rule establishes a presumption that the public water system controls every service line up to the wall of the building it serves; the system can rebut the presumption only by demonstrating that its control is limited by state statute, local ordinance, public service contract, or other legal authority. 40 C.F.R. §141.84(e). A public water system that controls only part of a service line must replace the portion under its control and must offer to replace the remaining portion, although not necessarily at the system's expense. 40 C.F.R. §141.84(d).

II. ANALYSIS

Together the petitioners raise four challenges to the EPA's final rule, which we review under the familiar framework of Chevron U.S.A., Inc. v. Natural Resources Defense Council, 467 U.S. 837 (1984). Where the "Congress has directly spoken to the precise question at issue," we must give effect to its "unambiguously expressed" intent; but where the Congress has been silent or its statement is ambiguous, we will defer to the EPA's interpretation if it is reasonable in view of the text, the structure, and the underlying purpose of the statute. Id. at 842-843; see also American Mining Congress v. United States EPA, 824 F.2d 1177, 1184 (D.C. Cir. 1987).

A. MCL for Lead at the Tap

The NRDC first contends that, because it is economically and technologically feasible to ascertain the level of lead in water, the Safe Drinking Water Act requires that the EPA set an MCL for lead. See 42 U.S.C. §300f(1)(C); 42 U.S.C. §300g-1(b)(7). Further, because the tap is the delivery point to the user of a public water system, the NRDC concludes that the MCL must be set at the tap.

At bottom the NRDC and the EPA disagree over the meaning of the word "feasible" as it applies to ascertaining the level of lead in drinking water. The NRDC argues that the Congress clearly expressed its intent that "feasible" be understood to mean "physically capable of being done at reasonable cost"; accordingly it argues that the EPA's rule is contrary to the plain meaning of the statute. See *Chevron*, 467 U.S. at 842-43. For its part, the EPA does not dispute that it is "feasible" to monitor lead under the definition advanced by the NRDC; instead the agency interprets "feasible" to mean "capable of being accomplished in a manner consistent with the Act." The agency argues that if public water systems were required to comply with an MCL for lead, they would have to undertake aggressive corrosion control techniques that might reduce the amount of lead leached from customers' plumbing but would also increase the levels of other contaminants. The EPA argues that because the Congress apparently did not anticipate a situation in which monitoring for one contaminant, although possible, is not conducive to overall water quality, it impliedly delegated to the agency the discretion to specify a treatment technique instead of an MCL.

We agree with the EPA that the meaning of "feasible" is not as plain as the NRDC suggests. Although we generally assume that the Congress intends the words it uses to have their ordinary meaning, see Securities Industry Assn v. Board of Governors of Federal Reserve System, 468 U.S. 137, 149 (1984), case law is replete with examples of statutes the ordinary meaning of which is not necessarily what the Congress intended. See, e.g., Young v. Community Nutrition Institute, 476 U.S. 974, 980 (1986) (EPA's interpretation of unclear statute held rational though not the "more natural interpretation"); *American Mining Congress*, 824 F.2d at 1185-1186. Indeed, where a literal reading of a statutory term would lead to absurd results, the term simply "has no plain meaning . . . and is the proper subject of construction by the EPA and the courts." Chemical Manufacturers Association v. Natural Resources Defense Council, Inc., 470 U.S. 116, 126 (1985). If the meaning of "feasible" suggested by the NRDC is indeed its plain meaning, then this is such a case; for it could lead to a result squarely at odds with the purpose of the Safe Drinking Water Act.

The Congress clearly contemplated that an MCL would be a standard by which both the quality of the drinking water and the public water system's efforts to reduce the contaminant could be measured. See 42 U.S.C. §300g-1(b)(5). Because lead generally enters drinking water from corrosion in pipes owned by customers of the water system, an MCL for lead would be neither; ascertaining the level of lead in water at the meter (i.e., where it enters the customer's premises) would measure the public water system's success in controlling the contaminant but not the quality of the public's drinking water (because lead may still leach into the water from the customer's plumbing), while ascertaining the level of lead in water at the tap would accurately reflect water quality but effectively hold the public water system responsible for lead leached from plumbing owned by its customers.

We must defer to the EPA's interpretation of "feasible" if it is reasonable, *Chevron,* 467 U.S. at 842-843, and we think that it is. A single national standard (i.e., an MCL) for lead is not suitable for every public water system because the condition of plumbing materials, which are the major source of lead in drinking water, varies across systems and the systems generally do not have control over the sources of lead in their water. In this circumstance the EPA suggests that requiring public water systems to design and implement custom corrosion control plans for lead will result in optimal treatment of drinking water overall, i.e., treatment that deals adequately with lead without causing public water systems to violate drinking water regulations for other contaminants. 56 Fed. Reg. 26,487.

Viewing the Act as a whole, we cannot say that the statute demonstrates a clear congressional intent to require that the EPA set an MCL for a contaminant merely because it can be measured at a reasonable cost. In light of the purpose of the Act to promote safe drinking water generally, we conclude that the EPA's interpretation of the term "feasible" so as to require a treatment technique instead of an MCL for lead is reasonable.

B. *Compliance Schedule*

We turn next to the NRDC's contention that the compliance schedule promulgated by the EPA is contrary to the statutory injunction that NPDWRs "shall take effect 18 months after the date of their promulgation." 42 U.S.C. §300g-1(b)(10). According to the petitioner, in "ordinary English" the phrase "shall take effect" means "shall be fully implemented and enforced against public water systems." Therefore, we are told, the meaning of the statute is plain and the EPA's interpretation to the contrary should be struck down, *Chevron,* 467 U.S. at 842-843, with the result that the rule must be fully implemented within 18 months of when it was promulgated.

The EPA, on the other hand, contends that the plain meaning of the statute is that the agency cannot impose the requirements of an NPDWR upon public water systems any earlier than eighteen months after promulgation. According to the agency, the Congress included the 18-month provision in the Act not in order to force the agency to adopt a hasty implementation schedule but in order to "constrain[ ] the Agency's authority under the Administrative Procedure Act, 5 U.S.C. §553(d), to make rules effective 30 days after their publication in the Federal Register." 56 Fed. Reg. at 26,494-26,495.

We start, as usual, with the terms of the statute. The spare mandate—that NPDWRs "shall take effect eighteen months after the date of their promulgation"—is in our view considerably less clear on its face than the NRDC suggests. As we only recently noted, depending upon the context, "take effect" can mean either "take legal effect" (as the EPA here suggests), or "produce results" (as the NRDC suggests). See Boehner v. Anderson, 30 F.3d 156, 161-162 (D.C. Cir. 1994); Natural Resources Defense Council v. Browner, 22 F.3d 1125, 1137-1140 (D.C. Cir. 1994). Because we must examine the effective date provision in its statutory context in order to determine which meaning the Congress intended, we cannot say that either the NRDC's or the EPA's reading is the uniquely "plain meaning" of the provision.

Turning to that context, we see first that the effective date provision refers only to drinking water regulations, not to their implementation and enforcement. The Act defines an NPDWR as a regulation that (1) applies to public water systems; (2) identifies a contaminant that could adversely affect human health; (3) specifies either an MCL or a treatment technique to control the contaminant; and (4) contains criteria and procedures, such as operating and maintenance standards, to assure a reasonably safe drinking water supply. 42 U.S.C. §300f(1). An NPDWR does not, however, set an implementation schedule or enforcement procedures for the MCL or treatment technique it specifies. On the contrary, the Act requires the States, which have primary enforcement responsibility, to promulgate regulations to implement and enforce the NPDWRs. See 42 U.S.C. §§300g-2, 300g-3. Clearly, therefore, the Congress contemplated that the date upon which a drinking water regulation takes effect under 42 U.S.C. §300g-1(b)(10) would not necessarily be the date upon which the regulation will be implemented or enforced. See, e.g., Boehner v. Anderson, 30 F.3d 156 (D.C. Cir. 1994) (law may have delayed effect).

4. Regulation of Toxic Substances

Second, the 18-month provision applies equally to all drinking water regulations, whether they promulgate a treatment technique or an MCL. Although it may be reasonable to assume that an MCL can be implemented and enforced 18 months after promulgation, we doubt that the Congress expected that each state could in 18 months approve the various treatment plans submitted by all the public water systems in the state; promulgate and implement enforcement regulations; grant exemptions and variances for public water systems that cannot comply with the NPDWR; and establish a reporting mechanism, which must be designed on a site-by-site basis in order to minimize exposure to the contaminant in drinking water without adversely affecting the public water system's compliance with other MCLs or treatment techniques. See 42 U.S.C. §§300g-2, 300g-4, 300g-5, 40 C.F.R. §§142.4-142.19; see also 56 Fed. Reg. at 26,487 (describing factors to take into account in designing treatment technique), 26,494-26,495 (describing actions by public water systems and States necessary to implement treatment technique). Compressing these activities into 18 months could compromise effective treatment for lead; it is surely not unreasonable, therefore, for the EPA to interpret the 18-month provision so as to prefer the Act's overall goal of safe drinking water over a hasty implementation and enforcement schedule. Accordingly, we conclude that the EPA's interpretation of the 18-month provision is reasonable.

NOTES AND QUESTIONS

1. Note that EPA conceded that it was physically possible to monitor lead levels at the tap at reasonable cost. Why then did the agency argue that it was not feasible to impose an at-the-tap MCL? Why did the court agree?

2. In a portion of the opinion not reproduced above, the court did agree with NRDC that EPA had failed to explain adequately why it declined to regulate transient noncommunity water systems. At the behest of the American Water Works Association, the court also struck down EPA's rebuttable presumption that a public water system "controls" the service line up to the wall of the building for purposes of requiring the system to replace them. The court stated that EPA had failed to provide adequate notice that it was considering such a provision.

3. As the court notes, chemicals used to treat the water supply to reduce corrosion of lead pipes can increase the levels of other contaminants in drinking water. EPA faces similar problems in considering exposure limits for chlorine and other chemicals used to disinfect drinking water. While epidemiological studies suggest that such chemicals

can increase the risk of bladder and rectal cancer, the chemicals are necessary to reduce the risk of pathogens such as protozoa giardia and cryptosporidium, a microbe that caused several deaths in Milwaukee in September 1993. EPA Queasy Over Chlorine Rule, 264 Science 1835 (1994).

4. In October 1992, EPA announced that levels of lead in excess of EPA's 15 ppb action level had been found in more than ten percent of the water samples taken by 130 of the nation's 659 major public water supply systems. One-Fifth of Big Municipal Suppliers Provide Water with Too Much Lead, EPA Says, 23 Env. Rep. 1636 (1992). As a result, these systems must begin to implement the corrosion control procedures required by EPA's regulations (parent text, p. 578). A total of 52 of the major water supply systems, including 46 in California, failed to perform the testing required by EPA's regulations. Id. In May 1993 EPA announced that more than 800 additional cities had elevated levels of lead in their water supplies.

3. Health-Based (Zero, Significant, or De Minimis) Risk

The Delaney Clause and De Minimis Risk (pp. 581-591). The Ninth Circuit decided the *Les* case (parent text, p. 591) in July 1992. The court rejected EPA's attempt to create a "de minimis" exception to the Delaney Clause that applies to food additives under section 409 of the federal Food, Drug, and Cosmetic Act (FDCA) (parent text, pp. 598-599). The court found that the reasoning employed by the D.C. Circuit in interpreting the color additives Delaney Clause in Public Citizen v. Young was "equally applicable" to the statutory language in section 409. Les v. Reilly, 968 F.2d 985, 989 (9th Cir. 1992). Finding the statutory language to be "clear and mandatory," the court explained that the legislative history indicates that "Congress intended the very rigidity that the language it chose commands." Id. at 988, 989. The court refused EPA's invitation to distinguish between the color additives Delaney Clause and the clause governing food additives. It found that "Congress intended to ban all carcinogenic food additives, regardless of amount or significance of risk, as the only safe alternative." Id. at 989.

Yet the court recognized that strict application of the Delaney Clause might not accomplish Congress's goal. It noted that consumers might switch to raw foods with pesticide residues that actually pose greater risks than the residues on processed foods that were at issue in the case. However, it stated that "[i]f there is to be a change, it is for Congress to direct." Id. at 990. The Clinton Administration announced in May 1993 that it will seek to develop new food safety legislation in response to the *Les* decision. In June 1993, EPA, FDA, and the Depart-

4. Regulation of Toxic Substances   Page 591

ment of Agriculture announced a major policy shift to promote reduced use of pesticides in food production. The agencies pledged a coordinated effort to remove high-risk pesticides from the market, and they endorsed integrated pest management, which emphasizes nonchemical pest-control alternatives. The new policy coincided with the release of a National Academy of Sciences report finding that existing regulatory policies fail to protect children adequately in light of their greater sensitivity to pesticide risks.

EPA already had begun to consider reforms in the process for registering pesticides under FIFRA. In July 1992, the Agency requested public comment on how to structure regulatory incentives to encourage the development of safer pesticides. 57 Fed. Reg. 32,140 (1992). EPA indicated that it was considering accelerating the registration process for lower-risk pesticides and the possible restriction or removal of higher-risk pesticides for which safer substitutes become available. EPA policy that prohibits safety claims for pesticides may also be reconsidered in order to harness market forces to encourage the development of safer alternatives.

Concerned that EPA was not implementing the *Les* decision, NRDC subsequently sued EPA to force the elimination of carcinogenic residues on processed foods. In October 1994 EPA settled the lawsuit by agreeing to conduct an expedited review of previously approved uses for 36 pesticides believed to contain carcinogens. Cushman, EPA Settles Suit and Agrees to Move Against 36 Pesticides, N.Y. Times, Oct. 13, 1994, at A24. In February 1995 EPA announced that it would require that 34 pesticides be phased out of processed foods within two years. EPA will also review data on 87 other pesticides during the next five years. EPA's decision is expected to increase pressure building in Congress to repeal the Delaney Clause. McCoy, EPA Agrees to Ban Pesticides, Comply with Rule in Food Act, Wall St. J., Feb. 9, 1995, at B16.

Naturally Occurring Carcinogens (pp. 590-591). Bruce Ames and his colleagues have revised and updated his comparison of the relative risks of naturally occurring carcinogens and synthetic chemicals. Gold, Slone, Stern, Manley, and Ames, Rodent Carcinogens: Setting Priorities, 258 Science 261 (1992). They maintain that residues of synthetic pesticides and environmental pollutants rank as a relatively low cancer hazard to humans when compared against the large background of naturally occurring carcinogens in common foods.

Section 112 of the Clean Air Act (p. 591). Citing the use of a "one-in-a-million" standard for additional risk reduction in the amended section 112 of the Clean Air Act, Alon Rosenthal, George Gray, and John Graham argue that Congress should use "bright line" levels of acceptable risk only as a tool for setting priorities for additional risk reduction. They explain that

> legislating bright lines [for acceptable risk] would do little to constrain agency discretion in risk management, since agencies would retain enormous discretion in the risk assessment process. In the face of profound uncertainty about cancer risk, agency risk assessors can make numerous quasi-policy judgments in deciding how chemical risks are calculated. Although Congress could constrain the discretion of risk assessors by mandating specific analytic methods and data sources, there is a real danger that such detailed legislative prescriptions would undermine scientific progress in risk assessment.

Rosenthal, Gray, and Graham, Legislating Acceptable Cancer Risk from Exposure to Toxic Chemicals, 19 Ecol. L.Q. 269 (1992).

Risk Assessment Legislation, The Contract With America, and Objections to Quantitative Risk Assessment (pp. 601-609). The controversy surrounding QRA has lately focused on the Congress. As of this writing a number of bills are pending before the 104th Congress to require QRA prior to issuing final rules. The most prominent proposals are contained in Title II of H.R. 9, which passed the House of Representatives by a vote of 286-141 on February 28, 1995. This legislation, called the Risk Communication Act of 1995, would require all agencies to base all regulatory decisions on risk assessment and cost-benefit criteria, overriding any conflicting criteria in existing laws. Detailed risk assessments and cost-benefit analyses would have to be prepared for all rules with an annual cost of $25 million or more. The legislation also would impose detailed statutory specifications on how agencies conduct risk assessments, including a requirement that "best estimates" and plausible lower bound estimates of risk be provided and that target risks be compared to other routine and familiar risks. Peer review panels that could include representatives of regulated industries would be required to review the scientific and economic data used in preparing risk assessments and parties unsatisfied by the results of risk assessments could seek judicial review of them.

Some supporters of this proposal candidly admit that its requirements are meant to make it far more difficult for federal agencies to promulgate additional health and safety rules. They maintain that past regulatory policies have exaggerated the seriousness of environmental risks and they support QRA for some or all of the reasons put forward by Administrator Ruckelshaus in the excerpt in the casebook, pp. 601-605.

Opponents of a one-size fits all legislative imposition of QRA con-

4. Regulation of Toxic Substances   Pages 601-609

tinue to advance counterarguments. EPA Administrator Carol Browner described the risk assessment legislation that passed the House as "a full frontal assault on our attempts to protect the nation's environment." Kenworthy, House Votes to Limit Health, Safety Rules, Wash. Post, Mar. 1, 1995, at A1. Terry Yosie, former director of EPA's Science Advisory Board and former vice president for Health and the Environment at the American Petroleum Institute, argues that risk assessment legislation may have unexpected side effects that would actually increase the burden on industry. He maintains that risk legislation "will push EPA to mandate expensive new testing mandates upon industry in order to supply the data necessary to conduct a voluminous number of new risk assessments." Yosie, Risk Assessment Legislation: Bad for Business?, Risk Policy Rep., Jan. 20, 1995, at 38. Yosie argues that EPA will be forced to expand greatly the use of default assumptions, particularly when assessing noncancer health effects and ecological effects. The peer review panels required by the legislation would compromise the integrity of risk assessments by combining policy and scientific considerations, while creating a "new and powerful and largely unaccountable bureaucracy to adjudicate risk decision-making." Id. The end result would be substantial delays in the regulatory process that will benefit lawyers and consultants, but not industries seeking clear rules.

New evidence continues to develop concerning whether the manner in which QRA compares the riskiness of various actions corresponds to the manner in which individuals assess the hazards of those actions. Consider the following comments that elaborate on some of the objections to risk assessment discussed in the parent text.

The Risk-Benefit Trade-offs Enabled by QRA Are Unjustified. At a conference on risk-based priority setting in EPA, Professor Mary O'Brien presented arguments in opposition to the proposition that such tradeoffs are necessary.

> She rejected the conclusion that we are near the limits of our resources to deal with environmental problems. She also rejected the very notion of risk-based priority setting, whether technocratic or based on public referendums, contending that any effort to rank risks is merely an environmental equivalent of Sophie's Choice: "Which child will you hand over to the Nazis?" This, she said, is a false and immoral choice that avoids the real solutions—to focus on how we can behave better towards the environment rather than how much damage we will permit, and to examine alternative products and processes rather than risks.
>
> Based on the assumption that we know many of the products and processes that are harmful to human health and the environment, O'Brien said, society should ask the more fundamental questions: Are these products essential? If so, are there environmentally less damaging

233

processes and products that can provide the same goods and services? If our goal is to have environmentally sound parks or agriculture, she argued, we should not try to rank the risks of different pesticides; rather, we should be looking for alternative ways to avoid or control pests.

O'Brien proposed that all sectors of society should be enrolled in the attempt to identify alternatives for all environmentally degrading activities, although we might begin with the relatively more tractable problems to build confidence, expertise, and momentum. EPA should facilitate this process, she said, and should take advantage of the knowledge and expertise of environmental groups in the United States and elsewhere in the world. O'Brien also proposed that all businesses should conduct biannual environmental audits aimed specifically at identifying alternative products and processes that are less environmentally damaging.

Resources for the Future, Conference Synopsis, Setting National Environmental Priorities: The EPA Risk-Based Paradigm and Its Alternatives, pp. 3-4 (Feb., 1993).

QRA Ignores Differences Among Risks. Results from experiments continue to confirm that people take account of more situational factors in evaluating different risky situations than are accounted for by QRA's analysis of the magnitude of harm and its probability. In particular, Sandman's concept of "outrage," which is used to distinguish the non-QRA aspects of risky situations from "hazard," or probability and magnitude of harm. (see p. 608 of the parent), has been studied in a number of different settings, as have similar concepts that use different labels. One such study asked different groups to read different newspaper accounts of the same interaction between a safety agency or company and a community at risk. The accounts contained the same QRA-relevant information, but portrayed different actions of the safety agency or company with respect to its willingness to disclose information, its responsiveness to community questions, and other actions that might affect an observer's sense of trust, control, and fairness. The study found that these differences, in situational factors the study authors termed the "outrage cluster" of factors, produced significant differences in risk assessment in a number of situations, although the authors cautioned that single hypothetical news accounts differ in several important respects from unfolding news coverage of actual events. Sandman, et al., Agency Communication, Community Outrage, and Perception of Risk: Three Simulation Experiments, 6 Risk Analysis 585 (1993).

Is Risk Assessment Too Conservative?: The Dioxin Reassessment (pp. 609-610). The controversy concerning reassessment of the risks posed by dioxin provides an excellent illustration of the uncertainties that surround risk assessment. In late 1989, EPA began reevaluating its

4. Regulation of Toxic Substances

Pages 609-610

estimate of the level of exposure to dioxin that poses a one-in-a-million risk (currently it equals .006 picograms per kilogram per day). In May 1991, EPA Administrator William Reilly announced that dioxin, once called the "most toxic compound known to mankind," would be subject to an official reassessment of risk. Although this review was undertaken in part in response to arguments based on mechanisms-of-action research, the discovery that dioxin contamination was more widespread than previously suspected (and thus would be extremely costly to remediate) also generated considerable pressure in favor of asking scientists for a second opinion.

Researchers initially had been impressed by how tightly dioxin binds to a protein (the Ah receptor) in mouse livers, setting off an enormous chain of unusual events. But human epidemiological data generally confirmed only that dioxin could cause a skin rash called chloracne. Some scientists hypothesized that there could be a safe level of exposure to dioxin if all the adverse effects caused by the substance required activation of the Ah receptor. Marshall, Toxicology Goes Molecular, 259 Science 1394-1395 (1993). While most scientists continue to subscribe to the one-hit hypothesis for mutagens (chemicals that operate by damaging DNA), dioxin is not a mutagen, but instead seems to operate by triggering reversible changes in the biological functioning of cells. For substances that function in this manner, some researchers believe there is likely to be a safe threshold level of human exposure below which dioxin is not capable of producing this biological alteration. Regulatory agencies in Canada, Australia, and several European countries have adopted more relaxed standards for dioxin exposure than the United States has. These countries have set limits in the range of 1 to 10 picograms per kilogram per day.

What are the stakes? One industry estimate is that $1 billion in waste site cleanup alone is at stake if the regulatory standard (the answer to the how-clean-is-clean question for dioxin) were changed to 5 picograms. Because dioxin is both pervasive and strictly regulated under many different regulatory statutes, avoided costs actually could be quite a bit higher. See generally Baker and Smith, Science Meets Policy—Dioxin Regulation in Flux, Environmental Law, Summer 1991 (quarterly newsletter of the Standing Committee on Environmental Law of the ABA).

With stakes this high, it is not surprising that industry groups have encouraged scientists to change their models in a manner that would generate a substantially lower risk assessment for dioxin. Early in 1990, the Chlorine Institute, a trade association whose members generate considerable dioxin, approached the nonprofit Danbury Center and suggested that it convene a meeting of scientists to reassess the risks of dioxin. The Institute persuaded an FDA scientist to chair the meeting and insisted only that one Institute consultant attend as an observer. The dioxin conference, funded by the Chlorine Institute in cooperation with EPA, was convened at the Banbury Center in October 1990. Many of the world's leading dioxin researchers attended along with the Chlorine Institute's observer. At the meeting many, but not all, participants expressed the view that EPA's model for assessing dioxin risks overestimated such risks. Following the meeting the Chlorine Institute hired a public relations firm to publicize a "consensus" summary of the meeting, prepared by the Chlorine Institute's representative. The summary stated that experts agreed that dioxin was not as harmful as previously thought. Stories then appeared in newspapers around the country announcing the new scientific findings, angering some scientists who had participated in the conference. The scientists protested that the meeting was being misrepresented by the Chlorine Institute. Roberts, Flap Erupts Over Dioxin Meeting, 251 Science 866 (1991).

Five months into EPA's reassessment of dioxin risks, a study by scientists at the National Institute of Environmental Health Sciences produced surprising new evidence suggesting that there may be no threshold for at least some effects of dioxin. Scientists who had argued against a linear model for dioxin risks thought that dioxin had to occupy a minimum number of receptors before it would activate adverse responses. However, an experiment in which rats were fed extremely low doses of dioxin every two weeks measured several dioxin-induced changes in enzyme activity and dioxin-induced alterations in the binding capacity of receptors that show "absolutely no deviation from linearity" at extremely low levels of exposure. Roberts, More Pieces in the Dioxin Puzzle, 254 Science 377 (1991).

EPA reviewed the results of its reassessment of dioxin risks and released a draft risk characterization report in September 1994. EPA reaffirmed its position that dioxin is a human carcinogen for which it has not been possible to demonstrate a safe threshold level of exposure. This conclusion was bolstered by a 1991 NIOSH study finding a significantly greater incidence of cancer in chemical workers exposed to dioxin. Dioxin Still Considered Major Health Threat, According to Early Findings of EPA Reassessment, 23 Env. Rep. 1504 (1992). However, the Agency also concluded that dioxin poses an even greater risk of adverse developmental, reproductive, and immune suppression effects than previously thought. Draft Dioxin Assessment Cites Health Risks: More Government Action Needed, Agency Says, 25 Env. Rep. 971 (1994). EPA estimated that 95 percent of known dioxin emissions were a product of combustion of medical and municipal waste. The agency pledged to explore new limits on dioxin emissions from such incinerators. Id. But it admitted that only between 10 and 50 percent of the sources of dioxins have been identified. Less Than Half of Dioxin Sources Identified, EPA Official Tells Seminar, 25 Env. Rep. 1132 (1994).

Reassessments of Radiation Risks (p. 610). Assessments of radiation risk are based in large part on epidemiological studies of workers exposed to radiation and victims of the atomic bombs dropped on Hiroshima and Nagasaki. Because it is difficult to determine these groups' actual levels of exposure and to track comprehensively the incidence of adverse health effects, risk assessments based on these studies are subject to great uncertainty. A study that argues that victims of the Hiroshima blast actually were exposed to significantly more radiation than previously thought is being cited as evidence that the risks of radiation exposure have been overestimated. Broad, New Study Questions Hiroshima Radiation, N.Y. Times, Oct. 13, 1992, at C1. Conversely, an epidemiological study that finds that workers at the Hanford nuclear reservation in Washington have suffered a substantially greater increase in radiation-induced cancer is being cited to argue that the risks of small doses of radiation have been underestimated by a factor of four to eight. Wald, Pioneer in Radiation Sees Risk Even in Small Doses, N.Y. Times, Dec. 8, 1992, at A1.

The Relationship Between Risk Assessment and Risk Management (p. 611). Arguing that the political process inevitably infects risk assessments performed by agencies, former FDA Commissioner Frank Young has proposed that an independent agency be formed to conduct risk assessment in a manner insulated from the political process. Based on his experience at FDA, Dr. Young, who endured the Alar controversy, deems it "extraordinarily difficult" to have the same agency perform both risk assessment and risk management because "there is an inevitable temptation for the political process to enter it." HHS Official Calls for Independent Unit to Do Risk Assessments, Deal with Public, 23 Env. Rep. 2727 (1993). Do you agree with Dr. Young? Is it naive to think that an independent agency would be insulated from the political process?

The Risk Assessment and Management Commission (pp. 611-612). The Risk Assessment and Management Commission created by the 1990 Clean Air Act Amendments held its first meetings in 1994. The Commission has scheduled 11 public meetings in 1995 and is expected to issue its final report in March 1996. ATSDR Future Dependent on Superfund Rewrite, Presidential Commission on Risk Assessment Told, 25 Env. Rep. 1478 (1994).

E. ALTERNATIVES TO CONVENTIONAL REGULATORY APPROACHES

1. *Informational and Burden-Shifting Approaches*

Informational Strategies and Agency Research Needs (pp. 612-614). As regulatory agencies place greater emphasis on nonregulatory approaches for reducing environmental risk, their research needs are likely to change. Former EPA Deputy Administrator Al Alm has argued that informational approaches will "require much more sophistication than choosing a regulatory limit or designating a technology." Instead, such approaches will require agencies to consider social science data to obtain "a basic understanding of how decisions are made in the private sector, what stimuli would change private sector behavior, and how public sector activities could make a difference." Alm, Science, Social Science, and the New Paradigm, 26 Envtl. Sci. Tech. 1123 (1992). Alm notes that when Congress enacted the EPCRTKA the debate focused not on how industry would react to disclosures of their chemical releases, but rather on how the public would react to such information. Yet it now has become clear that the most significant effect of the legislation has been to encourage companies to voluntarily reduce emissions of toxic substances.

In September 1994, EPA unveiled a program to encourage industry to design safer chemicals through expanded research into mechanisms of toxicity. Modeled on EPA's program to encourage source reduction, the program will assist industry in exploring alternative chemical designs that can perform the original function of a chemical in a manner that reduces its toxicity. Flam, EPA Campaigns for Safer Chemicals, 265 Science 1519 (1994). EPA scientists cite the example of a common pesticide toxic to fish that was redesigned to create an equally effective, fish-friendly compound by replacing some carbon atoms with silicon. To design safer chemicals it may be necessary to train "a new breed of chemist" with a broader understanding of both chemical synthesis and toxicology. Id.

The Nutrition Labeling and Education Act (p. 615). After a bitter battle with the Department of Agriculture that generated lengthy delays, the Food and Drug Administration in 1993 issued a series of regulations implementing the Nutrition Labeling and Education Act, Pub. L. No. 101-535. Occupying nearly 1,000 pages spread over two volumes of the Federal Register, the regulations require nutrition labeling on most foods and ban the making of all but four health claims on food labels.

4. Regulation of Toxic Substances   Pages 616-622

58 Fed. Reg. 2070 (1993). The regulations provide a complicated, but fascinating, case study of a host of regulatory policy issues, including the need to tailor informational regulation to take into account variations among members of the target audience (e.g., men and women have very different dietary requirements), the question of how to distill information into a form that will permit effective communication of complex concepts, and the need to anticipate potentially deceptive response strategies by the regulated community.

California's Proposition 65 (pp. 616-622). The California Superior Court decision ruling that grocers could not simply employ a toll-free telephone number to comply with Proposition 65 (parent text, p. 619) was affirmed on appeal by the California Court of Appeal. Ingredient Communication Council, Inc. v. Lungren, 4 Cal. Rptr. 2d 216 (1992). The court explained why the use of a toll-free number was insufficient to meet the law's requirement to provide "a clear and reasonable warning":

> The major conceptual problem was that the system proceeded on the assumption [that] most consumers before shopping sit down with the food section of the newspaper each week, see the advertised 800 number, make a list of the specific brand names of products they intend to buy, and then call to check whether these products carry a warning. This assumption is contradicted by the fact that about two-thirds of the buying decisions made by grocery consumers are made in the store on impulse. In addition, few consumers are willing to spend time researching and calling about those relatively inexpensive products they frequently buy in a grocery store; such purchases differ from those of automobiles or computers.

Id. at 225.

In March 1992, the Ninth Circuit held that Proposition 65 is not preempted by federal legislation, Chemical Specialties Manufacturing Assn. v. Allenby, 958 F.2d 941 (9th Cir. 1992), affirming the district court decision of the same name mentioned in the text on page 620. In October 1992, the Supreme Court declined to review the Ninth Circuit's decision. The day after the Ninth Circuit's decision was released, a group of large California hardware store chains settled a lawsuit brought by the Environmental Defense Fund (EDF) by agreeing not to sell paint removers and other household products that contain methylene chloride and to promote noncarcinogenic alternatives. In November 1992, Thompson & Formby became the twentieth maker of methylene chloride products to reach a similar settlement. Company to Take Products off California Market, 23 Env. Rep. 1881 (1992).

In December 1992, 16 faucet manufacturers were sued by the state of California and two environmental groups, who alleged that their faucets leached lead into drinking water in violation of Proposition 65. Suit Names 16 Faucet Manufacturers; Alleges Release of Lead in Drinking Water, 23 Env. Rep. 2106 (1992). A California court hearing the lawsuit ruled that the manufacturers must provide warnings concerning the lead content of the faucets, but that the faucets were not themselves sources of drinking water that would violate Proposition 65's separate ban on introducing toxics to drinking water sources. California v. American Standard, No. 9480178 (Calif. Super. Ct., May 5, 1994). In October 1994, 14 companies that manufacture submersible well pumps announced that they would virtually eliminate the use of lead in their products to avoid similar problems. Pump Makers Plan Phaseout of Brass Part Due to Lead Concerns, Wall St. J., Oct. 6, 1994, at A13.

As a result of a lawsuit filed by EDF and the California Attorney General, 10 leading china manufacturers agreed in January 1993 to reduce the amount of lead used in ceramic glazes by 50 percent and to place conspicuous warning labels on all tableware whose lead content poses a potential hazard. Lead can leach into food from ceramic glazes used on plates, cups, and bowls. The settlement agreement included a $2.3 million penalty.

California has repealed a regulation that had exempted from Proposition 65's coverage products regulated under the federal Food, Drug, and Cosmetic Act. However, a federal district court ruled in 1994 that Proposition 65's warning requirements could not be applied to dental mercury because they were preempted by the Medical Devices Amendments to the federal act. Committee of Dental Amalgam Alloy Mfrs. v. Henry, 871 F. Supp. 1278 (S.D. Cal. 1994).

Emergency Planning and Community Right-to-Know Act (pp. 622-628). The toxics release inventory (TRI) created by EPCRA continues to be viewed as a dramatic success that is being used to create new programs to encourage pollution prevention. As a result, efforts to broaden its coverage continue. In August 1993 President Clinton issued Executive Order 12,856, 58 Fed. Reg. 41,981, which directs federal facilities to comply with EPCRA's reporting requirements and to reduce their releases of toxics by 50 percent by 1999.

In November 1994 EPA added 286 additional toxic substances to the list of chemicals whose release must be reported under EPCRA. The new rule expands the number of chemicals on the TRI to 654 as of January 1, 1995. 59 Fed. Reg. 61,432 (1994). To make it easier for small companies to comply with EPCRA, EPA has issued a regulation allowing companies that do not release more than 500 pounds of any

4. Regulation of Toxic Substances

TRI chemical to use a simplified reporting form. 59 Fed. Reg. 61,488 (1994).

2. Common Law Liability

Asbestos Litigation (p. 630). A state trial court judge in Maryland has consolidated 8,555 tort actions filed against asbestos manufacturers. Judge Marshal A. Levin presided over a mass jury trial of the claims that culminated in a verdict finding the former asbestos firms liable for compensatory and punitive damages against. Judge Levin is now conducting mini-trials of sample plaintiffs in order to assess compensatory damages, and he has ruled that plaintiffs cannot collect any of the punitive damages until all compensatory damages are paid. Abate v. AC & S Inc., No. 89236704 (Baltimore City Circuit Court).

In January 1993, 20 former asbestos firms participating in the Center for Claims Resolution announced an unusual $1 billion settlement designed to cover at least 100,000 future asbestos-related claims during the next decade. The settlement is to be implemented with the filing of class actions on behalf of all workers injured by asbestos who have yet to file suit. Payments to victims would range from $2,000 to $300,000, based on the average of past awards in similar cases. Moses, Former Asbestos Makers, 2 Law Firms Map $1 Billion Pact to Curb Litigation, Wall St. J., Jan. 18, 1993, at A2. The settlement was approved by a federal district court in August 1994. Georgine v. Amchem Products, Inc., No. 93-0215 (E.D. Pa. 1994).

Santiago v. Sherwin-Williams Co. (p. 630). The decision by the federal district court in Massachusetts in Santiago v. Sherwin-Williams Co. (see parent at p. 630) is reported at 794 F. Supp. 29 (D. Mass. 1992). It was affirmed by the First Circuit in September 1993. Santiago v. Sherwin-Williams Co., 3 F.3d 546 (1st Cir. 1993). The court concluded that the plaintiff could not recover under a market share theory of liability, even if Massachusetts would accept such a doctrine, because she could not "pinpoint with any degree of precision the time the injury-causing paint was applied to [her] house." 3 F.3d at 550. It noted that several of the paint companies were not in the white lead pigment market for significant portions of the period between 1917 and 1970 when layers of paint were placed on the house. The court also held that the paint suppliers could not be held liable under a concert of action theory because there was no evidence that lead paint would not have been used on her house had the lead paint manufacturers not conducted a nationwide promotional campaign.

Agent Orange (pp. 636-638). In an effort to resolve the continuing controversy over the health effects of Agent Orange on Vietnam veterans, a new panel has been convened, under the auspices of the Institute of Medicine, to review all studies of Agent Orange and the health effects associated with exposure to it. IOM to Study Agent Orange, 257 Science 1335 (1992). While some scientists believe that studies conducted in Vietnam would help illuminate this question, their efforts are being hampered by the lack of diplomatic relations between the United States and Vietnam. Crossette, Study of Dioxin's Effect in Vietnam Is Hampered by Diplomatic Freeze, N.Y. Times, Aug. 18, 1992, at C4.

Radiation Exposure Compensation Act (p. 638). As of May 1, 1993, a total of 1,307 claims for compensation had been filed under the Radiation Exposure Compensation Act by persons who lived downwind from the Nevada test site; 348 of these claims had been approved and 267 had been rejected. Uranium miners had filed 1,125 claims under the Act; 341 of these claims had been approved and 131 rejected. Lippman, For Utah Fallout Victims, Money Is of Little Comfort, Wash. Post, May 18, 1993, at A1, A12.

Admission of Expert Testimony (p. 654). On the final day of its 1992-1993 Term, the Supreme Court decided an important case involving the admissibility of expert testimony in toxic tort litigation. In Daubert v. Merrell Dow Pharmaceuticals, 113 S. Ct. 2786 (1993), the Court reviewed a Ninth Circuit decision (951 F.2d 1128 (9th Cir. 1991)) upholding the exclusion of testimony plaintiffs sought to introduce to show that in utero exposure to the drug Bendectin caused birth defects. Bendectin, which had been approved by the FDA in 1956 to treat morning sickness, was removed voluntarily from the market in 1983 after more than 30 million women had used it.

The testimony excluded in *Daubert* was expert opinion that Bendectin had caused the plaintiff's birth defects, based on animal test data, chemical structure analyses, and the reanalysis of epidemiological studies that formerly had not shown a relationship between Bendectin exposure and birth defects. Like other courts that had rejected Bendectin claims, the Ninth Circuit found persuasive the fact that more than 30 published epidemiological studies had not linked Bendectin exposure with birth defects. The court had concluded that "[f]or expert opinion based on a given scientific methodology to be admissible, the methodology cannot diverge significantly from the procedures accepted by recognized authorities in the field." 951 F.2d at 1130. Because plaintiff's experts had not published their reanalysis of the epidemiological studies in a peer-reviewed journal, the Ninth Circuit concluded that the testimony should be excluded. The Supreme Court rendered the following decision.

Daubert v. Merrell Dow Pharmaceuticals, Inc.
113 S. Ct. 2786 (1993)

Justice BLACKMUN delivered the opinion of the Court.

In this case we are called upon to determine the standard for admitting expert scientific testimony in a federal trial.

I

Petitioners Jason Daubert and Eric Schuller are minor children born with serious birth defects. They and their parents sued respondent in California state court, alleging that the birth defects had been caused by the mothers' ingestion of Bendectin, a prescription anti-nausea drug marketed by respondent. Respondent removed the suits to federal court on diversity grounds.

After extensive discovery, respondent moved for summary judgment, contending that Bendectin does not cause birth defects in humans and that petitioners would be unable to come forward with any admissible evidence that it does. In support of its motion, respondent submitted an affidavit of Steven H. Lamm, physician and epidemiologist, who is a well-credentialed expert on the risks from exposure to various chemical substances. Doctor Lamm stated that he had reviewed all the literature on Bendectin and human birth defects—more than 30 published studies involving over 130,000 patients. No study had found Bendectin to be a human teratogen (i.e., a substance capable of causing malformations in fetuses). On the basis of this review, Doctor Lamm concluded that maternal use of Bendectin during the first trimester of pregnancy has not been shown to be a risk factor for human birth defects.

Petitioners did not (and do not) contest this characterization of the published record regarding Bendectin. Instead, they responded to respondent's motion with the testimony of eight experts of their own, each of whom also possessed impressive credentials. These experts had concluded that Bendectin can cause birth defects. Their conclusions were based upon "in vitro" (test tube) and "in vivo" (live) animal studies that found a link between Bendectin and malformations; pharmacological studies of the chemical structure of Bendectin that purported to show similarities between the structure of the drug and that

243

of other substances known to cause birth defects; and the "reanalysis" of previously published epidemiological (human statistical) studies.

The District Court granted respondent's motion for summary judgment. The court stated that scientific evidence is admissible only if the principle upon which it is based is " 'sufficiently established to have general acceptance in the field to which it belongs.' " 727 F. Supp. 570, 572 (SD Cal. 1989), quoting United States v. Kilgus, 571 F.2d 508, 510 (CA9 1978). The court concluded that petitioners' evidence did not meet this standard. Given the vast body of epidemiological data concerning Bendectin, the court held, expert opinion which is not based on epidemiological evidence is not admissible to establish causation. 27 F. Supp., at 575. Thus, the animal-cell studies, live-animal studies, and chemical-structure analyses on which petitioners had relied could not raise by themselves a reasonably disputable jury issue regarding causation. Ibid. Petitioners' epidemiological analyses, based as they were on recalculations of data in previously published studies that had found no causal link between the drug and birth defects, were ruled to be inadmissible because they had not been published or subjected to peer review. Ibid.

The United States Court of Appeals for the Ninth Circuit affirmed. 951 F.2d 1128 (1991). Citing Frye v. United States, 293 F. 1013, 1014 (1923), the court stated that expert opinion based on a scientific technique is inadmissible unless the technique is "generally accepted" as reliable in the relevant scientific community. 951 F.2d, at 1129-1130. The court declared that expert opinion based on a methodology that diverges "significantly from the procedures accepted by recognized authorities in the field . . . cannot be shown to be 'generally accepted as a reliable technique.' " Id., at 1130, quoting United States v. Solomon, 753 F.2d 1522, 1526 (CA9 1985).

The court emphasized that other Courts of Appeals considering the risks of Bendectin had refused to admit reanalyses of epidemiological studies that had been neither published nor subjected to peer review. 951 F.2d, at 1130-1131. Those courts had found unpublished reanalyses "particularly problematic in light of the massive weight of the original published studies supporting [respondent's] position, all of which had undergone full scrutiny from the scientific community." Id., at 1130. Contending that reanalysis is generally accepted by the scientific community only when it is subjected to verification and scrutiny by others in the field, the Court of Appeals rejected petitioners' reanalyses as "unpublished, not subjected to the normal peer review process and generated solely for use in litigation." Id., at 1131. The court concluded that petitioners' evidence provided an insufficient foundation to allow admission of expert testimony that Bendectin caused their injuries and,

4. Regulation of Toxic Substances

accordingly, that petitioners could not satisfy their burden of proving causation at trial.

We granted certiorari, 113 S. Ct. 320 (1992), in light of sharp divisions among the courts regarding the proper standard for the admission of expert testimony. Compare, e.g., United States v. Shorter, 809 F.2d 54, 59-60 (applying the "general acceptance" standard), cert. denied, 484 U.S. 817 (1987), with DeLuca v. Merrell Dow Pharmaceuticals, Inc., 911 F.2d 941, 955 (CA3 1990) (rejecting the "general acceptance" standard).

II

A

In the 70 years since its formulation in the *Frye* case, the "general acceptance" test has been the dominant standard for determining the admissibility of novel scientific evidence at trial. See E. Green & C. Nesson, Problems, Cases, and Materials on Evidence 649 (1983). Although under increasing attack of late, the rule continues to be followed by a majority of courts, including the Ninth Circuit.

The *Frye* test has its origin in a short and citation-free 1923 decision concerning the admissibility of evidence derived from a systolic blood pressure deception test, a crude precursor to the polygraph machine. In what has become a famous (perhaps infamous) passage, the then Court of Appeals for the District of Columbia described the device and its operation and declared:

> Just when a scientific principle or discovery crosses the line between the experimental and demonstrable stages is difficult to define. Somewhere in this twilight zone the evidential force of the principle must be recognized, and while courts will go a long way in admitting expert testimony deduced from a well-recognized scientific principle or discovery, *the thing from which the deduction is made must be sufficiently established to have gained general acceptance in the particular field in which it belongs.* [54 App. D.C., at 47, 293 F., at 1014 (emphasis added).]

Because the deception test had "not yet gained such standing and scientific recognition among physiological and psychological authorities as would justify the courts in admitting expert testimony deduced from the discovery, development, and experiments thus far made," evidence of its results was ruled inadmissible. Ibid.

The merits of the *Frye* test have been much debated, and scholarship on its proper scope and application is legion. Petitioners' primary attack, however, is not on the content but on the continuing authority of the rule. They contend that the *Frye* test was superseded by the adoption of the Federal Rules of Evidence. We agree.

We interpret the legislatively-enacted Federal Rules of Evidence as we would any statute. Beech Aircraft Corp. v. Rainey, 488 U.S. 153, 163 (1988). Rule 402 provides the baseline:

> All relevant evidence is admissible, except as otherwise provided by the Constitution of the United States, by Act of Congress, by these rules, or by other rules prescribed by the Supreme Court pursuant to statutory authority. Evidence which is not relevant is not admissible.

"Relevant evidence" is defined as that which has "any tendency to make the existence of any fact that is of consequence to the determination of the action more probable or less probable than it would be without the evidence." Rule 401. The Rule's basic standard of relevance thus is a liberal one.

Frye, of course, predated the Rules by half a century. In United States v. Abel, 469 U.S. 45 (1984), we considered the pertinence of background common law in interpreting the Rules of Evidence. We noted that the Rules occupy the field, id., at 49, but, quoting Professor Cleary, the Reporter, explained that the common law nevertheless could serve as an aid to their application:

> In principle, under the Federal Rules no common law of evidence remains. "All relevant evidence is admissible, except as otherwise provided. . . ." In reality, of course, the body of common law knowledge continues to exist, though in the somewhat altered form of a source of guidance in the exercise of delegated powers. [Id., at 51-52.]

We found the common-law precept at issue in the *Abel* case entirely consistent with Rule 402's general requirement of admissibility, and considered it unlikely that the drafters had intended to change the rule. Id., at 50-51. In Bourjaily v. United States, 483 U.S. 171 (1987), on the other hand, the Court was unable to find a particular common-law doctrine in the Rules, and so held it superseded.

Here there is a specific Rule that speaks to the contested issue. Rule 702, governing expert testimony, provides:

> If scientific, technical, or other specialized knowledge will assist the trier of fact to understand the evidence or to determine a fact in issue, a witness qualified as an expert by knowledge, skill, experience, training, or education, may testify thereto in the form of an opinion or otherwise.

4. Regulation of Toxic Substances

Nothing in the text of this Rule establishes "general acceptance" as an absolute prerequisite to admissibility. Nor does respondent present any clear indication that Rule 702 or the Rules as a whole were intended to incorporate a "general acceptance" standard. The drafting history makes no mention of *Frye*, and a rigid "general acceptance" requirement would be at odds with the "liberal thrust" of the Federal Rules and their "general approach of relaxing the traditional barriers to 'opinion' testimony." Beech Aircraft Corp. v. Rainey, 488 U.S., at 169 (citing Rules 701 to 705). See also Weinstein, Rule 702 of the Federal Rules of Evidence Is Sound; It Should Not Be Amended, 138 F.R.D. 631, 631 (1991) ("The Rules were designed to depend primarily upon lawyer-adversaries and sensible triers of fact to evaluate conflicts."). Given the Rules' permissive backdrop and their inclusion of a specific rule on expert testimony that does not mention "general acceptance," the assertion that the Rules somehow assimilated *Frye* is unconvincing. *Frye* made "general acceptance" the exclusive test for admitting expert scientific testimony. That austere standard, absent from and incompatible with the Federal Rules of Evidence, should not be applied in federal trials.

B

That the *Frye* test was displaced by the Rules of Evidence does not mean, however, that the Rules themselves place no limits on the admissibility of purportedly scientific evidence. Nor is the trial judge disabled from screening such evidence. To the contrary, under the Rules the trial judge must ensure that any and all scientific testimony or evidence admitted is not only relevant, but reliable.

The primary locus of this obligation is Rule 702, which clearly contemplates some degree of regulation of the subjects and theories about which an expert may testify. "*If scientific*, technical, or other specialized *knowledge will assist the trier of fact* to understand the evidence or to determine a fact in issue" an expert "may testify *thereto*." The subject of an expert's testimony must be "scientific . . . knowledge." The adjective "scientific" implies a grounding in the methods and procedures of science. Similarly, the word "knowledge" connotes more than subjective belief or unsupported speculation. The term "applies to any body of known facts or to any body of ideas inferred from such facts or accepted as truths on good grounds." Webster's Third New International Dictionary 1252 (1986). Of course, it would be unreasonable to conclude that the subject of scientific testimony must be "known" to a certainty; arguably, there are no certainties in science. See, e.g., Brief for Nicolaas Bloembergen et al. as Amici Curiae 9 ("Indeed, scientists do not assert that they know what is immutably 'true'—they are committed to searching for new, temporary theories to explain, as best they can, phenomena."); Brief for American Association for the Advancement of Science and the National Academy of Sciences as Amici Curiae 7-8 ("Science is not an encyclopedic body of knowledge about the universe. Instead, it represents a *process* for proposing and refining theoretical explanations about the world that are subject to further testing and refinement") (emphasis in original). But, in order to qualify as "scientific knowledge," an inference or assertion must be derived by the scientific method. Proposed testimony must be supported by appropriate validation—i.e., "good grounds," based on what is known. In short, the requirement that an expert's testimony pertain to "scientific knowledge" establishes a standard of evidentiary reliability.[9]

Rule 702 further requires that the evidence or testimony "assist the trier of fact to understand the evidence or to determine a fact in issue." This condition goes primarily to relevance. "Expert testimony which does not relate to any issue in the case is not relevant and, ergo, non-helpful." 3 Weinstein & Berger ¶702[02], pp. 702-718. See also United States v. Downing, 753 F.2d 1224, 1242 (CA3 1985) ("An additional consideration under Rule 702—and another aspect of relevancy—is whether expert testimony proffered in the case is sufficiently tied to the facts of the case that it will aid the jury in resolving a factual dispute."). The consideration has been aptly described by Judge Becker as one of "fit." Ibid. "Fit" is not always obvious, and scientific validity for one purpose is not necessarily scientific validity for other, unrelated purposes. See Starrs, Frye v. United States Restructured and Revitalized: A Proposal to Amend Federal Evidence Rule 702, 26 Jurimetrics J. 249, 258 (1986). The study of the phases of the moon, for example, may

---

9. We note that scientists typically distinguish between "validity" (does the principle support what it purports to show?) and "reliability" (does application of the principle produce consistent results?). See Black, A Unified Theory of Scientific Evidence, 56 Ford. L. Rev. 595, 599 (1988). Although "the difference between accuracy, validity, and reliability may be such that each is distinct from the other by no more than a hen's kick," Starrs, *Frye v. United States Restructured and Revitalized: A Proposal to Amend Federal Evidence Rule 702*, 26 Jurimetrics J. 249, 256 (1986), our reference here is to evidentiary reliability—that is, trustworthiness. Cf., e.g., Advisory Committee's Notes on Fed. Rule Evid. 602 (" 'The rule requiring that a witness who testifies to a fact which can be perceived by the senses must have had an opportunity to observe, and must have actually observed the fact' is a 'most pervasive manifestation' of the common law insistence upon 'the most reliable sources of information.' " (citation omitted)); Advisory Committee's Notes on Art. VIII of the Rules of Evidence (hearsay exception will be recognized only "under circumstances supposed to furnish guarantees of trustworthiness"). In a case involving scientific evidence, *evidentiary reliability* will be based upon *scientific validity*.

4. Regulation of Toxic Substances

provide valid scientific "knowledge" about whether a certain night was dark, and if darkness is a fact in issue, the knowledge will assist the trier of fact. However (absent creditable grounds supporting such a link), evidence that the moon was full on a certain night will not assist the trier of fact in determining whether an individual was unusually likely to have behaved irrationally on that night. Rule 702's "helpfulness" standard requires a valid scientific connection to the pertinent inquiry as a precondition to admissibility.

That these requirements are embodied in Rule 702 is not surprising. Unlike an ordinary witness, see Rule 701, an expert is permitted wide latitude to offer opinions, including those that are not based on first-hand knowledge or observation. See Rules 702 and 703. Presumably, this relaxation of the usual requirement of first-hand knowledge—a rule which represents "a 'most pervasive manifestation' of the common law insistence upon 'the most reliable sources of information,' " Advisory Committee's Notes on Fed. Rule Evid. 602 (citation omitted)—is premised on an assumption that the expert's opinion will have a reliable basis in the knowledge and experience of his discipline.

C

Faced with a proffer of expert scientific testimony, then, the trial judge must determine at the outset, pursuant to Rule 104(a), whether the expert is proposing to testify to (1) scientific knowledge that (2) will assist the trier of fact to understand or determine a fact in issue.[11] This entails a preliminary assessment of whether the reasoning or methodology underlying the testimony is scientifically valid and of whether that reasoning or methodology properly can be applied to the facts in issue. We are confident that federal judges possess the capacity to undertake this review. Many factors will bear on the inquiry, and we do not presume to set out a definitive checklist or test. But some general observations are appropriate.

Ordinarily, a key question to be answered in determining whether a theory or technique is scientific knowledge that will assist the trier of fact will be whether it can be (and has been) tested. "Scientific methodology today is based on generating hypotheses and testing them

---

11. Although the *Frye* decision itself focused exclusively on "novel" scientific techniques, we do not read the requirements of Rule 702 to apply specially or exclusively to unconventional evidence. Of course, well-established propositions are less likely to be challenged than those that are novel, and they are more handily defended. Indeed, theories that are so firmly established as to have attained the status of scientific law, such as the laws of thermodynamics, properly are subject to judicial notice under Fed. Rule Evid. 201.

to see if they can be falsified; indeed, this methodology is what distinguishes science from other fields of human inquiry." Green, at 645. See also C. Hempel, Philosophy of Natural Science 49 (1966) ("The statements constituting a scientific explanation must be capable of empirical test"); K. Popper, Conjectures and Refutations: The Growth of Scientific Knowledge 37 (5th ed. 1989) ("The criterion of the scientific status of a theory is its falsifiability, or refutability, or testability").

Another pertinent consideration is whether the theory or technique has been subjected to peer review and publication. Publication (which is but one element of peer review) is not a *sine qua non* of admissibility; it does not necessarily correlate with reliability, see S. Jasanoff, The Fifth Branch: Science Advisors as Policymakers 61-76 (1990), and in some instances well-grounded but innovative theories will not have been published, see Horrobin, The Philosophical Basis of Peer Review and the Suppression of Innovation, 263 J. Am. Med. Assn. 1438 (1990). Some propositions, moreover, are too particular, too new, or of too limited interest to be published. But submission to the scrutiny of the scientific community is a component of "good science," in part because it increases the likelihood that substantive flaws in methodology will be detected. See J. Ziman, Reliable Knowledge: An Exploration of the Grounds for Belief in Science 130-133 (1978); Relman and Angell, How Good Is Peer Review?, 321 New Eng. J. Med. 827 (1989). The fact of publication (or lack thereof) in a peer-reviewed journal thus will be a relevant, though not dispositive, consideration in assessing the scientific validity of a particular technique or methodology on which an opinion is premised.

Additionally, in the case of a particular scientific technique, the court ordinarily should consider the known or potential rate of error, see, e.g., United States v. Smith, 869 F.2d 348, 353-354 (CA7 1989) (surveying studies of the error rate of spectrographic voice identification technique), and the existence and maintenance of standards controlling the technique's operation. See United States v. Williams, 583 F.2d 1194, 1198 (CA2 1978) (noting professional organization's standard governing spectrographic analysis), cert. denied, 439 U.S. 1117 (1979).

Finally, "general acceptance" can yet have a bearing on the inquiry. A "reliability assessment does not require, although it does permit, explicit identification of a relevant scientific community and an express determination of a particular degree of acceptance within that community." United States v. Downing, 753 F.2d, at 1238. See also 3 Weinstein & Berger ¶702[03], pp. 702-41 to 702-42. Widespread acceptance can be an important factor in ruling particular evidence admissible, and "a known technique that has been able to attract only minimal support within the community," *Downing*, supra, at 1238, may properly be viewed with skepticism.

The inquiry envisioned by Rule 702 is, we emphasize, a flexible one. Its overarching subject is the scientific validity—and thus the evidentiary relevance and reliability—of the principles that underlie a proposed submission. The focus, of course, must be solely on principles and methodology, not on the conclusions that they generate.

Throughout, a judge assessing a proffer of expert scientific testimony under Rule 702 should also be mindful of other applicable rules. Rule 703 provides that expert opinions based on otherwise inadmissible hearsay are to be admitted only if the facts or data are "of a type reasonably relied upon by experts in the particular field in forming opinions or inferences upon the subject." Rule 706 allows the court at its discretion to procure the assistance of an expert of its own choosing. Finally, Rule 403 permits the exclusion of relevant evidence "if its probative value is substantially outweighed by the danger of unfair prejudice, confusion of the issues, or misleading the jury. . . ." Judge Weinstein has explained: "Expert evidence can be both powerful and quite misleading because of the difficulty in evaluating it. Because of this risk, the judge in weighing possible prejudice against probative force under Rule 403 of the present rules exercises more control over experts than over lay witnesses." Weinstein, 138 F.R.D., at 632.

III

We conclude by briefly addressing what appear to be two underlying concerns of the parties and amici in this case. Respondent expresses apprehension that abandonment of "general acceptance" as the exclusive requirement for admission will result in a "free-for-all" in which befuddled juries are confounded by absurd and irrational pseudoscientific assertions. In this regard respondent seems to us to be overly pessimistic about the capabilities of the jury, and of the adversary system generally. Vigorous cross-examination, presentation of contrary evidence, and careful instruction on the burden of proof are the traditional and appropriate means of attacking shaky but admissible evidence. See Rock v. Arkansas, 483 U.S. 44, 61 (1987). Additionally, in the event the trial court concludes that the scintilla of evidence presented supporting a position is insufficient to allow a reasonable juror to conclude that the position more likely than not is true, the court remains free to direct a judgment, Fed. Rule Civ. Proc. 50(a), and likewise to grant summary judgment, Fed. Rule Civ. Proc. 56. Cf., e.g., Turpin v. Merrell Dow Pharmaceuticals, Inc., 959 F.2d 1349 (CA6) (holding that scientific evidence that provided foundation for expert testimony, viewed in the light most favorable to plaintiffs, was not sufficient to allow a jury to find it more probable than not that defendant caused plaintiff's injury);

Brock v. Merrell Dow Pharmaceuticals, Inc., 874 F.2d 307 (CA5 1989) (reversing judgment entered on jury verdict for plaintiffs because evidence regarding causation was insufficient), modified, 884 F.2d 166 (CA5 1989); Green, 680-681. These conventional devices, rather than wholesale exclusion under an uncompromising "general acceptance" test, are the appropriate safeguards where the basis of scientific testimony meets the standards of Rule 702.

Petitioners and, to a greater extent, their amici exhibit a different concern. They suggest that recognition of a screening role for the judge that allows for the exclusion of "invalid" evidence will sanction a stifling and repressive scientific orthodoxy and will be inimical to the search for truth. See, e.g., Brief for Ronald Bayer et al. as Amici Curiae. It is true that open debate is an essential part of both legal and scientific analyses. Yet there are important differences between the quest for truth in the courtroom and the quest for truth in the laboratory. Scientific conclusions are subject to perpetual revision. Law, on the other hand, must resolve disputes finally and quickly. The scientific project is advanced by broad and wide-ranging consideration of a multitude of hypotheses, for those that are incorrect will eventually be shown to be so, and that in itself is an advance. Conjectures that are probably wrong are of little use, however, in the project of reaching a quick, final, and binding legal judgment—often of great consequence—about a particular set of events in the past. We recognize that in practice, a gatekeeping role for the judge, no matter how flexible, inevitably on occasion will prevent the jury from learning of authentic insights and innovations. That, nevertheless, is the balance that is struck by Rules of Evidence designed not for the exhaustive search for cosmic understanding but for the particularized resolution of legal disputes.

IV

To summarize: "general acceptance" is not a necessary precondition to the admissibility of scientific evidence under the Federal Rules of Evidence, but the Rules of Evidence—especially Rule 702—do assign to the trial judge the task of ensuring that an expert's testimony both rests on a reliable foundation and is relevant to the task at hand. Pertinent evidence based on scientifically valid principles will satisfy those demands.

The inquiries of the District Court and the Court of Appeals focused almost exclusively on "general acceptance," as gauged by publication and the decisions of other courts. Accordingly, the judgment of the Court of Appeals is vacated and the case is remanded for further proceedings consistent with this opinion.

NOTES AND QUESTIONS

1. After holding that the Federal Rules of Evidence supplanted the *Frye* rule, the Court majority in Parts II-B & II-C offers "general observations" concerning how judges should approach the admissibility of scientific evidence in the future. In a partial dissent Chief Justice Rehnquist and Justice Stevens refused to join Parts II-B and II-C of the majority opinion, which they criticized for offering "vague and abstract" dicta.

2. Will the Court's decision make it easier or more difficult for judges to determine whether scientific evidence is admissible than under the *Frye* test? Is a wider range of scientific evidence likely to be admissible in light of *Daubert* because general acceptance no longer will be required, or will *Daubert* actually be more restrictive because some evidence that is generally accepted may be unable to satisfy the Court's "scientific validity" standard? Would the evidence proffered by the plaintiffs in *Daubert* be admissible in light of the Court's decision?

3. How strictly should trial courts scrutinize scientific testimony to determine if it satisfies the standards of reliability and scientific validity discussed by Justice Blackmun? If the expert's methodology is sound, can the court second-guess the validity of the expert's conclusions? Will the *Daubert* decision require judges to create a kind of common law governing what constitutes scientifically valid evidence? How deferential should appellate courts be in reviewing trial court decisions on admissibility of scientific evidence?

4. The *Daubert* case attracted unusual interest in the scientific community. More than 20 amicus briefs were filed with the Court, many on behalf of scientific organizations. While some scientists supported the Ninth Circuit decision as a useful tool for excluding "junk science" from the courtroom, others feared that excessively rigid rules of evidence would discourage scientific inquiry.

5. A study published in August 1994 found that *Daubert* had not made it easier for plaintiffs to admit scientific testimony. It found that "over half of the reported post-*Daubert* decisions, both at the trial and appellate level, exclude expert testimony," Hoffman, Expert Testimony Since *Daubert:* A Major Shift, 25 Env. Rep. 252 (1994). "Despite *Daubert*'s lip service to increasing flexibility, its plea that the courts scrutinize the expert's methodology to screen out junk science has resulted in greater restriction upon expert testimony than before." 43 F.3d at 259.

6. On remand, the Ninth Circuit panel who had been reversed by the Supreme Court in *Daubert* again ruled that the plaintiffs' evidence must be excluded. Refusing the plaintiffs' request that the case be remanded to the trial court to apply the *Daubert* analysis, Judge Alex Kozinski harshly criticized the *Daubert* decision for saddling judges with

253

"a far more complex and daunting task" than under the *Frye* rule. Daubert v. Merrell Dow Pharmaceuticals, Inc., 43 F.3d 1311 (9th Cir. 1995). Judge Kozinski argued that *Daubert* will force judges "to resolve disputes among respected, well-credentialed scientists about matters squarely within their expertise, in areas where there is no scientific consensus as to what is and what is not 'good science,' and occasionally to reject such expert testimony because it was not 'derived by the scientific method.'" Id. at 1316. While describing this as a "heady task," Judge Kozinski had little trouble again finding that the plaintiffs' testimony must be excluded as a matter of law. Although he noted that "plaintiffs' scientists are all experts in their respective fields," Judge Kozinski emphasized that none "based his testimony on preexisting or independent research." Id. at 1317. Citing the absence of peer-reviewed publication or an explanation of precisely how plaintiffs' experts reached their conclusions based on some objective source, the court held that there was "no understandable scientific basis" for the conclusions of plaintiffs' experts. Id. at 1319.

7. Will *Daubert* encourage judges to make greater use of court-appointed experts, as authorized by Rule 706 of the Federal Rules of Evidence? Few judges have done so, although many seem favorably inclined to the idea. The Federal Judicial Center has prepared a 600-page primer for federal judges to help explain scientific issues to them. Woo, New Guide for Judges Tries To Clarify Scientific Issues, Wall St. J., Dec. 12, 1994, at B1.

Impact of the Jury System (p. 655). Some challenge the popular notion that the tort system does a poor job of weeding out frivolous claims and that juries are more sympathetic to plaintiffs in tort litigation. See Saks, Do We Really Know Anything About the Tort Litigation System—And Why Not?, 140 U. Pa. L. Rev. 1147 (1992); Clermont and Eisenberg, Trial by Jury or Judge: Transcending Empiricism, 77 Cornell L. Rev. 1124 (1992).

A study by Jury Verdict Research in 1994 found that the probability of recovery at trial in tort cases had declined steadily from 63 percent in 1989 to 58 percent in 1990 and 52 percent in 1992. Average levels of awards also declined, with only 30 percent of reported verdicts exceeding $200,000. Reske, Stingier Jurors Doling Out Fewer Awards, ABA J., Sept. 1994, p. 20. See also Moran, Juries Are Just Saying No, N.Y. Times, Jan. 16, 1995, at A16.

=5=
‖ *The Regulatory Process* ‖

> What is undermining and weakening environmental law in this country today is the fact that people are seeing too much of the absurdity and not enough of the benefits. . . . [The regulatory reform provisions in the Contract With America] will require the use of sound science and sound economic principles to determine if there is a rational basis for imposing new and costly regulations on the American people.
>
> —*Rep. Robert S. Walker, Feb. 28, 1995*

> This legislation is not reform; it is a full frontal assault on protecting public health and the environment. Protecting the health of the American people cannot be reduced to a game of numbers. Important public health decisions should not be based solely on mathematical calculations. This legislation would undermine virtually every health protection that the American people depend on.
>
> —*EPA Administrator Carol Browner, Feb. 28, 1995*

This chapter reviews important developments pertaining to the regulatory process that have occurred since publication of the parent text. While the Clinton Administration adopted a more sympathetic attitude toward environmental regulation by lifting the Bush Administration regulatory freeze and by instituting a more selective regulatory review process, the new Republic majority in Congress is considering legislation that would dramatically alter the regulatory process. The legislation is designed to make it far more difficult for agencies to issue regulations by imposing a host of elaborate analytical requirements while creating numerous new opportunities for industry to challenge regulatory decisions. The Clinton Administration has embarked upon its own program of more modest regulatory reform as part of its effort to "reinvent government" to make it operate more efficiently. This chapter considers these and other developments as well as providing extensive analysis of Lujan v. Defenders of Wildlife, the Supreme Court's immensely important environmental standing decision.

A. ESTABLISHING REGULATORY PRIORITIES

1. Reducing Risk as a Method for Setting Priorities

Reducing Risk (pp. 658-663). Risk reduction continues to be a popular theme in discussions of how to set agency priorities. For a discussion of the implications of a shift to risk-based priority setting for EPA's research budget, see Shifrin, Not by Risk Alone: Reforming EPA Research Priorities, 102 Yale L.J. 547 (1992). EPA is encouraging state regulatory agencies to use comparative risk assessment as a means for setting environmental protection priorities. Stone, California Report Sets Standard for Comparing Risks, 266 Science 214 (1994). A report prepared for California's Environmental Protection Agency has drawn widespread praise for its approach to ranking potential environmental hazards. California Comparative Risk Project, Toward the 21st Century: Planning for the Protection of California's Environment (1994).

Legislation to require some form of comparative risk assessment is currently being debated. The risk assessment legislation incorporated in the Republican's Contract With America would require agencies to conduct risk assessments prior to regulation, to compare the risks that are the target of contemplated regulation with other risks and to describe the risks of activities that may substitute for the regulated activity. Other legislation has been proposed that would require EPA to institutionalize the approach of the Agency's Reducing Risk report by having expert advisory committees report relative risk rankings of environmental problems every two years. Some argue that risk-based priority-setting is inconsistent with democratic values. For instance, then Senator Durenberger stated that "[t]here is no philospher-king or committee of Ph.D.s who can relieve the Congress of the difficult job of setting priorities in a world of competing interests and limited knowledge. And there is no reason to believe that Congress has chosen incorrectly in the past." Bill to Require EPA Risk-Ranking Receives Mixed Reaction at Hearing, 23 Env. Rep. 1467, 1468 (1992).

In a book published shortly before he became a Supreme Court Justice, Stephen Breyer argues that environmental priorities can be improved by creating a more centralized coordinating mechanism for setting such priorities staffed by a technically sophisticated elite. S. Breyer, Breaking the Vicious Cycle (1993). For a critique of Breyer's argument see Dana, Setting Environmental Priorities: The Promise of a Bureaucratic Solution, 74 B.U. L. Rev. 365 (1994).

Gregg Eastbrook argues that the environmental priorities of the developed world ignore far more serious environmental problems in

5. The Regulatory Process   Pages 666-671

less developed countries, where dirty air and water kill millions of people each year. G. Easterbrook, A Moment on the Earth (1995). Easterbrook maintains that it is irrational for the developed world to agree to spend billions to combat global warming when the same money could be used to save some of the millions of poor children who die from poor sanitation in the developing world.

Regulatory Priorities and Hazardous Waste Dumpsites (p. 663). The high level of public concern over hazardous waste disposal may result from the fact that more than 40 million Americans live within 4 miles of a site listed on EPA's National Priority List (NPL) for Superfund cleanups. Approximately 3.8 million of these people live within one mile of an NPL site. Poore and Davis, Where's the Waste?, Issues in Sci. & Tech. 78 (Spring 1992). See also National Research Council, Environmental Epidemiology: Public Health and Hazardous Wastes (1991).

One reason why remediation of contaminated dumpsites is a relatively low priority has been the absence of clear evidence that groundwater contamination has caused widespread harm to public health. However, new evidence of harm is now becoming available. An epidemiological study released in July 1992 found a statistically significant increase in birth defects in children born to mothers living within one mile of abandoned hazardous waste dumps. The study was based on examination of birth records for more than 27,000 New York children by researchers from Yale's School of Medicine and the New York Department of Health. They found that although the overall incidence of birth defects in New York is 30 per every 1,000 births, birth defects occurred at a rate of 34 per 1,000 in children born to mothers living within a mile of one of the state's 590 abandoned waste dumps. Geschwind, Stolwijk, Bracken, Fitzgerald, Stark, Olsen, and Melius, Risk of Congenital Malformations Associated with Proximity to Hazardous Waste Sites, 135 Am. J. Epidemiology 1197 (1992). EPA's Science Advisory Board found that the Agency's methodology for assessing health risks from Superfund sites did not adequately take into account "hot spots" of exposure. Risk Assessment Methodology Used by EPA Fails to Address Hot Spots at Sites, SAB Says, 23 Env. Rep. 2680 (1993).

2. *Agency-Forcing Mechanisms*

Citizen Suits and Statutory Deadlines (pp. 666-671). Citizen suits have continued to play a significant role in ensuring the implementation of regulatory statutes, particularly in the face of the Bush Administration's "regulatory moratorium." The Sierra Club and California Congressman Henry Waxman filed a series of "deadline suits" against EPA for its failure to meet statutory deadlines for regulatory action embodied in the 1990 Amendments to the Clean Air Act. In November 1992, the lawsuits were settled through a consent decree establishing a new timetable for EPA to complete 19 regulatory actions required by the 1990 Amendments. Waxman, Sierra Club Settle Lawsuits; Schedule Set for Issuing 19 Air Regulations, 23 Env. Rep. 1938 (1992). In October 1994 the Sierra Club and EPA settled another lawsuit against the Agency for missing additional Clean Air Act deadlines. 59 Fed Reg. 59,774 (1994).

Petitions to Initiate Rulemaking (pp. 671-673). The question of what obligations EPA has after it announces that it is "granting" a TSCA section 21 petition has been raised by another case. On October 22, 1992, EDF and three other environmental groups filed a section 21 petition asking EPA to require that the sale of lead fishing sinkers be accompanied by a label warning that such products are toxic to wildlife. On January 14, 1993, EPA responded that it would "grant" the petition and would conduct a "regulatory investigation to determine whether action is necessary under Section 6(a) of TSCA to address any unreasonable risk to waterfowl from ingestion of lead fishing sinkers." EDF maintains that this response is not adequate to satisfy the requirements of section 21 of TSCA because it does not involve a commitment to initiate rulemaking proceedings. Do you agree with EDF? On March 15, 1993, EDF sued EPA under section 21 of TSCA to seek a court order directing the Agency to commence rulemaking proceedings. Gugliotta, Swan Song Becomes a Call to Action, Wash. Post, May 18, 1993, at A19. EPA ultimately agreed to settle the suit by commencing a rulemaking.

A variation on TSCA's citizen petition procedure is the petition process created by section 606(b) of the Clean Air Act, 42 U.S.C. §7671e(b), which was added by the 1990 Amendments. Section 606(b) provides that any person may petition the EPA administrator to promulgate regulations for phasing out substances harmful to the stratospheric ozone layer. The EPA administrator is given 180 days to respond, and if she grants the petition she must promulgate final regulations within one year. While there is no judicial review provision authorizing de novo review of petition denials, the EPA administrator is required to publish an explanation of why the petition was denied, which presumably would give disappointed petitioners the right to judicial review under the Administrative Procedure Act.

5. The Regulatory Process   Pages 683-685

B. THE RULEMAKING PROCESS AND REGULATORY OVERSIGHT

1. The Rulemaking Process

Rulemaking Proceedings: Ossification and the Contract With America (pp. 674-681). The challenge of surmounting the difficulties agencies face in completing rulemakings in timely fashion was dubbed "deossification of rulemaking" by Professor Tom McGarity. McGarity, Some Thoughts on "Deossifying" the Rulemaking Process, 1992 Duke L.J. 1385. Studies continue to confirm this difficulty. See Administrative Conf. of the U.S. Comm. on Rulemaking, Improving the Environment for Agency Rulemaking (1993). In 1993 the Carnegie Commission noted that "agency officials about to embark upon an 'informal' rulemaking procedure in a complex, technical subject matter area may well face a four- or five-year rulemaking process." Carnegie Commission, Risk and the Environment: Improving Regulatory Decision Making 108 (1993). An empirical study of how well EPA kept to its own rulemaking schedules announced in its biannual regulatory agendas between 1989 and 1992 found that more than 80 percent of all schedules slipped and that the average slippage that occurred every six months was nearly six months in length. Groseclose, Reinventing the Regulatory Agenda: Conclusions from an Empirical Study of EPA's Clean Air Act Rulemaking Progress Projections, 53 Md. L. Rev. 521 (1994). For an analysis of how the judiciary has contributed to ossification of the rulemaking process see Pierce, Seven Ways to Deossify Agency Rulemaking, 47 Admin. L. Rev. 59 (1995).

Despite the well-documented difficulties agencies face in completing rulemakings under existing procedures, the Republican Contract With America proposes to impose a host of additional requirements on agencies before regulations can be issued. EPA believes that it would have to hire nearly a thousand new employees to undertake the 22 new analytical exercises that would be required and that the average rulemaking would be delayed by an additional two years. Wetstone, And Now, Regulatory Reform (See Above), N.Y. Times, Feb. 23, 1995, at A23.

Negotiated Rulemaking (pp. 683-685). EPA continues to conduct negotiated rulemakings, with a mixed record of success. One of the most successful regulatory negotiations produced agreement on a proposed national emissions standard for hazardous air pollutants for coke ovens under section 112 of the Clean Air Act. Year-Long Coke Oven Negotiations Yield Pact Between Steel Industry, Environmentalists, 23 Env. Rep. 1669 (1992). A regulatory negotiation involving the reformulated gasoline provisions of the 1990 Clean Air Act Amendments also produced an agreement on proposed regulations. However, representatives of ethanol interests who initially had agreed to the proposed rules later reneged on the agreement after discovering they could win special concessions from the White House during the presidential election campaign. A negotiated rulemaking to require recycling of lead acid batteries was terminated after the Bush Administration concluded that the costs of such an initiative exceeded the small risk reduction that would be obtained. A regulatory negotiation to consider limits on emissions of nitrogen oxide was canceled at the direction of the White House. Negotiations on standards under the Safe Drinking Water Act resulted in EPA publication of three proposed rules in 1994.

For discussion of how negotiated rulemakings are conducted see Siegler, Regulatory Negotiations: A Practical Perspective, 22 Env. L. Rep. 10647 (1992).

Generic Approaches to Rulemaking (pp. 685-688). As noted in Chapter 4 of this Supplement, OSHA's ambitious effort to use generic rulemaking to revise permissible exposure limits for more than 400 air contaminants (parent text, p. 686) was struck down by the Eleventh Circuit in AFL-CIO v. OSHA, 965 F.2d 962 (11th Cir. 1992). This decision is reproduced in Chapter 4 of this Supplement. You may wish to consult this now, particularly parts IIIA and IV of the decision, which discuss generic rulemaking.

2. Presidential Oversight of Rulemaking

Regulatory Review in the Clinton Administration (pp. 689-694). On its second full day in office, the Clinton Administration abolished the Council on Competitiveness (parent text, pp. 700-701) and directed the Federal Register not to publish more than 100 last-minute regulatory actions that had been completed by Bush Administration officials shortly before the change of administration. Tolchin, Last Minute Bush Proposals Rescinded, N.Y. Times, Jan. 23, 1993, at A10. President Clinton described the abolition of the Competitiveness Council as closing "the back door the polluters used to be able to use to get out from under our laws." Statement by President Clinton on New Environmental Policy, Feb. 8, 1993, at 1. Yet at the same time the Clinton Administration signalled that it planned to continue presidential oversight of rulemaking through the OMB review process supplemented by occasional White House intervention in rulemaking disputes. Vice President Gore stated:

5. The Regulatory Process   Pages 689-694

>   [T]here's not going to be a back door to hot-wire the regulatory process. The decisions in virtually all cases will be made at the OIRA office at OMB. We recognize, however, that there will be exceptions where, for a variety of reasons, conflicting viewpoints have to be heard on appeal, as it were, at the White House level. And the President has asked me to take charge of organizing that process.

Remarks by Vice President Al Gore on New Environmental Policy, Feb. 8, 1993, at 4.

In September 1993, President Clinton issued Executive Order 12,866, which established a new regulatory review process, replacing the process that had existed for 12 years under Executive Order 12,291. The new executive order establishing the Clinton Administration's regulatory review process is reproduced below.

Executive Order 12866
Regulatory Planning and Review
58 Fed. Reg. 51,735 (1993)

The American people deserve a regulatory system that works for them, not against them: a regulatory system that protects and improves their health, safety, environment, and well-being and improves the performance of the economy without imposing unacceptable or unreasonable costs on society; regulatory policies that recognize that the private sector and private markets are the best engine for economic growth; regulatory approaches that respect the role of State, local, and tribal governments; and regulations that are effective, consistent, sensible, and understandable. We do not have such a regulatory system today.

With this Executive order, the Federal Government begins a program to reform and make more efficient the regulatory process. The objectives of this Executive order are to enhance planning and coordination with respect to both new and existing regulations; to reaffirm the primacy of Federal agencies in the regulatory decision-making process; to restore the integrity and legitimacy of regulatory review and oversight; and to make the process more accessible and open to the public. In pursuing these objectives, the regulatory process shall be conducted so as to meet applicable statutory requirements and with due regard to the discretion that has been entrusted to the Federal agencies.

Accordingly, by the authority vested in me as President by the Constitution and the laws of the United States of America, it is hereby ordered as follows:

Section 1. Statement of Regulatory Philosophy and Principles

    (a) *The Regulatory Philosophy.* Federal agencies should promulgate only such regulations as are required by law, are necessary to interpret the law, or are made necessary by compelling public need, such as material failures of private markets to protect or improve the health and safety of the public, the environment, or the well-being of the American people. In deciding whether and how to regulate, agencies should assess all costs and benefits of available regulatory alternatives, including the alternative of not regulating. Costs and benefits shall be understood to include both quantifiable measures (to the fullest extent that these can be usefully estimated) and qualitative measures of costs and benefits that are difficult to quantify, but nevertheless essential to consider. Further, in choosing among alternative regulatory approaches, agencies should select those approaches that maximize net benefits (including potential economic, environmental, public health and safety, and other advantages; distributive impacts; and equity), unless a statute requires another regulatory approach.

(b) *The Principles of Regulation.* To ensure that the agencies' regulatory programs are consistent with the philosophy set forth above, agencies should adhere to the following principles, to the extent permitted by law and where applicable:

(1) Each agency shall identify the problem that it intends to address (including, where applicable, the failures of private markets or public institutions that warrant new agency action) as well as assess the significance of that problem.

(2) Each agency shall examine whether existing regulations (or other law) have created, or contributed to, the problem that a new regulation is intended to correct and whether those regulations (or other law) should be modified to achieve the intended goal of regulation more effectively.

(3) Each agency shall identify and assess available alternatives to direct regulation, including providing economic incentives to encourage the desired behavior, such as user fees or marketable permits, or providing information upon which choices can be made by the public.

(4) In setting regulatory priorities, each agency shall consider, to the extent reasonable, the degree and nature of the risks posed by various substances or activities within its jurisdiction.

(5) When an agency determines that a regulation is the best available method of achieving the regulatory objective, it shall design its regulations in the most cost-effective manner to achieve the regulatory objective. In doing so, each agency shall consider incentives for innovation, consistency, predictability, the costs of enforcement and compliance (to the government, regulated entities, and the public), flexibility, distributive impacts, and equity.

## 5. The Regulatory Process	Pages 689-694

(6) Each agency shall assess both the costs and the benefits of the intended regulation and, recognizing that some costs and benefits are difficult to quantify, propose or adopt a regulation only upon a reasoned determination that the benefits of the intended regulation justify its costs.

(7) Each agency shall base its decisions on the best reasonably obtainable scientific, technical, economic, and other information concerning the need for, and consequences of, the intended regulation.

(8) Each agency shall identify and assess alternative forms of regulation and shall, to the extent feasible, specify performance objectives, rather than specifying the behavior or manner of compliance that regulated entities must adopt.

(9) Wherever feasible, agencies shall seek views of appropriate State, local, and tribal officials before imposing regulatory requirements that might significantly or uniquely affect those governmental entities. Each agency shall assess the effects of Federal regulations on State, local, and tribal governments, including specifically the availability of resources to carry out those mandates, and seek to minimize those burdens that uniquely or significantly affect such governmental entities, consistent with achieving regulatory objectives. In addition, as appropriate, agencies shall seek to harmonize Federal regulatory actions with related State, local, and tribal regulatory and other governmental functions.

(10) Each agency shall avoid regulations that are inconsistent, incompatible, or duplicative with its other regulations or those of other Federal agencies.

(11) Each agency shall tailor its regulations to impose the least burden on society, including individuals, businesses of differing sizes, and other entities (including small communities and governmental entities), consistent with obtaining the regulatory objectives, taking into account, among other things, and to the extent practicable, the costs of cumulative regulations.

(12) Each agency shall draft its regulations to be simple and easy to understand, with the goal of minimizing the potential for uncertainty and litigation arising from such uncertainty.

Section 2. Organization

An efficient regulatory planning and review process is vital to ensure that the Federal Government's regulatory system best serves the American people.

(a) *The Agencies.* Because Federal agencies are the repositories of significant substantive expertise and experience, they are responsible for developing regulations and assuring that the regulations are consistent with applicable law, the President's priorities, and the principles set forth in this Executive order.

(b) *The Office of Management and Budget.* Coordinated review of agency rulemaking is necessary to ensure that regulations are consistent with applicable law, the President's priorities, and the principles set forth in this Executive order, and that decisions made by one agency do not conflict with the policies or actions taken or planned by another agency. The Office of Management and Budget (OMB) shall carry out that review function. Within OMB, the Office of Information and Regulatory Affairs (OIRA) is the repository of expertise concerning regulatory issues, including methodologies and procedures that affect more than one agency, this Executive order, and the President's regulatory policies. To the extent permitted by law, OMB shall provide guidance to agencies and assist the President, the Vice President, and other regulatory policy advisors to the President in regulatory planning and shall be the entity that reviews individual regulations, as provided by this Executive order.

(c) *The Vice President.* The Vice President is the principal advisor to the President on, and shall coordinate the development and presentation of recommendations concerning, regulatory policy, planning, and review, as set forth in this Executive order. In fulfilling their responsibilities under this Executive order, the President and the Vice President shall be assisted by the regulatory policy advisors within the Executive Office of the President and by such agency officials and personnel as the President and the Vice President may, from time to time, consult.

Section 3. Definitions. . . .

(e) "Regulatory action" means any substantive action by an agency (normally published in the Federal Register) that promulgates or is expected to lead to the promulgation of a final rule or regulation, including notices of inquiry, advance notices of proposed rulemaking, and notices of proposed rulemaking.

(f) "Significant regulatory action" means any regulatory action that is likely to result in a rule that may:

(1) Have an annual effect on the economy of $ 100 million or more or adversely affect in a material way the economy, a sector of the economy, productivity, competition, jobs, the environment, public health or safety, or State, local, or tribal governments or communities;

(2) Create a serious inconsistency or otherwise interfere with an action taken or planned by another agency;

(3) Materially alter the budgetary impact of entitlements,

grants, user fees, or loan programs or the rights and obligations of recipients thereof; or

(4) Raise novel legal or policy issues arising out of legal mandates, the President's priorities, or the principles set forth in this Executive order. . . .

Section 6. *Centralized Review of Regulations*

The guidelines set forth below shall apply to all regulatory actions, for both new and existing regulations, by agencies other than those agencies specifically exempted by the Administrator of OIRA:

(a) *Agency Responsibilities.*

(1) Each agency shall (consistent with its own rules, regulations, or procedures) provide the public with meaningful participation in the regulatory process. In particular, before issuing a notice of proposed rulemaking, each agency should, where appropriate, seek the involvement of those who are intended to benefit from and those expected to be burdened by any regulation (including, specifically, State, local, and tribal officials). In addition, each agency should afford the public a meaningful opportunity to comment on any proposed regulation, which in most cases should include a comment period of not less than 60 days. Each agency also is directed to explore and, where appropriate, use consensual mechanisms for developing regulations, including negotiated rulemaking.

(2) Within 60 days of the date of this Executive order, each agency head shall designate a Regulatory Policy Officer who shall report to the agency head. The Regulatory Policy Officer shall be involved at each stage of the regulatory process to foster the development of effective, innovative, and least burdensome regulations and to further the principles set forth in this Executive order.

(3) In addition to adhering to its own rules and procedures and to the requirements of the Administrative Procedure Act, the Regulatory Flexibility Act, the Paperwork Reduction Act, and other applicable law, each agency shall develop its regulatory actions in a timely fashion and adhere to the following procedures with respect to a regulatory action:

(A) Each agency shall provide OIRA, at such times and in the manner specified by the Administrator of OIRA, with a list of its planned regulatory actions, indicating those which the agency believes are significant regulatory actions within the meaning of this Executive order. Absent a material change in the development of the planned regulatory action, those not designated as significant will not be subject to review under this section unless, within 10 working days of receipt of the list, the Administrator of OIRA notifies the agency that OIRA has determined that a planned regulation is a significant regulatory action within the meaning of this Executive order. The Administrator of OIRA may waive review of any planned regulatory action designated by the agency as significant, in which case the agency need not further comply with subsection (a)(3)(B) or subsection (a)(3)(C) of this section.

(B) For each matter identified as, or determined by the Administrator of OIRA to be, a significant regulatory action, the issuing agency shall provide to OIRA:

(i) The text of the draft regulatory action, together with a reasonably detailed description of the need for the regulatory action and an explanation of how the regulatory action will meet that need; and

(ii) An assessment of the potential costs and benefits of the regulatory action, including an explanation of the manner in which the regulatory action is consistent with a statutory mandate and, to the extent permitted by law, promotes the President's priorities and avoids undue interference with State, local, and tribal governments in the exercise of their governmental functions.

(C) For those matters identified as, or determined by the Administrator of OIRA to be, a significant regulatory action within the scope of section 3(f)(1), the agency shall also provide to OIRA the following additional information developed as part of the agency's decision-making process (unless prohibited by law):

(i) An assessment, including the underlying analysis, of benefits anticipated from the regulatory action (such as, but not limited to, the promotion of the efficient functioning of the economy and private markets, the enhancement of health and safety, the protection of the natural environment, and the elimination or reduction of discrimination or bias) together with, to the extent feasible, a quantification of those benefits;

(ii) An assessment, including the underlying analysis, of costs anticipated from the regulatory action (such as, but not limited to, the direct cost both to the government in administering the regulation and to businesses and others in complying with the regulation, and any adverse effects on the efficient functioning of the economy, private markets (including productivity, employment, and competitiveness), health, safety, and the natural environment, together with, to the extent feasible, a quantification of those costs; and

5. The Regulatory Process — Pages 689-694

(iii) An assessment, including the underlying analysis, of costs and benefits of potentially effective and reasonably feasible alternatives to the planned regulation, identified by the agencies or the public (including improving the current regulation and reasonably viable nonregulatory actions), and an explanation why the planned regulatory action is preferable to the identified potential alternatives.

(D) In emergency situations or when an agency is obligated by law to act more quickly than normal review procedures allow, the agency shall notify OIRA as soon as possible and, to the extent practicable, comply with subsections (a)(3)(B) and (C) of this section. For those regulatory actions that are governed by a statutory or court-imposed deadline, the agency shall, to the extent practicable, schedule rulemaking proceedings so as to permit sufficient time for OIRA to conduct its review, as set forth below in subsection (b)(2) through (4) of this section.

(E) After the regulatory action has been published in the Federal Register or otherwise issued to the public, the agency shall:

(i) Make available to the public the information set forth in subsections (a)(3)(B) and (C);

(ii) Identify for the public, in a complete, clear, and simple manner, the substantive changes between the draft submitted to OIRA for review and the action subsequently announced; and

(iii) Identify for the public those changes in the regulatory action that were made at the suggestion or recommendation of OIRA.

(F) All information provided to the public by the agency shall be in plain, understandable language.

(b) *OIRA Responsibilities.* The Administrator of OIRA shall provide meaningful guidance and oversight so that each agency's regulatory actions are consistent with applicable law, the President's priorities, and the principles set forth in this Executive order and do not conflict with the policies or actions of another agency. OIRA shall, to the extent permitted by law, adhere to the following guidelines:

(1) OIRA may review only actions identified by the agency or by OIRA as significant regulatory actions under subsection (a)(3)(A) of this section.

(2) OIRA shall waive review or notify the agency in writing of the results of its review within the following time periods:

(A) For any notices of inquiry, advance notices of proposed

rulemaking, or other preliminary regulatory actions prior to a Notice of Proposed Rulemaking, within 10 working days after the date of submission of the draft action to OIRA;

(B) For all other regulatory actions, within 90 calendar days after the date of submission of the information set forth in subsections (a)(3)(B) and (C) of this section, unless OIRA has previously reviewed this information and, since that review, there has been no material change in the facts and circumstances upon which the regulatory action is based, in which case, OIRA shall complete its review within 45 days; and

(C) The review process may be extended (1) once by no more than 30 calendar days upon the written approval of the Director and (2) at the request of the agency head.

(3) For each regulatory action that the Administrator of OIRA returns to an agency for further consideration of some or all of its provisions, the Administrator of OIRA shall provide the issuing agency a written explanation for such return, setting forth the pertinent provision of this Executive order on which OIRA is relying. If the agency head disagrees with some or all of the bases for the return, the agency head shall so inform the Administrator of OIRA in writing.

(4) Except as otherwise provided by law or required by a Court, in order to ensure greater openness, accessibility, and accountability in the regulatory review process, OIRA shall be governed by the following disclosure requirements:

(A) Only the Administrator of OIRA (or a particular designee) shall receive oral communications initiated by persons not employed by the executive branch of the Federal Government regarding the substance of a regulatory action under OIRA review;

(B) All substantive communications between OIRA personnel and persons not employed by the executive branch of the Federal Government regarding a regulatory action under review shall be governed by the following guidelines:

(i) A representative from the issuing agency shall be invited to any meeting between OIRA personnel and such person(s);

(ii) OIRA shall forward to the issuing agency, within 10 working days of receipt of the communication(s), all written communications, regardless of format, between OIRA personnel and any person who is not employed by the executive branch of the Federal Government, and the dates and names of individuals involved in all substantive oral communications (including meetings to which an agency representative was invited, but did not attend, and telephone conversations between OIRA personnel and any such persons); and

(iii) OIRA shall publicly disclose relevant information about such communication(s), as set forth below in subsection (b)(4)(C) of this section.

(C) OIRA shall maintain a publicly available log that shall contain, at a minimum, the following information pertinent to regulatory actions under review:

(i) The status of all regulatory actions, including if (and if so, when and by whom) Vice Presidential and Presidential consideration was requested;

(ii) A notation of all written communications forwarded to an issuing agency under subsection (b)(4)(B)(ii) of this section; and

(iii) The dates and names of individuals involved in all substantive oral communications, including meetings and telephone conversations, between OIRA personnel and any person not employed by the executive branch of the Federal Government, and the subject matter discussed during such communications.

(D) After the regulatory action has been published in the Federal Register or otherwise issued to the public, or after the agency has announced its decision not to publish or issue the regulatory action, OIRA shall make available to the public all documents exchanged between OIRA and the agency during the review by OIRA under this section.

(5) All information provided to the public by OIRA shall be in plain, understandable language.

Section 7. Resolution of Conflicts

To the extent permitted by law, disagreements or conflicts between or among agency heads or between OMB and any agency that cannot be resolved by the Administrator of OIRA shall be resolved by the President, or by the Vice President acting at the request of the President, with the relevant agency head (and, as appropriate, other interested government officials). Vice Presidential and Presidential consideration of such disagreements may be initiated only by the Director, by the head of the issuing agency, or by the head of an agency that has a significant interest in the regulatory action at issue. Such review will not be undertaken at the request of other persons, entities, or their agents.

Resolution of such conflicts shall be informed by recommendations developed by the Vice President, after consultation with the Advisors (and other executive branch officials or personnel whose responsibilities to the President include the subject matter at issue).

The development of these recommendations shall be concluded within 60 days after review has been requested.

During the Vice Presidential and Presidential review period, communications with any person not employed by the Federal Government relating to the substance of the regulatory action under review and directed to the Advisors or their staffs or to the staff of the Vice President shall be in writing and shall be forwarded by the recipient to the affected agency(ies) for inclusion in the public docket(s). When the communication is not in writing, such Advisors or staff members shall inform the outside party that the matter is under review and that any comments should be submitted in writing.

At the end of this review process, the President, or the Vice President acting at the request of the President, shall notify the affected agency and the Administrator of OIRA of the President's decision with respect to the matter.

Section 8. Publication

Except to the extent required by law, an agency shall not publish in the Federal Register or otherwise issue to the public any regulatory action that is subject to review under section 6 of this Executive order until (1) the Administrator of OIRA notifies the agency that OIRA has waived its review of the action or has completed its review without any requests for further consideration, or (2) the applicable time period in section 6(b)(2) expires without OIRA having notified the agency that it is returning the regulatory action for further consideration under section 6(b)(3), whichever occurs first. If the terms of the preceding sentence have not been satisfied and an agency wants to publish or otherwise issue a regulatory action, the head of that agency may request Presidential consideration through the Vice President, as provided under section 7 of this order. Upon receipt of this request, the Vice President shall notify OIRA and the Advisors. The guidelines and time period set forth in section 7 shall apply to the publication of regulatory actions for which Presidential consideration has been sought.

Section 9. Agency Authority

Nothing in this order shall be construed as displacing the agencies' authority or responsibilities, as authorized by law.

Section 10. Judicial Review

Nothing in this Executive order shall affect any otherwise available judicial review of agency action. This Executive order is intended only to improve the internal management of the Federal Government and does not create any right or benefit, substantive or procedural, enforce-

5. The Regulatory Process   Pages 689-694

able at law or equity by a party against the United States, its agencies or instrumentalities, its officers or employees, or any other person.

NOTES AND QUESTIONS

1. In what respects is the Clinton Administration's regulatory review program different from that employed under the Reagan and Bush Administrations, as embodied in EO 12,291 (parent text, p. 690)? In what circumstances does the Clinton executive order require agencies to perform cost-benefit analyses? Does the executive order require agencies to base regulatory decisions on the results of cost-benefit analyses?

2. Under the Clinton Administrations' executive order, what authority does the Office of Management and Budget have to influence the substance of regulations? How are disputes between OMB and regulatory agencies to be resolved? Can OMB block the issuance of regulations that it disagrees with?

3. One of the most controversial aspects of regulatory review during the Reagan and Bush administrations was the secrecy of the process. How does EO 12,866 seek to ensure that the regulatory review process is open to public scrutiny?

4. Early data indicates that the regulatory review process is operating significantly faster under the Clinton program than during the previous administrations, in part because the greater selectivity of the Clinton program means that fewer rules need to be reviewed. EPA reports that the number of its rules that are reviewed by OMB has declined by 50 percent under the Clinton program since only significant rules are now subject to review. OMB Reviews Fewer EPA Rules Under Clinton Order, 25 Env. Rep. 742 (1994).

5. EO 12,866 gives the Vice President new authority over regulatory review. The executive order was developed in close coordination with the six-month National Performance Review Vice President Gore conducted to develop a plan for "reinventing government" to make it operate more efficiently. A. Gore, Creating a Government That Works Better and Costs Less (1993). One of the goals of the National Performance Review is to "eliminate regulatory overkill" by reducing unnecessary regulation. Agencies have been instructed to "identify regulations that are cumulative, obsolete, or inconsistent, and, where appropriate, eliminate or modify them." Id. at 42.

6. Faced with legislative proposals to drastically alter the regulatory process, President Clinton announced his own regulatory reform program in March 1995. The President directed agencies to intensify their efforts to identify and eliminate unnecessary regulations. He announced that fines for first-time violations by small businesses could be

271

waived and that reporting requirements imposed on small businesses will be simplified. Emissions trading programs will be expanded to include water pollutants and other air pollutants not covered by the current program. Regulators will select up to 50 companies who will be given the opportunity to demonstrate that they can reduce pollution more cheaply and more effectively through alternatives to compliance with existing rules.

Regulatory Review and the Clean Air Permit Regulations (pp. 700-701). While agency heads can try to resist directives from the Executive Office of the President, it is difficult to do so successfully. The controversy over the Clean Air Act permit rule (parent text, pp. 700-701) was precipitated by EPA's conviction that the changes in the permit rules dictated by OMB and the Competitiveness Council were illegal. After losing an appeal to President Bush, EPA Administrator William Reilly, despite rumors that he would resign in protest, agreed to promulgate the rule provided that the Justice Department issued an opinion stating that it was legal. The Justice Department eventually produced such an opinion, Memorandum for William K. Reilly from Barry M. Hartman, Acting Assistant Attorney General, U.S. Dept. of Justice, Environment and Natural Resources Division, May 27, 1992, though it was not issued by the Department's Office of Legal Counsel, the division normally responsible for providing legal advice in cases of interagency disputes. Davis, Formal Legal Opinion Backing Bush on EPA Came 2 Weeks After Decision, Wall St. J., June 2, 1992, at A16. Several environmental organizations and state attorneys general are now challenging the permit regulations in court. Clean Air Implementation Project v. United States EPA, No. 92-1303 and consolidated cases (D.C. Circuit).

Legal Bounds on Executive Oversight (pp. 701-712). Two court decisions help illuminate the murky boundaries of the president's authority to influence regulatory decisions by agencies. In Portland Audubon Society v. Oregon Lands Coalition, 988 F.2d 121 (9th Cir. 1993), environmentalists argued that improper ex parte contacts by the White House had tainted the decision by the Endangered Species Committee ("God Squad") to exempt certain timber sales from the requirements of the Endangered Species Act under §7(e), 16 U.S.C. §1536(e). Reportedly, three members of the committee had been summoned to the White House and pressured to vote for the exemptions. The Ninth Circuit decided that the committee's proceedings are subject to the Administrative Procedure Act's prohibition on ex parte communications, 5 U.S.C. §557(d)(1), because they are adjudicatory hearings. The court then rejected government's arguments that the prohibition does not apply to the President and his staff. The court distinguished Sierra Club v.

5. The Regulatory Process   Pages 712-713

Costle (parent text, p. 701) because it involved an informal rulemaking proceeding to which the APA's ban on ex parte communications did not apply. The court also rejected the government's claim that to apply the ban to the President and his staff would violate the separation of powers doctrine, noting that otherwise the President "could effectively destroy the integrity of all federal agency adjudications."

The Ninth Circuit's decision was made in response to plaintiffs' motion to permit discovery concerning contacts between the White House and the God Squad. After the court decided to appoint an administrative law judge (ALJ) to supplement the record, the new administration agreed not to pursue the timber sales exempted by the God Squad's decision. The government agreed to vacate the Squad's decision, and the Sierra Club's legal challenge was dismissed as moot.

As discussed on pp. 705-706 of the text, the Bush Administration's Competitiveness Council vetoed EPA's proposal to ban incineration of lead acid batteries and to impose a 25 percent recycling requirement on municipal incinerators in a new source performance standard. After the decision was challenged by NRDC, the D.C. Circuit struck down a portion of it in New York v. Reilly, 969 F.2d 1147 (D.C. Cir. 1992). The court upheld the decision not to include a 25 percent recycling requirement because it found that the record adequately supported EPA's change in position, which ostensibly was based on the argument that the costs and benefits of such a provision were too uncertain. The court rejected the claim that EPA had relied on the opinion of the Competitiveness Council and had not exercised its own expertise, noting that EPA's change of position "in light of the Council's advice . . . does not mean that EPA failed to exercise its own expertise in promulgating the final rules." However, the court found that EPA had not adequately explained why it declined to prohibit the burning of lead acid batteries and it remanded this portion of the rule to EPA for reconsideration. Does this experience suggest that an agency that loses a battle over regulatory review ultimately may prevail simply by failing adequately to justify the position foisted upon it by OMB?

The Bush Administration's Regulatory Freeze (pp. 712-713). As the 1992 elections approached, President Bush launched what appeared to be a major deregulation campaign. Ironically, this campaign substantially delayed implementation of the 1990 Amendments to the Clean Air Act, which the president had claimed as his principal environmental achievement. On April 29, 1992, the administration announced that its regulatory moratorium was being extended for an additional 120 days. The president also announced that he was directing federal agencies to conduct cost-benefit analyses of prospective legislation. The administration claimed that the initial 90-day moratorium had produced reforms that would save $15 billion to $20 billion per year. The only environmental initiative cited by the administration was the "cash for clunkers" program (announced just before the Michigan primary), which would provide emission reduction credits to companies that buy up old automobiles.

At the Republican Party Convention in August 1992, President Bush announced that he was extending the regulatory moratorium for an additional year. Despite the claim that regulations subject to statutory deadlines would be exempt from the moratorium, in practice the moratorium was cited by agencies as a reason for missing many statutory deadlines. While the Bush Administration claimed that the regulatory moratorium would save $20 to $30 billion, OMB, Budget Baselines, Historical Data and Alternatives for the Future 113 (1993), these estimates were greatly inflated. See Watzman and Triano, Voodoo Accounting: The Toll of President Bush's Regulatory Moratorium (1992).

Could a president philosophically opposed to regulation legally impose a permanent freeze on new regulations? If not, could such a president require that before any new regulations are promulgated they must be sequentially reviewed and approved by every federal agency, effectively blocking any regulatory action for years? Proposals have been made to adopt a regulatory budget limiting the amount agencies may "spend" by imposing new regulatory costs on industry. If adopted, would a regulatory budget be a reason to relax regulatory review in order to give agencies greater freedom in choosing where to allocate their regulatory energies?

C. JUDICIAL REVIEW AND THE REGULATORY PROCESS

Associational Standing (p. 737). Even national environmental organizations may face standing difficulties similar to those faced by the regional Conservation Law Foundation. In United States v. AVX Corp., 962 F.2d 108 (1st Cir. 1992), the First Circuit denied standing to the National Wildlife Federation (NWF), which was seeking to challenge the government's settlement of natural resources damages claims for pollution of New Bedford Harbor. The court held that an allegation that NWF had "79,000 members and supporters in Massachusetts" who "use and enjoy, through fishing, swimming, recreational and other uses, the environment and natural resources in the New Bedford Harbor" area was insufficient to establish standing. The court stated that "[t]he

5. The Regulatory Process   Page 738

averment has no substance: the members are unidentified; their places of abode are not stated; the extent and frequency of any individual use of the affected resources is left open to surmise." 962 F.2d at 117. It concluded that after Lujan v. National Wildlife Federation [parent text, p. 728] a plaintiff must show actual use of the specific property in question in order to establish standing for injury to natural resources. Id. at 118.

Lujan v. Defenders of Wildlife and the Future of Environmental Standing (p. 738). On June 12, 1992, the U.S. Supreme Court decided Lujan v. Defenders of Wildlife (parent text, p. 738). The decision, which we will refer to as *Lujan II* to distinguish it from Lujan v. National Wildlife Federation (parent text, p. 728), is immensely important to the future of environmental standing. Before presenting the decision, we apologize for a blatant bit of sexism in the second to the last sentence of Note 3 on page 727, where the masculine pronoun is used to refer to a member of Defenders. The member in question actually was Ms. Amy Skilbred, as indicated in the decision below. Ms. Joyce Kelly, president of Defenders of Wildlife, also submitted an affidavit in an effort to establish the organization's standing.

> *Lujan v. Defenders of Wildlife*
> 504 U.S. 555 (1992)

JUSTICE SCALIA, J., delivered the opinion of the Court with respect to Parts I, II, III-A, and IV, and an opinion with respect to Part III-B, in which the CHIEF JUSTICE and JUSTICE WHITE and JUSTICE THOMAS joined.

This case involves a challenge to a rule promulgated by the Secretary of the Interior interpreting §7 of the Endangered Species Act of 1973 (ESA), 87 Stat. 892, as amended, 16 U.S.C. §1536, in such fashion as to render it applicable only to actions within the United States or on the high seas. [Section 7 of the ESA requires all federal agencies, in consultation with the Secretary of the Interior, to insure that their actions do not jeopardize the continued existence of any endangered species.] The preliminary issue, and the only one we reach, is whether the respondents here, plaintiffs below, have standing to seek judicial review of the rule. . . .

II

. . . Over the years, our cases have established that the irreducible constitutional minimum of standing contains three elements: First, the

275

plaintiff must have suffered an "injury in fact"—an invasion of a legally-protected interest which is (a) concrete and particularized, see id., at 756; Warth v. Seldin, 422 U.S. 490, 508 (1975); Sierra Club v. Morton, 405 U.S. 727, 740-741, n. 16 (1972); and (b) "actual or imminent, not 'conjectural' or 'hypothetical,' " *Whitmore,* supra, at 155 (quoting Los Angeles v. Lyons, 461 U.S. 95, 102 (1983)). Second, there must be a causal connection between the injury and the conduct complained of—the injury has to be "fairly . . . trace[able] to the challenged action of the defendant, and not . . . th[e] result [of] the independent action of some third party not before the court." Simon v. Eastern Kentucky Welfare Rights Org., 426 U.S. 26, 41-42 (1976). Third, it must be "likely," as opposed to merely "speculative," that the injury will be "redressed by a favorable decision." Id., at 38, 43.

The party invoking federal jurisdiction bears the burden of establishing these elements. . . .

When the suit is one challenging the legality of government action or inaction, the nature and extent of facts that must be averred (at the summary judgment stage) or proved (at the trial stage) in order to establish standing depends considerably upon whether the plaintiff is himself an object of the action (or forgone action) at issue. If he is, there is ordinarily little question that the action or inaction has caused him injury, and that a judgment preventing or requiring the action will redress it. When, however, as in this case, a plaintiff's asserted injury arises from the government's allegedly unlawful regulation (or lack of regulation) of *someone else,* much more is needed. In that circumstance, causation and redressability ordinarily hinge on the response of the regulated (or regulable) third party to the government action or inaction—and perhaps on the response of others as well. The existence of one or more of the essential elements of standing "depends on the unfettered choices made by independent actors not before the courts and whose exercise of broad and legitimate discretion the courts cannot presume either to control or to predict," ASARCO Inc. v. Kadish, 490 U.S. 605, 615 (1989) (opinion of Kennedy, J.); and it becomes the burden of the plaintiff to adduce facts showing that those choices have been or will be made in such manner as to produce causation and permit redressability of injury. E.g., *Warth,* supra, at 505. Thus, when the plaintiff is not himself the object of the government action or inaction he challenges, standing is not precluded, but it is ordinarily "substantially more difficult" to establish. *Allen,* supra, at 758.

III

We think the Court of Appeals failed to apply the foregoing principles in denying the Secretary's motion for summary judgment. Respondents had not made the requisite demonstration of (at least) injury and redressability.

A

Respondents' claim to injury is that the lack of consultation with respect to certain funded activities abroad "increas[es] the rate of extinction of endangered and threatened species." Complaint para. 5. Of course, the desire to use or observe an animal species, even for purely aesthetic purposes, is undeniably a cognizable interest for purpose of standing. See, e.g., Sierra Club v. Morton, 405 U. S., at 734. "But the 'injury in fact' test requires more than an injury to a cognizable interest. It requires that the party seeking review be himself among the injured." Id., at 734-735. To survive the Secretary's summary judgment motion, respondents had to submit affidavits or other evidence showing, through specific facts, not only that listed species were in fact being threatened by funded activities abroad, but also that one or more of respondents' members would thereby be "directly" affected apart from their " 'special interest' in th[e] subject." Id., at 735, 739.

With respect to this aspect of the case, the Court of Appeals focused on the affidavits of two Defenders' members—Joyce Kelly and Amy Skilbred. Ms. Kelly stated that she traveled to Egypt in 1986 and "observed the traditional habitat of the endangered Nile crocodile there and intend[s] to do so again, and hope[s] to observe the crocodile directly," and that she "will suffer harm in fact as a result of [the] American . . . role . . . in overseeing the rehabilitation of the Aswan High Dam on the Nile . . . and [in] developing . . . Egypt's . . . Master Water Plan." Ms. Skilbred averred that she traveled to Sri Lanka in 1981 and "observed th[e] habitat" of "endangered species such as the Asian elephant and the leopard" at what is now the site of the Mahaweli Project funded by the Agency for International Development (AID), although she "was unable to see any of the endangered species"; "this development project," she continued, "will seriously reduce endangered, threatened, and endemic species habitat including areas that I visited . . . [, which] may severely shorten the future of these species"; that threat, she concluded, harmed her because she "intend[s] to return to Sri Lanka in the future and hope[s] to be more fortunate in spotting at least the endangered elephant and leopard." When Ms. Skilbred was asked at a subsequent deposition if and when she had any plans to return to Sri Lanka, she reiterated that "I intend to go back to Sri Lanka," but confessed that she had no current plans: "I don't know [when]. There is a civil war going on right now. I don't know. Not next year, I will say. In the future."

We shall assume for the sake of argument that these affidavits contain facts showing that certain agency-funded projects threaten listed species—though that is questionable. They plainly contain no facts, however, showing how damage to the species will produce "imminent" injury to Mss. Kelly and Skilbred. That the women "had visited" the areas of the projects before the projects commenced proves nothing. As we have said in a related context, " '[p]ast exposure to illegal conduct does not in itself show a present case or controversy regarding injunctive relief . . . if unaccompanied by any continuing, present adverse effects.' " *Lyons*, 461 U.S., at 102 (quoting O'Shea v. Littleton, 414 U.S. 488, 495-496 (1974)). And the affiants' profession of an "inten[t]" to return to the places they had visited before—where they will presumably, this time, be deprived of the opportunity to observe animals of the endangered species—is simply not enough. Such "some day" intentions—without any description of concrete plans, or indeed even any specification of *when* the some day will be—do not support a finding of the "actual or imminent" injury that our cases require.[2]

Besides relying upon the Kelly and Skilbred affidavits, respondents propose a series of novel standing theories. The first, inelegantly styled "ecosystem nexus," proposes that any person who uses *any part* of a "contiguous ecosystem" adversely affected by a funded activity has standing even if the activity is located a great distance away. This approach, as the Court of Appeals correctly observed, is inconsistent with our opinion in [Lujan v.] *National Wildlife Federation* [parent text, p. 728], which held that a plaintiff claiming injury from environmental damage must use the area affected by the challenged activity and not an area roughly "in the vicinity" of it. 497 U.S., at 887-889; see also *Sierra Club*, 405 U.S., at 735. It makes no difference that the general-

---

2. . . . There is no substance to the dissent's suggestion that imminence is demanded only when alleged harm depends upon "the affirmative actions of third parties beyond a plaintiff's control." Our cases *mention* third-party-caused contingency, naturally enough; but they also mention the plaintiff's failure to show that he will soon expose *himself* to the injury, see, e.g., *Lyons*, supra, at 105-106; O'Shea v. Littleton, 414 U.S. 488, 497 (1974); Ashcroft v. Mattis, 431 U.S. 171, 172-173, n. 2 (1977) *(per curiam)*. And there is certainly no reason in principle to demand evidence that third persons will take the action exposing the plaintiff to harm, while *presuming* that the plaintiff himself will do so. Our insistence upon these established requirements of standing does not mean that we would, as the dissent contends, "demand . . . detailed descriptions" of damages, such as a "nightly schedule of attempted activities" from plaintiffs alleging loss of consortium. That case and the others posited by the dissent all involve *actual* harm; the existence of standing is clear, though the precise extent of harm remains to be determined at trial. Where there is no actual harm, however, its imminence (though not its precise extent) must be established.

purpose section of the ESA states that the Act was intended in part "to provide a means whereby the ecosystems upon which endangered species and threatened species depend may be conserved," 16 U.S.C. §1531(b). To say that the Act protects ecosystems is not to say that the Act creates (if it were possible) rights of action in persons who have not been injured in fact, that is, persons who use portions of an ecosystem not perceptibly affected by the unlawful action in question.

Respondents' other theories are called, alas, the "animal nexus" approach, whereby anyone who has an interest in studying or seeing the endangered animals anywhere on the globe has standing; and the "vocational nexus" approach, under which anyone with a professional interest in such animals can sue. Under these theories, anyone who goes to see Asian elephants in the Bronx Zoo, and anyone who is a keeper of Asian elephants in the Bronx Zoo, has standing to sue because the Director of AID did not consult with the Secretary regarding the AID-funded project in Sri Lanka. This is beyond all reason. Standing is not "an ingenious academic exercise in the conceivable," United States v. Students Challenging Regulatory Agency Procedures (SCRAP), 412 U.S. 669, 688 (1973), but as we have said requires, at the summary judgment stage, a factual showing of perceptible harm. It is clear that the person who observes or works with a particular animal threatened by a federal decision is facing perceptible harm, since the very subject of his interest will no longer exist. It is even plausible—though it goes to the outermost limit of plausibility—to think that a person who observes or works with animals of a particular species in the very area of the world where that species is threatened by a federal decision is facing such harm, since some animals that might have been the subject of his interest will no longer exist, see Japan Whaling Assn. v. American Cetacean Soc., 478 U.S. 221, 231, n.4 (1986). It goes beyond the limit, however, and into pure speculation and fantasy, to say that anyone who observes or works with an endangered species, anywhere in the world, is appreciably harmed by a single project affecting some portion of that species with which he has no more specific connection.[3]

---

[3]. . . . The dissent may be correct that the geographic remoteness of those members (here in the United States) from Sri Lanka and Aswan does not *"necessarily"* prevent such a finding—but it assuredly does so when no further facts have been brought forward (and respondent has produced none) showing that the impact upon animals in those distant places will in some fashion be reflected here. The dissent's position to the contrary reduces to the notion that distance *never* prevents harm, a proposition we categorically reject. It cannot be that a person with an interest in an animal automatically has standing to enjoin federal threats to that species of animal, anywhere in the world. Were that the case, the plaintiff in *Sierra Club,* for example, could have avoided the necessity of establishing anyone's use of Mineral King by merely identifying one of its members interested in an endangered species of

B

Besides failing to show injury, respondents failed to demonstrate redressability. Instead of attacking the separate decisions to fund particular projects allegedly causing them harm, the respondents chose to challenge a more generalized level of government action (rules regarding consultation), the invalidation of which would affect all overseas projects.

. . . Since the agencies funding the projects were not parties to the case, the District Court could accord relief only against the Secretary: He could be ordered to revise his regulation to require consultation for foreign projects. But this would not remedy respondents' alleged injury unless the funding agencies were bound by the Secretary's regulation, which is very much an open question. Whereas in other contexts the ESA is quite explicit as to the Secretary's controlling authority, see, e.g., 16 U.S.C. §1533(a)(1) ("The Secretary shall" promulgate regulations determining endangered species); §1535(d)(1) ("The Secretary is authorized to provide financial assistance to any State"), with respect to consultation the initiative, and hence arguably the initial responsibility for determining statutory necessity, lies with the agencies, see §1536(a)(2) ("*Each Federal agency shall*, in consultation with and with the assistance of the Secretary, insure that any" funded action is not likely to jeopardize endangered or threatened species) (emphasis added)). . . .

Respondents assert that this legal uncertainty did not affect redressability (and hence standing) because the District Court itself could resolve the issue of the Secretary's authority as a necessary part of its standing inquiry. Assuming that it is appropriate to resolve an issue of law such as this in connection with a threshold standing inquiry, resolution by the District Court would not have remedied respondents' alleged injury anyway, because it would not have been binding upon the agencies. They were not parties to the suit, and there is no reason they should be obliged to honor an incidental legal determination the suit produced. The Court of Appeals tried to finesse this problem by simply proclaiming that "[w]e are satisfied that an injunction requiring the Secretary to publish [respondents' desired] regulatio[n] . . . would result in consultation." *Defenders of Wildlife*, 851 F.2d, at 1042, 1043-1044. We do not know what would justify that confidence, particularly when the Justice Department (presumably after consultation with the

---

flora or fauna at that location. Justice Blackmun's accusation that a special rule is being crafted for "environmental claims" is correct, but *he* is the craftsman . . .

agencies) has taken the position that the regulation is not binding.[5] The short of the matter is that redress of the only injury-in-fact respondents complain of requires action (termination of funding until consultation) by the individual funding agencies; and any relief the District Court could have provided in this suit against the Secretary was not likely to produce that action.

A further impediment to redressability is the fact that the agencies generally supply only a fraction of the funding for a foreign project. AID, for example, has provided less than 10% of the funding for the Mahaweli Project. Respondents have produced nothing to indicate that the projects they have named will either be suspended, or do less harm to listed species, if that fraction is eliminated. As in *Simon*, 426 U.S., at 43-44, it is entirely conjectural whether the nonagency activity that affects respondents will be altered or affected by the agency activity they seek to achieve. There is no standing.

IV

The Court of Appeals found that respondents had standing for an additional reason: because they had suffered a "procedural injury." The so-called "citizen-suit" provision of the ESA provides, in pertinent part, that "any person may commence a civil suit on his own behalf (A) to enjoin any person, including the United States and any other governmental instrumentality or agency . . . who is alleged to be in violation of any provision of this chapter." 16 U.S.C. §1540(g). The court held that, because §7(a)(2) requires interagency consultation, the citizen-suit provision creates a "procedural righ[t]" to consultation in all "persons"—so that *anyone* can file suit in federal court to challenge the Secretary's (or presumably any other official's) failure to follow the assertedly correct consultative procedure, notwithstanding their inability to allege any discrete injury flowing from that failure. To understand the remarkable nature of this holding one must be clear about what it does *not* rest upon: This is not a case where plaintiffs are seeking to enforce a procedural requirement the disregard of which could

---

5. Seizing on the fortuity that the case has made its way to this Court, Justice Stevens protests that no agency would ignore "an authoritative construction of the [ESA] by this Court." In that he is probably correct; in concluding from it that plaintiffs have demonstrated redressability, he is not. Since, as we have pointed out above, standing is to be determined as of the commencement of suit; since at that point it could certainly not be known that the suit would reach this Court; and since it is not likely that an agency would feel compelled to accede to the legal view of a district court expressed in a case to which it was not a party; redressability clearly did not exist.

impair a separate concrete interest of theirs (e.g., the procedural requirement for a hearing prior to denial of their license application, or the procedural requirement for an environmental impact statement before a federal facility is constructed next door to them).[7] Nor is it simply a case where concrete injury has been suffered by many persons, as in mass fraud or mass tort situations. Nor, finally, is it the unusual case in which Congress has created a concrete private interest in the outcome of a suit against a private party for the government's benefit, by providing a cash bounty for the victorious plaintiff. Rather, the court held that the injury-in-fact requirement had been satisfied by congressional conferral upon *all* persons of an abstract, self-contained, noninstrumental "right" to have the Executive observe the procedures required by law. We reject this view.[8]

---

7. There is this much truth to the assertion that "procedural rights" are special: The person who has been accorded a procedural right to protect his concrete interests can assert that right without meeting all the normal standards for redressability and immediacy. Thus, under our case-law, one living adjacent to the site for proposed construction of a federally licensed dam has standing to challenge the licensing agency's failure to prepare an Environmental Impact Statement, even though he cannot establish with any certainty that the Statement will cause the license to be withheld or altered, and even though the dam will not be completed for many years. (That is why we do not rely, in the present case, upon the Government's argument that, *even if* the other agencies were obliged to consult with the Secretary, they might not have followed his advice.) What respondents' "procedural rights" argument seeks, however, is quite different from this: standing for persons who have no concrete interests affected—persons who live (and propose to live) at the other end of the country from the dam.

8. The dissent's discussion of this aspect of the case, distorts our opinion. We do *not* hold that an individual cannot enforce procedural rights; he assuredly can, so long as the procedures in question are designed to protect some threatened concrete interest of his that is the ultimate basis of his standing. The dissent, however, asserts that there exist "classes of procedural duties . . . so enmeshed with the prevention of a substantive, concrete harm that an individual plaintiff may be able to demonstrate a sufficient likelihood of injury just through the breach of that procedural duty." If we understand this correctly, it means that the government's violation of a certain (undescribed) class of procedural duty satisfies the concrete-injury requirement by itself, without any showing that the procedural violation endangers a concrete interest of the plaintiff (apart from his interest in having the procedure observed). We cannot agree. The dissent is unable to cite a single case in which we actually found standing solely on the basis of "procedural right" unconnected to the plaintiff's own concrete harm. Its suggestion that we did so in *Japan Whaling Association,* supra, and Robertson v. Methow Valley Citizens Council, 490 U. S. 332 (1989), is not supported by the facts. In the former case, we found that the environmental organizations had standing because the "whale watching and studying of their members would be adversely affected by continued whale harvesting," see 478 U. S., at 230-231, n.4; and in the latter we did not so much as mention standing, for the very good reason that the plaintiff was a citizen's council for the area

We have consistently held that a plaintiff raising only a generally available grievance about government—claiming only harm to his and every citizen's interest in proper application of the Constitution and laws, and seeking relief that no more directly and tangibly benefits him than it does the public at large—does not state an Article III case or controversy. . . .

To be sure, our generalized-grievance cases have typically involved Government violation of procedures assertedly ordained by the Constitution rather than the Congress. But there is absolutely no basis for making the Article III inquiry turn on the source of the asserted right. Whether the courts were to act on their own, or at the invitation of Congress, in ignoring the concrete injury requirement described in our cases, they would be discarding a principle fundamental to the separate and distinct constitutional role of the Third Branch—one of the essential elements that identifies those "Cases" and "Controversies" that are the business of the courts rather than of the political branches. "The province of the court," as Chief Justice Marshall said in Marbury v. Madison, 1 Cranch, 137, 170 (1803) "is, solely, to decide on the rights of individuals." Vindicating the *public* interest (including the public interest in government observance of the Constitution and laws) is the function of Congress and the Chief Executive. The question presented here is whether the public interest in proper administration of the laws (specifically, in agencies' observance of a particular, statutorily prescribed procedure) can be converted into an individual right by a statute that denominates it as such, and that permits all citizens (or, for that matter, a subclass of citizens who suffer no distinctive concrete harm) to sue. If the concrete injury requirement has the separation-of-powers significance we have always said, the answer must be obvious: To permit Congress to convert the undifferentiated public interest in executive officers' compliance with the law into an "individual right" vindicable in the courts is to permit Congress to transfer from the President to the courts the Chief Executive's most important constitutional duty, to "take Care that the Laws be faithfully executed," Art. II, §3. It would enable the courts, with the permission of Congress, "to assume a position of authority over the governmental acts of another and co-equal department," Frothingham v. Mellon, 262 U. S., at 489, and to become " 'virtually continuing monitors of the wisdom and soundness of Executive action.' " *Allen,* 468 U.S., at 760 (quoting Laird v. Tatum, 408 U.S. 1, 15 (1972)). We have always rejected that vision of our role:

---

in which the challenged construction was to occur, so that its members would obviously be concretely affected, see Methow Valley Citizens Council v. Regional Forester, 833 F.2d 810, 812-813 (CA9 1987).

> When Congress passes an Act empowering administrative agencies to carry on governmental activities, the power of those agencies is circumscribed by the authority granted. This permits the courts to participate in law enforcement entrusted to administrative bodies only to the extent necessary to protect justiciable individual rights against administrative action fairly beyond the granted powers. . . . This is very far from assuming that the courts are charged more than administrators or legislators with the protection of the rights of the people. Congress and the Executive supervise the acts of administrative agents. . . . But under Article III, Congress established courts to adjudicate cases and controversies as to claims of infringement of individual rights whether by unlawful action of private persons or by the exertion of unauthorized administrative power.

Stark v. Wickard, 321 U.S. 288, 309-310 (1944). "Individual rights," within the meaning of this passage, do not mean public rights that have been legislatively pronounced to belong to each individual who forms part of the public. See also *Sierra Club,* 405 U.S., at 740-741, n.16.

Nothing in this contradicts the principle that "[t]he . . . injury required by Art. III may exist solely by virtue of 'statutes creating legal rights, the invasion of which creates standing.' " *Warth,* 422 U.S., at 500 (quoting Linda R. S. v. Richard D., 410 U.S. 614, 617, n.3 (1973)). Both of the cases used by *Linda R. S.* as an illustration of that principle involved Congress's elevating to the status of legally cognizable injuries concrete, *de facto* injuries that were previously inadequate in law (namely, injury to an individual's personal interest in living in a racially integrated community, see Trafficante v. Metropolitan Life Ins. Co., 409 U.S. 205, 208-212 (1972), and injury to a company's interest in marketing its product free from competition, see Hardin v. Kentucky Utilities Co., 390 U.S. 1, 6 (1968)). As we said in *Sierra Club,* "[Statutory] broadening [of] the categories of injury that may be alleged in support of standing is a different matter from abandoning the requirement that the party seeking review must himself have suffered an injury." 405 U.S., at 738. Whether or not the principle set forth in *Warth* can be extended beyond that distinction, it is clear that in suits against the government, at least, the concrete injury requirement must remain.

We hold that respondents lack standing to bring this action and that the Court of Appeals erred in denying the summary judgment motion filed by the United States. The opinion of the Court of Appeals is hereby reversed, and the cause remanded for proceedings consistent with this opinion.

JUSTICE KENNEDY, with whom JUSTICE SOUTER joins, concurring in part and concurring in the judgment.

Although I agree with the essential parts of the Court's analysis, I write separately to make several observations.

I agree with the Court's conclusion in Part III-A that, on the record before us, respondents have failed to demonstrate that they themselves are "among the injured." Sierra Club v. Morton, 405 U.S. 727, 735 (1972). This component of the standing inquiry is not satisfied unless

> [p]laintiffs . . . demonstrate a "personal stake in the outcome." . . . Abstract injury is not enough. The plaintiff must show that he has sustained or is immediately in danger of sustaining some direct injury as the result of the challenged official conduct and the injury or threat of injury must be both "real and immediate," not "conjectural" or "hypothetical." Los Angeles v. Lyons, 461 U.S. 95, 101-102 (1983) (citations omitted).

While it may seem trivial to require that Mss. Kelly and Skilbred acquire airline tickets to the project sites or announce a date certain upon which they will return, this is not a case where it is reasonable to assume that the affiants will be using the sites on a regular basis, see Sierra Club v. Morton, supra, at 735, n.8, nor do the affiants claim to have visited the sites since the projects commenced. With respect to the Court's discussion of respondents' "ecosystem nexus," "animal nexus," and "vocational nexus" theories, I agree that on this record respondents' showing is insufficient to establish standing on any of these bases. I am not willing to foreclose the possibility, however, that in different circumstances a nexus theory similar to those proffered here might support a claim to standing. See Japan Whaling Assn. v. American Cetacean Soc., 478 U.S. 221, 231, n.4 (1986) ("respondents . . . undoubtedly have alleged a sufficient 'injury in fact' in that the whale watching and studying of their members will be adversely affected by continued whale harvesting").

In light of the conclusion that respondents have not demonstrated a concrete injury here sufficient to support standing under our precedents, I would not reach the issue of redressability that is discussed by the plurality in Part III-B.

I also join Part IV of the Court's opinion with the following observations. As government programs and policies become more complex and far-reaching, we must be sensitive to the articulation of new rights of action that do not have clear analogs in our common-law tradition. Modern litigation has progressed far from the paradigm of Marbury suing Madison to get his commission, Marbury v. Madison, 1 Cranch 137 (1803), or Ogden seeking an injunction to halt Gibbons' steamboat operations. Gibbons v. Ogden, 9 Wheat. 1 (1824). In my view, Congress has the power to define injuries and articulate chains of causation that will give rise to a case or controversy where none existed before, and I do not read the Court's opinion to suggest a contrary view. See Warth v. Seldin, 422 U.S. 490, 500 (1975). In exercising this power, however, Congress must at the very least identify the injury it seeks to vindicate and relate the injury to the class of persons entitled to bring suit. The citizen-suit provision of the Endangered Species Act does not meet these minimal requirements, because while the statute purports to confer a right on "any person . . . to enjoin . . . the United States and any other governmental instrumentality or agency . . . who is alleged to be in violation of any provision of this chapter," it does not of its own force establish that there is an injury in "any person" by virtue of any "violation." 16 U.S.C. §1540(g)(1)(A).

The Court's holding that there is an outer limit to the power of Congress to confer rights of action is a direct and necessary consequence of the case and controversy limitations found in Article III. I agree that it would exceed those limitations if, at the behest of Congress and in the absence of any showing of concrete injury, we were to entertain citizen-suits to vindicate the public's nonconcrete interest in the proper administration of the laws. While it does not matter how many persons have been injured by the challenged action, the party bringing suit must show that the action injures him in a concrete and personal way. This requirement is not just an empty formality. It preserves the vitality of the adversarial process by assuring both that the parties before the court have an actual, as opposed to professed, stake in the outcome, and that "the legal questions presented . . . will be resolved, not in the rarefied atmosphere of a debating society, but in a concrete factual context conducive to a realistic appreciation of the consequences of judicial action." Valley Forge Christian College v. Americans United for Separation of Church and State, Inc., 454 U.S. 464, 472 (1982). In addition, the requirement of concrete injury confines the Judicial Branch to its proper, limited role in the constitutional framework of government.

An independent judiciary is held to account through its open proceedings and its reasoned judgments. In this process it is essential for the public to know what persons or groups are invoking the judicial power, the reasons that they have brought suit, and whether their claims are vindicated or denied. The concrete injury requirement helps assure that there can be an answer to these questions; and, as the Court's opinion is careful to show, that is part of the constitutional design.

With these observations, I concur in Parts I, II, III-A, and IV of the Court's opinion and in the judgment of the Court.

JUSTICE STEVENS, concurring in the judgment.

Because I am not persuaded that Congress intended the consultation requirement in §7(a)(2) of the Endangered Species Act of 1973 (ESA), 16 U.S.C. §1536(a)(2), to apply to activities in foreign countries, I concur in the judgment of reversal. I do not, however, agree with the Court's conclusion that respondents lack standing because the threatened injury to their interest in protecting the environment and studying endangered species is not "imminent." Nor do I agree with the plurality's additional conclusion that respondents' injury is not "redressable" in this litigation.

I

In my opinion a person who has visited the critical habitat of an endangered species, has a professional interest in preserving the species and its habitat, and intends to revisit them in the future has standing to challenge agency action that threatens their destruction. Congress has found that a wide variety of endangered species of fish, wildlife, and plants are of "aesthetic, ecological, educational, historical, recreational, and scientific value to the Nation and its people." 16 U.S.C. §1531(a)(3). Given that finding, we have no license to demean the importance of the interest that particular individuals may have in observing any species or its habitat, whether those individuals are motivated by aesthetic enjoyment, an interest in professional research, or an economic interest in preservation of the species. Indeed, this Court has often held that injuries to such interests are sufficient to confer standing, and the Court reiterates that holding today.

The Court nevertheless concludes that respondents have not suffered "injury in fact" because they have not shown that the harm to the endangered species will produce "imminent" injury to them. I disagree. An injury to an individual's interest in studying or enjoying a species and its natural habitat occurs when someone (whether it be the government or a private party) takes action that harms that species and habitat. In my judgment, therefore, the "imminence" of such an injury should be measured by the timing and likelihood of the threatened environmental harm, rather than—as the Court seems to suggest—by the time that might elapse between the present and the time when the individuals would visit the area if no such injury should occur. . . .

[W]e have denied standing to plaintiffs whose likelihood of suffering any concrete adverse effect from the challenged action was speculative. In this case, however, the likelihood that respondents will be injured by the destruction of the endangered species is not speculative. If respondents are genuinely interested in the preservation of the endangered species and intend to study or observe these animals in the future, their injury will occur as soon as the animals are destroyed. Thus the only potential source of "speculation" in this case is whether respondents' intent to study or observe the animals is genuine.[2] In my view, Joyce Kelly and Amy Skilbred have introduced sufficient evidence to negate petitioner's contention that their claims of injury are "speculative" or "conjectural." As Justice Blackmun explains, a reasonable finder of fact could conclude, from their past visits, their professional backgrounds, and their affidavits and deposition testimony, that Ms. Kelly and Ms. Skilbred will return to the project sites and, consequently, will be injured by the destruction of the endangered species and critical habitat. . . .

JUSTICE BLACKMUN, with whom JUSTICE O'CONNOR joins, dissenting.

I part company with the Court in this case in two respects. First, I believe that respondents have raised genuine issues of fact—sufficient to survive summary judgment—both as to injury and as to redressability. Second, I question the Court's breadth of language in rejecting standing for "procedural" injuries. I fear the Court seeks to impose fresh limitations on the constitutional authority of Congress to allow citizen-suits in the federal courts for injuries deemed "procedural" in nature. I dissent. . . .

I-A

1

Were the Court to apply the proper standard for summary judgment, I believe it would conclude that the sworn affidavits and deposi-

---

2. As we recognized in Sierra Club v. Morton, 405 U.S., at 735, the impact of changes in the aesthetics or ecology of a particular area does "not fall indiscriminately upon every citizen. The alleged injury will be felt directly only by those who use [the area,] and for whom the aesthetic and recreational values of the area will be lessened. . . ." Thus, respondents would not be injured by the challenged projects if they had not visited the sites or studied the threatened species and habitat. But, as discussed above, respondents did visit the sites; moreover, they have expressed an intent to do so again. This intent to revisit the area is significant evidence tending to confirm the genuine character of respondents' interest, but I am not at all sure that an intent to revisit would be indispensable in every case. The interest that confers standing in a case of this kind is comparable, though by no means equivalent, to the interest in a relationship among family members that can be immediately harmed by the death of an absent member, regardless of when, if ever, a family reunion is planned to occur. Thus, if the facts of this case had shown repeated and regular visits by the respondents, proof of an intent to revisit might well be superfluous.

tion testimony of Joyce Kelly and Amy Skilbred advance sufficient facts to create a genuine issue for trial concerning whether one or both would be imminently harmed by the Aswan and Mahaweli projects. In the first instance, as the Court itself concedes, the affidavits contained facts making it at least "questionable" (and therefore within the province of the factfinder) that certain agency-funded projects threaten listed species. The only remaining issue, then, is whether Kelly and Skilbred have shown that they personally would suffer imminent harm.

I think a reasonable finder of fact could conclude from the information in the affidavits and deposition testimony that either Kelly or Skilbred will soon return to the project sites, thereby satisfying the "actual or imminent" injury standard. The Court dismisses Kelly's and Skilbred's general statements that they intended to revisit the project sites as "simply not enough." But those statements did not stand alone. A reasonable finder of fact could conclude, based not only upon their statements of intent to return, but upon their past visits to the project sites, as well as their professional backgrounds, that it was likely that Kelly and Skilbred would make a return trip to the project areas. Contrary to the Court's contention that Kelly's and Skilbred's past visits "prove[] nothing," the fact of their past visits could demonstrate to a reasonable factfinder that Kelly and Skilbred have the requisite resources and personal interest in the preservation of the species endangered by the Aswan and Mahaweli projects to make good on their intention to return again. Cf. Los Angeles v. Lyons, 461 U.S. 95, 102 (1983) ("Past wrongs were evidence bearing on whether there is a real and immediate threat of repeated injury") (internal quotations omitted). Similarly, Kelly's and Skilbred's professional backgrounds in wildlife preservation also make it likely—at least far more likely than for the average citizen—that they would choose to visit these areas of the world where species are vanishing.

By requiring a "description of concrete plans" or "specification of *when* the some day [for a return visit] will be," the Court, in my view, demands what is likely an empty formality. No substantial barriers prevent Kelly or Skilbred from simply purchasing plane tickets to return to the Aswan and Mahaweli projects. This case differs from other cases in which the imminence of harm turned largely on the affirmative actions of third parties beyond a plaintiff's control. To be sure, a plaintiff's unilateral control over his or her exposure to harm does not *necessarily* render the harm non-speculative. Nevertheless, it suggests that a finder of fact would be far more likely to conclude the harm is actual or imminent, especially if given an opportunity to hear testimony and determine credibility.

I fear the Court's demand for detailed descriptions of future conduct will do little to weed out those who are genuinely harmed from those who are not. More likely, it will resurrect a code-pleading formalism in federal court summary ju-dgment practice, as federal courts, newly doubting their jurisdiction, will demand more and more particularized showings of future harm. Just to survive summary judgment, for example, a property owner claiming a decline in the value of his property from governmental action might have to specify the exact date he intends to sell his property and show that there is a market for the property, lest it be surmised he might not sell again. A nurse turned down for a job on grounds of her race had better be prepared to show on what date she was prepared to start work, that she had arranged daycare for her child, and that she would not have accepted work at another hospital instead. And a Federal Torts Claims Act plaintiff alleging loss of consortium should make sure to furnish this Court with a "description of concrete plans" for her nightly schedule of attempted activities.

2

The Court also concludes that injury is lacking, because respondents' allegations of "ecosystem nexus" failed to demonstrate sufficient proximity to the site of the environmental harm. To support that conclusion, the Court mischaracterizes our decision in Lujan v. National Wildlife Federation, —U.S.— (1990) [parent text, p. 728], as establishing a general rule that "a plaintiff claiming injury from environmental damage must use the area affected by the challenged activity." In *National Wildlife Federation*, the Court required specific geographical proximity because of the particular type of harm alleged in that case: harm to the plaintiff's visual enjoyment of nature from mining activities. One cannot suffer from the sight of a ruined landscape without being close enough to see the sites actually being mined. Many environmental injuries, however, cause harm distant from the area immediately affected by the challenged action. Environmental destruction may affect animals traveling over vast geographical ranges, see, e.g., Japan Whaling Assn. v. American Cetacean Soc., 478 U.S. 221 (1986) (harm to American whale watchers from Japanese whaling activities), or rivers running long geographical courses, see, e.g., Arkansas v. Oklahoma, —U.S.— (1992) (harm to Oklahoma residents from wastewater treatment plant 39 miles from border). It cannot seriously be contended that a litigant's failure to use the precise or exact site where animals are slaughtered or where toxic waste is dumped into a river means he or she cannot show injury.

The Court also rejects respondents' claim of vocational or professional injury. The Court says that it is "beyond all reason" that a zoo "keeper" of Asian elephants would have standing to contest his government's participation in the eradication of all the Asian elephants in another part of the world. I am unable to see how the distant location of the destruction necessarily (for purposes of ruling at summary judgment) mitigates the harm to the elephant keeper. If there is no more access to a future supply of the animal that sustains a keeper's livelihood, surely there is harm.

I have difficulty imagining this Court applying its rigid principles of geographic formalism anywhere outside the context of environmental claims. As I understand it, environmental plaintiffs are under no special constitutional standing disabilities. Like other plaintiffs, they need show only that the action they challenge has injured them, without necessarily showing they happened to be physically near the location of the alleged wrong. The Court's decision today should not be interpreted "to foreclose the possibility . . . that in different circumstances a nexus theory similar to those proffered here might support a claim to standing." (Kennedy, J., concurring in part and concurring in the judgment).

[I]-B

A plurality of the Court suggests that respondents have not demonstrated redressability: a likelihood that a court ruling in their favor would remedy their injury. The plurality identifies two obstacles. The first is that the "action agencies" (e.g., the Agency for International Development) cannot be required to undertake consultation with petitioner Secretary, because they are not directly bound as parties to the suit and are otherwise not indirectly bound by being subject to petitioner Secretary's regulation. Petitioner, however, officially and publicly has taken the position that his regulations regarding consultation under §7 of the Act are binding on action agencies. 50 CFR §402.14(a) (1991). And he has previously taken the same position in this very litigation, having stated in his answer to the complaint that petitioner "admits the Fish and Wildlife Service (FWS) was designated the lead agency for the formulation of regulations concerning section 7 of the ESA." I cannot agree with the plurality that the Secretary (or the Solicitor General) is now free, for the convenience of this appeal, to disavow his prior public and litigation positions. More generally, I cannot agree that the Government is free to play "Three-Card Monte" with its description of agencies' authority to defeat standing against the agency given the lead in administering a statutory scheme.

Emphasizing that none of the action agencies are parties to this suit (and having rejected the possibility of their being indirectly bound by petitioner's regulation), the plurality concludes that "there is no reason they should be obliged to honor an incidental legal determination the suit produced." I am not as willing as the plurality is to assume that agencies at least will not try to follow the law. Moreover, I wonder

291

if the plurality has not overlooked the extensive involvement from the inception of this litigation by the Department of State and the Agency for International Development. Under principles of collateral estoppel, these agencies are precluded from subsequently relitigating the issues decided in this suit. . . .

. . . As a result, I believe respondents' injury would likely be redressed by a favorable decision.

The second redressability obstacle relied on by the plurality is "that the [action] agencies generally supply only a fraction of the funding for a foreign project." What this Court might "generally" take to be true does not eliminate the existence of a genuine issue of fact to withstand summary judgment. Even if the action agencies supply only a fraction of the funding for a particular foreign project, it remains at least a question for the finder of fact whether threatened withdrawal of that fraction would affect foreign government conduct sufficiently to avoid harm to listed species.

The plurality states that "AID, for example, has provided less than 10% of the funding for the Mahaweli project." The plurality neglects to mention that this "fraction" amounts to $170 million, not so paltry a sum for a country of only 16 million people with a gross national product of less than $6 billion in 1986 when respondents filed the complaint in this action. Federal Research Division, Library of Congress, Sri Lanka: A Country Study (Area Handbook Series) xvi-xvii (1990).

. . . I do not share the plurality's astonishing confidence that, on the record here, a factfinder could only conclude that AID was powerless to ensure the protection of listed species at the Mahaweli project.

As for the Aswan project, the record again rebuts the plurality's assumption that donor agencies are without any authority to protect listed species. Kelly asserted in her affidavit—and it has not been disputed—that the Bureau of Reclamation was "overseeing" the rehabilitation of the Aswan project.

I find myself unable to agree with the plurality's analysis of redressability, based as it is on its invitation of executive lawlessness, ignorance of principles of collateral estoppel, unfounded assumptions about causation, and erroneous conclusions about what the record does not say. In my view, respondents have satisfactorily shown a genuine issue of fact as to whether their injury would likely be redressed by a decision in their favor.

II

The Court concludes that any "procedural injury" suffered by respondents is insufficient to confer standing. It rejects the view that the "injury-in-fact requirement. . . . [is] satisfied by congressional conferral upon *all* persons of an abstract, self-contained, noninstrumental 'right' to have the Executive observe the procedures required by law." Whatever the Court might mean with that very broad language, it cannot be saying that "procedural injuries" *as a class* are necessarily insufficient for purposes of Article III standing.

Most governmental conduct can be classified as "procedural." Many injuries caused by governmental conduct, therefore, are categorizable at some level of generality as "procedural" injuries. Yet, these injuries are not categorically beyond the pale of redress by the federal courts. When the Government, for example, "procedurally" issues a pollution permit, those affected by the permittee's pollutants are not without standing to sue. Only later cases will tell just what the Court means by its intimation that "procedural" injuries are not constitutionally cognizable injuries. In the meantime, I have the greatest of sympathy for the courts across the country that will struggle to understand the Court's standardless exposition of this concept today.

The Court expresses concern that allowing judicial enforcement of "agencies' observance of a particular, statutorily prescribed procedure" would "transfer from the President to the courts the Chief Executive's most important constitutional duty, to 'take Care that the Laws be faithfully executed,' Art. II, sec. 3." In fact, the principal effect of foreclosing judicial enforcement of such procedures is to transfer power into the hands of the Executive at the expense—not of the courts—but of Congress, from which that power originates and emanates.

Under the Court's anachronistically formal view of the separation of powers, Congress legislates pure, substantive mandates and has no business structuring the procedural manner in which the Executive implements these mandates. To be sure, in the ordinary course, Congress does legislate in black-and-white terms of affirmative commands or negative prohibitions on the conduct of officers of the Executive Branch. In complex regulatory areas, however, Congress often legislates, as it were, in procedural shades of gray. That is, it sets forth substantive policy goals and provides for their attainment by requiring Executive Branch officials to follow certain procedures, for example, in the form of reporting, consultation, and certification requirements. . . .

The consultation requirement of §7 of the Endangered Species Act is a similar, action-forcing statute. Consultation is designed as an integral check on federal agency action, ensuring that such action does not go forward without full consideration of its effects on listed species. . . . These action-forcing procedures are "designed to protect some threatened concrete interest" of persons who observe and work with endangered or threatened species. That is why I am mystified by the Court's unsupported conclusion that "[t]his is not a case where plaintiffs are seeking to enforce a procedural requirement the disregard of which could impair a separate concrete interest of theirs."

Congress legislates in procedural shades of gray not to aggrandize its own power but to allow maximum Executive discretion in the attainment of Congress' legislative goals. Congress could simply impose a substantive prohibition on executive conduct; it could say that no agency action shall result in the loss of more than 5% of any listed species. Instead, Congress sets forth substantive guidelines and allows the Executive, within certain procedural constraints, to decide how best to effectuate the ultimate goal. The Court never has questioned Congress' authority to impose such procedural constraints on executive power. Just as Congress does not violate separation of powers by structuring the procedural manner in which the Executive shall carry out the laws, surely the federal courts do not violate separation of powers when, at the very instruction and command of Congress, they enforce these procedures. . . .

It is to be hoped that over time the Court will acknowledge that some classes of procedural duties are so enmeshed with the prevention of a substantive, concrete harm that an individual plaintiff may be able to demonstrate a sufficient likelihood of injury just through the breach of that procedural duty. For example, in the context of the NEPA requirement of environmental-impact statements, this Court has acknowledged "it is now well settled that NEPA itself does not mandate particular results [and] simply prescribes the necessary process," but "*these procedures are almost certain to affect the agency's substantive decision.*" Robertson v. Methow Valley Citizens Council, 490 U.S., 332, 350 (1989) (emphasis added). This acknowledgement of an inextricable link between procedural and substantive harm does not reflect improper appellate factfinding. It reflects nothing more than the proper deference owed to the judgment of a coordinate branch—Congress—that certain procedures are directly tied to protection against a substantive harm.

In short, determining "injury" for Article III standing purposes is a fact-specific inquiry. "Typically . . . the standing inquiry requires careful judicial examination of a complaint's allegations to ascertain whether the particular plaintiff is entitled to an adjudication of the particular claims asserted." Allen v. Wright, 468 U.S., at 752. There may be factual circumstances in which a congressionally imposed procedural requirement is so insubstantially connected to the prevention of a substantive harm that it cannot be said to work any conceivable injury to an individual litigant. But, as a general matter, the courts owe substantial deference to Congress' substantive purpose in imposing a certain procedural requirement. In all events, "[o]ur separation-of-powers analysis does not turn on the labeling of an activity as 'substantive' as opposed to 'procedural.' " Mistretta v. United States, 488 U.S. 361, 393 (1989).

There is no room for a per se rule or presumption excluding injuries labeled "procedural" in nature.

III

In conclusion, I cannot join the Court on what amounts to a slash-and-burn expedition through the law of environmental standing. In my view, "[t]he very essence of civil liberty certainly consists in the right of every individual to claim the protection of the laws, whenever he receives an injury." Marbury v. Madison, 1 Cranch 137, 163 (1803).

NOTES AND QUESTIONS

1. Does Justice Scalia's majority opinion change in any way the nature of the injury that may be asserted by environmentalists to qualify for standing? Is injury to aesthetic values, as recognized in Sierra Club v. Morton, still a cognizable interest for purposes of standing? How do Justice Scalia and Justice Blackmun differ in their views concerning what plaintiffs must demonstrate about the imminence of harm in order to establish standing?

2. In order for a plaintiff to qualify for standing, how close must the connection be in space and time between the action challenged in a lawsuit and the plaintiff's asserted injury? Does the closeness of the geographic nexus required for standing vary with the type of harm alleged? How do Justice Scalia and Justice Blackmun differ in their interpretation of Lujan v. National Wildlife Federation [parent text, p. 728]? Why does the majority reject the ecosystem, animal, and vocational nexus theories offered by Defenders? Note that two members of the majority, Justices Kennedy and Souter, indicate in their concurrence that they are more sympathetic to these theories than the majority and that it may be possible to establish standing using similar nexus claims in different circumstances.

3. Justice Kennedy states that "Congress has the power to define injuries and articulate chains of causation that will give rise to a case or controversy where none existed before. . . ." Does this mean that Congress can affect who has standing to sue by making legislative determinations of what constitutes injury and who is harmed by certain actions? Cass Sunstein argues that when Congress creates a right of action enabling people to sue over "destruction of environmental assets, it is really giving people a kind of property right in a certain state of affairs. Invasion of the property right is the relevant injury." Sunstein, What's Standing After *Lujan*? Of Citizen Suits, "Injuries," and Article

III, 91 Mich. L. Rev. 163, 191 (1992). Can Congress create procedural rights whose injury can give rise to standing? Could it give anyone bringing a citizen enforcement action a financial stake in the outcome of the suit sufficient to confer standing simply by authorizing monetary rewards for successful plaintiffs?

4. What types of "procedural injury" does Justice Scalia recognize could give rise to standing? How does he attempt to distinguish the kind of procedural injury plaintiffs allege from the kind that he believes could give rise to standing? Why must Justice Scalia concede (in footnote 7 of his opinion) that in certain circumstances some "procedural rights" can be asserted "without meeting the normal standards for redressability and immediacy"?

5. Justice Scalia suggests that separation-of-powers principles limit the constitutional authority of Congress to open the courts to citizen enforcement suits. "To permit Congress to convert the undifferentiated public interest in executive officers' compliance with the law into an 'individual right' vindicable in the courts is to permit Congress to transfer from the President to the courts the Chief Executive's most important constitutional duty, to 'take Care that the Laws be faithfully executed.'" Does this call into question the constitutionality of the citizen suit provisions of the environmental laws? See Sunstein, supra, at 165-166, 221. Professor Sunstein asks, "[I]f a court could set aside executive action at the behest of plaintiffs with a plane ticket, why does the Take Care Clause forbid it from doing so at the behest of plaintiffs without a ticket?" Id. at 213. The editors of the New York Times decried Justice Scalia's "breathtaking vision of boundless executive power" as a "distorted view of power-sharing among the branches, hazardous to the environment—and democracy." No Day in Court, N.Y. Times, June 17, 1992, at A24.

6. Justices Kennedy and Souter suggest that plaintiffs in *Lujan II* could have established standing with relatively little extra effort by making specific travel plans. In his concurring opinion, Justice Kennedy concedes that "it may seem trivial to require that [the plaintiff's members] acquire airline tickets to the project site or announce a date certain upon which they will return." Because their votes were crucial to the majority in *Lujan II*, does this statement suggest that the decision will have relatively little impact on environmental litigation, aside from encouraging environmentalists to get to know their travel agents better? What purpose is served by requiring plaintiffs to buy plane tickets? Is Justice Blackmun right that "the Court's demand for detailed descriptions of future conduct . . . will do little to weed out those who are genuinely harmed from those who are not"?

7. After *Lujan II*, how do you think the plaintiffs in Portland Audubon Society v. Oregon Lands Coalition (9th Cir. 1993) established

5. The Regulatory Process

standing to challenge the God Squad's decision exempting from the ESA timber sales that could jeopardize the continued existence of the spotted owl? Under what rationale could the Ninth Circuit distinguish *Lujan II*? In another post-*Lujan II* decision, the Ninth Circuit upheld the standing of environmental groups to defend a regulation protecting sea otters. Beck v. United States Department of Commerce, 982 F.2d 1332 (9th Cir. 1992); see also Colorado Environmental Coalition v. Lujan, 803 F. Supp. 364 (D.C. Colo. 1992), another post-*Lujan II* decision.

8. Justice Scalia has been criticized for attempting to use standing doctrine to resurrect the very kind of private law notions of proof of causal injury that made the common law a poor vehicle for protecting the environment. Note, for example, that Justice Scalia believes that it should be much easier for regulated industries to establish standing to sue than for the beneficiaries of regulation because the former are "an object of the action at issue." Justice Kennedy's concurrence reflects a greater appreciation of the consequences of the shift from common law to public law. He emphasizes that courts need to "be sensitive to the articulation of new rights of action that do not have clear analogs in our common law tradition."

9. Note that because Justices Kennedy and Souter did not join the portion of Justice Scalia's opinion (Section II-B) discussing redressability, there is no majority opinion on this issue. Cass Sunstein emphasizes that the redressability of an injury is critically dependent on how broadly the injury is characterized. Sunstein, What's Standing After *Lujan*? Of Citizen Suits, "Injuries," and Article III, 91 Mich. L. Rev. 163, 207 (1992). Thus, narrow common law conceptions of injury are far less likely to be redressable than injuries characterized as reducing the risk of more particularized injury. As a result, Professor Sunstein concludes that redressability should be viewed "as a crude device for determining whether Congress intended to confer a cause of action." Id. at 209. "We should be asking whether the injury that Congress sought to prevent would likely be redressed by a favorable judgment." Id. at 229.

10. Cass Sunstein is sharply critical of the *Lujan II* decision and much of the Supreme Court's recent approaches to standing doctrine. Sunstein, supra. Reviewing the historical development of standing doctrine, Professor Sunstein traces its difficulties to the recently invented notion that injury in fact was a critical constitutional component of standing. He argues that the key question should be "whether Congress (or some other relevant source of law) has created a cause of action." Id. at 222. To prevent *Lujan II* from undercutting citizen access to the courts, Professor Sunstein proposes that Congress either authorize bounties for successful citizen plaintiffs or expressly "create a property

interest in the various regulatory 'goods' that it wants to authorize citizens to protect" (e.g., by stating that "citizens generally have a beneficial interest in certain endangered species that are at risk from acts of the U.S. government"). Id. at 225.

Chevron *Deference and the Scope of Judicial Review (pp. 746-752).* Professor Tom Merrill has found that the Supreme Court's increasing reliance on textualism in statutory interpretation has diminished the force of the *Chevron* doctrine. Under the influence of Justice Scalia, the Court now more frequently relies on dictionaries than legislative history in interpreting statutes and *Chevron*'s "deference doctrine appears to be playing an increasingly peripheral role in the decisions even when it is mentioned." Merrill, Textualism and the Future of the *Chevron* Doctrine, 72 Wash. U. L.Q. 351, 361 (1994). For an argument that courts should place greater emphasis on step two of the *Chevron* doctrine—assessing the reasonableness of agency interpretations of statutes—see Seidenfeld, A Syncopated *Chevron*: Emphasizing Reasoned Decisionmaking in Reviewing Agency Interpretations of Statutes, 73 Tex. L. Rev. 83 (1994).

Judicial Hostility to Environmental Concerns (p. 754). In his foreword to A Symposium on the United States Supreme Court's "Environmental Term" (1991-1992), Frank Grad finds that the Court has been remarkably unsympathetic to environmental concerns. Grad cites "the Court's hostility to citizen suits; the Court's preference for executive power to defeat legislative protections of the environment; the Court's use of federal preemption to thwart sound exercises of state police power; the Court's use of commerce power to favor the interest of major waste disposal businesses against state efforts to protect both the environment and health and safety in the workplace; the Court's narrow view of standing, preventing sound cases from ever being heard; and . . . the Court's attenuated view of sovereign immunity waivers reflecting intentional obtuseness to block the recognition of clear congressional intent to allow the full enforcement of environmental law even against the federal government itself." Grad, Foreword, 43 J. Urban & Cont. L. 3, 32-33 (1993).

=6=
‖ *Air Pollution Control* ‖

[T]he 1990 Clean Air Act Amendments set the course for many current and soon-to-be-introduced environmental improvements. Mobil opposed some of that legislation, because we thought it might be too costly for the consumer. In retrospect, we were wrong. Air quality is improving, at a cost acceptable to the motoring public.

—*Mobil Corporation, Oct. 27, 1994*

If we are to clean up our air, we need to move beyond the one-size-fits-all approach and work toward flexibility and innovation—solutions that work for real people, real communities.

—*EPA Administrator Carol Browner, Feb. 9, 1995*

While implementation of the 1990 Amendments to the Clean Air Act continues to be one of EPA's greatest challenges, it is becoming apparent that the Amendments are far less costly than their opponents feared, as reflected in the statement above by the Mobil Corporation. However, looming on the horizon are efforts in the 104th Congress to repeal or modify many of the Act's requirements. The new House majority whip, Rep. Thomas A. DeLay, has introduced eight bills to amend the act, including legislation that would repeal the 1990 Amendments in their entirety. While there is little chance that all the 1990 Amendments will be repealed, state officials and representatives of industry are lobbying aggressively for administrative and legislative fixes to make compliance easier. This chapter considers these and other developments including the D.C. Circuit's invalidation of EPA's policy of conditional SIP approvals and the Ninth Circuit's refusal to let EPA off the hook for promulgating a federal implementation for Southern California. It also discusses progress implementing Title IV's emissions trading program, efforts by northeastern states to adopt the California standards option, and how the Air Act is helping stimulating the development of electric car and cleaner fuels technology.

A. THE AIR POLLUTION PROBLEM

Air Pollution Trends (pp. 759-760). Continued progress has been made in reducing emissions of criteria air pollutants. Despite this progress, 54 million people still live in areas where pollution levels exceed at least one national air quality standard, with ozone nonattainment being the primary problem. Agency Reports Decreases in Pollution, But 54 Million People Still Breathe Unhealthy Air, 24 Env. Rep. 1312 (1993).

Epidemiological studies continue to associate air pollution with serious health consequences. In March 1995 the results of the most comprehensive epidemiological study of the impact of particulates on human health were released. The study of more than 550,000 people in 151 cities from 1982-1989 found that death rates increased by 15 to 17 percent in cities with the dirtiest air when factors other than levels of particulate pollution were controlled. P. Hilts, Dirty-Air Cities Far Deadlier Than Clean Ones, Study Shows, N.Y. Times, March 10, 1995, at A20. Even in cities that were in compliance with the NAAQS for particulates, death rates were three to eight percent higher than in cities with substantially lower levels of particulates. See also Dockery, et al., An Association Between Air Pollution and Mortality in Six U.S. Cities, 329 N.E. J. Med. 1753 (1993). EPA has pledged to consider the results of this study in completing its review of the adequacy of the existing NAAQS for particulates. The agency is under a court order requiring it to complete its review of the particulates NAAQS by January 31, 1997. Agency Will Consider Particulate Study As It Moves to Revise National Standard, 25 Env. Rep. 2290 (1994).

B. THE CLEAN AIR ACT: ORIGIN AND PRINCIPLES

Air Pollution Control: A Pathfinder (pp. 762-763). A useful, detailed guide to the structure of the Clean Air Act as modified by the 1990 Amendments is a three-part series of articles that appeared in the Environmental Law Reporter from April through June 1992. Garrett and Winner, A Clean Air Act Primer: Part I, 22 Env. L. Rep. 10159 (1992) (history and structure of the Act, NAAQSs, SIPs, nonattainment); Part II, 22 Env. L. Rep. 10235 (PSD, new and modified sources, acid deposition control, NESHAPs, mobile sources); Part III, 22 Env. L. Rep. 10301

6. Air Pollution Control

(new permit program, enforcement, judicial review, protection of the stratospheric ozone layer, legislative history).

The Clean Air Act and the 104th Congress (pp. 768-769). The Republican sweep of the 1994 congressional elections has produced a Congress with a decidedly less sympathetic attitude toward the Clean Air Act. The new House majority whip, Rep. Thomas A. DeLay, was one of only 30 members of Congress who voted against the 1990 Amendments. Thus, it is not surprising that he has introduced eight bills to relax or repeal provisions of the Act, including legislation that would repeal the 1990 Amendments in their entirety. House Majority Whip Introduces Legislation to Repeal Several Portions of Clean Air Act, 25 Env. Rep. 1787 (1995). The provisions of the Act most vulnerable to amendment appear to be those dealing with mobile sources. Oversight Chairman Say Air Act Likely to Be Reopened, Amended this Congress, 25 Env. Rep. 2121 (1995).

There is a possibility that the 1990 Amendments will be repealed.

C. NATIONAL AMBIENT AIR QUALITY STANDARDS

Efforts to Force Revision of the Ozone Standard (p. 777). EPA ultimately settled the lawsuit filed in 1991 (parent text, p. 777) that sought to force the Agency to revise the ozone standard. American Lung Association v. EPA, No. 91-4114 (E.D.N.Y.). The settlement agreement required EPA to make a final decision on promulgation of a revised NAAQS for ozone by March 1, 1993. On the day of the deadline, EPA announced that it had decided not to revise the ozone standard, but that its decision was based only on review of pre-1989 studies of the health effects of exposure to ozone. The Agency did not consider more recent studies because they had yet to be incorporated into the Agency's criteria document for ozone. EPA indicated that it eventually would consider these new studies. In February 1994 the agency announced that would complete another review of the NAAQS for ozone by mid-1997. 59 Fed. Reg. 5164 (1994). Studies of long-term animal exposure to high levels of ozone, which were released in February 1995, found remarkably little evidence of either damage to lung function or an association between ozone exposure and cancer. D. Stipp, Two Ozone Studies Find Little Evidence of Lung Damage or Cancer in Rodents, Wall St. J., Feb. 3, 1995, at B10.

The SO_2 Standard (pp. 778-783). EPA's proposal not to revise the NAAQS for SO_2 was issued in part to respond to a lawsuit seeking to force revision of the standard. In Environmental Defense Fund v. Thomas, 870 F.2d 892 (2d Cir. 1989), the Second Circuit held that although a court could not force EPA to revise the standard, it could require the Agency to make a formal decision either to revise the standard or to decline to revise it. Environmental groups were particularly interested in having EPA revise the secondary NAAQS for SO_2 in order to combat acid deposition. Settlement negotiations with EPA failed, and the Agency in November 1992 was sued again for failing to revise the SO_2 standard. American Lung Association v. EPA, No. 92-5316 (E.D.N.Y.). In addition to the American Lung Association, the plaintiffs in this new lawsuit included the states of Maine and New Jersey. The plaintiffs were particularly concerned about the effect of short-term exposure to SO_2 on asthmatics. In response to the lawsuit, a court ordered EPA to decide whether to revise the sulfur dioxide standard by April 1, 1994. In February 1994 EPA asked for a seven-month extension of the deadline to November 1, 1994. The court granted EPA the extension. In November, EPA again proposed not to revise the 24-hour standard, but it proposed three alternatives for protecting asthmatics from short-term peak exposures: (1) a five-minute standard of 0.60 parts per million, (2) a new state-administered regulatory program under §303 of the Act, which provides EPA with emergency powers, that would be triggered by exceedances of 0.60 ppm over a five-minute period, and (3) enhanced monitoring and enforcement of existing standards against sources likely to produce high five-minute concentrations of sulfur dioxide. 59 Fed. Reg. 58,958 (1994). A study released in January 1995 found that deaths from asthma have increased 40 percent since 1982. Forty Percent Rise Reported in Asthma and Asthma Deaths, N.Y. Times, Jan. 7, 1995, at 10.

Revisions of Other NAAQSs (p. 783). In August 1994 EPA announced that it would not revise the national ambient air quality standard (NAAQS) for carbon monoxide. 59 Fed. Reg. 38,906 (1994). In December 1994 the Clean Air Act Scientific Advisory Committee accepted a recommendation by EPA staff that there be no revision in the current NAAQS for nitrogen oxides. Advisory Panel Back Staff Recommendation on Retaining Current Nitrogen Oxide Standard, 25 Env. Rep. 1652 (1994). EPA is under a court-ordered deadline to complete its review of the PM-10 NAAQS by January 31, 1997.

D. STATE IMPLEMENTATION PLANS

In April 1992, EPA issued regulations outlining how the Agency plans to implement the requirements of the 1990 Amendments for new

6. Air Pollution Control   Pages 791-792

and revised state implementation plans (SIPs). 57 Fed. Reg. 13,498 (1992). The regulations focus largely on how the Agency will review SIP submissions for nonattainment areas and the requirements for review of new and modified sources in such areas. In November 1992, EPA supplemented these regulations with new controls on nitrogen oxide. 57 Fed. Reg. 55,620 (1992). The problems states are having in developing acceptable SIP revisions to comply with the 1990 Amendments are discussed in Section E below.

The Clean Air Act's National Permit System (pp. 791-792). After a bitter battle between EPA and the Competitiveness Council (see pp. 182-183 of this Supplement), regulations to implement the Clean Air Act's new national permit system were issued by EPA. 57 Fed. Reg. 32,250 (1992). States were required to submit proposed permit programs to EPA by November 15, 1993, and EPA had up to a year to approve or disapprove state programs. Many states missed these deadlines. Permit applications must be submitted by sources within a year after EPA approval of the program. EPA's permit regulations are being challenged in court by several states, environmental groups, and affected industries. Clean Air Implementation Project v. EPA, No. 92-1303 and consolidated cases (D.C. Circuit). EPA's permit regulations are reviewed in Novello, The New Clean Air Act Operating Permit Program: EPA's Final Rules, 23 Env. L. Rep. 10080 (1993). In August 1994 EPA issued proposed revisions to its permit regulations in response to concerns raised in the litigation. 59 Fed. Reg. 44,460 (1994).

One issue that is likely to be of importance for citizen participation in the permit process is the requirement that states provide an opportunity for judicial review in state courts of final permit actions by "any person who participated in the public comment process." This provision, which is found in section 70.4(b)(3)(x) of the permit regulations, is expressly required by section 502(b)(6) of the Act. Because many states restrict standing to sue to a narrower class of persons than federal law, see, e.g., Medical Waste Associates, Inc. v. Maryland Waste Coalition, Inc., 612 A.2d 241 (Md. 1992), state standing doctrine may have to be relaxed in order for certain states to qualify to administer the operating permit program of the federal Clean Air Act. In November 1994 EPA disapproved Virginia's operating permits program because it failed to provide adequate citizen access to judicial review of final permit decisions. Under Virginia law, only persons who can demonstrate an "immediate, pecuniary, and substantial interest" in permit decisions may seek judicial review. Virginia Operating Permit Plan Rejected on Basis of State Statute Limiting Lawsuits, 25 Env. Rep. 1559 (1994). In January 1995 Virginia sued EPA, alleging that the requirement that citizen access to courts be broadened was an unconstitutional condition infringing on state sovereignty in violation of the Tenth Amendment. Virginia Seeks to Block Federal Sanctions for Failure to Meet Clean Air Act Provisions, 25 Env. Rep. 1797 (1995).

As a result of inflation, EPA has increased the presumptive $25 per ton emissions fee that states are required to charge major sources for operating permits to $28.39 per ton. Emission Fees Rise to $28.39 Per Ton, EPA Says in Guidance on Operating Permits, 23 Env. Rep. 2252 (1993). Section 502(b)(3)(B)(v) of the Act requires EPA to adjust the emissions fee annually to track changes in the Consumer Price Index.

E. THE NONATTAINMENT PROBLEM

Air Quality Trends: A Clean Air Report Card (pp. 792-795). As noted above, continued progress was made in 1992 toward reducing ambient levels of criteria pollutants. In 1991 forty-one additional cities came into attainment with the ozone standard, based on statistics from the 1989-1991 period, though much of this progress was attributed to substituting the cooler weather that prevailed during the summer of 1991 for the hot summer of 1988 in the three-year averaging period for determining compliance. Gutfeld, In Many Areas, There's Improvement in the Air, Wall St. J., Oct. 16, 1992, at B1. Thirteen cities attained the NAAQS for carbon monoxide for the first time in 1991. A total of 56 cities violated the ozone NAAQS in 1991, while 29 cities violated the carbon monoxide NAAQS. Air Found Cleaner in 41 U.S. Cities, N.Y. Times, Oct. 20, 1992, at A24.

A FIP for the South Coast Basin (pp. 807-810). Even as it was urging Congress expressly to exempt it from its obligation to promulgate a federal implementation plan (FIP) for the South Coast Air Basin, EPA agreed to issue a proposed FIP as part of a settlement agreement with the Sierra Club and the Coalition for Clean Air in March 1989. The settlement required EPA to issue the FIP by April 30, 1990 and to take final action on the proposal by February 28, 1991. Even though EPA did not obtain the legislative relief it sought, the Agency sought to vacate the settlement agreement after the 1990 Clean Air Act Amendments were enacted. In Coalition for Clean Air v. Southern California Edison Co., 971 F.2d 219 (9th Cir. 1992), the Ninth Circuit held that the 1990 Amendments had not relieved EPA of its obligation to promulgate FIPs.

In dissent, Judge Noonan argued that the text of the 1990 Amend-

6. Air Pollution Control   Pages 807-810

ments clearly repealed EPA's previous obligation to prepare a FIP, and concluded his dissent with the following observation:

> There is no one, I suppose, who does not desire a cleaner, brighter, healthier South Coast. Attainment of that goal, however, is not without substantial costs. The conflict that the costs have caused is reflected in the actions of EPA and in the congressional legislation. . . . [E]ven if the courts could supply what the Coalition sees as the missing will in the agency, the court cannot supply a will that is not present in the legislation. In a major economic and political battle Congress has chosen the path of slow progress. It is not the task of judges to produce a different rate of attainment.

971 F.2d at 234 (Noonan, J., dissenting).

In a somewhat different context, the Second Circuit has held that the 1990 Amendments did relax an obligation contained in a SIP to take measures to meet a December 31, 1987 compliance deadline. In Coalition Against Columbus Center v. City of New York, 967 F.2d 764 (2d Cir. 1992), the court held that a commitment in a SIP to implement "mitigating measures" when an environmental impact statement finds that a proposed project would exacerbate a violation of a NAAQS was "an emissions standard or limitation" enforceable in a citizen suit under section 304(a)(1) of the Clean Air Act. However, the court then determined that because the commitment required implementation of such measures "so as to provide for attainment of the standard by December 31, 1987," the 1990 Amendments effectively extended the deadline for the commitment to achieve attainment to 1995. While the savings clause in section 110(n)(1) provides that provisions in existing SIPs "shall remain in effect," the court found that the very generality of the commitment at issue warranted finding that the deadline had been extended. The court explained that "Congress wanted citizens to be able to sue to enforce all SIP obligations relating to an emission standard or limitation, save only those that are . . . in effect an obligation to enforce the NAAQS." Id. at 773.

The Ninth Circuit also required EPA to prepare a FIP for the Sacramento, California area. Environmental Council of Sacramento, Inc. v. EPA, No. 92-15293 (9th Cir. 1992). EPA sought review of both of the Ninth Circuit's decisions in the U.S. Supreme Court. In February 1993, the Court denied review. This did not surprise Mark Abramowitz, who started the entire FIP process when he brought a citizen suit (parent text, pp. 809-810) and who is now working as a consultant. "It was clear to all of us that this was just EPA's recipe for another delay." High Court Denies Review of FIP Cases, Forcing EPA to Prepare California Plans, 23 Env. Rep. 2830, 2831 (1993).

Having lost in court, EPA in February 1994 proposed FIPs for three areas of California: Ventura County, the South Coast air basin, and the Sacramento area. Federal Implementation Plans Proposed by EPA for Los Angeles, Sacramento, Ventura Air Basins, 24 Env. Rep. 1780 (1994). The FIPs included several measures to reduce emissions of volatile organic compounds, including greater controls on leaks from piping at petroleum facilities, improved vapor recovery devices at service stations, and requirements that the VOC content in coatings and paints be reduced. The FIPs also proposed an enhanced vehicle inspection and maintenance program and requirements that businesses that provide free parking spaces to more than 25 employees offer cash or a transit voucher as an alternative. Among the provisions of the proposed FIPs that generated fierce opposition were proposals to require "no-drive days" and to charge fees for marine vessels and port operations and to limit strictly emissions from commercial airliners.

Faced with fierce opposition from business interests and state officials, EPA in January 1995 reached a settlement with environmentalists that delayed implementation of the FIPs for two years in order to give the state time to complete its own plans. EPA preapproved elements of the state's most recent SIP, while dropping some of the most controversial elements of the FIP, which was adopted in final form to serve as a backup plan. The new compliance deadline will be May 15, 1997. Two-Year Rule Delay in Federal Proposal Allows Time for Approval of State's Plan, 25 Env. Rep. 2134 (1995). The executive director of the Coalition for Clean Air explained that "[t]he FIP has become a symbol. We need to get back to the real issues that need to be solved, and we hope EPA and the state have the willingness to address those issues." Judge Says State May Not Delay FIPs But Can Put Off Regulations Two Years, 25 Env. Rep. 1920 (1995).

The SCAQMD's RECLAIM Program (p. 810). The incorporation of emissions trading in a state implementation plan is being tested in Southern California. In February 1995, EPA conditionally approved the Regional Clean Air Incentive Market, known as RECLAIM, which allows trading among facilities emitting more than four tons per year of nitrogen oxide or sulfur oxide. 60 Fed. Reg. 10,819 (1995). Facilities in the program are given emissions limits that are reduced by eight percent per year. Approximately 390 facilities are participating in the program's nitrogen dioxide market, while 40 facilities participate in the sulfur dioxide market. At an auction held in August 1994, more than 114,000 NOx allowances were sold at prices ranging from $334/ton for 1995 to $2,090/ton for the year 2003. Sulfur oxide allowances were sold at prices of $1,500/ton for 1995 and $1,900 for 1996. Emissions Credits

6. Air Pollution Control   Pages 810-814

Traded by Companies at RECLAIM Auction in Southern California, 25 Env. Rep. 717 (1994).

Facilities can comply either by reducing emissions or by purchasing emissions reduction credits on the open market. Agreeing on baseline emissions levels for sources proved to be the most difficult aspect of establishing the RECLAIM program. As one official notes, "[e]verybody wants to use a formula that naturally most advantages them." However, "if you let each [source] pick the most advantageous number," then the amount of allowable pollution will be "a lot more than what is being put into the air." Emission Baselines, Monitoring Critical to Success of Trading Program, Official Says, 24 Env. Rep. 18 (1993). For a description of the program see D. Selmi, Transforming Economic Incentives From Theory to Reality: The Marketable Permit Program of the South Coast Air Quality Management District, 24 Envtl. L. Rep. 10,695 (1994).

Illinois is developing a trading program for volatile organic compounds (VOCs). The program, called the Illinois Clean Air Market, is scheduled to begin operation in 1997. Nearly 300 stationary sources with annual VOC emissions of 10 tons or more (accounting for almost 90 percent of all VOC emissions) will be granted tradeable emissions allowances based on historical levels of emissions. New State VOC Emissions Trading Program Expected to Cut Ozone, Encourage Compliance, 25 Env. Rep. 2252 (1995). Permissible emissions levels will be lowered annually until they are at a level of 60 percent reduction in 2007. Smaller sources emitting 5 to 10 tons of VOCs per year will be allowed to participate in the program. Passell, Illinois Is Looking to Market Forces to Help Reduce Its Smog, N.Y. Times, Mar. 30, 1995, at D2.

Nonattainment, SIP Revisions, and the 1990 Amendments (pp. 810-814). The 1990 Amendments required states in serious or severe nonattainment areas to submit revised SIPs by November 15, 1992. These SIPs were to include enhanced vehicle inspection and maintenance (I/M) programs and the application of reasonably available control technology (RACT) for stationary sources of nitrogen oxide. EPA was nearly a year late in issuing guidance for the I/M plans, which the agency produced only ten days before the deadline for submitting revised SIPs. To give the states more time to develop revised SIPs, EPA announced that it would conditionally approve SIPs that promised to adopt adequate measures within a year. Conditional approval of SIPs had been authorized by §110(k)(4) of the Act, which was added by the 1990 Amendments. Arguing that EPA had acted illegally, the Natural Resources Defense Council brought suit, which produced the following decision.

Natural Resources Defense Council, Inc. v. EPA
22 F.3d 1125 (D.C. Cir. 1994)

Before MIKVA, Chief Judge, WALD and HENDERSON, Circuit Judges.
Opinion for the court filed PER CURIAM.
PER CURIAM Opinion:

The petitioners seek review of decisions of the Environmental Protection Agency ("EPA") implementing the 1990 Amendments to the Clean Air Act ("CAA"), 42 U.S.C. §§7401 et seq. First, petitioner Natural Resources Defense Council, Inc. ("NRDC") challenges the EPA's policy of permitting conditional approval of committal state implementation plan ("SIP") submissions. In addition, all petitioners challenge substantive agency decisions in the EPA's final rule on vehicle inspection and maintenance programs ("I/M"). . . .

I. CONDITIONAL APPROVAL OF SIPS

First, the NRDC challenges the EPA's use of a "conditional approval" procedure, under §110(k)(4) of the 1990 Amendments, Pub. L. No. 101-549, tit. I, §110(k)(4), 104 Stat. 2399, 2407 (codified at 42 U.S.C. §7410(k)(4)), to permit states to comply with statutory SIP deadlines by submitting "committal" SIPs that contain no specific remedial measures but merely promise to adopt such measures within a year. The NRDC contends this procedure is contrary to congressional intent and has impermissibly postponed the statutory deadlines for the affected SIP submittals. To remedy the delay caused by the EPA's conditional approval procedure, the NRDC asks that we require prompt submission and review of all overdue SIPs and immediate imposition of statutory sanctions on states that have not submitted adequate SIPs as of July 15, 1994. While we hold that the EPA misconstrued and misapplied §110(k)(4), we nevertheless conclude that equity and practicality require that we approve the extensions in part and that we adopt more moderate remedial measures, as set out below.

Since it was amended in 1970, the CAA has required states to adopt, after reasonable notice and public hearings and approval by the EPA, SIPs designed to attain and maintain "national ambient air quality standards" ("NAAQS"). See 42 U.S.C. §7410(a)(2)(A) (added by Pub. L. No. 91-604, §4(a), 84 Stat. 1980 (1970)). Not until 1990, however, did Congress establish specific deadlines for submitting SIPs and SIP

6. Air Pollution Control

revisions. As amended in 1990, the CAA now requires states encompassing "nonattainment" areas to submit particular SIPs or SIP revisions by fixed deadlines. Two of the deadlines are significant here: (1) November 15, 1990, the date on which the Amendments took effect and "immediately after" which date states were required thereunder to submit "basic" I/M submissions, see 42 U.S.C. §7511a(a)(2)(B)(i), (b)(4), and (2) November 15, 1992, the date by which states were required to submit SIPs addressing enhanced I/M, see id. §7511a(c)(3), and application of "reasonably available control technology" ("RACT") to stationary emission sources of nitrogen oxides ("NOx"), see id. §7511a(b)(2), (f). . . .

The 1990 CAA Amendments also established statutory teeth to enforce the new SIP deadlines. Initially, §110(k)(1)(B) requires the EPA to make a finding that the submittal is complete or incomplete within two months of submission or six months of the submission deadline. Id. §7410(k)(1)(B). If the EPA determines a submittal is incomplete, it is deemed not to have been made. Id. §7410(k)(1)(C). If the EPA finds the submittal complete, the agency has 12 months to approve, disapprove (in part or whole) or conditionally approve the submittal. Id. §7410(k)(2)-(4).[8] At any time after the EPA makes a whole or partial disapproval or an incompleteness finding, it "may apply" the two sanctions set out in 42 U.S.C. §7509(b), namely, withholding approval of highway projects and grants and imposing stricter permit requirements for new emission sources. Id. §7410(m). If a state fails to correct a deficiency within 18 months after a disapproval or finding of failure to submit, the EPA is *required* to impose one of the statutory sanctions. 42 U.S.C. §7509(a). Further, unless a complete SIP is approved within two years after such disapproval or finding, the state will be subject to an EPA-promulgated Federal Implementation Plan. 42 U.S.C. §7410(c)(1).

Although the statutory scheme set out above provides the EPA with clear submission and sanction schedules, the agency nevertheless strayed from Congress's directions in two relevant respects. First, the EPA waited until November 5, 1992 to publish the enhanced I/M guidance required under the Amendments to be provided no later than November 15, 1991. Second, in part to compensate for its dilatory promulgation of that guidance, the EPA decided to invoke the CAA conditional approval provision to afford states additional time, beyond the statutory submission deadlines, to develop and

---

8. If the EPA fails to make any determination at all within six months of submission, the submittal is deemed complete by operation of law. 42 U.S.C. §7410(k)(1)(B).

submit some of the required SIPs, notably here, those relating to I/M and NOx RACT.

The EPA first indicated its intent to permit conditional approval of the I/M submittals, both basic and enhanced, in its April 16, 1992 "General Preamble for the Implementation of Title I of the Clean Air Act Amendments of 1990" ("General Preamble"), 57 Fed. Reg. 13,498 (April 16, 1992).... The EPA later confirmed its intent to conditionally approve the I/M, as well as other, submittals in a memorandum to regional EPA directors dated July 22, 1992 ("Shapiro Memorandum") and in an August 26, 1992 letter to the NRDC ("Rosenberg Letter"). Subsequently, in a final rule on "Inspection/Maintenance Program Requirements," 57 Fed. Reg. 52,950, 52,970-52,971 (Nov. 5, 1992), the EPA codified the conditional approval policy for enhanced I/M submissions.... The NRDC filed three petitions challenging the EPA's conditional approval policy as set out in the Shapiro Memorandum and the Rosenberg Letter and as specifically applied in the NOx Supplement and the I/M Rule....

The Committal SIP Policy

Next, we address the merits of the EPA's construction of the conditional approval provision. We review the agency's construction of the provision under the framework set forth in Chevron USA, Inc. v. NRDC, 467 U.S. 837 (1984). NRDC v. Reilly, 976 F.2d 36, 40-41 (D.C. Cir. 1992). Given the express language of §110(k)(4), the CAA's general SIP approval scheme and the legislative history, we conclude the EPA's construction of the conditional approval provision is contrary to Congress's unambiguous intent and must therefore be rejected. Cf. id. (denying deference to and rejecting EPA construction of CAA which "both the language and the purpose of the Act and the 1990 Amendments preclude.").

Section 110(k)(4) provides:

(4) Conditional approval

The Administrator may approve a plan revision based on a commitment of the State to adopt specific enforceable measures by a date certain, but not later than 1 year after the date of approval of the plan revision. Any such conditional approval shall be treated as a disapproval if the State fails to comply with such commitment.

42 U.S.C. §7410(k)(4). The EPA has construed this provision to authorize conditional approval of a committal SIP that contains no specific

6. Air Pollution Control   Pages 810-814

substantive measures so long as it is submitted by one of the statutory deadlines and includes (1) a promise to adopt specific enforceable measures within a year and (2) a schedule of "interim milestones" in this future adoption process. . . . We believe the EPA's position reflects a strained construction of the statutory language. On its face, that language seems to authorize conditional approval of a substantive SIP or SIP revision which, although not approvable in its present form, can be made so by adopting specific EPA-required changes within the prescribed conditional period.

The statutory scheme confirms our interpretation of the statutory language. As already noted, the 1990 Amendments require that the EPA determine the completeness of each submission, that is, whether it contains "the information necessary to enable the Administrator to determine whether the plan submission complies with the provisions of [the CAA]," "within 60 days of the Administrator's receipt of a plan or plan revision, but no later than 6 months after the date, if any, by which a State is required to submit the plan or revision." 42 U.S.C. §7410(k)(1). Such a determination cannot reasonably be made unless the conditionally approved submittal contains something more than a mere promise to take appropriate but unidentified measures in the future. In addition, the statute appears to require that the *conditional* approval decision, like any approval or disapproval determination, be made within 12 months after the completeness finding, see 42 U.S.C. §7410(k)(2), (3), (4), which, as we noted, must follow the submission. In short, the CAA contemplates the following schedule: (1) submission of a SIP, (2) followed by a finding, within two to six months, that the SIP is complete, and (3) approval (whether absolute, partial, or conditional) or disapproval within 12 months thereafter. To permit conditional approval at the time of initial submission, without any completeness determination or substantive review, would turn the statutory timetable on its head.

Finally, our construction of §110(k)(4) is bolstered by the House Report on the 1990 Amendments, which explains that "section 110(k)(4) authorizes conditional approval of a SIP where the State commits to adopt such specific enforceable *additional* measures as EPA requires within one additional year," H.R. Rep. No. 490, 101st Cong., 2d Sess., pt. 1 at 220 (1990) (emphasis added). That the contemplated specific and enforceable measures are to be "additional" presupposes that the SIP already contains some specific enforceable measures before it can be conditionally approved.

For the preceding reasons, we conclude that the conditional approval mechanism was intended to provide the EPA with an alternative to disapproving substantive, but not entirely satisfactory, SIPs submitted by the statutory deadlines and not, as the EPA has used it, a means of circumventing those deadlines. Accordingly, we hold that §110(k)(4) does not authorize the EPA to use committal SIPs to postpone SIP deadlines. We must nevertheless decide whether the one-year extensions of the I/M and NOx RACT submission deadlines, which the EPA's conditional approval policy effected, can be sustained on some other basis. We conclude that the extension of the enhanced I/M and the NOx RACT deadlines can be upheld as necessary and appropriate under the particular circumstances here but that the basic I/M extension was entirely unjustified. . . .

Having concluded that the EPA properly extended the statutory enhanced I/M and NOx RACT deadlines, but not the basic I/M deadline, we must now consider what if any remedial measures to adopt. The NRDC asks that we take a strict approach and require the EPA to make immediate findings of noncompliance for all states that failed to meet the statutory deadlines, to approve or disapprove the submissions it has received within 120-180 days, and immediately thereafter to impose the statutory sanctions on those states that have not submitted fully approved SIPs. We believe the circumstances call for a less drastic remedy.

First, because the EPA, by ignoring the statutory deadline for promulgating guidance, was responsible for the tardy submission of enhanced I/M SIPs, we conclude that the EPA should be required to compensate for the delays it caused by accelerating its review of those submittals. It is for this reason that we have already ordered the EPA to propose either approval or disapproval of SIPs it has received no later than July 15, 1994 and to finally approve or disapprove them no later than September 15, 1994. See Amended Order, No. 92-1596 (filed April 22, 1994). On the other hand, we think it would be unfair to penalize states that reasonably relied on and complied with the EPA's extended deadlines by similarly accelerating the statutory sanction scheme. Accordingly, we direct that the sanction clock for I/M SIPs start, if necessary, from the time of SIP disapproval in accordance with the statutory scheme.

As for the NOx RACT SIPs, we find it undesirable to shorten the SIP review time for two reasons. First, the reason for extending the NOx RACT deadline was outside the EPA's control. As we explained above, some states simply needed more time for further grid modeling. Second, and more importantly, it is likely that the EPA will require the full statutory review period to make the necessary individual determinations whether each state granted a NOx RACT extension qualifies for any of the §182(f)(1) exemptions. Accordingly, we leave intact the NOx RACT timetable, under which the EPA must approve or disapprove submittals no later than May 15, 1995.

In summary, we hold that (1) the EPA's use of "committal" SIPs

6. Air Pollution Control   Pages 810-814

to extend the statutory submission deadlines is without statutory authority, (2) under the circumstances here the enhanced I/M and the NOx RACT deadlines were properly extended to further the CAA's purposes, (3) July 15, 1994 should be treated as the deadline for EPA approval or disapproval of basic and enhanced I/M submittals, with the statutory sanction clock running from that time, and (4) the statutory period for reviewing NOx RACT submittals should commence as of the extended submittal deadline of November 15, 1993, expiring 14-18 months as the Amendments require.

NOTES AND QUESTIONS

1. As the court notes, the 1990 Amendments added section 179 to the Clean Air Act, which requires EPA to impose sanctions on states that fail to rectify deficiencies in their SIP submissions within 18 months. In August 1994 EPA adopted final rules outlining the order in which sanctions would be imposed under section 179. 59 Fed. Reg. 39,832 (1994). EPA will require an increased emissions offset ratio of at least 2:1 in nonattainment areas 18 months after a finding of noncompliance and it will impose a ban on federal highway funds 24 months after such a finding. EPA also has the authority under section 110(m) to impose sanctions immediately after it determines that a state's SIP submission is inadequate. In January 1994 EPA issued a final rule outlining the criteria it will consider in using this authority, 59 Fed. Reg. 1476 (1994), which is conditioned by a requirement that sanctions not be applied on a statewide basis if one or more localities are principally responsible for the SIP's deficiency.

2. In an effort to give states more time to develop acceptable SIPs for ozone attainment, EPA announced in September 1994 that it would conditionally approve SIPs that contained commitments for measures that would produce at least 80 percent of the emissions reductions needed to attain the standard. After environmentalists sued the agency, EPA agreed to drop the policy. In February 1995 EPA announced a new policy designed to give states more flexibility in meeting ozone reduction deadlines in SIPs. New Policy Gives States Flexibility in Pursuing Implementation Plan Deadlines, 25 Env. Rep. 1919 (1995). While requiring states to continue making "reasonable further progress," the policy provides more time to states that convince EPA they are trying hard to deliver on their commitments.

3. Only a few states met the November 1994 deadline for submitting revising SIPs for the 44 serious, severe, or extreme ozone nonattainment areas. Among the reasons cited by states for missing the deadline were problems with regional transport of ozone, with modelling, and

with identifying sources of emissions reductions. Most Nonattainment Areas Miss EPA Deadline for Submitting Clean Air Act Attainment Plans, 25 Env. Rep. 1374 (1994). Environmentalists maintain that of the 35 states with ozone nonattainment areas, ten have made little or no progress, 17 are "proceeding cautiously," and eight have made significant progress. Action Needed to Force States to Comply with Clean Air Act Amendments, Groups Say, 25 Env. Rep. 1373 (1994).

4. In a portion of the decision not reproduced above, the court agreed with NRDC that the enhanced I/M program must include both emissions testing and a visual inspection for evidence of tampering or misfueling. The court also rejected a claim by automobile dealers that the model I/M program in EPA's guidance was unlawfully biased against decentralized testing and repair stations. EPA's requirements for I/M programs have been the subject of considerable controversy. The agency adopted rules that require separate testing and repair facilities and that virtually require centralized testing. 57 Fed. Reg. 52,950 (1992). After California and two other states refused to adopt such a program, EPA threatened to impose discretionary sanctions. Following the January 1994 earthquake in southern California, EPA announced that it would not impose such sanctions. Two months later the agency agreed to let California establish a "hybrid" I/M program that would not require separation of test and repair facilities. This touched off a parade of other states announcing that they would defy EPA. In response, EPA has promised more flexible rules that may require centralized testing only for the oldest and dirtiest vehicles, while permitting cars that fail centralized tests to be retested and repaired at neighborhood service stations. M. Wald, EPA to Allow Flexibility in Auto Emission Testing, N.Y. Times, Dec. 10, 1994, at 8. Arguing that the Clean Air Act violates the Tenth Amendment, Virginia is currently suing EPA to prevent enforcement of I/M program requirements, Verhovek, Texas Joins Parade of States Colliding with Clean Air Act, N.Y. Times, Feb. 14, 1995, at A1. Environmental and public health groups are suing EPA to require that sanctions be imposed upon Virginia. Cohn, Sierra Club, Health Group Sue EPA over Virginia Emissions Program, Wash. Post, Sept. 14, 1994, at D5. This experience is described in Dwyer, The Practice of Federalism Under the Clean Air Act, 54 Md. L. Rev. — (1995).

5. Mindful of the new political climate in Congress in the wake of the Republican sweep of the 1994 elections, state officials are pressing EPA for a variety of changes to relax SIP requirements. Among the changes they are seeking are a two-year moratorium on sanctions for missing SIP deadlines, a rollback of enhanced I/M requirements, and a repeal of mandatory trip reduction programs for certain areas. Moratorium on Sanction Under Clean Air Act Among Dozens of EPA Actions Sought by States, 25 Env. Rep. 1827 (1995). While EPA reportedly has

6. Air Pollution Control   Pages 824-825

rejected the two-year moratorium on sanctions, the agency has promised to develop far more flexible requirements for state I/M programs. States, EPA Moving Forward on Initiatives to Add Flexibility to Clean Air Act Rules, 25 Env. Rep. 1860 (1995). EPA also has announced that it will not sanction states for failure to implement and enforce trip reduction programs. State Must Enforce Trip-Reduction Plans, But EPA Says It Will Not Impose Sanctions, 25 Env. Rep. 1862 (1995).

6. The question of whether a state may make its SIP commitments conditional on obtaining funding was presented in Trustees for Alaska v. Fink, 17 F.3d 1209 (9th Cir. 1994). An environmental group sued the city of Anchorage, Alaska after it failed to expand its mass transit bus fleet as provided in Alaska's SIP. The Ninth Circuit held that Alaska had conditioned, and could legally condition, its commitment to expanding mass transit on finding the necessary funding to implement such a measure. Noting that there was no showing that Anchorage had failed to pursue state and federal grants, the court held that Alaska had not violated the Clean Air Act.

F. INTERSTATE AIR POLLUTION

The Acid Deposition Problem (pp. 820-821). In September 1992 the Nissan Motor Company announced that 11,000 new cars and trucks had been damaged by acid rain while sitting in a lot near the company's Smyrna, Tennessee plant. As a result, Nissan had to sell the vehicles as used cars at a substantial discount. The company stated that acid rain had caused the paint on the cars to look uneven in the past, but that this was the first time the damage had been so widespread. Nissan Will Sell Vehicles Damaged by Acid Rain, Wall St. J., Sept. 29, 1992, at B7.

The Acid Rain Control Program (pp. 824-825). Shortly before the Bush Administration left office, EPA issued the final regulations establishing the core framework of the acid rain control program mandated in Title IV of the 1990 Amendments. 58 Fed. Reg. 3590 (1993). The regulations implement the Act's requirements for a two-phased reduction in sulfur dioxide emissions to a level 10 million tons per year below 1980 levels. They incorporate the Amendments' emissions trading program and adopt final allocations of emissions allowances for the power plants subject to Phase I of the reduction program. The regulations implement the Act's mandate for continuous emissions monitoring with quarterly reporting to EPA. EPA also has proposed regulations to implement the Amendments' nitrogen oxide emissions limits.

Even before the core acid rain rules had been issued, EPA had been sued by a utility seeking to compel the Agency to process an application under section 404(d)(1) for a compliance extension and bonus emissions allowances. In Monongahela Power Co. v. Reilly, 980 F.2d 272 (4th Cir. 1992), the Fourth Circuit held that EPA was not required to process such applications until after the acid rain regulations had been issued. In Madison Gas & Electric Co. v. EPA, 25 F.3d 526 (7th Cir. 1994), the Seventh Circuit directed EPA to reconsider its allocation of emissions allowances to two utilities on the ground that EPA had failed to apply properly the allocation formula provided by section 405 of the Act.

EPA made revisions to its core rules governing Title IV's acid rain control program in November 1994. 59 Fed. Reg. 60,218 (1994). The revisions were a product of a settlement reached in May between EPA and representatives of electric utilities and environmental groups. Environmentalists had complained that EPA's previous regulations had made it possible for utilities to obtain emissions allowances in excess of what Congress had intended. In March 1994 EPA issued rules under section 407 of the Clean Air Act to limit emissions of nitrogen oxides from coal-fired powerplants. These rules were struck down by the D.C. Circuit in November 1994. Alabama Power Co. v. EPA, 40 F.3d 450 (D.C. Cir. 1994). The court ruled that EPA had adopted an unreasonably stringent emissions control technology when it sought to require utilities to use overfire air technology to control NOx.

The Emissions Trading Program: An Update (pp. 825-832). As of Spring 1995, the hoped-for market in pollution allowances was beginning to gain some momentum after a relatively slow start. A few private sales between individual utility companies had been announced, and most were accompanied by some controversy. In May 1992, the Tennessee Valley Authority (TVA) and Wisconsin Power & Light (WPL) made the first public announcement of an allowance purchase, with TVA buying 10,000 allowances per year from WPL to meet the January 1, 1995 Phase I requirements. The sale price was not disclosed, but informed sources put it at between $250 and $400 per allowance—substantially lower than the price initially anticipated. Some environmentalists protested the sale, condemning the transaction as "licensing pollution." In June 1992, Alcoa became the first non-utility to "opt in" to the emissions trading program. It sold 5,000 allowances per year for five years to Ohio Edison Co. for approximately $7.5 million, or about $300 per allowance.

Then, in January 1993, Long Island Lighting Company (LILCO) announced plans to sell allowances to an undisclosed company. Critics charged that utility companies should not be able to make such un-

6. Air Pollution Control   Pages 825-832

regulated, undisclosed sales, because such transactions might reduce pollution from LILCO's stacks—which usually drifts out over the Atlantic—while permitting pollution to continue from stacks upwind of New York, from states such as Ohio, and thus continue the ill effects of acid deposition over New York. State legislators in Albany responded by introducing legislation that would require New York utilities to disclose the purchasers in such transactions and to prepare environmental impact statements on those transactions.

Supporters of the trading program worried that such reactions by states would unnecessarily burden the free market in allowances. A spokesperson for the Environmental Defense Fund, an environmental organization supporting the trading program, said that trying to determine the environmental impact of a pollution trade would be futile. "Atmospheric chemistry doesn't allow you to know that emissions . . . from Plant A are going to fall on Area B. Believe me, we tried." United Press International, Inc., Feb. 10, 1993.

An EPA spokesperson also contended that the Adirondacks would benefit substantially from the overall reductions to be achieved under the 1990 provisions, even if individual trades might arguably fail to improve the region's air quality. This is because the midwest, which is thought to be the major source of Adirondacks acid deposition, produces about one-half of the total sulfur dioxide emissions covered by the acid deposition program. Achieving the major reductions in that overall total, as required by the Act, will necessarily require midwest utilities to cut their emissions substantially. For one thing, the rest of the nation simply could not produce enough credits for midwestern utilities to avoid emissions reductions. In addition, the older, coal-burning power plants of the midwest are so dirty now that they can achieve substantial reductions by installing even the most basic pollution control equipment, thus making it likely that they will be net sellers of allowances to utilities elsewhere, who can only reduce through more expensive compliance options, and thus will be interested in acquiring allowances on the open market. Dao, A New, Unregulated Market: Selling the Right to Pollute, N.Y. Times, Feb. 6, 1993, at A1.

A trade between utilities at opposite ends of the country that did not cause environmental concerns was announced in November 1994. An Arizona utility, Arizona Public Service, traded 25,000 allowances to emit sulfur dioxide to a utility in upstate New York, the Niagara Mohawk Power Corporation. Niagara Mohawk agreed to donate the allowances to an environmental group that would retire them unused, enabling the utility to take a $3.75 million tax deduction. Niagara Mohawk promised to use the money saved from the tax deduction (approximately $1 million) to fund projects to reduce emissions of greenhouse gases by 1.75 million tons. Niagara will transfer credit for such reductions to

317

Arizona Public Service to help that corporation satisfy its voluntary commitment to reduce carbon dioxide emissions. Passell, For Utilities, New Clean-Air Plan, N.Y. Times, Nov. 18, 1994, at D1. The commitment was part of the Climate Challenge Accord signed by several utilities in April 1994 to help the U.S. government meet its international commitment to reduce emissions of greenhouse gases.

In addition to private sales and swaps, allowances have now been traded for several years in an open auction. Over time this method of buying and selling allowances may become more frequent than private transactions. (For one thing, with trades in an open market, links between specific buyers and sellers are less visible, so that the sorts of comparisons between gainers and losers that stimulated the LILCO controversy are less likely.)

The 1990 provisions held back 2.8 percent of the allowances for EPA to sell in an auction, and in the Fall of 1992, the EPA selected the Chicago Board of Trade to administer annual auctions, the first one of which was held in March 1993, the second in March 1994 and the third in March 1995. CBOT trades both "spot" allowances, which can be used to meet the 1995 compliance levels by the 110 largest emitters, and "advance" allowances, which can be used to meet the tighter Phase II compliance levels that go into effect in the year 2000, and that will apply to an additional 700 emitters.

The 1993 and 1994 auctions involved exclusively the allowances withheld from assignment to private parties. In the 1995 auction CBOT for the first time sold a small quantity of privately-held allowances from parties participating in EPA's Allowance Tracking System. These were sold only after EPA's withheld allowances had been exhausted. In the first two auctions, the available withheld allowances were not exhausted. In 1993, for instance, EPA offered 145,010 spot allowances and 50,010 were purchased, at successful bids ranging from $131 to $450. In 1994, 108,001 spot allowances were offered, and 50,000 were sold at bids ranging from $150 to $400. In 1995, EPA offered 50,000 spot allowances and private parties offered 8,306. A total of 50,600 spot allowances were sold at prices ranging from $130 to $350. The average prices for spots in 1994 was $159, and for advance allowances the average was $148. The average prices for spots in 1995 was $132 and for advance allowances the averages were $131 (six-year advance) and $128 (seven-year advance). The first auction netted $21.7 million in sales; the second netted $26.7 million, and the third netted $22.8 million. CBOT has plans to offer quarterly sales and to establish a futures market.

One purpose envisioned by the 1990 provisions for auctioning withheld allowances was to assist in establishing a market price for them, and analysts believe that the auctions are having this desired effect, and that the additional price information supplied by each auction will work

6. Air Pollution Control

Pages 825-832

to increase volume. Some believe that the relatively small volume of sales so far also reflects an early utility compliance strategy emphasis on fuel switching and installing scrubbers. If so, as each compliance deadline nears, trading may increase.

Several other factors have contributed to the slow start of the allowance trading program, none of them wholly unanticipated by the drafters of the 1990 provisions. State public utility commisisions (PUCs) have not yet developed consistent methodologies for treating the expenses associated with acquiring allowances or the revenues associated with selling them. Among other things, it is conceivable that PUCs would disallow recovery of expenditures for allowances on the basis that the utility had paid "too much" for them. Conversely, if a PUC concludes a utility has been selling allowances for "too little," it might require pre-transfer approvals that would hamper the market.

The low price for which the allowances are selling has been viewed by many observers as confirming the impression that industry estimates of the cost of complying with Title IV were greatly exaggerated. When the Clean Air Act was enacted, early projections indicated that the allowances could sell for $1,000 to $1,500 per ton because of the high cost of installing pollution control equipment. Yet it now seems clear that these costs estimates were far too high. At a hearing held in February 1993, Donald A. Deieso, executive vice president of Air and Water Technologies Corporation, a firm that markets pollution control equipment, reminded Senators of industry estimates that compliance with the 1990 Amendments would cost up to $20 billion per year. "I would like to report to you now, 28 months after passage of the act, the U.S. air pollution control market was smaller in 1992 than it was in 1991 and these levels are as small as they have been for the past 10 years." Deieso charged that industry greatly exaggerates the cost of environmental regulations by including routine purchases such as new toilets in its cost calculations. Actual spending on air pollution control in the United States peaked at $2.2 to $3 billion in the early 1980s as a result of the requirements of the 1977 Clean Air Act Amendments, and air pollution control expenditures in 1992 were less than $1 billion. Senate Hearing Examines Technology Issues Related to Environmental Protection Rules, 23 Env. Rep. 2837 (1993). EPA acknowledges that the costs of complying with Title IV will be at least $2 billion less than previously forecast, savings attributed in part to the decreasing cost of scrubbers. Sulfur Dioxide Emissions Limited by New Rule; Market-Based Incentives Called "Sophisticated," 23 Env. Rep. 1667 (1992).

Controls on NOx emissions also are proving to be substantially cheaper than first forecast. Now that pollution control companies actually are "bidding on real jobs," NOx controls have been found to cost "only 20 percent to 50 percent of the costs states regulators have assumed they would be in determining reasonably available control technology." Cutting NOx Will Cost Less Than Predicted, Pollution Control Equipment Suppliers Say, 23 Env. Rep. 3196 (1993).

The low prices that emissions allowances are commanding even convinced one utility to cancel a pollution control investment. The Illinois Power Company stopped construction on a $350 million scrubber because it has determined that it can more cheaply stockpile emissions allowances. A utility spokesperson explains that "[u]sing the permits will save us at least $250 million over the next 20 years and save Illinois coal-mining jobs as well." Feder, Sold: $21 Million of Air Pollution, N.Y. Times, Mar. 30, 1993, at D1, D22.

To some observers, the regulated nature of the utility industry poses difficulties for the market in allowances. Because utility companies' profits are determined by PUC rate decisions, they have little or no profit incentive to explore potentially risky trades. "Utilities are looking at compliance, not profits," says one analyst. Hoarding may also be a problem, as highly risk-averse utility companies decide to save whatever excess allowances they obtain via over-compliance, so that they have them available for their own needs. Public relations difficulties, as experienced by both LILCO and TVA in the sales described above, may also discourage trades. Matthew Wald, Risk-Shy Utilities Avoid Trading Emissions Credits, N. Y. Times, Jan. 25, 1993, at A20.

Environmental and public health groups are just beginning to realize that they could use the market for emissions allowances to *reduce* pollution. Northeast Utilities announced in March 1993 that it was donating 10,000 tons' worth of emissions allowances to chapters of the American Lung Association in Connecticut, Massachusetts, and New Hampshire. The Lung Association will retire the allowances to guarantee that the 10,000 tons of pollution they represent will not be emitted. A utility spokesperson stated that "[i]n the great tradition of the United States, we will be taking a tax deduction" for the donation of $3 million worth of allowances. Wald, Lung Association Getting a Donation of Cleaner Air, N.Y. Times, Mar. 20, 1993, at A9. Environmentalists have formed a Cleveland-based nonprofit group called the National Healthy Air License Exchange, which purchased an emissions allowance at the March 1993 CBOT auction that it will allow to expire. Taylor and Kansas, Environmentalists Vie for Right to Pollute, Wall St. J., Mar. 26, 1993, at C1. Student environmental law societies also have gotten into the act. At the March 1994 auction, the Maryland Environmental Law Society (MELS) became the first student group to purchase an emissions allowance. MELS purchased four more allowances at the March 1995 auction where student groups from Duke, Hamline, Michigan, New England, and Thomas M. Cooley law schools also purchased allowances. Law

6. Air Pollution Control

Students Buy and Hold Pollution Rights, N.Y. Times, Mar. 31, 1995, at A28.

G. MOBILE SOURCE CONTROLS: A TECHNOLOGY-FORCING VENTURE

Clean Fuels Program (pp. 839-842). Beginning in November 1992, oxygenated gasoline was placed on the market in more than three dozen areas that do not meet the NAAQS for carbon monoxide (CO). In March 1993, EPA reported preliminary monitoring data indicating that the use of oxygenated gasoline sharply reduced the frequency of violations of the CO standard. Based on monitoring data from 20 areas from November 1, 1992 through January 31, 1993, EPA determined that there were only two instances in which the CO standard was violated, compared to 43 violations during the same period the year before. Noah, New Fuel Blend Apparently Helps Cities' Air Quality, Wall St. J., Mar. 12, 1993, at A4B. After investigating reports that use of MTBE in the oxygenated fuels program in Alaska has caused motorists to experience headaches and dizziness, EPA concluded that MTBE was not the culprit. Alaskan Illnesses Remain a Mystery, 263 Science 177 (1994). However, Alaskans' complaints disappeared when MTBE fuels were removed from the Alaskan market in 1993.

In February 1994 EPA adopted final rules requiring that reformulated gasoline be sold in areas with the most severe ozone nonattainment problems. The regulations, which implement section 211(k)(1) of the Clean Air Act, require that gasoline be reformulated to reduce emissions of toxics and ozone-forming compounds. Reformulated gasoline must be sold effective January 1, 1995 in the nine largest metropolitan areas with the most severe summertime ozone levels and in more than 160 other areas that have opted-in to the program as provided by §211(k)(6). 59 Fed. Reg. 7,716 (1994). These areas, which are in 17 different states, represent nearly 30 percent of the national gasoline market, and include the northeastern states that comprise the Ozone Transport Region, which had agreed in 1991 that all of their ozone nonattainment areas would participate in the program.

In 1994 EPA issued additional regulations requiring that, by 1996, at least 30 percent of the oxygen content of reformulated gasoline be derived from feedstocks that are produced from renewable resources (for example, ethanol). 59 Fed. Reg. 39,258 (1994). This regulation, which was quite controversial, has been stayed by the D.C. Circuit. 59 Fed. Reg. 60,715 (1994).

EPA estimates that the reformulated fuels program will reduce emissions of ozone-forming compounds by more than 15 percent, or more than 300,000 tons per year. This is the equivalent of removing 8 million cars from the road. The petroleum industry, which has invested nearly $14 billion to produce the gasoline, enthusiastically supports the program.

Fears that the reformulated gasoline (RFG) rules would result in sharply higher prices and spot shortages of gasoline appear to have been exaggerated. Southerland, Gas Prices Fall But Clean-Fuels Issue Burns Hot, Wash. Post, Dec. 22, 1994, at B9. Nevertheless motorists in many parts of the country complained about price increases (it costs about five cents more per gallon to make RFG than conventional gasoline), reduced vehicle mileage, and fears of adverse health effects from exposure to reformulated gas. Appel and Solomon, "Clean Air" Fuel Ignites Revolt Among Drivers, Wall St. J., Dec. 13, 1994, at B1. Some areas of the country that had chosen to opt into the program subsequently changed their minds. In December 1994 EPA agreed to let 28 Pennsylvania counties opt out of the program. Counties in Maine and New York followed suit in January 1995 after EPA adopted a new policy permitting such opt-outs upon 30 days notice.

Onboard Vapor Recovery Controls (p. 841). The question of how best to control evaporative emissions from refueling vehicles has generated spirited conflict between automobile manufacturers and oil companies. Not surprisingly, automobile manufacturers have long favored requiring vapor recovery devices on gas pumps (called "Stage II" controls), while oil companies have argued that vapor recovery devices installed onboard vehicles would be a more effective and more efficient strategy. Fierce lobbying by automobile manufacturers forced EPA to back off on efforts to require onboard controls prior to adoption of the 1990 Amendments. While each industry urged that the legislation target the other one, Congress dealt them both a setback by requiring that Stage II controls be implemented in most nonattainment areas and that EPA, after consulting with the Department of Transportation, promulgate standards for onboard vapor recovery devices as well.

While President Bush had been an enthusiastic supporter of the 1990 Amendments, he later changed his tune during the 1992 presidential campaign. Faced with a conservative primary opponent, the Bush Administration launched a deregulation campaign that featured a freeze on new regulations. Four days before the Michigan presidential primary, President Bush announced that EPA would not require automobile manufacturers to install onboard vapor recovery devices, a deci-

6. Air Pollution Control   Pages 844-845

sion designed to please that state's automobile industry. NRDC brought suit, arguing that this decision violated the plain language of the 1990 Amendments. The D.C. Circuit agreed in NRDC v. Reilly, 983 F.2d 259 (D.C. Cir. 1993). The court held that Congress had unambiguously intended to require EPA to issue regulations requiring onboard refueling vapor recovery (ORVR) systems. While the court noted that section 206(a)(6) of the Clean Air Act permitted EPA first to consult with the Department of Transportation regarding safety issues, it did not view this consultation as authorizing EPA to avoid requiring the use of ORVR systems.

In a concurring opinion, Judge Stephen Williams displayed his fondness for market-based alternatives to command-and-control regulation by noting that "[u]nder a system of either emissions fees or marketable permits, firms whose production or products pollute can be induced to invest in R & D for pollution-reducing devices under conditions substantially similar to those under which they invest in R & D for products whose demand is generated by consumers—investing up to the point where the marginal cost equals the marginal expected revenues." 983 F.2d at 274. Thus, Judge Williams argued, emissions fees or marketable permits would be a more efficient means for stimulating the development of technologies to control evaporative emissions.

In March 1993, EPA announced that it would not seek further judicial review of the court's decision. EPA believes that improved onboard vapor recovery technology are emerging as the prospects for regulation increase. Evaporative Emission Regulations Give Rise to Better Vapor Control Technology, EPA Says, 23 Env. Rep. 3227 (1993). In April 1994 EPA issued final rules requiring that the use of ORVR equipment on light-duty cars and trucks be phased in beginning with the 1998 model year. 59 Fed. Reg. 16,262 (1994).

Update on the California Standards Option (pp. 844-845). On January 7, 1993, outgoing EPA Administrator Reilly granted California a waiver for its Low Emission And Zero Emission Vehicle standards. The waiver, which long had been expected, will facilitate adoption of the California standards by other states. Automobile manufacturers have been lobbying vigorously to persuade northeastern states not to adopt the California standards option. Despite these efforts, the states are making progress toward implementing their joint agreement to adopt such standards. Maine, Massachusetts, and New York have enacted legislation adopting the California standards. To forestall a change of heart by the New York Legislature, EPA announced in April 1993 that it would permit auto dealers in New York and surrounding states to sell California cars to residents of any state. New Jersey and Maryland have voted to adopt the program provided that their neighboring states do so. Deprived of the classic argument that any state adopting strict standards will place its residents at a disadvantage relative to consumers in surrounding states, the auto industry now argues that the standards are not worth the cost outside of California. The industry has been using cost estimates considerably higher than those of state environmental officials.

Having lost in the legislatures, the auto industry turned to the courts, arguing that it is illegal for states to adopt the California LEV standards option without also adopting the California clean fuels standard. In Motor Vehicle Manufacturers Association v. New York State Department of Environmental Conservation, 810 F. Supp. 1331 (N.D.N.Y. 1993), a federal court agreed with the manufacturers that the state violated the uniformity requirements of section 177 in two respects. First, zero-emission vehicles in the colder climate of New York would have to incorporate heaters, a sufficiently different design to constitute a "third vehicle" (neither a federal nor a California car). Second, New York's decision not to adopt the California fuels program would allow higher sulfur content fuels that would require a different catalytic converter. New York appealed this decision to the Second Circuit, which reached the following decision.

> *Motor Vehicle Manufacturers Association v. New York State Department of Environmental Conservation*
> 17 F.3d 521 (2d Cir. 1994)

Before: NEWMAN, Chief Judge, CARDAMONE and JACOBS, Circuit Judges. CARDAMONE, Circuit Judge:

The plaintiffs associations of American and foreign automobile manufacturers contest on this appeal the legality of defendant New York State's newly adopted rules regulating automobile tailpipe emissions. The most controversial issues to be resolved are whether New York State, like California, will in the coming years have a fixed percentage of zero emission automobiles, most likely, electric cars, and whether New York State, unlike California, can adopt auto emission requirements without adopting clean fuel requirements.

The invention and proliferation of the automobile has been a mixed blessing: its advantages are obvious and need no chronicling; its disadvantages, most notably as a source of air pollution that threatens human health and well-being, have become more and more apparent. Automobiles are the primary agents of ground level ozone and carbon monoxide. Ground level ozone, a major component of the now familiar phenomenon of urban smog, inhibits the human immune system and

6. Air Pollution Control

damages otherwise healthy lung tissue. The State of New York estimates that ten million New Yorkers live in ozone nonattainment areas. Carbon monoxide, a killer poison that interferes with the transfer of oxygen to the blood stream, adversely affects the functions of the heart and brain.

In response to the serious public health problems caused by ozone and carbon monoxide and the enormous task of cleaning up the air we breathe, the federal government enacted the Clean Air Act, and New York State under that Act adopted California regulations that mandate low emission vehicles. New York's regulations fall heaviest on members of plaintiffs association, General Motors, Ford and Chrysler, and numerous international auto manufacturers, such as Honda, Nissan, Toyota, Volkswagen and Volvo. These manufacturers challenge on this appeal New York's adoption of California's standards. . . .

BACKGROUND

Developments Leading up to the Clean Air Act

The Clean Air Act (Act), 42 U.S.C. §§7401-7671q (1988 & Supp. III 1991), is one of the most comprehensive pieces of legislation in our nation's history. In order to better understand the issues it is helpful to trace briefly the development of that Act.

The original Clean Air Act, enacted by Congress in 1955, was aimed primarily at increasing federal research and assistance in air pollution prevention. It made no provision for federal motor vehicle emission standards. See Air Pollution Control-Research and Technical Assistance Act of 1955, Pub. L. No. 84-159, 69 Stat. 322. Because several states had begun to adopt their own motor vehicle emission standards, the Senate Committee on Public Works, after noting that California was the leader in regulating automotive pollutant emissions, decided that national standards were to be preferred over having each state go its own way, "which could result in chaos insofar as manufacturers, dealers, and users are concerned." S. Rep. No. 192, 89th Cong., 1st Sess. 5-6 (1965). As a result, the Committee proposed and Congress enacted in 1965 emission standards for new motor vehicle engines. See Motor Vehicle Air Pollution Control Act of 1965, Pub. L. No. 89-272, §202(a), 79 Stat. 992.

A number of states, in addition to California, nonetheless continued to develop separate emission programs. Congress thereupon promptly amended the Clean Air Act in 1967 to impose federal preemption over motor vehicle emission standards. See Air Quality Act of 1967, Pub. L. No. 90-148, §208, 81 Stat. 485. Over the adamant objection of the auto industry, which sought a single national standard to avoid undue economic strain for manufacturers, California was excepted from preemption as the only state regulating auto emissions "prior to March 30, 1966". Id. §208(b). The reason for this lone exception was because the Senate Committee on Public Works was persuaded by California's then Senator Murphy that his state's "unique problems and pioneering efforts" warranted a waiver from preemption. S. Rep. No. 403, 90th Cong. 1st Sess. 33 (1967).

Comprehensive revisions made to the Act in 1970 established national ambient air quality standards (NAAQS) and required even more stringent uniform emission standards for new motor vehicles. See Clean Air Amendments of 1970, Pub. L. No. 91-604, §§4, 6, 84 Stat. 1676. In further amendments to the Act in 1977, §209 (formerly §208) was amended to require the U.S. Environmental Protection Agency (EPA) to consider California's standards as a package, so that California could seek a waiver from preemption if its standards "in the aggregate" protected public health at least as well as federal standards. See Clean Air Act Amendments of 1977, Pub. L. 95-95, §207, 91 Stat. 685.

Significantly, for the issues on this appeal, the Clean Air Act Amendments of 1977 added §177, which permitted other states to "piggyback" onto California's standards, if the state's standards "are identical to the California standards for which a waiver has been granted for such model year." Pub. L. No. 95-95, §129(b), 91 Stat. 685, 750. In order for another state, here New York, to use California standards in a given model year, the House Committee on Interstate and Foreign Commerce made clear that California must adopt its standards two years in advance of such year, California must receive a waiver for its standards, and the adopting state must adopt California standards at least two years before the model year. See H.R. Rep. No. 294, 95th Cong., 1st Sess. 310 (1977).

Clean Air Act Amendments of 1990

. . . In Title II of the Act Congress endeavors to resolve the problems caused by moveable sources or vehicle emissions. The emission standards applicable to any given vehicle depend upon its weight and use classification, and its model year designation. See Act §§202, 207(c), 42 U.S.C. §§7521, 7541(c). Section 202 authorizes the Administrator to promulgate emission standards for motor vehicles sold in the United States. Motor vehicle emission standards primarily regulate emissions of carbon monoxide (CO), hydrocarbons or volatile organic compounds (VOCs) and nitrogen oxides (NOx). Hydrocarbons and nitrogen oxides are two classes of chemicals that combine in the presence of sunlight to form ozone, a major component of urban smog.

The cornerstone of Title II is Congress' continued express preemp-

6. Air Pollution Control   Pages 844-845

tion of state regulation of automobile emissions. See Act §209(a), 42 U.S.C. §7543(a). Pursuant to the Act, the great majority of states have chosen to rely on the federal emission standards as set forth in §202 of the Act, 42 U.S.C. §7521. Only California, because its unique Los Angeles smog problem caused it to begin regulating auto emissions "prior to March 30, 1966," enjoys a statutory exemption allowing it to promulgate its own emission standards. See Act §209(b), 42 U.S.C. §7543(b)(1). . . .

The effect of the Clean Air Act is that motor vehicles manufactured for sale in the United States must be either "federal cars"—certified to meet federal vehicle emission standards as set by the EPA—or "California cars"—certified to meet that state's standards. . . .

Many states, including New York, are in danger of not meeting increasingly stringent federal air pollution limits. Congress has directed the Administrator to impose mandatory sanctions on states failing to timely submit approvable SIPs or SIP revisions. See 42 U.S.C. §§7410(m), 7509(a). . . .

It was in an effort to assist those states struggling to meet federal pollution standards that Congress, as noted earlier, directed in 1977 that other states could promulgate regulations requiring vehicles sold in their state to be in compliance with California's emission standards or to "piggyback" onto California's preemption exemption. This opt-in authority, set forth in §177 of the Act, 42 U.S.C. §7507, is carefully circumscribed to avoid placing an undue burden on the automobile manufacturing industry. Specifically, (1) an opt-in state must adopt standards that are identical to California's; (2) California must receive a waiver from the EPA for the standards; and (3) both California and the opt-in state must adopt the standards at least two years before the beginning of the automobile model year to which they apply. See Act §177, 42 U.S.C. §7507.

In the 1990 sweeping amendments to the Act two further restrictions were added to the last paragraph of §177. First, Congress added new language providing that §177 shall not be construed as authorizing an opt-in state to limit the sale of California-certified vehicles. Second, it forbade opt-in states from taking any action that has the effect of creating a car different from those produced to meet either federal or California emission standards, a so-called "third vehicle." See Clean Air Act Amendments of 1990, Pub. L. No. 101-549, §232, 104 Stat. 2399, 2529. . . .

California's Plan

With the evolution and scope of the Clean Air Act in mind, we turn now to examine the development of California's emission limitation plan. In 1988 the California Legislature directed CARB [California

Air Resources Board] to adopt the most cost-effective combination of motor vehicle controls, vehicle fuel restrictions, and in-use vehicle control requirements so as to achieve a 55 percent reduction in organic gas emissions by December 31, 2000. See Cal. Health & Safety Code §§43018(b), (c). CARB proceeded to establish low-emission vehicles (LEV) and clean fuels (CF) requirements, which became effective on September 28, 1991.

California's LEV program applies to passenger cars and light-duty trucks (collectively light-duty vehicles) and medium-duty vehicles, and requires the creation of four classes of California light- and medium-duty vehicles, to be phased in over the next decade. The four categories are (1) Transitional Low-Emission Vehicles (TLEVs), (2) Low-Emission Vehicles (LEVs), (3) Ultra-Low-Emission Vehicles (ULEVs), and (4) Zero-Emission Vehicles (ZEVs). See Cal. Code Regs. tit. 13 §1960.1(g)(2). For each category a set of more stringent emission standards for carbon monoxide, nitrogen oxides and formaldehyde applies. The average emissions from the mix of these categories of vehicles produced by a given manufacturer in a given year must meet an overall "fleet average" requirement. See id.

In addition, the fleet average for allowable exhaust emissions beginning in 1994 declines each year until 2003. See id. Automobile manufacturers, under CARB's regulations, have the flexibility to decide how many vehicles of each type they manufacture and sell in order to meet the fleet average. Additional flexibility is provided through the establishment of a marketable credit system: manufacturers may earn credits if they sell more low-emission vehicles than needed to meet the fleet average. Credits many be banked internally to offset future shortfalls or sold to other manufacturers unable to meet their fleet average.

The only limitation on this fleet averaging approach is the sales quota established for ZEVs—vehicles with no tailpipe emissions of any pollutants throughout their lifetimes, which are presumably electric cars. By 1998, two percent of all vehicles certified for sale in California must be ZEVs, with the rate increasing to five percent in 2001 and to ten percent in 2003. See id. The ZEV quota initially applies to all manufacturers who sell annually more than 35,000 light- and medium-duty vehicles in California. But, beginning in 2003 that threshold drops to manufacturers who sell only 3,000 or more vehicles in California. See id. The ZEV quota also has a marketable credit system that works just like the fleet averaging credit system. See id.

The CF component of California's plan, see Cal. Code Regs. tit. 13 §§2300-2317, entails a two-step introduction of "reformulated gasoline," which is referred to as Phase 1 and Phase 2 gasoline. These fuels will have a lower sulfur content than gas sold in the rest of the nation, such as the Venezuelan gasoline sold on the east coast, which has a high sulphur content. With limited exceptions, gasoline sold in California after January 1, 1992 had to be Phase 1. Compliance with the Phase 2 gas requirements—which are considerably more stringent than the Phase 1 requirements—commences on March 1, 1996. Officials of CARB have frequently stated that "the primary purpose of the specifications will be to reduce emissions from pre-1993 and off-road vehicles."

Notwithstanding that fact, California will allow vehicle manufacturers to certify, both pre-sale and in-use, their new vehicles using a test fuel with properties of the Phase 2 reformulated gasoline. Manufacturers need not wait until the commercial introduction of these fuels; rather they can begin certifying vehicles on Phase 2 gas immediately. In fact, General Motors has already done so in an attempt to secure LEV credits for the upcoming years. Prior to this plan, California tested vehicles using Indolene, a special non-commercial certification fuel used by the EPA in the rest of the nation. The Chief Deputy Executive Officer of CARB has stated that "allowing vehicle manufacturers to certify gasoline-powered low-emission vehicles on Phase 2 reformulated gasoline certification fuel [is] an integral part of the CARB's new motor vehicle standards and test procedures."

In October 1991 California submitted its plan to the EPA for approval as required by §209(b). See 42 U.S.C. §7543(b). While the ability to use Phase 2 gas for certification was not in the waiver application, CARB intends to ask the EPA for a waiver or assurance that the Phase 2 amendments are within the scope of the October 1991 application. The EPA approved California's plan on January 7, 1993. Significantly, despite requests by automobile manufacturers, this approval was not conditioned on the commercial availability of Phase 2 gasoline.

New York's Adoption of California's Plan

According to DEC [New York State Department of Energy Conservation], New York currently has one of the most intractable air pollution problems in the nation due largely to automobile emissions. Mobile sources emit more than 90 percent of the carbon monoxide and nitrogen oxides that pollute its air. New York—like 39 other states and the District of Columbia—is not in compliance with the ozone NAAQS or carbon monoxide NAAQS established pursuant to the 1990 amendments to the Act. New York City suffers from serious carbon monoxide pollution and has been classified as a "moderate" nonattainment area. See 56 Fed. Reg. 56,694 (Nov. 6, 1991). In addition, eight counties in New York are not in compliance with the carbon monoxide NAAQS and 22 counties failed to meet the ozone requirements. See id. at 56,804.

Of these 22, the New York City area has been designated a "severe" nonattainment area.

New York therefore must prepare a SIP adequate to meet the federal air quality standards for carbon monoxide by the end of 1995 and for ozone by late 2007. See 42 U.S.C. §§7512(a)(1), 7511(a)(2). The SIP must demonstrate to the satisfaction of the EPA that New York (1) will meet the health-based standards by the dates specified in the Act, and (2) will achieve a 15 percent reduction in volatile organic compounds from 1990 baseline emissions by 1996, and a three percent reduction on average each year thereafter until the federal standard is achieved. See id. §§7511a(b), (c). Failure to meet these obligations will trigger the sanctions discussed earlier. See id. §7509.

In order to combat its serious persistent pollution problem, New York, pursuant to §177 and through regulations promulgated by the DEC, adopted California's LEV program on May 28, 1992. Although these regulations were filed on April 28, 1992, they did not become effective until May 28, 1992. For purposes of this opinion the term "adoption" refers to the latter date. New York's regulation applies at present only to light-duty vehicles and does not apply to medium-duty vehicles as in California. New York's adoption took place more than six months before the EPA granted California a waiver. The DEC acted under its rulemaking authority, and the regulations contain new standards for tailpipe and evaporative emissions for model year 1995. The regulations were published at 6 NYCRR Part 218.

New York did not adopt California's CF program, but the regulations do provide that motor vehicles sold in New York will be certified, both pre-sale and in-use, under the identical procedures used in California, which currently permit manufacturers to use the reformulated gasoline—Phase 1 and Phase 2—as noted above. See id. §218-5. Federal reformulated gasoline—while not as "clean" as California's Phase 2 gas—will be marketed in New York beginning January 1, 1995 in all ozone nonattainment areas classified marginal or worse. See 57 Fed. Reg. 7926, 7926-7927 (Mar. 5, 1992). New York says it elected not to adopt the California CF plan because it concluded the plan was not cost-effective.

In addition to New York's adoption of the California plan, a letter of understanding was signed by all the states of the Northeast Ozone Transport Commission—a group composed of 12 states along the eastern seaboard from Virginia to Maine and the District of Columbia—on October 29, 1991 pledging to adopt the LEV plan. Other than New York, so far only Massachusetts has promulgated regulations to this effect. The other states of the Commission, we are advised, are awaiting the outcome of this litigation.

6. Air Pollution Control — Pages 844-845

Prior Proceedings

We pass now to the proceedings held in the district court. The complaint alleges in six counts that DEC's adoption of the LEV standards violates §177 of the Act: (1) DEC's failure to adopt the CF component of California's regulations violates the "identicality" requirement and (2) violates the "undue burdens" and "third vehicle" prohibitions of §177; (3) DEC's adoption of California's regulations before California had received a waiver from the EPA violates §177 and (4) did not comply with the two year leadtime requirement; (5) DEC's ZEV sales quota contravenes the prohibition on all plans that limits the sales of California certified vehicles and (6) contravenes the prohibition against a "third vehicle." . . .

DISCUSSSION . . .

As the report of the House Committee on Interstate and Foreign Commerce demonstrates, §177 was inserted into the Act in 1977 so that states attempting to combat their own pollution problems could adopt California's more stringent emission controls. See H.R. Rep. No. 294, 95th Cong., 1st Sess. 309-310 (1977). An equally significant purpose evident in the statute and the legislative history is Congress' desire not to burden manufacturers unduly with myriad state emission regulations. See id. at 309. We endeavor in the discussion that follows to harmonize these sometimes disparate goals.

I. IDENTICALITY

The first issue addressed is whether the DEC's failure to adopt California's CF plan when it promulgated the LEV standards violates §177's requirement that State emission standards be "identical to the California standards for which a waiver has been granted." 42 U.S.C. §7507. Exactly what "California standards" New York must adopt to meet the identicality requirement is found in the plain language of the statute.

Section 177 refers to "standards relating to control of emissions . . . for which a waiver *has been granted*." Id. (emphasis added). In enacting §209(b), which establishes California's preemption exception, Congress uses the same words as it did when it allowed California to set its own "standards . . . for the control of emissions," provided the EPA approves a waiver application. Id. §7543(b)(1). Hence, the most

331

logical reading of §177 is that New York may adopt only those standards that, pursuant to §209(b), California included in its waiver application to the EPA.

California was not required to obtain an EPA waiver for its CF plan because Congress treated the two initiatives to clean up the air separately—one for engine emission and one for fuel—as shown by the fact that it granted California a fuels exemption under a separate provision of the Act, namely §211(c)(4)(B). Moreover, the Chief Deputy Officer of CARB stated that the CF plan was not included in the waiver application submitted by California in October 1991. California adopted its LEV standards over a year before it promulgated its final rule for Phase 2 reformulated gasoline, and the EPA's approval of the LEV plan, as already observed, was not conditioned on the commercial availability of the gasoline. Only the regulations allowing manufacturers to certify LEVs on reformulated gasoline are within the scope of the §209(a) preemption provision, and therefore require a §209(b) waiver, though California has yet to receive such a formal waiver. But because New York has adopted these certification standards by reference, see 6 NYCRR §218-5(b), manufacturers are not deprived of the ability to certify on reformulated gasoline the vehicles they sell in New York.

In sum, the plain language of §177 not only provides that New York need not adopt California's CF plan, it actually precludes New York's adoption of such plan under this provision, as the plan was not part of the waiver application. This view is entirely consistent with the reasoning of Motor & Equipment Manufacturers Association Inc. v. EPA, which held "the plain meaning of [§209] indicates that Congress intended to make the waiver power coextensive with the preemption provision." 627 F.2d 1095, 1107 (D.C. Cir. 1979), cert. denied, 446 U.S. 952 (1980). Since the preemption provision of §209 covers only automobile emission standards, the waiver provision of §209 must only apply to automobile emission standards. Consequently, California could not have obtained a preemption waiver for its CF plan under §209(b). Rather, California's exception from preemption for this program could only come from §211, which has no federal waiver review requirements analogous to those contained in §209.

At first glance this construction might appear to be at odds with the Act's overall emphasis on more stringent standards for improving the quality of our nation's air. In fact, the manufacturers ask why, when promulgating Part 218, the DEC did not impose regulations on the fuel burned as well as the emission control hardware, since tailpipe exhaust is a product of both. New York answers this query by saying regulation of fuel was not cost effective. In any event, whether to impose such regulation is a matter of policy confided to New York. The Part 218 Regulations do not preclude New York from adopting the CF plan and seeking a CF preemption waiver from the EPA under §211(c)(4)(C) of the Act, 42 U.S.C. §7545(c)(4)(C), should it choose to do so later. Thus, Congress' aim of improving air quality is not undermined by reading the CF plan out of the "identicality" requirement. Were we to hold otherwise, we would undermine Congress' scheme of treating emissions and fuel standards separately, in effect ruling in a manner outside our authority and substituting our judgment for that of the state regulatory body. . . .

[A]llowing the DEC to adopt only the emission standards plan does not defeat the two goals of §177. Our reading of §177 permits New York to adopt emission standards more stringent than those it would be left with under current federal law, and the LEV plan standing alone does not force auto manufacturers to do something more than they already have to do, that is, develop a plan to meet the fleet average requirement. After all, the manufacturers will presumably design and build the same cars for California as will be sold in New York. Most importantly, the auto industry will be allowed to certify vehicles as meeting emissions requirements using the same fuels that California uses for its certification. In this respect, whether New York's failure to adopt the CF plan somehow violates the "third vehicle" prohibition is not a question we need to reach on this appeal. That question is embodied in count two of the complaint, and it is proceeding to trial.

II. Timing

A. *DEC's Adoption Prior to EPA's Grant of California's Waiver*

The next issue for analysis is whether DEC violated §177 by adopting the Part 218 Regulations more than six months prior to EPA's having granted California a waiver pursuant to §209(b). Again, the plain language of §177, coupled with common sense, suggests how this issue should be resolved.

As related, §177 allows New York to "adopt and enforce" emission standards "identical to the California standards for which a waiver has been granted." 42 U.S.C. §7507. Plaintiffs insist this apparently plain language is not in fact so plain. All parties agree the EPA's grant of a waiver to California pursuant to §209(b) is a precondition to some type of action by the adopting state. But the manufacturers declare that New York was precluded from taking any action until the EPA actually granted California a waiver for the LEV plan—which it did on January 7, 1993—and that New York should not have been permitted to adopt California's LEV plan until that date.

The manufacturers wanted the DEC to withhold its action of adopting the regulations until January 7, 1993 because that date is when they believe the two year leadtime should have commenced running. They support their position by noting that this precondition was in the statute to insure that manufacturers had sufficient notice of future regulations affecting the auto industry. The DEC had of course adopted the Part 218 Regulations on May 28, 1992. It responds to the manufacturer's position by stating it was permitted to adopt the regulations prior to the EPA's having granted California's waiver, provided it did not enforce the regulations before January 7, 1993.

The issue is what do the above quoted words of §177 mean, that is to say, what is the waiver a precondition to—DEC's adoption of the LEV plan or DEC's enforcement of the LEV plan, or both. The most sensible response, it appears to us, is that the waiver is a precondition to enforcement of the standard that has been adopted. In other words, it is sensible for DEC to adopt the standards prior to the EPA's having granted a waiver, so long as the DEC makes no attempt to enforce the plan prior to the time when the waiver is actually obtained.

The result urged by the manufacturers ignores the fact that the need for adequate notice was addressed by Congress in the two year leadtime requirement discussed below. The manufacturers' suggestion that more than two years is required because of possible uncertainty in the approval of California's waiver is a bit disingenuous. Plaintiffs know that California's waiver applications are almost always approved, in light of Congress' decision "to permit California to blaze its own trail with a minimum of federal oversight." Ford Motor Co. v. EPA, 606 F.2d 1293, 1297 (D.C. Cir. 1979); see also *Motor & Equip. Mfrs. Ass'n*, 627 F.2d at 1121-1122 (California's emission standards "are presumed to satisfy the waiver requirements" and EPA may not disregard California's determination absent "clear and compelling evidence" to the contrary).

By adopting, without enforcing, the challenged Part 218 Regulations before the EPA ruled on the waiver application, the DEC put plaintiffs on notice that New York intended to take the same path as had California. The two year leadtime of §177 more than adequately ensures a sufficient period for manufacturers to prepare for an opt-in state's adoption of California's standards.

B. *Two Year Leadtime*

Given our holding that New York's adoption of the Part 218 Regulations was valid even though it occurred before California was granted

6. Air Pollution Control

a waiver, a third issue is whether DEC's adoption of California's standards—applicable to model year 1995 vehicles—provides manufacturers the two year leadtime required by §177. The critical date is May 28, 1992, the date when New York adopted the California standards. The district court ruled the Regulations would be unenforceable as against those manufacturers who commenced production of model year 1995 vehicles prior to May 28, 1994, because those manufacturers would have had less than two years from the 1992 adoption date. See Motor Vehicle Mfrs. Ass'n v. New York State Dep't. of Envtl. Conservation (*MVMA II*), 831 F. Supp. 57, 64 (N.D.N.Y. 1993). General Motors, for one, produced unrebutted evidence that it would commence production of all of its model year 1995 vehicles prior to May 28, 1994.

The trial court's ruling regarding the two year leadtime requirement satisfies neither side. DEC contends the leadtime requirement turns on a specific model's or engine family's first production within the model year. Under this interpretation, individual manufacturers could be subject to differing certification rules for different models or engine families. The manufacturers, similarly dissatisfied with the district court's decision, maintain that the manufacturer-by-manufacturer rule would create havoc in the automobile industry; they also reject DEC's engine-family-by-engine-family rule as having the potential to create even greater chaos in the industry.

To determine the proper application of the two year leadtime provision, we look again to the language of §177. It provides that states adopting California's standards must do so "at least two years before commencement of [the] model year." 42 U.S.C. §7507. Congress specifically stated in §177 that "model year" shall be "determined by regulations of the Administrator." Id. But such regulations have never been promulgated. For the purpose of federal automobile regulations, the EPA defines a model year as a manufacturer's annual production period. See 40 C.F.R. §86.082-2 (1992). The EPA issued an Advisory Circular that an annual production period for any specific model within an engine family commences (1) when a vehicle or engine designated for a particular year is "first produced," or (2) on January 2 of the calendar year prior to the model year, whichever date is later. Relying on this definition in its *amicus* brief, the EPA sides with the DEC, asserting that its definition means that "model year" should be applied on an engine-family-by-engine-family basis, not on a manufacturer-by-manufacturer basis. Moreover, the EPA believes its view is entitled to deference under Chevron, U.S.A., Inc. v. Natural Resources Defense Council, Inc., 467 U.S. 837, 843 (1984). We are unwilling to accept the proffered definition. Section 177 charges the EPA with the single, narrow responsibility to issue "regulations" in order to define the commencement of a model year under §177. The EPA Advisory Circular upon which the DEC relies is not a "regulation" for §177 purposes and was not promulgated specifically to implement this provision. . . .

Given the lack of EPA regulations for purposes of §177, a practical approach to interpreting this requirement is warranted and reveals the unreasonableness of the DEC's and EPA's view. The crux of the LEV plan is the fleet averaging concept. Fleet averaging is designed to give manufacturers sufficient flexibility to develop varying emissions within their entire fleet to meet the overall goal. Breaking down a particular manufacturer's fleet on an engine-family-by-engine-family or model-by-model basis would disserve the LEV plan itself by unduly complicating the fleet averaging plan. Moreover, the flexibility of the LEV plan allows manufacturers to buy and sell credits to meet their fleet average requirements. This feature would also be frustrated if all manufacturers were not playing by the same rules. Consequently, we hold that absent promulgated EPA regulations, "model year" is best read as applying on an industry-wide basis. Because model year 1995 commences prior to May 28, 1994, as demonstrated by the uncontroverted evidence submitted by General Motors, DEC should be enjoined from enforcing its LEV plan for model year 1995 as against all manufacturers.

Our holding accords with Congress' express inclusion of the leadtime requirement in §177 to protect the auto industry. This requirement must be construed for the plaintiffs' benefit, in contrast to the deferential approach—accruing to defendant's benefit—taken on the earlier issues addressed. The leadtime provision was specifically added to insure that manufacturers would have an ample amount of time to adjust to upcoming regulations. The district court's manufacturer-by-manufacturer rule might well impose different emission standards on different manufacturers within the same model year depending upon the date each manufacturer starts production of its model year 1995 vehicles or engines.

We do not believe Congress contemplated a "split" model year approach, differentiating manufacturers based on when each commences production. No set of regulations has sought to implement a "split" model year. Nor has any court ever applied emission standards on a manufacturer-by-manufacturer basis. The only court to have previously touched on this subject refused to differentiate among manufacturers because of the "competitive as well as statutory considerations." International Harvester Co. v. Ruckelshaus, 478 F.2d 615, 640 (D.C. Cir. 1973). Needless to say, imposing a manufacturer-by-manufacturer standard or, even worse, an engine-family-by-engine-family standard, would cause great confusion for the entire automobile industry, while being entirely impractical to enforce.

6. Air Pollution Control

III. THE ZEV SALES QUOTA

A. Limitation on the Sale of California-Certified Vehicles

Next we discuss whether DEC's ZEV sales quota violates §177 because, as the manufacturers point out, it will limit sales of other classes of California-certified cars. Pursuant to §177, New York cannot "prohibit or limit, directly or indirectly, the manufacture or sale of a [vehicle or engine] that is certified in California as meeting California standards." 42 U.S.C. §7507. The district court held that by requiring a certain percentage of California-certified vehicles sold in New York to be ZEVs, "DEC has effectively limited the sales of all other classes of California certified vehicles." Motor Vehicle Mfrs. Ass'n v. New York State Dep't of Envtl. Conservation (*MVMA I*), 810 F. Supp. 1331, 1346 (N.D.N.Y. 1993)....

The ZEV sales mandate was obviously included by California in the LEV plan to encourage the development, production, sale and use of ZEVs. The Act is concededly a "technology forcing" law. Equally obvious is the fact that ZEVs sold in New York will themselves be California-certified cars. Under the current ZEV plan, manufacturers may sell any number of California-certified vehicles other than ZEVs so long as they also sell the specified percentage of ZEVs. Hence, New York has not acted so as to limit (either directly or indirectly) the number of non-ZEV California-certified cars the manufacturers will sell. The more non-ZEV California-certified vehicles they sell, the more ZEVs they must sell. How the manufacturers will insure the sale of ZEVs is not a matter we must resolve; suffice it to say the sale of ZEVs will hinge on marketing and competitive factors, fields in which the manufacturers are experts.

Even though California and New York have not decided how they intend to penalize noncompliance, manufacturers would not be penalized *per se* for the sale of too many California-certified cars other than ZEVs. Rather, it would be their failure to sell the appropriate number of ZEVs (or purchase sufficient ZEV credits) that would lead to penalties. Thus, in our view the purpose of the sales limitation prohibition is to prohibit §177 opt-in states from attempting to regulate against the sale of a particular type, not number, of California-certified cars. It must be remembered that the manufacturer has already expended resources specifically for the design and certification of emissions hardware. There is no allegation in this record that New York has overtly limited the sale of any type of California vehicle.

It would be naive not to recognize that since the market for cars is not unlimited, the ZEV quota may affect the sale of non-ZEV California-certified cars. But "affect" is not the key word of §177, the catchword is "limit." See 42 U.S.C. §7507. The district court's holding that the DEC regulation respecting a percentage sale of ZEVs limited the sale of other classes of California vehicles skews Congress' purpose. Congress wanted the plans of opt-in states to be identical to those of California, as is evident from the identicality requirement. Ruling in effect that one portion of the plan adopted according to the specific instructions in §177 somehow at the same time violates §177, places New York or other potential opt-in states in a Catch-22 position. Like the third vehicle rule, the sales-limitation rule is designed to reinforce the identicality requirement. It would be incongruous for us to hold that the DEC wrongly mandated a ZEV sales percentage identical to California's mandate.

Moreover, under the trial court's view of this matter, the fleet averaging concept standing alone would have to be read as violating this same provision because it necessarily forces manufacturers to sell some unfixed number of lower emissions vehicles. The only difference between the fleet averaging and the ZEV quota notions is that with the ZEV quota the actual percentage of vehicles sold is fixed; while the number can fluctuate under the rest of the LEV plan, the fixed fleet average must also still be met.

In light of Congress' recognition, when it amended the Act in 1990, of California's LEV program, including the ZEV mandate, see, e.g., Act §§241(4), 243(f), 246(f)(4), 42 U.S.C. §§7581(4), 7583(f), 7586(f)(4), we are disinclined to pave the way for a nullification of New York's Part 218 Regulations or to impair any other state's ability to adopt California's LEV plan. It would be inappropriate to construe the 1990 amendments in a manner that would effectively prohibit any state from opting into the California program since Congress so obviously planned for the several states to have that option. See Lewis v. Grinker, 965 F.2d 1206, 1215 (2d Cir. 1992). Because the district court may unintentionally have laid the groundwork for an abrogation of the entire LEV plan, its decision on this issue must be reversed.

B. The Third Vehicle Prohibition

The remaining issue is whether summary judgment was properly granted to the manufacturers on the rationale that DEC's ZEV quota would inevitably cause production of a third vehicle in violation of §177. Obviously, the disposition of this issue turns on the meaning of the third vehicle bar that was added to §177 in 1990. Section 177 prohibits states from "taking any action of any kind to create, or have the effect of creating, a motor vehicle or motor vehicle engine different than a

6. Air Pollution Control   Pages 844-845

motor vehicle or engine certified in California under California standards (a 'third vehicle') or otherwise creating such a 'third vehicle'." 42 U.S.C. §7507. According to the district court, because ZEVs in New York would require distinct features to satisfy the demands of local climates, the ZEV quota violates this provision. See *MVMA I*, 810 F. Supp. at 1347. . . .

Resorting again to the plain language of the statute, it is clear that the third vehicle prohibition is not simply surplusage, but instead was meant to guard against several forms of state action. One clear purpose of the third vehicle prohibition is to bar a state from *administering and enforcing* standards identical to California's in such a burdensome way as to effectively require a third vehicle. For instance, a state that has met the identicality requirement cannot adopt imprecise testing procedures to check compliance with those standards, or require remedial action for noncompliance with identical California emission standards that have the effect of imposing an "undue burden" on the manufacturer. With respect to the ZEV quota, New York has adopted California's standard precisely and no party contends that New York is administering this standard or remedying its noncompliance in a manner or method different than California. Hence, the DEC regulation does not violate §177's third vehicle prohibition in respect to administration and enforcement.

Nor does the ZEV requirement violate the third-vehicle prohibition, apart from matters of administration and enforcement. It may be that a state would never violate the third vehicle prohibition so long as it meets the identicality requirement and does not administer or enforce the California emission standards in a manner more burdensome than what occurs in California. We need not go so far on this appeal in order to reject the manufacturers' claim. They contend that, even if New York is deemed to have met the identicality requirement by adopting the LEV standard without the CF standards, a third vehicle has been required because in New York's colder climate it will be necessary to install a more powerful heater than the one the manufacturers plan to use in California. The short answer is that whatever heater the manufacturers choose to install on cars sold in New York is a marketing choice for theirs and not a requirement imposed by DEC. We note in that connection that California recently amended its definition of a ZEV to permit the inclusion of a fuel fired heater without altering the zero-emission status of the vehicle. See Cal. Code Regs. tit. 13 §1900(b)(15).

Whether we could so easily reject a third-vehicle claim as to vehicles meeting California's requirements if some aspect of New York's climate required alteration to the emission control features of the automobile or substantially impaired the ability of the vehicle to perform basic transportation functions are issues we need not consider on this record. In the absence of facts even putting such claims in issue, the grant of summary judgment to the manufacturers based on the notion that the ZEV quota violates §177's third vehicle prohibition must be reversed, and summary judgment on this count must be entered for the DEC. No doubt as a result of the technology forcing nature of the Clean Air Act, today's automobile as we know it is passing away. But the manufacturers' argument with respect to the difficulty of building a viable ZEV is reminiscent of the view that 100 years ago some thought the U.S. Patent Office should be closed because anything that ever could be invented had already been invented.

NOTES AND QUESTIONS

1. *A LEV Program for the Northeastern States?* The court's opinion refers to the Northeast Ozone Transport Commission (OTC), an entity established by §184 of the Clean Air Act, consisting of representatives of the governors of 12 Northeastern states plus the government of the District of Columbia. The Commission was created in recognition of the fact that air pollution shows no respect for state boundaries, and that compliance with the national ambient air quality standards for ozone in any single jurisdiction in the densely populated northeast corridor of the country (the Ozone Transport Region, or OTR) may well depend upon air pollution control measures adopted outside that jurisdiction. The Commission is authorized to make recommendations for "additional control measures to be applied within all or a part of [the covered states] if the commission determines such measures are necessary to bring any area in such region into attainment," and to forward them to EPA for its consideration. §184(c)(1).

As the court indicates, all the jurisdictions in the OTC had signed a letter of understanding that each would adopt the California LEV plan, but eight days before the court issued its opinion that unanimity had officially disintegrated. On February 1, 1994, the Commission voted 9-4 to recommend to the EPA that the LEV plan be mandated by EPA as part of each Commission member's SIP. (Within a week, the state legislature of Pennsylvania adopted a resolution repudiating the affirmative vote of the Pennsylvania commissioner.)

2. The statute requires EPA to review any such Commission recommendation, §184(c)(2), and EPA issued a notice of proposed rulemaking to do just that. 59 Fed. Reg. 21,720 (1994). After public hearings and several supplemental notices of proposed rulemaking, the EPA issued a final rule requiring all thirteen OTC jurisdictions either to implement a LEV program for new cars and light-duty trucks or to

adopt a "LEV-equivalent" program, described by EPA as a "voluntary nationwide program that would achieve emission reductions from new motor vehicles in the OTR equivalent to or greater than would be achieved by the OTC LEV program and that would advance motor vehicle emission control technology." 60 Fed. Reg. 4712, 4715 (1995).

In performing the analyses necessary to reach its conclusion, EPA determined that reductions of between 50 percent and 75 percent from 1990 baseline levels of both NOx and VOCs would be necessary in all regions to the south, southwest, west and northwest of serious and severe nonattainment areas in order to bring those areas into compliance, and that vehicle emissions will account for approximately 38 percent of NOx and 22 percent of VOC emissions without the adoption of a LEV program or its equivalent.

3. The idea of a LEV-equivalent program emerged during the consideration of EPA's rule. It amounts to an automobile industry proposal to adopt emission reductions more stringent than the federal standards but without the LEV and ZEV fleet percentage requirements of the California approach. It is, in other words, a proposal for a "third vehicle." EPA clearly believes that a LEV-equivalent program "would be far better than OTC LEV," and "would have significant advantages when compared to an OTC LEV," in that would achieve the same or greater emission reductions within the OTR, it would provide significant health benefits to other regions of the country where the LEV-equivalent vehicles would be sold, and it would effectively lead to a harmonizing of California and federal standards over time. 60 Fed. Reg. at 4712, 4713 n.3. The auto industry continues to express a willingness to adopt such an approach, but industry members are unwilling to develop and commit to it without a concomitant commitment of OTC states to agree to accept such vehicles and to refrain from opting for the stricter California approach. Among other things, this would mean that New York and Massachusetts would need to drop their current ZEV requirements. Ironically, EPA can neither require the auto industry to develop such a "third vehicle" because of the Clean Air Act's limitation that only two government standards are allowed (the existing federal standards and the California standards, nor can it require any state to refrain from exercising the option to adopt the California standards), nor can it require any state to refrain from exercising the option to adopt the California standards, as was upheld in the case you have just read. Thus, EPA proceeded to issue its call for SIP revisions by the jurisdictions in the OTC, adopting the California LEV approach.

4. On remand, the district court dismissed the auto manufacturers' remaining claim that New York violated the third vehicle prohibition by failing to adopt California's clean fuels program to supplant New York's higher-sulfur gasoline. Motor Vehicle Manufacturers Assn. v. New York

Dept. of Environmental Conservation, No. 92-CV-869 (N.D.N.Y. Oct. 22, 1994). The court noted that New York was not mandating any modifications of catalytic converters to cope with the higher-sulfur gasoline.

5. The First Circuit has affirmed a district court's refusal to grant a preliminary injunction against the LEV program adopted by Massachusetts. American Automobile Manufacturers Assn. v. Commission, Massachusetts Dept. of Environmental Protection, 31 F.3d 18 (1st Cir. 1994). Unlike the Second Circuit, the First Circuit accepted EPA's interpretation of "model year" and ruled for the state on the two-year lead time issue.

6. As a result of the 1990 Amendments to the Clean Air Act, efforts to develop clean car technology are intensifying. In January 1995 the Honda Motor Company surprised many by announcing that it had developed an engine that reduces tailpipe emissions by 90 percent despite burning reformulated gasoline. Bennet, New Honda Engine a Threat to Natural Gas, N.Y. Times, Jan. 9, 1995, at D1. It previously had been anticipated that only cars running on an alternative fuel such as natural gas could satisfy the LEV program standards. However, even Honda's engine will not be sufficient to comply with the zero-emissions vehicle (ZEV) standards that will apply to two percent of the vehicle fleet in California, New York, and Massachusetts beginning in 1998. Only electric vehicles are expected to meet this standard.

7. The ZEV standards are generating considerable investment in electric car technology. While substantial progress is being made, the largest obstacle to producing economical electric vehicles seems to be limitations in battery performance. See Electric Cars, Business Week, May 30, 1994, at 36. Eyeing a new market for their product, electric utilities are getting involved in promoting the development of electric vehicles. Wald, Advances in Electric Cars for Masses, N.Y. Times, Dec. 2, 1994, at D5. Automobile manufacturers are trying to determine the best marketing strategy for vehicles that initially are likely to be substantially more costly, while offering more limited performance, than conventional models. Mathews, Generating a Market for Electric Cars, Wash. Post, Oct. 6, 1994, at D11; Stern, General Motors Says Saturn Division Is Likely to Market Electric Cars in U.S., Wall St. J., Mar. 8, 1995, at A5.

H. PREVENTION OF SIGNIFICANT DETERIORATION

The "Top-Down" Approach to BACT (p. 852). Despite intense pressure from the Competitiveness Council, outgoing EPA administrator

6. Air Pollution Control

William Reilly refused to modify EPA's "top-down" approach to BACT determinations (parent text, p. 852). The "top-down" approach was initially outlined in guidance issued by EPA in 1987. OMB and the Competitiveness Council at one point had held up all EPA rules in hopes of forcing Reilly to modify the "top-down" approach prior to the Bush Administration's leaving office. Instead, Reilly issued a memorandum on January 19, 1993 that suggested that the new administration should convene a regulatory negotiation to explore alternative approaches to BACT determination at some time in the future.

The "WEPCO Fix" (p. 852). In a controversial effort to clarify the application of preconstruction review requirements and new source performance standards to electric utility projects, EPA issued what has become known as the "WEPCO fix." 57 Fed. Reg. 32,314 (1992). The regulations respond to the decision in Wisconsin Electric Power Co. v. Reilly, 893 F.2d 901 (7th Cir. 1990). As predicted in the parent text (p. 852), the regulations provide that an "actual-to-future-actual" approach shall be used to assess whether or not modifications at an existing facility generate an emissions increase that triggers new source review. They also exempt certain pollution control projects from new source review.

Visibility Protection in National Parks (p. 852). In Central Arizona Water Conservation District v. EPA, 990 F.2d 1531 (9th Cir. 1993), the Ninth Circuit upheld EPA regulations requiring a power plant to reduce sulfur dioxide emissions by 90 percent in order to improve visibility in Grand Canyon National Park during the wintertime. The court held that EPA could address visibility impairment "reasonably attributable" to an individual source even if the regulations would produce less than a 10 percent improvement in visibility.

I. AIR TOXICS

Revisions to NESHAPs (p. 860). In March 1992, EPA issued a temporary stay of the effective date of the benzene NESHAP (parent text, pp. 860, 593-598) in order to give the Agency time to issue clarifying amendments. 57 Fed. Reg. 8017 (1992). The stay was lifted in December 1992 after clarifying amendments were promulgated by EPA. 58 Fed. Reg. 3072 (1993). Pursuant to section 112(d)(9) of the Clean Air Act, EPA proposed in September 1992 to stay application of its radionuclides NESHAP to facilities licensed by the Nuclear Regulatory Commission.

However, the D.C. Circuit held that EPA did not have the authority to stay the standards for facilities other than nuclear power plants. NRDC v. Reilly, 976 F.2d 36 (1992). As a result of a highly successful regulatory negotiation, EPA has promulgated a NESHAP for coke oven emissions. 58 Fed. Reg. 57,898 (1993).

EPA's Source Category List and Schedule for Issuance of Standards (p. 862). In July 1992, EPA published the list required by section 112(c) of categories of sources that emit any of the hazardous air pollutants identified in section 112(b) of the Act. 57 Fed. Reg. 31,576 (1992). EPA's list includes 174 source categories. In 1993, EPA published its schedule for issuing emissions standards for these source categories. 58 Fed. Reg. 63,941 (1993). This schedule arranged source categories into four classes, with emission standards to be issued for each no later than November 15th of 1992, 1994, 1997, and 2000. If an applicable emission standard is not promulgated on schedule for a listed category of sources, the sources become subject to case-by-case emission limits under section 112(j) of the Act, which must be equivalent to the limit that would have applied if the standards had been promulgated on schedule.

The Proposed HON Rule: MACT Regulations for SOCMI (p. 862). Will EPA's implementation of the revised section 112 provide more evidence bearing on the question of whether a health-based, a technology-based, or a balancing approach to toxic substances control is preferable? After a spirited battle with OMB and the Competitiveness Council and a deadline suit brought by NRDC, in November 1992 EPA administrator William Reilly issued the first proposed regulations to implement the technology-based provisions of the amended section 112. 57 Fed. Reg. 62,608 (1992). Known as the "HON" rule (for "hazardous organic NESHAP"), the proposal would establish MACT regulations for 149 organic hazardous air pollutants emitted by production processes of the synthetic organic chemical manufacturing industry (SOCMI). If finally adopted, these restrictions are estimated to reduce emissions of these hazardous air pollutants by 80 percent. The nature of the control technologies involved implies that volatile organic compounds, precursors to the production of ozone and other photochemical oxidants, will also be reduced by 71 percent. The hazardous air pollutant reductions would be approximately 50 percent of the levels of air emissions reported in the latest Toxics Release Inventory data. (Figures for 1991 air emissions were reported in May 1993 to be approximately 2 billion pounds per year.)

A major feature of the proposed HON rule is that companies would be allowed to average their emissions in meeting the MACT standard. MACT controls will apply to process vents, storage vessels, transfer racks, wastewater streams, and equipment leaks, but firms will be able to employ a bubble concept (called emissions averaging) under which sources can overcontrol at any of these specific sources to produce emissions credits, which can then be used to offset undercontrol at any other such specific source at the same facility covering a contiguous area and under common control. Critics of this proposal argue that it compromises health protection because it does not require each individual source to install maximum controls. At least "one of the sources in an averaging scheme would not be using state-of-the-art controls," and thus "we could not ensure the greatest protection to public health." Proposal on Hazardous Organic Emissions, Final Early Reduction Rules Issued by EPA, 22 Env. Rep. 1707 (1992) (quoting the co-chair of State and Territorial Air Pollution Program Administrators). They also argue that emissions averaging causes administrative and enforcement problems.

Basing their opinion on estimates that compliance with MACT would cost the industry more than $2,000 per ton of toxic emissions removed, OMB and Competitiveness Council officials had viewed EPA's initial proposals as too costly. An unidentified bush Administration source was quoted as saying that "[t]he risks involved only justify going to a $1,000" per ton level and that "[n]obody has demonstrated any health benefits from these reductions." OMB, EPA Discussing Differences on Rule to Control Emissions from Chemical Industry, 22 Env. Rep. 1583, 1584 (1992). The emissions averaging permitted under the proposed rule is expected to ease some of the costs of compliance, which EPA now estimates at $347 million in capital costs and $182 million in annual operating expenses. Proposal on Hazardous Organic Emissions, Final Early Reduction Rules Issued by EPA, 22 Env. Rep. 1707 (1992).

EPA adopted the HON rule in final form in April 1994. 59 Fed. Reg. 19,402 (1994). The final rule regulates emissions of 112 of the 189 hazardous air pollutants covered by §112. The emissions averaging provisions included in EPA's proposed rule were modified substantially in the final rule. Sources who wish to use emissions averaging must demonstrate that it will not result in greater risk or hazard than compliance without averaging. New sources are not allowed to use emissions averaging to comply with the regulations and the number of emissions points that can be included in emissions averaging was reduced to 20. The final rule was estimated to impose capital costs of $450 million and annual operating costs of $230 million, amounts greater than the proposed rule in part due to the restrictions on emissions averaging.

For a somewhat skeptical view of the impact of the 1990 Amendments on control of hazardous air pollutants, see Wichers, Cooke, Kramarz, and Brandon, Regulation of Hazardous Air Pollutants Under the New Clean Air Act: Technology-Based Standards at Last, 22 Env. L. Rep. 10717 (1992) (arguing that implementation of section 112 is likely to overtax EPA's limited resources and that even full implementation of MACT may not be any more effective than the pre-amendment section 112).

Incentives for Early Reduction (p. 862). EPA issued regulations governing the early reduction program of section 112(i) in December 1992. 57 Fed. Reg. 61,970 (1992). While the regulations allow facilities to treat diverse emissions as a single "source" for purposes of calculating emissions reductions, they identify 47 high-risk pollutants for which limits are established on the use of offsetting reductions from other sources. By October 1992, a total of 32 companies, including Allied Signal, American Cyanamid, DuPont, Monsanto, and Union Carbide, had pledged to qualify for the early reductions program by reducing emissions of hazardous air pollutants at 47 chemical plants more than 90 percent by January 1, 1994. Rosewicz, EPA Acts to Cut Toxic Emissions, Draws Criticism, Wall St. J., Oct. 30, 1992, at A4. For example, the Kalama Chemical Company reported that it would make "relatively simple changes" to reduce emissions of benzene and toluene from oxidation vents at its plant in Kalama, Washington. Plant officials said these changes will cut estimated releases of these two chemicals to 32 tons per year. In order to qualify for the early reductions program, Kalama is asking EPA to use its 1987 emissions estimate of 328 tons as the base year, rather than its 1986 estimate of 106 tons of emissions. Four Companies Commit to Early Reductions of Hazardous Air Pollutants, EPA Announces, 23 Env. Rep. 1461 (1992). Why would Kalama want EPA to use 1987 as the base year instead of 1986? Should EPA approve this request?

By December 1992, EPA had received 76 "enforceable commitments" for early reductions, and it had approved 12 of them as sufficient to demonstrate that the facilities will achieve the required 90 percent reductions. 57 Fed. Reg. 58,203 (1992).

=7=
Water Pollution Control

> Where the State seeks to sustain regulation that deprives land of all economically beneficial use, we think it may resist compensation only if the logically antecedent inquiry into the nature of the owner's estate shows that the proscribed use interests were not part of his title to begin with.
>
> —*Lucas v. South Carolina Coastal Council**

> The common law of nuisance is too narrow a confine for the exercise of regulatory power in a complex and interdependent society. The State should not be prevented from enacting new regulatory initiatives in response to changing conditions, and courts must consider all reasonable expectations whatever their source. The Takings Clause does not require a static body of state property law; it protects private expectations to ensure private investment.
>
> —*Id.***

Efforts to control water pollution continue to shift their focus toward control of nonpoint sources of pollution. Yet land use regulation and measures to protect wetlands continue to face vigorous political opposition from the emerging property rights movement. While the new Republican majority in Congress is moving legislation to relax major provisions of the Clean Water Act, the Supreme Court has energized opponents of land use regulation with its decisions in Lucas v. South Carolina Coastal Council and Dolan v. City of Tagard.

After reviewing developments in water pollution control and an important Supreme Court decision interpreting the Clean Water Act, this chapter focuses on the *Lucas* and *Dolan* decisions and their implications for the future of environmental regulation. It also discusses further developments concerning citizen enforcement actions and the enactment of the Federal Facility Compliance Act of 1992.

---

*112 S. Ct. 2886, 2899 (Scalia, J., majority opinion).
**Id. at 2903 (Kennedy, J., concurring in the judgment).

A. THE WATER POLLUTION PROBLEM

Water Quality Trends (pp. 866-867). The water pollution control effort can be viewed as a kind of good news/bad news story. The Clean Water Act has kept levels of many water pollutants substantially below what they otherwise would be. Yet severe water pollution problems remain, particularly as a result of nonpoint pollution, combined sewer overflows, and discharges from sewage treatment plants. This was vividly illustrated in April 1993 when Milwaukee's municipal water supply became contaminated with cryptosporidium, an intestinal parasite that apparently originated in runoff from dairy farms. Thousands of people experienced nausea, cramps, and diarrhea, and at least one elderly cancer patient may have died as a result of drinking the contaminated water. Hinds, '92 Study Hinted Milwaukee Had Parasite Present, N.Y. Times, April 10, 1993, at A6. In March 1995 EPA reported that in 1994 nearly 30 million Americans received drinking water from systems that failed to meet one or more public health standards. EPA, Strengthening the Safety of Our Drinking Water (1995). Microbial contaminants like cryptosporidium and giardia were found to be among the largest problems facing water suppliers. For an assessment of the impact of the Clean Water Act on water quality, see Knopman and Smith, Twenty Years of the Clean Water Act: Has U.S. Water Quality Improved? Environment 16 (Jan.-Feb. 1993); see also R. Adler, The Clean Water Act: 20 Years Later (1993).

It remains surprisingly difficult to make a comprehensive assessment of water quality in the United States. As the Council on Environmental Quality notes, "[d]espite decades of research and regulation, the federal government still lacks a comprehensive assessment of the quality of the nation's waters." CEQ, 23d Annual Report 225 (1993). What data are available from EPA's 1992 National Water Quality Inventory indicate that only 56 percent of river miles examined and 43 percent of lake acres assessed have water quality that fully supports their intended uses. However, water quality data are not available for nearly 80 percent of river miles and more than one half of lake and reservoir acres. EPA previously had explained that "many waters remain unassessed because States are generally constrained by diminishing resources and competing needs to monitor most often in those waters with known or suspected problems." EPA, National Water Quality Inventory—1990 Report to Congress xiv (1992). Moreover, the decentralized approach to water quality testing causes major problems of data quality and consistency. Data that were collected were "reported by States with differing monitoring

7. Water Pollution Control

capabilities, water quality standards, and assessment approaches." Id. Despite inadequacies in water quality monitoring, state agencies have issued approximately 1,500 fishing bans or restrictions throughout the country due to water pollution problems. EPA maintains a National Listing of Fish Consumption Advisories, which is available on computer disk by contacting Jeff Bigler of EPA at (202) 260-1305.

B. STATUTORY AUTHORITIES FOR CONTROLLING WATER POLLUTION

Clean Water Act Reauthorization (pp. 877-879). Although several congressional hearings were held on reauthorization of the Clean Water Act, no reauthorization bill reached the floor of either House in 1993 or 1994. But the new Republican majority in the 104th Congress rapidly moved reauthorization legislation. In May 1995 the House of Representatives, by a vote of 240-185 approved a comprehensive reauthorization bill, H.R. 961, that would dramatically weaken the Clean Water Act. The bill would drastically restrict the amount of wetlands protected by section 404 of the Act while making control of stormwater pollution essentially voluntary. It would relax technology-based effluent standards for certain industries and permit further water quality-based improvements only if it could be demonstrated that their benefits exceeded their costs. "Polluters wrote the bill," declared a New York Times editorial that described the process as "amount[ing] to an open house for the lobbyists and lawyers representing the special interests the 1972 Act is designed to regulate." Bud Shuster's Dirty Water Act, N.Y. Times, April 2, 1995, at E14. President Clinton has threatened to veto the legislation, which is not expected to move rapidly through the Senate. Senator John Chafee, who chairs the Senate Environment and Public Works Committee, does not favor relaxing the Clean Water Act.

C. EFFLUENT LIMITATIONS ON POINT SOURCE DISCHARGES

Defining Point Sources Subject to Permit Requirements (p. 885-893). As noted in the parent text, the Clean Water Act uses the NPDES permit system to apply effluent standards to point sources of water pollution and publicly owned treatment works. EPA reported in 1992 that a total of 7,102 major permits and 56,791 minor permits have been issued to point sources by EPA and state authorities under the NPDES program. EPA, National Water Quality Inventory—1990 Report to Congress 136 (1992).

Courts continue to grapple with the question of what constitutes a point source. In Committee to Save Mokelumne River v. East Bay Municipal Utility District, 13 F.3d 305 (9th Cir. 1993), the Ninth Circuit held that a series of surface impoundments designed to capture, contain and evaporate toxic runoff from an abandoned copper and zinc mine was a point source requiring an NPDES permit. The court distinguished cases holding that a dam was not a point source by noting that the facility did "not pass pollution from one body of navigable water into another," but rather allows it occasionally to spill from surface impoundments into a nearby river. In a concurring opinion Judge Fernandez suggested that because the facility was like a dam and had been constructed to help reduce pollution, he would have been willing to defer to an EPA determination that it was not a point source. EPA, however, had made no such finding.

In the case below the U.S. Court of Appeals for the Second Circuit addressed the question whether a person can be a point source for purposes of the Clean Water Act.

United States v. Plaza Health Laboratories, Inc.
3 F.3d 643 (2d Cir. 1993)

Before: OAKES, KEARSE, and PRATT, Circuit Judges.
GEORGE C. PRATT, Circuit Judge:

Defendant Geronimo Villegas appeals from a judgment entered in the United States District Court for the Eastern District of New York, Edward R. Korman, Judge, convicting him of two counts of knowingly discharging pollutants into the Hudson River in violation of the Clean Water Act ("CWA"). See 33 U.S.C.§§1311 and 1319(c)(2). . . .

FACTS AND BACKGROUND

Villegas was co-owner and vice president of Plaza Health Laboratories, Inc., a blood-testing laboratory in Brooklyn, New York. On at least two occasions between April and September 1988, Villegas loaded

7. Water Pollution Control — Pages 885-893

containers of numerous vials of human blood generated from his business into his personal car, and drove to his residence at the Admirals Walk Condominium in Edgewater, New Jersey. Once at his condominium complex, Villegas removed the containers from his car and carried them to the edge of the Hudson River. On one occasion he carried two containers of the vials to the bulkhead that separates his condominium complex from the river, and placed them at low tide within a crevice in the bulkhead that was below the high-water line.

On May 26, 1988, a group of eighth graders on a field trip at the Alice Austin House in Staten Island, New York, discovered numerous glass vials containing human blood along the shore. Some of the vials had washed up on the shore; many were still in the water. Some were cracked, although most remained sealed with stoppers in solid-plastic containers or ziplock bags. Fortunately, no one was injured. That afternoon, New York City workers recovered approximately 70 vials from the area.

On September 25, 1988, a maintenance worker employed by the Admirals Walk Condominium discovered a plastic container holding blood vials wedged between rocks in the bulkhead. New Jersey authorities retrieved numerous blood vials from the bulkhead later that day.

Ten of the retrieved vials contained blood infected with the hepatitis-B virus. All of the vials recovered were eventually traced to Plaza Health Laboratories.

Based upon the May 1988 discovery of vials, Plaza Health Laboratories and Villegas were indicted on May 16, 1989, on two counts each of violating §§1319(c)(2) and (3) of the Clean Water Act. 33 U.S.C. §§1251 et seq. A superseding indictment charged both defendants with two additional CWA counts based upon the vials found in September 1988.

In December of 1990 the district court granted the government's motion to sever all claims against Plaza Health Laboratories, apparently due to Plaza's participation in ongoing bankruptcy proceedings. The government then proceeded to trial against Villegas only.

Counts II and IV of the superseding indictment charged Villegas with knowingly discharging pollutants from a "point source" without a permit. See 33 U.S.C. §§1311(a), 1319(c)(2). Counts I and III alleged that Villegas had discharged pollutants, knowing that he placed others in "imminent danger of death or serious bodily injury." See 33 U.S.C. §1319(c)(3). On January 31, 1991, following a trial before Judge Korman, the jury found Villegas guilty on all four counts.

Renewing a motion made at trial, Villegas moved for a judgment of acquittal on all counts under rule 29 of the Federal Rules of Criminal Procedure. Judge Korman granted the motion on counts I and III, holding that he had incorrectly instructed the jury on the act's "knowing

351

endangerment" provisions. This ruling is reported at 784 F. Supp. 6, 13-14 (E.D.N.Y. 1991). The district judge denied the motion on counts II and IV, rejecting arguments that the act did not envision a human being as a "point source." 784 F. Supp. at 10-11.

Judge Korman sentenced Villegas on counts II and IV to two concurrent terms of twelve months' imprisonment, one year of supervised release, and a $100 special assessment. Execution of the sentence was stayed pending this appeal.

Villegas contends that one element of the CWA crime, knowingly discharging pollutants from a "point source," was not established in his case. He argues that the definition of "point source," 33 U.S.C. §1362(14), does not include discharges that result from the individual acts of human beings. Raising primarily questions of legislative intent and statutory construction, Villegas argues that at best, the term "point source" is ambiguous as applied to him, and that the rule of lenity should result in reversal of his convictions. . . .

DISCUSSION . . .

A. *Navigating the Clean Water Act*

The basic prohibition on discharge of pollutants is in 33 U.S.C. §1311(a), which states:

> Except as in compliance with this section and sections 1312, 1316, 1317, 1328, 1342, and 1344 of this title, the *discharge* of any *pollutant* by any person shall be unlawful.

Id. (emphasis added).

The largest exception to this seemingly absolute rule is found in 33 U.S.C. §1342, which establishes the CWA's national pollutant discharge elimination system, or NPDES:

> (a) Permits for discharge of pollutants
> (1) Except as provided in sections 1328 [aquaculture] and 1344 of this title [dredge and fill permits], the Administrator may, after opportunity for public hearing, issue a permit for the discharge of any pollutant . . . *notwithstanding section 1311(a) of this title*, upon condition that such discharge will meet . . . all applicable requirements under sections 1311, 1312, 1316, 1317, 1318, and 1343 of this title. . . .

33 U.S.C. §1342(a) (emphasis added).

Reading §1311(a), the basic prohibition, and §1342(a)(1), the

7. Water Pollution Control   Pages 885-893

permit section, together, we can identify the basic rule, our rhumb line to clean waters, that, absent a permit, "the discharge of any pollutant by any person" is unlawful. 33 U.S.C. §1311(a). *[Basic Rule]*

We must then adjust our rhumb line by reference to two key definitions—"pollutant" and "discharge." "Pollutant" is defined, in part, as "biological materials . . . *discharged* into water." 33 U.S.C. §1362(6) (emphasis added). "Discharge," in turn, is "any addition of any pollutant to navigable waters *from any point source*. . . ." (emphasis added). 33 U.S.C. §1362(12).

As applied to the facts of this case, then, the defendant "added" a "pollutant" (human blood in glass vials) to "navigable waters" (the Hudson River), and he did so without a permit. The issue, therefore, is whether his conduct constituted a "discharge," and that in turn depends on whether the addition of the blood to the Hudson River waters was "from any point source." For this final course adjustment in our navigation, we look again to the statute. *[Issue]*

> The term "point source" means any discernible, confined and discrete conveyance, including but not limited to any pipe, ditch, channel, tunnel, conduit, well, discrete fissure, container, rolling stock, concentrated animal feeding operation, or vessel or other floating craft, from which pollutants are or may be discharged. This term does not include agricultural stormwater discharges and return flows from irrigated agriculture.

33 U.S.C. §1362(14).

During and after Villegas's trial, Judge Korman labored over how to define "point source" in this case. At one point he observed that the image of a human being is not "conjured up" by Congress's definition of "point source." Ultimately, he never defined the "point source" element but he did charge the jury:

> Removing pollutants from a container, and a vehicle is a container, parked next to a navigable body of water and physically throwing the pollutant into the water constitutes a discharge from a point source.

In ruling on Villegas's rule 29 motion, however, Judge Korman held that the element "point source" may reasonably be read

> to include any discrete and identifiable conduit—*including a human being*—designated to collect or discharge pollutants produced in the course of a waste-generating activity. (emphasis added).

As the parties have presented the issue to us in their briefs and at oral argument, the question is "whether a human being can be a

353

point source." Both sides focus on the district court's conclusion in its rule 29 memorandum that, among other things, the requisite "point source" here could be Villegas himself. . . .

Far more fundamental than any error in jury instructions is the problem highlighted by the district court's analytical struggle to find somewhere in the Villegas transaction a "discernible, confined and discrete conveyance." Simply put, that problem is that this statute was never designed to address the random, individual polluter like Villegas. . . .

1. Language and Structure of Act

Human beings are not among the enumerated items that may be a "point source." Although by its terms the definition of "point source" is nonexclusive, the words used to define the term and the examples given ("pipe, ditch, channel, tunnel, conduit, well, discrete fissure," etc.) evoke images of physical structures and instrumentalities that systematically act as a means of conveying pollutants from an industrial source to navigable waterways.

In addition, if every discharge involving humans were to be considered a "discharge from a point source," the statute's lengthy definition of "point source" would have been unnecessary. It is elemental that Congress does not add unnecessary words to statutes. Had Congress intended to punish any human being who polluted navigational waters, it could readily have said: "any person who places pollutants in navigable waters without a permit is guilty of a crime."

The Clean Water Act generally targets industrial and municipal sources of pollutants, as is evident from a perusal of its many sections. Consistent with this focus, the term "point source" is used throughout the statute, but invariably in sentences referencing industrial or municipal discharges. See, e.g., 33 U.S.C. §1311 (referring to "owner or operator" of point source); §1311(e) (requiring that effluent limitations established under the Act "be applied to all point sources of discharge"); §1311(g)(2) (allows an "owner or operator of a point source" to apply to EPA for modification of its limitations requirements); §1342(f) (referring to classes, categories, types, and sizes of point sources); §1314(b)(4)(B) (denoting "best conventional pollutant control technology measures and practices" applicable to any point source within particular category or class); §1316 ("any point source . . . which is constructed as to meet all applicable standards of performance"); §1318(a) (administrator shall require owner or operator of any point source to install, use and maintain monitoring equipment or methods);

and §1318(c) (states may develop procedures for inspection, monitoring, and entry with respect to point sources located in state).

This emphasis was sensible, as "industrial and municipal point sources were the worst and most obvious offenders of surface water quality. They were also the easiest to address because their loadings emerge from a discrete point such as the end of a pipe." David Letson, Point/Nonpoint Source Pollution Reduction Trading: An Interpretive Survey, 32 Nat. Resources J. 219, 221 (1992).

Finally on this point, we assume that Congress did not intend the awkward meaning that would result if we were to read "human being" into the definition of "point source." Section 1362(12)(A) defines "discharge of a pollutant" as "any addition of any pollutant to navigable waters from any point source." Enhanced by this definition, §1311(a) reads in effect "the addition of any pollutant to navigable waters *from any point source by any person* shall be unlawful" (emphasis added). But were a human being to be included within the definition of "point source", the prohibition would then read: "the addition of any pollutant to navigable waters *from any person by any person* shall be unlawful," and this simply makes no sense. As the statute stands today, the term "point source" is comprehensible only if it is held to the context of industrial and municipal discharges.

2. Legislative History and Context

The broad remedial purpose of the CWA is to "restore and maintain the chemical, physical, and biological integrity of the Nation's waters." 33 U.S.C. §1251(a). The narrow questions posed by this case, however, may not be resolved merely by simple reference to this admirable goal. See National Wildlife Fed'n v. Gorsuch, 693 F.2d 156, 178 (D.C. Cir. 1982) ("it is one thing for Congress to announce a grand goal, and quite another for it to mandate full implementation of that goal"). We agree with the court in *National Wildlife Fed'n* that "even if we accept the purposes section at face value, it is only suggestive, not dispositive of [the issue before us]. Caution is always advisable in relying on a general declaration of purpose to alter the apparent meaning of a specific provision." Id.

The legislative history of the CWA, while providing little insight into the meaning of "point source," confirms the act's focus on industrial polluters. Congress required NPDES permits of those who discharge from a "point source." The term "point source," introduced to the act in 1972, was intended to function as a means of identifying industrial polluters—generally a difficult task because pollutants quickly

355

disperse throughout the subject waters. The Senate report for the 1972 amendments explains:

> In order to further clarify the scope of the regulatory procedures in the Act the Committee had added a definition of point source to distinguish between control requirements where there are *specific confined conveyances, such as pipes,* and control requirements which are imposed to control runoff. The control of pollutants from runoff is applied pursuant to section 209 and the authority resides in the State or other local agency.

S. Rep. No. 92-414, reprinted in 1972 U.S.C.C.A.N. 3668, 3744.

Senator Robert Dole added his comments to the committee report:

> Most of the problems of agricultural pollution deal with non-point sources. Very simply, a non-point source of pollution is one that does not confine its polluting discharge to one fairly specific outlet, such as a sewer pipe, a drainage ditch or a conduit; thus, a feedlot would be considered to be a non-point source as would pesticides and fertilizers.

Id. at 3760 (supplemental views). See also *National Wildlife Fed'n*, 693 F.2d at 175 (Congress's focus was on traditional industrial and municipal wastes); E.I. du Pont de Nemours & Co. v. Train, 430 U.S. 112, 118-121, 51 L. Ed. 2d 204, 97 S. Ct. 965 (1977) (outlines EPA scheme of effluent limitations for subject industrial groups).

We find no suggestion either in the act itself or in the history of its passage that Congress intended the CWA to impose criminal liability on an individual for the myriad, random acts of human waste disposal, for example, a passerby who flings a candy wrapper into the Hudson River, or a urinating swimmer. Discussions during the passage of the 1972 amendments indicate that Congress had bigger fish to fry.

The 1972 Congress modeled the NPDES, its aggressive new permitting program, after the Rivers and Harbors Act of 1899 ("RHA"; known also as the Refuse Act), 33 U.S.C. §401, et seq. See S. Rep. No. 92-414, reprinted in 1972 U.S.C.C.A.N. 3668, 3672 & 3738. The CWA's focus on transporting pollutants to navigable waters via the "point source" mechanism represented a departure from the RHA's more general approach:

> It shall not be lawful to throw, discharge, or deposit . . . any refuse matter of any kind or description whatever other than that flowing from streets and sewers and passing therefrom in a liquid state, into any navigable water of the United States. . . .

33 U.S.C. §407.

Unlike §§1311 and 1319(c)(2) of the CWA, the RHA's relevant

criminal provision, 33 U.S.C. §411, has been held to provide for strict liability, and the most severe criminal penalty is a misdemeanor. United States v. White Fuel Corp., 498 F.2d 619, 622 (1st Cir. 1974). Accordingly, we view with skepticism the government's contention that we should broadly construe the greatly magnified penal provisions of the CWA based upon RHA cases that did so in the context of strict-liability and misdemeanor penalties. See, e.g., United States v. Standard Oil Co., 384 U.S. 224, 229-230, 16 L. Ed. 2d 492, 86 S. Ct. 1427 (1966) (holding "refuse matter" in §407 includes commercially valuable gasoline accidentally discharged into navigable river); United States v. American Cyanamid Co., 354 F. Supp. 1202, 1205 (S.D.N.Y. 1973) (construing RHA broadly, court held that refuse discharged into tributary satisfied "navigable waters" requirement); see also United States v. Republic Steel Corp., 362 U.S. 482, 489-491, 4 L. Ed. 2d 903, 80 S. Ct. 884 (1960) (RHA construed broadly in injunction context; RHA "obstruction" included liquid matter discharged from mills which impaired navigation by settling in bottom of channel).

3. Caselaw

Our search for the meaning of "point source" brings us next to judicial constructions of the term.

The "point source" element was clearly established in the few CWA criminal decisions under §1319(c) that are reported. See United States v. Boldt, 929 F.2d 35, 37-38 (1st Cir. 1991) (discharge of partially untreated industrial wastewater from storage tank directly into municipal sewer); United States v. Frezzo Bros., Inc., 602 F.2d 1123, 1125 (3d Cir. 1979) (compost materials discharged from pipe into tributary of creek), cert. denied, 444 U.S. 1074, 62 L. Ed. 2d 756, 100 S. Ct. 1020 (1980); United States v. Hamel, 551 F.2d 107, 108 (6th Cir. 1977) (gasoline pumped into lake from underground tank); cf. United States v. Oxford Royal Mushroom Products, Inc., 487 F. Supp. 852, 854 (E.D. Pa. 1980) (overflow of spray-irrigation system discharging waste water into nearby stream is "point source" discharge).

With the exception of *Oxford Royal Mushroom*, supra, the cases that have interpreted "point source" have done so in civil-penalty or licensing settings, where greater flexibility of interpretation to further remedial legislative purposes is permitted, and the rule of lenity does not protect a defendant against statutory ambiguities. See, e.g., Avoyelles Sportsmen's League, Inc. v. Marsh, 715 F.2d 897, 922 (5th Cir. 1983) ("point source" includes bulldozing equipment that discharged dredged materials onto wetland).

For example, our circuit recently held in Dague v. City of Burlington, a civil-penalty case, that a discharge of pollutant-laden leachate into a culvert leading to navigable waters was through a "point source." 935 F.2d 1343, 1354-1355 (2d Cir. 1991), rev'd in part on other grounds, 112 S. Ct. 2638 (1992). But in *Dague*, unlike in this case, the city's discharge involved a culvert, one of the specifically enumerated examples of a "point source" set forth in §1362(14). *Dague*, 935 F.2d at 1354. *Dague* thus presented a classic "point source" discharge.

The government relies on broad dicta in another civil case, United States v. Earth Sciences, Inc., 599 F.2d 368, 373 (10th Cir. 1979), in which the court held "the concept of a point source was designed to further this [permit regulatory] scheme by embracing the broadest possible definition of any identifiable conveyance from which pollutants might enter the waters of the United States." We do not find this *Earth Sciences* dicta persuasive here, however, because that court found a "point source" in a ditch used in the mining operation—certainly not a far leap when "ditch" also is an expressly listed example of a "point source." We cannot, however, make the further leap of writing "human being" into the statutory language without doing violence to the language and structure of the CWA.

4. Regulatory Structure

Finally, not even the EPA's regulations support the government's broad assertion that a human being may be a "point source." Cf. National Wildlife Fed'n, 693 F.2d at 166-167 & 173 n.54 (as EPA has power to define point and nonpoint sources in CWA, courts must give great deference to EPA's construction of "point source"). The EPA stresses that the discharge be "through pipes, sewers, or other conveyances":

> *Discharge of a pollutant* means:
> (a) Any addition of any "pollutant" or combination of pollutants to "waters of the United States" from any "point source.". . .
> This definition includes additions of pollutants into waters of the United States from: surface runoff which is collected or channelled by man; *discharges through pipes, sewers, or other conveyances* owned by a State, municipality, or other person which do not lead to a treatment works; and discharges through pipes, sewers, or other conveyances, leading into privately owned treatment works. This term does not include an addition of pollutants by any "indirect discharger."

40 C.F.R. §122.2 (1992) (emphasis supplied).

In sum, although Congress had the ability to so provide, §1362(14) of the CWA does not expressly recognize a human being as a "point source"; nor does the act make structural sense when one incorporates a human being into that definition. The legislative history of the act adds no light to the muddy depths of this issue, and cases urging a broad interpretation of the definition in the civil-penalty context do not persuade us to do so here, where Congress has imposed heavy criminal sanctions. Adopting the government's suggested flexibility for the definition would effectively read the "point source" element of the crime out of the statute, and not even the EPA has extended the term "point source" as far as is urged here.

We accordingly conclude that the term "point source" as applied to a human being is at best ambiguous.

B. Rule of Lenity

In criminal prosecutions the rule of lenity requires that ambiguities in the statute be resolved in the defendant's favor. . . .

Since the government's reading of the statute in this case founders on our inability to discern the "obvious intention of the legislature," Huddleston, 415 U.S. at 831, to include a human being as a "point source," we conclude that the criminal provisions of the CWA did not clearly proscribe Villegas's conduct and did not accord him fair warning of the sanctions the law placed on that conduct. Under the rule of lenity, therefore, the prosecutions against him must be dismissed. . . .

OAKES, Circuit Judge, dissenting:

I agree that this is not the typical Clean Water Act prosecution—though, as criminal prosecutions under the Act are infrequent, or at least result in few published judicial opinions, what is "typical" is as yet ill-defined. I also agree that the prosecutors in this case may not have defined the theory of their case before proceeding to trial as well as they might have, thereby complicating the task of determining whether the jury was asked to resolve the proper factual questions. However, because I do not agree that a person can never be a point source, and because I believe that Mr. Villegas' actions, as the jury found them, fell well within the bounds of activity proscribed by the Clean Water Act's bar on discharge of pollutants into navigable waters, I am required to dissent. . . .

The key in this case is the definition of a point source. The term is introduced as part of the definition of "discharge of a pollutant": "any addition of any pollutant to navigable waters from any point source." 33 U.S.C. §1362(12)(A) (1988). The term "point source," in turn, is defined as *any discernible, confined and discrete conveyance, including but not limited* to any pipe, ditch, channel, tunnel, conduit, well, discrete fissure, container, rolling stock, concentrated animal feeding operation, or vessel or other floating craft, from which pollutants are or may be discharged. This term does not include agricultural stormwater discharges and return flows from irrigated agriculture.

33 U.S.C. §1362(14) (1988) (emphasis added).

The language of this definition indicates that it encompasses a wide range of means of placing pollutants into navigable waters. The question before us is what, in addition to the listed examples, is a "discernible, confined and discrete conveyance."

I begin with the obvious, in hopes that it will illuminate the less obvious: the classic point source is something like a pipe. This is, at least in part, because pipes and similar conduits are needed to carry large quantities of waste water, which represents a large proportion of the point source pollution problem. Thus, devices designed to convey large quantities of waste water from a factory or municipal sewage treatment facility are readily classified as point sources. Because not all pollutants are liquids, however, the statute and the cases make clear that means of conveying solid wastes to be dumped in navigable waters are also point sources. See, e.g., 33 U.S.C. §1362(14) ("rolling stock," or railroad cars, listed as an example of a point source); Avoyelles Sportsmen's League, Inc. v. Marsh, 715 F.2d 897, 922 (5th Cir. 1983) (backhoes and bulldozers used to gather fill and deposit it on wetlands are point sources).

What I take from this look at classic point sources is that, at the least, an organized means of channeling and conveying industrial waste in quantity to navigable waters is a "discernible, confined and discrete conveyance." The caselaw is in accord: courts have deemed a broad range of means of depositing pollutants in the country's navigable waters to be point sources. See, e.g., Rybachek v. EPA, 904 F.2d 1276 (9th Cir. 1990) (placer mining; sluice box from which discharge water is redeposited in stream is point source, despite provisions protecting some mining activities); United States v. M.C.C. of Fla., Inc., 772 F.2d 1501, 1505-1506 (11th Cir. 1985) (tugs redepositing dirt from bottom of water body onto beds of water grass are point sources discharging the dirt), vacated on other grounds, 481 U.S. 1034 (1987) (defendants' right to jury trial); Sierra Club v. Abston Constr. Co., 620 F.2d 41, 45 (5th Cir. 1980) (spill of contaminated runoff from strip mine, if collected or channeled by the operator, is point source discharge); United States v. Earth Sciences, Inc., 599 F.2d 368, 374 (10th Cir. 1979) (same); Appalachian Power Co. v. Train, 545 F.2d 1351, 1372 (4th Cir. 1976) (same); O'Leary v. Moyer's Landfill, Inc., 523 F. Supp. 642, 655 (E.D.

7. Water Pollution Control   Pages 885-893

Pa. 1981) (same). Nor have courts been inclined to exclude mining or agricultural point sources, despite the fact that portions of the Clean Water Act protect these industries to some extent. . . .

Further, the legislative history indicates that the Act was meant to control periodic, as well as continuous, discharges. S. Rep. No. 92-414, 92d Cong. 1st Sess. (1971), reprinted at 1972 U.S.C.C.A.N. 3668, 3705.

In short, the term "point source" has been broadly construed to apply to a wide range of polluting techniques, so long as the pollutants involved are not just humanmade, but reach the navigable waters by human effort or by leaking from a clear point at which waste water was collected by human effort. From these cases, the writers of one respected treatise have concluded that such a "man-induced gathering mechanism plainly is the essential characteristic of a point source" and that a point source, "put simply, . . . is an identifiable conveyance of pollutants." 5 Robert E. Beck, Waters & Water Rights §53.01(b)(3) at 216-17 (1991). . . .

In explaining why a broad definition was needed, the *Kennecott Copper* court, quoting American Petroleum Inst. v. EPA, 540 F.2d 1023, 1032 (10th Cir. 1976), cert. denied, 430 U.S. 922, 97 S. Ct. 1340, 51 L. Ed. 2d 601 (1977), noted that the statute sets as its goal the "attainment of the no discharge objective," and that this objective could not be achieved if the term "point source" were read narrowly. 612 F.2d at 1243. . . .

Nonetheless, the term "point source" sets significant definitional limits on the reach of the Clean Water Act. Fifty percent or more of all water pollution is thought to come from nonpoint sources. S. Rep. 99-50, 99th Cong., 1st Sess. 8 (1985); William F. Pedersen, Jr., Turning the Tide on Water Quality, 15 Ecol. L.Q. 69, n. 10 (1988). So, to further refine the definition of "point source," I consider what it is that the Act does not cover: nonpoint source discharges.

Nonpoint source pollution is, generally, runoff: salt from roads, agricultural chemicals from farmlands, oil from parking lots, and other substances washed by rain, in diffuse patterns, over the land and into navigable waters. The sources are many, difficult to identify and difficult to control. Indeed, an effort to greatly reduce nonpoint source pollution could require radical changes in land use patterns which Congress evidently was unwilling to mandate without further study. The structure of the statute—which regulates point source pollution closely, while leaving nonpoint source regulation to the states under the Section 208 program—indicates that the term "point source" was included in the definition of discharge so as to ensure that nonpoint source pollution would not be covered. Instead, Congress chose to regulate first that which could easily be regulated: direct discharges by identifiable parties, or point sources.

361

This rationale for regulating point and nonpoint sources differently—that point sources may readily be controlled and are easily attributable to a particular source, while nonpoint sources are more difficult to control without radical change, and less easily attributable, once they reach water, to any particular responsible party—helps define what fits within each category. Thus, Professor Rodgers has suggested, "the statutory 'discernible, confined and discrete conveyance' . . . can be understood as singling out those candidates suitable for control-at-the-source." 2 William H. Rodgers, Jr., Environmental Law: Air and Water §4.10 at 150 (1986). And, as Professor Rodgers notes, "case law confirms the controllability theory, adding to it a responsibility component, so that 'point sources' are understood both as sources that can be cleaned up and as sources where fairness suggests the named parties should do the cleaning." Id. . . .

While Villegas' activities were not prototypical point source discharges—in part because he was disposing of waste that could have been disposed of on land, and so did not need a permit or a pipe—they much more closely resembled a point source discharge than a nonpoint source discharge. First, Villegas and his lab were perfectly capable of avoiding discharging their waste into water: they were, in Professor Rodgers' terms, a "controllable" source.

Furthermore, the discharge was directly into water, and came from an identifiable point, Villegas. Villegas did not dispose of the materials on land, where they could be washed into water as nonpoint source pollution. Rather, he carried them, from his firm's laboratory, in his car, to his apartment complex, where he placed them in a bulkhead below the high tide line. I do not think it is necessary to determine whether it was Mr. Villegas himself who was the point source, or whether it was his car, the vials, or the bulkhead: in a sense, the entire stream of Mr. Villegas' activity functioned as a "discrete conveyance" or point source. The point is that the source of the pollution was clear, and would have been easy to control. Indeed, Villegas was well aware that there were methods of controlling the discharge (and that the materials were too dangerous for casual disposal): his laboratory had hired a professional medical waste handler. He simply chose not to use an appropriate waste disposal mechanism.

Villegas' method may have been an unusual one for a corporate officer, but it would undermine the statute—which, after all, sets as its goal the elimination of discharges, 33 U.S.C. §1311(a)—to regard as "ambiguous" a Congressional failure to list an unusual method of disposing of waste. I doubt that Congress would have regarded an army of men and women throwing industrial waste from trucks into a stream as exempt from the statute. Since the Act contains no exemption for de minimus violations—since, indeed, many Clean Water Act prosecu-

7. Water Pollution Control   Pages 885-893

tions are for a series of small discharges, each of which is treated as a single violation—I cannot see that one man throwing one day's worth of medical waste into the ocean differs (and indeed, with this type of pollution, it might be that only a few days' violations could be proven even if the laboratory regularly relied on Villegas to dispose of its waste by throwing it into the ocean). A different reading would encourage corporations perfectly capable of abiding by the Clean Water Act's requirements to ask their employees to stand between the company trucks and the sea, thereby transforming point source pollution (dumping from trucks) into nonpoint source pollution (dumping by hand). Such a method is controllable, easily identifiable, and inexcusable. To call it nonpoint source pollution is to read a technical exception into a statute which attempts to define in broad terms an activity which may be conducted in many different ways.

Having explained my own view of what a "point source" is, and why Villegas, or his activities in carrying waste from his lab to the ocean, was a point source, I will attempt to confront the majority's counterarguments. My colleagues suggest that a person can never be a point source, relying heavily on the supposed redundancy produced when the Act's language barring the "discharge of any pollutant by any person" is read with the definitional terms placed in terms of the linguistic variables, as follows: "any addition of any pollutant to navigable waters from a person by a person." Granted, this sounds odd. But I believe the oddity is an artifact of assuming that the term "person" means the same thing in both parts of the sentence, and that in both cases it means what it means in everyday language.

The apparent oddness disappears when one grasps that the first term "person" in the peculiar sentence means "a person acting as a point source"[6] and that the second term "person" has been defined, typically for statutes imposing responsibility on a variety of parties, but not typically for ordinary speech, as a responsible party. As the linguistic hint "any" before both "person" and "point source" suggests, the terms are to be construed broadly. Thus, for example, one could fill in the linguistic variables as follows: the Act bars the addition of any pollutant to navigable waters by an employee's throwing them there (a person acting as a point source) at the instruction of his or her employer (a corporation, or person capable of being held responsible) and in

---

6. In my view, persons can be both point and nonpoint sources of pollution. They may be point sources when they deposit waste directly into water; they may be nonpoint sources when they, for example, spread fertilizer on the ground or deposit oil in a driveway, leaving it to be washed into nearby rivers. Thus, to say that the Clean Water Act bars persons polluting, rather than point sources polluting, would be too broad.

particular of his or her supervisor (also a person capable of being held responsible). More specifically, the sentence could refer to an individual hired to convey, by hand, all of a corporation's toxic wastes from the company's back door to the Mississippi River, three feet away (the point source), by that individual and by the corporation which authorized the disposal (the potential defendants). I do not think technical arguments about whether the toxic substances were in discrete containers are fruitful when the activity is discrete, conveys pollutants, and is confined to a clear, traceable single source. When a company chooses to use the nation's waters as a dumpsite for waste it has created and gathered in a manageable place,[7] it should ask for a permit or face prosecution.

I am of course given pause, however, by the nature of the criminal sanctions attached to point source discharges under §1319. Given the broad statutory definitions of pollutant and point source, it would appear that a knowing violation would include intentionally throwing a candy wrapper into the ocean—and that this is an activity which could subject the thrower to a $25,000 fine and three years in jail. It seems improbable to me that this could have been Congress' intent. Consequently, I would with the majority read the statute as ambiguous as it pertains to individual litterers, as opposed to disposers of industrial and municipal waste.[8] The latter were the principal targets of the authors of the CWA, and, as professional creators of waste, charged with knowledge that disposal of waste into navigable waters is a crime. . . .

Rule of Lenity

My colleagues also suggest that the statute is sufficiently ambiguous that the rule of lenity requires resolving the ambiguity in Villegas' favor. However, as I have indicated, I do not think the Clean Water Act is ambiguous with respect to an individual physically disposing of medical wastes, in quantity, directly into navigable waters, by means of a controllable, discrete conveyance and course of action. . . .

---

7. I mean to distinguish a company whose agricultural or other activity leaves pollutants dispersed on the land, which may then find their way into the nation's waters.

8. An alternative—that the Act applies only to major discharges—seems to me both administratively unworkable (where does one draw the line?) and inconsistent with the statute and case law. The statutory definition of "discharge" refers to "any" addition of "any" pollutant from "any" point source, indicating a congressional intent to bar all, even minor, violations. Further, the D.C. Circuit has held that EPA has no discretion to limit regulation of point sources to those it deems most significant. National Resources Defense Council, Inc. v. Costle, 568 F.2d 1369, 1374 (D.C. Cir. 1977). This, too, indicates that small as well as large point sources are governed by the Act.

7. Water Pollution Control

Having resorted to the language and structure, legislative history and motivating policies of the Clean Water Act, I think it plain enough that Congress intended the statute to bar corporate officers from disposing of corporate waste into navigable waters by hand as well as by pipe. Further, I would note that this is not the sort of activity that Villegas could honestly have believed violated no statute, whether promulgated by federal, state, or local authorities. Thus, this is not a case in which the defendant had no fair warning that his actions were illegal. No compliance attorney here could have struggled with the difficulty of deciding whether this was activity for which a permit should be sought, as might be the case in a factory dealing with runoff that arguably was channelled and thereby transformed from nonpoint to point source pollution; rather, an attorney asked to advise Villegas whether his activity was permissible might say that there was as yet no case law indicating that such activity was point source pollution under the Clean Water Act, but that such a view was certainly consistent with the Act and that the behavior would almost certainly be proscribed by that Act or some other.

NOTES AND QUESTIONS

1. This case concerned events that took place during the summer of 1988, when beach closings caused by the discovery of medical waste received enormous publicity. Given the high level of public concern about contaminated blood at that time, it is not surprising that severe criminal penalties were sought. Did the fact that this case involved criminal charges have any bearing on how the court interpreted the term "point source"?

2. The court majority says that the Clean Water Act was never designed to address the random, individual polluter. Why not? Is the court majority correct when they argue that interpreting "point source" to embrace humans could subject to criminal penalties a urinating swimmer or a passerby who flings a candy wrapper into surface waters?

3. As the court notes, the Rivers and Harbors Act make it unlawful "to throw, discharge, or deposit . . . any refuse matter" into surface waters. Why do you think the government chose not to prosecute Mr. Villegas under this statute, which would not have presented the "point source" problem?

4. The court invokes the rule of lenity to resolve statutory ambiguities in favor of a defendant in a criminal case. The purpose of this rule is to ensure that individuals will have fair warning concerning what behavior is criminal. Do you think that most people would consider

the dumping of contaminated vials of blood into water where they could wash onto beaches on which children play to be a criminal act?

5. On what does Judges Oakes premise his dissenting view that persons are point sources? Is he right that under the majority's interpretation a company could avoid compliance with the Clean Water Act simply by having its employees hurl waste into water? How would Judge Oakes deal with the problem of criminalizing the urinating swimmer or the candy wrapper tosser?

6. The government was sufficiently upset about this decision to seek Supreme Court review, but the high court declined to review the case. United States v. Villegas, cert. denied, 114 S. Ct. 2764 (1994).

7. In a subsequent case, Judge Oakes, writing for a unanimous court, reversed a district court holding that a liquid manure spreading operation was not a point source for purposes of the Clean Water Act. In Concerned Area Residents for the Environment v. Southview Farm, 34 F.3d 114 (2d Cir. 1994), the Second Circuit held that because the liquid manure was collected by human effort and channelled through ditches that led to a stream, the operation was a point source. The court also held that manure spreading vehicles used by the operation were point sources because they collected liquid manure and discharged it on fields from which the manure directly flowed into navigable waters. It rejected arguments that the operation involved "agricultural stormwater discharges" exempted from the definition of "point source" in §502(14), finding that it instead involved the kind of "concentrated animal feeding operation" (CAFO) specifically listed in the point source definition. EPA has defined CAFOs to include facilities where more than 700 mature dairy cattle are kept in a confinement where crops are not sustained. Agricultural groups have reacted with alarm to this decision. The defendants' attorney argues that the case "means that if you don't grow crops in the barn, any farmer with more than 700 animals is subject to Clean Water Act sanctions," Appeals Court Rules Manure Discharges Make Farm "Point Source" Under Water Act, 25 Env. Rep. 973 (1994).

Storm Water Discharges (p. 893). In Natural Resources Defense Council v. United States EPA, 966 F.2d 1292 (9th Cir. 1992), the Ninth Circuit struck down some provisions of EPA's storm water discharge regulations (parent text, p. 893) while upholding others. The court held that it was unlawful for EPA to attempt administratively to extend the statutory deadlines for applications for, and approval of, storm water discharge permits and that the regulations must inform the regulated community of statutory compliance deadlines. The court also struck down EPA's effort to exempt certain light industry and construction sites of less than five acres from the regulations, but it upheld EPA's

7. Water Pollution Control

definition of "municipal separate storm sewer systems." In response to the court's decision, EPA issued new regulations specifying deadlines for the issuance of permits and compliance deadlines. 57 Fed. Reg. 60,444 (1992). EPA also issued regulations providing general permits for storm water discharges from more than 25,000 facilities in states that do not operate their own NPDES permit programs under delegated authority from EPA. 57 Fed. Reg. 41,236 (1992). EPA believes that the most important provision of the general permit is the requirement that facilities "implement a site-specific storm water pollution prevention plan." Storm Water General Permit Effort Focuses on Getting 25,000 Sites to Apply by Deadline, 23 Env. Rep. 1371 (1992).

EPA has completed the first phase of issuing regulations governing storm water discharges by large industrial facilities, cities with separate storm water sewer systems that serve populations of 100,000 or more, and construction projects that disturb more than five acres of land. Smaller dischargers will be regulated during the second phase. While the agency missed an October 1, 1994 deadline for issuing such regulations, EPA reportedly has developed a draft final rule that would use a two-tiered approach for regulating smaller dischargers. Dischargers determined to be significant contributors to water quality problems would have to apply for NPDES permits within 180 days, while other dischargers would be given six years to apply for such permits. Draft Storm Water Rule Shown to Groups: Agency Vows to Move Forward with Proposal, 25 Env. Rep. 2032 (1995).

Effluent Limitations: The State of the Art (p. 913). The NRDC consent decree outlining a new schedule for promulgating effluent guidelines (parent text, p. 913) was approved in Natural Resources Defense Council, Inc. v. Reilly, 781 F. Supp. 806 (D.D.C. 1992). In addition to the provisions outlined in the text, the decree requires EPA to establish an Effluent Guidelines Task Force to provide guidance to the Agency on the long-term implementation of the Act. 57 Fed. Reg. 19,748 (1992); 57 Fed. Reg. 41,000 (1992). This task force hopes to incorporate pollution prevention programs into effluent guidelines, building on the perceived success of EPA's 33/50 program. Effluent Control Program Should Use 33/50 as Model, Industry Official Says, 23 Env. Rep. 2681 (1993). In August 1994 EPA released its third biennial plan for developing new and revised effluent guidelines. 59 Fed. Reg. 44,234 (1994). EPA is continuing to develop rules for nine categories of industrial dischargers, which are to be adopted in final form at various dates between September 1995 and March 1999. Under the plan EPA will begin to develop phase two effluent guidelines for the metal products and machinery industry, which are to be adopted in final form in 1999. The agency also promises to begin development of rules for two new point source categories per year between 1996 and 1999, which it hopes to adopt in final form between the years 2000 and 2003.

Sewage Sludge Standards (p. 916). In February 1993, EPA finally published regulations governing the use and disposal of sewage sludge as required by §405(d) of the Clean Water Act. 58 Fed. Reg. 9248 (1993). The regulations establish numerical limits on concentrations of various heavy metals and pathogens in sewage sludge and they require that sewage use and disposal permits be obtained under the NPDES system. The numeric limits apply when sludge is incinerated, applied to land for a beneficial purpose, or disposed of at land disposal sites other than municipal solid waste landfills. In Sierra Club v. EPA, 992 F.2d 337 (D.C. Cir. 1993), the D.C. Circuit upheld EPA's decision to exempt sludge disposed of at municipal landfills from the numeric limits for toxic substances. The court found that EPA had insufficient information to establish numeric limits that could be justified scientifically. In November 1994 the D.C. Circuit struck down EPA's numerical limits on selenium and chromium in sludge, finding that they were insufficiently supported in the record. Leather Industries of America v. EPA, 40 F.3d 392 (D.C. Cir. 1994). However, the court upheld EPA's refusal to provide for site-specific variances and it confirmed that the agency has authority to regulate sludge to protect against phytotoxicity, the reduction in crop yields that occurs when plants absorb toxic metals.

Section 405(e) of the Clean Water Act specifies that "the manner of disposal or use of sludge is a local determination" so long as federal regulations are not violated. In Welch v. Board of Supervisors of Rappahannock County, 860 F. Supp. 328 (W.D. Va. 1994), a federal district court held that a county ordinance banning the application of sewage sludge to farmland was not preempted by federal law, because state and local governments may adopt more stringent limits on sludge disposal so long as they meet federal minimum standards.

Sewage Treatment (pp. 916-917). The cost of correcting Boston's notorious sewage disposal problems (parent text, p. 917) has become high enough that some businesses are reportedly drilling their own wells to avoid having to pay soaring water bills. Stuart, Latest Boston Revolt Goes Underground, Wash. Post, Dec. 26, 1992, at A11.

One reason why EPA has had difficulty obtaining compliance by municipalities is the inadequacy of sanctions imposed on government entities who violate the environmental laws. In 1995 the director of EPA's Office of Waste Water Compliance conceded that the agency "almost never" has penalized cities in an amount that recoups the economic benefit to them of violating the environmental laws. Indeed, EPA is now considering amending its municipal enforcement policy to

7. Water Pollution Control   Pages 924-928

remove the charade that it recoups the benefits of such violations. Possible Changes Being Considered by EPA to Municipal Enforcement Policy, Official Says, 25 Env. Rep. 1908 (1995). EPA seeks to justify its practice by arguing that money is better spent on building treatment works than on paying fines.

POTWs discharging into marine waters have been allowed to obtain waivers from treatment requirements. While the 1987 amendments to the Clean Water Act imposed several restrictions on such waivers, more than 50 POTWs have obtained them. Section 301(h) of the Clean Water Act, which was added by the 1987 amendments, provides that EPA may approve such waivers only with the concurrence of the state in which the POTW is located and only if the applicant meets certain conditions designed to prevent water quality-related problems. EPA issued regulations governing the section 301(h) waiver process in August 1994. 59 Fed. Reg. 40,642 (1994).

While the 1987 amendments imposed a deadline for POTWs to apply for section 301(h) waivers, Congress extended this deadline in 1994 to allow the City of San Diego to apply for such a waiver. Even though EPA already has indicated that it would approve a waiver for San Diego, the city is now seeking to have Congress amend the Clean Water Act to exempt it from treatment requirements. Speaker of the House Newt Gingrich has endorsed such an amendment as a forerunner of monthly "Corrections Days" when Congress will consider measures to repeal regulations to benefit individual members of the regulated community. Cushman, House to "Correct" San Diego Sewage Plan, N.Y. Times, Feb. 3, 1995, at B8.

D.   WATER QUALITY-BASED CONTROLS

Water Quality Standards (pp. 924-928). The D.C. Circuit has upheld EPA regulations requiring that narrative state water quality criteria (e.g., "no toxics in toxic amounts") be translated into numeric criteria when NPDES permits incorporate water quality-based effluent limits. American Paper Institute v. EPA, 996 F.2d 346 (D.C. Cir. 1993). Noting that there was no evidence that Congress was concerned only with violations of numeric standards, the court also held that section 304(l)(1)(B)'s requirement for listing waters that will not achieve "applicable standards" includes waters that will not meet narrative water quality standards.

The Fourth Circuit has upheld EPA's approval of state water quality standards that are dramatically more permissive than recommended by

EPA's criteria. Revised water quality standards for dioxin that were adopted by Maryland and Virginia were approved by EPA even though they allowed concentrations of dioxin nearly one thousand times greater than EPA's criteria. In Natural Resources Defense Council v. EPA, 16 F.3d 1395 (4th Cir. 1993), the court held that EPA could approve such standards so long as they were scientifically defensible and protective of designated uses, even though they were based on different assumptions from those employed by EPA in assessing the toxicity of dioxin. The court emphasized that states have the primary role in establishing water quality standards and that EPA's decision to approve them should be upheld if there is a rational basis for it in the record. The court also held that the availability of new data does not obligate EPA to update its water quality criteria guidance documents, and that such documents are not subject to judicial review under the Administrative Procedure Act because they do not represent final agency action.

Sediment Quality Criteria (pp. 927-928). In 1994 EPA released its internal strategy for coordinating agency action to control sediment contamination. 59 Fed. Reg. 44,880 (1994). EPA announced that it intended to develop a national inventory of sites with contaminated sediments and to assess sources of such contamination. EPA also indicated that it would consider developing effluent guidelines for industries that release significant amounts of pollutants that contaminate sediments.

Impact of Water Quality Standards on Permit Limits (pp. 928-929). In Northwest Environmental Advocates v. City of Portland, 11 F.3d 900 (9th Cir. 1993), the Ninth Circuit held that water quality standards cannot be enforced in citizen suits unless they have been translated into end-of-the-pipe effluent limitations. Even though the City of Portland's permit prohibited the discharge of wastes that would violate state water quality standards, the court held that this restriction was not enforceable until it had been embodied in specific effluent limits. While noting that the legislative history of the Clean Water Act suggested that citizen suits could be brought to enforce *any* permit condition, the court, over one dissent, found that Congress had relied on end-of-the-pipe effluent limitations to enforce water quality standards.

Total Maximum Daily Loadings (TMDLs) (pp. 929-930). In response to the district court's decision in *Alaska Center for the Environment* (text, pp. 929-930), EPA entered into a Memorandum of Understanding concerning the implementation of TMDLs. The memorandum provided that EPA and the state would complete watershed assessments for eight watersheds or water bodies by April 1993. Noting that the memorandum

7. Water Pollution Control

covered only eight water segments and provided no assurance that TMDLs would be promulgated for any of them, the court required EPA to conduct a more comprehensive assessment of water pollution and, on the basis of that assessment, to "propose a schedule for the establishment of TMDLs for all waters designated as water quality limited," Alaska Center for the Environment v. Reilly, 796 F. Supp. 1374, 1381 (W.D. Wash. 1992). In response to EPA's plea for deference to the Agency's interpretation of the law, the court observed that "[t]he only 'consistently held interpretation' that the EPA has demonstrated with respect to the CWA's TMDL requirements has been to ignore them." 796 F. Supp. at 1379. The district court's decision was affirmed by the Ninth Circuit in Alaska Center for the Environment v. Browner, 20 F.3d 981 (9th Cir. 1994).

In 1994 EPA proposed TMDLs for copper, lead, mercury, and nickel in New York Harbor. 59 Fed. Reg. 41,293 (1994). The agency acted to ensure that uniform standards applied to a water body under the jurisdiction of both New York and New Jersey.

Water Quality Certification Under Section 401 (p. 939). Section 401 of the Clean Water Act requires applicants for a federal license or permit that may result in a discharge into intrastate navigable waters to provide a certification from the state in which the discharge will occur that the discharge will comply with various provisions of the Act. Section 401(d) provides that such certifications "shall set forth any effluent limitations and other limitations, and monitoring requirements necessary to assure that" the applicant complies with the Act "and with any other appropriate requirement of State law set forth in" the certification, which then becomes a condition of the federal permit. In the case below the Supreme Court considered whether a state could condition certification of a hydroelectric dam on the imposition of minimum stream flow rates.

> *PUD No. 1 of Jefferson County v. Washington Department of Ecology*
> 114 S. Ct. 1900 (1994)

O'CONNOR, J., delivered the opinion of the Court, in which REHNQUIST, C. J., and BLACKMUN, STEVENS, KENNEDY, SOUTER, and GINSBURG, JJ., joined. STEVENS, J., filed a concurring opinion. THOMAS, J., filed a dissenting opinion, in which SCALIA, J., joined.

Justice O'CONNOR delivered the opinion of the Court.

Petitioners, a city and a local utility district, want to build a hydroelectric project on the Dosewallips River in Washington State. We must decide whether respondent, the state environmental agency, properly conditioned a permit for the project on the maintenance of specific minimum stream flows to protect salmon and steelhead runs.

I

This case involves the complex statutory and regulatory scheme that governs our Nation's waters, a scheme which implicates both federal and state administrative responsibilities. The Federal Water Pollution Control Act, commonly known as the Clean Water Act, 86 Stat. 816, as amended, 33 U.S.C. §1251 et seq., is a comprehensive water quality statute designed to "restore and maintain the chemical, physical, and biological integrity of the Nation's waters." §1251(a). The Act also seeks to attain "water quality which provides for the protection and propagation of fish, shellfish, and wildlife." §1251(a)(2).

To achieve these ambitious goals, the Clean Water Act establishes distinct roles for the Federal and State Governments. Under the Act, the Administrator of the Environmental Protection Agency is required, among other things, to establish and enforce technology-based limitations on individual discharges into the country's navigable waters from point sources. See §§1311, 1314. Section 303 of the Act also requires each State, subject to federal approval, to institute comprehensive water quality standards establishing water quality goals for all intrastate waters. §§1311(b)(1)(C), 1313. These state water quality standards provide "a supplementary basis . . . so that numerous point sources, despite individual compliance with effluent limitations, may be further regulated to prevent water quality from falling below acceptable levels." EPA v. California ex rel. State Water Resources Control Bd., 426 U.S. 200, 205, n.12 (1976).

A state water quality standard "shall consist of the designated uses of the navigable waters involved and the water quality criteria for such waters based upon such uses." 33 U.S.C. §1313(c)(2)(A). In setting standards, the State must comply with the following broad requirements:

> Such standards shall be such as to protect the public health or welfare, enhance the quality of water and serve the purposes of this chapter. Such standards shall be established taking into consideration their use and value for public water supplies, propagation of fish and wildlife, recreational [and other purposes.]" [Ibid. See also §1251(a)(2).]

A 1987 amendment to the Clean Water Act makes clear that §303 also contains an "antidegradation policy"—that is, a policy requiring

7. Water Pollution Control   Page 939

that state standards be sufficient to maintain existing beneficial uses of navigable waters, preventing their further degradation. Specifically, the Act permits the revision of certain effluent limitations or water quality standards "only if such revision is subject to and consistent with the antidegradation policy established under this section." §1313(d)(4)(B). Accordingly, EPA's regulations implementing the Act require that state water quality standards include "a statewide antidegradation policy" to ensure that "[e]xisting instream water uses and the level of water quality necessary to protect the existing uses shall be maintained and protected." 40 CFR §131.12 (1992). At a minimum, state water quality standards must satisfy these conditions. The Act also allows States to impose more stringent water quality controls. See 33 U.S.C. §§1311(b)(1)(C), 1370. See also 40 CFR §131.4(a) ("As recognized by section 510 of the Clean Water Act [33 U.S.C. §1370], States may develop water quality standards more stringent than required by this regulation").

The State of Washington has adopted comprehensive water quality standards intended to regulate all of the State's navigable waters. See Washington Administrative Code (WAC) 173-201-010 to 173-201-120 (1990). The State created an inventory of all the State's waters, and divided the waters into five classes. 173-201-045. Each individual fresh surface water of the State is placed into one of these classes. 173-201-080. The Dosewallips River is classified AA, extraordinary. 173-201-080(32). The water quality standard for Class AA waters is set forth at 173-201-045(1). The standard identifies the designated uses of Class AA waters as well as the criteria applicable to such waters.

In addition to these specific standards applicable to Class AA waters, the State has adopted a statewide antidegradation policy. That policy provides:

> (a) Existing beneficial uses shall be maintained and protected and no further degradation which would interfere with or become injurious to existing beneficial uses will be allowed.
>
> (b) No degradation will be allowed of waters lying in national parks, national recreation areas, national wildlife refuges, national scenic rivers, and other areas of national ecological importance. . . .
>
> (f) In no case, will any degradation of water quality be allowed if this degradation interferes with or becomes injurious to existing water uses and causes long-term and irreparable harm to the environment. [173-201-035(8).]

As required by the Act, EPA reviewed and approved the State's water quality standards. See 33 U.S.C. §1313(c)(3); 42 Fed. Reg. 56,792 (1977). Upon approval by EPA, the state standard became "the water

373

quality standard for the applicable waters of that State." 33 U.S.C. §1313(c)(3).

States are responsible for enforcing water quality standards on intrastate waters. 33 U.S.C. §1319(a). In addition to these primary enforcement responsibilities, §401 of the Act requires States to provide a water quality certification before a federal license or permit can be issued for activities that may result in any discharge into intrastate navigable waters. 33 U.S.C. §1341. Specifically, §401 requires an applicant for a federal license or permit to conduct any activity "which may result in any discharge into the navigable waters" to obtain from the state a certification "that any such discharge will comply with the applicable provisions of sections 1311, 1312, 1313, 1316, and 1317 of this title." 33 U.S.C. §1341(a). Section 401(d) further provides that "any certification . . . shall set forth any effluent limitations and other limitations, and monitoring requirements necessary to assure that any applicant . . . will comply with any applicable effluent limitations and other limitations, under section 1311 or 1312 of this title . . . and with any other appropriate requirement of State law set forth in such certification." 33 U.S.C. §1341(d). The limitations included in the certification become a condition on any Federal license. Ibid.

II

Petitioners propose to build the Elkhorn Hydroelectric Project on the Dosewallips River. If constructed as presently planned, the facility would be located just outside the Olympic National Park on federally owned land within the Olympic National Forest. The project would divert water from a 1.2-mile reach of the River (the bypass reach), run the water through turbines to generate electricity and then return the water to the River below the bypass reach. Under the Federal Power Act (FPA), 41 Stat. 1063, as amended, 16 U.S.C. §791 et seq., the Federal Energy Regulatory Commission has authority to license new hydroelectric facilities. As a result, the petitioners must get a FERC license to build or operate the Elkhorn Project. Because a federal license is required, and because the project may result in discharges into the Dosewallips River, petitioners are also required to obtain State certification of the project pursuant to §401 of the Clean Water Act, 33 U.S.C. §1341.

The water flow in the bypass reach, which is currently undiminished by appropriation, ranges seasonally between 149 and 738 cubic feet per second (cfs). The Dosewallips supports two species of salmon, Coho and Chinook, as well as Steelhead trout. As originally proposed, the project was to include a diversion dam which would completely

7. Water Pollution Control   Page 939

block the river and channel approximately 75 percent of the River's water into a tunnel alongside the streambed. About 25 percent of the water would remain in the bypass reach, but would be returned to the original riverbed through sluice gates or a fish ladder. Depending on the season, this would leave a residual minimum flow of between 65 and 155 cfs in the River. Respondent undertook a study to determine the minimum stream flows necessary to protect the salmon and steelhead fisheries in the bypass reach. On June 11, 1986, respondent issued a §401 water quality certification imposing a variety of conditions on the project, including a minimum stream-flow requirement of between 100 and 200 cfs depending on the season.

A state administrative appeals board determined that the minimum flow requirement was intended to enhance, not merely maintain, the fishery, and that the certification condition therefore exceeded respondent's authority under state law. On appeal, the state Superior Court concluded that respondent could require compliance with the minimum flow conditions. The Superior Court also found that respondent had imposed the minimum flow requirement to protect and preserve the fishery, not to improve it, and that this requirement was authorized by state law.

The Washington Supreme Court held that the antidegradation provisions of the State's water quality standards require the imposition of minimum stream flows. 849 P.2d 646, 650 (1993). The court also found that §401(d), which allows States to impose conditions based upon several enumerated sections of the Clean Water Act and "any other appropriate requirement of State law," 33 U.S.C. §1341(d), authorized the stream flow condition. Relying on this language and the broad purposes of the Clean Water Act, the court concluded that §401(d) confers on States power to "consider all state action related to water quality in imposing conditions on section 401 certificates." 849 P.2d, at 652. We granted certiorari to resolve a conflict among the state courts of last resort. See 849 P.2d 646 (1993); Georgia Pacific Corp. v. Dept. of Environmental Conservation, 628 A.2d 944 (1992) (table); Power Authority of New York v. Williams, 457 N.E.2d 726 (1983). . . .

III

The principal dispute in this case concerns whether the minimum stream flow requirement that the State imposed on the Elkhorn project is a permissible condition of a §401 certification under the Clean Water Act. To resolve this dispute we must first determine the scope of the State's authority under §401. We must then determine whether the

375

limitation at issue here, the requirement that petitioners maintain minimum stream flows, falls within the scope of that authority.

A

There is no dispute that petitioners were required to obtain a certification from the State pursuant to §401. Petitioners concede that, at a minimum, the project will result in two possible discharges—the release of dredged and fill material during the construction of the project, and the discharge of water at the end of the tailrace after the water has been used to generate electricity. Petitioners contend, however, that the minimum stream flow requirement imposed by the State was unrelated to these specific discharges, and that as a consequence, the State lacked the authority under §401 to condition its certification on maintenance of stream flows sufficient to protect the Dosewallips fishery.

If §401 consisted solely of subsection (a), which refers to a state certification that a "discharge" will comply with certain provisions of the Act, petitioners' assessment of the scope of the State's certification authority would have considerable force. Section 401, however, also contains subsection (d), which expands the State's authority to impose conditions on the certification of a project. Section 401(d) provides that any certification shall set forth "any effluent limitations and other limitations . . . necessary to assure that *any applicant*" will comply with various provisions of the Act and appropriate state law requirements. 33 U.S.C. §1341(d) (emphasis added). The language of this subsection contradicts petitioners' claim that the State may only impose water quality limitations specifically tied to a "discharge." The text refers to the compliance of the applicant, not the discharge. Section 401(d) thus allows the State to impose "other limitations" on the project in general to assure compliance with various provisions of the Clean Water Act and with "any other appropriate requirement of State law." Although the dissent asserts that this interpretation of §401(d) renders §401(a)(1) superfluous, we see no such anomaly. Section 401(a)(1) identifies the category of activities subject to certification—namely those with discharges. And §401(d) is most reasonably read as authorizing additional conditions and limitations on the activity as a whole once the threshold condition, the existence of a discharge, is satisfied.

Our view of the statute is consistent with EPA's regulations implementing §401. The regulations expressly interpret §401 as requiring the State to find that "there is a reasonable assurance that the *activity* will be conducted in a manner which will not violate applicable water

376

7. Water Pollution Control   Page 939

quality standards." 40 CFR §121.2(a)(3) (1992) (emphasis added). See also EPA, Wetlands and 401 Certification 23 (Apr. 1989) ("In 401(d), the Congress has given the States the authority to place any conditions on a water quality certification that are necessary to assure that the applicant will comply with effluent limitations, water quality standards, . . . and with 'any other appropriate requirement of State law.'"). EPA's conclusion that *activities*—not merely discharges—must comply with state water quality standards is a reasonable interpretation of §401, and is entitled to deference. See, e.g., Arkansas v. Oklahoma, 503 U.S. 91, 110 (1992); Chevron U.S.A., Inc. v. Natural Resources Defense Council, Inc., 467 U.S. 837 (1984).

Although §401(d) authorizes the State to place restrictions on the activity as a whole, that authority is not unbounded. The State can only ensure that the project complies with "any applicable effluent limitations and other limitations, under [33 U.S.C. §§1311, 1312]" or certain other provisions of the Act, "and with any other appropriate requirement of State law." 33 U.S.C. §1341(d). The State asserts that the minimum stream flow requirement was imposed to ensure compliance with the state water quality standards adopted pursuant to §303 of the Clean Water Act, 33 U.S.C. §1313.

We agree with the State that ensuring compliance with §303 is a proper function of the §401 certification. Although §303 is not one of the statutory provisions listed in §401(d), the statute allows states to impose limitations to ensure compliance with §301 of the Act, 33 U.S.C. §1311. Section 301 in turn incorporates §303 by reference. See 33 U.S.C. §1311(b)(1)(C); see also H. R. Conf. Rep. No. 95-830, p. 96 (1977) ("Section 303 is always included by reference where section 301 is listed"). As a consequence, state water quality standards adopted pursuant to §303 are among the "other limitations" with which a State may ensure compliance through the §401 certification process. This interpretation is consistent with EPA's view of the statute. See 40 CFR §121.2(a)(3) (1992); EPA, Wetlands and 401 Certification, supra. Moreover, limitations to assure compliance with state water quality standards are also permitted by §401(d)'s reference to "any other appropriate requirement of State law." We do not speculate on what additional state laws, if any, might be incorporated by this language.[3] But at a minimum,

---

3. The dissent asserts that §301 is concerned solely with discharges, not broader water quality standards. Infra, 8 n. 2. Although §301 does make certain discharges unlawful, see 33 U.S.C. §1311(a), it also contains a broad enabling provision which requires states to take certain actions, to wit: "In order to carry out the objective of this chapter [viz. the chemical, physical, and biological integrity of the Nation's water] there shall be achieved . . . not later than July 1, 1977, any more stringent limitation, including those necessary to meet water

377

limitations imposed pursuant to state water quality standards adopted pursuant to §303 are "appropriate" requirements of state law. Indeed, petitioners appear to agree that the State's authority under §401 includes limitations designed to ensure compliance with state water quality standards.

B

Having concluded that, pursuant to §401, States may condition certification upon any limitations necessary to ensure compliance with state water quality standards or any other "appropriate requirement of State law," we consider whether the minimum flow condition is such a limitation. Under §303, state water quality standards must "consist of the designated uses of the navigable waters involved and the water quality criteria for such waters based upon such uses." 33 U.S.C. §1313(c)(2)(A). In imposing the minimum stream flow requirement, the State determined that construction and operation of the project as planned would be inconsistent with one of the designated uses of Class AA water, namely "[s]almonid [and other fish] migration, rearing, spawning, and harvesting." The designated use of the River as a fish habitat directly reflects the Clean Water Act's goal of maintaining the "chemical, physical, and biological integrity of the Nation's waters." 33 U.S.C. §1251(a). Indeed, the Act defines pollution as "the man-made or man-induced alteration of the chemical, physical, biological, and radiological integrity of water." §1362(19). Moreover, the Act expressly requires that, in adopting water quality standards, the State must take into consideration the use of waters for "propagation of fish and wildlife." 33 U.S.C. §1313(c)(2)(A).

Petitioners assert, however, that §303 requires the State to protect designated uses solely through implementation of specific "criteria." According to petitioners, the State may not require them to operate their dam in a manner consistent with a designated "use"; instead, say petitioners, under §303 the State may only require that the project comply with specific numerical "criteria."

We disagree with petitioners' interpretation of the language of §303(c)(2)(A). Under the statute, a water quality standard must "consist of the designated uses of the navigable waters involved *and* the water quality criteria for such waters based upon such uses." 33 U.S.C. §1313(c)(2)(A) (emphasis added). The text makes it plain that water

---

quality standards . . . established pursuant to any State law or regulations." 33 U.S.C. §1311(b)(1)(C). This provision of §301 expressly refers to state water quality standards, and is not limited to discharges.

7. Water Pollution Control

quality standards contain two components. We think the language of §303 is most naturally read to require that a project be consistent with *both* components, namely the designated use *and* the water quality criteria. Accordingly, under the literal terms of the statute, a project that does not comply with a designated use of the water does not comply with the applicable water quality standards.

Consequently, pursuant to §401(d) the State may require that a permit applicant comply with both the designated uses and the water quality criteria of the state standards. In granting certification pursuant to §401(d), the State "shall set forth any . . . limitations . . . necessary to assure that [the applicant] will comply with any . . . limitations under [§303] . . . and with any other appropriate requirement of State law." A certification requirement that an applicant operate the project consistently with state water quality standards—i.e., consistently with the designated uses of the water body and the water quality criteria—is both a "limitation" to assure "compliance with . . . limitations" imposed under §303, and an "appropriate" requirement of State law.

EPA has not interpreted §303 to require the States to protect designated uses exclusively through enforcement of numerical criteria. In its regulations governing state water quality standards, EPA defines criteria as "*elements* of State water quality standards expressed as constituent concentrations, levels, or narrative statements, representing a quality of water that supports a particular use." §40 CFR 131.3(b) (1992) (emphasis added). The regulations further provide that "when criteria are met, water quality will *generally* protect the designated use." Ibid. (emphasis added). Thus, the EPA regulations implicitly recognize that in some circumstances, criteria alone are insufficient to protect a designated use.

Petitioners also appear to argue that use requirements are too open-ended, and that the Act only contemplates enforcement of the more specific and objective "criteria." But this argument is belied by the open-ended nature of the criteria themselves. As the Solicitor General points out, even "criteria" are often expressed in broad, narrative terms, such as "'there shall be no discharge of toxic pollutants in toxic amounts.'" See American Paper Institute, Inc. v. EPA, 996 F.2d 346, 349 (CADC 1993). In fact, under the Clean Water Act, only one class of criteria, those governing "toxic pollutants listed pursuant to section 1317(a)(1)" need be rendered in numerical form. See 33 U.S.C. §1313(c)(2)(B); 40 CFR §131.11(b)(2) (1992).

Washington's Class AA water quality standards are typical in that they contain several open-ended criteria which, like the use designation of the River as a fishery, must be translated into specific limitations for individual projects. For example, the standards state that "[t]oxic, radioactive, or deleterious material concentrations shall be less than those which may affect public health, the natural aquatic environment, or the desirability of the water for any use." WAC 173-201-045(c)(vii). Similarly, the state standards specify that "aesthetic values shall not be impaired by the presence of materials or their effects, excluding those of natural origin, which offend the senses of sight, smell, touch, or taste." 173-201-045(c)(viii). We think petitioners' attempt to distinguish between uses and criteria loses much of its force in light of the fact that the Act permits enforcement of broad, narrative criteria based on, for example, "aesthetics."

Petitioners further argue that enforcement of water quality standards through use designations renders the water quality criteria component of the standards irrelevant. We see no anomaly, however, in the State's reliance on both use designations and criteria to protect water quality. The specific numerical limitations embodied in the criteria are a convenient enforcement mechanism for identifying minimum water conditions which will generally achieve the requisite water quality. And, in most circumstances, satisfying the criteria will, as EPA recognizes, be sufficient to maintain the designated use. See 40 CFR §131.3(b) (1992). Water quality standards, however, apply to an entire class of water, a class which contains numerous individual water bodies. For example, in the State of Washington, the Class AA water quality standard applies to 81 specified fresh surface waters, as well as to all "surface waters lying within the mountainous regions of the state assigned to national parks, national forests, and/or wilderness areas," all "lakes and their feeder streams within the state," and all "unclassified surface waters that are tributaries to Class AA waters." WAC 173-201-070. While enforcement of criteria will in general protect the uses of these diverse waters, a complementary requirement that activities also comport with designated uses enables the States to ensure that each activity—even if not foreseen by the criteria—will be consistent with the specific uses and attributes of a particular body of water.

Under petitioners' interpretation of the statute, however, if a particular criterion, such as turbidity, were missing from the list contained in an individual state water quality standard, or even if an existing turbidity criterion were insufficient to protect a particular species of fish in a particular river, the State would nonetheless be forced to allow activities inconsistent with the existing or designated uses. We think petitioners' reading leads to an unreasonable interpretation of the Act. The criteria components of state water quality standards attempt to identify, for all the water bodies in a given class, water quality requirements generally sufficient to protect designated uses. These criteria, however, cannot reasonably be expected to anticipate all the water quality issues arising from every activity which can affect the State's hundreds of individual water bodies. Requiring the States to enforce only the criteria component of their water quality standards would in essence require the States to study to a level of great specificity each individual surface water to ensure that the criteria applicable to that water are sufficiently detailed and individualized to fully protect the water's designated uses. Given that there is no textual support for imposing this requirement, we are loath to attribute to Congress an intent to impose this heavy regulatory burden on the States.

The State also justified its minimum stream flow as necessary to implement the "antidegradation policy" of §303, 33 U.S.C. §1313(d)(4)(B). When the Clean Water Act was enacted in 1972, the water quality standards of all 50 States had antidegradation provisions. These provisions were required by federal law. See U.S. Dept. of Interior, Federal Water Pollution Control Administration, Compendium of Department of Interior Statements on Non-degradation of Interstate Waters 1-2 (Aug. 1968); see also Hines, A Decade of Nondegradation Policy in Congress and the Courts: The Erratic Pursuit of Clean Air and Clean Water, 62 Iowa L. Rev. 643, 658-660 (1977). By providing in 1972 that existing state water quality standards would remain in force until revised, the Clean Water Act ensured that the States would continue their antidegradation programs. See 33 U.S.C. §1313(a). EPA has consistently required that revised state standards incorporate an antidegradation policy. And, in 1987, Congress explicitly recognized the existence of an "antidegradation policy established under [§303]." §1313(d)(4)(B).

EPA has promulgated regulations implementing §303's antidegradation policy, a phrase that is not defined elsewhere in the Act. These regulations require States to "develop and adopt a statewide antidegradation policy and identify the methods for implementing such policy." 40 CFR §131.12 (1992). These "implementation methods shall, at a minimum, be consistent with the . . . existing instream water uses and the level of water quality necessary to protect the existing uses shall be maintained and protected." Ibid. EPA has explained that under its anti-degradation regulation, "no activity is allowable . . . which could partially or completely eliminate any existing use." EPA, Questions and Answers re: Antidegradation 3 (1985). Thus, States must implement their antidegradation policy in a manner "consistent" with existing uses of the stream. The State of Washington's antidegradation policy in turn provides that "existing beneficial uses shall be maintained and protected and no further degradation which would interfere with or become injurious to existing beneficial uses will be allowed." WAC 173-201-035(8)(a). The State concluded that the reduced streamflows would have just the effect prohibited by this policy. The Solicitor General, representing EPA, asserts, and we agree, that the State's minimum stream flow condition is a proper application of the state and federal antidegradation regulations, as it ensures that an "existing instream water use" will be "maintained and protected." 40 CFR §131.12(a)(1) (1992).

Petitioners also assert more generally that the Clean Water Act is only concerned with water "quality," and does not allow the regulation of water "quantity." This is an artificial distinction. In many cases, water quantity is closely related to water quality; a sufficient lowering of the water quantity in a body of water could destroy all of its designated uses, be it for drinking water, recreation, navigation or, as here, as a fishery. In any event, there is recognition in the Clean Water Act itself that reduced stream flow, i.e., diminishment of water quantity, can constitute water pollution. First, the Act's definition of pollution as "the man-made or man induced alteration of the chemical, physical, biological, and radiological integrity of water" encompasses the effects of reduced water quantity. 33 U.S.C. §1362(19). This broad conception of pollution—one which expressly evinces Congress' concern with the physical and biological integrity of water—refutes petitioners' assertion that the Act draws a sharp distinction between the regulation of water "quantity" and water "quality." Moreover, §304 of the Act expressly recognizes that water "pollution" may result from "changes in the movement, flow, or circulation of any navigable waters . . . including changes caused by the construction of dams." 33 U.S.C. §1314(f). This concern with the flowage effects of dams and other diversions is also embodied in the EPA regulations, which expressly require existing dams to be operated to attain designated uses. 40 CFR §131.10(g)(4). . . .

In summary, we hold that the State may include minimum stream flow requirements in a certification issued pursuant to §401 of the Clean Water Act insofar as necessary to enforce a designated use contained in a state water quality standard. The judgment of the Supreme Court of Washington, accordingly, is affirmed.

Justice STEVENS, concurring.

While I agree fully with the thorough analysis in the Court's opinion, I add this comment for emphasis. For judges who find it unnecessary to go behind the statutory text to discern the intent of Congress, this is (or should be) an easy case. Not a single sentence, phrase, or word in the Clean Water Act purports to place any constraint on a State's power to regulate the quality of its own waters more stringently than federal law might require. In fact, the Act explicitly recognizes States' ability to impose stricter standards. See, e.g., §301(b)(1)(C), 33 U.S.C. §1311(b)(1)(C).

Justice THOMAS, with whom Justice SCALIA joins, dissenting.

The Court today holds that a State, pursuant to §401 of the Clean Water Act, may condition the certification necessary to obtain a federal license for a proposed hydroelectric project upon the maintenance of a minimum flow rate in the river to be utilized by the project. In my view, the Court makes three fundamental errors. First, it adopts an interpretation that fails adequately to harmonize the subsections of §401. Second, it places no meaningful limitation on a State's authority under §401 to impose conditions on certification. Third, it gives little or no consideration to the fact that its interpretation of §401 will significantly disrupt the carefully crafted federal-state balance embodied in the Federal Power Act. Accordingly, I dissent.

I

A

. . . The terms of §401(a)(1) make clear that the purpose of the certification process is to ensure that discharges from a project will meet the requirements of the CWA. . . .

The minimum stream flow condition imposed by respondents in this case has no relation to any possible "discharge" that might "result" from petitioners' proposed project. The term "discharge" is not defined in the CWA, but its plain and ordinary meaning suggests "a flowing or issuing out," or "something that is emitted." Webster's Ninth New Collegiate Dictionary 360 (1991). Cf. 33 U.S.C. §1362(16) ("The term 'discharge' when used without qualification includes a discharge of a pollutant, and a discharge of pollutants"). A minimum stream flow requirement, by contrast, is a limitation on the amount of water the project can take in or divert from the river. That is, a minimum stream flow requirement is a limitation on intake—the opposite of discharge. Imposition of such a requirement would thus appear to be beyond a State's authority as it is defined by §401(a)(1).

The Court remarks that this reading of §401(a)(1) would have "considerable force" were it not for what the Court understands to be the expansive terms of §401(d). . . . According to the Court, the fact that §401(d) refers to an "applicant," rather than a "discharge," complying with various provisions of the Act "contradicts petitioners' claim that the State may only impose water quality limitations specifically tied to a 'discharge.'" In the Court's view, §401(d)'s reference to an applicant's compliance "expands" a State's authority beyond the limits set out in §401(a)(1), thereby permitting the State in its certification process to scrutinize the applicant's proposed "activity as a whole," not just the discharges that may result from the activity. The Court concludes that this broader authority allows a State to impose conditions on a §401 certification that are unrelated to discharges.

While the Court's interpretation seems plausible at first glance, it ultimately must fail. If, as the Court asserts, §401(d) permits States

383

to impose conditions unrelated to discharges in §401 certifications, Congress' careful focus on discharges in §401(a)(1)—the provision that describes the scope and function of the certification process—was wasted effort. The power to set conditions that are unrelated to discharges is, of course, nothing but a conditional power to deny certification for reasons unrelated to discharges. Permitting States to impose conditions unrelated to discharges, then, effectively eliminates the constraints of §401(a)(1).

Subsections 401(a)(1) and (d) can easily be reconciled to avoid this problem. To ascertain the nature of the conditions permissible under §401(d), §401 must be read as a whole. See United Savings Assn. of Texas v. Timbers of Inwood Forest Associates, Ltd., 484 U.S. 365, 371 (1988) (statutory interpretation is a "holistic endeavor"). As noted above, §401(a)(1) limits a State's authority in the certification process to addressing concerns related to discharges and to ensuring that any discharge resulting from a project will comply with specified provisions of the Act. It is reasonable to infer that the conditions a State is permitted to impose on certification must relate to the very purpose the certification process is designed to serve. Thus, while §401(d) permits a State to place conditions on a certification to ensure compliance of the "applicant," those conditions must still be related to discharges. In my view, this interpretation best harmonizes the subsections of §401. Indeed, any broader interpretation of §401(d) would permit that subsection to swallow §401(a)(1)....

II

The Washington Supreme Court held that the State's water quality standards, promulgated pursuant to §303 of the Act, 33 U.S.C. §1313, were "appropriate" requirements of state law under §401(d), and sustained the stream flow condition imposed by respondents as necessary to ensure compliance with a "use" of the river as specified in those standards. As an alternative to their argument that §401(d) conditions must be discharge-related, petitioners assert that the state court erred when it sustained the stream flow condition under the "use" component of the State's water quality standards without reference to the corresponding "water quality criteria" contained in those standards. As explained above, petitioners' argument with regard to the scope of a State's authority to impose conditions under §401(d) is correct. I also find petitioners' alternative argument persuasive. Not only does the Court err in rejecting that §303 argument, in the process of doing so it essentially removes all limitations on a State's conditioning authority under §401.

The Court states that, "at a minimum, limitations imposed pursuant to state water quality standards adopted pursuant to §303 are 'appropriate' requirements of state law" under §401(d).[2] A water quality standard promulgated pursuant to §303 must "consist of the designated uses of the navigable waters involved and the water quality criteria for such waters based upon such uses." 33 U.S.C. §1313(c)(2)(A). The Court asserts that this language "is most naturally read to require that a project be consistent with both components, namely the designated use and the water quality criteria." In the Court's view, then, the "use" of a body of water is independently enforceable through §401(d) without reference to the corresponding criteria.

The Court's reading strikes me as contrary to common sense. It is difficult to see how compliance with a "use" of a body of water could be enforced without reference to the corresponding criteria. In this case, for example, the applicable "use" is contained in the following regulation: "Characteristic uses shall include, but not be limited to . . . [s]almonid migration, rearing, spawning, and harvesting." Wash. Admin. Code (WAC) 173-201-045(1)(b)(iii) (1990). The corresponding criteria, by contrast, include measurable factors such as quantities of fecal coliform organisms and dissolved gases in the water. WAC 173-201-045(1)(c)(i) and (ii).[3] Although the Act does not further address (at least not expressly) the link between "uses" and "criteria," the regulations promulgated under §303 make clear that a "use" is an aspirational goal to be attained through compliance with corresponding "criteria." Those regulations suggest that "uses" are to be "achieved and protected," and that "water quality criteria" are to be adopted to "protect the designated uses." 40 CFR §§131.10(a), 131.11(a)(1) (1993).

The problematic consequences of decoupling "uses" and "criteria" become clear once the Court's interpretation of §303 is read in the context of §401. In the Court's view, a State may condition the §401 certification "upon *any limitations* necessary to ensure compliance" with the "uses of the water body" (emphasis added). Under the Court's interpretation, then, state environmental agencies may pursue, through §401, their water goals in any way they choose; the conditions imposed on certifications need not relate to discharges, nor to water quality

---

2. In the Court's view, §303 water quality standards come into play under §401(d) either as "appropriate" requirements of state law, or through §301 of the Act, which, according to the Court, "incorporates §303 by reference." The Court notes that through §303, "the statute allows states to impose limitations to ensure compliance with §301 of the Act." Yet §301 makes unlawful only "the [unauthorized] *discharge* of any pollutant by any person." 33 U.S.C. §1311(a). Thus, the Court's reliance on §301 as a source of authority to impose conditions unrelated to discharges is misplaced.

3. Respondents concede that petitioners' project "will likely not violate any of Washington's water quality criteria." Brief for Respondents 24.

criteria, nor to any objective or quantifiable standard, so long as they tend to make the water more suitable for the uses the State has chosen. In short, once a State is allowed to impose conditions on §401 certifications to protect "uses" in the abstract, §401(d) is limitless.

To illustrate, while respondents in this case focused only on the "use" of the Dosewallips River as a fish habitat, this particular river has a number of other "characteristic uses," including "recreation (primary contact recreation, sport fishing, boating, and aesthetic enjoyment)." WAC 173-201-045(1)(b)(v). Under the Court's interpretation, respondents could have imposed any number of conditions related to recreation, including conditions that have little relation to water quality. In Town of Summersville, 60 FERC ¶61,291, p. 61,990 (1992), for instance, the state agency required the applicant to "construct . . . access roads and paths, low water stepping stone bridges, . . . a boat launching facility . . . , and a residence and storage building." These conditions presumably would be sustained under the approach the Court adopts today.[4] In the end, it is difficult to conceive of a condition that would fall outside a State's §401(d) authority under the Court's approach.

NOTES & QUESTIONS

1. In his dissent Justice Thomas argues that §401(d) should not be interpreted to allow states to impose conditions unrelated to discharges. Why does Justice Thomas think that a minimum streamflow requirement is unrelated to a pollutant discharge? Why does the Court majority deem the minimum stream flow requirement an appropriate requirement? Does the majority view this requirement as unrelated to pollutant discharges? How does the majority's view in this regard differ from that of Justice Thomas?

2. Justice O'Connor's opinion for the Court states that while "§401(d) authorizes the State to place restrictions on the activity as a whole, that authority is not unbounded." Yet in his dissent Justice Thomas argues that the majority's decision "places no meaningful limitations on a State's authority under §401 to impose conditions on certification." What limits, if any, does the Court place on a state's ability to impose conditions on a §401 certification? How meaningful are they?

3. As noted in the opinions above, Washington state has not established any specific stream flow water quality criteria. Yet the Court

---

[4]. Indeed, as the §401 certification stated in this case, the flow levels imposed by respondents are "in excess of those required to maintain water quality in the bypass region" and therefore conditions not related to water quality must, in the Court's view, be permitted.

majority holds that §401(d) can be used to protect designated uses (here the protection of fish habitat) independent of specific criteria. In the majority's view, what is the relationship between designated uses and water quality criteria? How does this view differ from that of Justice Thomas in his dissent?

4. In Puerto Rico Sun Oil Co. v. EPA, 8 F.3d 73 (1st Cir. 1993), the First Circuit found that EPA had acted arbitrarily and capriciously in approving a §401 certification from Puerto Rico without waiting for the Commonwealth to complete an ongoing reconsideration of an important aspect of its certification. In a sharp departure from its prior practice, Puerto Rico's Environmental Quality Board (EQB) had issued a §401 certification that did not provide for a mixing zone for measuring the impact of a refinery's discharges. EPA had approved the certification despite the fact that the agency had been asked by the EQB to delay its decision while the EQB reconsidered its certification to incorporate new regulations governing mixing zones.

5. A §401 certification can be useful to dischargers in withstanding permit challenges. In Adams v. EPA, 38 F.3d 43 (1st Cir. 1994), the First Circuit rejected a challenge to EPA's issuance of an NPDES permit based on the presumption that the discharger's receipt of a §401 certification demonstrated that the discharge would not cause unreasonable degradation of receiving waters.

6. The Federal Energy Regulatory Commission (FERC) issues long-term licenses for hydroelectric projects. Because the licenses for many large hydroelectric projects will be expiring in coming years, the Court's decision in *PUD No. 1* offers states a significant tool for using §401 to protect water quality. Can you think of any conditions under which §401 certification could be required for applicants for federal grazing permits?

Water Quality Criteria for Toxics (p. 941). As noted in the text (p. 941), EPA had proposed to establish its own water quality criteria for toxics in 22 states that had failed to comply with section 303(c)(2)(b) of the Clean Water Act. After 8 states adopted their own criteria, EPA in December 1992 promulgated criteria for the remaining 14 states. 57 Fed. Reg. 60,848 (1992). The criteria promulgated by EPA cover 98 chemicals and include numeric criteria for protecting both human health and aquatic life. They were issued only after a nine-month dispute between EPA and OMB and the filing of a lawsuit to compel the Agency to act.

Judicial Review of Approval of State ICSs (p. 942). In Lake Cumberland Trust, Inc. v. EPA, 954 F.2d 1218 (6th Cir. 1992), the Sixth Circuit held that EPA approval of an individual control strategy (ICS) developed by a state pursuant to section 304(*l*) of the Act was not subject to judicial review. This decision is in accord with the decisions of the Third, Seventh, and Ninth Circuit cited in the parent text (p. 942). See also Hecla Mining Co. v. EPA, 12 F.3d 164 (9th Cir. 1993) (EPA's inclusion of additional waters on §304(l) list not subject to judicial review).

Lead Contamination from Gun Clubs (pp. 943-944). Lead contamination from gun clubs, the fact situation presented in the Problem Exercise (parent text, pp. 943-944), is a fairly common problem. See Berger, Gun Range Contends with Perils of Lead, N.Y. Times, Feb. 8, 1993, at B7. The case that inspired the Problem Exercise was decided by the Second Circuit in March 1993. Connecticut Coastal Fisherman's Association v. Remington Arms Co., 989 F.2d 1305 (2d Cir. 1993).

E. CONTROL OF POLLUTION FROM NONPOINT SOURCES

Nonpoint Pollution Problems (p. 944). A study by the Environmental Working Group found that runoff from agricultural areas has caused widespread contamination of drinking water by five commonly used herbicides. Lee, Farm Herbicides Foul Tap Water for 14 Million, Wash. Post, Oct. 19, 1994, at A3. As a result of this exposure, 14 million people are drinking water containing traces of the herbicides, resulting in a slight increase in their cancer risks. For example, the study estimated that citizens of Springfield, Illinois, will experience a 48 in 1 million chance of getting cancer from being exposed to the herbicides. Given the high background levels of cancer risks, one observer found the report "so underwhelming I must wonder why it was considered newsworthy." Noting that Americans already face a background risk of 1 in 4 of getting cancer, he observed that the herbicide exposure increased the risk from 250,000 in 1 million to 250,048 in 1 million," an increase he deemed "so insignificant as to be almost worthless," Heuchling, Responsible Environmental Activism, Wash. Post, Nov. 1, 1994, at A22 (letter to editor).

The Food Security Act of 1985 (pp. 946-947). The Conservation Reserve Program, another provision of the 1985 farm bill, provides subsidies to farmers who remove land from agricultural production to restore it to a natural state. Approximately 36 million acres of habitat has been enrolled in this program at a cost of $1.6 billion per year. Stevens, U.S. Effort to Return Farm Land to Natural State Wins Praise,

7. Water Pollution Control

N.Y. Times, Jan. 10, 1995, at C4. Wildlife experts believe that the program has helped reverse a sharp decline in duck populations in North America. The Soil Conservation Service reports that these and other programs have helped slow soil erosion, which has declined from 3.1 billion tons of soil in 1982 to 2.1 billion tons in 1992. Farm-Related Erosion Slows in Last Decade, Aug. 13, 1994, at E17. The most comprehensive assessment yet undertaken of the environmental and economic costs of soil erosion estimated that it costs nearly $44 billion per year in direct damage to farmland and indirect damage to waterways, public health, and infrastructure Pimentel, et al., Environmental and Economic Costs of Soil Erosion and Conservation Benefits, 267 Science 1117 (1995).

Section 1455b of the CZMA (pp. 948-951). In January 1993, EPA and NOAA finally issued the guidance documents governing how states with federally approved coastal zone management programs are to develop nonpoint source management programs pursuant to section 1455b of the CZMA. EPA, Guidance Specifying Management Measures for Sources of Nonpoint Pollution in Coastal Waters (1993); NOAA, Coastal Nonpoint Pollution Control Program: Program Development and Approval Guidance (1993). EPA estimated that the costs of adopting the measures recommended in the guidance documents would range from $390 million to $590 million. Yet only $50 million in grant money is available to the states through EPA, and less than $2 million is available directly from NOAA. Guidance Issued by EPA, NOAA to Curb Non-Point Source Pollution in Coastal Areas, 23 Env. Rep. 2489 (1993). As a result of the guidance, states must now submit their nonpoint source control programs to EPA and NOAA by July 1995.

State Land Use Controls and Water Quality (pp. 952-958). Robert Liberty has written a comprehensive review of the lessons of Oregon's growth management experience for other state land use control programs. Liberty, Oregon's Comprehensive Growth Management Program: An Implementation Review and Lessons for Other States, 22 Env. L. Rep. 10367 (1992). For a discussion of whether or not the federal government should enact national land use legislation, see Do We Need a Federal Land Act?, Envtl. Forum 28 (Jan.-Feb. 1993).

Lucas v. South Carolina Coastal Council (p. 965). On the last day of its 1992-1993 Term, the Supreme Court decided Lucas v. South Carolina Coastal Council, a significant decision, although perhaps less groundbreaking than the most ambitious proponents of invigorating takings analysis might have hoped.

Lucas v. South Carolina Coastal Council
112 S. Ct. 2886 (1992)

JUSTICE SCALIA delivered the opinion of the Court, in which REHNQUIST, C.J., and WHITE, O'CONNOR and THOMAS, JJ., joined.

In 1986, petitioner David H. Lucas paid $975,000 for two residential lots on the Isle of Palms in Charleston County, South Carolina, on which he intended to build single-family homes. In 1988, however, the South Carolina Legislature enacted the Beachfront Management Act (Act), which had the direct effect of barring petitioner from erecting any permanent habitable structures on his two parcels. A state trial court found that this prohibition rendered Lucas's parcels "valueless." This case requires us to decide whether the Act's dramatic effect on the economic value of Lucas's lots accomplished a taking of private property under the Fifth and Fourteenth Amendments requiring the payment of "just compensation."

I

A

[In 1977, South Carolina enacted a state coastal zone management act (the 1977 Act). The 1977 Act] required owners of coastal zone land that qualified as a "critical area" (defined in the legislation to include beaches and immediately adjacent sand dunes) to obtain a permit from the newly created South Carolina Coastal Council (respondent here) prior to committing the land to a "use other than the use the critical area was devoted to on [September 28, 1977]."

In the late 1970's, Lucas and others began extensive residential development of the Isle of Palms, a barrier island situated eastward of the City of Charleston. Lucas in 1986 purchased the two lots at issue in this litigation for his own account. No portion of the lots, which were located approximately 300 feet from the beach, qualified as a "critical area" under the 1977 Act; accordingly, at the time Lucas acquired these parcels, he was not legally obliged to obtain a permit from the Council in advance of any development activity. His intention with respect to the lots was to do what the owners of the immediately adjacent parcels had already done: erect single-family residences. He commissioned architectural drawings for this purpose.

The Beachfront Management Act brought Lucas's plans to an abrupt end. Under that 1988 legislation, the Council was directed to establish a "baseline" connecting the landward-most "[p]oints of ero-

7. Water Pollution Control

sion . . . during the past forty years" in the region of the Isle of Palms that includes Lucas's lots. In action not challenged here, the Council fixed this baseline landward of Lucas's parcels. That was significant, for under the Act construction of occupiable improvements was flatly prohibited seaward of a line drawn 20 feet landward of, and parallel to, the baseline. The Act provided no exceptions.

B

Lucas promptly filed suit in the South Carolina Court of Common Pleas, contending that the Beachfront Management Act's construction bar effected a taking of his property without just compensation. Lucas did not take issue with the validity of the Act as a lawful exercise of South Carolina's police power, but contended that the Act's complete extinguishment of his property's value entitled him to compensation regardless of whether the legislature had acted in furtherance of legitimate police power objectives. Following a bench trial, the court agreed. The trial court found that the Beachfront Management Act decreed a permanent ban on construction insofar as Lucas's lots were concerned, and that this prohibition "deprived Lucas of any reasonable economic use of the lots, . . . eliminated the unrestricted right of use, and rendered them valueless." The court thus concluded that Lucas's properties had been "taken" by operation of the Act, and it ordered respondent to pay "just compensation" in the amount of $1,232,387.50.

The Supreme Court of South Carolina reversed. It found dispositive what it described as Lucas's concession "that the Beachfront Management Act [was] properly and validly designed to preserve . . . South Carolina's beaches." Failing an attack on the validity of the statute as such, the court believed itself bound to accept the "uncontested . . . findings" of the South Carolina legislature that new construction in the coastal zone—such as petitioner intended—threatened this public resource. The Court ruled that when a regulation respecting the use of property is designed "to prevent serious public harm" (citing, inter alia, Mugler v. Kansas, 123 U.S. 623 (1887)), no compensation is owing under the Takings Clause regardless of the regulation's effect on the property's value. . . .

We granted certiorari. . . .

III

A

Prior to Justice Holmes' exposition in Pennsylvania Coal Co. v. Mahon, 260 U.S. 393 (1922), it was generally thought that the Takings

Clause reached only a "direct appropriation" of property, Legal Tender Cases, 12 Wall. 457, 551 (1871), or the functional equivalent of a "practical ouster of [the owner's] possession." Transportation Co. v. Chicago, 99 U.S. 635, 642 (1879). Justice Holmes recognized in *Mahon*, however, that if the protection against physical appropriations of private property was to be meaningfully enforced, the government's power to redefine the range of interests included in the ownership of property was necessarily constrained by constitutional limits. If, instead, the uses of private property were subject to unbridled, uncompensated qualification under the police power, "the natural tendency of human nature [would be] to extend the qualification more and more until at last private property disappeared." These considerations gave birth in that case to the oft-cited maxim that, "while property may be regulated to a certain extent, if regulation goes too far it will be recognized as a taking."

Nevertheless, our decision in *Mahon* offered little insight into when, and under what circumstances, a given regulation would be seen as going "too far" for purposes of the Fifth Amendment. In 70-odd years of succeeding "regulatory takings" jurisprudence, we have generally eschewed any " 'set formula' " for determining how far is too far, preferring to "engag[e] in . . . essentially ad hoc, factual inquiries," Penn Central Transportation Co. v. New York City, 438 U.S. 104 (1978). We have, however, described at least two discrete categories of regulatory action as compensable without case-specific inquiry into the public interest advanced in support of the restraint. The first encompasses regulations that compel the property owner to suffer a physical "invasion" of his property. In general (at least with regard to permanent invasions), no matter how minute the intrusion, and no matter how weighty the public purpose behind it, we have required compensation. For example, in Loretto v. Teleprompter Manhattan CATV Corp., 458 U.S. 419 (1982), we determined that New York's law requiring landlords to allow television cable companies to emplace cable facilities in their apartment buildings constituted a taking, id., at 435-440, even though the facilities occupied at most only 1 1/2 cubic feet of the landlords' property.

The second situation in which we have held categorical treatment appropriate is where regulation denies all economically beneficial or productive use of land. See *Agins*, 447 U. S., at 260.[6] As we have said

---

6. We will not attempt to respond to all of Justice Blackmun's mistaken citations of case precedent. Characteristic of its nature is his assertion that the cases we discuss here stand merely for the proposition "that proof that a regulation does *not* deny an owner economic use of his property is sufficient to defeat a facial taking challenge" and not for the point that "*denial* of such use is sufficient to establish a taking claim regardless of any other consideration." Post, at 2911, n. 11. The cases say, repeatedly and unmistakably, that

on numerous occasions, the Fifth Amendment is violated when land-use regulation "does not substantially advance legitimate state interests *or denies an owner economically viable use of his land.*" *Agins,* supra, at 260 (emphasis added).[7]

We have never set forth the justification for this rule. Perhaps it is simply, as Justice Brennan suggested, that total deprivation of benefi-

---

"the test to be applied in considering [a] facial [takings] challenge is fairly straightforward. A statute regulating the uses that can be made of property *effects a taking if it 'denies an owner economically viable use of his land.'* " *Keystone,* 480 U.S., at 495 (quoting *Hodel,* 452, U.S., at 295-296 (quoting *Agins,* 447 U.S., at 260)) (emphasis added).

Justice Blackmun describes that rule (which we do not invent but merely apply today) as "altering the long-settled rules of review" by foisting on the State "the burden of showing [its] regulation is not a taking." Post, at 11, 12. This is of course wrong. Lucas had to do more than simply file a lawsuit to establish his constitutional entitlement; he had to show that the Beachfront Management Act denied him economically beneficial use of his land. Our analysis presumes the unconstitutionality of state land-use regulation only in the sense that any rule-with-exceptions presumes the invalidity of a law that violates it. . . .

7. Regrettably, the rhetorical force of our "deprivation of all economically feasible use" rule is greater than its precision, since the rule does not make clear the "property interest" against which the loss of value is to be measured. When, for example, a regulation requires a developer to leave 90% of a rural tract in its natural state, it is unclear whether we would analyze the situation as one in which the owner has been deprived of all economically beneficial use of the burdened portion of the tract, or as one in which the owner has suffered a mere diminution in value of the tract as a whole. (For an extreme—and, we think, unsupportable—view of the relevant calculus, see Penn Central Transportation Co. v. New York City, 366 N.E. 2d 1271, 1276-1277 (1977), aff'd, 438 U.S. 104 (1978), where the state court examined the diminution in a particular parcel's value produced by a municipal ordinance in light of total value of the taking claimant's other holdings in the vicinity.) Unsurprisingly, this uncertainty regarding the composition of the denominator in our "deprivation" fraction has produced inconsistent pronouncements by the Court. Compare Pennsylvania Coal Co. v. Mahon, 260 U.S. 393, 414 (1922) (law restricting subsurface extraction of coal held to effect a taking), with Keystone Bituminous Coal Assn. v. DeBenedictis, 480 U.S. 470, 497-502 (1987) (nearly identical law held not to effect a taking); see also id., at 515-520 (Rehnquist, C.J., dissenting); Rose, *Mahon* Reconstructed: Why the Takings Issue is Still a Muddle, 57 S. Cal. L. Rev. 561, 566-569 (1984). The answer to this difficult question may lie in how the owner's reasonable expectations have been shaped by the State's law of property—i.e., whether and to what degree the State's law has accorded legal recognition and protection to the particular interest in land with respect to which the takings claimant alleges a diminution in (or elimination of) value. In any event, we avoid this difficulty in the present case, since the "interest in land" that Lucas has pleaded (a fee simple interest) is an estate with a rich tradition of protection at common law, and since the South Carolina Court of Common Pleas found that the Beachfront Management Act left each of Lucas's beachfront lots without economic value.

cial use is, from the landowner's point of view, the equivalent of a physical appropriation. See San Diego Gas & Electric Co. v. San Diego, 450 U.S., at 652 (Brennan, J., dissenting). "For what is the land but the profits thereof?" 1 E. Coke, Institutes ch. 1, §1 (1st Am. ed. 1812). Surely, at least, in the extraordinary circumstance when *no* productive or economically beneficial use of land is permitted, it is less realistic to indulge our usual assumption that the legislature is simply "adjusting the benefits and burdens of economic life," in a manner that secures an "average reciprocity of advantage" to everyone concerned. And the functional basis for permitting the government, by regulation, to affect property values without compensation—that "Government hardly could go on if to some extent values incident to property could not be diminished without paying for every such change in the general law," —does not apply to the relatively rare situations where the government has deprived a landowner of all economically beneficial uses.

On the other side of the balance, affirmatively supporting a compensation requirement, is the fact that regulations that leave the owner of land without economically beneficial or productive options for its use—typically, as here, by requiring land to be left substantially in its natural state—carry with them a heightened risk that private property is being pressed into some form of public service under the guise of mitigating serious public harm. . . . The many statutes on the books, both state and federal, that provide for the use of eminent domain to impose servitudes on private scenic lands preventing developmental uses, or to acquire such lands altogether, suggest the practical equivalence in this setting of negative regulation and appropriation. See, e.g., 16 U.S.C. 410ff-1(a) (authorizing acquisition of "lands, waters, or interests [within Channel Islands National Park] (including but not limited to scenic easements)"); §460aa-2(a) (authorizing acquisition of "any lands, or lesser interests therein, including mineral interests and scenic easements" within Sawtooth National Recreation Area); §§3921-3923 (authorizing acquisition of wetlands); N.C. Gen. Stat. §113A-38 (1990) (authorizing acquisition of, inter alia, "scenic easements" within the North Carolina natural and scenic rivers system); Tenn. Code Ann. §§11-15-101 [to] 11-15-108 (1987) (authorizing acquisition of "protective easements" and other rights in real property adjacent to State's historic, architectural, archaeological, or cultural resources).

We think, in short, that there are good reasons for our frequently expressed belief that when the owner of real property has been called upon to sacrifice *all* economically beneficial uses in the name of the common good, that is, to leave his property economically idle, he has suffered a taking.[8]

---

8. Justice Stevens criticizes the "deprivation of all economically beneficial use" rule as "wholly arbitrary," in that "[the] landowner whose property is

B

The trial court found Lucas's two beachfront lots to have been rendered valueless by respondent's enforcement of the coastal-zone construction ban.[9] Under Lucas's theory of the case, which rested upon our "no economically viable use" statements, that finding entitled him to compensation. Lucas believed it unnecessary to take issue with either the purposes behind the Beachfront Management Act, or the means chosen by the South Carolina Legislature to effectuate those purposes. The South Carolina Supreme Court, however, thought otherwise. In its view, the Beachfront Management Act was no ordinary enactment, but involved an exercise of South Carolina's "police powers" to mitigate the harm to the public interest that petitioner's use of his land might occasion. By neglecting to dispute the findings enumerated in the Act or otherwise to challenge the legislature's purposes, petitioner "conceded that the beach/dune area of South Carolina's shores is an extremely valuable public resource; that the erection of new construction, inter

---

diminished in value 95% recovers nothing," while the landowner who suffers a complete elimination of value "recovers the land's full value." Post, at 4. This analysis errs in its assumption that the landowner whose deprivation is one step short of complete is not entitled to compensation. Such an owner might not be able to claim the benefit of our categorical formulation, but, as we have acknowledged time and again, "the economic impact of the regulation on the claimant and . . . the extent to which the regulation has interfered with distinct investment-backed expectations" are keenly relevant to takings analysis generally. Penn Central Transportation Co. v. New York City, 438 U.S. 104, 124 (1978). It is true that in at least *some* cases the landowner with 95% loss will get nothing, while the landowner with total loss will recover in full. But that occasional result is no more strange than the gross disparity between the landowner whose premises are taken for a highway (who recovers in full) and the landowner whose property is reduced to 5% of its former value by the highway (who recovers nothing). Takings law is full of these "all-or-nothing" situations.

Justice Stevens similarly misinterprets our focus on "developmental" uses of property (the uses proscribed by the Beachfront Management Act) as betraying an "assumption that the only uses of property cognizable under the Constitution are developmental uses." Post, at 5, n. 3. We make no such assumption. Though our prior takings cases evince an abiding concern for the productive use of, and economic investment in, land, there are plainly a number of noneconomic interests in land whose impairment will invite exceedingly close scrutiny under the Takings Clause, See, e.g., Loretto v. Teleprompter Manhattan CATV Corp., 458 U.S. 419, 436 (1982) (interest in excluding strangers from one's land).

9. This finding was the premise of the Petition for Certiorari, and since it was not challenged in the Brief in Opposition we decline to entertain the argument in respondent's brief on the merits that the finding was erroneous. Instead, we decide the question presented under the same factual assumptions as did the Supreme Court of South Carolina. See Okalahoma City v. Tuttle, 471 U.S. 808, 816 (1985).

alia, contributes to the erosion and destruction of this public resource; and that discouraging new construction in close proximity to the beach/ dune area is necessary to prevent a great public harm." In the court's view, these concessions brought petitioner's challenge within a long line of this Court's cases sustaining against Due Process and Takings Clause challenges the State's use of its "police powers" to enjoin a property owner from activities akin to public nuisances. See Mugler v. Kansas, 123 U.S. 623 (1887) (law prohibiting manufacture of alcoholic beverages); Hadacheck v. Sebastian, 239 U.S. 394 (1915) (law barring operation of brick mill in residential area); Miller v. Schoene, 276 U.S. 272 (1928) (order to destroy diseased cedar trees to prevent infection of nearby orchards); Goldblatt v. Hempstead, 369 U.S. 590 (1962) (law effectively preventing continued operation of quarry in residential area).

It is correct that many of our prior opinions have suggested that "harmful or noxious uses" of property may be proscribed by government regulation without the requirement of compensation. For a number of reasons, however, we think the South Carolina Supreme Court was too quick to conclude that that principle decides the present case. The "harmful or noxious uses" principle was the Court's early attempt to describe in theoretical terms why government may, consistent with the Takings Clause, affect property values by regulation without incurring an obligation to compensate—a reality we nowadays acknowledge explicitly with respect to the full scope of the State's police power. We made this very point in *Penn Central Transportation Co.*, where, in the course of sustaining New York City's landmarks preservation program against a takings challenge, we rejected the petitioner's suggestion that Mugler and the cases following it were premised on, and thus limited by, some objective conception of "noxiousness":

> The uses in issue in *Hadacheck, Miller,* and *Goldblatt* were perfectly lawful in themselves. They involved no 'blameworthiness, . . . moral wrongdoing or conscious act of dangerous risk-taking which induce[d society] to shift the cost to a particular individual.' Sax, Takings and the Police Power, 74 Yale L. J. 36, 50 (1964). These cases are better understood as resting not on any supposed noxious quality of the prohibited uses but rather on the ground that the restrictions were reasonably related to the implementation of a policy—not unlike historic preservation—expected to produce a widespread public benefit and applicable to all similarly situated property. 438 U. S., at 133-134, n.30.

"Harmful or noxious use" analysis was, in other words, simply the progenitor of our more contemporary statements that " 'land-use regulation does not effect a taking if it substantially advances legitimate state interests' . . . ." *Nollan*, supra, at 834 (quoting *Agins*).

The transition from our early focus on control of "noxious" uses to our contemporary understanding of the broad realm within which government may regulate without compensation was an easy one, since the distinction between "harm-preventing" and "benefit-conferring" regulation is often in the eye of the beholder. It is quite possible, for example, to describe in *either* fashion the ecological, economic, and aesthetic concerns that inspired the South Carolina legislature in the present case. One could say that imposing a servitude on Lucas's land is necessary in order to prevent his use of it from "harming" South Carolina's ecological resources; or, instead, in order to achieve the "benefits" of an ecological preserve. Compare, e.g., Claridge v. New Hampshire Wetlands Board, 125 N.H. 745, 752, 485 A.2d 287, 292 (1984) (owner may, without compensation, be barred from filling wetlands because landfilling would deprive adjacent coastal habitats and marine fisheries of ecological support), with, e.g., Bartlett v. Zoning Comm'n of Old Lyme, 161 Conn. 24, 30, 282 A. 2d 907, 910 (1971) (owner barred from filling tidal marshland must be compensated, despite municipality's "laudable" goal of "preserving marshlands from encroachment or destruction"). Whether one or the other of the competing characterizations will come to one's lips in a particular case depends primarily upon one's evaluation of the worth of competing uses of real estate . . . .[12]

[N]oxious-use logic cannot serve as a touchstone to distinguish regulatory "takings"—which require compensation—from regulatory deprivations that do not require compensation. . . . None of them that employed the logic of "harmful use" prevention to sustain a regulation involved an allegation that the regulation wholly eliminated the value of the claimant's land.[13]

---

12. In Justice Blackmun's view, even with respect to regulations that deprive an owner of all developmental or economically beneficial land uses, the test for required compensation is whether the legislature has recited a harm-preventing justification for its action. See post, at 2906, 2910-2912. Since such a justification can be formulated in practically every case, this amounts to a test of whether the legislature has a stupid staff. We think the Takings Clause requires courts to do more than insist upon artful harm-preventing characterizations.

13. E.g., Mugler v. Kansas, 123 U.S. 623 (1887) (prohibition upon use of a building as a brewery; other uses permitted); Plymouth Coal Co. v. Pennsylvania, 232 U.S. 531 (1914) (requirement that "pillar" of coal be left in ground to safeguard mine workers; mineral rights could otherwise be exploited); Reinman v. Little Rock, 237 U.S. 171 (1915) (declaration that livery stable constituted a public nuisance; other uses of the property permitted); Hadacheck v. Sebastian, 239 U.S. 394 (1915) (prohibition of brick manufacturing in residential

Where the State seeks to sustain regulation that deprives land of all economically beneficial use, we think it may resist compensation only if the logically antecedent inquiry into the nature of the owner's estate shows that the proscribed use interests were not part of his title to begin with. This accords, we think, with our "takings" jurisprudence, which has traditionally been guided by the understandings of our citizens regarding the content of, and the State's power over, the "bundle of rights" that they acquire when they obtain title to property. It seems to us that the property owner necessarily expects the uses of his property to be restricted, from time to time, by various measures newly enacted by the State in legitimate exercise of its police powers; "as long recognized, some values are enjoyed under an implied limitation and must yield to the police power." *Pennsylvania Coal Co. v. Mahon,* 260 U.S., at 413. And in the case of personal property, by reason of the State's traditionally high degree of control over commercial dealings, he ought to be aware of the possibility that new regulation might even render his property economically worthless (at least if the property's only economically productive use is sale or manufacture for sale), see Andrus v. Allard, 444 U.S. 51, 66-67 (1979) (prohibition on sale of eagle feathers). In the case of land, however, we think the notion pressed by the Council that title is somehow held subject to the "implied limitation" that the State may subsequently eliminate all economically valuable use is inconsistent with the historical compact recorded in the Takings Clause that has become part of our constitutional culture. . . .[15]

---

area; other uses permitted); Goldblatt v. Hempstead, 369 U.S. 590 (1962) (prohibition on excavation; other uses permitted).

15. After accusing us of "launching a missile to kill a mouse," post, at 2904, Justice Blackmun expends a good deal of throw-weight of his own upon a noncombatant, arguing that our description of the "understanding" of land ownership that informs the Takings Clause is not supported by early American experience. That is largely true, but entirely irrelevant. The practices of the States *prior* to incorporation of the Takings and Just Compensation Clauses, see Chicago, B. & Q. R. Co. v. Chicago, 166 U.S. 226 (1897)—which, as Justice Blackmun acknowledges, occasionally included *outright physical appropriation* of land without compensation, see post, at 2915—were out of accord with *any* plausible interpretation of those provisions. Justice Blackmun is correct that early constitutional theorists did not believe the Takings Clause embraced regulations of property at all, see post, at 2915, and n. 23, but even he does not suggest (explicitly, at least) that we renounce the Court's contrary conclusion in *Mahon.* Since the text of the Clause can be read to encompass regulatory as well as physical deprivations (in contrast to the text originally proposed by Madison, see Speech Proposing Bill of Rights (June 8, 1789), in 12 J. Madison, The Papers of James Madison 201 (C. Hobson, R. Rutland, W. Rachal, & J. Sisson ed. 1979) ("No person shall be . . . obliged to relinquish his property,

7. Water Pollution Control   Page 965

We believe . . . confiscatory regulations, i.e., regulations that prohibit all economically beneficial use of land . . . cannot be newly legislated or decreed (without compensation), but must inhere in the title itself, in the restrictions that background principles of the State's law of property and nuisance already place upon land ownership. A law or decree with such an effect must, in other words, do no more than duplicate the result that could have been achieved in the courts—by adjacent landowners (or other uniquely affected persons) under the State's law of private nuisance, or by the State under its complementary power to abate nuisances that affect the public generally, or otherwise.[16]

On this analysis, the owner of a lake bed, for example, would not be entitled to compensation when he is denied the requisite permit to engage in a landfilling operation that would have the effect of flooding others' land. Nor the corporate owner of a nuclear generating plant, when it is directed to remove all improvements from its land upon discovery that the plant sits astride an earthquake fault. Such regulatory action may well have the effect of eliminating the land's only economically productive use, but it does not proscribe a productive use that was previously permissible under relevant property and nuisance principles. The use of these properties for what are now expressly prohibited purposes was *always* unlawful, and (subject to other constitutional limitations) it was open to the State at any point to make the implication of those background principles of nuisance and property law explicit. . . . When, however, a regulation that declares "off-limits" all economically productive or beneficial uses of land goes beyond what the relevant background principles would dictate, compensation must be paid to sustain it.

The "total taking" inquiry we require today will ordinarily entail (as the application of state nuisance law ordinarily entails) analysis of, among other things, the degree of harm to public lands and resources, or adjacent private property, posed by the claimant's proposed activities, see, e.g., Restatement (Second) of Torts §§826, 827, the social value of the claimant's activities and their suitability to the locality in question, see, e.g., id., §§828(a) and (b), 831, and the relative ease with which the alleged harm can be avoided through measures taken by the claim-

---

where it may be necessary for public use, without a just compensation"), we decline to do so as well.

16. The principal "otherwise" that we have in mind is litigation absolving the State (or private parties) of liability for the destruction of "real and personal property, in cases of actual necessity, to prevent the spreading of a fire" or to forestall other grave threats to the lives and property of others. Bowditch v. Boston, 101 U.S. 16, 18-19 (1880); see United States v. Pacific Railroad, 120 U.S. 227, 238-239 (1887).

ant and the government (or adjacent private landowners) alike, see, e.g., id., §§827(e), 828(c), 830. The fact that a particular use has long been engaged in by similarly situated owners ordinarily imports a lack of any common-law prohibition (though changed circumstances or new knowledge may make what was previously permissible no longer so, see Restatement (Second) of Torts, supra, §827, comment g). So also does the fact that other landowners, similarly situated, are permitted to continue the use denied to the claimant.

It seems unlikely that common-law principles would have prevented the erection of any habitable or productive improvements on petitioner's land; they rarely support prohibition of the "essential use" of land. The question, however, is one of state law to be dealt with on remand. We emphasize that to win its case South Carolina must do more than proffer the legislature's declaration that the uses Lucas desires are inconsistent with the public interest, or the conclusory assertion that they violate a common-law maxim such as *sic utere tuo ut alienum non laedas*. As we have said, a "State, by *ipse dixit*, may not transform private property into public property without compensation. . . ." Webb's Fabulous Pharmacies, Inc. v. Beckwith. Instead, as it would be required to do if it sought to restrain Lucas in a common-law action for public nuisance, South Carolina must identify background principles of nuisance and property law that prohibit the uses he now intends in the circumstances in which the property is presently found. Only on this showing can the State fairly claim that, in proscribing all such beneficial uses, the Beachfront Management Act is taking nothing. . . .[18]

The judgment is reversed and the cause remanded for proceedings not inconsistent with this opinion.

JUSTICE KENNEDY, concurring in the judgment.

. . . Petitioner has not applied for a special permit but may still do so. The availability of this alternative, if it can be invoked, may dispose of petitioner's claim of a permanent taking. As I read the Court's opinion, it does not decide the permanent taking claim, but neither does it foreclose the Supreme Court of South Carolina from considering

---

18. Justice Blackmun decries our reliance on background nuisance principles at least in part because he believes those principles to be as manipulable as we find the "harm prevention"/"benefit conferral" dichotomy. There is no doubt some leeway in a court's interpretation of what existing state law permits—but not remotely as much, we think, as in a legislative crafting of the reasons for its confiscatory regulation. We stress that an affirmative decree eliminating all economically beneficial uses may be defended only if an *objectively reasonable application* of relevant precedents would exclude those beneficial uses in the circumstances in which the land is presently found.

the claim or requiring petitioner to pursue an administrative alternative not previously available. . . .

The South Carolina Court of Common Pleas found that petitioner's real property has been rendered valueless by the State's regulation. The finding appears to presume that the property has no significant market value or resale potential. This is a curious finding, and I share the reservations of some of my colleagues about a finding that a beach front lot loses all value because of a development restriction. Post, at 2908 (Blackmun, J., dissenting); post, at 2919, n.3 (Stevens, J., dissenting); post, at 2925 (Statement of Souter, J.). While the Supreme Court of South Carolina on remand need not consider the case subject to this constraint, we must accept the finding as entered below. See Oklahoma City v. Tuttle, 471 U.S. 808, 816 (1985). Accepting the finding as entered, it follows that petitioner is entitled to invoke the line of cases discussing regulations that deprive real property of all economic value. See *Agins*.

The finding of no value must be considered under the Takings Clause by reference to the owner's reasonable, investment-backed expectations. . . .

There is an inherent tendency towards circularity in this synthesis, of course; for if the owner's reasonable expectations are shaped by what courts allow as a proper exercise of governmental authority, property tends to become what courts say it is. Some circularity must be tolerated in these matters, however, as it is in other spheres. E.g., Katz v. United States, 389 U.S. 347 (1967) (Fourth Amendment protections defined by reasonable expectations of privacy). The definition, moreover, is not circular in its entirety. The expectations protected by the Constitution are based on objective rules and customs that can be understood as reasonable by all parties involved.

In my view, reasonable expectations must be understood in light of the whole of our legal tradition. The common law of nuisance is too narrow a confine for the exercise of regulatory power in a complex and interdependent society. The State should not be prevented from enacting new regulatory initiatives in response to changing conditions, and courts must consider all reasonable expectations whatever their source. The Takings Clause does not require a static body of state property law; it protects private expectations to ensure private investment. I agree with the Court that nuisance prevention accords with the most common expectations of property owners who face regulation, but I do not believe this can be the sole source of state authority to impose severe restrictions. Coastal property may present such unique concerns for a fragile land system that the State can go further in regulating its development and use than the common law of nuisance might otherwise permit.

The Supreme Court of South Carolina erred, in my view, by reciting the general purposes for which the state regulations were enacted without a determination that they were in accord with the owner's reasonable expectations and therefore sufficient to support a severe restriction on specific parcels of property. The promotion of tourism, for instance, ought not to suffice to deprive specific property of all value without a corresponding duty to compensate. Furthermore, the means as well as the ends of regulation must accord with the owner's reasonable expectations. Here, the State did not act until after the property had been zoned for individual lot development and most other parcels had been improved, throwing the whole burden of the regulation on the remaining lots. This too must be measured in the balance. See *Mahon.*

JUSTICE BLACKMUN, dissenting.

Today the Court launches a missile to kill a mouse.

. . . According to the Court, [a case of total deprivation of value] never has arisen in any of our prior cases, and the Court imagines that it will arise "relatively rarely" or only in "extraordinary circumstances." Almost certainly it did not happen in this case.

Nonetheless, the Court presses on to decide the issue, and as it does, it ignores its jurisdictional limits, remakes its traditional rules of review, and creates simultaneously a new categorical rule and an exception (neither of which is rooted in our prior case law, common law, or common sense). I protest not only the Court's decision, but each step taken to reach it. More fundamentally, I question the Court's wisdom in issuing sweeping new rules to decide such a narrow case. Surely, as Justice Kennedy demonstrates, the Court could have reached the result it wanted without inflicting this damage upon our Takings Clause jurisprudence.

My fear is that the Court's new policies will spread beyond the narrow confines of the present case. For that reason, I, like the Court, will give far greater attention to this case than its narrow scope suggests—not because I can intercept the Court's missile, or save the targeted mouse, but because I hope perhaps to limit the collateral damage. . . .

I

C

. . . If the state legislature is correct that the prohibition on building in front of the setback line prevents serious harm, then, under this Court's prior cases, the Act is constitutional. "Long ago it was recognized that all property in this country is held under the implied obligation that the owner's use of it shall not be injurious to the community, and the Takings Clause did not transform that principle to one that requires compensation whenever the State asserts its power to enforce it." *Keystone*, 480 U.S. at 491-492 (1987). The Court consistently has upheld regulations imposed to arrest a significant threat to the common welfare, whatever their economic effect on the owner. See, e.g., *Goldblatt;* Euclid v. Ambler Realty Co., 272 U.S. 365 (1926); Gorieb v. Fox, 274 U.S. 603, 608 (1927); Mugler v. Kansas, 123 U.S. 623 (1887).

[After arguing that the case was not ripe for decision because Lucas had failed to exhaust available administrative remedies, and that the finding of total deprivation of value was contradicted by the record and "almost certainly erroneous," Justice Blackmun continued:]

IV

The Court does not reject the South Carolina Supreme Court's decision simply on the basis of its disbelief and distrust of the legislature's findings. It also takes the opportunity to create a new scheme for regulations that eliminate all economic value. From now on, there is a categorical rule finding these regulations to be a taking unless the use they prohibit is a background common-law nuisance or property principle.

A

I first question the Court's rationale in creating a category that obviates a "case-specific inquiry into the public interest advanced," if all economic value has been lost. . . .

This Court repeatedly has recognized the ability of government, in certain circumstances, to regulate property without compensation no matter how adverse the financial effect on the owner may be. More than a century ago, the Court explicitly upheld the right of States to prohibit uses of property injurious to public health, safety, or welfare without paying compensation: "A prohibition simply upon the use of property for purposes that are declared, by valid legislation, to be injurious to the health, morals, or safety of the community, cannot, in any just sense, be deemed a taking or an appropriation of property." Mugler v. Kansas. On this basis, the Court upheld an ordinance effectively prohibiting operation of a previously lawful brewery, although the "establishments will become of no value as property." Id.

Mugler was only the beginning in a long line of cases. In Powell v.

Pennsylvania, the Court upheld legislation prohibiting the manufacture of oleomargarine, despite the owner's allegation that "if prevented from continuing it, the value of his property employed therein would be entirely lost and he be deprived of the means of livelihood." In Hadacheck v. Sebastian, the Court upheld an ordinance prohibiting a brickyard, although the owner had made excavations on the land that prevented it from being utilized for any purpose but a brickyard. In Miller v. Schoene, the Court held that the Fifth Amendment did not require Virginia to pay compensation to the owner of cedar trees ordered destroyed to prevent a disease from spreading to nearby apple orchards. The "preferment of [the public interest] over the property interest of the individual, to the extent even of its destruction, is one of the distinguishing characteristics of every exercise of the police power which affects property." Again, in Omnia Commercial Co. v. United States, 261 U.S. 502 (1923), the Court stated that "destruction of, or injury to, property is frequently accomplished without a 'taking' in the constitutional sense."

More recently, in *Goldblatt*, the Court upheld a town regulation that barred continued operation of an existing sand and gravel operation in order to protect public safety. "Although a comparison of values before and after is relevant," the Court stated, "it is by no means conclusive." In 1978, the Court declared that "in instances in which a state tribunal reasonably concluded that the health, safety, morals, or general welfare would be promoted by prohibiting particular contemplated uses of land, this Court has upheld land-use regulation that destroyed . . . recognized real property interests." Penn Central Transp. Co. In First Lutheran Church v. Los Angeles County, the owner alleged that a floodplain ordinance had deprived it of "all use" of the property. The Court remanded the case for consideration whether, even if the ordinance denied the owner all use, it could be justified as a safety measure. And in *Keystone Bituminous Coal*, the Court summarized over 100 years of precedent: "the Court has repeatedly upheld regulations that destroy or adversely affect real property interests."

The Court recognizes that "our prior opinions have suggested that 'harmful or noxious uses' of property may be proscribed by government regulation without the requirement of compensation," but seeks to reconcile them with its categorical rule by claiming that the Court never has upheld a regulation when the owner alleged the loss of all economic value. Even if the Court's factual premise were correct, its understanding of the Court's cases is distorted. In none of the cases did the Court suggest that the right of a State to prohibit certain activities without paying compensation turned on the availability of some residual valuable use. Instead, the cases depended on whether the government interest was sufficient to prohibit the activity, given the significant private cost. . . .

B

Ultimately even the Court cannot embrace the full implications of its per se rule: it eventually agrees that there cannot be a categorical rule for a taking based on economic value that wholly disregards the public need asserted. Instead, the Court decides that it will permit a State to regulate all economic value only if the State prohibits uses that would not be permitted under "background principles of nuisance and property law."

Until today, the Court explicitly had rejected the contention that the government's power to act without paying compensation turns on whether the prohibited activity is a common-law nuisance. The brewery closed in *Mugler* itself was not a common-law nuisance, and the Court specifically stated that it was the role of the legislature to determine what measures would be appropriate for the protection of public health and safety. In upholding the state action in *Miller*, the Court found it unnecessary to "weigh with nicety the question whether the infected cedars constitute a nuisance according to common law; or whether they may be so declared by statute." Instead the Court has relied in the past, as the South Carolina Court has done here, on legislative judgments of what constitutes a harm.

The Court rejects the notion that the State always can prohibit uses it deems a harm to the public without granting compensation because "the distinction between 'harm-preventing' and 'benefit-conferring' regulation is often in the eye of the beholder." Since the characterization will depend "primarily upon one's evaluation of the worth of competing uses of real estate," the Court decides a legislative judgment of this kind no longer can provide the desired "objective, value-free basis" for upholding a regulation. The Court, however, fails to explain how its proposed common law alternative escapes the same trap.

The threshold inquiry for imposition of the Court's new rule, "deprivation of all economically valuable use," itself cannot be determined objectively. As the Court admits, whether the owner has been deprived of all economic value of his property will depend on how "property" is defined. The "composition of the denominator in our 'deprivation' fraction,'" is the dispositive inquiry. Yet there is no "objective" way to define what that denominator should be. "We have long understood that any land-use regulation can be characterized as the 'total' deprivation of an aptly defined entitlement. . . . Alternatively, the same regulation can always be characterized as a mere partial withdrawal from full, unencumbered ownership of the landholding affected by the regulation. . . ." Michelman, Takings, 1987, 88 Colum. L. Rev. 1600, 1614 (1988).

The Court's decision in *Keystone Bituminous Coal* illustrates this principle perfectly. In *Keystone*, the Court determined that the "support estate" was "merely a part of the entire bundle of rights possessed by the owner." Thus, the Court concluded that the support estate's destruction merely eliminated one segment of the total property. Ibid. The dissent, however, characterized the support estate as a distinct property interest that was wholly destroyed. The Court could agree on no "value-free basis" to resolve this dispute.

Even more perplexing, however, is the Court's reliance on common-law principles of nuisance in its quest for a value-free takings jurisprudence. In determining what is a nuisance at common law, state courts make exactly the decision that the Court finds so troubling when made by the South Carolina General Assembly today: they determine whether the use is harmful. Common-law public and private nuisance law is simply a determination whether a particular use causes harm. See Prosser, Private Action for Public Nuisance, 52 Va. L. Rev. 997, 997 (1966) ("*Nuisance* is a French word which means nothing more than harm"). There is nothing magical in the reasoning of judges long dead. They determined a harm in the same way as state judges and legislatures do today. If judges in the 18th and 19th centuries can distinguish a harm from a benefit, why not judges in the 20th century, and if judges can, why not legislators? There simply is no reason to believe that new interpretations of the hoary common law nuisance doctrine will be particularly "objective" or "value-free." Once one abandons the level of generality of sic utere tuo ut alienum non laedas, ante, at 26, one searches in vain, I think, for anything resembling a principle in the common law of nuisance.

C

Finally, the Court justifies its new rule that the legislature may not deprive a property owner of the only economically valuable use of his land, even if the legislature finds it to be a harmful use, because such action is not part of the "long recognized" "understandings of our citizens." These "understandings" permit such regulation only if the use is a nuisance under the common law. Any other course is "inconsistent with the historical compact recorded in the Takings Clause." It is not clear from the Court's opinion where our "historical compact" or "citizens' understanding" comes from, but it does not appear to be history.

The principle that the State should compensate individuals for property taken for public use was not widely established in America at the time of the Revolution.

The colonists . . . inherited . . . a concept of property which permitted extensive regulation of the use of that property for the public benefit—regulation that could even go so far as to deny all productive use of the property to the owner if, as Coke himself stated, "the regulation extends to the public benefit . . . for this is for the public, and every one hath benefit by it."

F. Bosselman, D. Callies & J. Banta, The Taking Issue 80-81 (1973), quoting The Case of the King's Prerogative in Saltpetre, 12 Co. Rep. 12-13 (1606) (hereinafter *Bosselman*). See also Treanor, The Origins and Original Significance of the Just Compensation Clause of the Fifth Amendment, 94 Yale L.J. 694, 697, n.9 (1985).

Even into the 19th century, state governments often felt free to take property for roads and other public projects without paying compensation to the owners. See M. Horwitz, The Transformation of American Law, 1780-1860, 63-64 (1977) (hereinafter Horwitz); Treanor, 94 Yale L. J., at 695. . . .

Nor does history indicate any common-law limit on the State's power to regulate harmful uses even to the point of destroying all economic value. Nothing in the discussions in Congress concerning the Takings Clause indicates that the Clause was limited by the common-law nuisance doctrine. Common law courts themselves rejected such an understanding. They regularly recognized that it is "for the legislature to interpose, and by positive enactment to prohibit a use of property which would be injurious to the public." Chief Justice Shaw explained in upholding a regulation prohibiting construction of wharves, the existence of a taking did not depend on "whether a certain erection in tide water is a nuisance at common law or not." *Alger*, 7 Cush., at 104; see also Commonwealth v. Parks, 155 Mass. 531, 532, 30 N.E. 174 (1892) (Holmes, J.) ("The legislature may change the common law as to nuisances, and may move the line either way, so as to make things nuisances which were not so, or to make things lawful which were nuisances").

In short, I find no clear and accepted "historical compact" or "understanding of our citizens" justifying the Court's new taking doctrine. Instead, the Court seems to treat history as a grab-bag of principles, to be adopted where they support the Court's theory, and ignored where they do not. If the Court decided that the early common law provides the background principles for interpreting the Taking Clause, then regulation, as opposed to physical confiscation, would not be compensable. If the Court decided that the law of a later period provides the background principles, then regulation might be compensable, but the Court would have to confront the fact that legislatures regularly determined which uses were prohibited, independent of the common law, and independent of whether the uses were lawful when the owner purchased. What makes the Court's analysis unworkable is its attempt to package the law of two incompatible eras and peddle it as historical fact. . . .

I dissent.

[The separate dissent by JUSTICE STEVENS is omitted.]

[JUSTICE SOUTER filed a statement stating that he would dismiss the writ of certiorari as improvidently granted on the ground that the trial court's conclusion that Lucas's land was totally deprived of value was extremely questionable viewing the record as a whole. In his view, this deprived the Court of the ability to clarify the meaning of "total taking," and thus so impaired the ability of the Court to proceed that it should dismiss.]

NOTES AND QUESTIONS

1. Total Takings. Justice Blackmun chides the majority for, among other things, articulating a rule of law applicable only in "extraordinary circumstances." These circumstances, namely, a statute's totally depriving property of value, rendering it "valueless," had never arisen in a Supreme Court decision before. (See text of the majority opinion at note 9.) Notice that courts have employed different terminology to describe deprivation so severe as to be constitutionally suspect, which Justice Scalia labels a case of "total takings": denied all "economically viable use of his land" (*Agins,* quoted by *Lucas*); "deprivation of all economically feasible use" (*Lucas,* note 7); "valueless"; "total deprivation of beneficial use" (*Lucas,* quoting *San Diego Gas and Electric*); "without economically beneficial or productive options for its uses" (*Lucas*); and there are other examples. In announcing a categorical approach to a certain class of takings cases, what precisely is the Court's definition of that category? Does Justice Scalia's reference to "beneficial or *productive* options" imply that complete destruction of the property's value may not be required for an action to fall within this category?

2. Other-than-total Takings. What formulation of takings doctrine does *Lucas* suggest is to be applied to regulatory situations that fall outside this category of severe limitations on property rights? Responding to an observation by Justice Stevens that it is anomalous that someone who loses 95 percent of a property's value is entitled to no compensation, Justice Scalia in note 8 states that it is erroneous to assume that a "landowner whose deprivation is one step short of complete is not entitled to compensation." He notes that "[s]uch an owner might not be able to claim the benefit of our categorical formulation," but he suggests that *Penn Central*'s "interfere[nce] with distinct investment-backed expectations" analysis might be "keenly relevant." In con-

7. Water Pollution Control   Page 965

sidering how the Court may approach the far more common less-than-total takings situation, consider Yee v. City of Escondido, 112 S. Ct. 1522 (1992). In that case, which involved a local rent control ordinance combined with restrictions on the ability of a mobile home park owner to terminate tenancies, Justice O'Connor, writing for the Court in an opinion joined by the Chief Justice and Justices White, Stevens, Scalia, Kennedy, and Thomas, states:

> [W]here the government merely regulates the use of property, compensation is required only if considerations such as the purpose of the regulation or the extent to which it deprives the owner of the economic use of the property suggest that the regulation has unfairly singled out the property owner to bear a burden that should be borne by the public as a whole. See, e.g., Penn Central Transp. Co. [This analysis] necessarily entails complex factual assessments of the purposes and economic effects of government actions.

Id. at 1526.

Insofar as Justice Scalia's opinion provides any clues about the jurisprudence outside the total takings category, it is truly delphic. Indeed, it is possible to read part of it as *relaxing* takings doctrine in cases of total takings. After quoting a portion of Justice Brennan's opinion in *Penn Central Transp. Co.,* in which the Court refuses to subject New York City's landmark preservation law to more severe scrutiny because it confers a benefit on society instead of preventing a harm to society (a nuisance), Justice Scalia writes that "harmful or noxious use" analysis was simply a progenitor of the Court's contemporary statements that "land-use regulation does not effect a taking if it substantially advances legitimate state interests," quoting from his own opinion in *Nollan* (which quotes from *Agins*). If that remark is to be taken literally, it means that a substantial connection to a legitimate state interest *always* saves a regulation from the requirement of compensation regardless of the extent of private deprivation or interference with reasonable investment backed expectations. It would thus seem to be at least a partial rejection of the three-factor formulation of takings doctrine enunciated in *Penn Central* itself, pursuant to which the takings question turned on the character of the governmental action, its interference with reasonable investment-backed expectations, and the economic impact of the action. Most analysts have interpreted this to mean that each of these factors is relevant in all takings analyses, save for those few areas where categorical analysis takes over (permanent physical occupations, *Teleprompter,* and total takings, *Lucas*).

This "relaxed" interpretation of *Lucas* is hard to square with Justice O'Connor's opinion in *Yee,* above.

409

3. Deprivation of Value and the "Nuisance Exception." Without saying so explicitly, Justice Scalia's opinion adopts major portions of Chief Justice Rehnquist's dissents in several important prior cases, especially *Penn Central Transp. Co.* and *Keystone Bituminous Coal*, thus indicating that the majority coalition on the Court has indeed shifted to a new, more property protecting, position. In each of these earlier decisions, the Chief Justice had urged that the so-called nuisance exception to the requirement to compensate for taking private property was narrower than that suggested by the Court majorities. In his view, the Court had become too lax in accepting government arguments that regulation was necessary to prevent a harm to the public, to the degree that the concept of harm prevention had become practically coterminous with the police power, insofar as anything that the government did under the police power to promote the public health, welfare, and morals could be articulated as a regulation preventing harm to the public health, welfare, and morals. He suggested that common law nuisance principles were the appropriate delimiters of the "nuisance exception."

The second objection the Chief Justice made in these two cases was to disagree with the premise that successfully invoking the nuisance exception meant that compensation never had to be paid. "Though nuisance regulations have been sustained despite a substantial reduction in value," he said in *Keystone*, "we have not accepted the proposition that the State may completely extinguish a property interest or prohibit all use without providing compensation."

It was this second objection of the Chief Justice's, coupled with the changed composition of the Court, that supplied Lucas's litigation strategy: In his brief, Lucas insisted that a person who has been deprived of all economically viable use of land is *always* entitled to compensation, whether or not the state is regulating a common law nuisance. This explains why he did not challenge the state's purposes in enacting the coastal zone protection legislation—debating the validity or nature of those purposes was irrelevant to his theory of the case.

In a significant amicus brief in *support* of Lucas written by Richard Epstein, the Institute for Justice rejected Lucas's theory and stressed the first of Justice Rehnquist's arguments: The "nuisance exception" had to be limited to traditional common law nuisances. Professor Epstein's theory was that compensation must be paid whenever government takes *any* "private property," unless it can justify the regulation as an exercise of common law nuisance principles. The extent of diminution is irrelevant; partial takings are as unconstitutional as total takings.

Justice Scalia's opinion for the *Lucas* majority is an interesting variation on these arguments. He announces that regulations that deprive owners of "all economically beneficial use of land" are a special category as to which the government must pay compensation unless it shows a justification under background principles of nuisance and property law, a category slightly larger than that proposed by Professor Epstein, but agrees with Epstein's position and Chief Justice Rehnquist's earlier opinions by taking the crucial issue of characterizing the government's purpose out of the hands of the legislature and placing it in the hands of the courts. In permitting a showing of consistency with background nuisance principles to obviate compensation, Justice Scalia's opinion appears to diverge from the Chief Justice's earlier views, which were that total deprivation always required compensation. However, it may be that the Chief Justice concluded that as a matter of actual application nuisance principles will never, or almost never, justify total deprivations, and thus that he was not shifting ground too much in signing onto Justice Scalia's opinion.

4. *The Remand in* Lucas. Because the case had not been litigated on the theory adopted by the Supreme Court, it was remanded for further proceedings. On remand, the lawyers for South Carolina Coastal Commission believed that they would not be precluded from litigating the issue of valuelessness, and were confident that Lucas would not be owed compensation. They also hoped that the coastal zone construction restrictions could satisfy the nuisance test laid down by the Court. Justice Stevens's opinion, which we omitted, stresses his belief that such restrictions may satisfy the majority's formulation, noting that the 29 deaths and more than $6 billion in property damage suffered in South Carolina from the effects of Hurricane Hugo in 1989—effects the state argues would have been mitigated if fewer coastal properties were developed—provide a substantial harm prevention justification, which may pass muster. However, a change in membership had occurred on the South Carolina Supreme Court since it first decided *Lucas,* and on remand the court brushed aside the arguments of the Coastal Council. Without discussing whether Lucas had been deprived of all the value of his property, the court stated in conclusory fashion:

> Coastal Council has not persuaded us that any common law basis exists by which it could restrain Lucas's desired use of his land; nor has our research uncovered any such common law principle. We hold that the sole issue on remand from this Court to the circuit level is a determination of the actual damages Lucas has sustained as the result of his being temporarily deprived of the use of his property.

Lucas v. South Carolina Coastal Council, 424 S.E.2d 484, 486 (S.C. 1992).

In 1993 the South Carolina Coastal Council agreed to grant Lucas conditional approval to build on his property. Nevertheless, he pursued a temporary takings claim in state court. In July 1993 the Coastal Council settled the litigation by agreeing to purchase Lucas's land for $850,000 plus $725,000 for interest, attorneys' fees, and costs, for a total settlement of $1,575,000. Two and one-half years before the Supreme Court's decision, Lucas had assigned the proceeds of the lawsuit to NationsBank, which held a mortgage on the property.

5. *Less-than-Total Takings after* Lucas. While *Lucas* is, by its terms, limited to enunciating the doctrine applicable to total takings, lower courts may well combine Justice Scalia's general logic with Justice Stevens's mocking of the distinction between 100 percent and 95 percent deprivation as arbitrary, to apply the same analysis outside the category. If that occurs, takings doctrine will be creeping toward Professor Epstein's position. Indeed, cases like *Whitney Benefits* and *Loveladies Harbor* (parent text, pp. 962-963) point in that direction already. Epstein, however, is not so confident. He believes that *Lucas* "appears to have adopted a powerful 'hands off' attitude to all forms of partial restriction on land use—a subject that dwarfs the importance of the peculiar circumstances of *Lucas*, the total wipeout of all land uses." Epstein, *Yee v. City of Escondido*: The Supreme Court Strikes Out Again, 26 Loyola L.A. L. Rev. 3 (1992). When *Lucas* is viewed together with *Yee*, Epstein despairs that "the inexorable flow of decided cases under the Takings Clause has been ever more supportive of big government and ever less respectful to the place of private property in our government regime." Id. at 22.

6. *Evolving Conceptions of Property Rights and Environmental Harm.* Recall from Chapter 2 that one of the motivations for legislation in the area of environmental degradation has been a dissatisfaction with the capacity of the common law to mediate between individual property rights and emerging environmental harm in a manner that adequately respects modern concerns about environmental quality. The 1973 CEQ report (text, pp. 964-965) emphasized the need for a changing understanding of what constitutes "reasonable use" of private property in light of environmental considerations. The idea that statutory law appropriately changes common law understanding is evident in decisions such as Weyerhaeuser v. Costle (parent text, p. 537). Does the majority opinion in *Lucas* inhibit the ability of legislatures legitimately to adjust private and public rights and responsibilities to accommodate changing conceptions of "reasonable use"?

Justice Scalia at least recognizes that common law notions of reasonable use must adjust to changed circumstances. He states that "[t]he fact that a particular use has long been engaged in by similarly situated owners ordinarily imports a lack of any common-law prohibition (though changed circumstances or new knowledge may make what was previously permissible no longer so, see Restatement (Second) of Torts, §827, comment g)." 112 S. Ct. at 2901. Comment g notes that changes in the character of a locality over time may make a particular land use "wholly unsuited to that locality twenty years later." It does not discuss the possibility that new scientific understanding (e.g., concerning the impact of development on nonpoint source pollution) might justify a finding that an activity long thought to be unobjectionable (e.g., building a home in a critical area) creates a nuisance.

Are only common law notions of harm worthy of the Court's respect? In his concurrence, Justice Kennedy states that "[t]he State should not be prevented from enacting new regulatory initiatives in response to changing conditions, and courts must consider all reasonable expectations whatever their source. The Takings Clause does not require a static body of state property law." 112 S. Ct. at 2903 (Kennedy, J., concurring).

7. *Burdens of Proof of Environmental Harm.* Justice Scalia's fondness for common law principles of nuisance seems to be founded on the notion that legislators are not to be trusted to make honest legislative findings of environmental harm. In footnote 12 he observes that since a "harm-preventing justification . . . can be formulated in practically every case, this amounts to a test of whether the legislature has a stupid staff." 112 S. Ct. at 2898 n. 12. Justice Kennedy seems willing to give legislators more leeway, though he does not think they acted properly in *Lucas*. After *Lucas*, under what circumstances could legislative findings that development in a critical area would create a nuisance avoid takings problems like those encountered by South Carolina's Beachfront Management Act?

8. *Real Property, Personal Property, and Investor Expectations.* Real estate is not the only kind of property whose value may be profoundly altered by government policy decisions. Investors foolish enough to place their entire investment portfolios in interest rate options could easily lose everything if they guess wrong about the Federal Reserve Board's future policies. Yet such investors clearly are not entitled to compensation even though the government's adjusting interest rates effectively can destroy the value of their property. Why then is real property entitled to special constitutional protection not afforded personal property? Justice Scalia appears to rely on investor expectations as the justification for this distinction. He states that "in the case of personal property, by reason of the State's traditionally high degree of control over commercial dealings, [the investor] ought to be aware of the possibility that new regulation might even render his property economically worthless," 112 S. Ct. at 2899. If investor expectations are the key to takings analysis, is a state free to change its conception of property law to alter what expectations concerning the risk of future regulation are reasonable? Richard Epstein argues that a major problem with *Lucas* is the Court's "failure to explain the relationship between expectations and entitlements" and that society should seek to deter-

mine what set of entitlements maximizes social welfare. Epstein, Lucas v. South Carolina Coastal Council: A Tangled Web of Expectations, 45 Stan. L. Rev. 1369, 1371 (1993).

In Just v. Marinette County (parent text, p. 964), the Wisconsin Supreme Court did not think it reasonable for property owners to expect that they could convert wetlands to a nonnatural state. In *Just*, a local ordinance allowed only limited use of wetlands surrounding a lake, such as harvesting of wild crops, forestry, hunting, and fishing. In holding that the ordinance was not an unconstitutional taking of property, the court noted that "[t]his is not a case where an owner is prevented from using his land for natural and indigenous uses. . . . The changing of wetlands and swamps to the damage of the general public by upsetting the natural environment and the natural relationship is not a reasonable use of that land." Just v. Marinette County, 201 N.W. 2d 761, 768-770 (Wis. 1972). How would *Just* be decided under the *Lucas* rationale? Joseph Sax argues that *Lucas* may "be viewed as the Court's long-delayed answer" to *Just*. In his view, Justice Scalia "recognizes the emerging view of land as part of an ecosystem, rather than as purely private property," but sought to send a "clear message" limiting its application: "States may not regulate land use solely by requiring landowners to maintain their property in its natural state as part of a functioning ecosystem, even though those natural functions may be important to the ecosystem." Sax, Property Rights and the Economy of Nature: Understanding Lucas v. South Carolina Coastal Council, 45 Stan. L. Rev. 1433, 1438 (1993).

9. *Statutes of Limitations and Takings Claims.* The Federal Circuit has ruled that a property owner may simultaneously challenge the validity of government action while pursuing a takings claim. Indeed, the court has indicated that the filing of a simultaneous challenge may be necessary to avoid the running of the statute of limitations. In Loveladies Harbor, Inc. v. United States, 27 F.3d 1545 (Fed. Cir. 1994) (en banc), the Federal Circuit ruled that because a district court might not adjudicate the validity of the government action prior to expiration of the six-year statute of limitations for filing a takings claim, a simultaneous filing of such a claim in the Court of Claims would toll the statute of limitations.

A Note on Post-*Lucas* Decisions by the Federal Circuit

In November 1993 the Federal Circuit held that the issuance of a cease and desist order by the Army Corps of Engineers, which was subsequently overturned by a federal court, did not constitute a temporary taking for which compensation was required. Tabb Lakes, Ltd. v.

7. Water Pollution Control

United States, 10 F.3d 796 (Fed. Cir. 1993). While the court noted that "a taking, even for a day, without compensation is prohibited by the Constitution," it found that "preliminary regulatory activity does not effect a taking in the constitutional sense." 10 F.3d at 800, 802. The court concluded that compensation need not be paid where the Corps made a mistake in asserting jurisdiction over isolated wetlands because mistakes may give rise to due process, but not takings claims. While leaving open the possibility that "extraordinary delay" in the permit process might create a taking, the court found nothing in the case law to suggest "that unreasonable delay converts the first preliminary act" into a taking. Id. at 803.

In March 1994 the Federal Circuit decided the appeal from the Court of Claims's decision in *Florida Rock Industries* (see p. 963 of the parent). The case involved a 1,560-acre parcel of wetlands purchased for $3 million for limestone mining just before the Clean Water Act had been enacted. The Army Corps of Engineers had been granting §404 permits to mine parcels only large enough to provide three years worth of extraction, which meant only 98 acres of Florida Rock's land. However, the Corps denied Florida Rock's application to mine a 98-acre parcel because of concerns about the impact of mining on water quality. The Court of Claims found that the permit denial was a regulatory taking and the government appealed. After an initial remand from the Federal Circuit, the Court of Claims again found that the permit denial had deprived Florida Rock of virtually all value in the 98-acre parcel because it had reduced its value from $10,500 per acre to a nominal $500 per acre (a loss of roughly 95 percent). The court awarded Florida Rock more than $1 million in damages plus compound interest.

In Florida Rock Industries, Inc. v. United States, 18 F.3d 1560 (Fed. Cir. 1994), the Federal Circuit vacated this judgment and again remanded the case to the Court of Claims. In light of evidence that Florida Rock had received and rejected offers of $4,000/acre for the property, the court found that the record did not support a finding that all economic use of the land had been taken by regulation. Thus, it returned the case to the Court of Claims to determine the property's fair market value. The Federal Circuit noted that the Supreme Court had not resolved the less-than-total takings issue in *Lucas* and it noted that if regulation works to preserve the reciprocity of advantages among property owners, thus protecting the property values of all, it would be less inclined to find a partial taking.

In June 1994 the Federal Circuit decided the government's appeal of the *Loveladies Harbor* decision (see p. 963 of the parent). In *Loveladies* a developer had sought to fill 50 acres of wetlands in a 51-acre parcel of land that had remained undeveloped after development of 199 acres of a 250-acre tract of property. While the state of New Jersey agreed to allowed development of 12.5 acres of the property, including 11.5 acres of wetlands, the Army Corps of Engineers denied the developer's application for a §404 permit. The Claims Court found that the permit denial was a regulatory taking because it had reduced the fair market value of the 12.5-acre parcel from $2.6 million to $12,500.

On appeal, the Federal Circuit affirmed. Loveladies Harbor, Inc. v. United States, 28 F.3d 1171 (Fed. Cir. 1994). The court outlined the following three-part test for determining whether a regulatory taking had occurred:

1. There was a denial of economically viable use of the property as a result of the regulatory imposition.
2. The property owner had distinct investment-backed expectations.
3. It was an interest vested in the owner, as a matter of state property law, and not within the power of the state to regulate under common law nuisance doctrine.

28 F.3d at 1179.

In determining whether the permit denial deprived Loveladies of all economically viable use, the court held that only the 12.5-acre parcel for which the permit was denied, and not the entire 250-acre property, should be considered. The court noted that development of the first 199 acres of the property occurred prior to the enactment of restrictions on the development of wetlands. The court observed that the other 38.5 acres should not be considered because it "for all practical purposes had been promised to New Jersey" in order to obtain the state's approval for developing the 12.5-acre tract. Having found that the relevant parcel was only the 12.5-acre tract, the court had little difficulty holding that denial of the permit had deprived the developer of all economically viable use.

The court viewed *Lucas* as having effected a dramatic change in the nuisance exception to takings doctrine by shifting the focus to state property law. It rejected the government's argument that filling the wetlands would constitute a nuisance because the state of New Jersey had approved the project. The court emphasized that the property had been purchased by Loveladies for development long before state and federal regulatory programs had been established and that the state had not restricted filling the 12.5 acres when it initially approved the project. Thus, it upheld the judgment against the government.

The possibility of windfall gains for developers when land use regulations are relaxed will always provide a powerful incentive for legal assaults on regulation. However, the Federal Circuit has made it clear that the "investment-backed expectations" prong of its takings analysis

7. Water Pollution Control

"limits recovery to owners who can demonstrate that they bought their property in reliance on the nonexistence of the challenged regulation." Creppel v. United States, 41 F.3d 627 (Fed. Cir. 1994). As the court explained: "One who buys with knowledge of a restraint assumes the risk of economic loss. In such a case, the owner presumably paid a discounted price for the property. Compensating him for a 'taking' would confer a windfall." 41 F.3d at 632. Thus, takings claims should remain a problem largely confined to whatever transitional period occurs when new regulations are imposed.

Regulatory Exactions and Takings Claims (p. 965). As discussed in the parent text on page 962, takings jurisprudence has been used to limit the ability of regulatory authorities to require exactions of property in return for approving development projects. In Nollan v. California Coastal Commission, 483 U.S. 825 (1987), the Supreme Court held that state regulators could not require a landowner to grant an easement over beachfront property as a condition for approving a building permit without providing compensation. At the close of its 1993-94 Term, the Court revisited this analysis in the decision below.

Dolan v. City of Tigard
114 S. Ct. 2309 (1994)

Chief Justice REHNQUIST delivered the opinion of the Court.

Petitioner challenges the decision of the Oregon Supreme Court which held that the city of Tigard could condition the approval of her building permit on the dedication of a portion of her property for flood control and traffic improvements. 854 P.2d 437 (Ore. 1993). We granted certiorari to resolve a question left open by our decision in Nollan v. California Coastal Comm'n, 483 U.S. 825 (1987), of what is the required degree of connection between the exactions imposed by the city and the projected impacts of the proposed developments.

I

The State of Oregon enacted a comprehensive land use management program in 1973. Ore. Rev. Stat. §§197.005-197.860 (1991). The program required all Oregon cities and counties to adopt new comprehensive land use plans that were consistent with the state-wide planning goals. §§197.175(1), 197.250. The plans are implemented by land use regulations which are part of an integrated hierarchy of legally binding goals, plans, and regulations. §§197.175, 197.175(2)(b). Pursuant to

417

the State's requirements, the city of Tigard, a community of some 30,000 residents on the southwest edge of Portland, developed a comprehensive plan and codified it in its Community Development Code (CDC). The CDC requires property owners in the area zoned Central Business District to comply with a 15 percent open space and landscaping requirement, which limits total site coverage, including all structures and paved parking, to 85 percent of the parcel. CDC, ch. 18.66. After the completion of a transportation study that identified congestion in the Central Business District as a particular problem, the city adopted a plan for a pedestrian/bicycle pathway intended to encourage alternatives to automobile transportation for short trips. The CDC requires that new development facilitate this plan by dedicating land for pedestrian pathways where provided for in the pedestrian/bicycle pathway plan.

The city also adopted a Master Drainage Plan (Drainage Plan). The Drainage Plan noted that flooding occurred in several areas along Fanno Creek, including areas near petitioner's property. The Drainage Plan also established that the increase in impervious surfaces associated with continued urbanization would exacerbate these flooding problems. To combat these risks, the Drainage Plan suggested a series of improvements to the Fanno Creek Basin, including channel excavation in the area next to petitioner's property. Other recommendations included ensuring that the floodplain remains free of structures and that it be preserved as greenways to minimize flood damage to structures. The Drainage Plan concluded that the cost of these improvements should be shared based on both direct and indirect benefits, with property owners along the waterways paying more due to the direct benefit that they would receive. CDC Chapters 18.84, 18.86 and CDC §18.164.100 and the Tigard Park Plan carry out these recommendations.

Petitioner Florence Dolan owns a plumbing and electric supply store located on Main Street in the Central Business District of the city. The store covers approximately 9,700 square feet on the eastern side of a 1.67-acre parcel, which includes a gravel parking lot. Fanno Creek flows through the southwestern corner of the lot and along its western boundary. The year-round flow of the creek renders the area within the creek's 100-year floodplain virtually unusable for commercial development. The city's comprehensive plan includes the Fanno Creek floodplain as part of the city's greenway system.

Petitioner applied to the city for a permit to redevelop the site. Her proposed plans called for nearly doubling the size of the store to 17,600 square feet, and paving a 39-space parking lot. The existing store, located on the opposite side of the parcel, would be razed in sections as construction progressed on the new building. In the second phase of the project, petitioner proposed to build an additional structure on the northeast side of the site for complementary businesses,

7. Water Pollution Control

and to provide more parking. The proposed expansion and intensified use are consistent with the city's zoning scheme in the Central Business District. CDC §18.66.030.

The City Planning Commission granted petitioner's permit application subject to conditions imposed by the city's CDC. The CDC establishes the following standard for site development review approval:

> Where landfill and/or development is allowed within and adjacent to the 100-year floodplain, the city shall require the dedication of sufficient open land area for greenway adjoining and within the floodplain. This area shall include portions at a suitable elevation for the construction of a pedestrian/bicycle pathway within the floodplain in accordance with the adopted pedestrian/bicycle plan. [CDC §18.120-180.A.8.]

Thus, the Commission required that petitioner dedicate the portion of her property lying within the 100-year floodplain for improvement of a storm drainage system along Fanno Creek and that she dedicate an additional 15-foot strip of land adjacent to the floodplain as a pedestrian/bicycle pathway. The dedication required by that condition encompasses approximately 7,000 square feet, or roughly 10 percent of the property. In accordance with city practice, petitioner could rely on the dedicated property to meet the 15 percent open space and landscaping requirement mandated by the city's zoning scheme. The city would bear the cost of maintaining a landscaped buffer between the dedicated area and the new store.

Petitioner requested variances from the CDC standards. Variances are granted only where it can be shown that, owing to special circumstances related to a specific piece of the land, the literal interpretation of the applicable zoning provisions would cause "an undue or unnecessary hardship" unless the variance is granted. CDC §18.134.010. Rather than posing alternative mitigating measures to offset the expected impacts of her proposed development, as allowed under the CDC, petitioner simply argued that her proposed development would not conflict with the policies of the comprehensive plan. The Commission denied the request.

The Commission made a series of findings concerning the relationship between the dedicated conditions and the projected impacts of petitioner's project. First, the Commission noted that "[i]t is reasonable to assume that customers and employees of the future uses of this site could utilize a pedestrian/bicycle pathway adjacent to this development for their transportation and recreational needs." City of Tigard Planning Commission Final Order No. 91-09 PC. The Commission noted that the site plan has provided for bicycle parking in a rack in front of the proposed building and "[i]t is reasonable to expect that some of the users of the bicycle parking provided for by the site plan will use the pathway adjacent to Fanno Creek if it is constructed." Ibid. In addition, the Commission found that creation of a convenient, safe pedestrian/bicycle pathway system as an alternative means of transportation "could offset some of the traffic demand on [nearby] streets and lessen the increase in traffic congestion." Ibid.

The Commission went on to note that the required floodplain dedication would be reasonably related to petitioner's request to intensify the use of the site given the increase in the impervious surface. The Commission stated that the "anticipated increased storm water flow from the subject property to an already strained creek and drainage basin can only add to the pubic need to manage the stream channel and floodplain for drainage purposes." Based on this anticipated increased storm water flow, the Commission concluded that "the requirement of dedication of the floodplain area on the site is related to the applicant's plan to intensify development on the site." The Tigard City Council approved the Commission's final order, subject to one minor modification; the City Council reassigned the responsibility for surveying and marking the floodplain area from petitioner to the city's engineering department.

Petitioner appealed to the Land Use Board of Appeals (LUBA) on the ground that the city's dedication requirements were not related to the proposed development, and, therefore, those requirements constituted an uncompensated taking of their property under the Fifth Amendment. In evaluating the federal taking claim, LUBA assumed that the city's findings about the impacts of the proposed development were supported by substantial evidence. Dolan v. Tigard, LUBA 91-161 (Jan. 7, 1992). Given the undisputed fact that the proposed larger building and paved parking area would increase the amount of impervious surfaces and the runoff into Fanno Creek, LUBA concluded that "there is a 'reasonable relationship' between the proposed development and the requirement to dedicate land along Fanno Creek for a greenway." With respect to the pedestrian/bicycle pathway, LUBA noted the Commission's finding that a significantly larger retail sales building and parking lot would attract larger numbers of customers and employees and their vehicles. It again found a "reasonable relationship" between alleviating the impacts of increased traffic from the development and facilitating the provision of a pedestrian/bicycle pathway as an alternative means of transportation.

The Oregon Court of Appeals affirmed, rejecting petitioner's contention that in Nollan v. California Coastal Comm'n, 483 U.S. 825 (1987), we had abandoned the "reasonable relationship" test in favor of a stricter "essential nexus" test. 832 P.2d 853 (Ore. 1992). The Oregon Supreme Court affirmed. 854 P.2d 437 (Ore. 1993). The court also disagreed with petitioner's contention that the *Nollan* Court abandoned the "reasonably related" test. Id., at 442. Instead, the court read *Nollan* to mean that an "exaction is reasonably related to an impact if the exaction serves the same purpose that a denial of the permit would serve." Id., at 443. The court decided that both the pedestrian/bicycle pathway condition and the storm drainage dedication had an essential nexus to the development of the proposed site. Id., at 443. Therefore, the court found the conditions to be reasonably related to the impact of the expansion of petitioner's business. Ibid. We granted certiorari, 114 S. Ct. 544 (1993), because of an alleged conflict between the Oregon Supreme Court's decision and our decision in *Nollan*, supra.

II

The Takings Clause of the Fifth Amendment of the United States Constitution, made applicable to the States through the Fourteenth Amendment, Chicago, B. & Q.R. Co. v. Chicago, 166 U.S. 226, 239 (1897), provides: "[N]or shall private property be taken for public use, without just compensation." One of the principal purposes of the Takings Clause is "to bar Government from forcing some people alone to bear public burdens which, in all fairness and justice, should be borne by the public as a whole." Armstrong v. United States, 364 U.S. 40, 49 (1960). Without question, had the city simply required petitioner to dedicate a strip of land along Fanno Creek for public use, rather than conditioning the grant of her permit to redevelop her property on such a dedication, a taking would have occurred. Nollan, supra, 483 U.S., at 831. Such public access would deprive petitioner of the right to exclude others, "one of the most essential sticks in the bundle of rights that are commonly characterized as property." Kaiser Aetna v. United States, 444 U.S. 164, 176 (1979).

On the other side of the ledger, the authority of state and local governments to engage in land use planning has been sustained against constitutional challenge as long ago as our decision in Euclid v. Ambler Realty Co., 272 U.S. 365 (1926). "Government hardly could go on if to some extent values incident to property could not be diminished without paying for every such change in the general law." Pennsylvania Coal Co. v. Mahon, 260 U.S. 393, 413 (1922). A land use regulation does not effect a taking if it "substantially advance[s] legitimate state interests" and does not "den[y] an owner economically viable use of his land." Agins v. Tiburon, 447 U.S. 225, 260 (1980).

The sort of land use regulations discussed in the cases just cited, however, differ in two relevant particulars from the present case. First, they involved essentially legislative determinations classifying entire areas of the city, whereas here the city made an adjudicative decision to condition petitioner's application for a building permit on an individual parcel. Second, the conditions imposed were not simply a limitation on the use petitioner might make of her own parcel, but a requirement that she deed portions of the property to the city. In *Nollan*, supra, we held that governmental authority to exact such a condition was circumscribed by the Fifth and Fourteenth Amendments. Under the well-settled doctrine of "unconstitutional conditions," the government may not require a person to give up a constitutional right—here the right to receive just compensation when property is taken for a public use—in exchange for a discretionary benefit conferred by the government where the property sought has little or no relationship to the benefit. See Perry v. Sindermann, 408 U.S. 593 (1972); Pickering v. Board of Ed. of Township High School Dist., 391 U.S. 563, 568 (1968).

Petitioner contends that the city has forced her to choose between the building permit and her right under the Fifth Amendment to just compensation for the public easements. Petitioner does not quarrel with the city's authority to exact some forms of dedication as a condition for the grant of a building permit, but challenges the showing made by the city to justify these exactions. She argues that the city has identified "no special benefits" conferred on her, and has not identified any "special burdens" created by her new store that would justify the particular dedications required from her which are not required from the public at large.

III

In evaluating petitioner's claim, we must first determine whether the "essential nexus" exists between the "legitimate state interest" and the permit condition exacted by the city. Nollan, 483 U.S., at 837. If we find that a nexus exists, we must then decide the required degree of connection between the exactions and the projected impact of the proposed development. We were not required to reach this question in *Nollan*, because we concluded that the connection did not meet even the loosest standard. 483 U.S., at 838. Here, however, we must decide this question.

A

We addressed the essential nexus question in *Nollan*. The California Coastal Commission demanded a lateral public easement across the Nollan's beachfront lot in exchange for a permit to demolish an existing bungalow and replace it with a three-bedroom house. 483 U.S., at 828. The public easement was designed to connect two public beaches that were separated by the Nollan's property. The Coastal Commission had asserted that the public easement condition was imposed to promote the legitimate state interest of diminishing the "blockage of the view of the ocean" caused by construction of the larger house.

We agreed that the Coastal Commission's concern with protecting visual access to the ocean constituted a legitimate public interest. Id., at 835. We also agreed that the permit condition would have been constitutional "even if it consisted of the requirement that the Nollans provide a viewing spot on their property for passersby with whose sighting of the ocean their new house would interfere." Id., at 836. We resolved, however, that the Coastal Commission's regulatory authority was set completely adrift from its constitutional moorings when it claimed that a nexus existed between visual access to the ocean and a permit condition requiring lateral public access along the Nollan's beachfront lot. Id., at 837. How enhancing the public's ability to "traverse to and along the shorefront" served the same governmental purpose of "visual access to the ocean" from the roadway was beyond our ability to countenance. The absence of a nexus left the Coastal Commission in the position of simply trying to obtain an easement through gimmickry, which converted a valid regulation of land use into "an out-and-out plan of extortion." Ibid., quoting J.E.D. Associates, Inc. v. Atkinson, 432 A.2d 12, 14-15 (N.H. 1981).

No such gimmicks are associated with the permit conditions imposed by the city in this case. Undoubtedly, the prevention of flooding along Fanno Creek and the reduction of traffic congestion in the Central Business District qualify as the type of legitimate public purposes we have upheld. *Agins,* supra, at 260-262. It seems equally obvious that a nexus exists between preventing flooding along Fanno Creek and limiting development within the creek's 100-year floodplain. Petitioner proposes to double the size of her retail store and to pave her now-gravel parking lot, thereby expanding the impervious surface on the property and increasing the amount of stormwater run-off into Fanno Creek.

The same may be said for the city's attempt to reduce traffic congestion by providing for alternative means of transportation. In theory, a pedestrian/bicycle pathway provides a useful alternative means of transportation for workers and shoppers: "Pedestrians and bicyclists occupying dedicated spaces for walking and/or bicycling . . . remove potential vehicles from streets, resulting in an overall improvement in total transportation system flow." A. Nelson, Public Provision of Pedestrian and Bicycle Access Ways: Public Policy Rationale and the Nature of Private Benefits 11, Center for Planning Development, Georgia Institute of Technology, Working Paper Series (Jan. 1994). See also, Intermodal Surface Transportation Efficiency Act of 1991, Pub. L. 102-240, 105 Stat. 1914 (recognizing pedestrian and bicycle facilities as necessary components of any strategy to reduce traffic congestion).

B

The second part of our analysis requires us to determine whether the degree of the exactions demanded by the city's permit conditions bear the required relationship to the projected impact of petitioner's proposed development. *Nollan,* supra, at 834, quoting *Penn Central,* 438 U.S. 104, 127 (1978) (" '[A] use restriction may constitute a taking if not reasonably necessary to the effectuation of a substantial government purpose' "). Here the Oregon Supreme Court deferred to what it termed the "city's unchallenged factual findings" supporting the dedication conditions and found them to be reasonably related to the impact of the expansion of petitioner's business. 854 P.2d, at 443.

The city required that petitioner dedicate "to the city as Greenway all portions of the site that fall within the existing 100-year flood plain [of Fanno Creek] and all property 15 feet above [the floodplain] boundary." In addition, the city demanded that the retail store be designed so as not to intrude into the greenway area. The city relies on the Commission's rather tentative findings that increased stormwater flow from petitioner's property "can only add to the public need to manage the [floodplain] for drainage purposes" to support its conclusion that the "requirement of dedication of the floodplain area on the site is related to the applicant's plan to intensify development on the site." City of Tigard Planning Commission Final Order No. 91-09 PC.

The city made the following specific findings relevant to the pedestrian/bicycle pathway:

> In addition, the proposed expanded use of this site is anticipated to generate additional vehicular traffic thereby increasing congestion on nearby collector and arterial streets. Creation of a convenient, safe pedestrian/bicycle pathway system as an alternative means of transportation could offset some of the traffic demand on these nearby streets and lessen the increase in traffic congestion. [Id.]

The question for us is whether these findings are constitutionally sufficient to justify the conditions imposed by the city on petitioner's building permit. Since state courts have been dealing with this question a good deal longer than we have, we turn to representative decisions made by them.

7. Water Pollution Control

Page 965

In some States, very generalized statements as to the necessary connection between the required dedication and the proposed development seem to suffice. See, e.g., Billings Properties, Inc. v. Yellowstone County, 394 P.2d 182 (Mont. 1964); Jenad, Inc. v. Scarsdale, 218 N.E. 2d 673 (N.Y. 1966). We think this standard is too lax to adequately protect petitioner's right to just compensation if her property is taken for a public purpose.

Other state courts require a very exacting correspondence, described as the "specific and uniquely attributable" test. The Supreme Court of Illinois first developed this test in Pioneer Trust & Savings Bank v. Mount Prospect, 176 N.E.2d 799, 802 (Ill. 1961). Under this standard, if the local government cannot demonstrate that its exaction is directly proportional to the specifically created need, the exaction becomes "a veiled exercise of the power of eminent domain and a confiscation of private property behind the defense of police regulations." Id., at 802. We do not think the Federal Constitution requires such exacting scrutiny, given the nature of the interests involved.

A number of state courts have taken an intermediate position, requiring the municipality to show a "reasonable relationship" between the required dedication and the impact of the proposed development. Typical is the Supreme Court of Nebraska's opinion in Simpson v. North Platte, 292 N.W.2d 297, 301 (Neb. 1980), where that court stated:

> The distinction, therefore, which must be made between an appropriate exercise of the police power and an improper exercise of eminent domain is whether the requirement has some reasonable relationship or nexus to the use to which the property is being made or is merely being used as an excuse for taking property simply because at that particular moment the landowner is asking the city for some license or permit.

Thus, the court held that a city may not require a property owner to dedicate private property for some future public use as a condition of obtaining a building permit when such future use is not "occasioned by the construction sought to be permitted." Id., at 302.

Some form of the reasonable relationship test has been adopted in many other jurisdictions. See, e.g., Jordan v. Menomonee Falls, 137 N.W.2d 442 (Wis. 1965); Collis v. Bloomington, 246 N.W.2d 19 (Minn. 1976) (requiring a showing of a reasonable relationship between the planned subdivision and the municipality's need for land); College Station v. Turtle Rock Corp., 680 S.W.2d 802, 807 (Tex. 1984); Call v. West Jordan, 606 P.2d 217, 220 (Utah 1979) (affirming use of the reasonable relation test). Despite any semantical differences, general agreement exists among the courts "that the dedication should have some reasonable relationship to the needs created by the [develop-

425

ment]." Ibid. See generally, Morosoff, Take My Beach Please!: Nollan v. California Coastal Commission and a Rational-Nexus Constitutional Analysis of Development Exactions, 69 B.U. L. Rev. 823 (1989); see also Parks v. Watson, 716 F.2d 646, 651-653 (CA9 1983).

We think the "reasonable relationship" test adopted by a majority of the state courts is closer to the federal constitutional norm than either of those previously discussed. But we do not adopt it as such, partly because the term "reasonable relationship" seems confusingly similar to the term "rational basis" which describes the minimal level of scrutiny under the Equal Protection Clause of the Fourteenth Amendment. We think a term such as "rough proportionality" best encapsulates what we hold to be the requirement of the Fifth Amendment. No precise mathematical calculation is required, but the city must make some sort of individualized determination that the required dedication is related both in nature and extent to the impact of the proposed development. . . .

It is axiomatic that increasing the amount of impervious surface will increase the quantity and rate of storm-water flow from petitioner's property. Record, Doc. No. F, ch. 4, p. 4-29. Therefore, keeping the floodplain open and free from development would likely confine the pressures on Fanno Creek created by petitioner's development. In fact, because petitioner's property lies within the Central Business District, the Community Development Code already required that petitioner leave 15 percent of it as open space and the undeveloped floodplain would have nearly satisfied that requirement. But the city demanded more—it not only wanted petitioner not to build in the floodplain, but it also wanted petitioner's property along Fanno Creek for its Greenway system. The city has never said why a public greenway, as opposed to a private one, was required in the interest of flood control.

The difference to petitioner, of course, is the loss of her ability to exclude others. As we have noted, this right to exclude others is "one of the most essential sticks in the bundle of rights that are commonly characterized as property." *Kaiser Aetna*, 444 U.S., at 176. It is difficult to see why recreational visitors trampling along petitioner's floodplain easement are sufficiently related to the city's legitimate interest in reducing flooding problems along Fanno Creek, and the city has not attempted to make any individualized determination to support this part of its request.

The city contends that recreational easement along the Greenway is only ancillary to the city's chief purpose in controlling flood hazards. It further asserts that unlike the residential property at issue in *Nollan*, petitioner's property is commercial in character and therefore, her right to exclude others is compromised. United States v. Orito, 413 U.S. 139, 142 (1973) (" 'The Constitution extends special safeguards to the privacy of the home' "). The city maintains that "there is nothing to suggest that preventing [petitioner] from prohibiting [the easements] will unreasonably impair the value of [her] property as a [retail store]." PruneYard Shopping Center v. Robins, 447 U.S. 74, 83 (1980).

Admittedly, petitioner wants to build a bigger store to attract members of the public to her property. She also wants, however, to be able to control the time and manner in which they enter. The recreational easement on the Greenway is different in character from the exercise of state-protected rights of free expression and petition that we permitted in *PruneYard*. In *PruneYard*, we held that a major private shopping center that attracted more than 25,000 daily patrons had to provide access to persons exercising their state constitutional rights to distribute pamphlets and ask passersby to sign their petitions. Id., at 85. We based our decision, in part, on the fact that the shopping center "may restrict expressive activity by adopting time, place, and manner regulations that will minimize any interference with its commercial functions." Id., at 83. By contrast, the city wants to impose a permanent recreational easement upon petitioner's property that borders Fanno Creek. Petitioner would lose all rights to regulate the time in which the public entered onto the Greenway, regardless of any interference it might pose with her retail store. Her right to exclude would not be regulated, it would be eviscerated.

If petitioner's proposed development had somehow encroached on existing greenway space in the city, it would have been reasonable to require petitioner to provide some alternative greenway space for the public either on her property or elsewhere. See *Nollan*, 483 U.S., at 836 ("Although such a requirement, constituting a permanent grant of continuous access to the property, would have to be considered a taking if it were not attached to a development permit, the Commission's assumed power to forbid construction of the house in order to protect the public's view of the beach must surely include the power to condition construction upon some concession by the owner, even a concession of property rights, that serves the same end"). But that is not the case here. We conclude that the findings upon which the city relies do not show the required reasonable relationship between the floodplain easement and the petitioner's proposed new building.

With respect to the pedestrian/bicycle pathway, we have no doubt that the city was correct in finding that the larger retail sales facility proposed by petitioner will increase traffic on the streets of the Central Business District. The city estimates that the proposed development would generate roughly 435 additional trips per day. Dedications for streets, sidewalks, and other public ways are generally reasonable exactions to avoid excessive congestion from a proposed property use. But on the record before us, the city has not met its burden of demonstrating that the additional number of vehicle and bicycle trips generated by the petitioner's development reasonably relate to the city's requirement for a dedication of the pedestrian/bicycle pathway easement. The city simply found that the creation of the pathway "could offset some of the traffic demand . . . and lessen the increase in traffic congestion."

As Justice Peterson of the Supreme Court of Oregon explained in his dissenting opinion, however, "the findings of fact that the bicycle pathway system '*could* offset some of the traffic demand' is a far cry from a finding that the bicycle pathway system *will*, or is *likely to*, offset some of the traffic demand." 854 P. 2d, at 447 (emphasis in original). No precise mathematical calculation is required, but the city must make some effort to quantify its findings in support of the dedication for the pedestrian/bicycle pathway beyond the conclusory statement that it could offset some of the traffic demand generated.

IV

Cities have long engaged in the commendable task of land use planning, made necessary by increasing urbanization particularly in metropolitan areas such as Portland. The city's goals of reducing flooding hazards and traffic congestion, and providing for public greenways, are laudable, but there are outer limits to how this may be done. "A strong public desire to improve the public condition [will not] warrant achieving the desire by a shorter cut than the constitutional way of paying for the change." *Pennsylvania Coal,* 260 U.S., at 416.

The judgment of the Supreme Court of Oregon is reversed, and the case is remanded for further proceedings consistent with this opinion.

Justice STEVENS, with whom Justice BLACKMUN and Justice GINSBURG join, dissenting. . . .

Certain propositions are not in dispute. The enlargement of the Tigard unit in Dolan's chain of hardware stores will have an adverse impact on the city's legitimate and substantial interests in controlling drainage in Fanno Creek and minimizing traffic congestion in Tigard's business district. That impact is sufficient to justify an outright denial of her application for approval of the expansion. The city has nevertheless agreed to grant Dolan's application if she will comply with two conditions, each of which admittedly will mitigate the adverse effects of her proposed development. The disputed question is whether the city has violated the Fourteenth Amendment to the Federal Constitution by refusing to allow Dolan's planned construction to proceed unless those conditions are met.

428

The Court is correct in concluding that the city may not attach arbitrary conditions to a building permit or to a variance even when it can rightfully deny the application outright. I also agree that state court decisions dealing with ordinances that govern municipal development plans provide useful guidance in a case of this kind. Yet the Court's description of the doctrinal underpinnings of its decision, the phrasing of its fledgling test of "rough proportionality," and the application of that test to this case run contrary to the traditional treatment of these cases and break considerable and unpropitious new ground.

I

Candidly acknowledging the lack of federal precedent for its exercise in rulemaking, the Court purports to find guidance in 12 "representative" state court decisions. To do so is certainly appropriate. The state cases the Court consults, however, either fail to support or decidedly undermine the Court's conclusions in key respects.

First, although discussion of the state cases permeates the Court's analysis of the appropriate test to apply in this case, the test on which the Court settles is not naturally derived from those courts' decisions. The Court recognizes as an initial matter that the city's conditions satisfy the "essential nexus" requirement announced in Nollan v. California Coastal Comm'n, 483 U.S. 825 (1987), because they serve the legitimate interests in minimizing floods and traffic congestions. The Court goes on, however, to erect a new constitutional hurdle in the path of these conditions. In addition to showing a rational nexus to a public purpose that would justify an outright denial of the permit, the city must also demonstrate "rough proportionality" between the harm caused by the new land use and the benefit obtained by the condition. The Court also decides for the first time that the city has the burden of establishing the constitutionality of its conditions by making an "individualized determination" that the condition in question satisfies the proportionality requirement.

Not one of the state cases cited by the Court announces anything akin to a "rough proportionality" requirement. For the most part, moreover, those cases that invalidated municipal ordinances did so on state law or unspecified grounds roughly equivalent to *Nollan's* "essential nexus" requirement. See, e.g., Simpson v. North Platte, 292 N.W.2d 297, 301-302 (Neb. 1980) (ordinance lacking "reasonable relationship" or "rational nexus" to property's use violated Nebraska constitution); J.E.D. Associates, Inc. v. Town of Atkinson, 432 A.2d 12, 14-15 (N.H. 1981) (state constitutional grounds). One case purporting to apply the strict "specifically and uniquely attributable" test established by Pioneer Trust & Savings Bank v. Mount Prospect, 176 N.E.2d 799 (Ill. 1961), nevertheless found that test was satisfied because the legislature had decided that the subdivision at issue created the need for a park or parks. Billings Properties, Inc. v. Yellowstone County, 394 P.2d 182, 187-188 (Mont. 1964). In only one of the seven cases upholding a land use regulation did the losing property owner petition this Court for certiorari. See Jordan v. Village of Menomonee Falls, 137 N.W.2d 442 (Wis. 1965), appeal dism'd, 385 U.S. 4 (1966) (want of substantial federal question). Although 4 of the 12 opinions mention the Federal Constitution—two of those only in passing—it is quite obvious that neither the courts nor the litigants imagined they might be participating in the development of a new rule of federal law. Thus, although these state cases do lend support to the Court's reaffirmance of *Nollan's* reasonable nexus requirement, the role the Court accords them in the announcement of its newly minted second phase of the constitutional inquiry is remarkably inventive.

In addition, the Court ignores the state courts' willingness to consider what the property owner gains from the exchange in question. The Supreme Court of Wisconsin, for example, found it significant that the village's approval of a proposed subdivision plat "enables the subdivider to profit financially by selling the subdivision lots as home-building sites and thus realizing a greater price than could have been obtained if he had sold his property as unplatted lands." Jordan v. Village of Menomonee Falls, 137 N.W.2d 442, 448 (Wis. 1965). The required dedication as a condition of that approval was permissible "in return for this benefit." Ibid. See also Collis v. Bloomington, 246 N.W.2d 19, 23-24 (Minn. 1976) (citing *Jordan*); College Station v. Turtle Rock Corp., 680 S.W.2d 802, 806 (Tex. 1984) (dedication requirement only triggered when developer chooses to develop land). In this case, moreover, Dolan's acceptance of the permit, with its attached conditions, would provide her with benefits that may well go beyond any advantage she gets from expanding her business. As the United States pointed out at oral argument, the improvement that the city's drainage plan contemplates would widen the channel and reinforce the slopes to increase the carrying capacity during serious floods, "conferring considerable benefits on the property owners immediately adjacent to the creek."

The state court decisions also are enlightening in the extent to which they required that the *entire parcel* be given controlling importance. All but one of the cases involve challenges to provisions in municipal ordinances requiring developers to dedicate either a percentage of the entire parcel (usually 7 or 10 percent of the platted subdivision) or an equivalent value in cash (usually a certain dollar amount per lot) to help finance the construction of roads, utilities, schools, parks and playgrounds. In assessing the legality of the conditions, the courts gave no indication that the transfer of an interest in realty was any more objectionable than a cash payment. See, e.g., Jenad, Inc. v. Scarsdale, 218 N.E.2d 673 (N.Y. 1966); *Jordan,* supra; *Collis,* supra. None of the decisions identified the surrender of the fee owner's "power to exclude" as having any special significance. Instead, the courts uniformly examined the character of the entire economic transaction.

II

It is not merely state cases, but our own cases as well, that require the analysis to focus on the impact of the city's action on the entire parcel of private property. In Penn Central Transportation Co. v. New York City, 438 U.S. 104 (1978), we stated that takings jurisprudence "does not divide a single parcel into discrete segments and attempt to determine whether rights in a particular segment have been entirely abrogated." Id., at 130-131. Instead, this Court focuses "both on the character of the action and on the nature and extent of the interference with rights in the parcel as a whole." Ibid. Andrus v. Allard, 444 U.S. 51 (1979), reaffirmed the nondivisibility principle outlined in *Penn Central,* stating that "at least where an owner possesses a full 'bundle' of property rights, the destruction of one 'strand' of the bundle is not a taking, because the aggregate must be viewed in its entirety." Id., at 65-66. As recently as last Term, we approved the principle again. See Concrete Pipe & Products, Inc. v. Construction Laborers Pension Trust, 508 U.S. —, (1993) (explaining that "a claimant's parcel of property [cannot] first be divided into what was taken and what was left" to demonstrate a compensable taking). Although limitation of the right to exclude others undoubtedly constitutes a significant infringement upon property ownership, Kaiser Aetna v. United States, 444 U.S. 164, 179-180 (1979), restrictions on that right do not alone constitute a taking, and do not do so in any event unless they "unreasonably impair the value or use" of the property. Pruneyard Shopping Center v. Robins, 447 U.S. 74, 82-84 (1980). . . .

The Court's assurances that its "rough proportionality" test leaves ample room for cities to pursue the "commendable task of land use planning"—even twice avowing that "no precise mathematical calculation is required"—are wanting given the result that test compels here. Under the Court's approach, a city must not only "quantify its findings," and make "individualized determinations" with respect to the nature and the extent of the relationship between the conditions and the impact, but also demonstrate "proportionality." The correct inquiry should instead concentrate on whether the required nexus is present and venture beyond considerations of a condition's nature or germaneness only if the developer establishes that a concededly germane condition is so grossly disproportionate to the proposed development's adverse effects that it manifests motives other than land use regulation on the part of the city. The heightened requirement the Court imposes on cities is even more unjustified when all the tools needed to resolve the questions presented by this case can be garnered from our existing case law.

III

Applying its new standard, the Court finds two defects in the city's case. First, while the record would adequately support a requirement that Dolan maintain the portion of the floodplain on her property as undeveloped open space, it does not support the additional requirement that the floodplain be dedicated to the city. Second, while the city adequately established the traffic increase that the proposed development would generate, it failed to quantify the offsetting decrease in automobile traffic that the bike path will produce. Even under the Court's new rule, both defects are, at most, nothing more than harmless error.

In her objections to the floodplain condition, Dolan made no effort to demonstrate that the dedication of that portion of her property would be any more onerous than a simple prohibition against any development on that portion of her property. Given the commercial character of both the existing and the proposed use of the property as a retail store, it seems likely that potential customers "trampling along petitioner's floodplain," are more valuable than a useless parcel of vacant land. Moreover, the duty to pay taxes and the responsibility for potential tort liability may well make ownership of the fee interest in useless land a liability rather than an asset. That may explain why Dolan never conceded that she could be prevented from building on the floodplain. The City Attorney also pointed out that absent a dedication, property owners would be required to "build on their own land" and "with their own money" a storage facility for the water runoff. Dolan apparently "did have that option," but chose not to seek it. If Dolan might have been entitled to a variance confining the city's condition in a manner this Court would accept, her failure to seek that narrower form of relief at any stage of the state administrative and judicial proceedings clearly should preclude that relief in this Court now.

The Court's rejection of the bike path condition amounts to nothing more than a play on words. Everyone agrees that the bike path "could" offset some of the increased traffic flow that the larger store will generate, but the findings do not unequivocally state that it *will* do so, or tell us just how many cyclists will replace motorists. Predictions on such matters are inherently nothing more than estimates. Certainly the assumption that there will be an offsetting benefit here is entirely reasonable and should suffice whether it amounts to 100 percent, 35 percent, or only 5 percent of the increase in automobile traffic that would otherwise occur. If the Court proposes to have the federal judiciary micromanage state decisions of this kind, it is indeed extending its welcome mat to a significant new class of litigants. Although there is no reason to believe that state courts have failed to rise to the task, property owners have surely found a new friend today.

IV. . . .

The Court has decided to apply its heightened scrutiny to a single strand—the power to exclude—in the bundle of rights that enables a commercial enterprise to flourish in an urban environment. That intangible interest is undoubtedly worthy of constitutional protection—much like the grandmother's interest in deciding which of her relatives may share her home in Moore v. East Cleveland, 431 U.S. 494 (1977). Both interests are protected from arbitrary state action by the Due Process Clause of the Fourteenth Amendment. It is, however, a curious irony that Members of the majority in this case would impose an almost insurmountable burden of proof on the property owner in the *Moore* case while saddling the city with a heightened burden in this case. . . .

In our changing world one thing is certain: uncertainty will characterize predictions about the impact of new urban developments on the risks of floods, earthquakes, traffic congestion, or environmental harms. When there is doubt concerning the magnitude of those impacts, the public interest in averting them must outweigh the private interest of the commercial entrepreneur. If the government can demonstrate that the conditions it has imposed in a land-use permit are rational, impartial and conducive to fulfilling the aims of a valid land-use plan, a strong presumption of validity should attach to those conditions. The burden of demonstrating that those conditions have unreasonably impaired the economic value of the proposed improvement belongs squarely on the shoulders of the party challenging the state action's constitutionality. That allocation of burdens has served us well in the past. The Court has stumbled badly today by reversing it.

I respectfully dissent.

Justice SOUTER, dissenting. . . .

I cannot agree that the application of *Nollan* is a sound one here, since it appears that the Court has placed the burden of producing evidence of relationship on the city, despite the usual rule in cases involving the police power that the government is presumed to have acted constitutionally. Having thus assigned the burden, the Court concludes that the City loses based on one word ("could" instead of "would"), and despite the fact that this record shows the connection the Court looks for. Dolan has put forward no evidence that the burden of granting a dedication for the bicycle path is unrelated in kind to the anticipated increase in traffic congestion, nor, if there exists a requirement that the relationship be related in degree, has Dolan shown that the exaction fails any such test. The city, by contrast, calculated the increased traffic flow that would result from Dolan's proposed development to be 435 trips per day, and its Comprehensive Plan, applied here, relied on studies showing the link between alternative modes of transportation, including bicycle paths, and reduced street traffic congestion. City of Tigard's Comprehensive Plan (" 'Bicycle and pedestrian pathway systems will result in some reduction of automobile trips within the community' "). *Nollan*, therefore, is satisfied, and on that assumption the city's conditions should not be held to fail a further rough proportionality test or any other that might be devised to give meaning to the constitutional limits.

NOTES & QUESTIONS

1. Unlike the situation in *Nollan*, the Court majority has no difficulty finding that an "essential nexus" exists between the legitimate state interests in preventing flooding and alleviating traffic congestion and the state's attempt to exact dedications of land for storm drainage and a bike pathway. Why then did the exactions fail to satisfy constitutional muster? What would the city have to do under the Court's decision to justify the exactions it sought? How detailed would the city's findings have to be in order to justify the exactions?

2. What test does the Court enunciate for determining whether the degree of exactions demanded bears the constitutionally required relationship to the projected impact of development? How does the Court derive this test? Who bears the burden of proof on this issue—the city or the developer? What test does Justice Stevens propose in dissent? How would it differ from the majority's test?

3. Suppose the city simply had denied the permit request without seeking any exaction. Would the permit denial give rise to any kind of takings claim? If instead of asking Dolan to dedicate her property to public use the city had simply imposed a zoning ordinance requiring that a certain percentage of a lot be maintained as a greenway buffer, would there have been any constitutional problem?

4. Does the Court's decision call into question the constitutionality of charging developers impact fees to help compensate for the increased demand for municipal services caused by development? After issuing the

7. Water Pollution Control

Dolan decision, the Court vacated and remanded a California decision requiring that required a developer to pay mitigation fees for the right to build condominiums on what formerly had been a tennis club. Ehrlich v. Culver City, 19 Cal. Rptr. 2d 468 (1993). The developer was required to pay a $280,000 fee for the loss of public recreational facilities, $30,000 as a park fee, and $33,220 for public art. On remand, the California Court of Appeals again upheld the fees as justified to compensate the city for diminished recreational, cultural, and artistic opportunities. See Kanner, In California, a Land Owner Loses Again, Wall St. J., Feb. 8, 1995, at A15.

    5. Note that *Dolan* was decided by a 5-4 majority, a narrower margin that the 6-3 split in *Lucas*. Justice Ginsburg, who had replaced Justice White on the Court, was in the dissent, while White had been in the majority in *Lucas*. This may indicate that the Court will become even more closely divided on future takings cases.

    6. Not content with gains made in court, property rights advocates are pushing for legislation that would expand takings doctrine far beyond constitutional confines. Legislation to provide compensation to property owners whose land values are diminished by government regulation is a prominent part of the Republican's Contract With America. In March 1995 the U.S. House of Representatives voted 277-148 to approve a bill requiring compensation when regulations reduce property values by 20 percent or more. The legislation would cover circumstances in which property values are adversely affected by regulations under the Endangered Species Act, the Clean Water Act's section 404 program, and regulatory changes in federal farm conservation and federal irrigation programs. The bill provides that if any of these regulations diminish property values by 50 percent or more, the federal government would be required to purchase the property if its owners so chose. Legislation introduced into the Senate by Senator Robert Dole, S. 605, which has 31 cosponsors, would provide compensation when regulation diminishes property values by 30 percent or more. In the November 1994 elections a property rights initiative that would have made it difficult for government to enact regulations that affect property values was soundly defeated by Arizona voters by a 60-40 margin.

F. WETLANDS PROTECTION AND THE SECTION 404 PERMIT PROGRAM

    Letting the Sea Back In (pp. 965-966). In what may be yet another indication of how attitudes toward wetlands have changed dramatically over time, the government of Holland is allowing large tracts of farmland reclaimed from the sea to revert to marshland. Simons, A Dutch Reversal: Letting the Sea Back In, N.Y. Times, Mar. 7, 1993, at A1.

Scope of the Section 404 Program (pp. 968-974). In April 1992, the Seventh Circuit flirted with a significantly more restrictive interpretation of the reach of section 404. The court briefly held that the jurisdiction of the Clean Water Act did not extend to what it called "intrastate, isolated wetlands." Hoffman Homes, Inc. v. Administrator, U.S. EPA, 961 F.2d 1310, *vacated,* 975 F.2d 1554 (7th Cir. 1992). In its initial decision, the court noted that the wetland in question "had no surface or groundwater connection to any other body of water," that it "did not perform sediment trapping or flood control purposes for any body of water, was not used for industrial or fishing purposes and was not visited by interstate travelers for recreational or other purposes." In an opinion by Judge Daniel Manion, the court distinguished *Riverside Bayview Homes* as involving wetlands that were adjacent to another body of water. While EPA has sought to defend federal jurisdiction over the wetland on the ground that migratory birds could use it as a place to feed or nest, the court concluded that there was "no evidence that migratory birds of any feather could actually use" the wetland. However, after EPA sought a rehearing en banc the decision was vacated by the Seventh Circuit. 975 F.2d 1554 (7th Cir. 1992). After settlement negotiations failed, the case was returned to the original Seventh Circuit panel. The court then issued a new decision upholding EPA's conclusion that a potential effect on interstate commerce was a sufficient basis for asserting jurisdiction under the Clean Water Act. However, the court found that EPA had failed to produce substantial evidence that the small, isolated wetland at issue in the case was a potential migratory bird habitat.

In Save Our Community v. EPA, 971 F.2d 1155 (5th Cir. 1992), the Fifth Circuit reversed a district court that had held that the draining of a wetland required a section 404 permit even in the absence of any finding that there had been a discharge into the waters of the United States. The Fifth Circuit concluded that "without an effluent discharge of some kind, there is no coverage under section 404." 971 F.2d at 1164.

While section 404(f) of the Clean Water Act exempts the discharge of dredged or fill material "from normal farming activities" from section 404's permit requirements, the exemption is only available to discharge activities that are part of an established farming operation. It does not authorize farmers to drain or fill wetlands into order to convert additional land into productive farmland. United States v. Brace, 41 F.3d 117 (3d Cir. 1994).

7. Water Pollution Control Pages 974-975

An analysis of criminal prosecutions for violations of section 404 has found that there have been a relatively limited number of reported cases, though they often have received considerable publicity. Dinkins & Bartman, Criminal Enforcement of Wetlands Protection Law, 25 Env. Rep. 1320 (1994). Most criminal cases have involved situations where developers deliberately ignored warnings, cease and desist orders, or notices of violations. For example, in United States v. Pozsgai, 999 F.2d 719 (3d Cir. 1993), a defendant received a three-year jail term for repeatedly dumping fill material into wetlands despite receiving cease and desist letters from the Corps and a temporary restraining order from a federal district court. The violations were so blatant that they were videotaped by government investigators.

In Save Our Community v. EPA, 971 F.2d 1155 (5th Cir. 1992), the Fifth Circuit reversed a district court that had held that the draining of a wetland required a section 404 permit even in the absence of any finding that there had been a discharge into the waters of the United States. The Fifth Circuit concluded that "without an effluent discharge of some kind, there is no coverage under section 404." 971 F.2d at 1164.

Wetland Identification and Delineation (pp. 974-975). The effort by the Competitiveness Council to revise the wetlands delineation manual generated such intense opposition from scientists and the environmental community that it was doomed to failure. Teams of scientists from federal and state agencies conducted a field assessment of the proposed revisions during the fall of 1991. Their reports provide a scathing denunciation of the proposed revisions as "without scientific basis." Efforts by the Competitiveness Council to exclude these reports from the public record were thwarted when a congressional Representative submitted a leaked copy to the public docket. For a summary of the impact of the proposed revisions, see Environmental Defense Fund & World Wildlife Fund, How Wet Is a Wetland?: The Impacts of the Proposed Revisions to the Federal Wetlands Delineation Manual (1992). See also Alper, War Over the Wetlands: Ecologists v. The White House, 257 Science 1043 (1992). EPA ultimately decided to return to the 1987 version of the wetlands delineation manual pending the completion of a study by the National Academy of Sciences 58 Fed. Reg. 4495 (1993). 1987 Delineation Manual Formally Adopted, Ending Battle over Changes Proposed in 1991, 23 Env. Rep. 2485 (1993).

Without waiting for release of the NAS report, a House committee in April 1995 approved H.R. 961, which would radically alter the Clean Water Act in part by sharply restricting the definition of wetlands protected by section 404. Under the bill, land must be covered with surface water for 21 consecutive days during summer months before it could be considered a wetland. Wetlands would then be ranked into three categories based on assessment of their ecological significance. Levels of protection for wetlands would vary depending upon the category in which the wetlands were placed. Type C wetlands—those serving marginal functions—could be developed without restriction, while Type B wetlands—those that perform "significant" ecological functions—could be developed if the Army Corps of Engineers deemed development to be in the "public interest." The most protection is reserved for Type A wetlands, those of "critical significance to the long-term conservation of the aquatic environment." But Type A wetlands would have to be at least 10 acres in size and could constitute no more than 20 percent of a given district or county. Stone, Wetlands Reform Bill Is All Wet, Say Scientists, 268 Science 970 (1995).

The report by the Committee on Wetlands Characterization of NAS's National Research Council was released in May 1995. The committee confirmed that existing procedures for delineating wetlands under the section 404 program were scientifically sound, but it recommended that a single wetlands delineation manual be adopted and that one federal agency be given the lead responsibility for wetlands regulation. Wetlands Provisions in CWA Legislation Lack Scientific Basis, Research Council Says, 26 Env. Rep. 182 (1995). The committee defined a wetland as "an ecosystem that depends on constant or recurrent, shallow inundation or saturation at or near the surface of the substrate." It recommended that delineation of wetlands be based on consideration of their hydrology, the type of plants present there, and soil characteristics.

The NAS report employs a much broader definition of wetlands than that included in H.R. 961. The scientists who prepared the NAS report are highly critical of the proposed legislation. They estimate that H.R. 961 would remove nearly half of all wetlands from protection under section 404 based on what they consider to be unscientific criteria. Stone, supra. The House committee bill would have prohibited an area from being designated a wetland "based solely on the fact that migratory birds use or could use" it. Because the Clean Water Act's jurisdictional requirements require a connection to interstate commerce that for noncoastal wetlands is often founded on their use by migratory birds, this provision would leave virtually all landlocked wetlands without federal protection. Despite the release of the NAS report, the House approved H.R. 961 on May 16, 1995, by a vote of 240-185. However, the House deleted the provision that would have prohibited an area from being delineated as a wetland based solely on its use by migratory birds.

The Section 404 Permit Process (p. 975). In August 1992, EPA and the Army Corps of Engineers adopted a revised memorandum of

7. Water Pollution Control   Pages 985-986

agreement governing procedures for consultation and resolution of disputed section 404 permit decisions.

"No Net Loss" and New Approaches to Wetlands Protection (pp. 983-984). In August 1993 the Clinton Administration unveiled its program for protecting wetlands. White House Office of Environmental Policy, Protecting America's Wetlands: A Fair, Flexible and Effective Approach (1993). The plan rescinded several Bush administration initiatives that would have reduced the coverage of the section 404 program, while endorsing the concept of "no net loss." To increase the flexibility and fairness of the permit process, the plan proposed new deadlines for permit decisions, a new appeal process, and the use of wetlands mitigation banks. For an analysis of the Clinton plan that concludes that it offers little additional protection for wetlands, see Blumm, The Clinton Wetlands Plan: No Net Gain in Wetlands Protection, 9 J. Land Use & Env. L. 203 (1994).

G. ENVIRONMENTAL ENFORCEMENT: THE CASE OF THE CLEAN WATER ACT

Environmental Enforcement (pp. 984-985). Problems with environmental enforcement were highlighted by a National Law Journal study finding that two-thirds of corporate lawyers admitted that their companies violated federal or state environmental laws. Natl. L.J., Aug. 30, 1993. Of the 233 corporate lawyers who responded to the survey, 66 percent asserted that it was not possible to achieve full compliance with the laws because of their complexity, cost, or the uncertainty that surrounded interpretation of them. Nearly 70 percent of the respondents agreed that greater attention to environmental concerns would improve their companies' long-term profitability. Virtually all agreed that environmental regulation is becoming more stringent throughout the world and 86 percent said that U.S. regulations had not caused their companies to consider shifting operations to other countries. Firms Violated Laws on the Environment, Many Lawyers Admit, Wall St. J., Aug. 23, 1993, at B2.

Monitoring and Detecting Violations (pp. 985-986). Technological innovations may permit the development of improved techniques for compliance monitoring. Researchers are exploring whether computed tomography—the technology used for CAT scans—can be harnessed to provide a cost-effective approach for continuous monitoring of emissions of nearly two hundred hazardous air pollutants. Brannigan, CAT Scan May Soon "Map" Air Pollution, Wall St. J., Nov. 10, 1994, at B7. Infrared light would be used with spectrometers to capture on computers a continous, moving image of pollutants as they leak from factories.

Borrowing a technique that has become prominent in criminal trials, researchers have used DNA testing to indicate that whale meat sold in Japan is not all from the southern minke whale, the only whale whose meat legally can be sold. Baker & Palumbi, Which Whales Are Hunted? A Molecular Genetic Approach to Monitoring Whaling, 265 Science 1538 (1994). Genetic analysis of 16 samples of whale meat purchased in Japan found that only seven were from southern minke whales, while several others were from protected species that cannot legally be harvested. In response to this evidence, the Japanese Fisheries Agency announced that it would create an enhanced reference library of DNA from coastal cetaceans to use in testing whale meat to help ensure compliance with legal requirements. Palumbi, DNA Labs vs. Whale Meat Smugglers, Wall St. J., Oct. 25, 1994, at A17. Efforts to develop isotopic "fingerprints" that would pinpoint sources of illegal ivory have been less successful. Researchers have discovered that when elephant habitats change, the isotopic composition of their ivory changes also, meaning that animals from a single place have a wide range of isotopic values. Koch, et al., Isotopic Tracking of Change in Diet and Habitat Use in African Elephants, 267 Science 1340 (1995).

Self-Monitoring and Environmental Audits (p. 986). Voluntary international standards for conducting environmental audits are being developed by the International Standards Organization (ISO) as part of a process known as ISO 14000 that will develop standards for corporate environmental management. Corporate counsel have become increasingly concerned that the results of environmental self-audits could be used to facilitate prosecutions of companies who perform such audits. They argue that companies will be discouraged from performing such audits and from voluntarily improving their compliance record if the results can be used in enforcement actions. As a result, they have advocated enactment of laws making the results of environmental self-audits privileged information. In 1993 Oregon enacted a law creating an environmental audit privilege. The law permits a company to keep the results of its environmental audits confidential so long as violations discovered in the audit are corrected reasonably promptly. As of March 1995, nine other states had enacted similar statutes. No Audit Privilege in Interim EPA Policy; Lack of Prosecution, Punitive Fines Possible, 25 Env. Rep. 2411 (1995). Virginia's new law actually provides immunity from civil and criminal penalties for violations discovered and corrected

7. Water Pollution Control   Pages 987-989

after environmental self-audits. EPA has threatened to withdraw delegation of program authority to states who adopt audit policies granting immunity from penalties.

While there is no indication that Oregon's privilege statute has spurred more firms to conduct audits, this may be due in part to the fact that the privilege does not extend to federal enforcement actions. Effects of State's Audit Privilege Law Still Unclear After First Year, Lawyers Say, 25 Env. Rep. 1621 (1994). In April 1995 EPA announced a new policy on how it will use the results of environmental self-audits. 60 Fed. Reg. 16,875 (1995). EPA announced that while it would not treat the results of environmental audits as privileged information, it would be more inclined to forego criminal prosecutions and waive punitive fines when violations discovered during such audits are reported and voluntarily corrected. The agency emphasized that it would continue to seek to recoup from companies the economic benefits of their violations.

Clean Air Act Bounty Provisions (p. 986). As discussed in the parent text, section 113(f) of the Clean Air Act authorizes the payment of rewards to those who furnish information concerning violations of the Act. EPA has proposed regulations outlining criteria and procedures for making such awards. See 59 Fed. Reg. 22,795 (1994).

Missing Data from Continuous Emissions Monitoring (pp. 986-987). As discussed in the parent text, section 412(d) of the Clean Air Act requires EPA to issue regulations specifying the consequences of breakdowns in continuous monitoring equipment required by section 412(a). In its final rules implementing this provision, EPA adopted a complicated procedure for supplying missing data when continuous emissions monitors (CEMs) break down. "The procedure is based on the premise that the longer the gap in recorded data and/or the lower the annual monitor availability, the more conservative the value to be substituted." 58 Fed. Reg. 3590, 3635 (1993). The value assumed for the missing data depends on the percentage of the prior year in which data was available from the CEM and the length of the current outage. Maximum emission levels are assumed for any outage from a CEM that has not achieved at least 90 percent availability in the prior year, while average values are assumed for outages of less than 24 hours from CEMs that have been available more than 95 percent of the time.

Enforcement Authorities and Policies (pp. 987-989). In March 1992, EPA created an Environmental Appeals Board to serve as the final forum for hearing appeals of administrative enforcement decisions. The Appeals Board is a three-person, permanent board designed to enhance EPA's administrative enforcement program. See Firestone, EPA's Environmental Appeals Board, 1 EPA Admin. L. Rep. 13 (1993).

EPA's enforcement program has been the subject of several major reorganizations since the early history of the agency. In October 1993 the Clinton Administration announced that it was reorganizing EPA's enforcement program to emphasize multimedia enforcement. The administration created a new Compliance Assurance office that was organized on an industrial sector basis. Under this approach teams of EPA enforcement personnel examine selected industries from a multimedia perspective. In August 1994 the Justice Department announced that it would return to U.S. attorneys offices the authority to approve indictments for environmental violations. McGee, Environmental Prosecutions Decentralized, Wash. Post, Aug. 26, 1994, at A23. This reversed a controversial Bush Administration policy designed to centralize authority for bringing environmental criminal prosecutions in the Justice Department.

Enforcement authorities have been exploring more innovative approaches to designing relief for environmental violations. Settlements that include provisions for environmental audits are being used to help violators prevent future violations. Supplemental environmental projects are being undertaken more frequently to settle enforcement cases. A total of $65 million was committed by companies to fund supplemental environmental projects during fiscal year 1994. New Records for Actions, Fines Set by EPA Despite Restructuring of Program, 25 Env. Rep. 1501 (1994). For example, the General Chemical Corp. of Richmond, California has agreed to contribute $600,000 for a health clinic and $200,000 to fund a mobile health van in partial settlement of charges that it released a cloud of sulfuric acid that made thousands of residents ill. Healthy Settlement, Calif. Lawyer, Apr., 1994, at 20.

Criminal Enforcement (pp. 993-995). In United States v. Borowski, 977 F.2d 27 (1st Cir. 1992), the First Circuit reversed the felony conviction of the owner of a company that had violated EPA's pretreatment standards for discharges of industrial waste. John Borowski had been convicted of knowing endangerment in violation of section 309(c)(3) of the Clean Water Act, which makes knowing violations of the Act a felony if they "place another person in imminent danger of death or serious bodily injury." Even though Borowski had placed his own employees in danger, the court held that a conviction "cannot be premised upon danger that occurs before the pollutant reaches a publicly-owned sewer or treatment works." 977 F.2d at 32.

In October 1994, a plant manager and an employee of Durex Industries, Inc., which had dumped toluene in a dumpster, were sentenced to 27 months in prison after being convicted of illegal disposal

7. Water Pollution Control

of hazardous waste in violation of RCRA. The two were acquitted of the more serious offense of knowing endangerment even though fumes from the tolulene killed two nine-year-old boys who climbed inside the dumpster. Durex pleaded no contest to charges of knowing endangerment and illegal waste disposal. United States v. William Recht Co., No. 94-70-CRT-17B (M.D. Fla. 1994).

Courts continue to wrestle with questions of how to interpret intent requirements for criminal violations of the environmental laws. In United States v. Weitzenhoff, 35 F.3d 1275 (9th Cir. 1994), the Ninth Circuit upheld the convictions of two managers of a sewage treatment plant who claimed that they believed that the discharges for which they were responsible were within limits permitted under the facility's NPDES permit. The court agreed with the government that it was not necessary to prove that the managers knew that the discharges exceeded permitted levels. Rather, the government need only prove that the defendants knew that they were discharging materials. Despite dissents from five Ninth Circuit judges to a petition for rehearing en banc, the Supreme Court denied review in January 1995.

Citizen Suits in the Aftermath of **Gwaltney** *(pp. 1008-1009).* In the wake of *Gwaltney*, most federal courts have held that ongoing violations can be established either by showing that violations continued on or after the filing of a complaint or by producing evidence from which a reasonable trier of fact could find a continuing likelihood that intermittent or sporadic violations would occur. See Connecticut Coastal Fisherman's Assn. v. Remington Arms Co., 989 F.2d 1305 (2d Cir. 1993); Natural Resources Defense Council v. Texaco, 2 F.3d 493 (3d Cir. 1993).

"Permit Shields" and the Clean Water Act (p. 1011). An important issue emerging in CWA enforcement actions is the question whether NPDES permits insulate dischargers from liability for discharges of pollutants not specifically regulated by their permits. In the case below a public interest group filed a citizen suit after discovering that a company's TRI report included surface water discharges of pollutants not covered by the company's NPDES permit. The trial court agreed with the defendant that the CWA does not prohibit discharges of pollutants by a permittee that do not violate specific limits established in the permit. The court stated that although section 301(a) of the Act generally prohibits unpermitted discharges, "the statutory and regulatory scheme of the Act takes enforcement actions against permit holders *outside* that general prohibition." Atlantic States Legal Foundation v. Eastman Kodak Co., 809 F. Supp. 1040, 1047 (W.D.N.Y. 1992). The decision was appealed to the Second Circuit, which reached the following decision.

Atlantic States Legal Foundation, Inc. v. Eastman Kodak Co.
12 F.3d 353 (2d Cir. 1994)

Before: WINTER, MCLAUGHLIN, and JACOBS, Circuit Judges.
WINTER, Circuit Judge:

ISSUE This appeal raises the issue of whether private groups may bring a citizen suit pursuant to Section 505 of the Federal Water Pollution Control Act (commonly known as the Clean Water Act), 33 U.S.C. §1365, to stop the discharge of pollutants not listed in a valid permit issued pursuant to the Clean Water Act ("CWA" or "the Act"), 33 U.S.C. §1342 (1988). . . .

BACKGROUND

Appellee Eastman Kodak Company ("Kodak") operates an industrial facility in Rochester, New York that discharges wastewater into the Genesee River and Paddy Hill Creek under a State Pollutant Discharge Elimination System ("SPDES") permit issued pursuant to 33 U.S.C. §1342. Appellant Atlantic States Legal Foundation, Inc. ("Atlantic States") is a not-for-profit environmental group based in Syracuse, New York.

Kodak operates a wastewater treatment plant at its Rochester facility to purify waste produced in the manufacture of photographic supplies and other laboratory chemicals. The purification plant employs a variety of technical processes to filter harmful pollutants before discharge into the Genesee River at the King's Landing discharge point (designated Outfall 001) pursuant to its SPDES permit.

Kodak first received a federal permit in 1975. At that time, the pertinent regulatory scheme was the National Pollutant Discharge Elimination System ("NPDES") that was administered directly by the federal Environmental Protection Agency ("EPA"). Subsequently, 33 U.S.C. §1342(b), (c) delegated authority to the states to establish their own programs in place of the EPA's. As a result, Kodak applied in July 1979 to renew its permit to the New York State Department of Environmental Conservation ("DEC"). The DEC declined to act on Kodak's renewal application, and Kodak's NPDES permit remained in effect. As part of the pending application for a SPDES permit, in April 1982 Kodak provided the DEC with a Form 2C describing estimated discharges of

7. Water Pollution Control   Page 1011

164 substances from each of its outfalls. Kodak also submitted an Industrial Chemical Survey ("ICS") disclosing the amounts of certain chemicals used in Kodak's facility and whether they might appear in the plant's wastewater. Although the ICS originally requested information on 144 substances, including some broad classes such as "unspecified metals," the DEC restricted the inquiry to chemicals used in excess of specified minimum levels.

On the basis of these disclosures, DEC issued Kodak a SPDES permit, number 000-1643, effective November 1, 1984, establishing specific effluent limitations for approximately 25 pollutants. The permit also included "action levels"[2] for five other pollutants as well as for three of the pollutants for which it had established effluent limits. DEC further required Kodak to conduct a semi-annual scan of "EPA Volatile, Acid and Base/Neutral Fractions and PCB's priority pollutants on a 24-hr. composite sample." In May 1989, Kodak applied to renew the SPDES permit submitting a new Form 2C and ICS, but the 1984 permit will continue to remain in effect until DEC issues a final determination. . . .

On November 14, 1991, Atlantic States filed the complaint in the instant matter. The complaint alleged that Kodak had violated Sections 301 and 402 of the Clean Water Act, 33 U.S.C. §§1311, 1342, by discharging large quantities of pollutants not listed in its SPDES permit.[4] . . .

After discovery, Atlantic States moved for partial summary judgment as to Kodak's liability in relation to the post-April 1, 1990 discharge of one or more of 16 of the 27 pollutants listed in the complaint. The 16 pollutants are all listed as toxic chemicals under Section 313(c) of the Emergency Planning and Community Right-to-Know Act, 42 U.S.C. §11023(c). Atlantic States argued that General Provision 1(b) of the SPDES permit and Section 301 of the CWA, 33 U.S.C. §1311, prohibit absolutely the discharge of any pollutant not specifically authorized under Kodak's SPDES permit.

On December 28, 1992, the district court denied Atlantic States' motion for partial summary judgment, granted Kodak's cross-motion for summary judgment, and dismissed the case. Atlantic States Legal Found., Inc. v. Eastman Kodak Co., 809 F. Supp. 1040 (W.D.N.Y. 1992). Atlantic States appealed from the judgment entered on that order. . . .

---

2. If the action level is exceeded, the permittee must undertake a "short-term, high-intensity monitoring program." If levels higher than the action levels are confirmed, the permit is reopened for consideration of revised action levels or effluent limits.

4. Specifically, the complaint alleged that Kodak had discharged "282,744 pounds of unpermitted pollutants in 1987, 308,537 pounds in 1988, 321,456 pounds in 1989[,] and 290,121 pounds in 1990," and that Atlantic States believed that Kodak continued to discharge such pollutants.

A. *"Standards and Limitations" of the Clean Water Act*

Atlantic States argues first that the plain language of Section 301 of the CWA, 33 U.S.C. §1311, prohibits the discharge of any pollutants not expressly permitted. With regard to this claim, therefore, Atlantic States' standing to bring this action turns on the merits of the action itself.

Section 301(a) reads: "Except as in compliance with this section and sections 1312, 1316, 1317, 1328, 1342, and 1344 of this title, the discharge of any pollutant by any person shall be unlawful." This prohibition is tempered, however, by a self-referential host of exceptions that allow the discharge of many pollutants once a polluter has complied with the regulatory program of the CWA. The exception relevant to the instant matter is contained in Section 402, which outlines the NPDES, 33 U.S.C. §1342(a), and specifies the requirements for suspending the national system with the submission of an approved state program, 33 U.S.C. §1342(b), (c). Section 402(k) contains the so-called "shield provision," 33 U.S.C. §1342(k), which defines compliance with a NPDES or SPDES permit as compliance with Section 301 for the purposes of the CWA's enforcement provisions. The Supreme Court has noted that "The purpose of [Section 402(k)] seems to be . . . to relieve [permit holders] of having to litigate in an enforcement action the question whether their permits are sufficiently strict." E.I. du Pont de Nemours & Co. v. Train, 430 U.S. 112 (1977).

Atlantic States' view of the regulatory framework stands that scheme on its head. Atlantic States treats permits as establishing limited permission for the discharge of identified pollutants and a prohibition on the discharge of unidentified pollutants. Viewing the regulatory scheme as a whole, however, it is clear that the permit is intended to identify and limit the most harmful pollutants while leaving the control of the vast number of other pollutants to disclosure requirements. Once within the NPDES or SPDES scheme, therefore, polluters may discharge pollutants not specifically listed in their permits so long as they comply with the appropriate reporting requirements and abide by any new limitations when imposed on such pollutants.[8]

---

8. The cases Atlantic States cites are therefore inapposite because each involves either a failure to correctly disclose accurately the discharge of pollutants and thus comply with regulation or a failure to secure the requisite NPDES or SPDES permit. Atlantic States Legal Found., Inc. v. Reynolds Metals Co., 31 Env't Rep. Cas. (BNA) 1156, 1158 (N.D.N.Y. 1990) (failing to "apply proper detection"); United States v. Tom-Kat Development, Inc., 614 F. Supp. 613 (D. Alaska 1985) (failing to obtain permit); Kitlutsisti v. ARCO Alaska, Inc., 592 F. Supp. 832 (D. Alaska 1984) (failing to obtain permit), vacated on other grounds,

7. Water Pollution Control   Page 1011

The EPA lists tens of thousands of different chemical substances in the Toxic Substances Control Act Chemical Substance Inventory pursuant to 15 U.S.C. §2607(b) (1988). However, the EPA does not demand even information regarding each of the many thousand chemical substances potentially present in a manufacturer's wastewater because "it is impossible to identify and rationally limit every chemical or compound present in a discharge of pollutants." Memorandum from EPA Deputy Assistant Administrator for Water Enforcement Jeffrey G. Miller to Regional Enforcement Director, Region V, at 2 (Apr. 28, 1976). "Compliance with such a permit would be impossible and anybody seeking to harass a permittee need only analyze that permittee's discharge until determining the presence of a substance not identified in the permit." Id. Indeed, Atlantic States conceded at oral argument that even plain water might be considered a "pollutant" under its view of the Act.

The EPA has never acted in any way to suggest that Atlantic States' absolutist and wholly impractical view of the legal effect of a permit is valid. In fact, the EPA's actions and policy statements have frequently contemplated discharges of pollutants not listed under a NPDES or SPDES permit. It has addressed such discharges by amending the permit to list and limit a pollutant when necessary to safeguard the environment without considering pre-amendment discharges to be violations calling for enforcement under the CWA. 33 U.S.C. §§1319, 1365. The EPA thus stated in its comments on proposed 40 C.F.R. §122.68(a), which applied the "application-based" limits approach to implementation of the CWA reporting scheme,

> There is still some possibility . . . that a [NPDES or SPDES] permittee may discharge a large amount of a pollutant not limited in its permit, and EPA will not be able to take enforcement action against the permittee as long as the permittee complies with the notification requirements [pursuant to the CWA].

45 Fed. Reg. 33,516, 33,523 (1980). The EPA's statement went on to note that this possibility constituted a "regulatory gap," and that, "the final regulations control discharges only of the pollutants listed in the [NPDES or SPDES] permit application, which consist primarily of the listed toxic pollutants and designated hazardous substances." Id. In a clarification of EPA policy on Section 304, 33 U.S.C. §1314, and

---

782 F.2d 800 (9th Cir. 1986); Love v. New York State Dep't of Envt'l Conservation, 429 F. Supp. 832 (S.D.N.Y. 1981) (failing to obtain proper permit).

water quality-based effluent limitations, an EPA official recently stated that:

> EPA did not intend to require water quality-based permit limitations on all pollutants contained in a discharge. . . . The proper interpretation of the regulations is that developing water quality-based limitations is a step-by-step process. . . . Water quality-based limits are established where the permitting authority reasonably anticipates the discharge of pollutants by the permittee at levels that have the reasonable potential to cause or contribute to an excursion above any state water quality criterion. . . .

Memorandum from Director, Office of Wastewater Enforcement and Compliance to Water Management Division Directors, Regions I-X, at 2-3 (Aug. 14, 1992).

The EPA is the federal agency entrusted with administration and enforcement of the CWA. 33 U.S.C. §1251(d). As such, EPA's reasonable interpretations of the Act are due deferential treatment in the courts. Chevron, U.S.A., Inc. v. Natural Resources Defense Council, 467 U.S. 837, 844 (1984). . . . Because the EPA's implementation of the CWA is entirely reasonable, we defer to it. . . .

Conclusion

For the reasons stated above, we affirm the order of the district court granting summary judgment to Kodak.

NOTES AND QUESTIONS

1. Does the court's decision mean that a discharger with an NPDES permit legally can discharge any material not specifically restricted in its permit? What, if anything, would prevent a discharger from dramatically changing the nature of its discharges once it has been granted an NPDES permit?

2. How did the court and Atlantic States differ in their interpretations of the effect of the language of section 301 providing that "the discharge of any pollutant by any person shall be unlawful" expect as in compliance with other provisions of the Clean Water Act? The court's decision, its interpretation of the statutory language, and EPA's history of implementation of the permit provisions of the Clean Water Act is criticized in Axline & McGinley, Universal Statutes and Planetary Programs: How EPA Has Diluted the Clean Water Act, 8 J. Env. L. & Litig. 253 (1993).

7. Water Pollution Control

3. The court suggests that its interpretation of the Clean Water Act is justified because it would be impossible for EPA to identify and to regulate every one of the thousands of chemicals that are discharged by industrial facilities. Is it true that compliance with the Act would be impossible if the court accepted Atlantic States' view that the discharge of unidentified pollutants is prohibited?

4. How realistic is the fear expressed by EPA that if Atlantic States' view were accepted, "anybody seeking to harass a permittee need only analyze that permittee's discharge until determining the presence of a substance not identified in the permit"? How difficult would it be for citizen groups to sample and analyze discharges and to prove that pollutants are being discharged that are unauthorized in a permit? If citizens were successful in proving such discharges, wouldn't permittees seek to have these discharges specifically addressed in their permits?

5. Does the court's decision preclude EPA from bringing an enforcement action against a permittee for discharges not addressed in an NPDES permit? In at least one other case a court has allowed the federal government to take enforcement action against discharges not regulated in an NPDES permit. United States v. Ketchikan Pulp Co., Civ. No. A92-587 (D. Alaska 1993).

6. In October 1994 Kodak agreed to pay a $5 million fine and to spend more than $60 million as a result of violations of federal hazardous waste laws at the plant that was the target of Atlantic States' citizen suit. McKinley, Kodak Fined $5 Million for Toxic Chemical Leaks, N.Y. Times, Oct. 8, 1994, at 29.

Federal Facilities Compliance Docket (p. 1012). In February 1993, EPA updated its Federal Agency Hazardous Waste Compliance Docket to add 263 new federal facilities to be evaluated for possible inclusion on the National Priorities List. 58 Fed. Reg. 7298 (1993). As a result there were 1,930 federal facilities in the docket, which EPA is required to maintain by section 120(c) of CERCLA.

The Federal Facility Compliance Act of 1992 (p. 1013). The Supreme Court's decision in United States Department of Energy v. Ohio, 112 S. Ct. 1627 (1992) (text, p. 1013), was overridden in large part when Congress enacted the Federal Facility Compliance Act of 1992 (FFCA), Pub. L. No. 102-386 (1992), which President Bush signed into law on October 6, 1992. The FFCA expressly waives the federal government's immunity from civil penalties for violations of RCRA. The legislation that became the FFCA had actually passed both houses of Congress during the previous session in 1991, prior to the Supreme Court's decision in Department of Energy v. Ohio. The Court's decision served as a catalyst for convening a conference committee and achieving final passage of the legislation.

The FFCA amends section 6001 of RCRA to waive federal sovereign immunity for civil or administrative penalties or fines, regardless of whether they are "punitive or coercive in nature or are imposed for isolated, intermittent, or continuing violations." This effectively overrides the Supreme Court's unanimous holding in Department of Energy v. Ohio that the previous version of section 6001 does not waive federal sovereign immunity for punitive penalties. The FFCA also amends the definition of "person" in section 1004(15) of RCRA to "include each department, agency, and instrumentality of the United States," thus effectively overriding the Court's holding that federal facilities are immune from civil penalties under RCRA's citizen suit provision. However, the FFCA does not address the Court's holdings with respect to waivers of sovereign immunity in the Clean Water Act.

Opponents of the legislation had maintained that states could abuse their civil penalty authority to line their coffers at federal expense. In response to this concern, the legislation requires that all funds collected by states for violations by federal agencies be used "only for projects designed to improve or protect the environment or to defray the costs of environmental protection or enforcement." While the term "environmental protection" is not defined in the FFCA, supporters of the Act maintained that it should be construed broadly to include wetlands protection and preservation of open space as well as pollution control. States with preexisting laws or constitutional provisions that bar earmarking of funds collected in enforcement actions are exempted from this limitation.

The Departments of Energy and Defense had opposed the legislation by arguing that their facilities produce so many diverse hazardous waste streams that full compliance with RCRA is impossible. These agencies maintained that the technology simply does not exist to ensure the safe treatment and disposal of many radioactive wastes they generate. To accommodate these concerns, the legislative waiver of sovereign immunity is not effective immediately for federal agencies whose violation of RCRA's prohibition on storage of land-banned hazardous waste (section 3004(j)) consists of storing radioactive waste that has been mixed with other hazardous waste ("mixed waste"). Federal agencies storing mixed wastes are given three years (or until October, 1995) before their immunity from civil penalties for storage violations will be waived, except for wastes subject to an approved treatment plan and compliance order. The waiver is effective immediately for violations of existing compliance agreements, permits, or orders governing the storage of mixed waste.

7. Water Pollution Control

The Federal Facility Compliance Act also includes provisions to force DOE to develop a plan for cleaning up the enormous quantities of mixed waste it has generated. The Secretary of Energy is required to provide a comprehensive state-by-state inventory of the sources and amounts of such wastes to EPA and to the governor of each state where DOE stores or generates mixed wastes. This inventory is to include estimates of the amount of each type of mixed waste that DOE expects to generate at each of its facilities during the next five years and information concerning the technology available for treating such wastes. DOE is required to submit a detailed description of its plans for treating mixed wastes and for identifying and developing treatment technologies for wastes for which no treatment technology exists. EPA or states with delegated RCRA program authority must review and approve the plans, which are then to be incorporated in administrative orders requiring compliance with the plans.

To improve EPA enforcement, the Act also amends section 3007(c) of RCRA to require EPA annually to inspect each federal facility used for the treatment, storage, or disposal of hazardous waste even in states authorized to administer the RCRA program. The 1984 Hazardous and Solid Waste Amendments had previously required such inspections only in states without delegated program authority. EPA is to be reimbursed for the costs of such inspection by the federal agency that owns or operates the facility. The initial EPA inspection must include groundwater monitoring unless it has been performed during the year prior to enactment.

A particularly significant provision in FFCA is its authorization of EPA to bring administrative enforcement actions against other federal agencies. While EPA had maintained that it had such authority under RCRA, the Justice Department maintained that it would violate constitutional principles of separation of powers for EPA to issue administrative orders against another executive agency, a position undermined by Morrison v. Olson, 487 U.S. 654, 695-96 (1988). The conference report describes the Act's express endorsement of EPA administrative enforcement actions against federal facilities as an effort "to reaffirm the original intent" of RCRA. 138 Cong. Rec. H8865 (Sept. 22, 1992 daily ed.). The report states that EPA should use its section 3008(a) administrative order authority against federal facilities for the same types of violations for which it is used against private parties. EPA had complained that other federal agencies were reluctant to negotiate compliance agreements with it because EPA had no credible threat of enforcement leverage to use against other federal agencies in the absence of such an agreement. With this new authority, EPA will be able to move more rapidly to penalize recalcitrant agencies. The FFCA requires that EPA give the defendant agency an opportunity to confer with the EPA Administrator before any administrative order can become final.

While the legislation effectively overrules the RCRA portion of the holding in Department of Energy v. Ohio, the scope of the congressional waiver of sovereign immunity is even broader than the penalties at issue in that decision. Because the federal government will be subject "to the full range of available enforcement tools . . . to penalize isolated, intermittent or continuing violations as well as to coerce future compliance," the legislation also effectively precludes assertion by federal defendants of a *Gwaltney* defense (see text, pp. 997-1011) in citizen suits alleging violations of RCRA. As the Conference report explains:

> By subjecting the federal government to penalties and fines for isolated, intermittent, or continuing violations, the waiver also makes it clear that the federal government may be penalized for any violation of federal, state, interstate or local law, whether a single or repeated occurrence, notwithstanding the holding of the Supreme Court in Gwaltney of Smithfield, Ltd. v. Chesapeake Bay Foundation, Inc., 484 U.S. 49 (1987).

Id. While the enactment of FFCA overrides the holding of Department of Energy v. Ohio with respect to RCRA, federal facilities may remain immune from civil penalties for violation of the Clean Water Act because the latter are not addressed by the FFCA. But see Pennsylvania Dept. of Environmental Resources v. U.S. Postal Service, 13 F.3d 62 (3rd Cir. 1993) (finding that the federal facilities provision of the Clean Water Act waives the Postal Service's immunity from civil penalties).

=8=
Protection of Public Resources

[U]seful products cannot be harvested from extinct species. If dwindling wildlands are mined for genetic material rather than destroyed for a few more boardfeet of lumber and acreage of farmland, their economic yield will be vastly greater over time. Salvaged species can help to revitalize timbering, agriculture, medicine, and other industries located elsewhere. The wildlands are like a magic well: the more that is drawn from them in knowledge and benefits, the more there will be to draw.

—*E. O. Wilson**

[When it comes to extinction] it matters little whether the fatal blow is delivered directly or indirectly, with malice aforethought or simple ignorance.†

Conflicts over public resource management, which were prominent issues during the 1992 presidential campaign, have intensified following the 1994 congressional elections. While the Clinton Administration has attempted to pursue more flexible policies for reconciling environmental and economic interests, the new Republican majority in Congress is pursuing legislation that would radically alter federal resource management policies. After making an ill-fated attempt to abolish the Council on Environmental Quality, the Clinton Administration has been more successful with its initiative to resolve the bitter controversy over logging old-growth forests in the Pacific Northwest. This chapter reviews these and other developments pertaining to NEPA, the Endangered Species Act, and public resource management policies. It examines the applicability of NEPA to international trade agreements, Public Citizen v. Office of the U.S. Trade Representative, 5 F.3d 549 (D.C. Cir. 1993), and it reviews the Supreme Court's *Sweet Home* decision

---

*The Diversity of Life 282 (1992).
† Amicus brief filed by 14 prominent scientists, including E.O. Wilson and Stephen Jay Gould, in Babbitt v. Sweet Home Chapter of Communities for a Great Oregon, — S. Ct. — (1995).

resolving a major controversy over interpretation of the Endangered Species Act.

A. THE NATIONAL ENVIRONMENTAL POLICY ACT

Proposed Abolition of the CEQ (p. 1025). The Clinton Administration surprised environmentalists by announcing in February 1993 that it planned to abolish the Council on Environmental Quality (CEQ) and to replace it with a new White House Office on Environmental Policy. The decision was widely viewed as a result of the president's campaign promise to reduce the White House staff by 25 percent. The administration proposed to transfer to EPA CEQ's responsibilities under NEPA. The proposal was abandoned after vigorous opposition from supporters of CEQ. Kenworthy, Clinton Plan on CEQ Sparks Tiff with Environmentalists, Wash. Post, Mar. 25, 1993, at A22.

Under What Circumstances Must an EIS Be Prepared?: Trade Agreements (p. 1033). The question of NEPA's applicability to international trade agreements has received considerable attention recently. It is widely recognized that trade liberalization can have significant environmental consequences for reasons explored in Chapter 9 (see parent, pp. 1189-1203). Beginning in 1990, the Office of the U.S. Trade Representative, which is responsible for negotiating trade agreements under the Trade Act of 1974, commenced negotiations on a North American Free Trade Agreement (NAFTA) between the U.S, Canada, and Mexico. During the negotiations, the Bush Administration openly acknowledged that it did not intend to prepare an EIS. As a result, Public Citizen filed suit on August 1, 1991, arguing that NEPA required the U.S. Trade Representative to prepare an EIS.

After losing in the district court for lack of standing, Public Citizen appealed to the D.C. Circuit. In August 1992 the D.C. Circuit held that there was no reviewable final agency decision not to prepare an EIS because the trade negotiations had not yet been concluded and the Trade Representative could always change her mind and agree to perform an EIS. Public Citizen v. Office of the U.S. Trade Representative, 970 F.2d 916 (D.C. Cir. 1992). Two months after the D.C. Circuit's decision, the Bush Administration announced in October 1992 that final agreement on NAFTA had been reached. The agreement was signed by the heads of state of the three countries in December 1992.

8. Protection of Public Resources

Public Citizen then filed a new lawsuit arguing that NEPA had been violated because of the Trade Representative's failure to prepare an EIS. On June 30, 1993, the district court ruled in favor of Public Citizen. The court held that NAFTA is in substantial part the result of work by the U.S. Trade Representative and that significant actions taken by her office, which is an agency subject to NEPA, were sufficient to trigger NEPA's EIS requirement.

Complaining that this "11th hour" decision could jeopardize ratification of NAFTA, the government sought an emergency appeal to the D.C. Circuit. The case was argued on August 24, 1993 by Solicitor General Drew Days, who made an unusual appearance outside of the Supreme Court in order to highlight the importance of the case. One month after argument the D.C. Circuit issued the following decision.

Public Citizen v. U.S. Trade Representative
5 F.3d 549 (D.C. Cir. 1993)

Before: MIKVA, Chief Judge, WALD and RANDOLPH, Circuit Judges.
MIKVA, Chief Judge:

Appellees Public Citizen, Friends of the Earth, Inc., and the Sierra Club (collectively "Public Citizen") sued the Office of the United States Trade Representative, claiming that an environmental impact statement was required for the North American Free Trade Agreement ("NAFTA"). The district court granted Public Citizen's motion for summary judgment and ordered that an impact statement be prepared "forthwith." In its appeal of that ruling, the government contends that the Trade Representative's preparation of NAFTA without an impact statement is not "final agency action" under the Administrative Procedure Act ("APA") and therefore is not reviewable by this court. Because we conclude that NAFTA is not "final agency action" under the APA, we reverse the decision of the district court and express no view on the government's other contentions.

I. BACKGROUND

In 1990, the United States, Mexico, and Canada initiated negotiations on the North American Free Trade Agreement. NAFTA creates a "free trade zone" encompassing the three countries by eliminating or reducing tariffs and "non-tariff" barriers to trade on thousands of items of commerce. After two years of negotiations, the leaders of the three countries signed the agreement on December 17, 1992. NAFTA has not yet been transmitted to Congress. If approved by Congress, NAFTA is scheduled to take effect on January 1, 1994.

Negotiations on behalf of the United States were conducted primarily by the Office of the United States Trade Representative ("OTR"). OTR, located "within the Executive Office of the President," 19 U.S.C. §2171(a) ("Trade Act of 1974" or "Trade Acts"), is the United States' chief negotiator for trade matters. OTR "reports directly to the President and the Congress, and [is] responsible to the President and the Congress for the administration of trade agreements. . . ." Id. §2171(c)(1)(B).

Under the Trade Acts and congressional rules, NAFTA is entitled to "fast-track" enactment procedures which provide that Congress must vote on the agreement, without amendment, within ninety legislative days after transmittal by the President. The current version of NAFTA, once submitted, will therefore be identical to the version on which Congress will vote. President Clinton has indicated, however, that he will not submit NAFTA to Congress until negotiations have been completed on several side agreements regarding, among other things, compliance with environmental laws.

Public Citizen first sought to compel OTR to prepare an environmental impact statement ("EIS") for NAFTA in a suit filed on August 1, 1991. Public Citizen v. Office of the United States Trade Representative, 782 F. Supp. 139 (D.D.C.), aff'd on other grounds, Public Citizen v. Office of the United States Trade Representative, 970 F.2d 916 (D.C. Cir. 1992) (*Public Citizen I*). The district court dismissed Public Citizen's claim for lack of standing. This court affirmed but did not reach the standing issue. *Public Citizen I*, 970 F.2d at 916. Instead, we ruled that because NAFTA was still in the negotiating stages, there was no final action upon which to base jurisdiction under the APA. Id. Public Citizen's current challenge is essentially identical, except that the President has now signed and released a final draft of NAFTA. The district court granted Public Citizen's motion for summary judgment and ordered OTR to prepare an EIS "forthwith." Public Citizen v. United States Trade Representative, 822 F. Supp. 21 (D.D.C. 1993). The government appeals.

II. Discussion

The National Environmental Policy Act ("NEPA") requires federal agencies to include an EIS "in every recommendation or report on proposals for legislation and other major Federal actions significantly affecting the quality of the human environment. . . ." 42 U.S.C. §4332(2)(C). In drafting NEPA, however, Congress did not create a

8. Protection of Public Resources   Page 1033

private right of action. Accordingly, Public Citizen must rest its claim for judicial review on the Administrative Procedure Act. Section 702 of the APA confers an action for injunctive relief on persons "adversely affected or aggrieved by agency action within the meaning of a relevant statute." 5 U.S.C. §702; see *Public Citizen I*, 970 F.2d at 918. Section 704, however, allows review only of "*final* agency action." 5 U.S.C. §704 (emphasis added); see Lujan v. National Wildlife Fed'n, 497 U.S. 871, 882 (1990). The central question in this appeal then is whether Public Citizen has identified some agency action that is final upon which to base APA review.

In support of its argument that NAFTA does not constitute "final agency action" within the meaning of the APA, the government relies heavily on Franklin v. Massachusetts, 112 S. Ct. 2767 (1992). *Franklin* involved a challenge to the method used by the Secretary of Commerce to calculate the 1990 census. The Secretary acted pursuant to a reapportionment statute requiring that she report the "tabulation of total population by States . . . to the President." 13 U.S.C. §141(b). After receiving the Secretary's report, the President must transmit to Congress the number of Representatives to which each state is entitled under the method of equal proportions. 2 U.S.C. §2(a)(2). The Supreme Court held that APA review was unavailable because the final action under the reapportionment statute (transmittal of the apportionment to Congress) was that of the President, and the President is not an agency. *Franklin*, 112 S. Ct. at 2773; see Armstrong v. Bush, 924 F.2d 282, 289 (D.C. Cir. 1991) (the President is not an "agency" within the meaning of the APA).

To determine whether an agency action is final, "the core question is whether the agency has completed its decisionmaking process, *and* whether the result of that process is one that will directly affect the parties.*" Franklin*, 112 S. Ct. at 2773 (emphasis added). The *Franklin* Court found that although the Secretary had completed her decisionmaking process, the action that would directly affect the plaintiffs was the President's calculation and transmittal of the apportionment to Congress, not the Secretary's report to the President. Id.

This logic applies with equal force to NAFTA. Even though the OTR has completed negotiations on NAFTA, the agreement will have no effect on Public Citizen's members unless and until the President submits it to Congress. Like the reapportionment statute in *Franklin*, the Trade Acts involve the President at the final stage of the process by providing for him to submit to Congress the final legal text of the agreement, a draft of the implementing legislation, and supporting information. 19 U.S.C. §2903(a)(1)(B). The President is not obligated to submit any agreement to Congress, and until he does there is no final action. If and when the agreement is submitted to Congress, it

457

will be the result of action by the President, action clearly not reviewable under the APA.

The district court attempts to distinguish *Franklin* by noting that unlike the census report (which the President was authorized to amend before submitting to Congress), NAFTA is no longer a "moving target" because the "final product . . . will not be changed before submission to Congress." 822 F. Supp. at 26. The district court goes on to say that NAFTA "shall" be submitted to Congress. Id. This distinction is unpersuasive. NAFTA is just as much a "moving target" as the census report in *Franklin* because in both cases the President has statutory discretion to exercise supervisory power over the agency's action. It is completely within the President's discretion, for example, to renegotiate portions of NAFTA before submitting it to Congress or to refuse to submit the agreement at all. In fact, President Clinton has conditioned the submission of NAFTA on the successful negotiation of side agreements on the environment, labor, and import surges. The President's position that the version of NAFTA negotiated by the OTR is the one that he "will" submit to Congress is irrelevant under *Franklin*. Indeed, in *Franklin* the President relied on the census report without making any changes, yet this did not affect the Court's analysis of whether the "final action" under the reapportionment statute was that of the President.

Public Citizen seeks to distinguish *Franklin* by arguing that the EIS requirement is an independent statutory obligation for the OTR and thus the agency's failure to prepare an EIS is reviewable final agency action. But the preparation of the census report in *Franklin* was also an "independent statutory obligation" for the Secretary of Commerce. The Court held nonetheless that because the report would have no effect on the plaintiffs without the President's subsequent involvement, the agency's action would not have the "direct effect" necessary for "final agency actions." Furthermore, although the argument that the absence of an EIS "directly affects" Public Citizen's ability to lobby Congress and disseminate information seems persuasive on its face, this court has stated that an agency's failure to prepare an EIS, by itself, is not sufficient to trigger APA review in the absence of identifiable substantive agency action putting the parties at risk. Foundation on Economic Trends v. Lyng, 943 F.2d 79, 85 (D.C. Cir. 1991).

Finally, Public Citizen argues that applying *Franklin* in this case would effectively nullify NEPA's EIS requirement because often "some other step must be taken before" otherwise final agency actions will result in environmental harm. In support of this position, it catalogs a number of cases in which courts have reviewed NEPA challenges to agency actions that require the involvement of some other governmental or private entity before becoming final. Although we acknowledge

8. Protection of Public Resources

the stringency of *Franklin*'s "direct effect" requirement, we disagree that it represents the death knell of the legislative EIS. *Franklin* is limited to those cases in which the President has final constitutional or statutory responsibility for the final step necessary for the agency action directly to affect the parties. Moreover, *Franklin* notes explicitly the importance of the President's role in the "integrity of the process" at issue. *Franklin*, 112 S. Ct. at 2775. Congress involved the President and the Secretary of Commerce in the reapportionment process to avoid stalemates resulting from congressional battles over the method for calculating reapportionment. Id. at 2771. Similarly, the requirement that the President, and not OTR, initiate trade negotiations and submit trade agreements and their implementing legislation to Congress indicates that Congress deemed the President's involvement essential to the integrity of international trade negotiations. When the President's role is not essential to the integrity of the process, however, APA review of otherwise final agency actions may well be available.

The government advances many other arguments opposing the preparation of an EIS, including weighty constitutional positions on the separation of powers and Public Citizen's lack of standing, as well as the inapplicability of NEPA to agreements executed pursuant to the Trade Acts in general, and NAFTA in particular. It also suggests that the judicial branch should avoid any conflict with the President's power by exercising the "equitable discretion" given it by §702 of the APA. We need not and do not consider such arguments in light of the clear applicability of the *Franklin* precedent.

The ultimate destiny of NAFTA has yet to be determined. Recently negotiated side agreements may well change the dimensions of the conflict that Public Citizen sought to have resolved by the courts. More importantly, the political debate over NAFTA in Congress has yet to play out. Whatever the ultimate result, however, NAFTA's fate now rests in the hands of the political branches. The judiciary has no role to play.

In sum, under the reasoning and language of Franklin v. Massachusetts, the "final agency action" challenged in this case is the submission of NAFTA to Congress by the President. Because the Trade Acts vest in the President the discretion to renegotiate NAFTA before submitting it to Congress or to refuse to submit it at all, his action, and not that of the OTR, will directly affect Public Citizen's members. The President's actions are not "agency action" and thus cannot be reviewed under the APA. The district court's grant of summary judgment in favor of Public Citizen is, therefore,

Reversed.

RANDOLPH, Circuit Judge, concurring:

8. Protection of Public Resources

I agree with my colleagues that the injunction against the United States Trade Representative must be set aside. The National Environmental Policy Act requires "all agencies of the Federal Government" to include an impact statement in "every recommendation or report on proposals for legislation and other major Federal actions significantly affecting the quality of the human environment. . . ." 42 U.S.C. §4332(2)(C). Private parties may sue to redress alleged violations of this provision only after there has been "final agency action" within the meaning of the Administrative Procedure Act, 5 U.S.C. §704. Public Citizen v. Office of the U.S. Trade Representative, 970 F.2d 916, 918 (D.C. Cir. 1992), citing Lujan v. National Wildlife Fed'n, 497 U.S. 871, 882 (1990). The majority holds that with respect to the North American Free Trade Agreement, there has been no "final" action because the President has not even transmitted NAFTA to Congress for its approval; and that if and when the President does submit the agreement and its implementing legislation, this would not qualify because, as Franklin v. Massachusetts, 112 S. Ct. 2767 (1992), decided, the President is not an "agency."

I do not quarrel with either one of these rationales. But I get a bit concerned when the opinion announces that it is too early to toll the bell for judicial review in a "legislative EIS" case and then starts trying to limit *Franklin*. The idea behind this is that proposing legislation to Congress can constitute "final . . . action," and that when an "agency" rather than the President does the proposing, §704 of the APA will be satisfied. I am not so sure. *Franklin* held not only that the President is outside the APA's definition of "agency," but also that "action" cannot be considered "final" under the APA unless it "will directly affect the parties." 112 S. Ct. at 2773. When the alleged "action" consists of a *proposal* for legislation, how can this condition for judicial review be satisfied? In *Franklin*, the President's submission to Congress directly affected the parties because, under the "automatic reapportionment statute," congressional action was not required. 112 S. Ct. at 2771. In general, however, it is difficult to see how the act of proposing legislation could generate direct effects on parties, or anyone else for that matter. The head of an independent agency, a member of the President's Cabinet, or the President himself may send a letter to the Speaker of the House and the President of the Senate transmitting a draft of proposed legislation. Such "executive communications" are commonplace. See How Our Laws Are Made, H.R. Doc. No. 139, 101st Cong., 2d Sess. 4 (1989). Yet only a Member of Congress may introduce a bill embodying the proposal, and even then no one will be affected, directly or otherwise, unless and until Congress passes the bill and the President signs it into law. If one takes *Franklin* at its word, a legislative proposal's lack of any direct effects would seem to mean that there can

8. Protection of Public Resources   Page 1033

be no final action sufficient to permit judicial review under the APA. Of course, there is a big difference between saying that APA review is unavailable and saying that officials do not have to comply with NEPA when they suggest legislation. If Congress believed an agency had not lived up to its obligation to prepare an impact statement, it could always refuse to consider the agency's proposal. Or, if Congress wanted to evaluate environmental impacts before putting the measure to a vote, congressional committees could hold hearings on the subject. This is how a large proportion of legislative proposals already must be treated. NEPA's impact statement requirement applies only to federal agencies. Members of Congress, who alone introduce bills and offer amendments, are not covered. Neither are private individuals, corporations, labor unions, citizen groups or other organizations, all of which frequently avail themselves of their First Amendment right to petition the government.

I am therefore not prepared to say whether in NEPA cases, the act of proposing legislation constitutes final action under §704 of the APA, as *Franklin* has interpreted that provision. This is a troublesome question, bound to arise in future cases, and we should not stake out a position on it here. The nub of the problem is that judicial review under the APA demands "final agency action" whereas the duty to prepare an impact statement arises earlier. The main objective of an impact statement is to ensure that the decisionmaker considers environmental effects prior to taking action. This is why in Kleppe v. Sierra Club, 427 U.S. 390, 406 n.15 (1976), the Court—without mentioning §704 of the APA—identified the "time at which a court enters the process" to be "when the report or recommendation on the proposal is made, and someone protests either the absence or the adequacy of the final impact statement." *Franklin*'s direct-effects-on-the-parties test, as applied to NEPA suits, may have to be reconciled with the portion of Kleppe v. Sierra Club just quoted. But there is no need to make the attempt in this case. It is enough to hold that regardless of whether the President's submission of NAFTA to Congress would be final action, there is no "final" action that can be attributed to an "agency."

NOTES & QUESTIONS

1. Environmental concerns were not entirely ignored while NAFTA was being negotiated. Indeed, they played a prominent role in the debate over NAFTA ratification. Few disagreed with the notion that NAFTA could have substantial environmental effects. The Bush administration prepared a Border Environmental Plan promising environmental cleanup measures along the U.S.-Mexican border. The ad-

ministration even solicited public comment on this plan before adopting in final form and it established an interagency review group to examine the environmental issues associated with NAFTA. Why then did the Bush Administration refuse to prepare an EIS for NAFTA?

2. Under the "fast track" provisions agreed to by Congress for treaty approval, Congress was required to vote on ratification of NAFTA without considering amendments within 90 legislative days of its transmittal by the President. When ruling on Public Citizen's first lawsuit in 1992, the D.C. refused to reach the merits of the group's NEPA claim on the ground that it was premature for the issue to be considered before an agreement actually was reached. Why do you think the government tried to avoid a decision on the merits of the plaintiff's NEPA claim? Did they gain anything by just postponing the litigation until after the agreement was finalized?

3. Does the D.C. Circuit ever decide whether NEPA requires preparation of an EIS for trade agreements? Under the D.C. Circuit's decision is there any way in which judicial review could be obtained for a claim that NEPA requires preparation of an EIS for a trade agreement? The court emphasizes that the "President has statutory discretion to exercise supervisory power over the agency's action." But doesn't the Constitution give the President supervisory power over all agency actions? Could the President avoid NEPA's EIS requirement by using this authority to require by executive order that all agency actions be submitted to him for final review and approval?

4. In his concurring opinion, is Judge Randolph suggesting that Congress, rather than the courts, is the appropriate institution for enforcing compliance with NEPA? Does this decision sound the "death knell" for legislative EISs?

5. After the Uruguay Round of GATT negotiations was finally concluded, Public Citizen again sued the U.S. Trade Representative. Relying on the D.C. Circuit's decision in Public Citizen v. U.S. Trade Representative, the district court held that judicial review is not available under the APA for NEPA claims relating to trade agreements. Public Citizen v. Kantor, 864 F. Supp. 208 (D.D.C. 1994).

Major Federal Action (pp. 1034-1035). Can a decision by a federal agency not to act trigger NEPA's requirements? Prior to 1990 the U.S. Forest Service used herbicides to control vegetation in the Lake States National Forests. In 1990, however, the Forest Service decided not to use herbicides. In Minnesota Pesticide Information and Education, Inc. v. Espy, 29 F.3d 442 (8th Cir. 1994), the Eighth Circuit held that the Forest Service was not required to prepare an EIS for deciding not to use herbicides. The court explained that "[t]his is not a decision to do something; rather it is a decision to *not* do something (namely, apply

8. Protection of Public Resources

herbicides), which does not trigger NEPA's requirements that an EIS be prepared." 29 F.3d at 443. The court explained that until the Forest Service actually decides upon an alternative method for controlling vegetation, "it has effectively elected a course of temporary inaction" to which NEPA does not apply.

In 1992 the U.S. government agreed to settle years of complex litigation against the Southern Florida Water Management District and the Florida Department of Environmental Regulation for contamination of a national wildlife refuge and a national park in the Everglades. The agreement requires the state to undertake remedial action to address the contamination and to restore the Everglades. In United States v. Southern Florida Water Management District, 28 F.3d 1563 (11th Cir. 1994), the Eleventh Circuit reversed a district court ruling that an EIS was required because of the federal government's participation in negotiating and implementing the settlement agreement. The Eleventh Circuit explained that a settlement "to compel a nonfederal party to undertake its legal responsibility does not convert the proposed state remedial measures into federal responsibilities for NEPA purposes." 28 F.3d at 1572. The court noted that NEPA obligations may arise in the future if federal agencies get involved in funding the restoration or issuing permits for activities undertaken to implement the settlement. But, it concluded, the mere fact that the federal government was involved in reaching the settlement was insufficient to trigger NEPA's requirements.

Significantly Affecting the Quality of the Environment (pp. 1050-1059). In Idaho v. I.C.C., 35 F.3d 585 (D.C. Cir. 1994), the D.C. Circuit held that the Interstate Commerce Commission had violated NEPA by failing to prepare an EIS before conditionally approving a proposal to abandon a portion of a railroad line. Even though it authorized salvage activities along a heavily contaminated track bed, the ICC had claimed that its decision would not significantly affect the environment because it required the railroad to consult with federal and state environmental agencies about the environmental effects of salvage operations. Citing its decision in *Calvert Cliffs* (text, p. 1025), the D.C. Circuit held that "[a]n agency cannot delegate its NEPA responsibilities in this manner," 35 F.3d at 595. The court concluded that the agency must take its own "hard look" at the environmental effects of its action, and cannot abdicate its NEPA responsibilities in favor of a regulated party.

Emergencies and the EIS Requirement (p. 1060). CEQ's regulations direct that when "emergency circumstances make it necessary to take an action with significant environmental impact without observing the provisions of these regulations, the Federal agency taking the action should consult with the Council about alternative arrangements." 40 C.F.R. §1506.11. Only "actions necessary to control the immediate impacts of the emergency" can be exempted from NEPA review. In October 1993 CEQ approved a proposal by the Department of Energy to permit an emergency shipment of 144 spent nuclear fuel rods to enter the United States from Belgium without preparing an EIS. Under the Reduced Enrichment for Research and Test Reactors program, the U.S. government has sought to promote nuclear nonproliferation by agreeing to reclaim used nuclear fuel provided by it to foreign countries who agree to stop using weapons-grade uranium.

While the Belgium government ultimately decided not to accept the U.S. offer to reclaim the fuel rods, a shipment of 153 fuel rods from other European reactors was allowed to enter the U.S. in September 1994. Over vigorous objections from the state of South Carolina, the Department of Energy shipped the fuel rods from Europe to its Savannah River nuclear reprocessing site. While South Carolina's efforts to block the shipment failed, in January 1995 a federal district court ruled that DOE violated NEPA by preparing only an environmental assessment and not a full EIS for such shipments. South Carolina v. O'Leary, No. 3:94-2419-0 (D.S.C. Jan. 27, 1995). The court has enjoined future shipments of spent fuel rods pending preparation of an EIS.

Is the EIS Adequate?: Consideration of Alternatives (pp. 1060-1067). In Resources Ltd., Inc. v. Robertson, 35 F.3d 1300 (9th Cir. 1993), the Ninth Circuit rejected a challenge to the adequacy of the analysis of alternatives in a forest-wide EIS prepared for a national forest land and resource management plan. While the plaintiffs argued that the Forest Service failed to consider timber harvest levels that were substantially lower than existing harvest levels, the court noted that five of the 17 alternatives considered included harvest levels more than 18 percent lower than existing levels. While no alternative in the plan allocated less than 75 percent of the harvest to cutting of even-aged trees, the court noted that there were relatively few stands of trees available that were suitable for uneven-aged cutting. "Alternatives that are unlikely to be implemented need not be considered," the court concluded. 35 F.3d at 1307.

Quality of the Analysis: Conservation Biology and the Ecosystems Approach (pp. 1060-1067). In 1990 a group of Wisconsin environmentalists and botanists launched an effort to use NEPA to improve the quality of the scientific analysis used by the Forest Service (FS). They sued the FS in an effort to require it to employ an ecosystems approach incorporating advanced principles of conservation biology when making forest management decisions to provide for diversity of plant and

8. Protection of Public Resources   Pages 1067-1074

animal communities. The plaintiffs argued that the FS should consider the relationships between differing landscape patterns and among various habitats rather than measuring vegetative diversity solely through analysis of the number of plants and animals and the variety of species in a given area. Because the size of a habitat tends to affect its chances of survival, the botanists argued that the FS should reserve larger, unfragmented tracts of forest rather than smaller, fragmented parcels. Despite presenting testimony from 13 highly distinguished scientists, the plaintiffs lost in the district court. The court found that "the agency's choice of methodology is entitled to considerable deference," and that the FS had not acted arbitrarily or capriciously. Sierra Club v. Marita, 845 F. Supp. 1317 (E.D. Wis. 1994), affd., 46 F.2d 606 (1995). See Versus a Lesson in Biodiversity Law, 264 Science 1078 (1994).

The botanists then took their case to the Seventh Circuit, which affirmed. Sierra Club v. Marita, 46 F.3d 606 (1995). The court noted that CEQ's regulations require agencies to insure the "scientific integrity" of their analyses, to use "high quality" science, and to integrate the natural and social sciences. However, the court found nothing in NEPA, the National Forest Management Act, or implementing regulations that dictates that the FS analyze diversity using any particular approach. Noting that the FS had considered, but rejected, using principles of conservation biology because of their uncertain application, the Seventh Circuit found that the FS had not acted arbitrarily or irrationally. The court refused to undertake a more detailed inquiry into the reliability of the Service's methodology under Daubert v. Merrell Dow Pharmaceuticals, Inc., 113 S. Ct. 2786 (1993), finding that "forcing an agency to make such a showing as a general rule is intrusive, undeferential, and not required." 46 F.3d at 622. The court concluded that "[t]he Service is entitled to use its own methodology, unless it is irrational," 46 F.3d at 621, and it upheld the agency's choice.

Adequacy of the Analysis in an EIS: Environmental Justice Concerns (pp. 1067-1074). As discussed in Chapter 1 of this Supplement, President Clinton's Executive Order 12,898 requires federal agencies to identify and to address disproportionate effects of their actions on minority and low-income populations. In October 1994 EPA challenged an EIS prepared by the Nuclear Regulatory Commission (NRC) that concluded that locating a uranium enrichment facility near a low-income, minority community in Louisiana would not raise environmental justice concerns. While the EIS incorporated demographic information about the parish where the facility would be located, EPA argued that it failed to analyze the demographic characteristics of the population in the immediate vicinity of the site and that it ignored the cumulative nature of the environmental burdens imposed on the community. Environmental Justice Concerns Caused EPA to Challenge Louisiana Uranium Plant's EIS, 25 Env. Rep. 1314 (1994). The Council on Environmental Quality is developing guidance to assist agencies in incorporating environmental justice concerns into their EISs.

"Tiering" (pp. 1078-1079). In Kelley v. Selin, 42 F.3d 1501 (6th Cir. 1995), the Sixth Circuit held that the Nuclear Regulatory Commission (NRC) had not violated NEPA by failing to prepare an EIS before approving the use of a new cask for dry storage of high-level radioactive waste at nuclear powerplants. Even though use of the new casks would enable utilities to expand significantly their capacity to store radioactive waste on-site, the court held that an EIS was not required because the NRC had conducted tiered analysis before approving the cask. Prior to approving use of the new cask, the NRC had prepared an environmental assessment (EA) finding that the new technology would have no significant impact on the environment. This finding was based in large part on the fact that EISs already had been prepared for each powerplant that would use the cask at the time the plant was licensed by the NRC. While plaintiffs argued that site-specific EAs should have been prepared, the court held that the NRC had properly relied on the prior site-specific EISs prepared for each plant as well as the NRC's previous generic analyses of the safety of on-site storage of radioactive waste.

NEPA Statistics: An Update (pp. 1081-1082). The Council on Environmental Quality reports that there were 512 EISs filed in 1992, an increase from the 456 filed in 1991. NEPA lawsuits decreased. A total of 81 NEPA cases were filed in 1992, a decline from 94 in 1991. Only five injunctions were issued. The most common complaint of litigants was a failure to prepare an EIS. Council on Environmental Quality, 24th Annual Report 350, 369 (1995).

B. CONSERVATION OF ENDANGERED SPECIES

Why Should We Conserve Endangered Species? (pp. 1085-1089). E. O. Wilson makes a powerful case for preserving endangered species in The Diversity of Life (1992).

Taxol (p. 1090). In December 1992, the Food and Drug Administration (FDA) approved the drug Taxol for treating advanced ovarian

8. Protection of Public Resources   Page 1103

cancer. Having developed an understanding of how taxol production occurs within the yew tree, researchers appear well on their way to being able to synthesize taxol using much smaller quantities of yew bark. Researchers Claim Way to Boost Taxol Output, Wall St. J., Apr. 15, 1992, at B5. Other scientists have discovered that taxol can be extracted from the leaves of a tree found widely in Himalayas, *Taxus baccata*, without killing the tree. Stipp, Himalayan Tree Could Serve as Source of Anti-Cancer Drug Taxol, Team Says, Wall St. J., Apr. 20, 1992, at B6. As a result, in December 1992 Bristol-Myers predicted that it would be able to produce all of its Taxol without using any Pacific yew bark by the year 1995. Leary, Drug Made from Rare Tree Is Approved to Treat Cancer, N.Y. Times, Dec. 30, 1992, at A10. In October 1994, the FDA approved a new, semi-synthetic version of Taxol that uses the Himalayan tree rather than the rare Pacific yew. New Version of Taxol Is Approved by FDA, N.Y. Times, Dec. 13, 1994, at C6. Environmentalists maintain that the Taxol experience demonstrates the importance of preserving endangered species.

The "God Squad" and the Spotted Owl (p. 1098). As noted in the text (p. 1135), in September 1991, Interior Secretary Manuel Lujan convened the God Squad to consider an exemption for 44 Bureau of Land Management timber sales in the habitat of the spotted owl. On May 15, 1992, the Committee approved an exemption for the BLM for 13 of 44 timber sales. It was the first exemption ever granted by the Committee. However, after losing the preliminary round of a lawsuit challenging the God Squad's decision, the Clinton Administration announced that it would not pursue the timber sales.

Species Listings (p. 1103). As of February 1995, there were 919 plants and animals on the endangered species list. The pace of species listing has accelerated in recent years due to a settlement the outgoing Bush Administration reached with environmentalists in December 1992. Under the terms of the settlement, the Interior Department agreed to propose listing 382 species "for which substantial information exists to warrant listing them as either endangered or threatened." The listing proposals were to be issued over a four-year period, which meant approximately 95 listings per year. Suggestions that the Bush Administration agreed to the settlement to create more political pressure to weaken the Endangered Species Act have been denied by former administration officials. Noah, Democrats Get Snared by GOP Pact on List of Endangered Species, Wall St. J., Feb. 17, 1995, at A1. However, the 104th Congress has responded to such pressures by passing an appropriations rider that forbids the Interior Department from listing any new species or designating critical habitat until the Endangered Species Act is reauthorized. Thus, despite the Interior Department's legal obligation to propose new species listings, Congress has placed a moratorium on them. Property Rights Measure Most Visible of Several Proposals to Curb Regulation, 25 Env. Rep. 2502, 2503 (1995).

What's Happened to Listed Species? (p. 1103). In March 1993, the Environmental Defense Fund released a report, Whatever Happened to the Class of '67?, that updated the status of the first endangered species list, released on March 11, 1967. The first list contained 78 species, all of which became subject to the comprehensive protections of the Endangered Species Act when it was enacted in 1973. The report found that most of the original species placed on the list had stable or increasing populations as a result of the ESA's protection. While 17 members of the initial class were still in decline, 44 had recovered or were improving. Eight of the species on the initial list had become extinct, but only three of those eight were still in existence when the ESA was enacted. Two species on the list (the gray whale and the American alligator) had fully recovered. Environmental Defense Fund, Whatever Happened to the Class of '67? 2 (1993). The report emphasized the importance of listing species early, before they reach such low numbers that recovery is virtually impossible. It noted that in recent years many species have been listed only after they have become so rare that their recovery is very doubtful (e.g., 39 Hawaiian plant species listed when 10 or fewer members of their species remained in existence). In June 1994 the American bald eagle was reclassified from "endangered" to "threatened" as a result of its remarkable recovery. During the 1960s, the eagle population had declined to a point where there were only 400 pairs of them in the lower 48 states. Today there are more than 8,000 pairs in the wild. Macintyre, American Eagle Soars Out of Danger's Reach, Times (London), June 30, 1994, at 14. While environmentalists point to the bald eagle's recovery as an example that the Endangered Species Act (ESA) is working, others argue that the high ratio of listings to delistings indicates that the Act is a failure.

By the end of 1994, the Fish and Wildlife Service had added 833 U.S. species to the original list of 122, while removing only 21 species. Seven of the species removed from the endangered species list were delisted because they had become extinct, though only one of these had a realistic chance of survival at the time of their listing. Another eight were removed from the list because they were discovered to exist in a wider range than previously thought. Mann & Plummer, Is Endangered Species Act in Danger? 267 Science 1256 (1995). Critics of the ESA claim that this track record is pitiful, while

8. Protection of Public Resources

environmentalists argue that it reflects tardy listings and an inadequate budget for enforcement.

Review of Federal Actions: Section 7 and Endangered Salmon (pp. 1103-1114). A dramatic decline in the stocks of salmon in the Pacific Northwest has resulted in the addition of five Pacific salmon species to the endangered species list during the past four years. As a result, federal and state agencies in the area are struggling to develop plans for protecting the salmon. In December 1994 the Northwest Power Planning Council approved a plan to require the release of more water from behind the dams at hydroelectric plants in order to help speed the passage of salmon. McCoy, Pacific Northwest Regulators Approve Plan to Cut Dam Power to Save Salmon, Wall St. J., Dec. 15, 1994, at B7. The plan is controversial because it will raise the cost of hydropower in the area. In January 1995 the National Marine Fisheries Service (NMFS) proposed a more modest strategy that would focus on making it easier for salmon to pass by dams through physical improvements in them, while conducting further study of the reservoir draw-down strategy. Kenworthy, Northwest Salmon Plan Is Outlined, Wash. Post, Jan. 26, 1995, at A3. Federal and state agencies are spending nearly $70 million to help restore critical habitat for salmon species. Stevens, Dwindling Salmon Spur West to Save Rivers, N.Y. Times, Nov. 15, 1994, at C1.

In Pacific Rivers Council v. Thomas, 30 F.3d 1050 (9th Cir. 1994), the Ninth Circuit required a district court to enjoin all federal logging, grazing, and road construction projects in two national forests pending consultations between the Forest Service and the National Marine Fisheries Services concerning efforts to protect the Snake River salmon. However, in Pacific Northwest Generating Cooperative v. Brown, 25 F.3d 1443 (9th Cir. 1994), the Ninth Circuit held that commercial and sport fishing for salmon could continue as an "incidental" taking because it was impossible to distinguish visually between listed and unlisted species of salmon.

An Ecosystem Approach to Species Management (p. 1114). In response to criticism that listing decisions are made too late to prevent development conflicts, Secretary of the Interior Bruce Babbitt has proposed a shift to an "ecosystem-wide" approach to species conservation. He explained that "[i]nstead of focusing on a single species, we have to look at the entire ecosystem and look at habitat management to prevent crisis." Interior to Take Ecosystem Approach to Species Management, Babbitt Tells Panel, 23 Env. Rep. 2728 (1993). The basic idea is to determine how to preserve entire ecosystems and the species that depend on them, rather than focusing on species-by-species protection.

In March 1993, Secretary Babbitt proposed to test this new policy by issuing a special rule under section 4(d) of the ESA to define circumstances under which certain land use activities that otherwise would violate section 9 by harming the California gnatcatcher could be permitted. 58 Fed. Reg. 16,758 (1993). Section 4(d) of the Act provides that when species are listed as threatened, special regulations can be issued to protect the species. The Interior Department is interpreting this to authorize the issuance of regulations designed to preserve healthy ecosystems to support the species, while permitting actions that otherwise would violate section 9 pursuant to conservation guidelines developed by a scientific review panel. The proposal was designed to support California's ecosystem planning effort, under which developers have agreed to make 200,000 acres off-limits to development while scientists map out the habitat of threatened species.

A federal district court has ordered the delisting of the California gnatcatcher because of concerns about the data relied upon by the Fish & Wildlife Service (FWS) in making its listing decision. When consultants for the building industry sought to review the data underlying the scientific report used as the basis for the listing, the author of the report refused to release the data. In Endangered Species Committee v. Babbitt, 852 F. Supp. 32 (D.D.C. 1994), the court held that it was arbitrary and capricious and a violation of the Administrative Procedure Act for the data to be withheld from public review and comment. The court, however, stayed its delisting order pending reconsideration of the listing by the FWS.

One obstacle to an "ecosystem-wide" approach to species conservation is that it is much easier for scientists to identify species than to identify ecosystems. To combat this problem, the Clinton Administration announced in April 1993 that the Interior Department would establish a National Biological Survey. The survey would seek to consolidate information about U.S. ecosystems in order to create an inventory of biodiversity that could assist policymakers in preventing future conflicts between development and species preservation. Yoon, Counting Creatures Great and Small, 260 Science 620 (1993). Many members of the new Republican majority in Congress have been critical of the ecosystem approach to species protection. While the Clinton Administration has renamed the National Biological Survey the National Biological Service, efforts to eliminate funding for virtually all scientific activities by the Interior Department are progressing in Congress. Cushman, Timber! A New Idea Is Crashing, N.Y. Times, Jan. 22, 1995, at E5.

Extraterritorial Application of the ESA (p. 1114). As mentioned above, nearly half of all species listed under the ESA are found only outside the United States. Extension of section 7 review to U.S. govern-

8. Protection of Public Resources   Pages 1114-1120

ment actions that might affect such species is thus not a trivial issue. In June 1992, the Supreme Court held in Lujan v. Defenders of Wildlife (see p. 275 of this Supplement) that Defenders lacked standing to challenge the Secretary of the Interior's decision that section 7 did not apply to actions outside the United States. The Court did not reach the merits of the controversy, though Justice Stevens in a separate opinion opined that Congress had not intended for the ESA to have extraterritorial application.

Protection Against Private Action: Section 9 (pp. 1114-1120). As noted in the parent text (p. 1114), one of the most important provisions of the Endangered Species Act adopted by Congress in 1973 is section 9(a)(1)(B), which makes it illegal for any person to "take" any endangered species of fish or wildlife listed under the Act. The Act defines "take" to mean "to harass, harm, pursue, hunt, shoot, wound, kill, trap, capture, or collect, or to attempt to engage in any such conduct." §3(19). Since virtually the inception of the Act, the U.S. Fish & Wildlife Service (FWS) has defined "take" to include "significant habitat modification or degradation where it actually kills or injures wildlife by significantly impairing essential behavioral patterns, including breeding, feeding or sheltering." 50 C.F.R. §17.3.

In July 1993 a D.C. Circuit panel narrowly rejected a facial challenge to this regulation by a 2-to-1 vote. Sweet Home Chapter of Communities for a Great Oregon v. Babbitt, 1 F.3d 1 (D.C. Cir. 1993), vacated on petition for rehearing, 17 F.3d 1463 (1994). Joining Judge Mikva in the majority, Judge Williams emphasized that the deciding factor in his vote to uphold the regulations was that Congress appeared to ratify the FWS's interpretation in 1982 by amending the Act to authorize the issuance of permits for incidental takings, including some habitat modification.

Six months later, however, Judge Williams changed his mind. In a surprising turnabout, the original panel granted a petition for rehearing and issued a new decision. Sweet Home Chapter of Communities for a Great Oregon v. Babbitt, 17 F.3d 1463 (D.C. Cir. 1994). Now writing for a 2-to-1 majority invalidating the regulations, Judge Williams held that they were facially invalid because the "harm" in the statutory language could not be interpreted to embrace habitat modifications. Invoking the principle of *noscitur a sociis* (that words are know by the company they keep), Judge Williams concluded that the Act forbade only actions that involve a substantially direct application of force against an animal and not habitat modifications that cause death or injury to a member of an endangered species. Judge Mikva dissented from the new decision.

After its petition for rehearing en banc was denied, the govern-

Pages 1114-1120   8. Protection of Public Resources

ment sought Supreme Court review, arguing that the Court's decision was inconsistent with the *Palila* case (text, pp. 1114-1120). The Court granted review and heard oral argument in the case in April 1995. In June 1995 the Court issued the following decision.

Babbitt v. Sweet Home Chapter of Communities for a Great Oregon
115 S. Ct. — (1995)

JUSTICE STEVENS delivered the opinion of the Court.

The Endangered Species Act of 1973, 87 Stat. 884, 16 U.S.C. §1531 (1988 ed. and Supp. V) (ESA or Act), contains a variety of protections designed to save from extinction species that the Secretary of the Interior designates as endangered or threatened. Section 9 of the Act makes it unlawful for any person to "take" any endangered or threatened species. The Secretary has promulgated a regulation that defines the statute's prohibition on takings to include "significant habitat modification or degradation where it actually kills or injures wildlife." This case presents the question whether the Secretary exceeded his authority under the Act by promulgating that regulation.

[handwritten: The Sec of I defined the term "harm" on its own, can the Dept of I do this?]

I

Section 9(a)(1) of the Endangered Species Act provides the following protection for endangered species:

> Except as provided in sections 1535(g)(2) and 1539 of this title, with respect to any endangered species of fish or wildlife listed pursuant to section 1533 of this title it is unlawful for any person subject to the jurisdiction of the United States to — . . .
> (B) take any such species within the United States or the territorial sea of the United States[.]" [16 U.S.C. §1538(a)(1).]

Section 3(19) of the Act defines the statutory term "take":

> The term "take" means to harass, harm, pursue, hunt, shoot, wound, kill, trap, capture, or collect, or to attempt to engage in any such conduct. [16 U.S.C. §1532(19).]

The Act does not further define the terms it uses to define "take." The Interior Department regulations that implement the statute, however, define the statutory term "harm":

8. Protection of Public Resources   Pages 1114-1120

Harm in the definition of "take" in the Act means an act which actually kills or injures wildlife. Such act may include significant habitat modification or degradation where it actually kills or injures wildlife by significantly impairing essential behavioral patterns, including breeding, feeding, or sheltering. [50 CFR §17.3 (1994).]

This regulation has been in place since 1975.[2]

A limitation on the §9 "take" prohibition appears in §10(a)(1)(B) of the Act, which Congress added by amendment in 1982. That section authorizes the Secretary to grant a permit for any taking otherwise prohibited by §9(a)(1)(B) "if such taking is incidental to, and not the purpose of, the carrying out of an otherwise lawful activity." 16 U.S.C. §1539(a)(1)(B).

In addition to the prohibition on takings, the Act provides several other protections for endangered species. Section 4, 16 U.S.C. §1533, commands the Secretary to identify species of fish or wildlife that are in danger of extinction and to publish from time to time lists of all species he determines to be endangered or threatened. Section 5, 16 U.S.C. §1534, authorizes the Secretary, in cooperation with the States, see 16 U.S.C. §1535, to acquire land to aid in preserving such species. Section 7 requires federal agencies to ensure that none of their activities, including the granting of licenses and permits, will jeopardize the continued existence of endangered species "or result in the destruction or adverse modification of habitat of such species which is determined by the Secretary . . . to be critical." 16 U.S.C. §1536(a)(2).

Respondents in this action are small landowners, logging companies, and families dependent on the forest products industries in the Pacific Northwest and in the Southeast, and organizations that represent their interests. They brought this declaratory judgment action against petitioners, the Secretary of the Interior and the Director of the Fish and Wildlife Service, in the United States District Court for the District of Columbia to challenge the statutory validity of the Secretary's regulation defining "harm," particularly the inclusion of habitat modification and degradation in the definition. Respondents challenged the regulation on its face. Their complaint alleged that application of the "harm" regulation to the red-cockaded woodpecker, an endangered species, and the northern spotted owl, a threatened species, had injured them economically. . . .

---

2. The Secretary, through the Director of the Fish and Wildlife Service, originally promulgated the regulation in 1975 and amended it in 1981 to emphasize that actual death or injury of a protected animal is necessary for a violation. See 40 Fed. Reg. 44,412, 44,416 (1975); 46 Fed. Reg. 54,748, 54,750 (1981).

473

Pages 1114-1120   8. Protection of Public Resources

II

Because this case was decided on motions for summary judgment, we may appropriately make certain factual assumptions in order to frame the legal issue. First, we assume respondents have no desire to harm either the red-cockaded woodpecker or the spotted owl; they merely wish to continue logging activities that would be entirely proper if not prohibited by the ESA. On the other hand, we must assume *arguendo* that those activities will have the effect, even though unintended, of detrimentally changing the natural habitat of both listed species and that, as a consequence, members of those species will be killed or injured. Under respondents' view of the law, the Secretary's only means of forestalling that grave result—even when the actor knows it is certain to occur[9]—is to use his §5 authority to purchase the lands on which the survival of the species depends. The Secretary, on the other hand, submits that the §9 prohibition on takings, which Congress defined to include "harm," places on respondents a duty to avoid harm that habitat alteration will cause the birds unless respondents first obtain a permit pursuant to §10.

The text of the Act provides three reasons for concluding that the Secretary's interpretation is reasonable. First, an ordinary understanding of the word "harm" supports it. The dictionary definition of the

---

9. As discussed above, the Secretary's definition of "harm" is limited to "acts which actually kill or injure wildlife." 50 CFR §17.3 (1994). In addition, in order to be subject to the Act's criminal penalties or the more severe of its civil penalties, one must "knowingly violate" the Act or its implementing regulations. 16 U.S.C. §§1540(a)(1), (b)(1). Congress added "knowingly" in place of "willfully" in 1978 to make "criminal violations of the act a general rather than a specific intent crime." H. R. Conf. Rep. No. 95-1804, p. 26 (1978). The Act does authorize up to a $500 civil fine for "any person who otherwise violates" the Act or its implementing regulations. 16 U.S.C. §1540(a)(1). That provision is potentially sweeping, but it would be so with or without the Secretary's "harm" regulation, making it unhelpful in assessing the reasonableness of the regulation. We have imputed scienter requirements to criminal statutes that impose sanctions without expressly requiring scienter, see, e.g., Staples v. United States, 511 U.S.—(1994), but the proper case in which we might consider whether to do so in the §9 provision for a $500 civil penalty would be a challenge to enforcement of that provision itself, not a challenge to a regulation that merely defines a statutory term. We do not agree with the dissent that the regulation covers results that are not "even foreseeable . . . no matter how long the chain of causality between modification and injury." Post, at 2. Respondents have suggested no reason why either the "knowingly violates" or the "otherwise violates" provision of the statute—or the "harm" regulation itself—should not be read to incorporate ordinary requirements of proximate causation and foreseeability. In any event, neither respondents nor their amici have suggested that the Secretary employs the "otherwise violates" provision with any frequency.

474

8. Protection of Public Resources — Pages 1114-1120

verb form of "harm" is "to cause hurt or damage to: injure." Webster's Third New International Dictionary 1034 (1966). In the context of the ESA, that definition naturally encompasses habitat modification that results in actual injury or death to members of an endangered or threatened species. Respondents argue that the Secretary should have limited the purview of "harm" to direct applications of force against protected species, but the dictionary definition does not include the word "directly" or suggest in any way that only direct or willful action that leads to injury constitutes "harm."[10] Moreover, unless the statutory term "harm" encompasses indirect as well as direct injuries, the word has no meaning that does not duplicate the meaning of other words that §3 uses to define "take." A reluctance to treat statutory terms as surplusage supports the reasonableness of the Secretary's interpretation. See, e.g., Mackey v. Lanier Collection Agency & Service, Inc., 486 U.S. 825, 837 (1988).[11]

Second, the broad purpose of the ESA supports the Secretary's decision to extend protection against activities that cause the precise harms Congress enacted the statute to avoid. In TVA v. Hill, 437 U.S. 153 (1978), we described the Act as "the most comprehensive legislation for the preservation of endangered species ever enacted by any nation." Id., at 180. Whereas predecessor statutes enacted in 1966 and 1969 had

---

10. Respondents and the dissent emphasize what they portray as the "established meaning" of "take" in the sense of a "wildlife take," a meaning respondents argue extends only to "the effort to exercise dominion over some creature, and the concrete effect of [sic] that creature." Brief for Respondents 19; see post, at 4-5. This limitation ill serves the statutory text, which forbids not taking "some creature" but "taking any [endangered] species"—a formidable task for even the most rapacious feudal lord. More importantly, Congress explicitly defined the operative term "take" in the ESA, no matter how much the dissent wishes otherwise, thereby obviating the need for us to probe its meaning as we must probe the meaning of the undefined subsidiary term "harm." Finally, Congress' definition of "take" includes several words—most obviously "harass," "pursue," and "wound," in addition to "harm" itself—that fit respondents' and the dissent's definition of "take" no better than does "significant habitat modification or degradation."

11. In contrast, if the statutory term "harm" encompasses such indirect means of killing and injuring wildlife as habitat modification, the other terms listed in §3—"harass," "pursue," "hunt," "shoot," "wound," "kill," "trap," "capture," and "collect"—generally retain independent meanings. Most of those terms refer to deliberate actions more frequently than does "harm," and they therefore do not duplicate the sense of indirect causation that "harm" adds to the statute. In addition, most of the other words in the definition describe either actions from which habitat modification does not usually result (e.g., "pursue," "harass") or effects to which activities that modify habitat do not usually lead (e.g., "trap," "collect"). To the extent the Secretary's definition of "harm" may have applications that overlap with other words in the definition, that overlap reflects the broad purpose of the Act. See infra, at 9-11.

475

not contained any sweeping prohibition against the taking of endangered species except on federal lands, see id., at 175, the 1973 Act applied to all land in the United States and to the Nation's territorial seas. As stated in §2 of the Act, among its central purposes is "to provide a means whereby the ecosystems upon which endangered species and threatened species depend may be conserved. . . ." 16 U.S.C. §1531(b).

In *Hill*, we construed §7 as precluding the completion of the Tellico Dam because of its predicted impact on the survival of the snail darter. See 437 U.S., at 193. Both our holding and the language in our opinion stressed the importance of the statutory policy. "The plain intent of Congress in enacting this statute," we recognized, "was to halt and reverse the trend toward species extinction, whatever the cost. This is reflected not only in the stated policies of the Act, but in literally every section of the statute." Id., at 184. Although the §9 "take" prohibition was not at issue in *Hill*, we took note of that prohibition, placing particular emphasis on the Secretary's inclusion of habitat modification in his definition of "harm." In light of that provision for habitat protection, we could "not understand how TVA intends to operate Tellico Dam without 'harming' the snail darter." Id., at 184, n. 30. Congress' intent to provide comprehensive protection for endangered and threatened species supports the permissibility of the Secretary's "harm" regulation.

Respondents advance strong arguments that activities that cause minimal or unforeseeable harm will not violate the Act as construed in the "harm" regulation. Respondents, however, present a facial challenge to the regulation. Thus, they ask us to invalidate the Secretary's understanding of "harm" in every circumstance, even when an actor knows that an activity, such as draining a pond, would actually result in the extinction of a listed species by destroying its habitat. Given Congress' clear expression of the ESA's broad purpose to protect endangered and threatened wildlife, the Secretary's definition of "harm" is reasonable.[13]

---

13. The dissent incorrectly asserts that the Secretary's regulation (1) "dispenses with the foreseeability of harm" and (2) "fails to require injury to particular animals." As to the first assertion, the regulation merely implements the statute, and it is therefore subject to the statute's "knowingly violates" language, see 16 U.S.C. §§1540(a)(1), (b)(1), and ordinary requirements of proximate causation and foreseeability. See n. 9, supra. Nothing in the regulation purports to weaken those requirements. To the contrary, the word "actually" in the regulation should be construed to limit the liability about which the dissent appears most concerned, liability under the statute's "otherwise violates" provision. See n. 9, supra. The Secretary did not need to include "actually" to connote "but for" causation, which the other words in the definition obviously require. As to the dissent's second assertion, every term in the

8. Protection of Public Resources
Pages 1114-1120

<u>Third</u>, the fact that Congress in 1982 authorized the Secretary to issue permits for takings that §9(a)(1)(B) would otherwise prohibit, "if such taking is incidental to, and not the purpose of, the carrying out of an otherwise lawful activity," 16 U.S.C. §1539(a)(1)(B), strongly suggests that Congress understood §9(a)(1)(B) to prohibit indirect as well as deliberate takings. The permit process requires the applicant to prepare a "conservation plan" that specifies how he intends to "minimize and mitigate" the "impact" of his activity on endangered and threatened species, 16 U.S.C. §1539(a)(2)(A), making clear that Congress had in mind foreseeable rather than merely accidental effects on listed species.[14] No one could seriously request an "incidental" take permit to avert §9 liability for direct, deliberate action against a member of an endangered or threatened species, but respondents would read "harm" so narrowly that the permit procedure would have little more than that absurd purpose. "When Congress acts to amend a statute, we presume it intends its amendment to have real and substantial effect." Stone v. INS, 514 U.S. —, — (1995). Congress' addition of the §10 permit provision supports the Secretary's conclusion that activities not intended to harm an endangered species, such as habitat modification, may constitute unlawful takings under the ESA unless the Secretary permits them.

The Court of Appeals made three errors in asserting that "harm" must refer to a direct application of force because the words around it do.[15] First, the court's premise was flawed. Several of the words that

---

regulation's definition of "harm" is subservient to the phrase "an act which actually kills or injures wildlife."

14. The dissent acknowledges the legislative history's clear indication that the drafters of the 1982 amendment had habitat modification in mind, but argues that the text of the amendment requires a contrary conclusion. This argument overlooks the statute's requirement of a "conservation plan," which must describe an alternative to a known, but undesired, habitat modification.

15. The dissent makes no effort to defend the Court of Appeals' reading of the statutory definition as requiring a direct application of force. Instead, it tries to impose on §9 a limitation of liability to "affirmative conduct intentionally directed against a particular animal or animals." Under the dissent's interpretation of the Act, a developer could drain a pond, knowing that the act would extinguish an endangered species of turtles, without even proposing a conservation plan or applying for a permit under §9(a)(1)(B); unless the developer was motivated by a desire "to get at a turtle," no statutory taking could occur. Because such conduct would not constitute a taking at common law, the dissent would shield it from §9 liability, even though the words "kill" and "harm" in the statutory definition could apply to such deliberate conduct. We cannot accept that limitation. In any event, our reasons for rejecting the Court of Appeals' interpretation apply as well to the dissent's novel construction.

accompany "harm" in the §3 definition of "take," especially "harass," "pursue," "wound," and "kill," refer to actions or effects that do not require direct applications of force. Second, to the extent the court read a requirement of intent or purpose into the words used to define "take," it ignored §9's express provision that a "knowing" action is enough to violate the Act. Third, the court employed *noscitur a sociis* to give "harm" essentially the same function as other words in the definition, thereby denying it independent meaning. The canon, to the contrary, counsels that a word "gathers meaning from the words around it." Jarecki v. G. D. Searle & Co., 367 U.S. 303, 307 (1961). The statutory context of "harm" suggests that Congress meant that term to serve a particular function in the ESA, consistent with but distinct from the functions of the other verbs used to define "take." The Secretary's interpretation of "harm" to include indirectly injuring endangered animals through habitat modification permissibly interprets "harm" to have "a character of its own not to be submerged by its association." Russell Motor Car Co. v. United States, 261 U.S. 514, 519 (1923).[16]

Nor does the Act's inclusion of the §5 land acquisition authority and the §7 directive to federal agencies to avoid destruction or adverse modification of critical habitat alter our conclusion. Respondents' argument that the Government lacks any incentive to purchase land under §5 when it can simply prohibit takings under §9 ignores the practical considerations that attend enforcement of the ESA. Purchasing habitat lands may well cost the Government less in many circumstances than pursuing civil or criminal penalties. In addition, the §5 procedure allows for protection of habitat before the seller's activity has harmed any endangered animal, whereas the Government cannot enforce the §9 prohibition until an animal has actually been killed or injured. The Secretary may also find the §5 authority useful for preventing modification of land that is not yet but may in the future become habitat for an endangered or threatened species. The §7 directive applies only to the Federal Government, whereas the §9 prohibition applies to "any person." Section 7 imposes a broad, affirmative duty to avoid adverse

---

16. Respondents' reliance on United States v. Hayashi, 22 F.3d 859 (CA9 1993) is also misplaced. *Hayashi* construed the term "harass," part of the definition of "take" in the Marine Mammal Protection Act of 1972, 16 U.S.C. §1361 et seq., as requiring a "direct intrusion" on wildlife to support a criminal prosecution. 22 F.3d, at 864. *Hayashi* dealt with a challenge to a single application of a statute whose "take" definition includes neither "harm" nor several of the other words that appear in the ESA definition. Moreover, *Hayashi* was decided by a panel of the Ninth Circuit, the same court that had previously upheld the regulation at issue here in Palila v. Hawaii Dept. of Land and Natural Resources, 852 F.2d 1106 (1988) *(Palila II)*. Neither the *Hayashi* majority nor the dissent saw any need to distinguish or even to cite *Palila II*.

habitat modifications that §9 does not replicate, and §7 does not limit its admonition to habitat modification that "actually kills or injures wildlife." Conversely, §7 contains limitations that §9 does not, applying only to actions "likely to jeopardize the continued existence of any endangered species or threatened species," 16 U.S.C. §1536(a)(2), and to modifications of habitat that has been designated "critical" pursuant to §4, 16 U.S.C. §1533(b)(2). Any overlap that §5 or §7 may have with §9 in particular cases is unexceptional, and simply reflects the broad purpose of the Act set out in §2 and acknowledged in *TVA v. Hill.*

We need not decide whether the statutory definition of "take" compels the Secretary's interpretation of "harm," because our conclusions that Congress did not unambiguously manifest its intent to adopt respondents' view and that the Secretary's interpretation is reasonable suffice to decide this case. See generally Chevron U.S.A. Inc. v. Natural Resources Defense Council, Inc., 467 U.S. 837 (1984). The latitude the ESA gives the Secretary in enforcing the statute, together with the degree of regulatory expertise necessary to its enforcement, establishes that we owe some degree of deference to the Secretary's reasonable interpretation. See Breyer, Judicial Review of Questions of Law and Policy, 38 Admin. L. Rev. 363, 373 (1986).

III

Our conclusion that the Secretary's definition of "harm" rests on a permissible construction of the ESA gains further support from the legislative history of the statute. The Committee Reports accompanying the bills that became the ESA do not specifically discuss the meaning of "harm," but they make clear that Congress intended "take" to apply broadly to cover indirect as well as purposeful actions. The Senate Report stressed that " 'take' is defined . . . in the broadest possible manner to include every conceivable way in which a person can 'take' or attempt to 'take' any fish or wildlife." S. Rep. No. 93-307, p. 7 (1973). The House Report stated that "the broadest possible terms" were used to define restrictions on takings. H. R. Rep. No. 93-412, p. 15 (1973). The House Report underscored the breadth of the "take" definition by noting that it included "harassment, *whether intentional or not.*" Id., at 11 (emphasis added). The Report explained that the definition "would allow, for example, the Secretary to regulate or prohibit the activities of birdwatchers where the effect of those activities might disturb the birds and make it difficult for them to hatch or raise their young." Ibid. These comments, ignored in the dissent's welcome but selective foray into legislative history, support the Secretary's interpretation that the term "take" in §9 reached far more than the deliberate actions of hunters and trappers. . . .

The history of the 1982 amendment that gave the Secretary authority to grant permits for "incidental" takings provides further support for his reading of the Act. The House Report expressly states that "by use of the word 'incidental' the Committee intends to cover situations in which it is known that a taking will occur if the other activity is engaged in but such taking is incidental to, and not the purpose of, the activity." H. R. Rep. No. 97-567, p. 31 (1982). This reference to the foreseeability of incidental takings undermines respondents' argument that the 1982 amendment covered only accidental killings of endangered and threatened animals that might occur in the course of hunting or trapping other animals. Indeed, Congress had habitat modification directly in mind: both the Senate Report and the House Conference Report identified as the model for the permit process a cooperative state-federal response to a case in California where a development project threatened incidental harm to a species of endangered butterfly by modification of its habitat. See S. Rep. No. 97-418, p. 10 (1982); H. R. Conf. Rep. No. 97-835, pp. 30-32 (1982). Thus, Congress in 1982 focused squarely on the aspect of the "harm" regulation at issue in this litigation. Congress' implementation of a permit program is consistent with the Secretary's interpretation of the term "harm."

IV

When it enacted the ESA, Congress delegated broad administrative and interpretive power to the Secretary. See 16 U.S.C. §§1533, 1540(f). The task of defining and listing endangered and threatened species requires an expertise and attention to detail that exceeds the normal province of Congress. Fashioning appropriate standards for issuing permits under §10 for takings that would otherwise violate §9 necessarily requires the exercise of broad discretion. The proper interpretation of a term such as "harm" involves a complex policy choice. When Congress has entrusted the Secretary with broad discretion, we are especially reluctant to substitute our views of wise policy for his. See *Chevron*, 467 U.S., at 865-866. In this case, that reluctance accords with our conclusion, based on the text, structure, and legislative history of the ESA, that the Secretary reasonably construed the intent of Congress when he defined "harm" to include "significant habitat modification or degradation that actually kills or injures wildlife."

In the elaboration and enforcement of the ESA, the Secretary and all persons who must comply with the law will confront difficult questions of proximity and degree; for, as all recognize, the Act encompasses a vast range of economic and social enterprises and endeavors. These questions must be addressed in the usual course of the law, through case-by-case resolution and adjudication.

The judgment of the Court of Appeals is reversed.

JUSTICE O'CONNOR, concurring.

My agreement with the Court is founded on two understandings. First, the challenged regulation is limited to significant habitat modification that causes actual, as opposed to hypothetical or speculative, death or injury to identifiable protected animals. Second, even setting aside difficult questions of scicnter, the regulation's application is limited by ordinary principles of proximate causation, which introduce notions of foreseeability. These limitations, in my view, call into question Palila v. Hawaii Dept. of Land and Natural Resources, 852 F.2d 1106 (CA9 1988) (*Palila II*), and with it, many of the applications derided by the dissent. Because there is no need to strike a regulation on a facial challenge out of concern that it is susceptible of erroneous application, however, and because there are many habitat-related circumstances in which the regulation might validly apply, I join the opinion of the Court.

In my view, the regulation is limited by its terms to actions that actually kill or injure individual animals. Justice Scalia disagrees, arguing that the harm regulation "encompasses injury inflicted, not only upon individual animals, but upon populations of the protected species." At one level, I could not reasonably quarrel with this observation; death to an individual animal always reduces the size of the population in which it lives, and in that sense, "injures" that population. But by its insight, the dissent means something else. Building upon the regulation's use of the word "breeding," Justice Scalia suggests that the regulation facially bars significant habitat modification that actually kills or injures *hypothetical* animals (or, perhaps more aptly, causes potential additions to the population not to come into being). Because "impairment of breeding does not 'injure' living creatures," Justice Scalia reasons, the regulation *must* contemplate application to "a *population* of animals which would otherwise have maintained or increased its numbers."

I disagree. As an initial matter, I do not find it as easy as Justice Scalia does to dismiss the notion that significant impairment of breeding injures living creatures. To raze the last remaining ground on which the piping plover currently breeds, thereby making it impossible for any piping plovers to reproduce, would obviously injure the population (causing the species' extinction in a generation). But by completely preventing breeding, it would also injure the individual living bird, in the same way that sterilizing the creature injures the individual living bird. To "injure" is, among other things, "to impair." Webster's Ninth

New Collegiate Dictionary 623 (1983). One need not subscribe to theories of "psychic harm" to recognize that to make it impossible for an animal to reproduce is to impair its most essential physical functions and to render that animal, and its genetic material, biologically obsolete. This, in my view, is actual injury. . . .

By the dissent's reckoning, the regulation at issue here, in conjunction with 16 U.S.C. §1540(1), imposes liability for any habitat-modifying conduct that ultimately results in the death of a protected animal, "regardless of whether that result is intended or even foreseeable, and no matter how long the chain of causality between modification and injury." Even if §1540(1) does create a strict liability regime (a question we need not decide at this juncture), I see no indication that Congress, in enacting that section, intended to dispense with ordinary principles of proximate causation. Strict liability means liability without regard to fault; it does not normally mean liability for every consequence, however remote, of one's conduct. See generally W. Keeton, D. Dobbs, R. Keeton, & D. Owen, Prosser and Keeton on Law of Torts 559-560 (5th ed. 1984) (describing "practical necessity for the restriction of liability within some reasonable bounds" in the strict liability context). I would not lightly assume that Congress, in enacting a strict liability statute that is silent on the causation question, has dispensed with this well-entrenched principle. In the absence of congressional abrogation of traditional principles of causation, then, private parties should be held liable under §1540(1) only if their habitat-modifying actions proximately cause death or injury to protected animals. Cf. Benefiel v. Exxon Corp., 959 F 2d 805, 807-808 (CA9 1992) (in enacting the Trans-Alaska Pipeline Authorization Act, which provides for strict liability for damages that are the result of discharges, Congress did not intend to abrogate common-law principles of proximate cause to reach "remote and derivative" consequences); New York v. Shore Realty Corp., 759 F.2d 1032, 1044, and n. 17 (CA2 1985) (noting that "traditional tort law has often imposed strict liability while recognizing a causation defense," but that, in enacting CERCLA, Congress "specifically rejected including a causation requirement"). The regulation, of course, does not contradict the presumption or notion that ordinary principles of causation apply here. Indeed, by use of the word "actually," the regulation clearly rejects speculative or conjectural effects, and thus itself invokes principles of proximate causation.

Proximate causation is not a concept susceptible of precise definition. See Keeton, supra, at 280-281. It is easy enough, of course, to identify the extremes. The farmer whose fertilizer is lifted by tornado from tilled fields and deposited miles away in a wildlife refuge cannot, by any stretch of the term, be considered the proximate cause of death or injury to protected species occasioned thereby. At the same time,

8. Protection of Public Resources   Pages 1114-1120

the landowner who drains a pond on his property, killing endangered fish in the process, would likely satisfy any formulation of the principle. We have recently said that proximate causation "normally eliminates the bizarre," Jerome B. Grubart, Inc. v. Great Lakes Dredge & Dock Co., 513 U.S. —, — (1995), and have noted its "functionally equivalent" alternative characterizations in terms of foreseeability, see Milwaukee & St. Paul R. Co. v. Kellogg, 94 U.S. 469, 475 (1877) ("natural and probable consequence"), and duty, see Palsgraf v. Long Island R. Co., 162 N.E. 99 (1928). Consolidated Rail Corp. v. Gottshall, 512 U.S. —, — (1994). Proximate causation depends to a great extent on considerations of the fairness of imposing liability for remote consequences. The task of determining whether proximate causation exists in the limitless fact patterns sure to arise is best left to lower courts. But I note, at the least, that proximate cause principles inject a foreseeability element into the statute, and hence, the regulation, that would appear to alleviate some of the problems noted by the dissent. See, e.g., infra (describing "a farmer who tills his field and causes erosion that makes silt run into a nearby river which depletes oxygen and thereby [injures] protected fish").

In my view, then, the "harm" regulation applies where significant habitat modification, by impairing essential behaviors, proximately (foreseeably) causes actual death or injury to identifiable animals that are protected under the Endangered Species Act. Pursuant to my interpretation, *Palila II*—under which the Court of Appeals held that a state agency committed a "taking" by permitting feral sheep to eat mamanenaio seedlings that, when full-grown, might have fed and sheltered endangered palila—was wrongly decided according to the regulation's own terms. Destruction of the seedlings did not proximately cause actual death or injury to identifiable birds; it merely prevented the regeneration of forest land not currently inhabited by actual birds. . . .

JUSTICE SCALIA, with whom THE CHIEF JUSTICE and JUSTICE THOMAS join, dissenting.

I think it unmistakably clear that the legislation at issue here (1) forbade the hunting and killing of endangered animals, and (2) provided federal lands and federal funds *for the acquisition of private lands,* to preserve the habitat of endangered animals. The Court's holding that the hunting and killing prohibition incidentally preserves habitat on private lands imposes unfairness to the point of financial ruin—not just upon the rich, but upon the simplest farmer who finds his land conscripted to national zoological use. I respectfully dissent. . . .

The regulation has three features which, for reasons I shall discuss at length below, do not comport with the statute. First, it interprets the statute to prohibit habitat modification that is no more than the cause-

483

in-fact of death or injury to wildlife. Any "significant habitat modification" that in fact produces that result by "impairing essential behavioral patterns" is made unlawful, regardless of whether that result is intended or even foreseeable, and no matter how long the chain of causality between modification and injury. See, e.g., Palila v. Hawaii Dept. of Land and Natural Resources (*Palila II*), 852 F.2d 1106, 1108-1109 (CA9 1988) (sheep grazing constituted "taking" of palila birds, since although sheep do not destroy full-grown mamane trees, they do destroy mamane seedlings, which will not grow to full-grown trees, on which the palila feeds and nests). See also Davison, Alteration of Wildlife Habitat as a Prohibited Taking under the Endangered Species Act, 10 J. Land Use & Envtl. L. 155, 190 (1995) (regulation requires only causation-in-fact).

Second, the regulation does not require an "act": the Secretary's officially stated position is that an omission will do. The previous version of the regulation made this explicit. See 40 Fed. Reg. 44,412, 44,416 (1975) (" 'Harm' in the definition of 'take' in the Act means an act or omission which actually kills or injures wildlife . . ."). When the regulation was modified in 1981 the phrase "or omission" was taken out, but only because (as the final publication of the rule advised) "the [Fish and Wildlife] Service feels that 'act' is inclusive of either commissions or omissions which would be prohibited by section [1538(a)(1)(B)]." 46 Fed. Reg. 54,748, 54,750 (1981). In its brief here the Government agrees that the regulation covers omissions, see Brief for Petitioners 47 (although it argues that "an 'omission' constitutes an 'act' . . . only if there is a legal duty to act"), ibid.

The third and most important unlawful feature of the regulation is that it encompasses injury inflicted, not only upon individual animals, but upon populations of the protected species. "Injury" in the regulation includes "significantly impairing essential behavioral patterns, including *breeding*," 50 CFR §17.3 (1994) (emphasis added). Impairment of breeding does not "injure" living creatures; it prevents them from propagating, thus "injuring" a *population* of animals which would otherwise have maintained or increased its numbers. What the face of the regulation shows, the Secretary's official pronouncements confirm. The Final Redefinition of "Harm" accompanying publication of the regulation said that "harm" is not limited to "direct physical injury to an individual member of the wildlife species," 46 Fed. Reg. 54,748 (1981), and refers to "injury to a *population*," id., at 54,749 (emphasis added).

None of these three features of the regulation can be found in the statutory provisions supposed to authorize it. The term "harm" in §1532(19) has no legal force of its own. An indictment or civil complaint that charged the defendant with "harming" an animal protected under the Act would be dismissed as defective, for the only operative term in the statute is to "take." If "take" were not elsewhere defined in the

8. Protection of Public Resources   Pages 1114-1120

Act, none could dispute what it means, for the term is as old as the law itself. To "take," when applied to wild animals, means to reduce those animals, by killing or capturing, to human control. See, e.g., 11 Oxford English Dictionary (1933) ("Take . . . To catch, capture (a wild beast, bird, fish, etc.)"); Webster's New International Dictionary of the English Language (2d ed. 1949) (take defined as "to catch or capture by trapping, snaring, etc., or as prey"); Geer v. Connecticut, 161 U.S. 519, 523 (1896) ("All the animals which can be taken upon the earth, in the sea, or in the air, that is to say, wild animals, belong to those who take them") (quoting the Digest of Justinian); 2 W. Blackstone, Commentaries 411 (1766) ("Every man . . . has an equal right of pursuing and taking to his own use all such creatures as are *ferae naturae*"). This is just the sense in which "take" is used elsewhere in federal legislation and treaty. See, e.g., Migratory Bird Treaty Act, 16 U.S.C. §703 (1988 ed., Supp. V) (no person may "pursue, hunt, take, capture, kill, [or] attempt to take, capture, or kill" any migratory bird); Agreement on the Conservation of Polar Bears, Nov. 15, 1973, Art. I, 27 U.S.T. 3918, 3921, T.I.A.S. No. 8409 (defining "taking" as "hunting, killing and capturing"). And that meaning fits neatly with the rest of §1538(a)(1), which makes it unlawful not only to take protected species, but also to import or export them (§1538(a)(1)(A)); to possess, sell, deliver, carry, transport, or ship any taken species (§1538(a)(1)(D)); and to transport, sell, or offer to sell them in interstate or foreign commerce (§§1538(a)(1)(E), (F). The taking prohibition, in other words, is only part of the regulatory plan of §1538(a)(1), which covers all the stages of the process by which protected wildlife is reduced to man's dominion and made the object of profit. It is obvious that "take" in this sense—a term of art deeply embedded in the statutory and common law concerning wildlife—describes a class of acts (not omissions) done directly and intentionally (not indirectly and by accident) to particular animals (not populations of animals). . . .

The verb "harm" has a *range* of meaning: "to cause injury" at its broadest, "to do hurt or damage" in a narrower and more direct sense. See, e.g., 1 N. Webster, An American Dictionary of the English Language (1828) ("Harm, v.t. To hurt; to injure; to damage; *to impair soundness of body, either animal* or vegetable") (emphasis added); American College Dictionary 551 (1970) ("harm . . . n. injury; damage; hurt: *to do him bodily harm*"). In fact the more directed sense of "harm" is a somewhat more common and preferred usage; "*harm* has in it a little of the idea of specially focused hurt or injury, as if a personal injury has been anticipated and intended." J. Opdycke, Mark My Words: A Guide to Modern Usage and Expression 330 (1949). See also American Heritage Dictionary of the English Language (1981) ("*Injure* has the widest range. . . . *Harm* and *hurt* refer principally to what causes physical or mental distress to living things"). To define "harm" as an act or omission that, however remotely, "actually kills or injures" a population of wildlife through habitat modification, is to choose a meaning that makes nonsense of the word that "harm" defines—requiring us to accept that a farmer who tills his field and causes erosion that makes silt run into a nearby river which depletes oxygen and thereby "impairs [the] breeding" of protected fish, has "taken" or "attempted to take" the fish. It should take the strongest evidence to make us believe that Congress has defined a term in a manner repugnant to its ordinary and traditional sense.

Here the evidence shows the opposite. "Harm" is merely one of 10 prohibitory words in §1532(19), and the other 9 fit the ordinary meaning of "take" perfectly. To "harass, pursue, hunt, shoot, wound, kill, trap, capture, or collect" are all affirmative acts (the provision itself describes them as "conduct," see §1532(19)) which are directed immediately and intentionally against a particular animal—not acts or omissions that indirectly and accidentally cause injury to a population of animals. The Court points out that several of the words ("harass," "pursue," "wound," and "kill") "refer to actions or effects that do not require direct *applications of force.*" Ante, at 13 (emphasis added). That is true enough, but force is not the point. Even "taking" activities in the narrowest sense, activities traditionally engaged in by hunters and trappers, do not all consist of direct applications of force; pursuit and harassment are part of the business of "taking" the prey even before it has been touched. What the nine other words in §1532(19) have in common—and share with the narrower meaning of "harm" described above, but not with the Secretary's ruthless dilation of the word—is the sense of affirmative conduct intentionally directed against a particular animal or animals. . . .

[T]he Court's contention that "harm" in the narrow sense adds nothing to the other words underestimates the ingenuity of our own species in a way that Congress did not. To feed an animal poison, to spray it with mace, to chop down the very tree in which it is nesting, or even to destroy its entire habitat in order to take it (as by draining a pond to get at a turtle), might neither wound nor kill, but would directly and intentionally harm.

The penalty provisions of the Act counsel this interpretation as well. Any person who "knowingly" violates §1538(a)(1)(B) is subject to criminal penalties under §1540(b)(1) and civil penalties under §1540(a)(1); moreover, under the latter section, any person "who otherwise violates" the taking prohibition (i.e., violates it *un*knowingly) may be assessed a civil penalty of $500 for each violation, with the stricture that "each such violation shall be a separate offense." This last provision should be clear warning that the regulation is in error, for when com-

8. Protection of Public Resources — Pages 1114-1120

bined with the regulation it produces a result that no legislature could reasonably be thought to have intended: A large number of routine private activities—farming, for example, ranching, roadbuilding, construction and logging—are subjected to strict-liability penalties when they fortuitously injure protected wildlife, no matter how remote the chain of causation and no matter how difficult to foresee (or to disprove) the "injury" may be (e.g., an "impairment" of breeding). The Court says that "[the strict-liability provision] is potentially sweeping, but it would be so with or without the Secretary's 'harm' regulation." Ante, at 8, n. 9. That is not correct. Without the regulation, the routine "habitat modifying" activities that people conduct to make a daily living would not carry exposure to strict penalties; only acts directed at animals, like those described by the other words in §1532(19), would risk liability.

The Court says that "[to] read a requirement of intent or purpose into the words used to define 'take' . . . ignores [§1540's] express provision that a 'knowing' action is enough to violate the Act." Ante, at 13. This presumably means that because the reading of §1532(19) advanced here ascribes an element of purposeful injury to the prohibited acts, it makes superfluous (or inexplicable) the more severe penalties provided for a "knowing" violation. That conclusion does not follow, for it is quite possible to take protected wildlife purposefully without doing so knowingly. A requirement that a violation be "knowing" means that the defendant must "know the facts that make his conduct illegal," Staples v. United States, 511 U.S. —, — (1994). The hunter who shoots an elk in the mistaken belief that it is a mule deer has not knowingly violated §1538(a)(1)(B)—not because he does not know that elk are legally protected (that would be knowledge of the law, which is not a requirement, see ante, at 8, n. 9), but because he does not know what sort of animal he is shooting. The hunter has nonetheless committed a purposeful taking of protected wildlife, and would therefore be subject to the (lower) strict-liability penalties for the violation. . . .

[T]he Court seeks support from a provision which was added to the Act in 1982, the year after the Secretary promulgated the current regulation. The provision states:

> "The Secretary may permit, under such terms and conditions as he shall prescribe—. . . "any taking otherwise prohibited by section 1538(a)(1)(B) . . . if such taking is incidental to, and not the purpose of, the carrying out of an otherwise lawful activity." [16 U.S.C. §1539(a)(1)(B).]

This provision does not, of course, implicate our doctrine that reenactment of a statutory provision ratifies an extant judicial or ad-

487

ministrative interpretation, for neither the taking prohibition in §1538(a)(1)(B) nor the definition in §1532(19) was reenacted. See Central Bank of Denver, N. A. v. First Interstate Bank of Denver, N. A., 511 U.S. —, — (1994). The Court claims, however, that the provision "strongly suggests that Congress understood [§1538(a)(1)(B)] to prohibit indirect as well as deliberate takings." Ante, at 12. That would be a valid inference if habitat modification were the only substantial "otherwise lawful activity" that might incidentally and nonpurposefully cause a prohibited "taking." Of course it is not. This provision applies to the many otherwise lawful takings that incidentally take a protected species—as when fishing for unprotected salmon also takes an endangered species of salmon, see Pacific Northwest Generating Cooperative v. Brown, 38 F.3d 1058, 1067 (CA9 1994). Congress has referred to such "incidental takings" in other statutes as well—for example, a statute referring to "the incidental taking of . . . sea turtles in the course of . . . harvesting [shrimp]" and to the "rate of incidental taking of sea turtles by United States vessels in the course of such harvesting," 103 Stat. 1038 §609(b)(2), note following 16 U.S.C. §1537 (1988 ed., Supp. V); and a statute referring to "the incidental taking of marine mammals in the course of commercial fishing operations," 108 Stat. 546, §118(a). The Court shows that it misunderstands the question when it says that "no one could seriously request an 'incidental' take permit to avert . . . liability for direct, deliberate action *against a member of an endangered or threatened species.*" Ante, at 12-13 (emphasis added). That is not an *incidental* take at all. . . .

[T]he Court and the concurrence suggest that the regulation should be read to contain a requirement of proximate causation or foreseeability, principally *because the statute does*—and "nothing in the regulation purports to weaken those requirements [of the statute]." See ante, at 8, n. 9; 11-12, n. 13; see also ante, at 4-6 (O'Connor, J., concurring). I quite agree that the statute contains such a limitation, because the verbs of purpose in §1538(a)(1)(B) denote action directed at animals. *But the Court has rejected that reading.* The critical premise on which it has upheld the regulation is that, despite the weight of the other words in §1538(a)(1)(B), "the statutory term 'harm' encompasses indirect as well as direct injuries," ante, at 9. See also ante, at 9-10, n. 11 (describing "the sense of indirect causation that 'harm' adds to the statute"); ante, at 14 (stating that the Secretary permissibly interprets " 'harm' " to include "indirectly injuring endangered animals"). Consequently, unless there is some strange category of causation that is indirect and yet also proximate, the Court has already rejected its own basis for finding a proximate-cause limitation in the regulation. In fact "proximate" causation simply *means* "direct" causation. See, e.g., Black's Law Dictionary 1103 (5th ed. 1979) (defining "proximate" as

8. Protection of Public Resources Pages 1114-1120

"Immediate; nearest; *direct*") (emphasis added); Webster's New International Dictionary of the English Language 1995 (2d ed. 1949) ("proximate cause. A cause which *directly,* or with no mediate agency, produces an effect") (emphasis added). The only other reason given for finding a proximate-cause limitation in the regulation is that "by use of the word 'actually,' the regulation clearly rejects speculative or conjectural effects, and thus itself invokes principles of proximate causation." Ante, at 5 (O'Connor, J., concurring); see also ante, at 11-12, n. 13 (majority opinion). *Non sequitur,* of course. That the injury must be "actual" as opposed to "potential" simply says nothing at all about the length or foreseeability of the causal chain between the habitat modification and the "actual" injury. It is thus true and irrelevant that "the Secretary did not need to include 'actually' to connote 'but for' causation," ante, at 11-12, n. 13; "actually" defines the requisite *injury,* not the requisite *causality.* The regulation says (it is worth repeating) that "harm" means (1) an act which (2) actually kills or injures wildlife. If that does not dispense with a proximate-cause requirement, I do not know what language would. And changing the regulation by judicial invention, even to achieve compliance with the statute, is not permissible. . . .

But since the Court is reading the regulation and the statute incorrectly in other respects, it may as well introduce this novelty as well—law a la carte. As I understand the regulation that the Court has created and held consistent with the statute that it has also created, habitat modification can constitute a "taking," but only if it results in the killing or harming of *individual animals,* and only if that consequence is the direct result of the modification. This means that the destruction of privately owned habitat that is essential, not for the feeding or nesting, but for the *breeding,* of butterflies, would not violate the Act, since it would not harm or kill any living butterfly. I, too, think it would not violate the Act—not for the utterly unsupported reason that habitat modifications fall outside the regulation if they happen not to kill or injure a living animal, but for the textual reason that only action directed at living animals constitutes a "take."

NOTES & QUESTIONS

1. Justice Scalia argues that the Interior Department regulation defining "harm" is unlawfully broad because it prohibits any habitat modification that is the cause-in-fact of injury or death to wildlife, omissions as well as acts, and acts that impair breeding. How does the majority's interpretation of the regulation differ from Justice Scalia's. Is *Palila II* still good law under the majority's interpretation?

2. In light of the Court's decision, what must the government

prove to establish a violation of §9(a)(1)(B)'s prohibition on takings? Must the government prove that the defendant's actions actually resulted in the death or injury of a particular member of an endangered species? If so, must the harm that actually occurred have been foreseeable at the time of the defendent's act? How direct must the chain of causation be between the defendant's act and the injury to the endangered species?

3. United States v. Hayashi, 22 F.3d 859 (9th Cir. 1993), involved an appeal of a conviction under the Marine Mammal Protection Act of a fisherman who fired a rifle at porpoises to scare them away from eating tuna on his line. As the Court notes in footnote 16, while the Marine Mammal Protection Act prohibits the taking of marine mammals in U.S. waters, 16 U.S.C. §1372(a)(2)(A), the Act does not include "harm" in the definition of "take," unlike the ESA. Hayashi was prosecuted for "harassing" a marine mammal. While the Ninth Circuit found a variety of errors that required reversal of the conviction, it also interpreted "harassment" to require "a direct and significant intrusion" that involves "a serious diversion of the mammal from its natural routine." 22 F.3d at 864. The court concluded that Hayashi's firing of the rifle was only an "isolated interference with abnormal marine mammal activity" that did not violate the Act.

4. Concern about the potential reach of the ESA has been fueled by conflicts involving species that are very sensitive to human intrusions. While there once were more than 50,000 grizzly bears in the lower 48 states, there are now less than 1,000 present in small, isolated populations. Kenworthy, Wrestling with a Bear of a Problem in the Western Wilderness, Wash. Post, Nov. 21, 1994, at A3. Because researchers have found that "bears and roads don't mix," id., managers of national forests are under pressure to block and close roads in bear habitat. Railroads also interfere with the survival of the grizzly. In National Wildlife Federation v. Burlington Northern Railroad, 23 F.3d 1508 (9th Cir. 1994), the Ninth Circuit held that a railroad's accidental spillage of corn along tracks running through bear habitat and the killing of seven grizzlies who were struck by trains did not warrant the issuance of an injunction. While the court conceded that the killing of the grizzlies was a "taking" in violation of the ESA, it noted that the railroad had undertaken extensive cleanup operations to avoid similar incidents and that no bears had been hit by trains in more than three years. Thus, it upheld a district court's finding that plaintiffs had failed to show irreparable injury to justify issuance of an injunction.

5. In February 1995 a federal district judge prohibited the Pacific Lumber Company from logging in an ancient redwood grove because of the presence of the marbled murrelet. The court refused to apply the D.C. Circuit's *Sweet Home* decision and rejected the company's claim

8. Protection of Public Resources Pages 1126-1127

that logging would not significantly harm the birds. The court also found "clear evidence" that company officials had sought to mislead government regulators concerning the presence of the murrelet by deleting or altering reports of murrelet sightings. McCoy, Protected Birds Prohibit Pacific Lumber from Logging in Its Grove, Judge Rules, Wall St. J., Feb. 28, 1995, at B5.

6. Section 9 of the ESA has been criticized as creating an incentive for private landowners to destroy habitat that might attract endangered species. To respond to this concern, Interior Secretary Bruce Babbitt announced a new program called "Safe Harbors" in March 1995. The program is designed to encourage large private landowners to create habitat for endangered species by promising in return that they will not be penalized with future development restrictions. Kenworthy, Deal Gives Woodpeckers Golf Habitat, Wash. Post, Mar. 2, 1995, at A19. Landowners who enroll in the program will sign agreements with the Fish & Wildlife Service (FWS) that will allow them later to develop the land after giving notice to the FWS so that it can attempt to relocate the endangered species.

C. PUBLIC RESOURCE MANAGEMENT AND THE ENVIRONMENT

Private Development of Public Resources (pp. 1126-1127). While the Clinton Administration vowed to reform federal resource management policies by charging royalties for mineral extraction and raising fees for logging and grazing on public lands, these efforts have not been successful. Each house of Congress passed a different version of mining reform legislation in 1993, but a conference committee was unable to agree on an acceptable compromise. A one-year moratorium on the patenting of claims under the Mining Act of 1872 was imposed, effective September 30, 1994. Support for the moratorium was fueled by the revelation that a Canadian company had used the Act to purchase 1,949 acres of federal land that may contain $10 billion worth of gold for the princely sum of $8,965. Kenworthy, Solid-Gold U.S. Bargain for Canadian Mining Firm, Intl. Herald Trib., Apr. 18, 1994, at 3. Efforts to raise grazing fees were dropped after opposition from western ranching interests. Indeed, grazing fees actually declined in 1995 because of the formula established by the Public Rangeland Improvement Act that ties them to the price of beef. Kenworthy, Proposal to Raise Grazing Fees Is Sinking Slowly in the West, Wash. Post, Jan. 19, 1995, at A23. In 1994 the Clinton Administration did cancel the 50-year contract that had required the harvest of five billion board feet of timber from the Tongass National Forest (text, p.1127), but this ultimately has produced a backlash from the new Republican majority in Congress, as described below. Kenworthy, Temperate Forest Teeters On the Ecological Edge, Wash. Post, Aug. 25, 1994, at 1.

The 104th Congress is moving in a distinctly different direction from the Clinton Administration's proposed reforms. Appropriations riders that would double the harvest of timber from public lands under the guise of "salvage" operations have passed both houses of Congress and are awaiting the outcome of a conference committee. The bills would exempt the harvest from virtually all existing environmental laws while barring court challenges to its implementation. Olmsted & Hanson, The Gorton-Hatfield Forest Giveaway, N.Y. Times, Apr. 30, 1995, at E15. In addition, a Senate committee has approved a bill that would temporarily prohibit any federal agency from taking action that "restricts recreational, subsistence or commercial use of any land under the control of a federal agency." This amendment was introduced by Senator Ted Stevens of Alaska, who was angered by what he called "dictatorial" decisions to restrict logging in the Tongass National Forest. Kenworthy, Senate Panel Votes to Lift Curbs on Federal Land Use, Wash. Post, Mar. 8, 1995, at A7.

The Spotted Owl Controversy, the God Squad, and the Pacific Forest Plan (pp. 1135). As noted in the text, in late 1991 then-Secretary of the Interior Lujan convened the Endangered Species Committee ("God Squad") to consider exempting from the ESA certain sales of old-growth timber on public lands. Under the procedures established in the ESA, the Secretary initially considered the BLM's exemption application, published a notice and summary of the application in the Federal Register, and determined that certain threshold requirements of the ESA had been met. §§7(g)(1)-(3). Then, in consultation with the other members of the God Squad, the Secretary was required to hold a hearing, which was conducted by an ALJ. The members of the God Squad include the Secretary of Agriculture, the Secretary of the Army, the Chairman of the Council of Economic Advisors, the Administrator of EPA, the Secretary of the Interior, the Administrator of the National Oceanic and Atmospheric Administration, and "one individual from each affected State" appointed by the president. 16 U.S.C. §1536(e)(3). The Committee members from the affected states have one collective vote. 50 C.F.R. §453.05(d) (Oct. 1, 1991).

The hearing convened in January 1992. The Secretary of the Interior prepared a written report to the Committee, which then made a final determination on the application for an exemption. §7(h)(1)(A); 50 C.F.R. §453.04. An exemption requires the approval of five of the

8. Protection of Public Resources

seven members of the Committee. §2536(h)(1). On May 15, 1992, the Committee issued its decision. By a vote of 5-to-2, the Committee granted BLM an exemption for 13 of the 44 proposed sales.

The written justification for the exemption decision was remarkably cryptic. It references various tables in the Report of the Secretary of the Interior to the Endangered Species Committee, April 29, 1992. Table 1.2 of the report compares the size (in millions of board feet) of timber sales proposed in FY 1992 that were not thought to jeopardize the owl in each of nine BLM resource areas with the size of the sales proposed to be exempted in each area. Based on these comparisons, the Committee determined that in areas for which the size of the proposed "no jeopardy" sales is small, there are no reasonable and prudent alternatives. Thus, in framing the alternatives to be considered, the Committee assumed that large quantities of public timber must be made available for sale in each BLM resource area.

Table 2.1 of the report lists the economic benefits of the timber sales to the nation and the region in three categories: timber production benefits, employment benefits, and sociological benefits. Table 2.2 lists the economic costs as "recreation costs," "decreased existence values experienced," and "other environmental costs." For recreation costs, it states that the regional costs are "small" and that national recreation costs are "[s]maller than regional." The report then notes that "decreased existence values experienced regionwide" are "[s]maller than national" and that other environmental costs are "unpriced." Table 3.1 summarizes the costs and benefits in a remarkable fashion. For costs it states only that national and regional recreation costs are "small," that decreased existence values experienced are "[c]lose to $0" (both regionally and nationally) and that other environmental costs are "[l]ikely to be small."

In June 1992, the Sierra Club Legal Defense Fund and ten other environmental organizations filed suit in the U.S. Court of Appeals for the Ninth Circuit, challenging the God Squad's decision. In addition to alleging that the Secretary had illegally invoked the exemption process, the lawsuit alleged that BLM failed to satisfy the stringent requirements for an exemption. Specifically, the lawsuit claimed that BLM failed to show (1) that the sales were of regional or national significance, (2) that there were no alternatives with lesser effects on the spotted owl, (3) that the benefits of the sales clearly outweighed the costs of more protective alternatives, and (4) that the public interest supported proceeding with the sales. After the Ninth Circuit ordered that an administrative hearing be held to determine whether White House officials engaged in improper ex parte contacts with members of the God Squad, Portland Audubon Society v. Oregon Lands Coalition, 984 F.2d 1534 (9th Cir. 1993), the Clinton Administration informed the court that it did not wish to go forward with the timber sales exempted by the God Squad. The government agreed to vacate the God Squad's decision, and the Ninth Circuit dismissed the Sierra Club's lawsuit as moot.

In an effort to resolve the spotted owl controversy, President Clinton convened a forest conference in Portland on April 2, 1993 to hear the views of environmental leaders, timber industry representatives, the public, and government officials. On July 1, 1993, President Clinton proposed to reduce sales of public timber to 1.2 billion board feet per year (approximately one third of previous levels) and to provide more than $1 billion in economic assistance to displaced loggers. The Pacific Forest Plan includes a system of interconnected reserves of old growth forest, a system of stream buffers to protect aquatic species, and new rules for timber harvests outside the core reserves that will require logging operations to be more selective. Babbitt, Science: Opening the Next Chapter of Conservation History, 267 Science 1954 (1995).

In December 1994 the Pacific Forest plan was approved by Judge Dwyer in Seattle Audubon Society v. Lyons, 871 F. Supp. 1291 (D. Ore. 1994). He noted that the plan was "the result of a massive effort by the executive branch of the federal government to meet the legal and scientific needs of forest management." Even though another federal district court had found that the Forest Eco-System Management Assessment Team (FEMAT) had violated the Federal Advisory Committee Act (FACA) by refusing to hold open meetings during the development of the Pacific Forest Plan, Northwest Forest Resource Council v. Espy, 846 F. Supp. 1009 (D.D.C. 1994), Judge Dwyer found that this did not invalidate the plan. However, he concluded that if the *Sweet Home* decision is upheld by the Supreme Court, the plan would have to be revised because private landowners no longer would have to protect habitat under the Endangered Species Act.

In February 1995 the FWS proposed to relax restrictions on logging on private lands in the range of the spotted owl. The proposal was prepared under section 4(d) of the ESA, as part of the administration's three-part strategy. Recovery measures contained in the Pacific Forest Plan and the negotiation of habitat conservation plans with large private landowners are the other parts of the strategy. FWS Announces Proposal to Ease Restriction on Logging on Nonfederal Lands in Northwest, 25 Env. Rep. 1919 (1995). The Weyerhaeuser Company has agreed to a habitat conservation plan that will set aside 2,000 acres of a 209,000-acre tract of land to provide habitat for the spotted owl. The company also has agreed to leave corridors of older trees that can be use by the owls to move between forest segments. McCoy, Regulators' Pact with Weyerhaeuser Allows Logging in Spotted-Owl Habitat, Wall St. J., Feb. 13, 1995, at C11.

8. Protection of Public Resources

The Oregon economy is thriving in spite of sharp reductions in the timber harvest, confounding forecasts of economic gloom. Unemployment is at its lowest level in years as the economy shifts away from its dependence on the timber industry. Egan, Oregon, Foiling Forecasters, Thrives as It Protects Owls, N.Y. Times, Oct. 11, 1994, at A1. While some timber workers have been disappointed with the results of the promised readjustment assistance, Clairborne, Nurturing New Jobs in a Land of Old Forests, Feb. 28, 1995, at A3, the overall economy of Oregon remains in excellent shape.

Assessment of the Endangered Species Act (pp. 1138-1139). For a comprehensive assessment of how the ESA has worked in practice, see Houck, The Endangered Species Act and Its Implementation by the U.S. Departments of Interior and Commerce, 64 Univ. Colo. L. Rev. 277 (1993). Professor Houck argues that the Act "is not what it seems— either in the media or in the United States Code" because it effectively has been transformed from a set of seemingly absolute protections into a "discretionary permit system." Id. at 358. As a result, virtually all conflicts between development and species protection have been avoided, indicating that the Act does not threaten economic development.

In May 1995 the National Research Council of the National Academy of Sciences released a report evaluating experience under the Endangered Species Act. The report, which had been commissioned by Congress in 1991, found that the ESA is a "critically important" and successful tool for promoting biological diversity. The report recommends that critical habitat for the survival of threatened or endangered species be designated immediately upon their listing, rather than waiting for years after the listing as typically occurs at present. Kenworthy, Panel Supports Stronger Species Act, Washington Post, May 25, 1995 at A3. The report also endorses the ESA's current protection of distinct subpopulations of species, such as grizzly bears and gray wolves who are endangered in the lower 48 states but not in Alaska.

Approaches to Protection of Biodiversity, the Earth Summit, and the Biodiversity Convention (p. 1139). Some environmental economists argue that we need to develop better mechanisms for providing financial incentives to preserve biodiversity. One group has proposed that legislation be enacted creating biodiversity trust funds to be funded from the royalties received by the federal government from activities such as grazing, logging, mining, and recreation that may damage wildlife habitat. The trust fund would then be used to provide tax credits to private landowners who agree to preserve their lands and to provide grants to private conservation groups who would submit competitive bids for projects to preserve habitat. The funds could be used to buy conservation easements or to reward those on whose land endangered species breed. Baden, Species Preservation Without Tears, Wall St. J., June 2, 1992, at A14. The idea behind this proposal is that private landowners would have a financial incentive to preserve endangered species (because the presence of such species would make their land valuable to preservation groups) rather than fear that the presence of such species would destroy the value of their land. John Baden argues that this would produce the following simple result: "More species would be protected, and at less cost." Id.

The Fish and Wildlife Service and the Environmental Defense Fund are trying to develop a credit-trading scheme to help preserve the habitat of the endangered red-cockaded woodpecker in the southeastern United States. Under the plan, landowners could earn "marketable transferable endangered species conservation certificates" if they allow a pair of such birds to breed on their land and then send their babies to live on federal lands. The certificate, which could be traded or sold to other landowners, would enable the property owner to cut trees or otherwise alter bird habitat. Gutfeld, New Schemes Are Tried to Assist Woodpecker, Wall St. J., Apr. 5, 1993, at B1.

One of the most interesting new approaches to biodiversity preservation is a private contract between a pharmaceutical manufacturer, Merck, Sharp & Dohme, and a nonprofit institute in Costa Rica. In return for a "prospecting fee" of $1 million paid by the company, Costa Rica has agreed to provide thousands of samples of plant species to be screened for their potential pharmaceutical properties. The agreement specifies that if the company makes any commercially useful discoveries from the screening process, it will pay royalties to Costa Rica on sales of the products developed from the discoveries. The funds received by Costa Rica are to be used to preserve biodiversity in that country. The purpose of the agreement is to provide a financial incentive for developing countries to preserve biodiversity. This idea is incorporated in the biodiversity treaty signed at the Earth Summit in June 1992.

In June 1992, nearly a hundred countries signed an international convention of biological diversity at the U.N. Conference on Environment and Development (UNCED), called the "Earth Summit." The convention provides that

- all signatories must take steps to (1) inventory the species and ecosystems within their borders and develop programs to conserve those resources; (2) establish a system of preserves to protect areas important to biological diversity; and (3) incorporate biodiversity into environmental impact assessments;
- developed countries must share the benefits of biotechnology

8. Protection of Public Resources

and other uses of biodiversity resources with the countries in which those resources originate, under terms to be worked out by mutual agreement; and
- the parties are to establish a financial mechanism to fund biodiversity conservation efforts in developing countries.

The United States was the only major country that refused to sign the convention. President Bush objected that the convention posed an open-ended financial obligation on the developed countries and that the convention would compromise the patent rights of the biotechnology industry. On the first point, U.S. interests were in fact fully protected, as the convention requires unanimous consent for adoption of the voting procedures that will govern funding decisions. On the second point, the convention specifically affirms "effective protection of intellectual property rights."

In his 1993 Earth Day speech, President Clinton announced that the U.S. government intended to sign the Biodiversity Treaty. The president called the treaty "critically important not only to our future, but to the future of the world . . . not only because of what it will do to preserve species, but because of opportunities it offers for cutting-edge companies whose research creates new medicines, new products, and new jobs." While acknowledging that the treaty "had some flaws," President Clinton stated that the administration had worked with business and environmental groups to reach an understanding concerning how to protect "both American interests and the world environment."

By 1995, 73 nations had signed the biodiversity treaty. However, the U.S. Senate failed to ratify the treaty in 1994 and it now is unlikely to do so. For a discussion of the bizarre politics behind the Senate's failure to ratify the treaty, see Ross, Biodiversity Bashing, Wash. Post, April 23, 1995, at C2.

9
International Environmental Law

> If we protect them too much, the oceans will eventually be full of whales.
>
> —*Masami Tanabu**

> Applying the presumption against extraterritoriality here would result in a federal agency being allowed to undertake actions significantly affecting the human environment in Antarctica . . . without ever being held accountable for its failure to comply with the decisionmaking procedures instituted by Congress—even though such accountability, if it was enforced, would result in no conflict with foreign law or threat to foreign policy. NSF has provided no support for its proposition that conduct occurring within the United States is rendered exempt from otherwise applicable statutes merely because the effects of its compliance would be felt in the global commons.
>
> —*Environmental Defense Fund v. Massey***

In the years since the Rio Earth Summit, environmental concerns have continued to occupy a prominent place on the international diplomatic agenda. Having accelerated the phaseout of ozone-depleting chemicals, the international community now grapples with even more difficult challenges in responding to global warming and climate change. The Clinton administration has become a more vigorous advocate of international environmental protection measures. In his 1993 Earth Day speech, President Clinton endorsed the Biodiversity Treaty and committed the United States to reducing emissions of greenhouse gasses to 1990 levels by 2000. The administration also has reorganized high-level policy positions to ensure that environmental concerns play a greater role in foreign and national security policy. Ratification of

---
*Masami Tanabu, Japanese Minister of Fisheries, on the eve of the International Whaling Commission meeting, April 1993.
**986 F.2d 528, 536-537 (D.C. Cir. 1993).

9. International Environmental Law

the North American Free Trade Agreement (NAFTA) and the new world trading system established by the Uruguay Round of GATT negotiations has not quelled the fierce debate over the environmental impacts of trade liberalization. This chapter reviews these and other recent developments in international environmental law. It examines the Framework Convention on Climate Change and early progress toward implementation of it. It also considers GATT decisions challenging environmental regulations as trade restrictions and the D.C. Circuit's decision on the extraterritorial application of NEPA. Environmental Defense Fund v. Massey, 986 F.2d 528 (D.C. Cir. 1993).

A. INTRODUCTION TO INTERNATIONAL ENVIRONMENTAL LAW

The Rio "Earth Summit" (p. 1142). The Earth Summit held in Rio de Janeiro in June 1992 was an event of unprecedented size and complexity, an Olympics of international environmental negotiation larger than any previous international summit. More than 40,000 persons attended a collection of events that included the nongovernmental Global Forum and the largely corporate displays of Eco-Tech. Three English-language daily newspapers were created for the purpose of giving exclusive coverage to Summit events and issues. More than 9,000 journalists attended, twice as many as at any previous UN conference. In addition to the expected government leaders and environmentalists, attendees included members of native tribes, representatives of religious organizations, and not a few entertainers, from the Beach Boys to Placido Domingo.

Surprisingly, understanding such an unusual and complex event is not proving difficult. At one level the meeting was a success simply because it was not, as some had expected, an obvious failure. Agreements were signed. No one walked out. Almost every important government leader attended. The 178 nations that attended approved a declaration of environmental principles called the "Rio Declaration" (text, pp. 1145-1147) and adopted treaties that addressed global warming and the loss of biological diversity as well as a nonbinding declaration of forest conservation principles. The most ambitious document, Agenda 21, which was also nonbinding, in 800 pages addressed almost every aspect of environment and development. For a general summation and overview, see Storm in Rio: Morning After, N.Y. Times, June 15, 1992, at 1.

9. International Environmental Law

There is also no question that the Rio Conference served to focus enormous attention on the seriousness of global environmental problems and their connection to economic development. These themes were introduced in the 1987 report Our Common Future (text, p. 1145), the first high-level UN report to recognize the concept of "sustainable development" and the relationship between poverty and environmental degradation. For some observers the Conference was a validation of worries about "limits to growth" first expressed by Donella and Dennis Meadows in 1972 and conveniently updated in their 1992 book Beyond the Limits. Growth vs. Environment: The Push for Sustainable Development, Bus. Week, May 11, 1992, at 66-75. However, in his Rio speech President Bush argued that "growth is the engine of change and a friend of the environment. . . . To sustain development, we must protect the environment and to protect the environment, we must sustain development."

Given the proximity of the Conference to the presidential election, the U.S. media not surprisingly focused primarily on the politics of the U.S. position and the appearance by President Bush. The United States was widely portrayed as the villain (or "Darth Vader," as the New York Times put it) because of its (successful) efforts to weaken the climate convention and its unwillingness to sign the biological diversity treaty due to concerns that general language could be construed to require transfer of intellectual property interests by U.S. biotechnology companies. One senior delegate noted that perhaps one lesson from the experience was that the U.N. should never again have a major conference in a U.S. election year.

The agreements reached at the Earth Summit are comprised mainly of broadly worded principles with little force, from the perspective of an American lawyer. As one environmental lawyer said of the climate convention, "The foundation for meeting the challenge is there, but it needs the mortar and the bricks to get beyond the basement." Yet it is telling that U.S. economic interests were considered sufficiently threatened to convince the president to oppose the biological diversity treaty. While a few other developed countries expressed reservations about some aspects of the treaty, they dealt with the problem by issuing separate statements interpreting controversial clauses while signing the overall document. But the United States refused to sign because "instead of going the extra mile to protect global resources, the Administration [found] fearsome risks everywhere." The Courage to Bend in Rio, N.Y. Times, June 12, 1992, at A24. Indeed, EPA Administrator William Reilly's last-minute appeal to the president to negotiate a compromise on the biodiversity treaty became a major embarrassment for him when a White House critic of the Earth Summit gleefully leaked the news that the overture had been rejected immediately.

501

It is too early to tell whether the agreements reached in Rio will have a profound impact on international environmental policy or whether other countries eventually will embrace the U.S. position as an excuse not to take them seriously. Such framework agreements have led surprisingly quickly to more action-oriented agreements in the past, as illustrated by the evolution of the Montreal Protocol (text, pp. 1155-1167). On the other hand, Maurice Strong, the Conference chairman, questioned whether the framework will lead to meaningful followup: "I sat at a podium in Stockholm 20 years ago. I heard most of the same things. Most were not translated into action." U.N. Chief Closes Summit with an Appeal for Action, N.Y. Times, June 15, 1992, at A8.

The meeting did produce some specific agreements to increase environmental aid to developing countries. The major donor nations, including Japan, Germany, and the United States, each agreed to increases. Altogether, more than $6 billion a year in new funds was pledged. The UNCED Secretariat estimated that developing countries will require something on the order of $125 billion in foreign aid to implement the Agenda 21 programs, almost entirely to address local pollution problems. For a discussion of this estimate, see Petesch, North-South Environmental Strategies, Costs, and Bargains 52-57 (1992).

One view of the outcome suggested by then-EPA administrator William Reilly, head of the U.S. delegation, was that the agreements could be compared with the nonbinding Helsinki Accords on human rights. The Accords have served as widely respected norms and arguably have advanced standards for human rights—despite the lack of direct enforcement procedures. Just as the Accords created watchdogs to monitor human rights violations, the Earth Summit created a Sustainable Development Commission to monitor progress toward the promises made at Rio. The Commission, which will meet annually, is comprised of 53 representatives elected by the Economic and Social Council (ECOSOC) of the United Nations. Its first meeting was held in New York in May 1993 in an atmosphere of optimism spawned by the Clinton Administration's interest in the global environment.

The presence of such a large nongovernmental community was also a notable accomplishment, and perhaps a turning point in international politics (heretofore virtually the exclusive domain of diplomats). The involvement of this community was a procedural and technological achievement. As Jessica Mathews of the World Resources Institute noted, "UNCED has for the first time opened international diplomacy to the direct scrutiny and pressures of public opinion. . . . Lengthy daily bulletins written by these groups and distributed simultaneously by global electronic mail broadened the audience and spurred diplomats' normally lethargic pace." Wash. Post, June 14, 1992, at C7.

The private sector also organized and achieved some significant

9. International Environmental Law

independent agreements. For example, 48 CEOs of major international corporations signed a set of principles prepared by the Business Council for Sustainable Development titled "Changing Course." The document calls for a partnership among government, business, and the public to achieve sustainable development. See generally Schmidheiny, A Business Agenda for Rio, 9 Envtl. Forum 24 (May-June 1992).

On the process leading up to the Summit see Adams and Martinez-Aragon, Setting the Stage for the Earth Summit: Brazil 1992, 22 Env. L. Rep. 10190 (1992), and Nitze, The Road Starts at Rio, 9 Envtl. Forum 10 (1992). For some perspectives from other countries, see Saving the Earth: Economic Development vs. a Clean World, World Press Review, June 1992, at 9. See also Yost, Rio and the Road Beyond, 11 Env. Law: Newsletter of the Standing Comm. on Env. L. of the ABA (Summer 1992). For an assessment of the Rio Declaration, see Wirth, "The Rio Declaration on Environment and Development: Two Steps Forward and One Back, or Vice-Versa?" 30 Ga. L. Rev. 599 (1995).

International Environmental Law: A Pathfinder (pp. 1142-1143). Additional basic sources on international environmental law include G. Handl, ed., Yearbook of International Environmental Law (1992) and E. Weiss, ed., Environmental Change and International Law (1992). For a guide to the documents that resulted from the Earth Summit and information on how to obtain them, see Parson, Haas, and Levy, A Summary of the Major Documents Signed at the Earth Summit and the Global Forum, 34 Environment 12 (Oct. 1992).

UNCED, Draft Declaration of Principles (p. 1145). The excerpt published in the text was taken from the April 1992 draft agreed to by all countries in negotiations preceding the June 1992 Earth Summit. Fortunately, despite some last-minute posturing by the United States concerning the possibility of reopening the draft, it was adopted at the Earth Summit in the exact form as it appears in the text. As a result, it is now generally referred to as the "Rio Declaration." Following in the venerable tradition of the 1972 Stockholm Declaration, the Rio Declaration embodies the consensus of the world community on the principles that should govern global environmental protection.

The International Whaling Commission (p. 1152). The International Whaling Commission was established in 1946 pursuant to the International Convention for the Regulation of Whaling. Efforts by Japan and Norway to lift the moratorium on commercial whaling proved unsuccessful at ICW meetings in Kyoto, Japan in May 1993 and in Puerto Vallarta, Mexico in May 1994. Arguing that minke whales have become so abundant that they can be harvested without jeopardy, Japan and

Norway sought permission to resume limited commercial whaling near their own shores. The proposal was defeated and the IWC voted overwhelmingly to create an 11.8-million-square-mile whale sanctuary in the oceans surrounding Antarctica. Adopting tactics formerly used by environmentalists to pack the Commission with anti-whaling forces, Japan had recruited three small Caribbean nations (Dominica, Grenada, and St. Lucia) to support its position. (Ironically, some of these countries originally joined the IWC at the behest of environmentalists.) Pollack, Commission to Save Whales Endangered, Too, N.Y. Times, May 18, 1993, at C4. Environmentalists countered by threatening tourist boycotts of these countries. Whale of a Story, Financial Times (London), May 23, 1994, at 15.

Japanese whalers have been taking more than 300 minke whales per year from waters now covered by the Southern Ocean sanctuary, ostensibly for purposes of scientific research, though whale meat is featured in gourmet restaurants in Tokyo. While Japanese public opinion is becoming more hostile toward whaling, Japan's delegate to the IWC argued that eating whale meat actually may save some tropical rainforests by reducing the demand for beef from cattle that might have grazed on land where rainforest was cleared.

Japanese officials maintain that whale stocks have recovered to the point at which whaling can be resumed and that controlled harvesting of whales creates better economic incentives for whale preservation than does a total ban on harvesting. Weisman, A Whale: Food for Deep Thought, or Just Food? N.Y. Times, April 6, 1993, at A4. They argue that it is "cultural imperialism" for other nations to dictate what foods Japanese should not eat. While privately conceding that minke whale stocks probably are large enough to permit commercial harvesting without jeopardy, U.S. officials opposed all efforts to lift the seven-year-old global moratorium. Reid, World Whaling Body Riven by Dispute, Wash. Post, May 15, 1993, at A17. Scientists agree that the moratorium on commercial whaling has contributed to a significant increase in whale populations, and many believe that it would be desirable to permit small-scale harvesting of minke whales. Schmidt, Scientists Count a Rising Tide of Whales in the Seas, 263 Science 25 (1994). However, environmentalists argue that considerable uncertainty surrounds estimates of current whale stocks and that it is impossible for the IWC to ensure that quotas are observed. They note that the Soviet Fisheries Ministry has revealed that between 1948 and 1973 it actually harvested nearly 50,000 whales, while officially reporting only 2,700 to the IWC.

The bitter split between pro-whaling and anti-whaling nations is now threatening the future of the IWC. Iceland has withdrawn from the organization to protest the whaling moratorium and Norway resumed limited commercial whaling in 1993 (taking 160 whales for commercial purposes and 136 for research). Greenland, Iceland, and Norway have formed their own rival organization, the North Atlantic Marine Mammal Commission, to regulate the management of marine mammals in North Atlantic waters. While Japanese officials have threatened to follow Iceland's lead, many observers question whether Japan would risk the enmity of the anti-whaling nations by resuming commercial whaling. The IWC has no enforcement authority and members states may opt out of the moratorium simply by objecting to it, as Norway has done. The willingness of the United States to act unilaterally to sanction countries not complying with IWC rules has provided a powerful incentive for compliance, but to date it has taken no action to punish Norway for its resumption of whaling. For a discussion of the history and structure of the IWC see Caron, The International Whaling Commission and the North Atlantic Marine Mammal Commission: The Institutional Risks of Coercion in Consensual Structures, 89 Am. J. Intl. L. 154 (1995).

B. PROTECTION OF THE GLOBAL ATMOSPHERE

1. *Ozone Depletion*

Accelerating the Phaseout (p. 1162). At a meeting in Copenhagen in November 1992, the parties to the Montreal Protocol adopted amendments to accelerate the phaseout of ozone-depleting compounds because of evidence indicating that depletion continues to occur faster than expected. The decision to accelerate the phaseout was facilitated by steady reductions in estimates of its cost. Greater attention is now being given to additional sources of ozone depletion not yet regulated, particularly methyl bromide. These developments have illustrated the importance of building flexibility into international agreements, as emphasized by Benedick (text, p. 1159).

The EPA had announced plans to accelerate the phaseout of ozone-depleting substances in the U.S. in February, 1992 (text, p. 1167). This action was taken shortly after the Senate voted 96-0 for a resolution urging that the phaseout be accelerated to 1995.

In November 1992, the World Meteorological Organization announced that stratospheric ozone values had reached record lows in Antarctica and the high and middle latitudes of the northern and southern hemispheres. This announcement helped convince the parties to the Montreal Protocol to further accelerate the timetable for reducing emissions of ozone-depleting compounds. Under the terms of the agreement reached in Copenhagen, production of halons is to end by 1994, while production of chlorofluorocarbons, carbon tetrachloride, and methyl chloroform is to end by 1996. Rosewicz, Industrialized Nations to Hasten End to Use of Ozone-Damaging Chemicals, Wall St. J., Nov. 27, 1992, at B6. A safety valve is allowed for "essential uses" approved by a Technology and Economic Assessment panel. Such uses must be necessary for health or safety or "critical for the functioning of society," and it must also be shown that there are no acceptable substitutes.

The parties also proposed amendments to the Protocol restricting two additional ozone-depleting compounds. The hydrochlorofluorocarbons (HCFCs), chemicals that also damage the ozone layer but that are relatively less harmful due to shorter atmospheric lifetimes, would be capped beginning in 1996 and gradually reduced under a schedule for interim targets, resulting in a 90 percent reduction by 2015 and a phaseout by 2030. In addition, after intense debate the parties agreed to cap use of methyl bromide, a widely used pesticide, at 1991 levels by 1995. The United States supported more aggressive action, but Israel and some developing countries were opposed because of economic concerns. The parties also agreed to a nonbinding resolution supporting adoption of methyl bromide controls by 1995 and an eventual phaseout. The New Ozone Accord: The Strongest Package of Law . . . But Not Enough, 4 Global Environmental Change Report 1 (Dec. 4, 1992).

Important decisions were also made in Copenhagen concerning the Multilateral Fund to assist developing countries in reducing their use of ozone-depleting chemicals. An interim fund was created by the parties in 1990. The Fund will now be permanent and will receive an additional $400 to $600 million for 1993-1996.

The amendments continue the trend of prompt governmental response to scientific reports of worsening environmental conditions. With the possible exception of methyl bromide, agreements have been achieved that will eliminate the vast majority of uses of all nontrivial ozone-depleting compounds over the next decade. Nevertheless, Mostafa Tolba, director of UNEP, noted in his closing remarks in Copenhagen that "[t]he question remains . . .: Is it enough? We are in the hands of the scientists. From them . . . we know that the answer is 'no.' . . . The process of protecting the ozone layer is not at an end."

In March 1993 the World Meteorological Organization reported that stratospheric ozone levels over much of Northern Europe and Canada had reached a record low for the second year in a row. Ozone levels were more than 20 percent below long-term normal values. Three days later the Du Pont Company announced that it would cease production of CFCs by the end of 1994, a full year before the legal deadline. McMurray, Du Pont to Speed up Phaseout of CFCs as Ozone Readings Post Record Lows, Wall St. J., Mar. 9, 1993, at B5.

CFC Tax and Freon Smuggling (pp. 1165-1166). Retail prices of CFCs have skyrocketed to $15 per pound in 1995 from $1 per pound in 1989. A huge black market has developed as CFCs purchased abroad are smuggled into the United States to avoid the $5.35 per pound federal tax. Halpert, Freon Smugglers Find Big Market, N.Y. Times, Apr 30, 1995, at A1. In October 1994 EPA, the Customs Service and the IRS formed a joint task force to combat illegal imports of CFCs. In December 1994 the owner of a San Diego automotive air-conditioning repair business was convicted for smuggling CFCs from Mexico. In January 1995 two men were indicted for illegally importing more than 100 tons of CFCs from Europe. Id.

The Ozone Backlash (pp. 1166-1167). The scientific community has been perplexed by the wide publicity received by recent claims that the theory of ozone depletion by CFCs is a hoax perpetrated by environmentalists in collusion with greedy scientists. This claim, which apparently originated in a magazine published by supporters of Lyndon LaRouche, received wide circulation after it was endorsed in former Washington governor Dixie Lee Ray's book Trashing the Planet, which was then enthusiastically embraced by talk show host Rush Limbaugh. Taubes, The Ozone Backlash, 260 Science 1580 (1993). They argue that CFCs cannot be threatening the ozone layer because far more chlorine is placed in the atmosphere by natural sources such as seawater, volcanoes, and the burning of biomass than is placed there by CFCs. This argument, however, was long ago dismissed by atmospheric scientists, who point out that significant quantities of chlorine from natural sources have not been found in the stratosphere. This is no surprise to scientists because chlorine from natural sources is soluble and is largely washed out in the lower atmosphere, unlike insoluble and inert CFCs, which reach the stratosphere. Id. at 1582. It is particularly ironic to scientists that these arguments "focus on the least uncertain aspect of ozone depletion science," id. at 1583, reinforcing the need for better communication between scientists and the public. See Rowland, President's Lecture: The Need for Scientific Communication with the Public, 260 Science 1571 (1993).

Formal scientific opinion and empirical evidence continues to indicate the seriousness of the ozone depletion problem. The most authoritative summary of scientific opinion is an international consensus report prepared under the auspices of NOAA, NASA, the United Nations Environment Programme, and the World Meteorological Organization at the request of the parties to the Montreal Protocol. The most recent edition, Scientific Assessment of Ozone Depletion: 1994 (released in early 1995) was prepared by 295 scientists from more than 30 countries. The report concludes that:

- Record low global ozone levels were measured over the past two years.
- Downward trends in ozone continue to be observed over much of the globe but models underestimate their magnitudes by factors of up to three.
- Ozone losses have been detected in the Arctic and linked to CFCs and other manmade compounds.
- Pollution and measurement difficulties have made it difficult to establish changes in ultraviolet radiation predicted as a consequence of ozone depletion. However, two unpolluted sites appear to show UV increases consistent with observed ozone trends.
- Peak ozone losses are expected to occur during the next several years, after which reductions in emissions of ozone-depleting compounds brought about by the Montreal Protocol should gradually restore the ozone layer to pre-CFC conditions.

An additional interesting feature of the report is the inclusion of a question and answer section that rebuts many of the most common statements made by skeptics, such as how we know that the chlorine in the stratosphere is due to human sources, how the effect of solar cycles on ozone has been ruled out as an explanation for the downward trend in ozone, and what we know about the link between ozone depletion and an increase in ground-level ultraviolet radiation.

Still more recent reports indicate that the Arctic ozone layer continued to shrink over the winter of 1994-1995, down by about a third of normal levels. Arctic Ozone Layer Shrinks, N.Y. Times, Apr. 4, 1995, at C5.

An Alternative Explanation for Ozone Depletion (p. 1167). For an alternative explanation of ozone depletion from a supermarket tabloid, see McGuire, UFOs Are Stealing Our Ozone Layer! Scientists Beg U.S. to Attack Space Intruder, Weekly World News, Mar. 9, 1993, at 6.

2. Global Climate Change

Intergovernmental Panel on Climate Change, Scientific Assessment (p. 1171). An updated consensus report on the science of climate change

9. International Environmental Law   Page 1174

by the Intergovernmental Panel on Climate Change has been published as Climate Change 1992: The Supplementary Report to the IPCC Scientific Assessment (Cambridge U. Press, 1992). Another useful overview of the subject is Mintzer, ed., Confronting Climate Change: Risks, Implications, and Responses (1992). See also Kerr, Greenhouse Science Survives Skeptics, 256 Science 1138 (1992).

The Intergovernmental Panel on Climate Change is scheduled to report next in the fall of 1995. This report will be the first major statement by the IPCC since 1992. An interim report, "Radiative Forcing of Climate Change," was released by the Scientific Assessment Working Group of the IPCC in 1994 and contained several important findings. One is that stabilization of atmospheric carbon dioxide concentrations at even twice current levels could only be achieved by reducing emissions "substantially below 1990 levels." This is because of the long atmospheric lifetime of carbon dioxide and most of the other significant greenhouse gases.

A second important finding in the interim report concerns the negative radiative forcing (the technical term for the warming effect) associated with aerosols from sulfates and biomass burning. These aerosols reduce the transmission of sunlight and change the earth's albedo, offsetting much of the warming otherwise predicted from greenhouse gases. "However, the estimates of the aerosol radiative forcing are highly uncertain, moreover the forcing is highly regional and cannot be regarded as a simple offset to greenhouse gas forcing."

A third interesting assessment is the role of volcanos and the eruption of Mt. Pinatubo in the Philippines in June 1991. The radiative forcing from aerosols emitted by this eruption was comparable in magnitude but of opposite sign to the cumulative greenhouse gas forcing this century and caused a cooling of global surface temperature of 0.3 to 0.5 degrees Centigrade during 1992. However, this effect is transitory and as of 1995 has largely disappeared. For a readable overview of recent scientific developments, see Reading the Patterns, 335 Economist 65-67 (1995).

The Long-term Impact of Climate Change (p. 1174).   The significance of taking a longer-term view of the risks of climate change is explored by economist William Cline in The Economics of Global Warming (1992). Cline argues that the risks are non-linear and likely to accelerate significantly at higher temperatures, so that projecting costs over several hundred years results in much greater estimates.

EPA has begun a program to estimate the cumulative macroeconomic effects of climate change on different sectors of the economy. A preliminary assessment of the potential effects on agriculture, electricity demand, and coastlines indicates a discounted value of cumulative reductions in U.S. consumption through 2060 of $200 billion. Scheraga et al., Macroeconomic Modeling and the Assessment of Climate Change Impacts (EPA Climate Change Division, Jan. 1993).

Legal and Policy Responses to Global Warming (p. 1176). In June 1992, more than 150 governments attending the Rio Earth Summit signed a Framework Convention on Climate Change. The Convention calls for the "stabilization of greenhouse-gas concentration in the atmosphere at a level that would prevent dangerous anthropogenic interference with the climate system . . . within a time frame sufficient to allow ecosystems to adapt naturally." However, as discussed below, the Convention reflects an inability of the parties to agree on specific commitments and begins a process of reporting, analysis, and no doubt lengthy further negotiations.

In pre-summit negotiations in May 1992, the United States insisted on the deletion of a firm requirement that nations stabilize their emissions of greenhouse gases at 1990 levels by 2000. The United States took the position that while it hoped to be able to achieve such a goal, it would be difficult to avoid exceeding the ceiling as the economy grew in subsequent years. At the Earth Summit, several European nations pushed for an endorsement of a nonbinding statement calling for stronger action. The European Commission has proposed an escalating tax on all carbon fuels that would rise from approximately $3 per barrel of oil to $10 by the end of the 1990s. However, fearing damage to their international competitive position, European governments will not pursue this idea until the United States and Japan agree to a similar carbon tax. Feldstein, The Case for a World Carbon Tax, Wall St. J., June 4, 1992, at A8. The Rio Climate Convention is discussed in greater detail below.

The Rio Climate Convention (p. 1187). The science of global warming remains controversial, but the official U.S. position moved much closer toward an international consensus in the weeks before the Rio Earth Summit. A paper titled "U.S. Views on Global Climate Change" distributed to delegations at the climate negotiations in April 1992 stated: "The best scientific information indicates that if greenhouse gas concentrations in the atmosphere continue to increase as a result of human activities, significant changes in the climate system are likely." The paper went on to state that the United States supports taking actions justified by multiple benefits, including responding to climate change, and that actions already taken for reasons of energy or environmental policy are expected to come close to stabilizing total U.S. emissions of greenhouse gases. The difference between the United States and other nations at Rio was a refusal to accept targets and timetables that would *require* stabilizing greenhouse gases and opposition to the European approach (which would impose specific requirements on carbon dioxide as opposed to total greenhouse gas emissions).

Excerpts from the Framework Convention on Climate Change signed at the Rio Earth Summit in June 1992 are reproduced below.

> *Framework Convention on Climate Change*
> 31 I.L.M. 849 (1992)

Article 2. Objective

The ultimate objective of this Convention and any related legal instruments that the Conference of the Parties may adopt is to achieve, in accordance with the relevant provisions of the Convention, stabilization of greenhouse gas concentrations in the atmosphere at a level that would prevent dangerous anthropogenic interference with the climate system. Such a level should be achieved within a time frame sufficient to allow ecosystems to adapt naturally to climate change, to ensure that food production is not threatened and to enable economic development to proceed in a sustainable manner. . . .

Article 4. Commitments

1. All Parties, taking into account their common but differentiated responsibilities and their specific national and regional development priorities, objectives and circumstances, shall:

   (a) Develop, periodically update, publish and make available to the Conference of the Parties, in accordance with Article 12, national inventories of anthropogenic emissions by sources and removals by sinks of all greenhouse gases not controlled by the Montreal Protocol, using comparable methodologies to be agreed upon by the Conference of the Parties;

   (b) Formulate, implement, publish and regularly update national and, where appropriate, regional programmes containing measures to mitigate climate change by addressing anthropogenic emissions by sources and removals by sinks of all greenhouse gases not controlled by the Montreal Protocol, and measures to facilitate adequate adaptation to climate change;

   (c) Promote and cooperate in the development, application and diffusion, including transfer of technologies, practices and processes that control, reduce or prevent anthropogenic emissions of greenhouse gases not controlled by the Montreal Protocol in all relevant sectors, including the energy, transport, industry, agriculture, forestry and waste management sectors;

(d) Promote sustainable management, and promote and cooperate in the conservation and enhancement, as appropriate, of sinks and reservoirs of all greenhouse gases not controlled by the Montreal Protocol, including biomass, forests and oceans as well as other terrestrial, coastal and marine ecosystems;

(e) Cooperate in preparing for adaptation to the impacts of climate change; develop and elaborate appropriate and integrated plans for coastal zone management, water resources and agriculture, and for the protection and rehabilitation of areas, particularly in Africa, affected by drought and desertification, as well as floods;

(f) Take climate change considerations into account, to the extent feasible, in their relevant social, economic and environmental policies and actions, and employ appropriate methods, for example impact assessments, formulated and determined nationally, with a view to minimizing adverse effects on the economy, on public health and on the quality of the environment, of projects or measures undertaken by them to mitigate or adapt to climate change;

(g) Promote and cooperate in scientific, technological, socio-economic and other research, systematic observation and development of data archives related to the climate system and intended to further the understanding and to reduce or eliminate the remaining uncertainties regarding the causes, effects, magnitude and time of climate change and the economic and social consequences of various response strategies;

(h) Promote and cooperate in the full, open and prompt exchange of relevant scientific, technological, technical, socio-economic and legal information related to the climate system and climate change, and to the economic and social consequences of various response strategies;

(*i*) Promote and cooperate in education, training and public awareness related to climate change and encourage the widest participation in this process, including that of nongovernmental organizations; and

(j) Communicate to the Conference of the Parties information related to implementation, in accordance with Article 12.

2. The developed country Parties and other Parties included in annex I commit themselves specifically as provided for in the following:

(a) Each of these Parties shall adopt national policies and take corresponding measures on the mitigation of climate change, by limiting its anthropogenic emissions of greenhouse gases and protecting and enhancing its greenhouse gas sinks and reservoirs. These policies and measures will demonstrate that developed countries are taking the lead in modifying longer-term trends in anthropogenic emissions consistent with the objective of the Convention, recognizing that the return by the end of the present decade to earlier levels of anthropogenic emissions of carbon dioxide and other greenhouse gases not controlled by the Montreal Protocol would contribute to such modification, and taking into account the differences in these Parties' starting points and approaches, economic structures and resources bases, the need to maintain strong and sustainable economic growth, available technologies and other individual circumstances, as well as the need for equitable and appropriate contributions by each of these Parties to the global effort regarding that objective. These Parties may implement such policies and measures jointly with other Parties and may assist other Parties in contributing to the achievement of the objective of the Convention and, in particular, that of this subparagraph;

(b) In order to promote progress to this end, each of these Parties shall communicate, within six months of the entry into force of the Convention for it and periodically thereafter, and in accordance with Article 12, detailed information on its policies and measures referred to in subparagraph (a) above, as well as on its resulting projected anthropogenic emissions by sources and removals by sinks of greenhouse gases not controlled by the Montreal Protocol for the period referred to in subparagraph (a) with the aim of returning individually or jointly to their 1990 levels of these anthropogenic emissions of carbon dioxide and other greenhouse gases not controlled by the Montreal Protocol. This information will be reviewed by the Conference of the Parties, at its first session and periodically thereafter, in accordance with Article 7;

(c) Calculations of emissions by sources and removals by sinks of greenhouse gases for the purposes of subparagraph (b) above should take into account the best available scientific knowledge, including of the effective capacity of sinks and the respective contributions of such gases to climate change. The Conference of the Parties shall consider and agree on methodologies for these calculations at its first session and review them regularly thereafter;

(d) The Conference of the Parties shall, at its first session, review the adequacy of subparagraphs (a) and (b) above. Such review shall be carried out in the light of the best available scientific information and assessment on climate change and its impacts, as well as relevant technical, social and economic information. Based on this review, the Conference of the Parties shall take appropriate action, which may include the adoption of amendments to the commitments in subparagraphs (a) and (b) above. The Conference of the Parties, at its first session, shall also take decisions regarding criteria for joint implementation as indicated in subparagraph (a) above. A second review of subparagraphs (a) and (b) shall take place not later than 31 December 1998, and thereafter at regular intervals determined by the Conference of the Parties, until the objective of the Convention is met;

    (e) Each of these Parties shall:

        (i) coordinate as appropriate with other such Parties, relevant economic and administrative instruments developed to achieve the objective of the Convention; and

        (ii) identify and periodically review its own policies and practices which encourage activities that lead to greater levels of anthropogenic emissions of greenhouse gases not controlled by the Montreal Protocol than would otherwise occur;

    (f) The Conference of the Parties shall review, not later than 31 December 1998, available information with a view to taking decisions regarding such amendments to the lists in annexes I and II as may be appropriate, with the approval of the Party concerned;

    (g) Any Party not included in annex I may, in its instrument of ratification, acceptance, approval or accession, or at any time thereafter notify the Depositary that it intends to be bound by subparagraphs (a) and (b) above. The Depositary shall inform the other signatories and Parties of any such notification.

3. The developed country Parties and other developed Parties included in annex II should provide new and additional financial resources to meet the agreed full costs incurred by developing country Parties in complying with their obligations under Article 12, paragraph 1. They shall also provide such financial resources, including for the transfer of technology, needed by the developing country Parties to meet the agreed full incremental costs of implementing measures that are covered by paragraph 1 of this Article and that are agreed between a developing country Party and the international entity or entities referred to in Article 11, in accordance with that Article. The implementation of these commitments shall take into account the need for adequacy and predictability in the flow of funds and the importance of appropriate burden sharing among the developed country Parties.

4. The developed country Parties and other developed Parties included in Annex II shall also assist the developing country Parties that are particularly vulnerable to the adverse effects of climate change in meeting costs of adaptation to those adverse effects.

5. The developed country Parties and other developed Parties included in annex II shall take all practicable steps to promote, facilitate and finance, as appropriate, the transfer of, or access to, environmentally sound technologies and knowhow to other Parties, particularly

9. International Environmental Law

developing country Parties, to enable them to implement the provisions of the Convention. In this process, the developed country Parties shall support the development and enhancement of endogenous capacities and technologies of developing country Parties. Other Parties and organizations in a position to do so may also assist in facilitating the transfer of such technologies.

6. In the implementation of their commitments under paragraph 2 above, a certain degree of flexibility shall be allowed by the Conference of the Parties included in annex I undergoing the process of transition to a market economy, in order to enhance the ability of these Parties to address climate change, including with regard to the historical level of anthropogenic emissions of greenhouse gases not controlled by the Montreal Protocol chosen as a reference.

7. The extent to which developing country Parties will effectively implement their commitments under the Convention will depend on the effective implementation by developed country Parties of their commitments under the Convention related to financial resources and transfer of technology and will take fully into account that economic and social development and poverty eradication are the first and overriding priorities of the developing country Parties.

8. In the implementation of the commitments in this Article, the Parties shall give full consideration to what actions are necessary under the Convention, including actions related to funding insurance and the transfer of technology, to meet the specific needs and concerns of developing country Parties arising from the adverse effects of climate change and/or the impact of the implementation of response measures, especially on:

- (a) Small island countries;
- (b) Countries with low-lying coastal areas;
- (c) Countries with arid and semi-arid areas, forested areas and areas liable to forest decay;
- (d) Countries with areas prone to natural disasters;
- (e) Countries with areas liable to drought and desertification;
- (f) Countries with areas of high urban atmosphere pollution;
- (g) Countries with areas with fragile ecosystems, including mountainous ecosystems;
- (h) Countries whose economies are highly dependent on income generated from the production, processing and export, and/or consumption of fossil fuels and associated energy-intensive products; and
- (i) Land-locked and transit countries.

Further, the Conference of the Parties may take actions, as appropriate, with respect to this paragraph.

9. The Parties shall take full account of the specific needs and special situations of the least developed countries in their actions with regard to funding and transfer of technology.

10. The Parties shall, in accordance with Article 10, take into consideration in the implementation of the commitments of the Convention the situation of Parties, particularly developing country Parties, with economies that are vulnerable to the adverse effects of the implementation of measures to respond to climate change. This applies notably to Parties with economies that are highly dependent on income generated from the production, processing and export, and/or consumption of fossil fuels and associated energy-intensive products and/or the use of fossil fuels for which such Parties have serious difficulties in switching to alternatives.

NOTES AND QUESTIONS

1. The Climate Convention is, as the discussion of the Rio Summit notes, the beginning of a process more than a legally binding mechanism for reducing greenhouse gas emissions. The Montreal Protocol, which followed from the Vienna Convention, offers a possible comparison; recall Benedick's references to the contribution that the process begun in Vienna in 1985 made to the eventual commitment to an action-oriented agreement two years later. This illustrates the importance of understanding the reasons for the success at Montreal: If, as some argue, the discovery of the ozone hole and industry's willingness to embrace substitutes were critical factors, then perhaps further progress toward greenhouse gas reductions will not be comparable.

2. The Climate Convention incorporates many of the concepts identified by Sand (text, p. 1148), including provisions for an upward ratchet and frequent scientific feedback on the need for further action. You may find it useful to compare his ideas with the agreement. The climate treaty will result in a much more detailed picture of the sources and quantity of greenhouse gas emissions as well as national strategies for cost-effective reductions. The opportunity for cross-country comparisons could prove a very fruitful source of moral suasion for further progress.

3. Does the Climate Convention appear to require any implementing legislation? The official U.S. position is that it does not. Might it be relevant to the operation of any existing environmental laws? One possibility is in the context of NEPA litigation, in which the Convention might be construed as further evidence that agencies must consider the implications of climate change.

4. In October 1992, the Senate ratified the Climate Convention.

The Convention entered into force on March 21, 1994, 90 days after having been ratified by 50 signatories. Prior to leaving office, the Bush Administration released two final statements summarizing U.S. policy on climate change. The State Department had released "Environmental Documentation: United Nations Framework Convention on Climate Change" in September 1992 as background for assessing the implications of ratifying the Convention. On December 8, the State Department published a "National Action Plan for Global Climate Change" describing the status of U.S. greenhouse gas emissions and existing policies expected to reduce them. The Plan indicates that implementation of the Clean Air Act and the Energy Policy Act of 1992, Pub. L. No. 102-486, may keep total U.S. emissions of greenhouse gases close to 1990 levels by 2000. A separate analysis published by the Energy Information Administration released in January 1993, Annual Energy Outlook 1993 with Projections to 2010, indicates a "reference case" that U.S. emissions of carbon dioxide from fossil fuel combustion are expected to increase over 20 percent by 2010 relative to 1990.

5. Several provisions directed to climate change were included in Title 16 of the Energy Policy Act of 1992. Section 1605 creates a voluntary system for tracking industry reductions in greenhouse emissions that could establish the baseline for a future system of emission trading akin to that used in the acid rain program. See Greenhouse Gas Offset Bank Sets Stage for Tradeable Permits, 4 Global Environmental Change Report 1 (Oct. 9, 1992). Such a system could also be incorporated in any international trading scheme; note the potential for "joint implementation" arrangements discussed in the article by Grubb. Other provisions in the Act require preparation of a "least-cost" energy plan for reducing greenhouse gas emissions and the designation of a Director of Climate Protection at the Department of Energy.

6. U.S. policy concerning climate change changed substantially under the Clinton Administration. In his 1993 Earth Day speech the president announced that the United States would seek to reduce greenhouse gas emissions to 1990 levels by 2000. In October 1993 the United States released its Climate Change Action Plan. As required by the Climate Convention, the plan was formally submitted in the Fall of 1994. Climate Action Report: Submission of the United States of America Under the United Nations Framework Convention on Climate Change (1994). The plan relies heavily on voluntary measures such as EPA's "Green Lights" program to achieve cost-saving reductions in greenhouse gas emissions. With only modest exceptions, the plan requires no legislative action. It also contains no measures to improve the efficiency of U.S. automobiles, an issue that President Clinton has so far addressed only through another voluntary collaboration, the so-called "green car" initiative with U.S. auto manufacturers to introduce

a super-efficient (80 mpg) car by 2010. For a description of the U.S. plan and a comparison of it with those submitted by other countries, see Stone, Most Nations Miss the Mark on Emission-Control Plans, 266 Science 1939 (1994).

Environmentalists have been highly critical of the U.S. plan and the plans submitted by most other countries. Id. The U.S. Submission recognizes that the Plan may fall short because since it was prepared "the economy has grown more rapidly than anticipated, the price of oil fell sharply . . . and the U.S. Congress . . . does not, for now, appear likely to provide full funding for the actions contained in the Plan." Climate Action Report at 14. As a consequence, the Administration plans a full review of its progress toward meeting the goals in late 1995, with the possibility of adopting additional measures if necessary. The Submission also indicates that even if the Plan meets the year 2000 target, continued economic growth will cause greenhouse gas emissions to grow again thereafter, increasing by more than 10 percent in 2010. Id at 190.

7. The first meeting of the parties to the Climate Convention took place in Berlin in late March and early April 1995. The first Conference of Parties (COP-1) was attended by more than 115 Parties to the Convention (out of the 127 nations that have so far ratified), 1,000 NGOs, and over 100 media representatives. For a description of the political context of nations at the meeting, see Global Warming and Cooling Enthusiasm, 335 Economist 33-34 (1995).

There were numerous issues to be resolved from the relatively trivial (where to locate the Secretariat: the COP settled on Bonn) to the most difficult (what aims, if any, should be adopted for the post-2000 period). Island nations proposed that a new protocol be negotiated that would require developing countries to make additional reductions in carbon dioxide emissions by the year 2005 to 20 percent below 1990 levels. Representatives of China argued that it was premature to negotiate a new protocol until existing commitments had been carried out. The Russian Federation and Saudi Arabia stated that a negotiation of a new protocol should await the release of the second IPCC assessment. The COP ultimately agreed to establish an ad hoc process for negotiating a protocol or other legal instrument to set quantified limits and emissions reduction objectives for developed countries for the years 2005, 2010, and 2020.

The COP also addressed criteria for joint implementation. The parties agreed to establish a pilot phase for joint implementation between developed countries that could include developing countries on a voluntary basis. It was agreed that the Global Environmental Facility (GEF) would continue to function as the interim financial mechanism for the Convention. The schedule for the second Conference of Parties

9. International Environmental Law

will be announced in October 1995. COP-2 is likely to be held in Uruguay sometime before October 1996.

8. The future of the Climate Convention is increasingly tied to North-South debates about access to technology and responsibility for past misdeeds. Developing countries have aggressively argued that they not be subjected to any obligations for reducing their emissions until significant steps have been taken by the industrialized nations primarily responsible for current concentrations of greenhouse gases. The affected industries in the industrialized nations have in turn argued that it makes no sense to impose strong measures on them when most of the projected growth in emissions over the next century will be in developing nations; for example, future growth in China alone could more than offset significant (and costly) emission reductions by the U.S.

One response to this tension has been growing interest in "joint implementation," a concept introduced with considerable ambiguity in Article 4.2(d) of the Convention. By some interpretations, this provision allows for trade in greenhouse gas mitigation projects from countries with high abatement costs to countries with lower costs. In practice, this emission trading scheme might make possible large investments in clean—or at least cleaner—energy in developing countries. However, many environmental organizations and developing countries have expressed serious reservations "because the economic benefits are unproven in practice, because the existence of such economic benefits are seen as the result of inequitable patterns of development which need to be addressed rather than used as arguments for industrialized countries to avoid their responsibilities, and because numerous technical problems need to be resolved if Joint Implementation is to become a significant factors in the international response to climate change." Von Moltke, Turning Up the Heat: Next Steps on Climate Change, a Report based on a Workshop at the Pontico Conference Center of the Rockefeller Brothers Fund, April 6-8, 1994, at 17. See generally Loske and Oberthur, Joint Implementation Under the Climate Change Convention, 6 Intl. Env. Aff. 45 (1994).

9. The majority of parties at COP-1 acknowledged that existing commitments to control greenhouse gas emissions will be inadequate even to achieve the existing goal of reducing emissions to 1990 levels by the year 2000. Shortly after the Berlin conference the International Energy Agency released a report predicting that increased global demand for energy will lead to a ten percent increase in greenhouse gas emissions by the year 2000 and a possible 40 percent increase by the year 2010. International Watchdog Agency Sees Rise in Energy Use, Global Warming, Wash. Post, Apr. 25, 1995, at A3.

10. State governments have also implemented some policies re-

sponding to climate change. See generally EPA, Office of Policy, Planning & Evaluation, Selected Summary of Current State Responses to Climate Change (1992). Most state climate policy is concerned with evaluating localized risks and potential strategies for adaptation. However, several state public utility commissions have adopted "adders" to reflect the risk of climate change when comparing alternative technologies for meeting the demand for electricity. The result is to increase the effective cost of fossil fuel projects relative to investments in efficiency, renewable energy, and nuclear power. Even some local governments are beginning to address the greenhouse problem. Toronto is one of several cities that have adopted goals for reducing CO_2 emissions. EPA and American Forests, an organization that sponsors tree planting programs, are implementing a program in seven U.S. localities that involves tree planting and lightening surface colors to reduce temperatures and the amount of energy needed for air conditioning. The "cool communities" program will test the potential for CO_2 reduction and evaluate its overall costs and benefits.

11. The extent of the opportunity for cost-effective reductions in greenhouse gas emissions was emphasized in a study by the OECD. It found that energy subsidies worldwide were in excess of $235 billion in 1985, equivalent to an implicit carbon subsidy of $90 per ton ($10 per barrel of oil), and that most countries have large opportunities to reduce their greenhouse gas emissions and make their economies work more efficiently. Cool Costing, The Economist, Mar. 6, 1993, at 86-87.

C. INTERNATIONAL TRADE AND THE ENVIRONMENT

The Environmental Impact of Trade Liberalization (pp. 1190-1195). Economist Herman Daly maintains that international free trade is in fundamental conflict with five important domestic policies: (1) getting prices right (by making it more difficult for a country to use regulation to internalize the external costs of pollution), (2) moving toward a more just distribution of income between labor and capital (by reducing returns to domestic labor), (3) fostering community (by forcing greater labor mobility and further separating ownership from the community as foreign investment occurs), (4) controlling the macroeconomy (by creating huge international payment imbalances), and (5) keeping scale within ecological limits (as more nations seek to live in excess of a sustainable development path by importing carrying capacity from others). Daly,

9. International Environmental Law   Pages 1195-1200

From Adjustment to Sustainable Development: The Obstacle of Free Trade, 15 Loyola of L.A. Intl. & Comp. L.J. 33 (1993).

In contrast to Daly, a report prepared by the GATT Secretariat for the Rio Summit not surprisingly adopts the view that trade makes countries richer and less polluting. It also argues in favor of consensual multilateral environmental agreements and environmental aid and technology transfer as an alternative to trade sanctions or other penalties against countries with lax environmental standards. GATT Secretariat, Trade and the Environment (Feb. 1992). See also OTA, Trade and Environment: Conflicts and Opportunities 4-6, 22-24 (1992); and Environmental Imperialism, The Economist, Feb. 15, 1992, at 78. Judge Stephen Williams of the D.C. Circuit speculates that trade liberalization may help the environment by reducing poverty. He cites data suggesting that because "low-income persons tend to buy in much smaller quantities than persons of higher income buying economy-size packages, they impose a heavier per capita load of packaging waste." Public Citizen v. Office of the U.S. Trade Representative, 970 F.2d 916, 921 n.6 (D.C. Cir. 1992).

Trade restrictions to protect natural resources may be as self-defeating if they reduce the value of the resources they are intended to protect to the point at which there is little incentive to preserve them. For example, the Netherlands has banned the import of tropical woods in a move designed to reduce deforestation in Southeast Asia. However, economists maintain that if such measures succeed in preventing trade in tropical hardwoods, the economic value of such forests will be destroyed, which could lead to more extensive forest clearing to make room for agriculture. Yet efforts to determine sustainable levels of resource exploitation have been fraught with difficulty; uncertainties are routinely used to justify overexploitation. Ludwig, Hilborn, and Walters, Uncertainty, Resource Exploitation, and Conservation: Lessons from History, 260 Science 17 (1993).

The Tuna-Dolphin Controversy and the GATT (pp. 1195-1200). The United States reached a compromise to defuse the tuna-dolphin dispute with Mexico. In June 1992 the United States reached an agreement with Mexico, Vanuatu, and Venezuela to ban the practice of setting purse seine nets around schools of tuna swimming with dolphins. The Earth Island Institute, the group that initiated the lawsuit that required the embargo, supported the compromise, Pro-Dolphin Accord Made, N.Y. Times, June 16, 1992, at D9, which was implemented through amendments to the MMPA approved by Congress in October 1992. The amendments, Pub. L. No. 102-523, authorize the Secretary of State to negotiate a five-year moratorium on the use of purse seine nets that encircle dolphins or other marine mammals during the harvesting of tuna. The amendments also ban the sale of any tuna product that is not "dolphin safe" effective June 1, 1994. Does the ban on the sale of such tuna indicate that the labeling approach was a failure? Does the settlement of the tuna-dolphin dispute indicate that, GATT notwithstanding, for certain countries and certain products trade with the United States is so important that unilateral trade sanctions by the United States can be effective in changing how other countries use the global commons?

Despite the settlement of the tuna-dolphin dispute between the United States and Mexico, a second GATT panel was convened to determine whether the broadened U.S. embargo on imports of tuna from intermediary nations who dealt with Mexico (see note 7 on p. 1200 of the parent) was a violation of GATT. That panel reached the following decision.

> *General Agreement on Tariffs and Trade: Dispute Settlement Panel Report on United States Restrictions on Imports of Tuna*
> 33 I.L.M. 839 (1994)

3. United States restrictions affecting indirect imports of tuna ("intermediary nation embargo")

5.5 The Act provides that any nation ("intermediary nation") that exports yellowfin tuna or yellowfin tuna products to the United States, and that imports yellowfin tuna or yellowfin tuna products that are subject to a direct prohibition on import into the United States, must certify and provide reasonable proof that it has not imported products subject to the direct prohibition within the preceding six months. This provision, effective 26 October 1992, is an amendment of an earlier provision, interpreted by a United States court to require that proof be made that each country identified as an intermediary nation had itself prohibited the import of any tuna that was barred from direct importation into the United States. Subsequent to the entry into force of the new provision France, the Netherlands Antilles and the United Kingdom were withdrawn from the list of intermediary nations. Costa Rica, Italy, Japan and Spain remained on the list. . . .

5.10 The Panel then examined whether the United States measures were consistent with Article XI:1, which reads in part:

> No prohibitions or restrictions other than duties, taxes or other charges, whether made effective through quotas, import or export licences or other measures, shall be instituted or maintained by any contracting party on the importation of any product of the territory of any other contracting party.

9. International Environmental Law

The Panel noted that the embargoes imposed by the United States were "prohibitions or restrictions" in the terms of Article XI, since they banned the import of tuna or tuna products from any country not meeting certain policy conditions. They were not "duties, taxes or other charges." The Panel therefore concluded that the measures were inconsistent with Article XI:1.

C. Article XX(g)

5.11 The Panel noted the United States argument that both the primary and intermediary nation embargoes, even if inconsistent with Articles III or XI, were justified by Article XX(g) as measures relating to the conservation of dolphins, an exhaustible natural resource. The United States argued that there was no requirement in Article XX(g) for the resources to be within the territorial jurisdiction of the country taking the measure. The United States further argued that the measures were taken in conjunction with restrictions on domestic production and consumption. Finally, it argued that the measures met the requirement of the preamble to Article XX. The EEC and the Netherlands disagreed, stating that the resource to be conserved had to be within the territorial jurisdiction of the country taking the measure. The EEC and the Netherlands were further of the view that the United States measures were not related to the conservation of an exhaustible natural resource under Article XX(g), and were not taken in conjunction with domestic restrictions on production or consumption.

5.12 The Panel proceeded first to examine the text of Article XX(g), which, together with its preamble, states:

> Subject to the requirement that such measures are not applied in a manner which would constitute a means of arbitrary or unjustifiable discrimination between countries where the same conditions prevail, or a disguised restriction on international trade, nothing in this Agreement shall be construed to prevent the adoption or enforcement by any contracting party of measures:
>
> (g) relating to the conservation of exhaustible natural resources if such measures are made effective in conjunction with restrictions on domestic production or consumption.

The Panel observed that the text of Article XX(g) suggested a three-step analysis:

> First, it had to be determined whether the policy in respect of which these provisions were invoked fell within the range of policies to conserve exhaustible natural resources.

Second, it had to be determined whether the measure for which the exception was being invoked—that is the particular trade measure inconsistent with the obligations under the General Agreement—was "related to" the conservation of exhaustible natural resources, and whether it was made effective "in conjunction" with restrictions on domestic production or consumption.

Third, it had to be determined whether the measure was applied in conformity with the requirement set out in the preamble to Article XX, namely that the measure not be applied in a manner which would constitute a means of arbitrary or unjustifiable discrimination between countries where the same conditions prevail or in a manner which would constitute a disguised restriction on international trade.

1. Conservation of an exhaustible natural resource

5.13 Concerning the first of the above three questions the Panel noted that the United States maintained that dolphins were an exhaustible natural resource. The EEC disagreed. The Panel, noting that dolphin stocks could potentially be exhausted, and that the basis of a policy to conserve them did not depend on whether at present their stocks were depleted, accepted that a policy to conserve dolphins was a policy to conserve an exhaustible natural resource.

5.14 The Panel noted that the EEC and the Netherlands argued that the exhaustible natural resource to be conserved under Article XX(g) could not be located outside the territorial jurisdiction of the country taking the measure. It based this view on an examination of the Article XX(g) in its context, and in light of the object and purpose of the General Agreement. The United States disagreed, pointing out that there was no textual or other basis for reading such a requirement into Article XX(g).

5.15 The Panel observed, first, that the text of Article XX(g) does not spell out any limitation on the location of the exhaustible natural resources to be conserved. It noted that the conditions set out in the text of Article XX(g) and the preamble qualify only the trade measure requiring justification ("related to") or to the manner in which the trade measure is applied ("in conjunction with," "arbitrary or unjustifiable discrimination," "disguised restriction on international trade"). The nature and precise scope of the policy area named in the Article, the conservation of exhaustible natural resources, is not spelled out or specifically conditioned by the text of the Article, in particular with respect to the location of the exhaustible natural resource to be conserved. The Panel noted that two previous panels have considered Article XX(g) to be applicable to policies related to migratory species of fish, and had made no distinction between fish caught within or outside the territorial jurisdiction of the contracting party that had invoked this provision.

5.16 The Panel then observed that measures providing different treatment to products of different origins could in principle be taken under other paragraphs of Article XX and other Articles of the General Agreement with respect to things located, or actions occurring, outside the territorial jurisdiction of the party taking the measure. An example was the provision in Article XX(e) relating to products of prison labour. It could not therefore be said that the General Agreement proscribed in an absolute manner measures that related to things or actions outside the territorial jurisdiction of the party taking the measure.

5.17 The Panel further observed that, under general international law, states are not in principle barred from regulating the conduct of their nationals with respect to persons, animals, plants and natural resources outside of their territory. Nor are states barred, in principle, from regulating the conduct of vessels having their nationality, or any persons on these vessels, with respect to persons, animals, plants and natural resources outside their territory. A state may in particular regulate the conduct of its fishermen, or of vessels having its nationality or any fishermen on these vessels, with respect to fish located in the high seas.

5.18 The Panel noted that the parties based many of their arguments on the location of the exhaustible natural resource in Article XX(g) on environmental and trade treaties other than the General Agreement. . . .

5.20 . . . The Panel also found that the statements and drafting changes made during the negotiation of the Havana Charter and the General Agreement cited by the parties did not provide clear support for any particular contention of the parties on the question of the location of the exhaustible natural resource in Article XX(g). In view of the above, the Panel could see no valid reason supporting the conclusion that the provisions of Article XX(g) apply only to policies related to the conservation of exhaustible natural resources located within the territory of the contracting party invoking the provision. The Panel consequently found that the policy to conserve dolphins in the eastern tropical Pacific Ocean, which the United States pursued within its jurisdiction over its nationals and vessels, fell within the range of policies covered by Article XX(g).

2. **"Related to" the conservation of an exhaustible natural resource; made effective "in conjunction" with restrictions on domestic production or consumption.** . . .

5.23 The Panel then proceeded to examine whether the embargoes imposed by the United States could be considered to be primarily aimed at the conservation of an exhaustible natural resource, and primarily aimed at rendering effective restrictions on domestic production or consumption. In particular, the Panel examined the relationship of the United States measures with the expressed goal of dolphin conservation. The Panel noted that measures taken under the intermediary nation embargo prohibited imports from a country of any tuna, whether or not the particular tuna was harvested in a manner that harmed or could harm dolphins, and whether or not the country had tuna harvesting practices and policies that harmed or could harm dolphins, as long as it was from a country that imported tuna from countries maintaining tuna harvesting practices and policies not comparable to those of the United States. The Panel then observed that the prohibition on imports of tuna into the United States taken under the intermediary nation embargo could not, by itself, further the United States conservation objectives. The intermediary nation embargo could achieve its intended effect only if it were followed by changes in policies or practices, not in the country exporting tuna to the United States, but in third countries from which the exporting country imported tuna.

5.24 The Panel noted also that measures taken under the primary nation embargo prohibited imports from a country of any tuna, whether or not the particular tuna was harvested in a way that harmed or could harm dolphins, as long as the country's tuna harvesting practices and policies were not comparable to those of the United States. The Panel observed that, as in the case of the intermediary nation embargo, the prohibition on imports of tuna into the United States taken under the primary nation embargo could not possibly, by itself, further the United States conservation objectives. The primary nation embargo could achieve its desired effect only if it were followed by changes in policies and practices in the exporting countries. In view of the foregoing, the Panel observed that both the primary and intermediary nation embargoes on tuna implemented by the United States were taken so as to force other countries to change their policies with respect to persons and things within their own jurisdiction, since the embargoes required such changes in order to have any effect on the conservation of dolphins.

5.25 The Panel then examined whether, under Article XX(g), measures primarily aimed at the conservation of exhaustible natural resources, or primarily aimed at rendering effective domestic restrictions on their production or consumption, could include measures taken so as to force other countries to change their policies with respect to persons or things within their own jurisdictions, and requiring such changes in order to be effective. The Panel noted that the text of Article XX does not provide a clear answer to this question. It therefore proceeded to examine the text of Article XX(g) in the light of the object and purpose of the General Agreement.

5.26 The Panel observed that Article XX provides for an exception to obligations under the General Agreement. The long-standing practice of panels has accordingly been to interpret this provision narrowly, in a manner that preserves the basic objectives and principles of the General Agreement. If Article XX were interpreted to permit contracting parties to deviate from the obligations of the General Agreement by taking trade measures to implement policies, including conservation policies, within their own jurisdiction, the basic objectives of the General Agreement would be maintained. If however Article XX were interpreted to permit contracting parties to take trade measures so as to force other contracting parties to change their policies within their jurisdiction, including their conservation policies, the balance of rights and obligations among contracting parties, in particular the right of access to markets, would be seriously impaired. Under such an interpretation the General Agreement could no longer serve as a multilateral framework for trade among contracting parties.

5.27 The Panel concluded that measures taken so as to force other countries to change their policies, and that were effective only if such changes occurred, could not be primarily aimed either at the conservation of an exhaustible natural resource, or at rendering effective restrictions on domestic production or consumption, in the meaning of Article XX(g). Since an essential condition of Article XX(g) had not been met, the Panel did not consider it necessary to examine whether the United States measures had also met the other requirements of Article XX. The Panel accordingly found that the import prohibitions on tuna and tuna products maintained by the United States inconsistently with Article XI:1 were not justified by Article XX(g).

D. *Article XX(b)*

5.28 The Panel noted the United States argument that both the primary and intermediary nation embargoes, even if inconsistent with Articles III or XI, were justified by Article XX(b) as measures necessary to protect the life and health of dolphins. The United States argued that there was no requirement in Article XX(b) that the animals whose life or health was to be protected had to be within the jurisdiction of the country taking the measure. The United States further argued that the measures were necessary to fulfill the policy goal of protecting the life and health of dolphins. Finally, it argued that the measures met the requirement of the preamble to Article XX. The EEC and the Netherlands disagreed, stating that the animals whose life or health was to be protected had to be within the jurisdiction of the country taking the measure. The EEC and the Netherlands were further of the view that the United States measures were not necessary within the meaning of Article XX(b).

5.29 The Panel proceeded first to examine the text of Article XX(b), which, together with its preamble, states:

> Subject to the requirement that such measures are not applied in a manner which would constitute a means of arbitrary or unjustifiable discrimination between countries where the same conditions prevail, or a disguised restriction on international trade, nothing in this Agreement shall be construed to prevent the adoption or enforcement by any contracting party of measures:
> (b) necessary to protect the human, animal, or plant life or health

The Panel observed that the text of Article XX(b) suggested a three-step analysis:

> First, it had to be determined whether the policy in respect of which these provisions were invoked fell within the range of policies referred to in these provisions, that is policies to protect human, animal or plant life or health;
> Second, it had to be determined whether the measure for which the exception was being invoked—that is the particular trade measure inconsistent with the obligations under the General Agreement—was "necessary" to protect human, animal or plant life or health;
> Third, it had to be determined whether the measure was applied in a manner consistent with the requirement set out in the preamble to Article XX, namely that the measure not be applied in a manner which would constitute a means of arbitrary or unjustifiable discrimination between countries where the same conditions prevail or in a manner which would constitute a disguised restriction on international trade.

1. To protect human, animal or plant life and health

5.30 Turning to the first of the above three questions, the Panel noted that the parties did not disagree that the protection of dolphin life or health was a policy that could come within Article XX(b). The EEC argued, however, that Article XX(b) could not justify measures taken to protect living things located outside the territorial jurisdiction of the party taking the measure. The United States disagreed. The arguments on this issue advanced by the parties were similar to those made under Article XX(g).

5.31 The Panel recalled its reasoning under Article XX(g). It observed that the text of Article XX(b) does not spell out any limitation on the location of the living things to be protected. It noted that the conditions set out in the text of Article XX(b) and the preamble qualify only the trade measure requiring justification ("necessary to") or the manner in which the trade measure is applied ("arbitrary or unjustifiable discrimination," "disguised restriction on international trade"). The nature and precise scope of the policy area named in the Article, the protection of living things, is not specified in the text of the Article, in particular with respect to the location of the living things to be protected.

5.32 The Panel further recalled its observation that elsewhere in the General Agreement measures according different treatment to products of different origins could in principle be taken with respect to things located, or actions occurring, outside the territorial jurisdiction of the party taking the measure. It could not therefore be said that the General Agreement proscribed in an absolute manner such measures. The Panel further recalled its observation that, under general international law, states are not in principle barred from regulating the conduct of their nationals with respect to persons, animals, plants and natural resources outside of their territory (see paragraph 5.17 above). . . .

5.33 . . . The Panel therefore found that the policy to protect the life and health of dolphins in the eastern tropical Pacific Ocean, which the United States pursued within its jurisdiction over its nationals and vessels, fell within the range of policies covered by Article XX(b).

2. **"Necessary"**

5.34 The Panel then examined the second of the above three questions, namely whether the primary and intermediary nation embargoes imposed by the United States on yellowfin tuna could be considered to be "necessary" for the protection of the living things within the meaning of Article XX(b). The United States argued that its measures met this requirement, since "necessary" in this sense simply meant "needed." The EEC disagreed, stating that the normal meaning of the term "necessary" was "indispensable" or "unavoidable." The EEC further argued that adopted panel reports had stated that a measure otherwise inconsistent with the General Agreement could only be justified as necessary under Article XX(b) if no other consistent measure, or more consistent measure, were reasonably available to fulfil the policy objective.

5.35 The Panel proceeded first to examine the relationship established by Article XX(b) between the trade measure and the policy of protecting living things. It noted that, in the ordinary meaning of the term, "necessary" meant that no alternative existed. A previous panel, in discussing the use of the same term in Article XX(d), stated that

> a contracting party cannot justify a measure inconsistent with another GATT provision as "necessary" in terms of Article XX(d) if an alternative

measure which it could reasonably be expected to employ and which is not inconsistent with other GATT provisions is available to it. By the same token, in cases where a measure consistent with other GATT provisions is not reasonably available, a contracting party is bound to use, among the measures reasonably available to it, that which entails the least degree of inconsistency with other GATT provisions.[85]

This interpretation had also been accepted by another panel specifically examining Article XX(b).[86] The Panel agreed with the reasoning of these previous panels. The Panel then proceeded to examine whether the trade embargoes imposed by the United States could be considered to be "necessary" in this sense to protect the life or health of dolphins.
5.36 The Panel noted that measures taken under the intermediary nation embargo prohibited imports from a country of any tuna, whether or not the particular tuna was harvested in a manner that harmed or could harm dolphins, and whether or not the country had tuna harvesting practices and policies that harmed or could harm dolphins, as long as it was from a country that imported tuna from countries maintaining tuna harvesting practices and policies not comparable to those of the United States. The Panel observed that the prohibition on imports of tuna into the United States taken under the intermediary nation embargo could not, by itself, further the United States conservation objectives. The intermediary nation embargo would achieve its intended effect only if it were followed by changes in policies or practices, not in the country exporting tuna to the United States, but in third countries from which the exporting country imported tuna.
5.37 The Panel also recalled that measures taken under the primary nation embargo prohibited imports from a country of any tuna, whether or not the particular tuna was harvested in a way that harmed or could harm dolphins, as long as the country's tuna harvesting practices and policies were not comparable to those of the United States. The Panel observed that, as in the case of the intermediary nation embargo, the prohibition on imports of tuna into the United States taken under then primary nation embargo could not possibly, by itself, further the United States objective of protecting the life and health of dolphins. The primary nation embargo could achieve its desired effect only if it were followed by changes in policies and practices in the exporting countries. In view of the foregoing, the Panel observed that both the primary and intermediary nation embargoes on tuna were taken by the United States

---

85. Report of the Panel on United States-Section 337 of the Tariff Act of 1930, adopted 7 November 1989, L/6439, 36S/345, 392, par. 5.26.

86. Report of the Panel on Thailand - Restrictions on importation of and internal taxes on cigarettes, DS10/R, adopted 7 November 1990, 37S/200, 223 [30 I.L.M. 1122 (1991)].

so as to force other countries to change their policies with respect to persons and things within their own jurisdiction, since the embargoes required such changes in order to have any effect on the protection of the life or health of dolphins.

5.38 The Panel then examined whether, under Article XX(b), measures necessary to protect the life or health of animals could include measures taken so as to force other countries to change their policies within their own jurisdictions, and requiring such changes in order to be effective. The Panel noted that the text of Article XX is not explicit on this question. The Panel then recalled its reasoning under its examination of Article XX(g) that Article XX, as a provision for exceptions, should be interpreted narrowly and in a way that preserves the basic objectives and principles of the General Agreement. If Article XX(b) were interpreted to permit contracting parties to deviate from the basic obligations of the General Agreement by taking trade measures to implement policies within their own jurisdiction, including policies to protect living things, the objectives of the General Agreement would be maintained. If however Article XX(b) were interpreted to permit contracting parties to impose trade embargoes so as to force other countries to change their policies within their jurisdiction, including policies to protect living things, and which required such changes to be effective, the objectives of the General Agreement would be seriously impaired.

5.39 The Panel concluded that measures taken so as to force other countries to change their policies, and that were effective only if such changes occurred, could not be considered "necessary" for the protection of animal life or health in the sense of Article XX(b). Since an essential condition of Article XX(b) had not been met, the Panel did not consider it necessary to examine the further issue of whether the United States measures had also met the other requirements of Article XX. The Panel accordingly found that the import prohibitions on tuna and tuna products maintained by the United States inconsistently with Article XI:1 were not justified by Article XX(b). . . .

F. *Concluding Observations*

5.42 The Panel noted that the objective of sustainable development, which includes the protection and preservation of the environment, has been widely recognized by the contracting parties to the General Agreement. The Panel observed that the issue in this dispute was not the validity of the environmental objectives of the United States to protect and conserve dolphins. The issue was whether, in the pursuit of its environmental objectives, the United States could impose trade embargoes to secure changes in the policies which other contracting parties pursued within their own jurisdiction. The Panel therefore had to resolve whether the contracting parties, by agreeing to give each other in Article XX the right to take trade measures necessary to protect the health and life of plants, animals and persons or aimed at the conservation of exhaustible natural resources, had agreed to accord each other the right to impose trade embargoes for such purposes. The Panel had examined this issue in the light of the recognized methods of interpretation and had found that none of them lent any support to the view that such an agreement was reflected in Article XX. . . .

VI. CONCLUSIONS

6.1 In the light of its findings above, the Panel concluded that the United States import prohibitions on tuna and tuna products under Section 101(a)(2) and Section 305(a)(1) and (2) of the Marine Mammal Protection Act (the "primary nation embargo") and under Section 101(a)(2)(C) of the Marine Mammal Protection Act (the "intermediary nation embargo") did not meet the requirements of the Note at Article III, were contrary to Article XI:1, and were not covered by the exceptions in Article XX(b), (g) or (d) of the General Agreement.

6.2 The Panel recommends that the CONTRACTING PARTIES request the United States to bring the above measures into conformity with its obligations under the General Agreement.

NOTES & QUESTIONS

1. Unlike the panel in *Tuna/Dolphin I*, the *Tuna/Dolphin II* panel suggests that the resources covered by Article XX(g)'s exemption of measures to conserve exhaustible natural resources do not have to be located within the jurisdiction of the country adopting the conservation measure. Why did the panels reach a different conclusion in this regard?

2. While the United States believed that the embargo on intermediary nations was necessary to prevent "tuna laundering" from undermining the effectiveness of its sanctions, the *Tuna/Dolphin II* panel finds it objectionable because it seeks to encourage other governments to adopt trade policies similar to those of the United States. Can you think of any circumstances under which an embargo on intermediary nations could be upheld in light of the decision in *Tuna/Dolphin II*?

3. In September 1994 another GATT panel upheld key provisions of U.S. fuel economy measures that had been challenged by the European Union (EU) as violative of GATT. General Agreement on Tariffs and Trade: Dispute Settlement Panel Report on United States—Taxes

on Automobiles (Sept. 29, 1994). The panel held that U.S. Corporate Average Fuel Economy (CAFE) requirements, a "gas guzzler" tax, and a luxury tax on expensive cars did not discriminate against Mercedes and BMW. However, the panel did strike down one aspect of the regulations—CAFE accounting rules that establish separate "domestic" and "import" fleets for determining overall fuel economy. This panel decision is noteworthy because it may suggest latitude within GATT principles for regulations on imports based on more than differences in their physical characteristics or end uses. The two previous panel decisions finding U.S. regulations on the importation of tuna designed to protect dolphins inconsistent with GATT caused significant concern that nations could not regulate imports based on the manner in which they were produced, a potentially serious obstacle to environmental regulation. (Note that none of these panel decisions has been formally adopted, and that there is no stare decisis in GATT/WTO decisions.)

The *Auto Taxes* panel was still concerned that any discrimination due to an environmental regulation be "based on factors directly relating to the product as such." Differential taxes based on fuel economy passed the test, but the CAFE regulations did not. "Thus, the Auto Taxes Panel seems to have expanded the leeway for measures that are closely related to, but do not strictly effect, the product; however, it is impossible to say just how broad or narrow that expansion is." R. Housman et al., The Use of Trade Measures in Select Multilateral Environmental Agreements (paper prepared for the United Nations Environment Programme, 1995). See also Lee, Process and Product: Making the Link Between Trade and the Environment, 6 Intl. Envt. Aff. 320 (1994).

4. The *Auto Taxes* and *Tuna/Dolphin* decisions all concerned the GATT consistency of unilateral legislative acts. The issue might have been very different if presented in conjunction with a bilateral or multilateral environmental agreement. With the increasing number and importance of such agreements, the application of GATT rules to actions taken pursuant to multilateral agreements is of considerable importance. R. Housman, et al., argue that Tuna/Dolphin I implied that measures operating under the authority of an international agreement would be covered by the Article XX exceptions to the GATT. Id. The *Tuna/Dolphin II* panel employed a three-part test for determining the applicability of Article XX, which subsequently was followed by the Auto Taxes panel.

> First, the *policy* upon which the measure is based must fall within the range of policies covered by the relevant article XX provisions.
> Second, the *measure* must be either "necessary" to protect human, animal or plant life or health under XX(b), or "related to" the conserva-

tion of exhaustible natural resources, and made effective "in conjunction" with restrictions on domestic production or consumption under XX(g).

Third, the measure must be applied in a manner consistent with the requirements of article XX's preamble; specifically, the measure cannot be applied in a manner that would constitute a means of arbitrary or unjustifiable discrimination between countries where the same conditions prevail or in a manner that would constitute a disguised restriction on international trade.

Measures taken to protect the environment outside of a country's territorial jurisdiction were acceptable to the *Tuna/Dolphin II* panel. However, measures to change the policies of other countries, acting within their own jurisdiction, were not acceptable if such measures would achieve their intended effect only if they were followed by such changes. The *Tuna/Dolphin II* panel stated that such measures would "seriously impair the objectives of the GATT" and, thus, could neither be considered "necessary" as required by the article XX(b) exception nor "primarily aimed at" legitimate conservation goals as required by article XX(g). Multilateral environmental agreements that seek to alter the policies of other countries, acting within their own jurisdiction, thus could be vulnerable under the reasoning of the *Tuna/Dolphin II* panel.

Housman, et al. argue that both the history of GATT and strong policy arguments support treating multilateral protections differently than unilateral protections. They maintain that "broad-based multilateral protections are the only effective means of addressing problems that spill over borders, affect the global commons, or are global in nature" and that they "serve to harmonize measures within their purview," thus reducing trade barriers. Id.

5. The Uruguay Round of GATT negotiations was successfully concluded in December 1993. Congress approved the agreement in December 1994. As a result, a new World Trade Organization (WTO) came into being on January 1, 1995. The new GATT/WTO changes the context for trade-environment issues in some important and as yet unpredictable ways. The preamble provides some helpful language: "no country shall be prevented from taking measures . . . for the protection of human, animal or plant life or health, or the environment." A new Committee on Trade and Environment is established. Also, the dispute resolution procedure now allows for (but does not require) consultation with outside experts and might open the process to greater environmental input. However, the public is still largely denied access to information on disputes. See generally D. Esty, Greening the GATT (1994); Shaw and Cosbey, GATT, the World Trade Organization, and Sustainable

9. International Environmental Law

Development, 6 Intl. Envtl. Aff. 245 (1994); Kennedy, Reforming U.S. Trade Policy to Protect the Global Environment: A Multilateral Approach, 18 Harv. Env. L.R. 185 (1993); Garvey, The GATT/WTO Committee on Trade and the Environment—Toward Environmental Reform, 89 Am. J. Intl. L. 423 (1995).

NAFTA and the Environment (p. 1200). The North American Free Trade Agreement (NAFTA) was signed in December 1992 and ratified by Congress in 1993. It took effect on January 1, 1994. Environmental concerns played a prominent role in the debate over ratification of NAFTA. While former EPA administrator William Reilly described NAFTA as the "greenest" trade agreement ever negotiated, environmental and labor groups expressed serious reservations. Schneider, Senate Panel Democrats Attack Free-Trade Pact, N.Y. Times, Sept. 17, 1992, at D2. Under Article 712.2 of NAFTA, each country reserves the right to establish the "appropriate level of protection" for life or health within its territory "notwithstanding any other provision" of NAFTA. However, the countries are directed to "avoid arbitrary or unjustifiable distinctions" in levels of health or environmental protection that would cause "unjustifiable discrimination" against goods from another country or that would "constitute a disguised restriction on trade." How do these provisions differ from GATT's treatment of health and environmental standards? How would the tuna-dolphin dispute have been affected if it were subject to the provisions of NAFTA instead of the GATT? For a more detailed analysis of NAFTA's environmental provisions, see Charnovitz, NAFTA: An Analysis of Its Environmental Provisions, 23 Env. L. Rep. 10067 (1993).

The Clinton administration endorsed NAFTA on the condition that supplemental agreements be reached with Canada and Mexico to allay concerns expressed by environmental and labor groups. Supplemental agreements covering environmental and labor issues were subsequently negotiated. The side agreement on environmental issues, North American Agreement on Environmental Cooperation, creates a tripartite Commission on Environmental Cooperation (CEC) with the power to investigate environmental compliance in each of the three countries. Citizens or governments may forward complaints to the CEC, which can appoint a five-member panel to hold hearings and issue judgments. If the panel finds "a persistent pattern of failure to effectively enforce environmental laws," fines or trade sanctions may be imposed.

Progress implementing the environmental side agreements to NAFTA has been slow. As of the fall of 1994, the Border Environment Cooperation Commission was barely operational and no cleanup projects were even close to beginning. Concerns were also being expressed about the announcement of Border Commission procedures, which limited public participation. See Myerson, Trade Pact's Environmental Efforts Falter, N.Y. Times, Oct. 17, 1994, at D1. See also Kublicki, The Greening of Free Trade: NAFTA, Mexican Environmental Law, and Debt Exchanges for Mexican Environmental Infrastructure Development, 19 Colum. J. Envtl. L. 59 (1994); Schoenbaum, The North American Free Trade Agreement (NAFTA): Good for Jobs, for the Environment, and for America, 23 Ga. J. Intl. & Comp. L. 461 (1993).

2. International Trade in Hazardous Substances

Policy Issues (pp. 1201-1203). International publicity has proved to be one of the few effective means for combatting efforts to export hazardous substances to developing countries. See Greenpeace, The International Trade in Wastes: A Greenpeace Inventory (1990). In March 1993, Germany announced that it would retrieve 468 tons of pesticide waste illegally dumped in Romania by a former secret police official. The official, who had claimed to be shipping "humanitarian aid" to Romania, shipped the waste for over four months before his operation was exposed by Greenpeace. Germany Will Take Back Pesticides Sent to Romania, Wall St. J., Mar. 2, 1993, at A15. In June 1993 the owners of the *Khian Sea* (text, p. 1201) were convicted of one count of illegal ocean dumping and two counts of perjury for telling a federal grand jury that the incinerator ash the boat was carrying had not been dumped at sea. At trial crew members testified that they were ordered to dump the ash in the Indian Ocean while the ship was en route to Singapore.

Even when principles of informed consent are honored, it is disturbing to many to permit the export of U.S. products banned or restricted domestically. Yet developing countries need not be helpless pawns in the face of aggressive marketing by U.S. chemical exporters. The Indonesian government, in cooperation with the U.N. Food and Agriculture Organization (FAO), is successfully promoting integrated pest management (IPM) as an alternative to pesticide use by Indonesian rice farmers. Recognizing that growing pesticide use was encouraging the development of pesticide-resistant strains of the brown planthopper and contaminating water supplies, Indonesian president Suharto in 1986 "banned 57 of the 63 pesticides used on rice and began diverting millions of dollars from pesticide subsidies to the country's until then largely quiescent IPM program." Stone, Researchers Score Victory Over Pesticides—and Pests—in Asia, 256 Science 1272 (1992). In two years, the FAO-run program taught nearly 200,000 farmers how to use IPM techniques. As a result, rice production has increased by approximately 10 percent since 1986, while pesticide use is down sharply. "The key

9. International Environmental Law

commodity, many scientists say, was the political will to risk enraging farmers who had long depended on pesticides" by banning their use. Id. Does this imply that it would be more difficult to implement such a program in a more democratic country?

The Basel Convention (pp. 1205-1210). The Basel Convention entered into force on May 5, 1992 after 20 countries ratified it. The U.S. Senate ratified the Convention on August 11, 1992, but Congress has not yet adopted the legislation necessary for implementing it. Murphy, The Basel Convention on Hazardous Wastes, 35 Environment 42-44 (Mar. 1993). EPA has outlined the implications of the Basel Convention for U.S. policy in a Federal Register notice. 57 Fed. Reg. 20,602 (1992). To implement the Convention, Congress will have to amend section 3017 of RCRA to grant EPA the authority to prohibit waste exports that it believes will be mismanaged, to require exporters to retrieve waste shipments that go awry, and to control waste imports. At the first meeting of parties to the Basel Convention, held in Uruguay in December 1992, industrialized nations agreed to pursue a ban on exports of hazardous waste for disposal in developing countries.

Multinational Corporate Policies (p. 1216). A study by Business International and Arthur D. Little, Managing the Global Environmental Challenge, has found that a surprising number of U.S. companies are adhering to higher environmental standards than required by host countries in operations outside of the United States. For example, because Nigeria has no hazardous waste disposal facilities, Chevron reportedly uses only water-based lubricating fluids in its drilling operations there. IBM recycles three-quarters of the hazardous waste it generates in Argentina because it cannot find a satisfactory local disposal site. The Freedom to Be Dirtier Than the Rest, The Economist, May 30, 1992, at 9 (special section).

Dow Chemical Co. v. Alfaro (p. 1217). The *Alfaro* case was settled shortly before it was scheduled to go to trial in Texas state court in August 1992. Terms of the settlement were not disclosed, but plaintiffs are thought to have received close to $50 million. One factor leading to the settlement was the plaintiffs' concern that the Texas legislature or supreme court would overturn *Alfaro* and reinstate the forum non conveniens doctrine in Texas. The business community expected a change in the membership of the Texas Supreme Court to reinstate the doctrine. When that did not occur, overturning *Alfaro* through legislation became the business lobby's top priority for the 1993 legislative session. In February 1993, the Texas legislature passed a bill reinstating the forum non conveniens doctrine. The legislation will take effect on September 1, 1993. Ironically, after the *Alfaro* case was decided by the Texas Supreme Court, but before the new legislation was enacted, Exxon moved its corporate headquarters from New York to Texas.

D. INTERNATIONAL DEVELOPMENT POLICY AND THE ENVIRONMENT

Effect of Development on Environmental Quality (p. 1224). The link between development and environmental quality was central to the Bruntland Report, *Our Common Future,* and the 1992 Earth Summit. Some economists and the World Bank have consistently argued that development is inherently good for the environment; despite an initial period of environmental degradation associated with development, they assert, increasing affluence brings both the means and the desire for improved environmental quality. However, some pollution (e.g., municipal solid waste and carbon dioxide) does not seem to decline when per capita income increases and the record of currently industrialized countries does not suggest any single, clear path to a sustainable society. For a useful overview, see Forrest, A Turning Point?, 12 Envtl. F. 25 (1995).

1. Federal Agencies and the Extraterritorial Application of Environmental Law

Extraterritorial Application of NEPA (p. 1225). The district court decision in Environmental Defense Fund v. Massey was appealed to the D.C. Circuit, which rendered the following decision.

Environmental Defense Fund, Inc.
v. Massey
986 F.2d 528 (D.C. Cir. 1993)

Before: MIKVA, Chief Judge, WALD and EDWARDS, Circuit Judges.
MIKVA, Chief Judge:
    The Environmental Defense Fund ("EDF") appeals the district court's order dismissing its action seeking declaratory and injunctive relief under the National Environmental Policy Act ("NEPA"). EDF alleges that the National Science Foundation ("NSF") violated NEPA

9. International Environmental Law   Page 1225

by failing to prepare an environmental impact statement ("EIS") in accordance with Section 102(2)(C) before going forward with plans to incinerate food wastes in Antarctica. The district court dismissed EDF's action for lack of subject matter jurisdiction. The court explained that while Congress utilized broad language in NEPA, the statute nevertheless did not contain "a clear expression of legislative intent through a plain statement of extraterritorial statutory effect"; consequently, the court was compelled by the recent Supreme Court decision in Equal Employment Opportunity Commission v. Arabian American Oil Co., 111 S. Ct. 1227 (1991) ("*Aramco*") to conclude that NEPA does not apply to NSF's decision to incinerate food wastes in Antarctica. See Environmental Defense Fund, Inc. v. Massey, 772 F. Supp. 1296, 1297 (D.D.C. 1991). . . .

I

As both parties readily acknowledge, Antarctica is not only a unique continent, but somewhat of an international anomaly. Antarctica is the only continent on earth which has never been and is not now, subject to the sovereign rule of any nation. Since entry into force of the Antarctic Treaty in 1961, the United States and 39 other nations have agreed not to assert any territorial claims to the continent or to establish rights of sovereignty there. *See* The Antarctica Treaty, 12 U.S.T. 794 (Dec. 1, 1959). Hence, Antarctica is generally considered to be a "global common" and frequently analogized to outer space. See Beattie v. United States, 756 F.2d 91, 99 (D.C. Cir. 1984).

Under the auspices of the United States Antarctica Program, NSF operates the McMurdo Station research facility in Antarctica. McMurdo Station is one of three year-round installations that the United States has established in Antarctica, and over which NSF exercises exclusive control. All of the installations serve as platforms or logistic centers for U.S. scientific research; McMurdo Station is the largest of the three, with more than 100 buildings and a summer population of approximately 1200.

Over the years, NSF has burned food wastes at McMurdo Station in an open landfill as a means of disposal. In early 1991, NSF decided to improve its environmental practices in Antarctica by halting its practice of burning food wastes in the open by October, 1991. After discovering asbestos in the landfill, however, NSF decided to cease open burning in the landfill even earlier, and to develop quickly an alternative plan for disposal of its food waste. NSF stored the waste at McMurdo Station from February, 1991 to July, 1991, but subsequently decided to resume incineration in an "interim incinerator" until a state-of-the-art

539

incinerator could be delivered to McMurdo Station. EDF contends that the planned incineration may produce highly toxic pollutants which could be hazardous to the environment, and that NSF failed to consider fully the consequences of its decision to resume incineration as required by the decisionmaking process established by NEPA. . . .

II

A. *The Presumption Against Extraterritoriality*

As the district court correctly noted, the Supreme Court recently reaffirmed the general presumption against the extraterritorial application of statutes in [*Aramco*]. Extraterritoriality is essentially, and in common sense, a jurisdictional concept concerning the authority of a nation to adjudicate the rights of particular parties and to establish the norms of conduct applicable to events or persons outside its borders. More specifically, the extraterritoriality principle provides that "[r]ules of the United States statutory law, whether prescribed by federal or state authority, apply only to conduct occurring within, or having effect within, the territory of the United States." Restatement (Second) of Foreign Relations Law of the United States §38 (1965) [hereinafter Restatement (Second)]; Restatement (Third) of Foreign Relations Law of the United States §403, Com. (g) (1987) [hereinafter Restatement (Third)]. As stated by the Supreme Court in *Aramco*, the primary purpose of this presumption against extraterritoriality is "to protect against the unintended clashes between our laws and those of other nations which could result in international discord." *Aramco*, 111 S. Ct. at 1230. . . .

There are at least three general categories of cases for which the presumption against the extraterritorial application of statutes clearly does not apply. First, as made explicit in *Aramco*, the presumption will not apply where there is an "affirmative intention of the Congress clearly expressed" to extend the scope of the statute to conduct occurring within other sovereign nations. Id. at 1230 (quoting Benz v. Compania Naviera Hidalgo, S.A., 353 U.S. 138, 147 (1957)).

Second, the presumption is generally not applied where the failure to extend the scope of the statute to a foreign setting will result in adverse effects within the United States. Two prime examples of this exception are the Sherman Anti-Trust Act, 15 U.S.C. §§1-7 (1976), and the Lanham Trade-Mark Act, 15 U.S.C. §1051 (1976), which have both been applied extraterritorially where the failure to extend the statute's reach would have negative economic consequences within the United States. . . .

Finally, the presumption against extraterritoriality is not applicable when the conduct regulated by the government occurs within the United States. By definition, an extraterritorial application of a statute involves the regulation of conduct beyond U.S. borders. Even where the significant effects of the regulated conduct are felt outside U.S. borders, the statute itself does not present a problem of extraterritoriality, so long as the conduct which Congress seeks to regulate occurs largely within the United States. See generally Laker Airways, 731 F.2d at 921; Restatement (Second) §38 (rules of U.S. statutory law apply "to conduct occurring within, or having effect within the territory of the United States"); Restatement (Second) §17 (1965); Restatement (Third) §492(1)(a),(b) (1987).

Despite these well-established exceptions to the presumption against extraterritoriality, the district court below bypassed the threshold question of whether the application of NEPA to agency actions in Antarctica presents an extraterritoriality problem at all. In particular, the court failed to determine whether the statute seeks to regulate conduct in the United States or in another sovereign country. It also declined to consider whether NEPA would create a potential for "clashes between our laws and those of other nations" if it was applied to the decisionmaking of federal agencies regarding proposed actions in Antarctica. *Aramco,* 111 S. Ct. at 1230. After a thorough review of these relevant factors, we conclude that this case does not present an issue of extraterritoriality.

B. *Regulated Conduct Under NEPA*

NEPA is designed to control the decisionmaking process of U.S. federal agencies, not the substance of agency decisions. By enacting NEPA, Congress exercised its statutory authority to determine the factors an agency must consider when exercising its discretion, and created a process whereby American officials, while acting within the United States, can reach enlightened policy decisions by taking into account environmental effects. In our view, such regulation of U.S. federal agencies and their decisionmaking processes is a legitimate exercise of Congress' territoriality-based jurisdiction, and does not raise extraterritoriality concerns.

Section 102(2)(C) lies at the heart of NEPA and is often considered the "action-forcing" element of the statute. See S. Rep. No. 91-296, 91st Cong., 1st Sess. 19 (1969); Robertson v. Methow Valley Citizens Council, 490 U.S. 332, 350 (1989). This section requires "all agencies of the Federal Government" to prepare a detailed environmental impact statement for every "major Federal action[]" which has the potential to significantly affect the human environment. 42 U.S.C. §4332(2)(C). Section 102(2)(C) binds only American officials and controls the very essence of the government function: decisionmaking. Because the decisionmaking processes of federal agencies take place almost exclusively in this country and involve the workings of the United States government, they are uniquely domestic. . . .

In many respects, NEPA is most closely akin to the myriad laws directing federal decisionmakers to consider particular factors before extending aid or engaging in certain types of trade. See Comment, NEPA's Role in Protecting the World Environment, 131 U. Pa. L. Rev. 353, 371 (1982). For example, the Foreign Assistance Act of 1961 requires the Agency for International Development, before approving developmental assistance, to consider the degree to which programs integrate women into the economy, as well as the possibility of using aid to "support democratic, social and political trends in recipient countries." 22 U.S.C. §§2151(k), 2218(c) (1976). Similarly, the Nuclear Nonproliferation Act requires the Nuclear Regulatory Commission to consider a nation's willingness to cooperate with American nonproliferation objectives before approving a nuclear export license. 22 U.S.C. §§3201-3282 (1976); 42 U.S.C. §§2156, 2157 (Supp. III 1979). Just as these statutes fall short of prescribing action in foreign jurisdictions, and are instead directed at the regulation of agency decisionmaking, NEPA also creates no substantive environmental standards and simply prescribes by statute the factors an agency must consider when exercising its discretionary authority.

Moreover, NEPA would never require enforcement in a foreign forum or involve "choice of law" dilemmas. This factor alone is powerful evidence of the statute's domestic nature, and distinguishes NEPA from Title VII as well as the Federal Tort Claims Act—two statutes that have been limited in their effect by the presumption against extraterritoriality. See *Aramco*, 111 S. Ct. at 1234 (presumption against extraterritoriality applies where Congress failed to provide for overseas enforcement and failed to address the potential conflicts of law issue). . . .

In sum, since NEPA is designed to regulate conduct occurring within the territory of the United States, and imposes no substantive requirements which could be interpreted to govern conduct abroad, the presumption against extraterritoriality does not apply to this case.

C. *The Unique Status of Antarctica*

Antarctica's unique status in the international arena further supports our conclusion that this case does not implicate the presumption against extraterritoriality. The Supreme Court explicitly stated in *Aramco*

9. International Environmental Law Page 1225

that when applying the presumption against extraterritoriality, courts should look to see if there is any indication that Congress intended to extend the statute's coverage "beyond places over which the United States has sovereignty *or some measure of legislative control.*" *Aramco*, 111 S. Ct. at 1230 (quoting *Foley Bros.*, 336 U.S. at 285 (emphasis added)). Thus, where the U.S. has some real measure of legislative control over the region at issue, the presumption against extraterritoriality is much weaker. See, e.g. Sierra Club v. Adams, 578 F.2d 389 (D.C. Cir. 1978) (NEPA assumed to be applicable to South American highway construction where the United States had two-thirds of the ongoing financial responsibility and control over the highway construction); People of Entewatak v. Laird, 353 F. Supp. 811 (D. Hawaii 1973) (concluding that NEPA applies to the United States trust territories in the Pacific). And where there is no potential for conflict "between our laws and those of other nations," the purpose behind the presumption is eviscerated, and the presumption against extraterritoriality applies with significantly less force. *Aramco*, 111 S. Ct. at 1230.

Indeed, it was the general understanding that Antarctica "is not a foreign country," but rather a continent that is most frequently analogized to outer space, that led this Court to conclude in Beattie v. United States, 756 F.2d 91 (D.C. Cir. 1984), that the presumption against extraterritoriality should not apply to cases arising in Antarctica. But cf. Smith v. United States, 932 F.2d 791 (9th Cir. 1991). The *Beattie* Court noted that Antarctica is not a "country" at all, as it has no sovereign, and stated that "to the extent that there is an assertion of governmental authority in Antarctica, it appears to be predominately that of the United States." *Beattie*, 756 F.2d at 99.

Even aside from this Court's holding in *Beattie*, it cannot be seriously suggested that the United States lacks some real measure of legislative control over Antarctica. The United States controls all air transportation to Antarctica and conducts all search and rescue operations there. Moreover, the United States has exclusive legislative control over McMurdo Station and the other research installations established there by the United States Antarctica Program. This legislative control, taken together with the status of Antarctica as a sovereignless continent, compels the conclusion that the presumption against extraterritoriality is particularly inappropriate under the circumstances presented in this case. As stated aptly by a State Department official in congressional testimony shortly following the enactment of NEPA,

> application of [NEPA] to actions occurring outside the jurisdiction of any State, including the United States, would not conflict with the primary purpose underlying this venerable rule of interpretation—to avoid ill-

543

will and conflict between nations arising out of one nation's encroachments upon another's sovereignty. . . . There are at least three general areas: The high seas, outer space and Antarctica.

See Memorandum of C. Herter, Special Assistant to the Secretary of State for Environmental Affairs, *reprinted in Administration of the National Environmental Policy Act: Hearing Before the Subcommittee on Fisheries and Wildlife Conservation of the House Committee on Merchant Marine and Fisheries*, 91st Cong., 2d Sess. 551 (1970) [hereinafter cited as State Department Memo].

While the State Department memo is hardly a part of appropriate legislative history, and is not entitled to any particular deference, the memo does reflect the general understanding by those intimately involved in the creation and execution of U.S. foreign policy that the global commons, including Antarctica, do not present the challenges inherent in relations between sovereign nations. Thus, in a sovereignless region like Antarctica, where the United States has exercised a great measure of legislative control, the presumption against extraterritoriality has little relevance and a dubious basis for its application.

D. *Foreign Policy Considerations*

Although NSF concedes that NEPA only seeks to regulate the decisionmaking process of federal agencies, and that this case does not present a conflict between U.S. and foreign sovereign law, NSF still contends that the presumption against extraterritoriality controls this case. In particular, NSF argues that the EIS requirement will interfere with U.S. efforts to work cooperatively with other nations toward solutions to environmental problems in Antarctica. In NSF's view, joint research and cooperative environmental assessment would be "placed at risk of NEPA injunctions, making the U.S. a doubtful partner for future international cooperation in Antarctica." Appellee's Brief at 45.

NSF also argues that the Protocol on Environmental Protection to the Antarctic Treaty, which was adopted and opened for signature on October 4, 1991, would, if adopted by all the proposed signatories, conflict with the procedural requirements adopted by Congress for the decisionmaking of federal agencies under NEPA. See Protocol on Environmental Protection to the Antarctic Treaty, with Annexes, XI ATSCM, reprinted in 30 Int'l Legal Materials 1461 (1991). According to NSF, since NEPA requires the preparation of an EIS for actions with potentially "significant" impacts, while the Protocol requires an environmental analysis even for actions with "minor or transitory" impacts on the Antarctic environment, the two regulatory schemes are incompatible and will result in international discord. We find these arguments unpersuasive. First, it should be noted that the Protocol is not in effect in any form and is years away from ratification by the United States and all 26 signatories. Second, we are unable to comprehend the difficulty presented by the two standards of review. It is clear that NSF will have to perform *fewer* studies under NEPA than under the Protocol, and where an EIS is required under NEPA, it would not strain a researcher's intellect to indicate in a single document how the environmental impact of the proposed action is more than "minor" and also more than "significant."

More importantly, we are not convinced that NSF's ability to cooperate with other nations in Antarctica in accordance with U.S. foreign policy will be hampered by NEPA injunctions. . . .

[T]he government may avoid the EIS requirement where U.S. foreign policy interests outweigh the benefits derived from preparing an EIS. Since NEPA imposes no substantive requirements, U.S. foreign policy interests in Antarctica will rarely be threatened, except perhaps where the time required to prepare an EIS would itself threaten international cooperation, see Flint Ridge Development Co. v. Scenic Rivers Association, 426 U.S. 776, 791 (1976) (EIS requirement must yield where a clear conflict in statutory authority is unavoidable, including conflicts which arise out of timetables imposed by statute), or where the foreign policy interests at stake are particularly unique and delicate. See *NRDC,* 647 F.2d at 1348. Thus, contrary to NSF's assertions, where U.S. foreign policy interests outweigh the benefits of the EIS requirement, NSF's efforts to cooperate with foreign governments regarding environmental practices in Antarctica will not be frustrated by forced compliance with NEPA. . . .

Conclusion

Applying the presumption against extraterritoriality here would result in a federal agency being allowed to undertake actions significantly affecting the human environment in Antarctica, an area over which the United States has substantial interest and authority, without ever being held accountable for its failure to comply with the decisionmaking procedures instituted by Congress—even though such accountability, if it were enforced, would result in no conflict with foreign law or threat to foreign policy. NSF has provided no support for its proposition that conduct occurring within the United States is rendered exempt from otherwise applicable statutes merely because the effects of this compliance would be felt in the global commons. We therefore reverse the district court's decision, and remand for a determination of whether the environmental analyses performed by NSF, prior to its decision to resume incineration, failed to comply with Section 102(2)(c) of NEPA.

We find it important to note, however, that we do not decide today how NEPA might apply to actions in a case involving an actual foreign sovereign or how other U.S. statutes might apply to Antarctica. We only hold that the alleged failure of NSF to comply with NEPA before resuming incineration in Antarctica does not implicate the presumption against extraterritoriality.

NOTES AND QUESTIONS

1. As the court notes, Antarctica's legal status is relatively unusual because it has no sovereign and because the United States exercises a good deal of control over the continent. To what extent, if any, does the court's decision suggest that NEPA may have extraterritorial impact outside the context of Antarctica? A federal district court has held that NEPA does not apply to operations at three U.S. naval bases in Japan. In NEPA Coalition of Japan v. Aspin, 837 F. Supp. 466 (D.D.C. 1993), the court distinguished EDF v. Massey on the ground that it involved actions by a federal agency in Antarctica rather than on the soil of a foreign sovereign. In the alternative, the court held that even if NEPA applied, an EIS need not be prepared because it might interfere with U.S. foreign policy interests that outweigh the benefits of preparing an EIS.

2. Efforts to apply other U.S. laws to Antarctica have met with less success. Several weeks after the D.C. Circuit's decision, the Supreme Court held that the Federal Tort Claims Act (FTCA) did not apply to conduct occurring in Antarctica. Smith v. United States, 113 S. Ct. 1178 (1993). Noting that the language of the FTCA expressly excludes claims "arising in a foreign country," 28 U.S.C. §2680(k), the Court found that the ordinary meaning of "foreign country" includes Antarctica even though it has no recognized government. The Court also cited the principle that waivers of sovereign immunity should be narrowly construed and the presumption against extraterritorial application of U.S. statutes.

3. As noted above, a federal district court ruled in June 1993 that NEPA requires that an EIS be prepared for the North American Free Trade Agreement. Ironically, the government is seeking to expedite its appeal of this ruling even though it had previously convinced the D.C. Circuit not to hear the challenge because no final agency action had taken place until the agreement was finalized. Public Citizen v. Office of the U.S. Trade Representative, 970 F.2d 916 (D.C. Cir. 1992), repro-

9. International Environmental Law Page 1227

duced on p. 455 of this Supplement. Despite the new district court ruling, could Congress still ratify NAFTA even if an EIS has not yet been completed?

4. If domestic law is not applied in an extraterritorial fashion, it may become more difficult to enforce the provisions of international agreements. For example, the environmental provisions of the Antarctic Treaty were strengthened by a protocol adopted in 1991. Under the protocol, so-called Specially Protected Areas were created to recognize the need for measures to protect the unusual ecosystem and to prevent contamination of long-term monitoring studies. In late 1991, without notice, New Zealand Telecom installed a satellite earth station on the boundary of a crater area reserved for scientific investigations. According to scientists working in the area, the satellite transmissions will interfere with highly sensitive radio measurements. How might scientists and environmentalists attempt to enforce the Treaty?

5. After vigorous lobbying by environmentalists and the intervention of the White House's Office of Environmental Policy, the Clinton Administration decided not to seek further review of the D.C. Circuit's decision in Environmental Defense Fund v. Massey.

Extraterritorial Application of the Endangered Species Act (pp. 1225-1226). In Lujan v. Defenders of Wildlife, 112 S. Ct. 2130 (1992), the Supreme Court reversed the Eighth Circuit decision mentioned on pages 1225-1226 on the ground that plaintiffs lacked standing. This decision is reproduced beginning on page 197 of this Supplement. Because the case was decided on standing grounds, Justice Stevens was the only justice to address the merits of the claim of extraterritorial application of the ESA. He expressed the view that section 7(a)(2)'s requirement that federal agencies consult with the Secretary of the Interior to ensure that activities funded by them are not likely to jeopardize endangered species did not apply to activities in foreign countries. In light of the fact that other sections of the ESA expressly deal with protection of species in foreign countries, Justice Stevens deemed it "particularly significant" that nothing in the text of section 7(a)(2) indicates that it applies abroad.

2. *International Financial Institutions and the Environment*

A. DEBT-FOR-NATURE SWAPS AND THE PRESERVATION OF TROPICAL FORESTS

The Rio Earth Summit (p. 1227). At the Rio Earth Summit, the U.S. delegation made international agreement on measures to protect forests its top priority. On the eve of the Earth Summit the United States announced that it would increase U.S. aid to foreign forestry programs from $120 million to $270 million per year starting in fiscal year 1993. Wines, Bush Offers Plan to Save Forests, N.Y. Times, June 2, 1992, at A1. The Bush Administration also announced that the U.S. Forest Service will sharply curtail clear-cutting of timber on federal lands managed by the agency. Clear-cutting, which had been used for 70-80 percent of the federal timber harvest, is considered particularly damaging to the environment because it involves cutting down every tree on large swaths of land. While the new policy will still permit clear-cutting in certain circumstances (e.g., for stands of timber damaged by wind or fire, or to open up scenic vistas), selective cutting is expected to become the norm, with clear-cutting reduced by 70 percent from 1988 levels. This policy change will raise the cost of harvesting timber on federal lands and may reduce by 10 percent the total timber harvested from federal lands. Ingersoll, Bush to Curtail Clear-Cutting of U.S. Forests, Wall St. J., June 4, 1992, at B1.

Developing countries maintained that the United States was being hypocritical by targeting this issue in order to deflect attention away from U.S. efforts to weaken the climate change and biodiversity conventions. They noted that satellite photos indicated that clear-cutting of patches of the old-growth forests of the Pacific Northwest has progressed to the point at which the biological integrity of the forest as an ecosystem is in far greater jeopardy than the tropical rainforests of the Amazon.

Noting that the annual rate of deforestation in the Amazon area of Brazil had dropped by 63 percent since 1985, the Brazilian government agreed to support the Earth Summit's "Statement of Principles on Forests." Using satellite photos, Brazilian officials have calculated that the annual rate of deforestation has declined from 30,000 square kilometers in 1985 to 11,000 square kilometers in 1991. Brooke, Brazil's News for Earth: Loss of Amazon Rain Forest Is Slowing Steadily, Intl. Herald Trib., May 23-24, 1992, at 3.

Nations at the Earth Summit ultimately agreed to a Statement of Principles on Forests that calls for the use of sustainable forestry management practices and urges efforts to avoid excessive timber harvesting. The statement acknowledges the link between forest protection and protection of biodiversity and the role of forests in combatting the buildup of greenhouse gases. At April 1993 talks to renegotiate the International Tropical Timber Agreement, the Clinton Administration sought to do some fence-mending to open the way for negotiation of a world forest treaty. Stevens, U.S. Cracks Door to World Forest Agreement, N.Y. Times, April 13, 1993, at C4. In January 1994 agreement was reached on a new version of the International Tropical Timber Agreement. Pitt, Accord Is Reached on Use of Forests, N.Y. Times, Jan. 23, 1994, at 7.

Debt-for-Nature Swaps (p. 1227). The Enterprise for the Americas Initiative, enacted into law in 1992, Pub. L. No. 102-440, seeks to facilitate debt-for-nature swaps. It permits other countries to redeem on favorable terms federally guaranteed debts incurred in purchasing U.S. agricultural commodities. To qualify for the program, the countries must agree to devote to environmental projects either 40 percent or more of the price paid for the debt or the difference between the price paid for the debt and its face value. For a proposal to expand the debt-for-nature concept into even more productive technology-for-nature exchanges, see O'Neill and Sunstein, Economics and the Environment: Trading Debt and Technology for Nature, 17 Colum. J. Envtl. L. 93 (1992).

Preservation of Tropical Forests (p. 1227). Experts continue to disagree about the adequacy of methods for achieving sustainable harvests from tropical forests. Evidence of success is so limited that some authorities suggest a ban on logging in tropical forests, confining forestry to plantations. Because of the economic implications of this conclusion, research on effective strategies continues. A range of innovative strategies to promote good management practices is also being tested, including certification programs to verify that tropical hardwood has been obtained using sustainable cutting methods. See N. Johnson and B. Cabarle, Surviving the Cut: Natural Forest Management in the Humid Tropics (1993).

B. MULTILATERAL DEVELOPMENT BANKS

Brazil's Polonoroeste Project (p. 1230). One of the most notorious World Bank projects, which Aufderheide and Rich allude to at the bottom of parent text page 1231, was the Polonoroeste project in Brazil's Amazon watershed. The project, which aimed to colonize an area of Amazon rainforest, lured one million settlers into the area where the soils beneath the rainforest were so poor that the area became "a 15,000 square mile wasteland." Adams, Rio Agenda: Soak the West's Taxpayers, Wall St. J., June 3, 1992, at A14. In an effort to make the proverbial silk purse out of an environmental sow's ear, the World Bank's first annual report claimed that the outcry generated by the Polonoroeste project "fostered a growing political and public commitment to preserve the Amazon's remaining natural resources." Id.

The Global Environmental Facility (p. 1234). Global Environment Facility (GEF) is evolving into a mechanism for subsidizing environmentally desirable expenditures in developing countries that could become a focal point for efforts to address North-South differences. The structure of the GEF is a critical issue. Industrialized countries do not want to create another international lending institution, but developing countries are insisting on a greater voice in international aid for the environment. In response to concerns from developing countries, changes may be made in the voting structure of the GEF and the scope of projects it funds.

The Global Environmental Facility completed its initial three-year pilot phase. A detailed and highly critical assessment of the pilot was prepared by an independent evaluation committee as the basis for a decision about restructuring and further financing. UN Development Programme, UN Environment Programme, and the World Bank, Global Environmental Facility: Independent Evaluation of the Pilot Phase (1994). See also I. Bowles and G. Prickett, Reframing the Green Window: An Analysis of the GEF Pilot Phase Approach to Biodiversity and Global Warming and Recommendations for the Operational Phase (1994); Jordan, Financing the UNCED Agenda: The Controversy over Additionality, 36 Envt. 16 (1994); A. Wolf and D. Reed, Incremental Cost Analysis in Addressing Global Environmental Problems (1994); Wells, "The Global Environmental Facility and Prospects for Biodiversity Conservation," 6 Intl. Envtl. Affairs 69 (1994).

Based on the evaluation, participating governments agreed in March 1994 to restructure the GEF. Twenty-six countries pledged to provide $2 billion for three years. Decisions will now be supervised by a council of 32 nations—18 from recipients and 14 from developed countries. Voting is by a "double majority" system and requires a 60 percent majority of both groups. Global Environmental Facility, Instrument for the Establishment of the Restructured Global Environmental Facility (1994).

For discussion of the Green Fund and other multilateral development bank issues, see Wold and Zaelke, Establishing an Independent Review Board at the European Bank for Reconstruction and Development: A Model for Improving MDB Decisionmaking, 2 Duke Env. L. & Poly. Forum 59 (1992); Hidyard, Green Dollars, Green Menace, 22 Ecologist 82 (May-June 1992). On the evolution of NGO participation in the UN system and its influence on the World Bank, see World Resources 1992-93, 215-234. The effort to give a greater voice to previously unrepresented indigenous peoples is causing some dilemmas for environmental groups, since the former sometimes support development as a source of income. NRDC found itself attacked by other environmental groups for working with indigenous tribes in Ecuador that favored negotiation with a U.S. oil company that had been granted development rights in a national park. Other U.S. environmental organizations were allied with more urban environmental interests opposed to allowing any development within park boundaries.

The Evolution of World Bank Environmental Policy (p. 1234-1235). Environmental policy at the World Bank continues to be a controversial topic. As discussed on text page 1203, Lawrence Summers, when he served as the Bank's senior economist, wrote a memorandum suggesting that the transfer of polluting industries to developing countries may be economically efficient because of the lower life expectancy in these countries. Let Them Eat Pollution, The Economist, Feb. 8, 1992, at 66; The In-Your-Face Economist at the World Bank, Bus. Week, May 11, 1992, at 76. On the other hand, the Bank's most important annual publication, the World Development Report, focused on the need for environmental protection for the first time in 1992. In an unprecedented action, the Bank also created an outside expert committee to review the Narmada River Dam project planned in India with Bank support. In June 1992 the committee issued its report, which recommended that the project not go forward without significantly increased planning and evaluation. In March 1993, the Indian government canceled the World Bank loan for the project after concluding that it could not meet the Bank's new environmental "benchmarks." Holmes, India Cancels Dam Loan from World Bank, N.Y. Times, Mar. 31, 1993, at A5.

In September 1992, the Bank issued the third in a series of annual "World Bank and the Environment" reports. This edition emphasized its growing use of environmental country studies to identify environmental investment priorities on a detailed, country-by-country basis.

A major critique of the World Bank's impact on the environment was published in 1994. B. Rich, Mortgaging the Earth: The World Bank, Environmental Impoverishment, and the Crisis of Development (1994). Rich is a lawyer with the Environmental Defense. In response, the Bank issued a strongly worded, 30-page rebuttal, The World Bank's Response to Bruce Rich's "Mortgaging the Earth." The Bank's most recent description of its environmental efforts is Making Development Sustainable: The World Bank Group and the Environment (1994).

E. FUTURE DIRECTIONS FOR INTERNATIONAL ENVIRONMENTAL LAW

Linking the International Environmental Agenda with Human Rights (p. 1236). An April 1992 conference at Yale Law School on human rights and environmental protection is summarized in a conference report published by the American Association for the Advancement of Science, Earth Rights and Responsibilities: Human Rights and Environmental Protection (1992). In opening remarks at the conference, Dean Guido Calabresi addressed the significance of adopting the language of "rights": "Much of law is a fight over the words we use to describe things, and if you have the right words, you are two-thirds of the way to winning the battle. If the environment is something to be traded off, . . . then it is very easy when the economy is going bad, or when a president finds it expedient, to have [it] thrown away. If [environmental concerns] are called rights, it is a very different matter."

What practical significance might follow from linking human rights and environmental concerns? Some leading human rights advocates argue that environmentalists have already established the beginning of much stronger international regimes than would be provided by the use of human rights arguments. They are also worried that extending the language of rights to conservation objectives might undercut the strength of concerns framed around *human* interests. On the other hand, it may also be possible to advance *both* agendas more effectively by recognizing areas of overlapping, mutual interest. For example, both communities share an interest in protecting freedom of expression for environmentalists in developing countries and the rights of indigenous peoples to maintain sustainable lifestyles.

Population, the Environment, and the Cairo Conference (p. 1236). The steady increase in global population is a contributor to many environmental problems. However, the effect of population size on the environment is determined by consumption patterns, technology, and income distribution. Criticism of population growth without respect to these other factors has not been well received by developing countries. Moreover, although global population growth may be relevant to assessing general trends, it is an issue that is extremely difficult to address through the traditional mechanisms of international law but rather requires the creative use of strategies for building international cooperation and improved national capabilities for family planning. See generally Dasgupta, Population, Poverty and the Local Environment, 272 Scientic Am. 40-45 (1995).

The link between population and global environmental problems received renewed attention with the September 1994 International Conference on Population and Development, held in Cairo, Egypt. The conference was the third international population conference. Two previous population policy conferences, the first in 1974 in Bucharest and a second in Mexico City a decade later, were characterized by sharp divisions between developed and developing country governments, and highlighted the sensitive ethical, sexual, and religious overtones inherent in the population debate. In contrast, the Cairo Conference witnessed an emerging consensus on the role of population policy in sustainable development.

International attention to rapid population growth heightened in the late 1960s. Believing a crisis was looming, the United States, joined by several Nordic countries, led the drive to create the United Nations Fund for Population Activities (UNFPA) and to organize international consensus around a policy agenda. But the governments of developing countries balked at the North's focus on fertility control, arguing that because population growth was a consequence of underdevelopment, it must be addressed via the underlying socioeconomic factors affecting fertility levels. Although the United States was disappointed with the Bucharest conference document because it failed to emphasize the need for governmental support of family planning programs, the "World Population Plan of Action" was considered a significant victory for developing nations.

Over the next decade, international agencies began to link population activities with other development and education initiatives, and developing country governments came to appreciate the importance of fertility control. The North-South conflict that had dominated Bucharest was largely absent from Mexico City, despite a dramatic reversal from the United States whose internal politics forced a withdrawal of funding for organizations that offered information on abortion. The Bucharest Plan was strengthened and expanded by the Mexico City declaration, which reflected an integrated, development-oriented approach to population policy and featured strong references to the links between the status of women and fertility.

With the 1994 Cairo Conference, both developed and developing country governments set a new tone and scope for population-related policies and activities for the next decades. Unlike previous documents which have focused on demographic objectives, Cairo's "World Programme of Action" (WPOA) centers on the reproductive rights and health needs of women. Though not binding on governments, the WPOA provides an overall perspective both to national programs and international assistance.

A shift in the international population debate to women's rights and health may signal a new level of power and effectiveness for the international women's movement. The three preparatory meetings (Prepcoms) leading up to Cairo were dominated by women's groups, and the WPOA sends a powerful signal about the relationships among women's empowerment, reproductive health, and family planning. This agenda contrasts with the more traditional priorities of family planning organizations and their donor and agency supporters.

While the Cairo Conference signaled the ability of women to interest governments in supporting better population policies, success or failure of the WPOA will depend a great deal on the level of effort put behind implementing the WPOA's recommendations. Among the elements crucial to its success will be the mechanisms that are put into place for monitoring and accountability at the national level.

Despite demonstrated political commitment, the greatest challenge facing the implementation of effective reproductive policies will center around resources. Initial estimates produced during the Prepcoms as to the resources required to implement the program of action ranged from between 10 and 20 billion dollars. While these numbers reflect more a political target than any firm sense of what will be needed, donor governments and agencies will nevertheless need to make stronger budgetary commitments if the goals of the WPOA are to be pursued effectively. Among the assignments for population activists will be to increase pressure for more resources targeted at enhancing the socioeconomic development agenda.

WPOA opens up the possibility of monitoring donor assistance vis-á-vis stated commitments to women's empowerment and health. Although donor assistance accounts at present for only 20 to 25 percent of all population expenditures, it has considerable leverage in determining the direction of national programs.

The attractiveness of the WPOA is that it is an enabling document, one that gives activists a basis for moving programs in particular directions. The Programme explicitly defines the role of NGOs in monitoring programs and calls for putting systems in place to detect and control abuses. Though few governments may automatically do what they have agreed in WPOA is worth doing, nations at least may be asked to justify action and inaction in terms of the WPOA.

For a review of the Cairo Conference, see Sen, The World Programme of Action: A New Paradigm for Population Policy, 37 Envt. 10 (1995). For a review of the evidence concerning the links between population, poverty, and environmental issues, see R. Cassen et al., Population and Development: Old Debates, New Conclusions (1994).

10
Conclusion

> Environmentalists, who are surely on the right side of history, are increasingly on the wrong side of the present, risking their credibility by proclaiming emergencies that do not exist. What some doctrinaire environmentalists wish were true for reasons of ideology has begun to obscure the view of what is actually true in "the laboratory of nature." It's time we began reading from a new script, one that reconciles the ideals of environmentalism with the observed facts of the natural world. . . . Ecorealism will be the next wave of environmental thinking. The core principles of ecorealism are these: that logic, not sentiment, is the best tool for safeguarding nature; that accurate understanding of the actual state of the environment will serve the Earth bettter than expressions of panic; that in order to form a constructive alliance with nature, men and women must learn to think like nature.
>
> —*Gregg Easterbrook*[*]

Earth Day 1995: The 25th Anniversary (p. 1239). The 25th anniversary of the first Earth Day was celebrated on April 22, 1995. The event was pushed to the back pages by the terrorist bombing that killed 167 people in Oklahoma City. The theme of the National Earth Day Rally, which drew more than 120,000 people to the Mall in Washington, D.C. was "Don't Turn Back the Clock on Environmental Protection"—a sign of how dramatically the political climate in Congress has changed with respect to environmental issues. Gaylord Nelson, who had organized the first Earth Day while a U.S. senator, complained that the new Republican majority in Congress was "using the anti-government mood as a club to destroy the environmental achievements of the last 25 years." Achenbach, Earth Day Birthday Bash, Wash. Post, Apr. 22, 1995, at D1. Complaining that the tradition of bipartisan support for environmental protection "is hanging by a thread," Vice President Al Gore vowed to "prevent the rollback of the gains we have made" and "to reinvent environmental protection in order to make further gains." Gore, Earth

---

[*]A Moment on the Earth: The Coming Age of Environmental Optimism xvi, xvii (1995).

Page 1239

Days Have Become Earth Years, N.Y. Times, Apr. 23, 1995, at 17. Predictably, skirmishes between corporate interests and environmentalists occurred over sponsorship of Earth Day events as marketing agencies offered companies "very special business building and marketing opportunities" by involvement in an "accepted credible cause: to better our environment." Cushman, Tug-of-War Develops over Earth Day in '95, N.Y. Times, Oct. 29, 1994, at 10. For an assessment of the state of the environment and a history of environmental politics since the first Earth Day, see Riordan et al., The Legacy of Earth Day: Reflections at a Turning Point, 37 Env. 6 (Apr. 1995).

A. ENVIRONMENTAL PROGRESS

A Moment on the Earth and "Ecorealism" (pp. 1239-1263). Environmental journalist Gregg Easterbrook has written a major new book arguing that environmentalists have been unduly alarmist about the state of the planet. G. Easterbrook, A Moment on the Earth: The Coming Age of Environmental Optimism (1995). Easterbrook makes the following provocative arguments:

- That in the Western world pollution will end within our lifetimes, with society almost painlessly adapting a zero-emissions philosophy.
- That several categories of pollution have *already* ended.
- That the environments of Western countries have been growing cleaner during the very period the public has come to believe they are growing more polluted.
- That First World industrial countries, considered the scourge of the global environment, are by most measures much cleaner than developing nations.
- That most feared environmental catastrophes, such as runaway global warming, are almost certain to be avoided.
- That far from becoming a new source of global discord, environmentalism, which binds nations to a common concern, will be the best thing that's ever happened to international relations.
- That nearly all technical trends are toward new devices and modes of production that are more efficient, use fewer resources, produce less waste, and cause less ecological disruption than technology of the past.
- That there exists no fundamental conflict between the artificial and the natural.

556

10. Conclusion

- That artificial forces which today harm nature can be converted into allies of nature in an incredibly short time by natural standards.
- Most important, that humankind, even a growing human population of many billions, can take a constructive place in the natural order.

Id. at xvi-xvii. Easterbrook advocates a new way of looking at environmental issues, which he dubs "ecorealism." He defines its "core principles" to be "that logic, not sentiment, is the best tool for safeguarding nature; that accurate understanding of the actual state of the environment will serve the Earth better than expressions of panic; that in order to form a constructive alliance with nature, men and women must learn to think like nature." Id. at xvii. While claiming that this philosophy is not the equivalent of "don't worry, be happy," Easterbrook maintains that for millions of years nature has been creating worse ecological problems than mankind.

Not surprisingly, Easterbrook's views have generated considerable controversy. Environmentalists maintain that he does not fully appreciate that many of the positive environmental trends he cites are due to hard fought battles waged by them. As one reviewer writes, "He wants it both ways—to condemn professional enviros and other doomsayers and at the same time to champion nature. This amounts to ecosophistry and ignores the fact that what are often perceived as extreme positions effect moderate, positive gains in any field." Conaway, Mother Nature's Prospects, Wash. Post Book World, April 23, 1995, at 5. Easterbrook may be guilty of the same hyperbolizing for which he condemns environmentalists, but in a very different direction that is likely to receive an enthusiastic reception from opponents of environmental regulation.

B. ENVIRONMENTAL PROSPECTS

The Valdez Principles Become the CERES Principles (p. 1263). In response to objections that the name "Valdez Principles" had a pejorative association with the *Exxon Valdez* oil spill, the Coalition for Environmentally Responsible Economies (CERES) has renamed them the CERES Principles. After the name change, one major oil company, the Sun Oil Company, agreed to sign the CERES principles. Mathews, Sun Co. Agrees to Take Environmental Pledge, Wash. Post, Feb. 11, 1993, at B11. Although the company's shareholders had defeated a resolution to adopt the CERES Principles by a vote of 94 percent to 6 percent, the company eventually became convinced that the principles were consistent with its own efforts to reduce pollution. As of May 1995, 60 corporations had signed the CERES Principles, including five Fortune 500 firms (Arizona Public Service Co., General Motors, H.B. Fuller, Polaroid Corp., and the Sun Oil Co.).

Most companies object to the notion of agreeing to make environmental disclosures to CERES, a private group with its own reporting requirements, and to submitting to a CERES audit concerning compliance with the principles. A spokesperson for Exxon maintains that the CERES Principles "do not recognize the need to balance environmental protection with the importance of adequate energy resources and a stable, healthy economy." Id. Many companies have adopted their own corporate environmental policies, in part to bolster their argument that they need not sign the CERES Principles. While some of these policies are little more than window dressing, more companies appear to be taking the environment seriously. See Popoff, Companies Change Course, EPA J. 26 (Sept.-Oct. 1992); Woolard, An Industry Approach to Sustainable Development, Issues in Science & Technology 29 (Spring 1992).

Consensus-Building Partnerships & EPA's "Common Sense" Initiative (pp. 1263-1266). When EPA released its five-year strategic plan in August 1994, one of its seven major principles was the development of partnerships with industry, the public, and state and local governments. Strategic Plan Shifts EPA's Focus to Needs of Ecosystems, Communities, 25 Env. Rep. 737 (1994). One part of this effort that already is underway is EPA's "Common Sense Initiative," launched in November 1993. The program is designed to develop ways to streamline and consolidate environmental regulations that affect certain industries. EPA has assembled teams of senior-level agency officials and representatives from industry, environmental groups, state and local officials and labor unions to focus on the development of consensus-building approaches for more efficiently achieving environmental protection goals. The teams are examining how six industry groups currently are regulated with a view to developing more cost-effective, multimedia approaches to regulation as an alternative to the pollutant-by-pollutant approach. Industries involved in the early phases of the program include the auto industry, metal plating and finishing, oil refining, iron and steel, the electronics and computer industries, and the printing industry.

Securities Law and the Environment (p. 1266). SEC Commissioner Richard Roberts has warned that the Securities and Exchange Commission will intensify its scrutiny of company disclosures to shareholders of the short-term and long-term effects of environmental regulation.

10. Conclusion

Scrutiny of Environmental Liability Disclosures Will Intensify, SEC Commissioner Tells Companies, 25 Env. Rep. 2071 (1994). While many companies are disclosing that they have been named as potentially responsible parties under CERCLA, few are disclosing estimates of their potential liability. Securities Official Renews Call for Disclosure of Companies' Possible Environmental Liabilities, 23 Env. Rep. 1646 (1992); see also Geltman, Disclosure of Contingent Environmental Liabilities by Public Companies under the Federal Securities Laws, 16 Harv. Env. L. Rev. 129 (1992).

In August 1992, a federal district court heard a lawsuit charging that the International Paper Company had materially misrepresented its environmental record in responding to a shareholder resolution urging the company to adopt the Valdez Principles. Excerpts from the court's decision are reproduced below.

> *United Paperworkers International Union v. International Paper Co.*
> 801 F. Supp. 1134 (S.D.N.Y. 1992),
> aff'd, 985 F.2d 1190 (2d Cir. 1993)

BRIEANT, Chief Judge.

On April 23, 1992, plaintiff brought an Order To Show Cause and a Temporary Restraining Order, seeking to enjoin further solicitation and voting of proxies in connection with defendant International Paper's Annual Meeting. That meeting was scheduled to take place on May 12, 1992. Specifically, the plaintiff alleged that the defendant's Board of Directors, in response to a shareholders' proposal, authorized and included in its proxy materials a statement which contained false and misleading representations, intended to procure the defeat of the proposal, as well as material omissions. . . .

Defendant International Paper is a New York corporation whose shares are publicly traded on the New York Stock Exchange. On May 31, 1992, the Company sent its shareholders a Notice of Annual Meeting and a Proxy Statement. Included in the proxy materials was a "Shareholder Proposal Concerning the Valdez Principles." This proposal, denominated as Item No. 6, has been submitted to the Company by the Presbyterian Church (USA) pursuant to Rule 14a-8 of the Securities Exchange Act of 1934. 17 C.F.R. §240.14a-8 (1992). This rule was promulgated by the Securities and Exchange Commission under its rulemaking authority, 15 U.S.C. §78n(a) (1981). It permits shareholders who have owned either 1% of the company's equity securities or $1,000 worth of its stock for a specified period of time to submit proposals for a vote of the Company's shareholders. 17 C.F.R. §240.14a-8(a)(1) (1992).

559

The text of proposal #6 was as follows:

RESOLVED, that the shareholders request our company to:
  1. sign and implement the Valdez Principles; and
  2. engage with shareholders, CERES, and affected communities in a continuing process to achieve a genuine and publicly trusted measure of public environmental accountability.

The sponsors of this proposal also appended a statement in support of their resolution. The statement outlines the Valdez Principles, which were developed by CERES, and recommends inter alia that the Company report its compliance with these principles to the CERES group.

Applicable regulations, specifically 17 C.F.R. §240.14a-8(e), permit the Company's Board of Directors to offer a written response to such shareholder proposals. Thus, immediately following the sponsors' statement in support of Item No. 6 is a statement describing the position of the Company's Board on this proposal. That statement, which is the focal point of this litigation, states in full:

Position of the Company's Board of Directors

Your Board of Directors recommends that the shareholders vote AGAINST the proposal for the reasons set forth below:

The Board, at the recommendation of Company management, has adopted a comprehensive statement of Environmental, Health and Safety Principles and implementing guidelines (set forth in Appendix B). This statement of Principles is the most recent articulating of the company's longstanding commitment to the protection of the environment, which has been an explicit Company policy for many years. We believe that the company's environmental conduct code in fact is both more stringent and more industry specific than the Valdez Principles. In the areas of waste disposal, air emissions and groundwater, the Company has invested hundreds of millions of dollars ($100 million in 1991 alone) in technology, equipment, facilities and personnel to be at the forefront in the enhancement and protection of the environment. An environmental staff was formed by the Company many years ago to maintain compliance with environmental laws and regulations as well as Company policy. The Company regularly audits each operating unit for compliance with the letter and spirit of those rules. A committee of the Board, the Environment, Health & Technology Committee, meets regularly to review environmental, safety and health policies and programs throughout the Company, and advise the Board of the effectiveness of these policies and programs.

The Board believes the Valdez principles, though well-intentioned, are in many respects ambiguous and certain of them may not be applicable

10. Conclusion

to the Company. The Board does not believe, for example, that the Company and its shareholders should be burdened with duplicative independent audit requirements and costs associated with additional reports, as called for by the Principles. Moreover, the Board believes that the Principles calling as they do for the selection of one director 'qualified to represent environmental interests' are inappropriate since there are many and varied interests which shareholders have that should be the concern of all directors. Finally, the Board believes that implementation of the proposal would not provide any greater environmental protection than now exists and could be significantly more costly.

In summary, the Board believes that protection of the environment is critical to any business today, but that the environmental affairs of the Company and the interests of our shareholders are already being addressed in an appropriate and timely manner. . . .

International Paper's Board had, as required by applicable regulations, submitted this response to proposal #6 to the proposal's sponsors, the Presbyterian Church (USA) and the Sisters of Saint Dominic, for their review. Neither sponsor objected to it, so it was included in the proxy materials sent to all shareholders on March 31, 1992.

However, the plaintiff Union, which owns twenty-five shares of International Paper's stock, did object to the Board's response to the proposal. It contends that the statement contains false and misleading representations and omissions, in violation of both section 14(a) of the Securities Exchange Act of 1934, 15 U.S.C. §78n(a) (1981) and Rule 14a-9 of the Securities and Exchange Commission, 17 C.F.R. §240, 14a-9 (1992).

Specifically, the plaintiff claims that the following undisputed facts about the Company's environmental record belie the breezy assertions found in its response to the shareholder proposal:

- On July 3, 1991, the Company pled guilty to five felonies, relating both to violations of hazardous waste laws and falsification of required environmental reports, in the United States District Court for the District of Maine. The company agreed to pay a criminal fine of $2.2 million, the second largest fine ever assessed for violations of the hazardous waste laws.
- In February 1992, the Environmental Protection Agency initiated proceedings to debar International Paper from doing business with the federal government for a period of three years.
- In April 1991, the company settled a civil suit brought by the State of Maine and the Maine Board of Environmental Protection for violations of state environmental laws and regulations. In October 1991, the State returned to Superior Court in Maine to seek $700,000 in stipulated penalties for the Company's al-

leged failure to comply with this settlement. On April 21, 1992, a Superior Court judge assessed penalties against International Paper in the amount of $85,000.
- In 1990, the State of Missouri notified International Paper that it was preparing an enforcement action against the Company for violations of hazardous waste regulations at a Company facility in Joplin, Missouri. Settlement negotiations are proceeding in this dispute.
- On August 9, 1991, the company entered into a consent decree with the State of New York. This settlement requires the Company to remedy air, water and soil pollution at a Company facility in Binghamton, New York.
- In December 1991, the EPA requested information from the Company relating to air pollution at a Company facility in Ukiah, California. The Company has stated that it anticipates the EPA will seek penalties in excess of $100,000 in this action.
- The Company has also stated that the EPA will likely seek penalties in excess of $100,000 in an anticipated action relating to 104 PCB facilitators in Longview, Washington.
- The Company is currently a party to approximately fifty administrative proceedings, brought under the Comprehensive Environmental Response, Compensation and Liability Act, which relate to the cleanup of hazardous wastes at commercial landfills.
- As of January 31, 1992, the Company is a defendant in 43 civil actions, involving 1,565 plaintiffs, relating to the pollution of three rivers in Mississippi. A codefendant in two of these cases, the Georgia-Pacific Corporation, has already suffered substantial jury verdicts in similar actions.

The totality of this environmental record, the Union contends, renders false and misleading numerous statements in the Board's response to shareholder proposal #6. It also contends that the Board's failure to mention these matters in its response to the proposal constituted omission of material facts, which is, of course, unlawful under the statute and rules promulgated thereunder.

Rule 14a-9, promulgated by the Securities and Exchange Commission pursuant to section 14(a) of the Securities Exchange Act of 1934, states:

> No solicitation subject to this regulation shall be made by means of any proxy statement, form of proxy, notice of meeting or other communication, written or oral, containing any statement which, at the time and [in] the light of the circumstances under which it is made, is false or misleading with respect to any material fact, or which omits to state any

10. Conclusion

material fact necessary in order to make the statements therein not false or misleading or necessary to correct any statement in any earlier communication with respect to the solicitation of a proxy for the same meeting or subject matter which has become false or misleading. 17 C.F.R. §240.14a-9 (1992).

In order to establish liability under this Rule, a plaintiff must establish 1) that the proxy materials contain a false or misleading statement of a material fact, or omit to state a material fact necessary in order to make the statement made not false or misleading; 2) that the misstatement or omission of a material fact was the result of knowing, reckless or negligent conduct; and 3) that the proxy solicitation was an essential link in effecting the proposed corporate action. E.g., Gerstle v. Gamble-Skogmo, Inc., 478 F.2d 1281, 1298-1301 (2d Cir. 1973). A fact is "material" if there is "a substantial likelihood that the disclosure of the omitted fact would have been viewed by the reasonable investor as having significantly altered the total mix of information made available." TSC Industries, Inc. v. Northway, Inc., 426 U.S. 438, 449 (1976). . . .

Our analysis of whether the defendant's Board made material misstatements or omissions must begin with the recent case of Virginia Bankshares v. Sandberg, 111 S. Ct. 2749 (1991). The *Bankshares* case involved a challenge by minority shareholders of the defendant Bank to representations made by the defendant's Board about the fairness of [a] proposed merger. Rejecting the Board's arguments that misrepresentations about "soft" information were never actionable, the Supreme Court held that conclusory statements that the merger was "fair" or that it created a "high value," were actionable if the plaintiff could prove, as it had in *Bankshares,* that the Board knowingly offered false reasons in support of its conclusions: "Under §14(a), then, a plaintiff is permitted to prove a specific statement of reason knowingly false or misleadingly incomplete, even when stated in conclusory terms." 111 S. Ct. at 2759 (per Souter, J.). In this case, the plaintiff contends, International Paper's Board knowingly misrepresented the Company's environmental record, with the aim of defeating shareholder proposal #6.

Defendant replies first that the Board's response to shareholder proposal #6, even viewed in isolation, is not misleading. This argument is palpably without merit. Specific statements in both the Board's response to the proposal, such as the representation that the Company has "a long standing commitment to the protection of the environment," and the Company's "Environmental, Health and Safety Principles," such as the representation that the Company has "a strong environmental compliance program," are, to put it charitably, inconsistent with the serious and ongoing environmental challenges the Company has endured. See Cooke v. Teleprompter Corp., 334 F. Supp. 467, 470 (S.D.N.Y. 1971) (granting relief to plaintiff when proxy statement "incomplete, slanted and misleading").

Moreover, even if the Court could not identify specific statements that are at variance with the facts, the total impression conveyed by the Board's glib response to this proposal is that the Company is a model of environmental rectitude. Nowhere in any of these materials is there even a bare acknowledgment that the company has had its share of difficulties in this area. As our Court of Appeals has held: "A proxy statement should honestly, openly and candidly state all the material facts . . . Unlike poker where a player must conceal his unexposed cards, the object of a proxy statement is to put all of one's cards on the table face-up." Mendell v. Greenberg, 927 F.2d 667, 670 (2d Cir. 1990), corrected, 938 F.2d 1528 (2d Cir. 1991). See also Mills v. Electric Auto-Lite, 396 U.S. 375, 381 (1970) (section 14(a) intended to ensure "that proxies would be solicited with 'explanation to the stockholder of the real nature of the questions for which authority to cast his vote is sought") (quoting J.I. Case Co. v. Borak, 377 U.S. 426 (1964)).

More substantial is the defendant's argument that the Court should consider the Proxy Statement's accuracy in light of its Annual Report and media coverage of the Company's environmental difficulties. The defendant avers that details of its environmental record had been disclosed adequately in its Annual Report, which was mailed to all holders prior to the Annual Meeting, and that several articles and news reports had likewise focused attention on the Company's environmental record. Thus, in the defendant's view, its failure to mention in its Proxy Statement proceedings pending against it cannot, as a matter of law, constitute a material omission. . . .

Furthermore, the defendant notes that shareholders concerned about environmental affairs could have consulted the Company's most recent Form 10-K, which did disclose fully all material facts regarding the Company's environmental record. But see *Bertoglio*, 488 F. Supp. at 643 (press release and Form 10-Q not type of information of which shareholders presumably aware).

Whether disclosure of material facts in other media satisfies the duty to disclose in a proxy statement depends on the facts of each particular case, and is subject to an "overriding principle" of "reasonableness." Powell v. American Bank & Trust Co., 640 F. Supp. 1568, 1579 (N.D. Ind. 1986). The proper analysis, this Court concludes, is that articulated in somewhat tortured fashion in the *Powell* case: " a public disclosure of information relieves the duty to disclose if it is

10. Conclusion

reasonable to conclude that the plaintiff should have been made aware of the fact as a result of that disclosure." Id.

In this case, the Court holds as a matter of law that neither the Company's Form 10-K nor the press reports about International Paper's environmental record should be included as part of the "total mix" of information available to shareholders. The Form 10-K, though publicly available, is not mailed to shareholders, and, as the *Bertoglio* court noted, is not information reasonably within the constructive knowledge of the typical security holder.

Likewise, though widespread press reports theoretically may put shareholders on constructive notice, the eight news articles cited by the Company span a period of over one year; the most recent article cited appeared some four months prior to the Annual Meeting. Furthermore, the only matters mentioned in these articles are the Company's guilty plea in District Court in Maine and the Mississippi dioxin litigation. This is hardly the type of thorough and intensive news reporting that is required for media coverage to be included in the "total mix" of information available to shareholders. GAF Corp. v. Heyman, 724 F. 2d 727, 729 (2d Cir. 1983) (proper to include media coverage in "total mix" when contest for corporate control generated "many news stories" and was "closely watched").

Thus, the question that the Court must answer is whether the Proxy Statement and the Annual Report, the only items to which all shareholders manifestly had access, accurately portrayed the Company's environmental record. Ash v. LFE Corp., 525 F.2d 215, 221 (3d Cir. 1975) ("Fair accuracy, not perfection, is the appropriate standard" in judging truthfulness of proxy statement). Under all the circumstances, the Court believes that they did not, for the following reasons.

First, there is *no* mention in either the statement in opposition to proposal #6 or in the annexed appendix of "Principles" of any of the recent or pending proceedings against the Company; nor is the relevant section of the Annual Report, which does discuss the Company's environmental record in a somewhat more balanced fashion, even referred to. Cf. Goldsmith v. Rawl, 755 F. Supp. 96, 96 (S.D.N.Y. 1991) (defendant's failure to disclose in proxy materials litigation related to grounding of Exxon *Valdez* and formation of independent litigation committee actionable under section 14(a)).

Second, the Board's discussion of environmental issues in the Annual Report simply does not disclose information sufficient to enable a shareholder to make a reasoned judgment on whether proposal #6 merits support. Thus, defendant's argument that the Annual Report "cures" any misstatements or omissions in the Proxy Statement must fail. *Bankshares,* 111 S. Ct. at 2760 ("only when the inconsistency [between conflicting statements] would exhaust the misleading conclusion's capacity to influence the reasonable shareholder would a §14(a) action fail on the element of materiality"). For example, though the Company's guilty plea in the District Court in Maine is mentioned, the fact that the crimes were felonies, two of which involved knowingly illegal conduct, is not disclosed. There is no mention of the pending EPA debarment action. Beyond the bland statement that "International Paper is also a party to other environmental remedial actions under various federal and state laws," there is no discussion of the actions initiated by the State of Maine and the State of Missouri, nor are the PCB enforcement action in Washington State and the fifty administrative proceedings under CERCLA disclosed.

Furthermore, even concerning those proceedings that *are* discussed, the Board's statement withholds critical facts from the shareholders. For instance, with respect to the State of New York's action against the Company, the Board stated that:

> [T]he Imaging Products Division is currently conducting soil, groundwater and air testing at its Binghamton, New York Anitec facility under a consent order with the State of New York to determine the extent of contamination and remedial action required due to accidental discharges. The Division's film base production process, which was a principal source of the environmental impact, was shut down in 1991. Ex. A to May 4 Wilderotter Affidavit at 36.

Undisclosed in this statement, as the plaintiff notes, are the facts that a) the tests alluded to were conducted only after the State of New York sought an injunction against the Company and b) as the Company did disclose in its Form 10-K, "It is expected that there will be additional orders and possible fines relating to environmental matters at that [Anitec] facility." Ex. B to May 4 Wilderotter Affidavit at 6. Cf. Gould v. American-Hawaiian S.S. Co., 535 F.2d 761, 773 (3d Cir. 1976) (summary judgment for securities law plaintiff proper when "reasonable minds could not differ" as to materiality of false statements).

The Court understands that many major American corporations which produce tangible goods have had serious environmental problems, and intends no criticism of the defendant in this regard. The Board was under no obligation to discuss its environmental record in responding to the shareholder proposal: it could simply have stated that it opposed the proposal, or that it opposed the proposal solely as a matter of corporate governance. Cf. Amalgamated Clothing & Textile Workers Union v. J.P. Stevens & Co., 475 F. Supp. 328, 331-32 (S.D.N.Y. 1979) (proxy regulations "simply do not require management to accuse itself of antisocial or illegal policies"), *vacated*

10. Conclusion

as moot, 638 F.2d 7 (2d Cir. 1980) (per curiam). However, since the Board chose to offer specific representations about the Company's environmental record and policies, it was obligated to portray that record fairly. *Bankshares,* 111 S. Ct. at 2761 n. 7 ("Once the proxy statement purported to disclose the factors considered . . . there was an obligation to portray them accurately") (quoting Berg v. First American Bankshares, 796 F.2d 489, 496 (D.C. Cir. 1986)); Schlanger v. Four-Phase Systems, Inc., 582 F. Supp. 128, 132-33 (S.D.N.Y. 1984); Tanzer v. Haynie, 405 F. Supp. 650, 654 (S.D.N.Y. 1976) ("When there is, as here, an affirmative representation by fiduciaries that they have determined a price to be fair and equitable, matters that might not otherwise have to be disclosed may require airing") (citation omitted). This it did not do.

Since we have concluded that the Board's response to shareholder proposal #6 contained material misstatements and omissions, we must now consider whether the Board acted with the requisite culpability. Regrettably, it is entirely unclear what degree of culpability is necessary for liability under Rule 14a-9. The Supreme Court in *Bankshares* expressly stated that "In TSC Industries, Inc. v. Northway, 426 U.S. 438 (1976), we reserved the question whether *scienter* was necessary for liability generally under §14(a). We reserve it still." *Bankshares,* 111 S. Ct. at 2757 n. 5. . . .

Even assuming a section 14(a) plaintiff must demonstrate *scienter,* the Court believes that this plaintiff has satisfied its burden of proof on this point. Defendant cannot argue with any rationality that the Board's response to the shareholder proposal was anything but a calculated attempt to mislead the shareholders and induce them to cast a negative vote. The Board was presumptively and constructively aware of all relevant details of the Company's environmental record; rather than portraying that record accurately, or remaining silent, it chose instead to engage in flowery corporate happy-talk in order to defeat the proposal. The undisputed evidence compels a finding that the Board acted with the requisite knowledge and intent in making the misstatements and omissions detailed above. Vucinich v. Paine, Webber, Jackson & Curtis, Inc., 739 F.2d 1434, 1436 (9th Cir. 1984) (summary judgment appropriate in securities fraud case when "no reasonable inference supports the adverse party's claim"). . . .

Accordingly, the Court concludes that the Board's response to shareholder proposal #6 contained both misleading statements and omissions, that such statements and omissions were made knowingly, and that they had a "significant propensity" to affect the vote on the proposal. The plaintiff's motion for summary judgment is therefore granted. The result of the shareholders' vote on proposal #6 must be, and hereby is, voided, and the Board is directed to resubmit the proposal to a vote of the shareholders at the Company's next Annual Meeting.

NOTES AND QUESTIONS

1. Would International Paper have been better off if it had said nothing about its environmental record or policies in its response to the shareholders' proposal? If you were counsel for International Paper, what would you advise them to say in a future proxy statement opposing adoption of the CERES Principles in light of the court's decision?

2. On appeal, the Second Circuit affirmed the district court's decision. United Paperworkers Intl. Union v. International Paper Co., 985 F.2d 1190 (2d Cir. 1993). The court found no serious question that the company's proxy statement was materially misleading because it conveyed an impression that was entirely false. Id. at 1200. The court also ruled that the union could alert shareholders to the district court's decision when it resubmitted its shareholder resolution. The case is discussed in Note, United Paperworkers International Union v. International Paper Company: Environmental Disclosure and the "Total Mix" Concept of Materiality, 49 Bus. Law. 1225 (1994).

3. In Roosevelt v. E. I. DuPont de Nemours & Co., 958 F.2d 416 (D.C. Cir. 1992), a shareholder challenged a corporation's refusal to include in the proxy materials for its annual meeting a proposal urging the company to accelerate plans to phase out production of ozone-depleting compounds. The company defended its refusal on the grounds that the proposal did not involve "significant policy" matters, but rather matters relating to the conduct of "ordinary business operations" for which shareholder proposals may be excluded under SEC Rule 14a-8(c)(7), 17 C.F.R. §240.141-8(c)(7). Emphasizing that the company already had agreed to phase out CFC production and had even accelerated its planned phase-out during the litigation, the court concluded that the more rapid schedule sought by the shareholder was not a matter of "significant policy." Thus, it upheld the company's decision not to include the shareholder's proposal in the proxy materials.

4. Consider the following response to a shareholder proposal urging the Exxon Corporation voluntarily to report to foreign authorities releases of toxic chemicals from its operations outside the United States, as it does for domestic releases as part of the TRI reporting required by the EPCRTKA. "To assume that all communities' needs and interests are the same as in the U.S. is presumptuous and insensitive to the views of those local communities outside the U.S. where Exxon operates. . . . To assemble and report such data outside the U.S. where it

10. Conclusion Page 1266

is not needed, in addition to that which is necessary to comply with local regulations, would impose inappropriate, costly, and excessive reporting requirements. This would extend the heavy burden of U.S. requirements to all operations of the Corporation, making it even more difficult for Exxon to compete in world markets." Exxon Corporation, Proxy Statement, Mar. 5, 1993, at 20. Do you agree with the company's rationale for rejecting the shareholder proposal?

The Greening of American Business? (p. 1266). Signs of change in corporate attitudes toward environmental protection policy are growing. The Business Council for Sustainable Development, a coalition of 48 multinational corporations, has issued a report called Changing Course, which advocates that business take the lead in the "new industrial revolution" that is being driven by environmental concerns. Chaired by a Swiss industrialist, the Council made a highly publicized appearance at the Earth Summit to promote "eco-efficiency," the notion that the most efficient businesses in the future will be those that are most environmentally responsible. Schmidheiny, Earth-Friendliness Is Going to Be Good Business, Intl. Herald Trib., May 27, 1992, at 4. See also The Greening of American Business (T. Sullivan, ed. 1992).

As the elements of the global economy becomes increasingly interdependent, international standard-setting organizations are acquiring greater influence on business practices. The International Organization for Standardization, located in Geneva, Switzerland, has announced that it is developing environmental management guidelines to be issued in 1996. Known as ISO 14000, these guidelines will create a set of minimum requirements for corporate environmental management systems. Ready for ISO 14000?, Wall St. J., Mar. 9, 1995, at A1. These guidelines may encourage companies to improve their environmental practices in ways that go beyond existing local and national regulations.

General Motors has signed an unusual agreement with the Environmental Defense Fund to participate in a cooperative venture to determine if common ground can be found between environmentalists and the auto industry on issues of environmental policy. Wald, G.M. Signs an Accord with Environmentalists, N.Y. Times, July 9, 1992, at D4. EDF and GM cooperated in the development of the cash-for-clunkers policy that was endorsed by the Bush Administration in 1992 as a means for encouraging the retirement of old, high-polluting automobiles. EDF previously collaborated with the McDonald's Corporation on an unusual project that produced many significant changes in the company's policies in order to substantially reduce the amount of waste it generated.

Another group of corporate leaders is advocating changes in companies' internal pricing policies to ensure that the price of the goods they sell reflects their full environmental costs. Hamilton, Making a Product's Cost Reflect Pollution's Costs, Wash. Post, Nov. 29, 1992, at H1. This concept of "full-cost pricing" is likely to be controversial, since it seems vulnerable either to being undercut by less responsible competitors or to being challenged by consumers on antitrust grounds.

In similar fashion the Clinton Administration is moving to revise national income accounting in order to take into account environmental conditions. In his 1993 Earth Day speech, President Clinton announced that he had directed the Commerce Department's Bureau of Economic Analysis to develop a new measure of gross domestic product to incorporate the costs of pollution and the value of environmental resources. For decades economists have criticized the current method used to calculate economic growth because it fails to reflect changes in environmental conditions. For example, the current methodology assumes that an oil spill increases national wealth since it requires greater expenditures on cleanup operations. For a discussion of the ways national income accounts can be revised to incorporate environmental considerations, see Repetto, Earth in the Balance Sheet: Incorporating Natural Resources in National Income Accounts, 34 Environment 12 (Sept. 1992).

For businesses to respond effectively to the environmental challenge, it is clear that the next generation of environmental lawyers will need to be able to think creatively about nonlegal as well as legal solutions to environmental problems.